HISTORY OF THE OTTOMAN TURKS

Edward S. Creasy

HISTORY OF THE OTTOMAN TURKS

With a new Introduction by ZEINE N. ZEINE

Beirut
1961
KHAYATS

Oriental Reprints No. 1

KHAYATS, 92-4 Rue Bliss Beirut Lebanon

INTRODUCTION

IN HIS *A Generall Historie of the Ottoman Empire*, which was first published in 1603, Richard Knolles wrote : "At this present if you consider the beginning, progress and perpetual felicity of this the Ottoman Empire, there is in this world nothing more admirable and strange ; if the greatness and lustre thereof, nothing more magnificent and glorious; if the Power and Strength thereof, nothing more Dreadful and Dangerous, which... holdeth all the world in scorn thundering out nothing but Blood and War, with a full persuasion in time to Rule over all. prefixing unto itself no other limits than the uttermost bounds of the Earth, from the rising of the Sun unto the going down of the same".[1]

The Turks are the third Islamic peoples of the Middle East, the first two being the Arabs and the Persians. But they established the largest and strongest Muslim Empire, known as the Ottoman Empire, since the rise of Islam. A series of decisive victories in a

[1] *Paul Rycaut reissued Richard Knolles HISTORIE in 1679 with several continuations of his own which appeared in successive editions until 1700, when an additional volume appeared bringing the history up to 1699. Rycaut's editions were entitled: THE TURKISH HISTORY, FROM THE ORIGINAL OF THAT NATION TO THE GROWTH OF THE OTTOMAN EMPIRE and were published in London.*

long chain of conquests led the Turks to the zenith of their military power and glory. An unbroken succession of ten brilliant and great Sultans led the Ottomans to acquire in the fourteenth, fifteenth and sixteenth centuries a vast empire "embracing many of the richest and most beautiful regions of the world" and stretching from the gates of Vienna to the straits of Bab-el-Mandib, and from the Caucasus across North Africa, almost to the Atlantic Ocean.

It has been very difficult — and the difficulty continues to the present time — to write a satisfactory and comprehensive one-volume history of the Ottoman Turks. To begin with, a knowledge of the Turkish language and Turkish literature is necessary for any historian who aspires to write a history of the Ottoman Empire. Then, in the second place, a study of Turkish manners, customs, social institutions and religious beliefs becomes equally necessary and unavoidable. Even after a historian has fulfilled the above two conditions, he needs a stout heart and a steady hand when he approaches the problem of sources and documents needed for the writing of his history. For here, only the bravest of the brave can step over the threshold into the immense treasure-house of materials available for the building of the Turkish past. This treasure-house includes numerous Turkish records, accounts and books, and the vast quantity of state papers, despatches and memoranda in the National Archives of every European or neighbouring country with which the Ottoman Sultans had either friendly or hostile relations. Professor Bernard Lewis writes : "The Ottoman archives of Istanbul have for long been one of the great unknowns of historical scholarship... A first classification of papers was made in 1918-1921 by a committee under the direction of Ali Emiri, which sorted about 180,000 documents in chronological order. In 1921 a second committee, under Ibnulemin Mahmud Kemal, sorted about 45,000 documents, from the fifteenth to the nineteenth centuries, into 23 subject groups with a rough chronological sequence in each group. A third team, under Muallim Cevdet, worked from 1932 to 1937 on much the same lines as Ibnulemin, and sorted some 185,000 documents into 16 subject categories".[2]

No historian has undertaken this formidable task ever since the famous Austrian author, Joseph Von Hammer-Purgstall laid down his pen on September 28, 1830 after having worked for thirty years painstakingly, meticulously and conscientiously at writing his *Geschichte des Osmanischen Reiches*[3], a monumental and majestic work on the Ottoman Empire which still remains the standard European book on this subject.

In the third place, most of those who have written on Turkish history have not only been ignorant of the vast amount of sources that exist for such a task but have generally clung to one prejudice or another. The late and deeply lamented Harold Bowen, that quiet, modest and painstaking scholar of the School of Oriental and African Studies, University of London, has written "For various obvious reasons, Turkey and the

---

[2] See *"Archives" — The Journal of the British Record Association, Vol. IV, No. 24 Michaelmas 1960*, p. 228.

[3] *French translation by J. J. Hellert, HISTOIRE DE L'EMPIRE OTTOMAN (Paris, 1835-1841).*

Turks have aroused passionate feelings in those who have written, about them. Exaggerated denunciation has been answered by indignant defence. Those who have suffered from Turkish ruthlessness and prevarication have been contradicted by others subjected by Turkish magnificence, courtesy and charm. Misunderstandings have been countless ; and on any fact capable of being variously interpreted controversy has raged. In the realm of generalisation it is quite evident that many of the writers knew little of what they were talking about, or were blinded by prejudice of one kind or another".[4] Hence, the impossibility of finding in the English language, or, indeed, in any other language, a one-volume history of the Ottoman Empire completely satisfactory in all respects.

There is one important book, however, which may be placed in a class by itself. It is this present 1878 edition of Edward Shepherd Creasy's *History of the Ottoman Turks.*

Harold Bowen in his delightful and fascinating essay in a brochure entitled *British Contributions to Turkish Studies* and published in 1945 lists over one hundred works on Ottoman history, in English, from 1625 to the fall of that Empire at the end of the First World War in 1918. After referring to the fact that much interest in Turkish history was stimulated in Great Britain by the Crimean War, Bowen says that Creasy's *History of the Ottoman Turks* was the most important work which appeared at that time. "This", adds Bowen, completed by 1856, came quickly to be regarded

[4] *Bowen, Harold, BRITISH CONTRIBUTIONS TO TURK- ISH STUDIES (London, 1945) p. 8.*

as a standard work ; and the author, who at the time of its first appearance was Professor of Modern and Ancient History in the University of London, subsequently brought out several further editions in which he added to and modified the original text ; so that the edition of 1878 carries us on as far as the settlement arrived at in that year at Berlin. Creasy made good use of the authorities available, principally of course Von Hammer, and was well aware of the Turks' cultural achievements. He, therefore, presents a much fairer and more complete picture than any of his predecessors".

Creasy himself has stated in the Preface of his 1878 edition that while his book is "chiefly founded on Von Hammer" (who "does not bring the Turkish history lower down than to the treaty of Kainardji, 1774"), he has consulted and sought information from other sources. "I have not made a mere abridgment of Von Hammer" he writes ; "but I have sought to write an independent work, for which his volumes have supplied me with the largest store of materials".

Creasy's work stops with the Treaty of San Stefano of March 3, 1878, which ended the Russo-Turkish war of 1877-78. As he could not use the documents available now in the Ottoman archives, his treatment of Ottoman history is, obviously, incomplete and imperfect, and particularly since the Crimean War, is brief and rather fragmentary. However, we have a number of good works in English on the different phases of the latter period.

Actually, the history of the Ottoman Empire in the nineteenth century is one of increasing internal weakness and deterioration in the machinery of Government and of sustained external pressure by the Great Powers, which ultimately led to the dissolution of that Empire. If the Empire was "on the edge of disruption and collapse" who would inherit its vast territories in Europe, Asia and Africa ? The history of the Ottomans and their relations with Europe in this century were dominated by the major and vital question known generally as the Eastern Question. In a letter to *The Times* on September 9, 1876, Lord Stratford de Redcliffe wrote : "The Eastern Question has by degrees assumed such large proportions that no one can be surprised at the space it occupies in all public discussions whether of the tongue or of the pen". The following very brief summary of this period will help to bring to the attention of the reader its major events and outstanding features.

With the opening of the nineteenth century, the Ottoman Empire became subject to a series of political pressures and military blows from friends and foes alike among the European Powers. All these Powers tried to find in the vast dominions of Turkey an outlet for their territorial ambitions, commercial expansion, national prestige, jealousies and fears. The capital of that Empire became the focal point of a sinister game of power-politics played by the Ambassadors of the Great Powers will all the astuteness of nineteenth century diplomacy. To Great Britain, the maintenance of the "Balance of Power" in Europe became more vital than ever, and for the maintenance of this balance, it became imperative to preserve the integrity of the Ottoman Empire.

During the first half of the nineteenth century, two major events greatly affected the Eastern Question. The first was the invasion of Egypt and Syria by Napoleon (1798-1801) and, the second, the occupation of Syria by Muhammad Ali Pasha's troops (1830-1840). Both brought French, Russian and British intervention in the Near East. The advance of Muhammad 'Ali Pasha's forces in Anatolia, as far as Kutahia, forced Sultan Mahmud to accept Russian aid for the defence of Constantinople (Istanbul); hence, the signing of the Treaty of Unkiar Skelessi (July 8, 1833). Napoleon and Muhammad Ali Pasha were both defeated. Turkey was saved, albeit it had grown weaker. Indeed, in 1827, as a result of the war of Greek independence Turkey lost Greece and the latter became a self-governing nation.

The events leading up to the Protocol of London in 1841 convinced Tsar Nicholas that Turkey was dying and he made no secret of his views. In 1843, he visited Vienna and Berlin and in 1844, London. In all these capitals, he told the responsible Governments that the downfall of Turkey was imminent. All that he wanted was to "come to an understanding" over the property of the dying man, particularly Constantinople, "before it is too late". In England, he told the Aberdeen Government: "In my Cabinet there are two opinions about Turkey: one is that she is dying; the other is that she is already dead".

Tsar Nicholas waited for nine years hoping that Britain would change her policy towards Turkey, *l'homme malade*, — the "sick man" of Europe. Exasperated by the attitude of the British Government and tired of waiting, the Tsar finally took the matter into his own hands. The result was the Crimean War of 1854-1856.

The Treaty of Paris which ended the Crimean War in 1856 guaranteed "the Independence and the Territorial Integrity of the Ottoman Empire". Russia was once more prevented from achieving her favourite object of conquering Istanbul. "This declaration of the independence of Turkey", wrote the Duke of Argyll "was the best form in which they (the Powers) could repel and condemn the attempt of Russia to establish the special dependence of Turkey upon herself..."

The twenty years which followed the Crimean War were a period of comparative calm in the field of international rivalry in the Ottoman Empire, with two exceptions : the civil war of 1860 in Lebanon and the sanguinary insurrections of 1866-1868 in Crete, an island with a Christian majority of Greeks and a privileged Muslim minority. The events in Lebanon led to the intervention of five Powers in Istanbul. These Powers, Great Britain, Russia, France, Austria and Prussia submitted a "Protocole" to the Porte which was accepted by the latter. According to this "Protocole", Mount Lebanon was detached from the vilayet of Syria and became an autonomous Province (*Sanjak*) ruled over by a Christian Governor (*Mutasarrif*) and an Administrative Council of twelve members. This led to the further weakening of the government machinery of the Ottoman Empire.

Meanwhile, an outstanding event took place in the Near East, which probably more than any other decided the fate of the Arab world as far as West European

imperialism was concerned, namely, the opening of the
Suez Canal in 1869. This 101-mile waterway brought
London nearer to Bombay by 4500 miles and to Aba-
dan by 4800 miles. When in November 1875, Khedive
Isma'il wanted to sell his 176,602 shares for £ 4,000,000,
Lord Derby, the Foreign Secretary, and Disraeli acted
quickly and bought them. Meanwhile, Russia was preparing herself to make one more attempt to solve the
Eastern Question in her favour. In July of that same
year, the spark of rebellion set Bosnia and Herzegovina
on fire. The revolt spread to Bulgaria.

The Russo-Turkish war of 1877-1878 which followed
brought the Russians dangerously close to Istanbul
— at San Stefano. But the firm attitude of the British
Government and the presence of the British fleet in
the sea of Marmara, near Istanbul, led to the signing
of the peace treaty of San Stefano in March 1878. This
treaty was shortly afterwards modified at the Congress
of Berlin in favour of Turkey and a new treaty, the
Treaty of Berlin, was signed in July 1878. The Ottoman Empire in Europe was saved from utter destruction and Istanbul continued to remain in Turkish
hands.

This was the first disastrous event to mark the long
reign of Sultan Abdu'l Hamid's thirty-three years
which began in August 1876. During this time, the
interests and rivalries of the various great Powers in
the Ottoman Empire became sharper and more clearly defined. It now became evident that the "sick man"
was, indeed, very dangerously sick and could not be
saved. The downfall of "the Ottoman ramshackle and
worm-eaten state" was no more a remote contingency.

The Ottomans had practically lost the greater part of their European Empire. The new and crucial question of the day was how were they going to keep their Asiatic Empire, i. e. mainly the Arab lands of the Near East. This question became one of the main preoccupations of British foreign policy after 1878. Hence, the secret Convention which Disraeli concluded with Turkey on June 4 1878 as a result of which Great Britain was "to occupy and administer" the island of Cyprus — to defend and protect the Asiatic possessions of the Sultan against Russia. Cyprus was an island which strategically commanded at once "the coast of Syria and Egypt".

A little over four years later, in September 1882, Britain occupied Egypt, an event which was closely related to the acquisition of Cyprus and the opening of the Suez Canal in 1869, the possession of which as "the Key of India", was essential for the protection of that sub-continent.

The occupation of Cyprus and Egypt transformed the situation in the Near East. As a Power ruling over India and as a Mediterranean Power, it was necessary for Great Britain to have a secure position in the Asiatic possessions of the Ottoman Empire.

Before the end of the century, another turning point in the history of the Eastern Question was marked by the growth of German influence in the Ottoman Empire. The German policy of penetration and of "Drang nach osten" was viewed with alarm by England, France and Russia. The visit of Emperor William II to Palestine, Lebanon and Syria at the end of October and beginning of November, 1898, inspired Professor

Hasse, the Chief of the 'Pan-Germanic Union' to write:
"Full steam ahead! Foward to the Euphrates and
to the Tigris and to the Persian Gulf! And let us have
the land route to India in the hands of those to
whom alone it ought to belong — in the hands of Germans who rejoice in battle and in toil".[5]

At the beginning of the twentieth century, the ever
growing fear of Germany produced a number of *mar-
riages de convenance* among the Powers. The menace
to British interests of the aggressive policy of the new
German Empire led Great Britain, in the words of
Harold Bowen, "to seek the friendship of Russia and,
consequently, to modify the long-standing British policy
of opposing Russia's designs of expansion at the expense of the Ottoman Empire". Actually, the conflicting interests of Great Britain, France and Russia were
temporarily reconciled by various accords and alliances,
such as the Entente Cordiale of 1904 between France
and Britain and the Anglo-Russian Entente of 1907.

Meanwhile, towards the end of the nineteenth
century, the internal situation of the Ottoman Empire
had been deteriorating rapidly. Discontent, corruption
and anarchy were spreading with alarming speed. It
had been known for sometime that both Arab and
Turkish reformers were planning and plotting to curb
the autocratic powers of Abd'ul Hamid. After the deposition of Sultan Abdu'l Aziz on May 30, 1876 and
of Sultan Murad on August 31, 1876, Abdu'l Hamid
was proclaimed Sultan, having given a prior pledge to
Midhat Pasha, a most enlightened and courageous

5 *THE TIMES, London, Friday November 11, 1898.*

reformer, that he would support the Pasha's Constitution and promulgate it. And so it was that on December 23, 1876, in an imposing ceremony held at Istanbul, the Imperial Rescript (Hatti Humayun) of Abdu'l Hamid addressed to the grand vezir Midhat Pasha, followed by the text of the Constitution, were read.

Actually, the Constitution of 1876 was itself the outcome of the many attempts made at reforming or "westernizing" the institutions of the Ottoman Empire since the beginning of the 19th century. It was in a sense a child of the *Tanzimat* and the third in a series of Imperial Rescripts, the first being the Hatti Sherif of Gulhane of November 3, 1839 which promised to procure for the provinces of the Ottoman Empire the benefits of a good administration by means of new institutions.

Elections were held on the basis of a Provisional Electoral Law and the inauguration of the first historic Ottoman Parliament took place on March 19, 1877. On February 14, 1878, it was dissolved *sine die* by the Sultan's command. All anti-Hamidian opposition and reform movements were driven either underground in the form of secret societies or beyond the boundaries of the Empire, particularly to Paris, London, Geneva and Cairo.

At the turn of the century, when Abdu'l Hamid celebrated on August 31, 1900, the twenty-fifth anniversary of his accession to the throne, Turkey's cup of misfortunes was already overflowing. The "Young Turks", successors to the "New Ottomans" were stirred to action to save Turkey from decay and ruin. The Young Turks' movement had branches in different parts of the Ottoman Empire but its nerve-centre was at Salonika, in Macedonia. The eventful years of 1905-08 gave this revolutionary movement a tremendous impetus. The Young Turks' Revolution of July 1908 restored the Constitution of 1876. Abdu'l Hamid, temporarily, gained much popularity. Elections were held for a new Parliament and the latter held its first meeting on Thursday, December 17, 1908 in the presence of the Sultan and the Ottoman princes. But while the democratic machinery had been introduced in the Empire of the Ottoman sultans, democracy itself with all its implications and philosophy of life, had few roots in that Empire. The masses were in almost complete ignorance of what a constitution meant. The sultan and the ruling class whether civilian or the religious hierarchy were, at heart, opposed to any system of Government that would curtail their powers and abolish their privileges. On April 13, 1909, there was an attempt at a counter-revolution in Istanbul. However, the Turkish army in Macedonia was ready. It marched on the capital and laid siege to the Sultan's palace at Yildiz. On April 27, Abdu'l Hamid was deposed in favour of his brother Muhammad Rashad, as Muhammad V, and was immediately exiled that evening to Salonika, where he has interned in Villa Alatini.

When the First World War burst forth upon Europe on August 1, 1914, the Young Turks, in the grip of William II's Germany, could not keep a helpless and practically disintegrating Ottoman Empire out of the conflict. On November 5, 1914, Turkey entered the war on the side of the Central Powers. Almost exactly four years later, on October 30, 1918, Turkey signed an armistice with the Allied Powers on board the British battleship *Agamemnon,* in the harbour of Mudros at Lemnos, in the Aegean Sea.

With the collapse of the Ottoman Empire, the Eastern Question, as far as it concerned the question of which Power or Powers would inherit the vast and rich possessions of the "Sick man" upon its dissolution, i. e. which Power or Powers would take the place of the Ottoman Empire and fill the "vacuum" created by its disappearance — in this specific sense, the Eastern Question ceased to exist. On the other hand, in its broadest sense, as an international question which dealt with the conflicting interests and rivalries of the Great Powers in the political and economic fields, in the Near and Middle East, the Eastern Question had by no means been settled. It had, in reality, become a western question and, indeed, a world question.

The subsequent history of the Near East after the defeat and dismemberment of the Ottoman Empire, was the miraculous birth of modern Turkey, the Turkish Republic of Mustafa Kemal Pasha, or Ataturk, and the gradual emergence of the independent Arab states in this area. But this is not, obviously, within the scope of Ottoman history, which is the subject-matter of this work.

Until a new and sound presentation of the Ottoman past is undertaken, Creasy's *History of the Ottoman Turks* will remain the standard work and the best general account of Ottoman history yet composed in English. The publishing firm of Khayat has rendered a signal service in the field of Middle Eastern studies

by making this valuable book available to students
and specialists in Turkish history.

ZEINE N. ZEINE

American University of Beirut
October 1961

HISTORY

OF

THE OTTOMAN TURKS:

FROM THE BEGINNING OF THEIR EMPIRE TO THE PRESENT TIME.

By SIR EDWARD S. CREASY, M.A.,

(Late Chief Justice of Ceylon),

EMERITUS PROFESSOR OF HISTORY IN UNIVERSITY COLLEGE, LONDON; LATE FELLOW OF
KING'S COLLEGE, CAMBRIDGE.
AUTHOR OF "THE FIFTEEN DECISIVE BATTLES OF THE WORLD," "RISE AND PROGRESS
OF THE ENGLISH CONSTITUTION," ETC.

LONDON:

1878.

PREFACE TO POPULAR EDITION.

HAVING been requested to prepare a Second Edition of this work, which has long been out of print, I have made in it many corrections, and some curtailments. I have added a few pages as to events subsequent to the Crimean War; but these are written with studious brevity.

The book (as I stated when it first appeared) is chiefly founded on Von Hammer. I have also carefully sought information from Knolles, Rycaut, Montecuculi, Roe, Hanway, Manstein, D'Ohsson Thornton, Eton, Ubicini, Porter, Marmont, Sir F. Smith, Col. Chesney, Urquhart, Möltke, Hamel, Sismondi, Ranke, Finlay, Tricoupi, Campbell, Bosworth Smith, and others. I have also availed myself of the fragmentary wealth that lies heaped up in the back numbers of our periodical literature. The indices to both the "Quarterly" and the "Edinburgh" point out several articles on Turkish subjects, from which I have repeatedly gained intelligence and warnings. I have also consulted some admirable papers entitled "Chapters on Turkish History," which were contributed about thirty years ago to "Blackwood" by the late Mr. Hulme, a profound Oriental scholar, and a writer of such taste and vigour, that if he had lived to complete the work, portions of which were then sketched out by him, a full, accurate, and brilliant History of the Turks would have ceased to be one of the desiderata in our literature.

Von Hammer's "History of the Ottoman Empire" will always be the standard European book on this subject. That history was the result of the labours of thirty years, during which Von Hammer explored, in addition to the authorities which his predecessors had made use of, the numerous works of the Turkish and other Oriental writers on the Ottoman history, and other rich sources of intelligence which are to be found in the archives of Venice, Austria, and other states, that have been involved in relations of hostility or amity with the Sublime Porte. Von Hammer's long residence in the East, and his familiarity with the institutions and habits, as well as with the language and the literature of the Turks, give an additional attractiveness and value to his volumes. His learning is as accurate as it is varied ; his honesty and candour are unquestioned; and his history is certainly one of the best productions of the first half of our century.

This great work has never been translated into English. Its length has probably caused it to be thus neglected, while the historical productions of other German writers, though of less merit, have been eagerly translated and extensively read in this country. The first edition of Von Hammer (published at Pesth) consists of ten thick closely-printed volumes. The second and smaller edition occupies four. This second edition omits the notes and observations, many of which are highly instructive and valuable. And Von Hammer does not bring the Turkish history lower down than to the treaty of Kainardji, 1774. A translation of his entire work, with a continuation of equal copiousness, would make up at least twenty octavo volumes, such as are usually printed in this country. Both writers and publishers have evidently feared that such a work would lack readers among our busy and practical population.

I have not made a mere abridgment of Von Hammer; but I have sought to write an independent work, for which his volumes have supplied me with the largest store of materials. In using them I have arranged, and amplified, and omitted, and added at discretion, so as to assume general responsibility for comments and opinions. Where I have adopted those of Von Hammer, I have generally referred to him as their author. My intention was always to do so, but there may be instances where this has been omitted.

The references to the pages of Von Hammer, in the notes, apply to the second edition of the German.

E. S. CREASY.

ATHENÆUM CLUB,
 March 10*th*, 1877.

CONTENTS.

CONTENTS.

CHAPTER V.

CHAPTER VI.

CHAPTER VII.

CHAPTER VIII.

CHAPTER IX.

CHAPTER X.

CHAPTER XI.

CONTENTS.

CHAPTER XII.

CHAPTER XIII.

CHAPTER XIV.

CHAPTER XV.

CHAPTER XVI.

CONTENTS.

CHAPTER XVII.

CHAPTER XVIII.

CHAPTER XIX.

CHAPTER XX.

CHAPTER XXI.

CONTENTS.

CONTENTS.

CHAPTER XXV.

HISTORY OF THE OTTOMAN TURKS.

CHAPTER I.

FIRST APPEARANCE AND EXPLOITS OF THE OTTOMAN TURKS
UNDER ERTOGHRUL IN ASIA MINOR—THEIR SETTLEMENT AT
SULTAN-ŒNI—REIGN OF OTHMAN I.—HIS DREAM—HIS CON-
QUESTS—DEATH AND CHARACTER.[1]

ABOUT six centuries ago, a pastoral band of four hundred Turkish
families was journeying westward from the upper streams of the
river Euphrates. Their armed force consisted of four hundred
and forty-four horsemen; and their leader's name was Ertoghrul,
which means "The Right-Hearted Man." As they travelled
through Asia Minor, they came in sight of a field of battle, on
which two armies of unequal numbers were striving for the
mastery. Without knowing who the combatants were, The
Right-Hearted Man took instantly the chivalrous resolution to
aid the weaker party : and charging desperately and victoriously
with his warriors upon the larger host, he decided the fortune of
the day. Such, according to the Oriental historian Neschri,[2] is
the first recorded exploit of that branch of the Turkish race,
which from Ertoghrul's son, Othman,[3] has been called the nation
of the Ottoman Turks.

[1] See Von Hammer, books 1 and 2.
[2] Neschri states this on the authority of Mewlana Ayas, who had heard
the battle narrated by the stirrup-holder of Ertoghrul's grandson Orchan,
who had heard it from Ertoghrul himself, and had told it to his followers.
See Von Hammer's note to p. 62 of his first volume.
[3] "Osman" is the real Oriental name of the Eponymus hero, and the
descendants of his subjects style themselves "Osmanlis." But the corrupted forms "Othman" and "Ottoman" have become so fixed in our language and literature, that it would be pedantry to write the correct
originals. I follow the same principle in retaining "Amurath" for "Murad,"
"Bajazet" for "Bayezid," "Spahi" for "Sipahi," &c., &c.

1

The little band of Ertoghrul was a fragment of a tribe of Oghouz Turks, which, under Ertoghrul's father, Solyman Shah, had left their settlements in Khorassan, and sojourned for a time in Armenia. After a few years, they left this country also; and were following the course of the Euphrates towards Syria, when their leader was accidentally drowned in that river. The greater part of the tribe then dispersed; but a little remnant of it followed two of Solyman's sons, Ertoghrul and Dundar, who determined to seek a dwelling-place in Asia Minor, under the Seljukian Turk, Alaeddin, the Sultan of Iconium. It so happened, that it was Alaeddin himself who commanded the army, to which Ertoghrul and his warriors brought such opportune succour on the battle-field, whither their march in quest of Alaeddin had casually led them. The adversaries, from whose superior force they delivered him, were a host of Mongols, the deadliest enemies of the Turkish race. Alaeddin, in gratitude for this eminent service, bestowed on Ertoghrul a principality in Asia Minor, near the frontiers of the Bithynian province of the Byzantine Emperors.

The rich plains of Saguta along the left bank of the river Sakaria, and the higher districts on the slopes of the Ermeni mountains, became now the pasture-grounds of the father of Othman. The town of Saguta, or Sægud, was his also. Here he, and the shepherd-warriors who had marched with him from Khorassan and Armenia, dwelt as denizens of the land. Ertoghrul's force of fighting men was largely recruited by the best and bravest of the old inhabitants, who became his subjects; and, still more advantageously, by numerous volunteers of kindred origin to his own. The Turkish race[1] had been extensively spread through Lower Asia long before the time of Ertoghrul. Quitting their primitive abodes on the upper steppes of the Asiatic continent, tribe after tribe of that martial family of nations had poured down upon the rich lands and tempting wealth of the southern and western regions, when the power of the early Khalifs had decayed, like that of the Greek Emperors. One branch of the Turks, called the Seljukian, from their traditionary patriarch Seljuk Khan, had acquired and consolidated a mighty empire, more than two centuries before the name of the Ottomans was heard. The Seljukian Turks were once masters of nearly all Asia Minor, of Syria, of Mesopotamia, Armenia, part of Persia, and

---

[1] See, for the ethnology of the Turks, Dr. Latham's work on Russia. According to that high authority, all the early great Asiatic conquerors from the parts north of the Oxus have been of Turkish race, except Zenghis Khan and his descendants, and except the Mantchoo conquerors of China.

Western Turkestan : and their great Sultans, Toghrul Beg, Alp
Arslan, and Melek Shah, are among the most renowned conquerors
that stand forth in Oriental and in Byzantine history.   But, by
the middle of the thirteenth century of the Christian era, when
Ertoghrul appeared on the battle-field in Asia Minor, the great
fabric of Seljukian dominion had been broken up by the assaults of
the conquering Mongols, aided by internal corruption and civil
strife.   The Seljukian Sultan Alaeddin reigned in ancient pomp
at Koniah, the old Iconium ; but his effective supremacy extended
over a narrow compass, compared with the ample sphere throughout which his predecessors had exacted obedience.   The Mongols
had rent away the southern and eastern acquisitions of his race.
In the centre and south of Asia Minor other Seljukian chiefs
ruled various territories as independent princes; and the Greek
Emperors of Constantinople had recovered a considerable portion
of the old Roman provinces in the north and east of that peninsula.   Amid the general tumult of border warfare, and of ever-
recurring peril from roving armies of Mongols, which pressed upon
Alaeddin, the settlement in his dominions of a loyal chieftain and
hardy clan, such as Ertoghrul and his followers, was a welcome
accession of strength ; especially as the new comers were, like the
Seljukian Turks, zealous adherents of the Mahometan faith.   The
Crescent was the device that Alaeddin bore on his banners;
Ertoghrul, as Alaeddin's vicegerent, assumed the same standard ;
and it was by Ertoghrul's race that the Crescent was made for
centuries the terror of Christendom, as the sign of aggressive
Islam, and as the chosen emblem of the conquering Ottoman
power.

There was little peace in Ertoghrul's days on the frontier near
which he had obtained his first grants of land.   Ertoghrul had
speedy and frequent opportunities for augmenting his military
renown, and for gratifying his followers with the spoils of successful forays and assaults.   The boldest Turkish adventurers
flocked eagerly to the banner of the new and successful chieftain
of their race ; and Alaeddin gladly recognised the value of his
feudatory's services by fresh honours and marks of confidence, and
by increased donations of territory.

In a battle which Ertoghrul, as Alaeddin's lieutenant, fought
against a mixed army of Greeks and Mongols, between Brusa and
Yenischeer, he drew up his troops so as to throw forward upon the
enemy a cloud of light cavalry, called Akindji ; thus completely
masking the centre of the main army, which, as the post of honour,
was termed the Sultan's station.   Ertoghrul held the centre him-

self, at the head of the four hundred and forty-four horsemen, who were his own original followers, and whose scimetars had won the day for Alaeddin, when they first charged unconsciously in his cause. The system now adopted by Ertoghrul of wearying the enemy by collision with a mass of irregular troops, and then pressing him with a reserve of the best soldiers, was for centuries the favourite tactic of his descendants. The battle in which he now employed it was long and obstinate; but in the end the Turkish chief won a complete victory. Alaeddin, on being informed of this achievement of his gallant and skilful vassal, bestowed on him the additional territory of Eskischeer, and in memory of the mode in which Ertoghrul had arrayed his army, Alaeddin gave to his principality the name of Sultan-Œni, which means "Sultan's Front."

The territory which received that name, and still bears it, as one of the Sanjaks, or minor governments of the Ottoman Empire, is nearly identical with the ancient Phrygia Epictetos. It was rich in pasturage, both in its alluvial meadows and along its mountain slopes. It contained also many fertile cornlands and vineyards; and the romantic beauty of every part of its thickly wooded and well-watered highlands still attracts the traveller's admiration.[1]

Besides numerous villages, it contained, in Ertoghrul's time, the strongholds of Karadjahissar, Biledjik, Inæni, and others; and the cities or towns of Eskischeer (so celebrated in the history of the crusades under its old name of Dorylæum), Seid-e-ghari, Lefke, and Sægud, near which is the domed tomb of Ertoghrul, an object still of the deepest veneration to frequent pilgrims from all parts of the Ottoman Empire. Many of the places that have been mentioned were, at the time when Alaeddin, as their titular sovereign, made grant of them to Ertoghrul, held by chieftains, who were practically independent, and who little heeded the sovereign's transfer of their lands and towns. It was only after long years of warfare carried on by Ertoghrul and his more renowned son, Othman, that Sultan-Œni became the settled possession of their house.

Othman, or, according to the Oriental orthography, Osman, is regarded as the founder of the Ottoman Empire; and it is from him that the Turks, who inhabit it, call themselves Osmanlis, the only national appellation which they recognise.[2] Ertoghrul never

---

[1] "Anadol," p. 274.
[2] They consider that the name of Turk implies rudeness and barbarism.

professed to act save as the vassal and lieutenant of the Sultan of
Iconium. But Othman, after the death of the last Alaeddin
in 1307, waged wars and accumulated dominions as an independent potentate. He had become chief of his race twelve
years before, on Ertoghrul's death, in 1288. Othman, at his
succession, was twenty-four years of age, and was already of
proved skill as a leader, and of tried prowess as a combatant.
His early fortunes and exploits are favourite subjects with the
Oriental writers, especially his love adventures in wooing and
winning the fair Malkhatoon. These legends have probably been
coloured by the poetical pens, that have recorded them in later
years ; but it is less improbable that they should be founded on
fact, than that no similar traditions should have been handed
down by the children and followers of so renowned a chief, as the
founder of the Ottoman Empire.

The Scheikh Edebali, celebrated for his piety and learning, had
come, while Othman was very young, to Itbourouni, a village
near Eskischeer. Othman used often to visit the holy man, out
of respect for his sanctity and learning ; and the young prince's
visits became still more frequent, after he had one evening accidentally obtained a view of the Scheikh's fair daughter, Malkhatoon, a name which means " Treasure of a Woman." Othman
confessed his love ; but the old man thought that the disparity of
station made a marriage imprudent, and refused his consent.
Othman sought consolation for his disappointment in the society
of his friends and neighbours, to whom he described with a lover's
inspiration, the beauty of Malkhatoon. He discoursed so eloquently on this theme to the young chief of Eskischeer, that the
listener fell in love with Malkhatoon upon hearsay ; and, going to
her father, demanded her hand for himself. Edebali refused him
also ; but fearing his vengeance more than that of Othman, the
old man removed from the neighbourhood of Eskischeer to a
dwelling close to that of Ertoghrul. The chief of Eskischeer
now hated Othman as his rival. One day when Othman and his
brother Goundonroulp were at the castle of their neighbour, the
lord of Inæni, an armed force suddenly appeared at the gate, led
by the chieftain of Eskischeer and his ally, Michael of the Peaked
Beard, the Greek lord of Khirenkia, a fortified city at the foot of
the Phrygian Olympus. They demanded that Othman should be
given up to them ; but the lord of Inæni refused to commit such
a breach of hospitality. While the enemy lingered irresolutely
round the castle wall, Othman and his brother seized an advantageous moment for a sudden sally at the head of a few com-

panions. They chased the chief of Eskischeer off the field in disgrace, and took Michael of the Peaked Beard prisoner. The captive an the captors became staunch friends; and in after times, when Othman reigned as an independent prince, Michael left the Christian for the Mussulman creed to join him, and was thenceforth one of the strongest supporters of the Ottoman power.[1]

Othman had by this encounter at Inæni, triumphed over his rival, and acquired a valuable friend; but he could not yet gain the maiden of his heart. For two more years the course of his true love ran through refusal and anxiety, until at length, old Edebali was touched by the young prince's constancy, and he interpreted a dream as a declaration of Heaven in favour of the long-sought marriage.

One night, when Othman was resting at Edebali's house (for the shelter of hospitality could never be denied even to the suitor whose addresses were rejected), the young prince, after long and melancholy musing on her whom he loved, composed his soul in that patient resignation to sorrow, which, according to the Arabs, is the key to all happiness. In this mood he fell asleep, and he dreamed a dream.

He saw himself and his host reposing near each other. From the bosom of Edebali rose the full moon (emblem of the beauteous Malkhatoon), and inclining towards the bosom of Othman, it sank upon it, and was lost to sight. Thence sprang forth a goodly tree, which grew in beauty and in strength ever greater and greater. Still did the embracing verdure of its boughs and branches cast an ampler and an ampler shade, until they canopied the extreme horizon of the three parts of the world. Under the tree stood four mountains, which he knew to be Caucasus, Atlas, Taurus, and Hæmus. These mountains were the four columns, that seemed to support the dome of the foliage of the sacred tree, with which the earth was now pavilioned. From the roots of the tree gushed forth four rivers, the Tigris, the Euphrates, the Danube, and the Nile. Tall ships and barks innumerable were on the waters. The fields were heavy with harvest. The mountain sides were clothed with forests. Thence in exulting and fertilising abundance sprang fountains and rivulets, that gurgled through thickets of the cypress and the rose. In the valleys glittered stately cities, with domes and cupolas, with pyramids and obelisks, with minarets and towers. The Crescent shone on

[1] Von Hammer, vol. i. p. 66.

their summits : from their galleries sounded the Muezzin's call to prayer. That sound was mingled with the sweet voices of a thousand nightingales, and with the prattling of countless parrots of every hue. Every kind of singing bird was there. The winged multitude warbled and flitted round beneath the fresh living roof of the interlacing branches of the all-overarching tree ; and every leaf of that tree was in shape like unto a scimetar. Suddenly there arose a mighty wind, and turned the points of the sword-leaves towards the various cities of the world, but especially towards Constantinople. That city, placed at the junction of two seas and two continents, seemed like a diamond set between two sapphires and two emeralds, to form the most precious stone in a ring of universal empire. Othman thought that he was in the act of placing that visioned ring on his finger, when he awoke.[1]

Othman related this dream to his host; and the vision seemed to Edebali so clearly to presage honour, and power, and glory, to the posterity of Othman and Malkhatoon,[2] that the old Scheikh no longer opposed their union. They were married by the saintly Dervise Touroud, a disciple of Edebali. Othman promised to give the officiating minister a dwelling-place near a mosque, and on the bank of a river. When Othman became an independent prince, he built for the dervise a convent, which he endowed richly with villages and lands, and which remained for centuries in the possession of the family of Touroud.

The Ottoman writers attach great importance to this dream of the founder of their empire. They dwell also on the prophetic significance of his name, signifying the resistless energy with which he and his descendants were to smite the nations of the earth. "Othman" means the "Bone-breaker." It is also a name given to a large species of vulture, commonly called the royal

---

[1] See Von Hammer, vol. i., p. 49. The author of "Anadol" recounts this dream, and remarks on the part of it respecting Constantinople :— "That link, Constantinople, fell into the hands of Osman Bey's descendant, Sultan Mohammed II., and the Turkish Empire was constituted. It is, indeed, an aggregation of many nations, and the prophetic allegory of the multitudes of foreign birds gathering under the Ottoman tent has been fully realised. For in a population of thirty-five millions, upwards of seven are Sclavonians, four claim Roman origin, two assert their Greek descent, the Arabs number nearly five, and there are two millions and a half of Armenians, fifteen hundred thousand Albanians, and a million of Kurds."—"Anadol," p. 45.

[2] Some of the Ottoman historians call her "Kameriyé," which means "Beautiful Moon."—Von Hammer, vol. i. p. 86.

vulture, and which is, in the East, the emblem of sovereignty and warlike power, as the eagle is with the nations of the West.

Othman is celebrated by the Oriental writers for his personal beauty, and for "his wondrous length and strength of arm." Like Artaxerxes Longimanus, of the old dynasty of Persian kings, and like the Highland chieftain of whom Wordsworth sang, Othman could touch his knees with his hands when he stood upright. He was unsurpassed in his skill and graceful carriage as a horseman; and the jet black colour of his hair, his beard, and eyebrows, gained him in youth the title of "Kara," that is to say, "Black" Othman. The epithet "Kara," which we shall often find in Turkish history,[1] is, when applied to a person, considered to imply the highest degree of manly beauty. His costume was simple as that of the first warriors of Islam. Like them he wore a turban of ample white linen, wreathed round a red centre. His loose flowing kaftan was of one colour, and had long open hanging sleeves. Such in outward appearance was the successful lover of the fair Malkhatoon, whose lineal descendant still rules the Ottoman Empire.

Othman's conquests were soon extended beyond the limits of Sultan-Œni, partly at the expense of rival Turkish chieftains, but principally by wresting fortress after fortress, and region after region from the Greek Empire. At the close of the thirteenth century of our era, the Ottoman head-quarters of empire were advanced as far north-westward as the city of Yenischeer, within a short march of the important Greek cities of Brusa and Nicæa, which were now the special objects of Turkish ambition.

It would, however, be unjust to represent Othman as merely an ambitious military adventurer, or to suppose that his whole career was marked by restless rapacity and aggressive violence against the neighbouring states. From 1291 A.D. to 1298, he was at peace; and the war that next followed was, at its commencement, a defensive one on his part, caused by the jealous aggressions of other Turkish Emirs, who envied his prosperity, and who were aided by some of the Greek commandants in the vicinity. Thus roused into action, Othman showed that his power had been strengthened, not corrupted by repose, and he smote his enemies in every direction. The effect of his arms in winning new subjects to his sway was materially aided by the reputation which he had honourably acquired, as a just lawgiver and judge, in whose dominions Greek

---

[1] E. g. Karadhissar, "The Black Castle;" Kara-Denis, "The Black Sea;" Kara Mustapha, "Black Mustapha;" Karadagh, "Black Mountain;" Kara-Su, "Black Water."

and Turk, Christian and Mahometan, enjoyed equal protection for property and person. It was about this time, A.D. 1299, that he coined money with his own effigy, and caused the public prayers to be said in his name. These among the Oriental nations are regarded as the distinctive marks of royalty.[1] The last prince of the family of Alaeddin, to which that of Othman had been indebted for its first foundation in Asia Minor, was now dead. There was no other among the various Emirs of that country who could compete with Othman for the headship of the whole Turkish population, and dominion over the whole peninsula, save only the Emir of Caramania.[2] A long and fierce struggle between the Ottoman and Caramanian princes for the ascendency, commenced in Othman's lifetime, and was protracted during the reigns of many of his successors. Othman himself had gained some advantages over his Caramanian rival; but the weak and wealthy possessions of the Byzantine Emperor in the north-east of Asia Minor were more tempting marks for his ambition than the Caramanian plains : and it was over Greek cities and armies that the chief triumphs of the last twenty-six years of Othman's life were achieved.

Some of Othman's counsellors hesitated at the entrance of the bold path of conquest on which their chief strode so firmly; but Othman silenced all remonstrance, and quelled all risk of dissension and mutiny by an act of prompt ferocity, which shows that the great ancestor of the Ottoman Sultans had, besides the traits of chivalrous and noble feelings which we have recorded, a full share of the ruthless cruelty, that has been the dark characteristic of the Turkish Royal House. Othman's uncle, the aged Dundar, who had marched with Ertoghrul from the Euphrates, seventy years before, was still alive, when Othman, in 1299, summoned a council of his principal followers, and announced to them his intention to attack the lord of the important Greek fortress of Kœprihissar. The old uncle opposed the enterprise; and urged the danger of provoking by such ambitious aggrandisement all the neighbouring princes, Turkish as well as Greek, to league against them for the destruction of their tribe. Enraged at the chilling caution of the grey-headed man, and, observing probably that others were beginning to share in it, Othman met the arrows of the tongue by the arrows of the bow. He spake not a word in

---

[1] Von Hammer discusses (vol. i. pp. 75, and 593) the question, whether these marks of sovereignty were assumed by Othman or his son Orchan. He comes to a different conclusion from that adopted above.

[2] Von Hammer, vol. i. p. 72.

reply, but he shot his old uncle dead upon the spot—a bloody lesson to all who should harbour thoughts of contradiction to the fixed will of so stern a lord.   The modern German historian, who recounts this scene, well observes that "This uncle's murder marks with terror the commencement of the Ottoman dominion, as the brother's murder that of Rome ; only the former rests on better historical evidence.   Edris, justly esteemed the most valuable historian of the Turks, who, at the beginning of his work, openly declares that, passing over in silence all that is reprehensible, he will only hand down to posterity the glorious deeds of the royal race of Othman, relates among the latter the murder of Dundar, with all the circumstances detailed above.   If then such murderous slaughter of their kindred be reckoned by the panegyrists of the Osmanlies among their praiseworthy acts, what are we to think of those which cannot be praised, and of which their history is there- fore silent ?"[1]

Kœprihissar was attacked, and fell ; and numerous other strong- holds in the vicinity of Nice soon shared the same fate.   In 1301, Othman encountered for the first time a regular Greek army, which was led against him by Muzaros, the commander of the guards of the Byzantine Emperor.   This important battle took place at Koyounhissar (called Baphœum by the Greeks) in the vicinity of Nicomedia.   Othman gained a complete victory ; and in the successful campaigns of the six following years, he carried his arms as far as the coast of the Black Sea, securing fortress after fortress, and hemming in the strong cities of Brusa, Nice, and Nicomedia (which yet were retained by the Greeks), with a chain of fortified posts, where his garrisons, under bold and skilful chiefs, were ever on the watch for the chance of a surprise or the mate- rial for a foray.   It was in vain that the Byzantine court sought to avert the pressure of this ever-active enemy, by procuring a Mongol army to attack Othman's southern dominions.   Othman sent his son Orchan against the invaders, and the young prince utterly defeated them.   Age and infirmity began now to press upon Othman, but his gallant son filled his place at the head of the troops with undiminished energy and success.   In 1326, the great city of Brusa surrendered to the Ottomans.   Othman was on his death-bed, at Sægud, the first town that his father Erto- ghrul had possessel, when his son effected this important con- quest ; but he lived long enough to hear the glad tidings, and to welcome the young hero.   The Oriental writers narrate the last

[1] Von Hammer, vol. i. p. 78.

scene of Othman's life, and profess to record his dying advice to his successor. The fair Malkhatoon had gone before him to the grave; but the two brave sons whom she had borne him, Orchan and Alaeddin, and a few of his veteran captains and sages, were at the monarch's death-bed. "My son," said Othman to Orchan, "I am dying; and I die without regret, because I leave such a successor as thou art. Be just; love goodness, and show mercy. Give equal protection to all thy subjects, and extend the law of the Prophet. Such are the duties of princes upon earth; and it is thus that they bring on them the blessings of Heaven." Then, as if he wished to take actual seisin of Brusa, and to associate himself with his son's glory, he directed that he should be buried there; and advised his son to make that city the seat of empire.[1] His last wishes were loyally complied with; and a stately mausoleum, which stood at Brusa until its destruction by fire in the present age, marked the last resting-place of Othman, and proved the pious reverence of his descendants. His banner and his sabre are still preserved in the treasury of the empire: and the martial ceremony of girding on that sabre is the solemn right, analogous to the coronations of Christendom, by which the Turkish Sultans are formally invested with sovereign power.

Othman is commonly termed the first Sultan of his race; but neither he nor his two immediate successors assumed more than the title of Emir. He had, at the time of his death, reigned as an independent Emir twenty-seven years, and had been chief of his tribe for thirty-nine years of his life of sixty-eight. His career fully displays the buoyant courage, the subtle watchfulness, the resolute decision, the strong common-sense, and the power of winning and wielding the affections and energies of other men, which are the usual attributes of the founders of empires. And, notwithstanding his blood-guiltiness in his uncle's death, we must believe him to have been eminently mild and gracious for an Oriental sovereign, from the traditional attachment with which his memory is still cherished by his nation, and which is expressed at the accession of each new Sultan by the formula of the people's prayer, "May he be as good as Othman."

[1] Von Hammer, vol. i. p. 86.

CHAPTER II.

ACCESSION OF ORCHAN—HIS VIZIER ALAEDDIN'S LEGISLATION—
THE JANISSARIES—CAPTURE OF NICE AND NICOMEDIA—DE-
SCENT ON EUROPE—CONQUEST OF SOLYMAN PACHA—HIS DEATH
AND ORCHAN'S DEATH.[1]

EMIR OTHMAN now slept at Brusa, and Emir Orchan reigned in
his stead.   Fratricide was not yet regarded as the necessary safeguard of the throne ; and Orchan earnestly besought his brother
Alaeddin to share with him his sovereignty and his wealth.
Alaeddin firmly refused to consent to any division of the empire,
and so contravene the will of their father, who had addressed
Orchan only as his successor.   Nor would Alaeddin accept more
of the paternal property than the revenues of a single village, near
Brusa.   Orchan then said to him, "Since, my brother, thou wilt
not take the flocks and the herds that I offer thee, be thou the
shepherd of my people ; be my Vizier."   The word "Vizier," in
the Ottoman language, means the bearer of a burden ; and
Alaeddin, in accepting the office, took on him, according to the
Oriental historians, his brother's burden of power.   Alaeddin did
not, like many of his successors in that office, often command in
person the armies of his race ; but he occupied himself most
efficiently with the foundation and management of the civil and
military institutions of his country.

According to some authorities, it was in his time, and by his
advice, that the semblance of vassalage to the ruler of Koniah, by
stamping money with his effigy, and using his name in the public
prayers, was discontinued by the Ottomans.[2]   These changes are
more correctly referred by others to Othman himself ; but all the
Oriental writers concur in attributing to Alaeddin the introduction
of laws, which endured for centuries, respecting the costume of the
various subjects of the empire, and of laws which created a stand-

[1] See Von Hammer, books 3, 4.
[2] See the authorities collected in Von Hammer, as cited in note to p. 9,
supra.

ing army of regular troops, and provided funds for its support. It was, above all, by his advice and that of a contemporary Turkish statesman, that the celebrated corps of Janissaries was formed, an institution which European writers erroneously fix at a later date, and ascribe to Amurath I.

Alaeddin, by his military legislation, may be truly said to have organised victory for the Ottoman race. He originated for the Turks a standing army of regularly paid and disciplined infantry and horse, a full century before Charles VII. of France established his fifteen permanent companies of men-at-arms, which are generally regarded as the first standing army known in modern history. Orchan's predecessors, Ertoghrul and Othman, had made war at the head of the armed vassals and volunteers, who thronged on horseback to their prince's banner, when summoned for each expedition, and who were disbanded as soon as the campaign was over. Alaeddin determined to ensure and improve future successes, by forming a corps of paid infantry, which should be kept in constant readiness for service. These troops were called Yaya, or Piadé; and they were divided into tens, hundreds, and thousands, under their respective decurions, centurions, and colonels. Their pay was high; and their pride soon made them objects of anxiety to their sovereign. Orchan wished to provide a check to them, and he took counsel for this purpose with his brother Alaeddin and Kara Khalil Tschendereli, who was connected with the royal house by marriage. Tschendereli laid before his master and the vizier a project, out of which arose the renowned corps of the Janissaries, so long the scourge of Christendom; so long, also, the terror of their own sovereigns; and which was finally extirpated by the Sultan himself, in our own age. Tschendereli proposed to Orchan to create an army entirely composed of Christian children, who should be forced to adopt the Mahometan religion. Black[1] Khalil argued thus: "The conquered are the property of the conqueror, who is the lawful master of them, of their lands, of their goods, of their wives, and of their children. We have a right to do what we will with our own; and the treatment which I propose is not only lawful, but benevolent. By enforcing the conversion of these captive children to the true faith, and enrolling them in the ranks of the army of the true believers, we consult both their temporal and eternal interests; for, is it not written in the Koran that all children are, at their birth, naturally disposed to Islam?" He also alleged that the for-

---

[1] See note, p. 8.

mation of a Mahometan army out of Christian children would
induce other Christians to adopt the creed of the Prophet; so
that the new force would be recruited, not only out of the children
of the conquered nations, but out of a crowd of their Christian
friends and relations, who would come as volunteers to join the
Ottoman ranks.

Acting on this advice, Orchan selected out of the families of the
Christians whom he had conquered, a thousand of the finest boys.
In the next year a thousand more were taken; and this annual
enrolment of a thousand Christian children was continued for three
centuries, until the reign of Sultan Mahomet IV., in 1648. When
the prisoners made in the campaign of the year did not supply a
thousand serviceable boys, the number was completed by a levy
on the families of the Christian subjects of the Sultan. This
was changed in the time of Mahomet IV., and the corps was
thenceforth recruited from among the children of Janissaries
and native Turks; but during the conquering period of the Ottoman power, the institution of the Janissaries, as designed by
Alaeddin and Tschendereli, was maintained in full vigour.

The name of Yeni Tscheri, which means "new troops," and
which European writers have turned into Janissaries, was given to
Orchan's young corps by the Dervish Hadji Beytarch. This dervish was renowned for sanctity; and Orchan, soon after he had
enrolled his first band of involuntary boyish proselytes, led them
to the dwelling-place of the saint, and asked him to give them his
blessing and a name. The dervish drew the sleeve of his mantle
over the head of one in the first rank, and then said to the Sultan,
"The troop which thou hast created shall be called Yeni Tscheri.
Their faces shall be white and shining, their right arms shall be
strong, their sabres shall be keen, and their arrows sharp. They
shall be fortunate in fight, and they shall never leave the battle-
field save as conquerors." In memory of that benediction, the
Janissaries ever wore, as part of their uniform, a cap of white felt,
like that of the dervish, with a strip of woollen hanging down
behind, to represent the sleeve of the holy man's mantle, that had
been laid on their comrade's neck.

The Christian children, who were to be trained as Janissaries,
were usually chosen at a tender age. They were torn from their
parents, trained to renounce the faith in which they were born and
baptised, and to profess the creed of Mahomet. They were then
carefully educated for a soldier's life. The discipline to which
they were subjected was severe. They were taught the most
implicit obedience; and they were accustomed to bear without

repining fatigue, pain, and hunger. But liberal honours and prompt promotion were the sure rewards of docility and courage. Cut off from all ties of country, kith, and kin, but with high pay and privileges, with ample opportunities for military advancement, and for the gratification of the violent, the sensual, and the sordid passions of their animal natures amid the customary atrocities of successful warfare, this military brotherhood grew up to be the strongest and fiercest instrument of imperial ambition, which remorseless fanaticism, prompted by the most subtle statecraft, ever devised upon earth.

The Ottoman historians eulogise with one accord the sagacity and piety of the founders of this institution. They reckon the number of conquerors whom it gave to earth, and of heirs of paradise whom it gave to heaven, on the hypothesis that, during three centuries, the stated number of a thousand Christian children, neither more nor less, was levied, converted, and enlisted. They boast, accordingly, that three hundred thousand children were delivered from the torments of hell by being made Janissaries. But Von Hammer calculates, from the increase in the number of these troops under later Sultans, that at least half a million of young Christians must have been thus made, first the helpless victims, and then the cruel ministers of Mahometan power.

After the organisation of the Janissaries, Alaeddin regulated that of the other corps of the army. In order that the soldier should have an interest, not only in making, but in preserving conquests, it was determined that the troops should receive allotments of land in the subjugated territories. The regular infantry, the Piadé, had at first received pay in money ; but they now had lands given to them on tenure of military service, and they were also under the obligation of keeping in good repair the public roads that led near their grounds. The irregular infantry, which had neither pay like the Janissaries, nor lands like the Piadé, was called Azab, which means "light." The lives of these undisciplined bands were held of little value ; and the Azabs were thrown forward to perish in multitudes at the commencement of a battle or a siege. It was over their bodies that the Janissaries usually marched to the decisive charge or the final assault.

The cavalry was distributed by Alaeddin, like the infantry, into regular and irregular troops. The permanent corps of paid cavalry was divided into four squadrons, organised like those which the Caliph Omar instituted for the guard of the Sacred Standard. The whole corps at first consisted of only 2400 horsemen ; but under Solyman the Great the number was raised to

4000. They marched on the right and left of the Sultan; they camped round his tent at night, and they were his body-guard in battle. One of these regiments of Royal Horse-guards was called the Turkish Spahis, a term applied to cavalry soldiers generally, but also specially denoting these select horse-guards. Another regiment was called the Silihdars, meaning the "vassal cavalry." A third was called the Ouloufedji, meaning the "paid horsemen;" and the fourth was called Ghoureba, meaning "the foreign horse." Besides this permanently embodied corps of paid cavalry, Alaeddin formed a force of horsemen, who received grants of land like the Piadé. As they paid no taxes for the lands which they thus held, they were termed Moselliman, which means "tax-free." They were commanded by Sandjak Beys (princes of standards), by Binbaschi (chiefs of thousands), and Soubaschi (chiefs of hundreds). There were other holders of the grand and petty fiefs which were called Ziamets and Timars. These terms will be adverted to hereafter, when we reach the period at which the Turkish feudal system was more fully developed and defined. But in the earliest times, their holders were bound to render military service on horseback, when summoned by their sovereign; and they were arrayed under banners, in thousands and in hundreds, like the Mosellimans. In addition to the regular and feudal cavalry, there were the Akindji, or irregular light horse, receiving neither pay nor lands, but dependent on plunder, who were still called together in multitudes, whenever an Ottoman army was on the march; and the terror which these active and ferocious marauders spread far and wide beyond the regular line of operations, made the name of the Akindji as much known and dreaded in Christendom, as that of the Janissaries and Spahis.

Orchan had captured the city of Nicomedia in the first year of his reign (1326); and with the new resources for warfare which the administrative genius of his brother placed at his command, he speedily signalised his reign by conquests still more important. The great city of Nice (second to Constantinople only in the Greek Empire) surrendered to him in 1330. Orchan gave the command of it to his eldest son, Solyman Pacha, who had directed the operations of the siege. Numerous other advantages were gained over the Greeks: and the Turkish prince of Karasi (the ancient Mysia), who had taken up arms against the Ottomans, was defeated; and his capital city, Berghama (the ancient Pergamus), and his territory, annexed to Orchan's dominions. On the conquest of Karasi, in the year 1336 of our era, nearly the whole of the north-west of Asia Minor was included in the Ottoman

Empire; and the four great cities of Brusa, Nicomedia, Nice, and Pergamus had become strongholds of its power.

A period of twenty years, without further conquests, and without war, followed the acquisition of Karasi. During this time the Ottoman sovereign was actively occupied in perfecting the civil and military institutions which his brother had introduced; in securing internal order, in founding and endowing mosques and schools, and in the construction of vast public edifices, which yet attest the magnificence and piety of Orchan. It is indeed a remarkable trait in the characters of the first princes of the Ottoman dynasty, that, unlike the generality of conquerors, especially of Asiatic conquerors, they did not hurry on from one war to another in ceaseless avidity for fresh victories and new dominions; but, on the contrary, they were not more eager to seize, than they were cautious and earnest to consolidate. They paused over each subdued province, till, by assimilation of civil and military institutions, it was fully blended into the general nationality of their empire. They thus gradually moulded, in Asia Minor, an homogeneous and a stable power; instead of precipitately heaping together a motley mass of ill-arranged provinces and discordant populations. To this policy the long endurance of the Ottoman Empire, compared with other Oriental empires of both ancient and modern times, is greatly to be ascribed. And the extent to which this policy was followed in Asia Minor, compared with their subsequent practice in European Turkey, in Syria, and in Egypt, may have conduced in giving to the Ottomans a firmer hold on the first-named country, than they possess on their territories westward of the Hellespont and southward of Mount Taurus. Every traveller notes the difference; the Ottomans themselves acknowledge it; and Anatolia (a name generally though not accurately used as co-extensive with that of Asia Minor) is regarded by the modern Turks as their stronghold in the event of further national disasters. They call it emphatically, "The last Home of the Faithful."[1] The facts (which have been already mentioned) of the general diffusion of Turkish populations over Asia Minor, before Othman's time, must unquestionably have greatly promoted the solidity as well as the extent of the dominion which he and his successor there established; but the far-sighted policy, with which they tempered their ambition, was also an efficient cause of permanent strength; and their remote descendants still experience its advantageous operation.

[1] See "Anadol," p. 228; and Ubicini, vol. ii. p. 523.

2

The friendly relations which Orchan formed with the Emperor Andronicus, and maintained (though not uninterruptedly) with that prince and some of his successors, contributed to give a long period of twenty years general repose to the Ottoman power. But in the civil wars which distracted the last ages and wasted the last resources of the Greek Empire, the auxiliary arms of the Turkish princes were frequently called over and employed in Europe. The Emperor Cantacuzene, in the year 1346, recognised in Orchan the most powerful sovereign of the Turks; and he hoped to attach the Ottoman forces permanently to his interests by giving his daughter in marriage to their ruler, notwithstanding the difference of creed, and the disparity of years between the young princess and the old Turk, who was now a widower of the age of sixty. The pomp of the nuptials between Orchan and Theodora is elaborately described by the Byzantine writers; but in the next year, during which the Ottoman bridegroom visited his imperial father-in-law at Scutari, the suburb of Constantinople on the Asiatic side of the Bosphorus, scenes of a less pleasing character to the Greeks ensued. Orchan's presence protected the Greek Emperor and his subjects during the display of festive splendour which Scutari exhibited at the meeting of the sovereigns; but when Orchan had returned to his Bithynian capital, some Ottoman bands crossed the Hellespont, and pillaged several towns in Thrace; but they were at last, after a series of sanguinary encounters, all killed or taken by the superior forces sent against them.

Not long afterwards, the war that raged between the two great maritime republics of Venice and Genoa along almost every coast of the Mediterranean and its connected seas, was the immediate cause of hostilities between the troops of Orchan and those of his father-in-law; and led to the settlement of the Ottomans in Europe. The Genoese possessed the European suburb of Constantinople, called Galata; and the Bosphorus was one of the scenes on which the most obstinate contests were maintained between their fleets and those of their rivals. Orchan hated the Venetians, whose fleets had insulted his seaward provinces, and who had met his diplomatic overtures with contempt, as if coming from an insignificant barbarous chieftain. The Venetians were allies of Cantacuzene; but Orchan sent an auxiliary force across the straits to Galata, which there co-operated with the Genoese. Orchan also aided the Emperor's other son-in-law, John Palæologus, in the civil war that was kept up between him and the Greek Emperor. In the midst of the distress and confusion with which the Byzantine Empire was now oppressed, Orchan's eldest son, Solyman Pacha, struck a bold blow in behalf of his own race, which gave the Turks a permanent establishment on the European side of the Hellespont. This important event in the world's history took place in 1356. The Ottoman writers pass over in silence the previous incursions of the Turks into Europe, which gained no conquest and led to no definite advantage ; but they dwell fully on this expedition of Solyman, and adorn it with poetic legends of the vision that appeared to the young chieftain as he mused on the sea-shore near the ruins of Cyzicus. They tell how the crescent of the moon rose before him as the emblem of his race, and united the continents of Europe and Asia with a chain of silver light, while temples and palaces floated up out of the great deep, and mysterious voices blended with the sounding sea, exciting in his heart a yearning for predestined enterprise, and a sense of supernatural summons.[1] The dream may have been both the effect of previous schemings, and the immediate stimulant that made Solyman put his scheming into act. With but thirty-nine of his chosen warriors, he embarked at night in a Genoese bark on the Asiatic side of the Hellespont, and surprised the Castle of Tzympe, on the opposite coast. Reinforcements soon pushed across to the adventurers ; and in three days Tzympe was garrisoned by three thousand Ottoman troops.

At this crisis, Cantacuzene was so severely pressed by his rival John Palæologus, that, instead of trying to dislodge the invaders from Tzympe, or even remonstrating against their occupation of that fortress, he implored the help of Orchan against his domestic enemy. Orchan gave up his brother-in-law's cause, and provided assistance to the old Emperor. But he ordered that assistance to be administered by Solyman, the conqueror of Tzympe, an auxiliary the most formidable to those with whom he was to co-operate. Ten thousand more Turks were sent across to Solyman, who defeated the Sclavonic forces which Palæologus had brought into the empire : but the victors never left the continent on which they had conquered.

Cantacuzene offered Solyman ten thousand ducats to retire from Tzympe. The sum was agreed on ; but before the ransom was paid, a terrible earthquake shook the whole district of Thrace, and threw down the walls of its fenced cities. The Greeks trembled at this visitation of Providence ; and the Turks saw in it the interposition of Heaven in their favour, and thought that

[1] Von Hammer, vol. i. p. 132.

the hand of God was smoothing the path for their conquest of the Promised Land. Two of Solyman's captains, Adjé Bey, and Ghasi Fasil, instantly occupied the important town of Gallipoli, marching in over the walls which the earthquake had shattered, and unresisted by the awe-struck inhabitants. The fields in the neighbourhood still are called after Adjé; and the tombs of these two captains of the Ottoman host are yet to be seen in Gallipoli. They were buried on the scene of their great exploit; and Turkish pilgrims throng hither in veneration of the warriors, who gave to their race the strong city, the key of the Hellespont, the gate of easy passage into Europe.

Solyman, on hearing that his troops had occupied Gallipoli, refused to give up Tzympe; and threw large colonies of Turks and Arabs across the straits, which he planted in the territory which had been thus acquired. The fortifications of Gallipoli were repaired, and that important post was strongly garrisoned. Solyman took possession of other places in the Thracian Chersonese, which he strengthened with new walls and secured with detachments of his best troops. The Greek Emperor made a formal complaint of these aggressions to Orchan, who replied that it was not the force of arms that had opened the Greek cities to his son, but the will of God, manifested in the earthquake. The Emperor rejoined that the question was not how the Turks had marched into the cities, but whether they had any right to retain them. Orchan asked time to consider the subject; and afterwards made some proposals for negotiating the restoration of the cities; but he had firmly resolved to take full advantage of the opportunities for aggrandising the Ottoman power, which now were afforded by the basis for operations in Europe which had been acquired, and by the perpetual dissensions that raged between Cantacuzene and his son-in-law Palæologus; each of whom was continually soliciting Orchan's aid against the other, and obtaining that aid according to what seemed best for the interests of the Turkish sovereign—the real enemy of them both.

Orchan only lived three years after the capture of Tzympe and Gallipoli: his son Solyman, to whom he owed those conquests, and in whom he had hoped to leave a successor who should surpass all the glories hitherto won by the house of Othman, had died before him. An accidental fall from his horse, while he was engaged in the favourite Turkish sport of falconry, caused the young conqueror's death. Solyman was not buried at Brusa; but, by Orchan's order, a tomb was built for him on the shore of the Hellespont, over which he had led his race to a second empire.

Orchan died in the year 1359 of our era, at the age of seventy-five, after a reign of thirty-three years, during which the most important civil and military institutions of his nation were founded, and the Crescent was not only advanced over many of the fairest provinces of Asia, but was also planted on the European continent, whence its enemies have hitherto vainly sought to dislodge it during five centuries.

CHAPTER III.

AMURATH I.—CAPTURE OF ADRIANOPLE—BATTLE OF THE MARIZZA
—CONQUESTS IN EUROPE AND ASIA—VICTORY OF KOSSOVA—
DEATH OF AMURATH—BAJAZET'S ACCESSION—CONQUESTS—
DEPRAVITY OF MANNERS—VICTORY OF NICOPOLIS—TIMOUR
—DEFEAT OF BAJAZET AT ANGORA.[1]

THE death of Solyman Pacha had opened to his younger brother
Amurath (or, as the Orientals name him, Murad), the inheritance
of the Ottoman throne. Amurath was forty years of age when
he succeeded his father, Orchan; and he reigned thirty years over
the Ottomans in prosperity and glory. His first projects after his
accession were to extend the European conquests of his father and
brother; but he was checked for a time by the enmity of the
Prince of Caramania, who stirred up a revolt in the Ottoman
dominions in the centre of Asia Minor. Amurath marched an
army rapidly to the scene of the insurrection, which he completely
quelled. He then (in 1360) led his troops to the passage of the
Hellespont; and commenced a series of victories in Europe, which
were only terminated by his death on the field of battle at Kossova
in 1389. Besides wresting from the Greeks numerous places of
secondary value, Amurath captured, in 1361, the great city of
Adrianople, which thenceforth became the capital of the Ottoman
dominions in Europe, until Constantinople fell before Mahomet
II. Pushing his conquests towards Macedonia and the Hæmus,
Amurath next took Sagræ and Philippopolis.

The Turkish armies, like the ancient Roman legions, found a
principal part of their booty in the prisoners they made, and who
were all destined for sale as slaves. The number of prisoners had
increased to such a multitude during these campaigns of Amurath,
that one of his statesmen pointed out to him the importance of
steadily enforcing the royal prerogative (neglected by his predecessors) of taking a fifth part of the spoil. This was thenceforth
exercised by the Sultans, who sometimes took their double tithe

See Von Hammer, books v. vi. vii. viii.

in kind; but more frequently received a stated sum per head, as the fifth of the value of each slave.   In after ages, when a Christian nation remonstrated against this practice, a formal stipulation, excepting prisoners of war of that nation from such liability, was usually established by express treaty.

Hitherto the Turkish victories in Europe had been won over the feeble Greeks; but the Ottomans now came in contact with the far more warlike Sclavonic tribes, which had founded kingdoms and principalities in Servia and Bosnia.   Amurath also menaced the frontiers of Wallachia and Hungary.   The Roman See, once so energetic in exciting the early crusades, had disregarded the progress of the new Mahometan power, so long as the heretical Greeks were the only sufferers beneath its arms.   But Hungary, a country that professed spiritual obedience to the Pope, a branch of Latin Christendom, was now in peril; and Pope Urban V. preached up a crusade against the infidel Turks.   The King of Hungary, the princes of Servia, of Bosnia and Wallachia, leagued together to drive the Ottomans out of Europe; and their forces marched towards Adrianople until they crossed the river Marizza at a point not more than two days' journey from that city.   Lalaschahin, who then was in command of the Ottoman forces in Europe, was unable to assemble an army equal in numbers to that of the confederate chieftains, who mustered more than twenty thousand men.   But the Christians, in the pride of assured victory, neglected all military precautions against their enemy; and suddenly, while they were all engaged in a nightly revel, the sound of the Turkish drums and fifes,[1] and the shouts of "Allah" were heard amid the darkness.   Their active enemy was on them; and they fled in panic rout.   "They were caught," says Seadeddin, the Oriental historian, "even as wild beasts in their lair.   They were driven before us as flames are driven before the wind, till plunging into the Marizza they perished in its waters."   Such was the issue of the first encounter of the Hungarians and Servians with the Turks; and centuries of further disaster and suffering to the Christians were to follow.

A long list of battles won, and towns taken by Amurath or his generals between the year of the battle of Marizza, in 1363, and the year 1376, may be found in the Turkish historians.   In the last-mentioned year, the capture of the strong city of Nissa by the Ottomans, forced the Prince of Servia to beg peace, which was granted to him on the condition of supplying a tribute of a thou-

[1] All the European nations have borrowed their military music from the Turks.   See Von Hammer, Supplement.

sand pounds of silver, and a thousand horse-soldiers every year. Sisvan, the King of the Bulgarians, had also taken part in the hostilities waged by the European Christians against Amurath, and he also was compelled to sue for mercy. Sisvan disliked paying money, and preferred to obtain peace by giving up his daughter in marriage to the conqueror.

Amurath now rested from warfare for six years, during which time he employed himself unremittingly in the internal affairs of his state. He improved the organisation of his military force, and completed the feudal system by which grants of land in each conquered country were made to Mahometans, on condition that each district so granted should supply one or more Spahis or armed horsemen in time of war. These granted districts, or fiefs (as we may term them by applying the phraseology of mediæval Europe) were classified into minor fiefs, called Timars; and grand fiefs, called Ziamets. We shall revert hereafter to the consideration of the effect of these feudal institutions both on the conquering and the conquered races. Amurath also formed out of the Christian subjects of his dominions a corps of camp-followers called Woinaks; on whom devolved all the humble and laborious duties of the barracks, the encampment, and the march; such as cleaning the stables and attending to the baggage-wagons. The red colour was now chosen for the banner of the Spahis, and became the national colour of the Ottoman armies.

During this season of peace Amurath was still solicitous to extend his dominions; and he used for that purpose his political and diplomatic skill in forming such matrimonial alliances for members of his family, as seemed to promise the future acquisition of new provinces. He married his eldest son Bajazet to the daughter of the Prince of Kermian, a Turkish state in Asia Minor, that adjoined the Ottoman territories in that country. The bride brought as her dowry a new kingdom to the throne of Othman. Amurath's own daughter Nifisay was given in marriage to the powerful Turkish Prince of Caramania. Amurath himself, and two of his sons, at a later period, permitted each a Byzantine princess to be added to their list of wives. Ever since the capture of Adrianople the Greek Emperor had cringed to the Ottoman sovereign, and sought eagerly to keep up such treaties with his infidel neighbour, as would promise him a quiet reign, though upon mere sufferance, at Constantinople. But Palæologus hated him whom he feared; and the Greek Emperor vainly, in 1380, underwent the expense and ignominy of a voyage from Constantinople to Rome, where he sought, by the most abject submissions to the papacy, to obtain a new crusade by the Frankish kings of Christendom against the Mahometan invaders of its eastern regions. In terror at the wrath which this attempt was likely to excite in Amurath, Palæologus sent his third son Theodorus to the Ottoman court, with a humble request that he might be allowed to serve in the ranks of the Turkish army. This servile humility allayed the anger of Amurath. Andronicus, another son of the Greek Emperor, formed about the same time a friendship with Prince Saoudji, Amurath's eldest son, which led to fatal results. The two young princes persuaded each other, and themselves, that they were neglected by their fathers, and that their brethren were unduly preferred to them. They seized an opportunity for insurrection, given by the absence of Amurath from Adrianople, whence he had been summoned by the tidings of disturbances in Asia, and during which he had left Saoudji in command of all the Ottoman dominions in Europe. They openly revolted, and established their joint camp near Constantinople, where Palæologus lay trembling at their threats. Amurath, on hearing of the insurrection, instantly hurried back across the straits, and summoned the Greek Emperor to appear before him to answer for his son's conduct. Palæologus earnestly disavowed all participation in his schemes; and, that he might completely allay the suspicions of Amurath, he promised to join him in acting against their sons, and agreed that the rebels should lose their eyes for their crime. The Ottoman army then advanced to a little stream near Apicidion, behind which the insurgent princes had taken post. At nightfall, without any escort, Amurath spurred his horse across the water, and called out to the soldiery in the rebel camp to return to their duty upon promise of pardon. At the sound of the well-known voice of their old sovereign, which had so often cheered them to victory, the troops of Saoudji deserted the two princes, and flocking round Amurath, implored forgiveness for the treason which they had been led into by his viceroy. Saoudji and Andronicus escaped into the town of Didymoticha with a small band of Turks and of young Greek nobles, who had taken part in their plot. They were besieged, and starved into surrender. Amurath had his own son led before him; and after the prince's eyes had been put out, so that the agreement between the imperial sires might be kept, Saoudji was beheaded in his father's presence. The young Greek nobles were tied together in knots of two or three at a time, and flung into the river Marizza, while Amurath sat by, and smiled with grim satisfaction at the rapidity with which they sank beneath the waves.

3

Having found the fathers of some of the youthful rebels, he made
them kill their children with their own hands. Two parents refused the horrible office, and were themselves slain for their disobedience. When his vengeance had been satiated by these
spectacles, Amurath sent young Andronicus in chains to his father,
and bade Palæologus deal with him as he himself had dealt with
Saoudji. The Greek Emperor, dreading his stern ally, caused his
child's eyes to be scalded with burning vinegar. Amurath was
pleased to consider this a sufficient obedience to his behest ; and
did not take notice that Andronicus's life was spared, or that the
horrid puishment of blinding was so imperfectly performed, as to
leave the wretched prisoner some faint power of vision.

Notwithstanding the Ottoman ruler's policy in forming a bond
of marriage between his house and that of the Turkish ruler of
Caramania, a war broke out in 1387 between these two powerful
rivals for the headship of the Turkish race in Asia Minor. A
great battle was fought between them at Iconium, in which the
valour of Prince Bajazet on the side of the Ottomans was particularly signalised. He is said, by the lightning-like rapidity and
violence of his charge upon the enemy on that day, to have
acquired the surname of Yilderim, or "the Lightning," by which
he is known in history. It is an appellation that will remind
the classical reader of the Ptolemy Ceraunus of the Græco-Mace-
donian era ; and still more appropriately of Hamilcar Barcas, the
father of the great Hannibal.

The Caramanian prince was utterly defeated at Iconium, and
owed the preservation of his life and kingdom to the interposition
of his wife, who succeeded in calming the anger of her victorious
father, and induced him to be satisfied with his defeated rival
acknowledging his superiority, and kissing his hand in token of
submission. Amurath dismissed his army and repaired to Brusa,
where he hoped to enjoy a period of repose. He refused to be
roused again by the temptation of conquering and annexing the
little independent territory of Tekké, that lay near his Asiatic
dominions. One of his generals advised an expedition against
that place ; but Amurath rejected the proposal with disdain.
"The Prince of Tekké," said he, "is too poor and feeble. I
should feel ashamed in making war on him. A lion does not
hunt flies." But the old lion was soon roused from his rest, to
encounter far more formidable foes, who were leagued together to
tear his European conquests from his grasp.

The Ottoman dominions in Europe at this time (1388) comprised nearly the whole of ancient Thrace and modern Roumelia.

Some important acquisitions beyond the boundary of this province had also been effected ; and the conquerors pursued the system of planting colonies of Turks and Arabs from Asia in the conquered districts, while they removed large portions of the old population. By this, and by their custom of recruiting their Janissaries from the flower of the Christian children, they excited the alarm of the neighbouring Christian states, who saw a fierce race, alien to them in blood and in creed, thus taking root on their frontier, and organising the resources of the subdued country for future military enterprises.   The Bulgarians, the Servians, the Bosnians, all of Sclavonic blood,[1] now united in one great national effort against the intrusive Turks.   Servia was chief of the movement.   She could not forget her proud position, which she had held before the Ottomans had come into Europe, when her great King Stephen Dushan ruled victoriously, from Belgrade to the Marizza, from the Black Sea to the Adriatic, and assumed the high title of " Emperor of the Roumelians, the Macedonian Christ-loving Czar."[2] Beside these Sclavonic nations, the Skipetars,[3] of Albania now armed against the common enemy from Asia.   The powers thus allied against Amurath expected also and received assistance from the semi-Roman population of Wallachia and from the Magyars of Hungary, who, like their kinsmen the Ottoman Turks,[4] had won by force a settlement in Europe ; but who, unlike the Turks, adopted the creed and the civilisation of European Christendom, and became for ages its chivalrous defenders. Sclavonic Poland also sent aid to her sister Sclavonic kingdom of the south.   No further succour was obtainable.   The other great kingdom of that family of nations, Russia, lay at this time in wretched slavery under the Mongols.   The great kingdoms of western Christendom heard with indifference the sufferings and the perils, to which its eastern portions were exposed by the new Mahometan power.   The old crusading enthusiasm had faded away ; nor could, indeed, the immediate stimulant of a cry to the rescue of the Holy Land be employed against the Ottomans, who had not yet approached the Syrian territory.   The internal condition, at the latter part of the fourteenth century, of each of the great European states, which had supplied the heroes of the early crusades, was peculiarly unfavourable for the efforts of those who

[1] For their ethnology, see Latham's " Ethnology of Europe."
[2] See Ranke's " History of Servia," p. 16.
[3] See Latham, p. 13.
[4] For the connection between the Magyars, the Huns of Attila, and the Ottoman Turks, see Latham.

strove to arouse their descendants to a similar expedition. And
the personal character of the sovereigns of England, France, and
Germany, in 1388, forbade all hopes of seeing the examples of
Richard Cœur de Lion, of Edward I., of Philip Augustus,
of St. Louis, of Conrad, and Frederick II., imitated by
their successors. The weak and worthless Richard II. was
sovereign of England; the imbecile Charles VI. was enthroned
at Paris. Both countries were the scenes of perpetual strife
between powerful nobles, and of general confusion and lawlessness. The German Empire, under the coarse and dissolute
Wenceslaus, was in a still more wretched condition : and the great
civil war between the confederations of brigand knights and the
burghers of the free cities was raging from the Danube to the
Rhine. The Christian princes of Spain were still fully occupied
with their long struggles against their own Moorish invaders. The
difficulty of uniting the powers of the West in any enterprise
against the common foe of their religion was augmented tenfold
by the schism in the Papacy, which divided the whole of Western
Christendom. Consciences were perplexed, zeal was distracted
and chilled, scepticism and indifference were created by the conflicting pretensions and behests of two Popes, one at Avignon,
and one at Rome ; each of whom anathematised the other and his
adherents with assiduity and animosity at least equal to any that
could be displayed against the Ottomans.

But although the great powers of Western Christendom stood
aloof from the struggle made by the Christian nations of the East
to free themselves from the pressure of the Ottoman conquests,
Amurath saw that the league which the ruler of Servia had succeeded in organising against him, was one which it would tax his
utmost energies to encounter. He made full and cautious arrangements for the military protection and civil government of the
Asiatic states, and then recrossed the Hellespont, with the design
of baffling the superior resources of his enemies by the celerity of
his operations. The Bulgarians and Servians had commenced the
war by falling upon an Ottoman army which was moving through
Bosnia. They destroyed fifteen out of twenty thousand Turks by
the impetuous suddenness of their attack, and the great superiority
of their numbers. After this vigorous blow, the Christians relaxed in their exertions. The vacillations and delays, which
usually mark the movements of a confederacy, kept the forces of
the greater number of the allies inactive during several months of
the year 1389 ; while their vigorous and resolute adversary was
pouring his forces into Bulgaria, and completing the conquest of

that important member of their league. Amurath was especially
incensed against Sisvan, the Bulgarian King, who had kept up the
appearance of submissive devotion to the Turkish interests, until
he suddenly joined the Servians in the attack upon his son-in-law's
forces in Bosnia. The necessity of making regulations for the defence and internal government of Roumelia during the war, and
of calling into active service and arranging the full military force
of the province, detained Amurath himself for a short time in
Adrianople; but he sent his general, Ali Pacha, forward into Bulgaria with an army of thirty thousand men. The Turks now
(1389) marched northward to conquest across that mountain chain
of the Balkan, which their descendants in the present century
trust to so earnestly, as a barrier against attacks upon themselves.
Ali Pacha advanced with the main army through the passes of
Nadir Derbend [1] upon Schumla, so celebrated in modern Russian
wars. Schumla surrendered to the Turks, nor has it yet ever
been retaken from them. Tirnova and Pravadi were also captured by Ali Pacha and his lieutenant, Yakshibey; and the Bulgarian King took refuge in Nicopolis on the Danube. Ali Pacha
besieged him there, and Sisvan begged for peace. Amurath
granted it, on condition that Silistria should be ceded to him, and
that the conquered Sisvan should pay him a regular tribute. But
disputes broke out as to the fulfilment of the terms of peace; the
war was recommenced, and the Turks stormed the strong places of
Dridja and Hirschova. Besieged again in Nicopolis, the Bulgarian
King surrendered at discretion. His life was spared; but Bulgaria
was now annexed to the Ottoman Empire, which thus advanced
its northern frontier to the Danube.

The Servian King Lazarus, alarmed at the destruction of his
confederate, now earnestly collected the forces of the remaining
members of the anti-Turkish league, and prepared for a resolute
struggle. So large was the force which he drew around him, that
in the pride and confidence of his heart he sent Amurath a formal
challenge to a decisive battle. Amurath had now taken in person
the command of the Turkish army, and continued his policy of
acting on the offensive, and making his enemy's territory the seat
of war. He marched westward from Bulgaria through a difficult
and mountainous country to the neighbourhood of Kossova, on
the frontiers of Servia and Bosnia, where his enemies had collected
their troops. The plain of Kossova, on which the fate of Servia

---

[1] See the excellent description of the passes of the Balkan and the fortresses near them, in Colonel Chesney's "Narrative of the Turko-Russian
Campaigns of 1828-29."

was decided on the 27th of August, 1389, is traversed by the little stream of the Schinitza. On the north side of this rivulet the combined levies of Servia, Bosnia, and Albania, with their auxiliaries from Poland, Hungary, and Wallachia, were arrayed, in numbers far exceeding those of the troops which Amurath had in hand for battle. According to the Ottoman historians, Amurath summoned a council of war to deliberate whether he should attack the enemy that seemed so superior in force. Several of the Turkish chiefs advised that he should draw up all the camels of their baggage-train in a line before the army, so as to serve as a living rampart, and to disorder the enemy's horse by the sight and smell of those animals.[1] Amurath's eldest son, Prince Bajazet, opposed this project : he fiercely urged that Heaven had ever manifestly favoured the arms of the house of Othman, and that to employ such artifices would show a distrust of Providence. "The honour of our flag," said he, "requires that those who march beneath the Crescent, should meet their enemy face to face, let that enemy be who he will." The grand vizier gave his vote also for open fighting, on the authority of what he believed to be a supernatural warning. He had opened the Koran at random, and had fallen upon the verse, "O Prophet, fight the unbelievers and the hypocrites." He had tried these *sortes Koranicas* again, and the verse which then presented itself was, "Verily a large host is often beaten by a weaker one." Another officer, the Beylerbey (lord of lords) Timourtash, also opposed the scheme of the camels, on reasons not of religion, but of common sense. He said that it was probable that the camels themselves would take fright at the sight and sound of the hostile cavalry, and that then they would rush back on the Turkish ranks, and create there the confusion which it was wished to cause amid the enemy. Night put an end to the deliberations of the council, without any settled plan being formed. Amurath had observed that the wind blew from the side of the enemy, wafting clouds of dust, which threatened to cause serious disadvantage to his troops in the action. He spent the whole night in earnest prayer for the aid of Heaven,[2] and asked that it might be vouchsafed him to close his life in fighting for the true faith ;—the only death that ensures the martyr's prize of eternal felicity.

In the other camp the discussions of the confederate princes

---

[1] See Herodotus, Clio, 78, 80, for the employment of this very stratagem by Cyrus against the Lydian cavalry at the battle of Sardis, B.C. 546.

[2] Von Hammer, vol. i. p. 176, cites the Turkish historians who narrate the council of war, Amurath's prayer, &c.

were equally long and uncertain.   Some advised an attack on the
Turks by night, in revenge probably for the disaster of the
Marizza, twenty-six years before.   Others opposed this plan as
full of risk and confusion, and also because the enemy would have
a better chance of escaping in the night, than if they waited for
daylight for the victory which they deemed secure.   The morning
at last broke upon the two camps ; and with the dawn there came
a heavy fall of rain, which completely laid the dust, and seemed
to Amurath and his followers to be an express sign that God was
with them.

The rain ceased after a while, and the two armies came forth
from their tents on a fair and open field, and drew themselves up
for battle.   The Turks were arranged in their customary order.
As the battle was in Europe, the European feudatory troops were
on the right wing ; and those of Asia on the left.   Prince Bajazet
commanded on the right ; the other wing was led by Amurath's
other surviving son, Prince Yacoub.   Amurath himself was in the
centre with the Janissaries, and the cavalry regiments of his guard.
The irregulars, horse and foot, the Akindji, and the Azabs,
skirmished in the van.   On the Christian side, King Lazarus
commanded the centre.   His nephew, Vuk Brankowich, led the
right, and the King of Bosnia the left wing.   Both armies advanced
resolutely to the charge, encountered each other fiercely, stood
their ground firmly ; and the event of the day was long doubtful.
The Asiatic troops in the left wing of the Mahometan army began
at last to give way before the warriors of Servia and Albania, who
pressed them on the Christians' right.   Prince Bajazet brought
succour from the right wing of the Ottomans, and restored the
fight.   Armed with a heavy mace of iron, he fought in person in
the thick of the battle, and smote down all who dared to cross his
path.   While the two armies thus strove together, and the field
was heaped thickly with carnage, a Servian nobleman, Milosch
Kabilovitsch, rode to the Ottoman centre, pretending that he was
a deserter, and had important secrets to reveal to Amurath in
person.   He was led before the Turkish sovereign ; he knelt as if
in homage before him, and then stabbed Amurath with a sudden
and mortal stroke of his dagger.   Milosch sprang up from his
knees, and, gifted with surprising strength and activity, he thrice
cleared himself from the vengeful throng of the Ottomans who
assailed him, and fought his way to the spot where his horse had
been left ; but ere he could remount, the Janissaries overpowered
him, and hewed him into pieces.   Amurath knew that his wound
was mortal ; but he had presence of mind sufficient to give the

orders for a charge of his reserve, which decided the victory in his favour. His rival, the Servian King, was brought captive into his presence, and Amurath died in the act of pronouncing the death-doom of his foe.

The execution of King Lazarus was not the only one of which the royal Ottoman tent was the scene before the close of that day. Prince Bajazet, when the victory over the Christians was secure, returned to the Turkish camp, and was acknowledged by his father's generals as their sovereign. Forthwith, and in the very presence of his father's lifeless remains, Bajazet ordered his brother Yacoub, who had fought valiantly through the battle, to be seized and put to death. This fratricide (according to the historian of the empire, Seadeddin), was committed in pursuance of the maxim of the Koran, "Disquiet is worse than putting to death." It was, according to the same authority, rendered particularly proper by the evil example of revolt which their brother Saoudji had given in Amurath's lifetime, which proved the necessity of cutting off those, who were likely to imitate such conduct. The death of Yacoub was also, according to Seadeddin, justifiable, because the Sultan, the shadow of God upon earth, and the Lord of all true believers, ought to reign in conformity with the ever-to-be-imitated example of God, alone upon the throne, and without the possibility of any one revolting against him.

According to some authorities it was from Bajazet's deadly rapidity in securing his accession by his brother's death that he acquired the surname of "Yilderim;" but his energy in war may well have been the more honourable cause of his obtaining this designation. His reign commenced in the camp, and he followed up the war against the Servians with vigour and success, that showed him to be the heir of his father's valour as well as of his throne. Stephen Lasarevich, the new King of Servia, found that it was hopeless to continue the struggle, and entered into a treaty by which Servia became the vassal state of the Ottomans. Lasarevich gave the Sultan his sister to wife, and agreed to pay as tribute-money a certain portion of the produce of all the silver mines in his dominions. He undertook also to render, in person, military service to the Sultan in all his campaigns ; and throughout his life he honourably performed his portion of the compact. In the great battles of Nicopolis and Angora, Lasarevich fought by the side of his brother-in-law. He was (says the modern historian of Servia) apparently bound to this house by an oath, and with the zeal of a kinsman he exerted himself in the adjustment of quarrels that broke out in the Ottoman family.[1]

Having successfully concluded the Servian war, Bajazet passed over to his Asiatic dominions, which he increased by fresh conquests over the neighbouring states. In 1390 the Turkish "Lightning" was again in Europe, waging war on Wallachia, Bosnia, Hungary, and the wretched remnants of the Byzantine Empire. Myrtchè, the Prince of Wallachia, submitted to Bajazet in 1391, and thenceforth Wallachia was for centuries in the list of the tributary states of the Ottoman Porte. The Bosnians, aided by the Hungarians, offered a more obstinate resistance. In 1392 the Hungarian King, Sigismund, advanced into Bulgaria and gained several advantages, but was at last overpowered by the superior forces of the Turks, and driven in utter rout back into his own kingdom. It was while King Sigismund in the course of his retreat from the campaign traversed the county of Huniadé, that he saw and became enamoured of the fair Elizabeth Morsiney. It is said and sung that monarchs seldom sigh in vain; and from this love-passage of the fugitive Sigismund ensued the birth of Hunyades the Great, the conqueror of the Turks in many a well-fought field.

Bajazet's European enemies obtained a seasonable relief from the pressure of his arms, by the sudden attack which the Prince of Caramania made in 1392 upon the Ottoman possessions in Asia. The Caramanian armies were at first so far successful that the Ottoman troops suffered a complete overthrow between Angora and Brusa; and Timourtash, Bajazet's viceroy in Asia, was taken prisoner. But on the arrival of Bajazet himself in Asia, the fortune of the war was speedily changed. The Caramanian prince was defeated and captured, and placed in the custody of his own former prisoner, Timourtash. Without waiting for orders from Bajazet, Timourtash put the unhappy Caramanian to death. Bajazet was at first angry at such an act having been done on the general's own authority, but he excused it on consideration of high state policy, and justified it by the maxim that "The death of a prince is not so bad as the loss of a province." That maxim was afterwards regularly quoted by the Turkish rulers when they ordered the execution of any prince.

Caramania now submitted to the Ottomans, and all the south of Asia Minor acknowledged Bajazet as sovereign. He then sent his armies into the east and north of that country, and annexed

---

[1] Ranke's "History of Servia," p. 25. Mrs. Kerr's translation.

Sivas (the ancient Sebaste) Kastemouni, Samsoun and Amassia, with their territories to his dominions. Bajazet disdained the title of Emir, which his three predecessors had borne ; and obtained from the successor of the caliphs (who was maintained in empty state by the Mameluke sovereign of Egypt, but still recognised as the religious chief of the Mahometan world) the superior title of Sultan. Proud of his numerous victories and rapidly augmented power, Bajazet now gave himself up for a time to luxurious ease and to sensual excesses of the foulest description. He is the first of the Ottoman princes who infringed the law of the Prophet which forbids the use of wine. His favourite general, Ali Pasha, had set his master the example of drunkenness ; and Bajazet debased himself by sharing and imitating his subject's orgies. The infamy with which their names are sullied even in the pages of Oriental writers does not end here : they introduced among the Ottoman grandees (and the loathsome habit soon spread far and wide) the open and notorious practice of those unutterable deeds of vice and crime, which the natural judgment of mankind in every age and among every race has branded as the most horrible of all offences against God and man. The Koran is explicit in its denunciation of such acts ; but the Turks, though in other respects faithful observers of the law of the Prophet, on this point compromised with their consciences and their creed. The pen recoils from this detestable subject ; and it is indeed one of the shameful peculiarities of such vice, that its very enormity secures to a great extent its oblivion. But it is the stern duty of History not to flinch from the facts, which prove how fearful a curse the Ottoman power was to the lands which it overran during the period of its ascendency. It became a Turkish practice to procure by treaty, by purchase, by force, or by fraud, bands of the fairest children of the conquered Christians, who were placed in the palaces of the Sultan, his viziers, and his pachas, under the title of pages, but too often really to serve as the helpless materials of abomination. Frequently wars were undertaken and marauding inroads made into other states to collect this most miserable human spoil for purposes at which humanity shudders. Sufficiently appalling is the institution of the Janissaries, by which the Christian boy was taken from his home, and trained to deadly service against his father's race and his father's faith. It might seem worthy of having been suggested by the fiend, whom Milton describes as—

" The strongest and the fiercest spirit
That fought in heaven."

" Moloch, horrid king, besmear'd with blood
   Of human sacrifice and parents' tears :"

but infinitely more detestable is the Belial spirit that prompted
these other ineffable atrocities of Turkish rule. We find an
aggravation, not a mitigation of such crimes, when we read that
the wretched beings, the promise of whose youth was thus turned
into infamy, were frequently, when they grew to manhood, placed
by their masters in posts of importance ; and that the Ottoman
Empire has owed many of her ablest generals and statesmen to
this foul source. Pity must be blended with the loathing with
which we regard the dishonest splendours of these involuntary
apostates ; but as unmixed as inexpressible is our abhorrence of
the authors of their guilt and shame.

Bajazet was startled from his flagitious revels by a crusade of
the Christian chivalry of Frankistan (A.D. 1396). Sigismund the
King of Hungary felt deeply after the day of Kossova and the
fall of Servia, the imminence of the peril to which his own country
was exposed ; and he succeeded in moving the sympathies of other
members of the Latin Church into active enterprise on his behalf.
Pope Boniface IX., in the year 1394, proclaimed a crusade against
the Ottomans, with plenary indulgence to all Christians who should
forthwith repair to the rescue of Hungary and the neighbouring
kingdoms. Sigismund was especially earnest in his endeavours to
move the Court of France to send troops to his assistance. The
cessation of hostilities between France and England, about this
time, favoured the grant of the Hungarian request; and many of
the martial youth of France and Burgundy were now eager for
new adventures and fresh scenes of distinction. It was resolved
that the Count de Nevers, the son of the Duke of Burgundy,
should lead a body of men-at-arms to the aid of the Hungarian
King, and that he should be commander-in-chief of the French and
other chivalry, "who" (in the words of the contemporary chronicler) "were to break the force of Bajazet in Hungary, and when
this was done, were to advance to Constantinople, cross the
Hellespont, enter Syria, gain the Holy Land, and deliver Jerusalem
and the holy sepulchre from the hands of the infidels."[1] Knights
and squires began now to gather together, with other gentlemen
who were desirous of renown. The chief commanders, under the
Count de Nevers, were the Count de la Manche and the three
cousins of the French King, James of Bourbon, and Henri and
Philippe de Bar. Among other chiefs who joined this crusade,

[1] Froissart.

3—2

were Philippe of Artois, Count of Eu, prince of the blood' royal, and Constable of France ; the Lord de Courcy, Sir Guy de la Tremouille, Sir John de Vienne, Admiral of France, Boucicault, Marshal of France, Sir Reginald de Roye, the Lords of St. Pol, de Montmorel, and Sampi, and many more, the very flower of the French chivalry.   They marched from France in companies, about the middle of March, 1396 ; and as they traversed Germany, they were joined by Frederic, Count of Hohenzollern, Grand Prince of the Teutonic Order, and the Grand Master Philibert de Naillac, who came from Rhodes at the head of a strong body of the Knights of St. John of Jerusalem.   Besides this splendid auxiliary force, the King of Hungary had obtained the services of a body of Bavarian knights, commanded by the Elector Palatine and the Count of Munspelgarde ; and he had also been joined by a band of the chivalry of Styria, headed by Herman, second Count de Cilly. Altogether, the crusaders of Western Christendom who marched to the Danube against the Ottomans in 1396, appear to have been from ten to twelve thousand in number,[1] all men " of tried courage and enterprise," as the old chronicler calls them, full of confidence in their cause and in their own valour, and who boasted in the pride of their hearts that "if the sky were to fall, they would uphold it on the points of their lances."   Sigismund had collected the full strength of his own kingdom, and had also prevailed on Myrtchè, the Prince or Voivode of Wallachia, to join him in this grand combined attack on the Ottoman power, although Wallachia had some time before obtained peace from the Turks on condition of paying a stipulated tribute.

The confederate Christian army marched in divisions, partly through Transylvania and Wallachia, and partly through Servia, against the Ottoman dominions.   The Servian prince remained faithful to his alliance with Bajazet, and his subjects were there-fore visited with merciless pillage and devastation by the army of fellow-Christians who marched through their land.   The first Turkish town that Sigismund attacked was Widdin, which sur-rendered immediately.   Orsova yielded after five days' resistance. Raco was taken by assault, and the garrison put to the sword, though they laid down their arms and asked for quarter.   The practice of refusing mercy to a fallen enemy was by no means confined to the Turkish side : and, indeed, even in the hostilities of one Christian nation against another, no law or custom of war

---

[1] Von Hammer collects careful and full data for this enumeration, which differs from that of Gibbon.

against butchering defeated and unresisting enemies was yet recognised. When lives were spared, it was generally from the
hope of obtaining ransom, or from sheer weariness and satiety of
slaughter. The Christian army marched next against Nicopolis,
which was closely invested. The commander of the Turkish
garrison, Yoglan Bey, made a gallant and obstinate resistance, in
the full hope that Bajazet would not suffer so important a city to
fall without making an effort for its relief. The Sultan had
indeed now crossed the Bosphorus from Asia, and was leading
the best troops of his empire to encounter these new foes from
the Far West. The stubborn valour of the commander of Nicopolis was of the utmost value to his sovereign, by giving him time
to concentrate and bring up his forces to the scene of action.
Bajazet's generalship was far superior to the military conduct on
the side of the Christians. They, and especially the French, in
arrogant confidence of their invincibility, gave themselves up to
riotous carousals, and neglected the most ordinary precautions to
ascertain whether any enemy was advancing. "Bajazet would
not dare to come across the Bosphorus." Such was their boast,
at the very time when Bajazet was swiftly and silently approaching with his well-appointed and well-disciplined army within six
leagues of their camp. The Count de Nevers and his French
chivalry were at table on the 24th of September, 1396, when
messengers hurried in with the tidings that some marauders from
the camp had come upon a great army of Turks, which was even
then close at hand. The young paladins of France rose hot and
flushed at the tidings, and ran to arms, demanding that they
should be led instantly to battle. The Turkish irregular troops,
the Azabs and the Akindji, were now seen hovering near ; and
the Count de Nevers, while his French cavalry was forming
hastily in line, required of King Sigismund that they should be
the van of the Christian army, and fill the post of honour in the
battle. Sigismund, who knew well the Turkish tactics, urged on
the Count that it would be wiser to send some light troops against
the half-armed and undisciplined hordes, which they saw before
them, and to reserve the French chivalry, as the flower of the
Christian army, to meet the Janissaries and Spahis, the best troops
on the other side. The Sire de Courcy and the Admiral advised
compliance with the King's advice, but the Constable and the
Maréchal Boucicault opposed it, out of a spirit of rivalry, and
insisted that the French cavalry should not suffer any Hungarians
to precede them to battle. The young knights all applauded
these proud words ; and in ferocious insolence of spirit, they

massacred some Turkish prisoners, whom they had in their power, and who had surrendered on promise of quarter—an act of useless perfidy and cruelty, which was soon to receive its chastisement.

Bajazet had halted his main army in a plain at a short distance from the Christian camp. There was some rising ground in the interval, which screened the Turks from the enemy's observation. The Sultan sent his irregular troops forward and supported them by a body of Janissaries, and by a large division of his cavalry ; but he reserved forty thousand of his best troops, and kept them under arms, and drawn up in perfect order on the plain. On the other side the French cavalry, about six thousand strong, galloped impetuously onward, disdaining to wait for the co-operation of the main Hungarian army, with which King Sigismund moved forward more slowly. The French rode the Turkish irregulars down like reeds, and then with levelled spears they charged the advanced division of the Janissaries. They broke this redoubtable infantry ; and next encountered with equal success the foremost squadrons of the Turkish regular cavalry that attempted to cover the retreat of their comrades. The triple success which the fiery valour of the young French nobles had thus achieved was splendid, and might have led to a complete victory, had they listened to the sage advice of the Sire de Courcy and the Admiral, who earnestly implored the Count de Nevers to order a halt, and wait for the Hungarians to come up ; or at least to give time enough for the horses to recover their wind, and for rearranging their disordered ranks. But carried away by the excitement of the strife, and the intoxication of their partial triumph, the French knights and their young commander continued to chase the flying Spahis, till, on gaining the summit of the high ground, they saw before them, not as they expected, a scared remnant of the defeated Turks, but a steady forest of hostile spears, and the Sultan himself at the head of his chosen troops, which soon began to extend, and wheel their enclosing lines round the scanty band of the rash assailants. The Turkish troops, which they had defeated in the first part of their advance, had now rallied, and formed in the rear of the French knights, cutting off all hope of retreat. In this extremity, charged furiously in every quarter by superior numbers, obliged to combat in confusion and disorder, and with their own strength and that of their horses exhausted by their previous efforts, the Christian chevaliers fought on heroically till they were nearly all cut down or made prisoners. A few only made their way back to the main army of the confederates, into which they carried the disheartening tidings of defeat. Bajazet, after the French were overpowered, restored the regular formation of his troops, and then moved forward against King Sigismund. The two wings of the Christian main army fled at once without striking a blow. The central division of Hungarians, which the king himself commanded, and the Bavarians and the Styrians, who also were posted in the centre, stood firm. They repulsed the Turkish charge, and advanced in turn against the Janissaries and Spahis, forcing these chosen troops of the Ottomans to recoil, when they were themselves fiercely charged by the Servians, who, under their king, Stephen Lasarevich, fought as allies of Bajazet in this battle. The overthrow of the Christian army was now complete. Sigismund's Hungarian division was almost destroyed; all the Bavarian knights and many of the Styrians died gloriously around their standards. King Sigismund and a few more of the leaders escaped with difficulty from the field; but nearly all the best and bravest of the gallant army which had marched on that crusade, lay stark on the bloody field of Nicopolis, or were helplessly waiting for the doom which it might please the triumphant Sultan to pass upon his captive foes.

After the conflict, Bajazet fixed his camp in front of the rescued city of Nicopolis, and then rode over the field of battle. He was enraged to find from the number of his men who lay dead, how dear the victory had cost him. He said, "This has been a cruel battle for our people : the Christians have defended themselves desperately ; but I will have this slaughter well avenged on those who are prisoners." Accordingly on the next morning the whole Turkish army was drawn up in the form of a crescent, the Sultan being in the centre. He commanded the Christian prisoners to be brought before him, and they were led out to the number of ten thousand, with their hands bound behind them, and with halters round their necks. Among them was a youth of Munich, named Schildberger, who had gone to that campaign as attendant on a Bavarian nobleman who fell in the battle. Schildberger, more fortunate than his lord, escaped death in the conflict and in the massacre that followed. He lived to witness and to share the captivity of his first captors ; and, after thirty-four years of slavery, returned to his home and wrote there a memoir of his own life, which is the most interesting and most trustworthy narrative that we possess of the campaign of Nicopolis, and of many of the subsequent scenes of Turkish history. The commander of the French chivalry, the Count de Nevers, had been taken in the battle. Bajazet ordered that he should be spared, and permitted him to select twenty-four more of the Christian nobles from among the prisoners, whose lives were also granted. The Sultan then gave the signal for the slaughter of the rest to commence ; and the unhappy captives were led in detachments before the royal tent, at the entrance of which Bajazet stood with the Count de Nevers and the twenty-four other Christian nobles who had been spared, but who were forced to witness the fate of their comrades and fellow-Christians. The contemporaneous chronicler of chivalry, old Froissart, tells the fate of the martyred chevaliers with natural sympathy :

" Many excellent knights and squires of France and other nations, who had been taken in battle or in the pursuit, were now brought forth in their shirts, one after another, before Bajazet, who eyeing them a little, they were led on ; and as he made a signal were instantly cut to pieces by those waiting for them with drawn swords. Such was the cruel justice of Bajazet this day, when upwards of three hundred gentlemen of different nations were thus pitilessly murdered. It was a cruel case for them to suffer for the love of our Saviour Jesus Christ, and may he receive their souls !

" Among the murdered of that day was the gallant knight Sir Henry d'Antoing : may God show gracious merit to his soul! The Lord Boucicault, Marshal of France, was led naked like the others, before Bajazet, and would have suffered the same cruel death, had not the Count de Nevers left his companions, who were motionless at the sad sight, and flung himself on his knees to the Sultan, entreating him to spare the Lord Boucicault, who was much beloved by the King of France, and well able to pay a considerable ransom ; and the Count made signs, as paying from one hand to the other, that he would give a large sum of money, to soften the anger of the Sultan. Bajazet consented to the request of the Count de Nevers, and the Lord Boucicault was put aside with those who were not to be killed. Others were brought forward, until the number I have mentioned was completed ; such was the cruel revenge the infidels had on the Christians. It seems, according to what I heard, that Bajazet took delight that the victory he had gained over the Christians, and the capture of the Count de Nevers, should be known in France, and carried thither by a French knight. Three knights, of whom Sir James de Helly was one, were brought before Bajazet and the Count de Nevers, who was asked which of the three he wished should go to the King of France and to his father the Duke of Burgundy. Sir

James de Helly had the good fortune to be made choice of, because the Count de Nevers was before acquainted with him : he
therefore said to the Sultan—'Sir, I wish that this person may
go to France from you and from me.' This was accepted by
Bajazet, and Sir James de Helly remained with him and the other
French lords; but the two unsuccessful knights were delivered over
to the soldiery, who massacred them without pity."

It is truly characteristic of Froissart and his age, that while he
thus bewails the slaughter which befell the three hundred captives
of gentle birth, he says not a word respecting the thousands of
the common soldiery of the Christian army, who were massacred
at the same time. It is from the lowly-born Bavarian that we
learn the extent and the cruelty of the carnage of that day.
Schildberger saw his comrades cut down in heaps by the scimetars
of the Turkish executioners, or battered to death by the maces of
the Janissaries, who were called forward to join in the bloody
work. He himself was saved by the intercession of Bajazet's son,
who was moved to pity by the evident youth of the captive. The
Sultan sate there from daybreak till four in the afternoon enjoying
with inexorable eye the death-pangs of his foes, when at last the
pity or the avarice of his grandees made them venture to come
between him and his prey, and implore that the Christians who
yet remained alive might be made slaves of, instead of being slain.
Bajazet assented, and the surviving captives, after the Sultan had
chosen his fifth part from among them, were given up, each to the
Mahometan who had taken him in battle. The Count de Nevers
and the other lords were ransomed after a long captivity, during
which Bajazet carried them about his dominions as trophies of his
power and glory, little thinking that he himself was soon to drink
still deeper of the same bitter cup of defeat and shame, and to
furnish a still more memorable spectacle of baffled ambition and
fallen pride.

Bajazet and his captives were at Brusa, in 1397, when the money
for their ransom arrived. Before he dismissed them, he gave them
an opportunity of witnessing both his barbaric magnificence and
his barbaric justice. Froissart thus relates the two scenes, and
the haughty leave-taking which the Sultan accorded to the Christian
lords :

"The Sultan had at this time seven thousand falconers, and as
many huntsmen: you may suppose from this the grandeur of his
establishments. One day, in the presence of the Count de Nevers,
he flew a falcon at some eagles; the flight did not please him;
and he was so wroth, that, for this fault he was on the point of

beheading two thousand of his falconers, scolding them exceedingly for want of diligence in their care of his hawks, when the one he was fond of behaved so ill. Another time, when the Count de Nevers and the French barons were with the Sultan, a poor woman came to him in tears, to demand justice against one of his servants, and said—'Sultan, I address myself to thee, as my sovereign, and complain of one of thy servants, who is, I understand, attached to thy person. He, this morning, entered my house, and seized by force the goat's milk I had provided for myself and children, and drank it against my will. I told him that I should complain to thee of this outrage, but I had no sooner uttered the words, than he gave me two great cuffs, and would not leave me, though I ordered him in thy name. Sultan, do me justice, as thou hast sworn to thy people thou wouldest, that I may be satisfied, this injury be punished, and that every one may know thou wilt see the meanest of thy subjects righted.'

"The Sultan was very rigidly determined that all crimes committed within his dominions should be severely punished : he therefore listened to her attentively, and said he would do her justice. He then ordered the varlet to be brought, and confronted with the woman, who repeated her complaint. The varlet, who dreaded Bajazet, began to make excuses, saying it was all false. The woman told a plain tale, and persisted in its truth. The Sultan stopped her, and said—'Woman, consider well thy accusation ; for, if I find thou hast told me a lie, thou shalt suffer death.' 'Sir,' replied the woman, 'I consent to it ; for were it not true, I could have no reason to come before thee, and I only ask for justice.' 'I will do it,' answered the Sultan, 'for I have so sworn, and indiscriminately to every man or woman within my dominions.' He then ordered the varlet to be seized, and to have his belly opened, for otherwise he would not have known if he had drank the milk or not. It was there found, for it had not had time to be digested ; and the Sultan, on seeing it, said to the woman, 'Thou hadst just cause of complaint : now go thy way, for the injury done thee has been punished.' She was likewise paid for her loss. This judgment of Bajazet was witnessed by the French lords, who were at the time in his company.[1]

"When the Count de Nevers and the lords of France who were made prisoners at the battle of Nicopolis (excepting the Count

---

[1] Dr. Newman, in his lectures on the Turks, when he relates this instance of the judicial system which makes the punishment supply the evidence, quotes appropriately Virgil's description of Rhadamanthus:

"Castigatque auditque dolos."

d'Eu and the Lord de Courcy, who had died), had been some time entertained by the Sultan, and had seen great part of his state, he consented they should depart, which was told them by those who had been ordered to attend to their personal wants. The Count and his companions waited on the Sultan in consequence, to thank him for his kindness and courtesy. On taking his leave, the Sultan addressed him, by means of an interpreter, as follows:—' John, I am well informed that in thy country thou art a great lord, and son to a powerful prince. Thou art young, and hast many years to look forward to; and, as thou mayest be blamed for the ill success of thy first attempt in arms, thou mayest perchance, to shake off this imputation and regain thine honour, collect a powerful army to lead against me, and offer battle. If I feared thee, I would make thee swear, and likewise thy companions, on thy faith and honour, that neither thou nor they would ever bear arms against me. But no: I will not demand such an oath: on the contrary, I shall be glad that when thou art returned to thy country, it please thee to assemble an army, and lead it hither. Thou wilt always find me prepared, and ready to meet thee in the field of battle. What I now say, do thou repeat to any person, to whom it may please thee to repeat it; for I am ever ready for, and desirous of deeds of arms, as well as to extend my conquests.'

"These high words the Count de Nevers and his companions understood well, and never forgot them as long as they lived."

Nothing indeed could surpass the arrogant confidence in the strength of his arms with which Bajazet was inspired by this victory over the chosen warriors of the Christian nations. It was his common boast, that he would conquer Italy, and that his horse should eat his oats on the high altar of St. Peter's. From his capital at Brusa, he sent vaunting messages to the princes of Asia and Egypt, announcing his victory at Nicopolis; and the messengers to each Mahometan court took with them a chosen band of the Christians who had been taken in the battle, as presents from the conqueror, and as attesting witnesses of his exploits. Nor was it in words only that Bajazet showed his unceasing energy against the yet unsubdued nations of the West. His generals overran and devastated Styria, and the south of Hungary; and the Sultan himself led the Turkish armies to the conquest of Greece. He marched through Thessaly, as Xerxes had marched nearly nineteen centuries before. But no modern Leonidas guarded Thermopylæ; and Locris, Phocis, and Bœotia fell almost without resistance into the Turkish power. Bajazet's lieutenants passed with equal celerity across the isthmus of Corinth, and subdued the whole Peloponnesus. Thirty thousand Greeks were removed thence by Bajazet's order, and transported into Asia; and Turco- man and Tartar colonies were settled in their stead in the classic regions of Laconia, Messenia, Achaia, Argolis, and Elis. Athens was taken in 1397, and the Turkish Crescent waved over "The City of the Wise," as she is termed by the Oriental historians who narrate the triumphs of Bajazet.

Constantinople had more than once been menaced, and had been pressed with actual siege by Bajazet, from which the Greek Emperor obtained a temporary respite by turning one of the churches of Constantinople into a mosque, and by binding him- self to pay the Sultan an annual tribute of 10,000 ducats. But, in 1400, Bajazet, no longer sated in his ambition with such conces- sions, commanded the Greek Emperor to surrender his crown to him, threatening extermination to all the inhabitants of the city in case of refusal. The Byzantines nobly replied—"We know our weakness, but we trust in the God of justice, who protects the weak and lowly, and puts down the mighty from on high." Bajazet was preparing to execute his threats, when the desolater was laid desolate and the victor overthrown, not by any efforts of European statesmanship or violence, but by the superior might of another Asiatic conqueror, before whom the spirit of the Ottoman power, high and unmatchable where Timour's was not, "became a Fear as being overpowered."

Timour the Tartar, as he is usually termed in history, was called by his countrymen Timourlenk, that is, Timour the Lame, from the effects of an early wound; a name which some European writers have converted into Tamerlane, or Tamberlaine. He was of Mongol origin, and a direct descendant, by the mother's side, of Zenghis Khan. He was born at Sebzar, a town near Samar- cand, in Transoxiana, in 1336, and was consequently nearly seventy years of age, when his conquests clashed with those of Bajazet, and the Ottoman power was struck by him to the dust. Timour's early youth was passed in struggles for ascendency with the petty chiefs of rival tribes, but at the age of thirty-five, he had fought his way to undisputed pre-eminence, and was proclaimed Khan of Zagatai by the *couroultai*, or general assembly of the warriors of his race. He chose Samarcand as the capital of his dominion, and openly announced that he would make that dominion comprise the whole habitable earth. When he took possession of the throne of Samarcand, he assumed, in addition to his name of Timour (which means "Iron," and which typified, in the eyes of the Orientals, the resistless might with which he subdued all things), the titles of the Great Wolf (Gurgan), the Lord of the Age (Sahet Kiwan), and Conqueror of the World (Jehargyr). The boastful appellations of Eastern sovereigns are frequently as ridiculous as they are pompous; but those which Timour bore were emblems of fearful truths; for in the thirty-six years of his reign he raged over the world from the great wall of China to the centre of Russia on the north; and the Mediterranean and the Nile were the western limits of his career, which was pressed eastward as far as the sources of Ganges. He united in his own person the sovereignties of twenty-seven countries, and he stood in the place of nine several dynasties of kings. He was often heard to quote a passage of an Eastern poet, which declares that as there is but one God in heaven, so there ought to be but one lord on earth, and that all the kingdoms of the universe could not satiate the ambition of one great sovereign.

The career of Timour as a conqueror, is unparalleled in history; for neither Cyrus, nor Alexander, nor Cæsar, nor Attila, nor Zenghis Khan, nor Charlemagne, nor Napoleon, ever won by the sword so large a portion of the globe, or ruled over so many myriads of subjugated fellow-creatures. Timour's triumphs were owing not only to personal valour and to high military genius, but to his eminent skill as a politician and a ruler. His code of laws, which he drew up for the regulation of his army, for the administration of justice, and for the finances of his empire, shows keen observation, and deep and sound reflection. The chief force of his art of government, and of his foreign policy, was derived from the admirable system, which he established of gaining accurate and full intelligence from the reports of emissaries, who were sent by him to travel in all directions, under various disguises, and especially as pilgrims or dervises. He thus knew the strength and the weakness of his enemies in each place, and at each crisis. Whatever information he obtained from his agents was by his orders carefully collected in registers and delineated on maps, which were kept ready for immediate reference. Thoughtful and provident in balancing probabilities, and guarding well against each contingency before he undertook an enterprise, he was unshaken in his resolution when his plans were matured. He countermanded no order which had once been issued; and it was a maxim with him never to repent, and never to regret. He had such an ascendency over his soldiers, that they not only underwent the severest privations, and lavished their lives at his bidding, but would, if Timour ordered, abstain from plunder in the hour of victory, and give up the spoils of war without a murmur. He was a generous master; but his cruelty to those who ventured to resist him surpasses all the similar horrors with which military history is so rife. Timour evidently employed terror as one of his principal instruments of conquest; and the punishments which he inflicted on whole populations often show the cold calculating subtilty of a practised tormentor, rather than the mere savage ferocity of an irritated despot.

Bajazet had, by his generals, extended the frontier of his empire in the east of Asia Minor during the three years that followed the battle of Nicopolis. Timour's dominions were already spread over Georgia, and other countries west of the Caspian Sea, so that a collision between these two great potentates of the Mahometan world became inevitable. Each sheltered the princes whom the other had dethroned, and a series of angry complaints and threats followed, which soon led to open insult and actual war. The strong city of Sivas (the ancient Sebaste in Cappadocia) near the Armenian frontier, which had submitted to Bajazet, was the first place in the Ottoman dominions which Timour assailed; and it was by the tidings of the fall of Sivas that Bajazet was recalled from the siege of Constantinople. Bajazet had sent Ertoghrul, the bravest of his sons, with a chosen force to protect Sivas; and the strength of the fortifications, the number and spirit of the population, and the military skill with which they were directed, had seemed to set the threats of its Tartar assailants at defiance. But Timour employed thousands of miners in digging huge cavities beneath the foundations of the city walls, taking care to prop up the walls with timber planking and piles until the excavations were complete. When this was done, the miners set fire to the timber, and the walls sank down by their own weight. The defenders of Sivas saw their town and ramparts thus swallowed up by the earth before their eyes, and implored in despair the mercy of the conqueror. Never had Timour shown himself so merciless. Four thousand Christian warriors from Armenia, who had formed part of the garrison, were buried alive by his orders. Their heads were tied down by cords lashed tightly round the neck and under the thighs, so as to bring the face between the legs. Bound in this agonising posture, they were flung into graves, which were planked over before the earth was thrown back, so as to prolong the torture of the wretched victims as long as possible. Prince Ertoghrul, and the Turkish part of the garrison were put to the sword. The fall of Sivas delayed that of Constantinople. Bajazet proceeded to Asia Minor in bitterness of heart for the blow that had been struck at his empire, and in deep affliction for the loss

of the best beloved of his sons.   One day, on his march, he passed
near where a shepherd was singing merrily, and he exclaimed,
" Sing me this burden :

> " Leave not Sivas to be taken,
> And thy son to die forsaken."

Before Bajazet had reached the eastern provinces of his dominions, Timour had marched southward from Sivas, spreading devastation far and wide through the southern regions of Asia Minor.
An insult from the Sultan of Egypt had drawn the wrath of the
Tartar conqueror in a southern direction, and Syria experienced
for two years the terror and the cruelty of his arms.   In the
spring of 1402 Timour marched again against the Ottomans.   A
new interchange of letters and embassies had taken place between
him and Bajazet, which had only incensed still more each of these
haughty conquerors against the other.   But though professing the
utmost scorn for his adversary, Timour knew well how formidable
were the Turkish arms, and he carefully drew together for this
campaign the best-appointed, as well as the most numerous army,
that his vast dominions could supply.   He practised also the subtle
policy of weakening his enemy by sowing discontent and treachery
among Bajazet's troops.   Timour's secret agents were sent to the
Ottoman camp, and urged on the numerous soldiers of Tartar race
who served there, that they ought not to fight against Timour,
who was the true chief of all Tartar warriors, and that Bajazet
was unworthy to command such brave men.   The efforts of these
spies and emissaries were greatly aided by the dissatisfaction
which Bajazet's ill-judged parsimony and excessive severity in
discipline had already created in his army.   His best generals
observed the bad spirit which was spreading among the men, and
implored their Sultan not to risk a decisive encounter with the
superior forces of Timour, or at least to regain the good-will of his
soldiers by judicious liberality.   Bajazet was both arrogant and
avaricious ; he determined to attack his enemy, but to keep back
his treasures ; reserving them, as one of his generals bitterly remarked, as certainly for Timour's use, as if the Turkish bullion
was already stamped with Tartar coinage.   Bajazet advanced with
about 120,000 men against the far superior forces of Timour,
which were posted near Sivas.   The Mongol Emperor did not immediately encounter the Ottomans ; but manœuvred so as to ensure
that the battle should take place on ground most advantageous for
the action of cavalry, and on which he could avail himself most
fully of his numerical superiority.   By an able forced march

through Kaisyraiah and Kirschehr he evaded Bajazet, and **reached**
the city and plain of Angora.   He immediately formed the siege
of the city, knowing that Bajazet would not suffer the shame of
letting so important a place fall without an effort to relieve it.   As
he expected, the Ottoman Sultan hurried to the rescue of Angora,
and Timour then took up an advantageous position on the broad
plain of Tchibukabad, to the north-west of the town.   Notwithstanding the immense preponderance of numbers which he possessed, the Mongol sovereign observed all military precautions.
One of his flanks was protected by the little river Tchibukabad,
which supplies Angora with water; on the other he had secured
himself by a ditch and strong palisade.   Bajazet, blinded by his
former successes, seemed to have lost all the generalship which he
usually exhibited, and to have been seized at Angora by the same
spirit of rashness which possessed the Frankish chivalry whom he
overthrew five years before at Nicopolis.   He camped first to the
north of Timour's position; and then, to show his contempt for
his enemy, he marched his whole army away to the high grounds
in the neighbourhood, and employed them in a grand hunting.
The troops were drawn out, according to the Asiatic custom, in a
vast circle, enclosing many miles; and they then moved in towards
the centre, so as to drive the game to where the Sultan and his
officers were posted.   Unfortunately the districts in which Bajazet
made this, his last chase, were destitute of water, and the sufferings of his troops whom he thus devoted to the image of war,
equalled those which an army ordinarily endures in war's stern
reality.   Five thousand of the Ottoman soldiers perished with
thirst and fatigue to promote their Sultan's fatal sport.   After
this imperial folly, Bajazet marched back to his enemy; but he
found that the camp which he had left was now occupied by the
Tartars, and that the only stream of water to which the Ottoman
army could gain access, had been turned and filled up by Timour's
orders, so as to be almost unserviceable.   Bajazet was thus obliged
to seek a battle, nor would he have declined it even if he had the
choice, such was his pride and confidence in his power.   On the
20th of July, 1402, the decisive conflict took place.   The Mongol
army is said to have exceeded 800,000 men, and it certainly was
far more numerous than that led by Bajazet, who could not have
brought more than 100,000 into the field; and not only in
numbers, but in equipment, in zeal, and in the skill with which
they were directed, the superiority was on the side of the Mongols.
Except the corps of Janissaries, who were under the Sultan's immediate orders, and the Servian auxiliaries who fought gallantly

for the Ottomans under their king, Stephen Lasarevich, Bajazet's
troops showed little prowess or soldiership at Angora. The arts
of Timour's emissaries had been effective; and, when the action
commenced, large numbers of the Tartars who were in Bajazet's
service, passed over to the ranks of his enemies. The contingents
of several of the Asiatic tributary princes took the same course;
and it was only in the Ottoman centre, where Bajazet and his
Janissaries stood, and in the left centre, where the Servians fought,
that any effective resistance was made to the fierce and frequent
charges of the Mongol cavalry. Bajazet saw that the day was
irreparably lost, but he rejected the entreaties of his officers to fly
while escape was yet practicable. He led his yet unbroken
veterans to some rising ground, which he occupied with them, and
there beat off all the attacks of the enemy throughout the day.
But his brave Janissaries were sinking beneath thirst, fatigue, and
wounds; and it was evident that the morning would see them a
helpless prey to the myriad enemies who swarmed around them.
At nightfall Bajazet attempted to escape from the field, but he
was marked and pursued; his horse stumbled and fell with him;
and Mahmoud, the Titular Khan of Jagetai, who served in
Timour's army, had the glory of taking the great Sultan of the
Ottomans prisoner. Of his five sons who had been in the battle,
three had been more fortunate than their father. Prince Solyman
had escaped towards the Ægean Sea, Prince Mahomet to Amassia,
and Prince Issa towards Caramania. Prince Musa was taken
prisoner; and the fifth, Prince Mustapha, disappeared in the
battle, nor was his fate ever certainly known.

Bajazet was at first treated by Timour with respect and kindness; but an ineffectual attempt to escape incensed the conqueror,
and increased the rigour of the Sultan's captivity. Thenceforth
Bajazet was strictly watched by a numerous guard, and was placed
in fetters every night. When the Mongol army moved from place
to place, Timour took his captive with him; but, in order to avoid
the hateful sight of his enemies, Bajazet travelled in a covered
litter with iron lattice-work. The similarity of sound between
two Turkish words caused the well-known story that the Tartar
king carried the captive Sultan about in an iron cage.[1] The real

---

[1] In Marlowe's play of "Tamburlaine," Bajazet and "the Turkess," his
wife, brain themselves against the bars of the cage on the stage. Though
he stoops to much bombast and extravagance, Marlowe breathes nobly the
full spirit of the ferocious energy and fiery pride of the great Oriental conquerors. His "Tamburlaine" is immeasurably superior to the benevolent
Tamerlane of Rowe, both as a dramatic character, and as an image of historic
truth.

4

ignominy which Bajazet underwent was sufficient to break a proud
heart, and he died in March, 1403, eight months after the battle
of Angora. Timour had sufficient magnanimity to set at liberty
Prince Musa, Bajazet's son, and to permit him to take the dead
body to Brusa for honourable interment in the burial-place of the
Ottoman sovereigns. He himself did not long survive his fallen
rival. He died at Otrar, on the 1st of February, 1405, while on
his march to conquer China. In the brief interval between his
victory at Angora and his death, he had poured his desolating
armies throughout the Ottoman dominions into Asia Minor, sack-
ing the Turkish cities of Brusa, Nice, Khemlik, Akshehr, Kara-
hissar, and many more, and then assailing the great city of
Smyrna, which had escaped the Ottoman power, and had been for
half a century held by the Christian Knights of St. John of Jerusalem. Timour directed the siege of Smyrna in person. In fifteen
days a mole had been thrown across the harbour, which deprived
the besieged of all succour, and brought the Mongol troops close
to the seaward parts of the city ; large portions of the landward
walls had been undermined ; huge movable towers had been constructed, from which the besiegers boarded the city's battlements,
and Smyrna was taken by storm, notwithstanding the heroic defence of the Christian knights. Timour ordered a general massacre
of the inhabitants without mercy to either age or sex.

It was the custom of the Tartar Conqueror to rear a vast
pyramid of human heads, when any great city had been captured
by his troops. The garrison and population of Smyrna proved
insufficient to supply materials for one of these monuments on his
accustomed scale of hideous grandeur. But Timour was resolved
not to leave the site of Smyrna without his wonted trophy ; and
he ordered that the supply of heads should be economised, by
placing alternate layers of mud between the rows of heads in the
pyramid. After other similar acts of gigantic cruelty in Asia
Minor, he marched into Georgia to punish the prince of that
country for not having come in person when required to the
Tartar camp. The unhappy Georgians perished by thousands for
the imputed fault of their sovereign, and seven hundred towns
and villages were destroyed by the troops of Timour. In 1404,
the Conqueror rested for a short time from blood-shedding, and
displayed his magnificence in his capital city of Samarkand, which
he had not seen for seven years. But the unslaked thirst of conquest and slaughter urged him onward to the attack of the Chinese
Empire before the year was closed ; and that wealthy and populous
realm must have been swept by his destroying hordes, had it not

been saved by the fever which seized him at Otrar, after his passage of the river Sihoon on the ice in February, 1405. Timour died in that city, at the age of seventy-one, having reigned thirty-six years, during which he shed more blood and caused more misery than any other human being that ever was born upon the earth.

CHAPTER IV.

INTERREGNUM AND CIVIL WAR—MAHOMET I. REUNITES THE
EMPIRE—HIS SUCCESSFUL REIGN—HIS DEATH AND CHARACTER
—ACCESSION OF AMURATH II.—SIEGE OF CONSTANTINOPLE—
CIVIL WAR IN ASIA—WARS WITH THE SERVIANS, HUNGARIANS,
AND OTHER NATIONS—VICTORIES OF HUNYADES—TREATY OF
SZEGEDDIN—BROKEN BY THE CHRISTIANS—BATTLE OF VARNA
—SCANDERBEG—SECOND BATTLE OF KOSSOVA—DEATH OF
AMURATH.[1]

THE Ottoman Empire, which during the fourteenth century had
acquired such dimensions and vigour, lay at the beginning of the
fifteenth century in apparently irretrievable ruin. Besides the
fatal day at Angora, when its veteran army was destroyed, and its
long-victorious sovereign taken captive, calamity after calamity
had poured fast upon the house of Othman. Their ancient rivals
in Asia Minor, the Seljukian princes of Caramania, Aidian, Kermian, and other territories which the three first Ottoman sovereigns had conquered, were reinstated by Timour in their
dominions. In Europe the Greek Empire accomplished another
partial revival, and regained some of its lost provinces. But the
heaviest and seemingly the most fatal of afflictions was the civil war
which broke out among the sons of Bajazet, and which threatened
the utter disintegration and destruction of the relics of their
ancestral dominions. At the time of Bajazet's death, his eldest
son, Solyman, ruled at Adrianople. The second son, Prince
Issa, established himself as an independent ruler at Brusa,
after the Mongols retired from Asia Minor. Mahomet, the
youngest and the ablest of the brothers, formed a petty kingdom
at Amassia. War soon broke out between Mahomet and Issa, in
which Mahomet was completely successful. Issa fled to Europe,
where he sought protection and aid from Solyman, who forthwith
attacked Mahomet, so that European Turkey and Asiatic Turkey
were now arrayed against each other. At first Solyman was suc-

[1] See Von Hammer, books 8, 9, 10, 11.

cessful. He invaded Asia, and captured Brusa and Angora. Meanwhile the other surviving son of Bajazet, Prince Musa, had, after his liberation by Timour, been detained in custody by the Seljukian Prince of Kermian, through whose territories he was passing with the remains of Bajazet, which he was to bury at Brusa. The interposition of Mahomet had put an end to this detention, and Prince Musa fought on Mahomet's side against Solyman in Asia. After some reverses which they sustained from Solyman in the first campaign, Musa persuaded Mahomet to let him cross over to Europe with a small force, and effect a diversion in Mahomet's favour by attacking the enemy in his own territories. This manoeuvre soon recalled Solyman to Europe, where a short but sanguinary contest between him and Musa ensued. At first Solyman had the advantage; but the better qualities of this prince were now obscured by the debasing effects of habits of debauchery. He treated his troops with savage cruelty, and heaped the grossest insults on his best generals. The result was that his army passed over to the side of Musa, and Solyman was killed while endeavouring to escape to Constantinople (1410).

Musa was now master of the Ottoman dominions in Europe, and speedily showed that he inherited a full proportion both of the energy and of the ferocity of his father Bajazet. In an expedition which he undertook against the Servian Prince, whom he accused of having treacherously aided Solyman in the civil war, he is said to have not only practised the customary barbarities of ravaging the country, carrying off the male youth as captives, and slaughtering the rest of the population; but according to the Byzantine writer Ducas, Musa caused the carcasses of three Servian garrisons to be arranged as tables, and a feast to be spread on them, at which he entertained the generals and chief captains of the Ottoman army.

The Greek Emperor, Manuel Palæologus, had been the ally of Solyman; Musa therefore attacked him, and besieged his capital. Palæologus called over Mahomet to protect him, and the Asiatic Ottomans now garrisoned Constantinople against the Ottomans of Europe. Mahomet made several gallant but unsuccessful sallies against his brother's troops, and was obliged to recross the Bosphorus, to quell a revolt that had broken out in his own territories. Musa now pressed the siege of the Greek capital; but Mahomet speedily returned to Europe, and obtained the assistance of Stephen, the Servian King. The armies of the rival Ottoman brethren were at last arrayed for a decisive conflict on the plain of Chamurli, near the southern Servian frontier. But Musa had alienated the loyalty of his soldiers by conduct similar to that by which Solyman's desertion and destruction had been caused, while Mahomet was as eminent for justice and kindness towards those who obeyed him, as for valour and skill against those who were his opponents. When the two armies were about to close in battle, Hassan, the Aga of the Janissaries on the side of Mahomet, stepped out before the ranks, and exhorted his old comrades, who were on the part of Musa, to leave the cause of a madman from whom they met with constant outrage and humiliation, and to range themselves among the followers of the most just and virtuous of the princes of the house of Othman. Enraged at hearing his troops thus addressed, Musa rushed against Hassan, and cut him down with his own hand, but was himself wounded by an officer who had accompanied Hassan. Musa reeled back bleeding towards his own soldiers, who were seized with a panic, and broke their ranks, and fled in all directions. Musa endeavoured to escape, but was found by the pursuers lying dead in a marsh near the field where the armies had met. His death ended the war of succession in the Ottoman Empire, for Prince Issa had disappeared some years before, during the hostilities between Solyman and Mahomet in Asia; and Mahomet was now, after Musa's death, the sole known surviving son of Bajazet.

Sultan Mahomet I. was surnamed by his subjects Pehlevan, which means the Champion, on account of his personal activity and prowess. His graciousness of disposition and manner, his magnanimity, his love of justice and truth, and his eminence as a discerning patron of literature and art, obtained for him also the still more honourable title of Tschelebi, which, according to Von Hammer, expresses precisely the same idea which is conveyed by the English word "gentleman." Other Turkish sovereigns have acquired more celebrity; but Mahomet, the Champion and the Gentleman, deserves to be cited as one of the noblest types of the Ottoman race. His humanity and his justice are attested by Greek as well as by Oriental historians. He was through life the honourable and firm ally of the Byzantine Emperor; the dreaded foe of the rebellious Turcomans; the glorious bulwark of the throne of Othman; and, as his country's histories term him, "The Noah who preserved the ark of the empire, when menaced by the deluge of Tartar invasions."

After the fall of Musa, Mahomet received at Adrianople the ready homage of the European subjects of the Ottoman Empire, and the felicitations of the neighbouring rulers. The Emperor Palæologus and Mahomet had reciprocally aided each other against

Musa; and Mahomet honourably showed his gratitude and good faith by restoring according to promise to the Greek Empire the strong places on the Black Sea and the Propontis, and the Thessalian fortresses which had been previously wrested from it by the Turks. A treaty of amity was also concluded between the Sultan and the Venetians. The little republic of Ragusa had in the reign of Mahomet's grandfather placed itself by treaty under the protection of the Turks, and that treaty was now renewed with Sultan Mahomet. The Ambassadors of the Princes of Servia, of Wallachia, of the Albanian Prince who reigned at Yanina, of the petty sovereigns or despots of the Morea, who after Bajazet's ruin had established themselves at Lacedæmon and in Achaia, came also before Mahomet at Adrianople. The Sultan received them all with friendly courtesy; and on their departure he said to them, "Forget not to tell your masters that peace I grant to all, peace I accept from all. May the God of peace be against the breakers of peace!"

A brief season of unusual calm was thus obtained for the countries westward of the Bosphorus and the Hellespont; but Asia was seething with insurrection and war, and Mahomet was speedily obliged to quit his feast of peace at Adrianople to reconquer and secure the ancient possessions of his house. The important city of Smyrna and the adjacent territory were at this period commanded by an Ottoman governor of the name of Djouneid, who had resumed possession of them after the Mongols had withdrawn from Asia Minor, and who had succeeded afterwards in making himself also master of the principality of Aidin. Djouneid had submitted first to Solyman, and afterwards to Mahomet, as his Sultan; but during the last civil war he had openly revolted against Mahomet and he now aspired to make himself an independent sovereign. At the same time the Prince of Caramania had taken advantage of the absence of Mahomet and his best troops from Asia to attack the very heart of the Ottoman Asiatic dominions, and had laid siege to Brusa. The city was well garrisoned, and held out firmly against him; but he burnt to the ground the mosques and other public buildings of the suburbs; and, in the rage of his heart against the race of Othman, he ordered the tomb of Bajazet, which was outside the city walls, to be opened, and the remains of that Sultan to be given to the flames. While the Caramanians were thus engaged in profaning the sanctuaries of their own creed, and in violating the repose of the dead, they suddenly saw approaching them from the west the funeral procession of Prince Musa, whose body had been borne by

Mahomet's orders from Europe to Asia for burial in the mosque of Amurath at Brusa. The besiegers were panic-stricken at this unexpected spectacle : and the Caramanian Prince, thinking possibly that Sultan Mahomet with an army was close at hand, or perhaps seized with remorse and ghostly terror at the sepulchral apparition, fled from Brusa, unchecked by the bitter reproach of one of his own followers, who said to him, "If thou fliest before the dead Ottoman, how wilt thou stand against the living one ?"

The Sultan, when he had crossed over from Europe to Asia with his forces, marched first against his rebellious vassal. He besieged Smyrna, and compelled it to surrender ; and Djouneid was soon reduced to beg for mercy, which Mahomet, moved by the tears of the fallen rebel's family, accorded him. He then marched against the Caramanians. He captured many towns in person ; but was obliged to leave his army by a sudden and severe malady, which baffled the skill of all his physicians save one, the celebrated Sinan, who prescribed the news of a victory as the best medicine that the Sultan could receive. His favourite general, Bajezid Pacha, soon supplied the desired remedy by completely defeating the Caramanians, and taking their Prince, Moustapha Bey, prisoner. Mahomet recovered his health at the joyous intelligence of this success. The Caramanians now sued for peace, which the Ottoman Sultan generously granted. The captive Caramanian Prince in Mahomet's presence placed his right hand within the robe on his own bosom, and solemnly pronounced the oath, "I swear that so long as there is breath in this body I will never attack or covet the Sultan's possessions." Mahomet set him at liberty with every mark of honour ; but while he was yet in sight of the conqueror's camp, the Prince, who held that between the Caramanians and the Ottomans war ought to reign from the cradle to the grave, commenced marauding on some of the herds that were grazing on the plain round him. His officers reminded him of the oath which he had just taken ; but he drew from his bosom a dead pigeon squeezed tightly in his right hand, and sarcastically repeated the words of his oath, "So long as there shall be breath in *this* body."

Incensed at this perfidy, Mahomet renewed the war, and gained great advantages ; but he again was generous enough to grant peace on the reiterated entreaties of the Caramanians. They had received such severe blows in the last war, that terror now kept them quiet for several years, and the Asiatic dominions of the Sultan enjoyed peace and tranquillity ; which Mahomet further secured by entering into friendly diplomatic relations with the various princes of Upper Asia, so as to avert further invasions like those of Timour.

On his return to Europe, in 1416, Mahomet became involved in a war with the Venetians. The petty lords of many of the islands of the Ægean Sea were nominal vassals of the Republic of Venice; but, in disregard of the treaty between that power and the Sultan, they continued to capture the Turkish shipping and to plunder the Turkish coasts. Mahomet fitted out a squadron of galleys to retaliate for their injuries, and this led to an encounter with the Venetian fleet, which, under their Admiral, Loredano, completely defeated the Turks off Gallipoli, on the 29th May, 1416. Peace was soon restored; and a Turkish ambassador appeared at Venice in the same year, with a new treaty between his master and the Republic. Mahomet's troops sustained some severe reverses in expeditions undertaken against Styria and Hungary between 1416 and 1420; but no very important hostilities were waged between him and his neighbours in European Christendom. A far more serious peril to the Sultan was a revolt of the Dervishes, which broke out both in Europe and Asia; and was only quelled by the Sultan's troops after several sanguinary battles. This insurrection was organised by the judge of the army, Bedreddin, aided by an apostate Jew, named Tirlak. The nominal chief of the fanatics was a Turk of low birth, named Bærekludye Mustapha, whom they proclaimed as their spiritual lord and father. All these three perished either in battle or by the executioner, and their sect was extinguished with them. Their revolt is remarkable, as being, with the exception of the Wahabite rebellion in the last and present centuries, the only religious war by which the Ottoman Empire has ever been troubled.

After this formidable peril had passed away, Mahomet was called on to defend his throne from another domestic enemy. It has been mentioned, that one of Bajazet's sons, Prince Mustapha, who was present on the day of Angora, disappeared after the defeat of the Turks in that battle. His body was not found among the slain, though Timour caused diligent search to be made for it; nor was the mode of his escape (if he escaped) ever ascertained. Certain it is, that, in 1420, a claimant to the Ottoman sovereignty appeared in Europe, who asserted that he was Mustapha, the son of Sultan Bajazet, and who was recognised as such by many of the Turks. Supported by the Prince of Wallachia, and by Djouneid, the old rebel against Mahomet, the pretender penetrated into Thessaly with a large army. Mahomet met him with his customary vigour, and a pitched battle was fought near Salonica, in which the claimant was utterly defeated, and fled for protection to the Greek commandant of that city. The Byzantine Emperor refused to surrender the suppliant fugitive, but consented to keep him in strict custody on condition of Mahomet paying annually a large sum of money, ostensibly for the captive's maintenance, but in reality as the wages for his imprisonment.

There was one other son of Sultan Bajazet, who figures little in history, but whose melancholy lot must not be passed over for the sake of uniformly preserving the bright colour, in which we would gladly represent the character of Mahomet I. Prince Kasimir does not appear to have fought at Angora, like his five brethren, or to have taken any part in the subsequent civil wars between them. He came into Mahomet's power; and though he was not put to death in conformity with the precedent which Bajazet had established, he was deprived of sight by his brother's order. The blinded prince received the grant of a domain near Brusa, where he resided; and Turkish historians praise the good-nature of Sultan Mahomet, who, whenever he visited his Asiatic capital, sent for his sightless brother to the palace and treated him with benevolence truly fraternal. Another stain on the memory of Mahomet the Gentleman is his guilty weakness in seeking to strengthen his sovereignty by the death of the son of his brother Solyman. But in this case, as in his conduct towards Prince Kasimir, Mahomet recoiled from following out to its full extent the stern principle of extinguishing in the blood of those nearest to the throne all risk of their rivalry with its occupant. He spared a daughter whom Solyman had also left; and when that daughter was married, and bore a son, Mahomet conferred ample wealth on the child, so that it should be maintained in a manner worthy of its rank. Mahomet indeed showed on his death-bed, that no sophistry or statecraft could blind his natural sense to the heinous guilt of fratricide. He was stricken with apoplexy near the close of the year 1421; and though he partially recovered, he knew that his end was approaching, and earnestly implored his favourite general, Bajezid Pacha, to place his two infant sons under the protection of the Greek Emperor, lest their elder brother, Prince Amurath, on becoming Sultan, should imitate the crimes of his grandfather and his father, and study his own security by their destruction. Mahomet did not long survive the shock which his system had received; but his death was concealed from the public by his general and chief officers of state for more than forty days, while intelligence of the event was sent to Prince

Amurath, who, at the time of his father's mortal illness, held a command on the frontiers of Asia Minor.

Mahomet I. was but forty-seven years of age at the time of his death; and his reign, as Sultan of the re-united empire, had lasted only eight years. But he had been an independent prince for nearly the whole preceding period of eleven years that passed between his father's captivity at Angora and his own final victory over his brother Musa at Chamurli. For nineteen years, therefore, he was a ruler over his people; and his memory is still deservedly cherished and honoured among them. He was buried at Brusa, in a mausoleum erected by himself near the celebrated mosque which he built there, and which, from its decorations of green porcelain, is called the Green Mosque. This edifice is said to be the most beautiful specimen of Saracenic architecture and carving that is in existence. Mahomet I. also completed the vast and magnificent mosque at Brusa, which his grandfather Amurath I. had commenced, but which had been neglected during the reign of Bajazet. It is deserving of mention that Mahomet founded in the vicinity of his own mosque and mausoleum two characteristic institutions, one a school, and one a refectory for the poor, both of which he endowed with royal munificence. The reign of this Sultan is cited by Von Hammer as the period when a taste for literature and fondness for poetry first prevailed among the Ottomans. He was a liberal patron of intellectual merit; and the name of an early literary Turkish politician, Sehiri, is preserved in honourable reputation for having, while Mahomet was Governor of Amassia, and Sehiri his Defterdar or Chancellor of the Exchequer, inspired the young prince with an enduring zeal for the advancement of literature and art, and for the generous patronage of their professors.

Amurath II., when called from his vice-royalty in Asia Minor to become the sovereign of the Turkish Empire, was only eighteen years of age. He was solemnly recognised as Sultan, and girt with the sabre of Othman, at Brusa; and the troops and officers of state paid willing homage to him as their sovereign. But his reign was soon troubled by insurrection. The Greek Emperor, despising the youth of Amurath, released the pretender Mustapha from confinement, and acknowledged him as the legitimate heir to the throne of Bajazet; having first stipulated with him that he should, if successful, repay the Greek Emperor for his liberation by the cession of a large number of important cities. The pretender was landed by the Byzantine galleys in the European dominions of the Sultan, and for a time made rapid progress.

Large bodies of the Turkish soldiery joined him, and he defeated and killed the veteran general Bajezid Pacha, whom Amurath first sent against him. He then crossed the Dardanelles to Asia, with a large army; but the young Sultan showed in this emergency that he possessed military and political abilities worthy of the best of his ancestors. Mustapha was out-manœuvred in the field; and his troops, whose affection to his person and confidence in his cause he had lost by his violence and incapacity, passed over in large numbers to Amurath. Mustapha took refuge in the strong city of Gallipoli; but the Sultan, who was greatly aided by a Genoese commandant named Adorno, beseiged him there, and stormed the place. Mustapha was taken and put to death; and the Sultan then turned his arms against the Greek Emperor, and declared his resolution to punish the unprovoked enmity of Palæologus by the capture of Constantinople.

The embassies, charged with abject apology, by which the Greeks now sought to appease the Sultan's wrath, were dismissed with contempt; and in the beginning of June, 1422, Amurath was before the trembling capital with twenty thousand of his best troops. Ten thousand of the dreaded Akindji, under their hereditary commander, Michael Bey, had previously been let loose by the Sultan upon the lands which the Greek Emperor yet retained beyond the city walls, and had spread fire and desolation through the doomed territory, without any attempt being made by the Byzantines to check or to avenge their ravages. Amurath's own army seemed still more irresistible; and the Sultan carried on the siege with a degree of skill as well as vigour, rarely to be found in the military operations of that age. He formed a line of embankment only a bowshot from the city wall, and extended it from the sea to the Golden Horn, so as to face the whole landward side of the city. This rampart was formed of strong timber. with a thick mound of earth heaped up along its front; and it received uninjured the discharges of firearms and the shocks of the heaviest stones that the ballistas of the Greeks could hurl against it. Under cover of this line, Amurath's army urged on the work of attack. Movable towers were built to convey storming parties to the summits of the city wall; mines were laboriously pushed forward; and breaching cannon were now for the first time employed by the Ottomans, but with little effect. Wishing to increase the zeal and the number of the assailants, Amurath proclaimed that the city and all its treasures should be given up to the true believers who would storm it; and crowds of fanatic volunteers flocked to the camp to share in the harvest of piety and plunder. Among the recruits were a large number of dervishes, headed by a renowned saint named Seid Bokhari, who announced the day and the hour at which it was fated for him to lead the Mahometans to the capture of Constantinople. Accordingly, at the appointed time, one hour after noon on Monday, the 25th of August, 1422, Seid Bokhari led on the Ottoman army to the assault. 500 dervishes, who had stipulated that the Christian nuns of Constantinople should be assigned as their particular share of the booty, formed the forlorn hope of the stormers. The Ottomans attacked vehemently, and the Greeks resisted steadily along the whole length of the city wall; but it was near the gate of St. Romanus that the combat raged most fiercely. The Christians as well as the Mahometans were animated by religious enthusiasm, and by the assurance that their arms were aided by the interposition of supernatural power. At last some said that they beheld, and all believed that there was seen on the outer bastions a bright apparition of a virgin robed in garments of violet hue and dazzling lustre, whose looks darted panic amid the assailing columns. This was the Panagia, the Holy Virgin, who had descended for the special protection of the sacred maids of the Christian city from the boastful impiety of the monks of Mahomet. The besiegers themselves (not unwilling perhaps to find some pretext for their defeat, besides the strength of the fortifications and the bravery of the defenders) gave credit and confirmation to this legend. It is certain that the attack failed, and that the siege was soon afterwards raised. But it is little consonant with the character of Amurath, that a single repulse, in which the loss of life was inconsiderable, should have made him abandon a siege for which he had made such ample and scientific preparations. The intrigues of the Byzantine Emperor had lit up a new civil war in his enemy's Asiatic dominions; and Amurath, like his grandfather Bajazet, was obliged to relinquish Constantinople, when the prize seemed to be within his grasp, and to fight for safety as well as for empire on the eastern side of the Bosphorus.

Besides the two infant brothers, of whom mention has already been made, Amurath had another brother named Mustapha, who was in Asia Minor at the time of their father's death. Prince Mustapha was of the age of thirteen when that event occurred; and his attendants, ignorant of the character of Amurath, fled with their princely charge into Caramania. He had grown up to manhood there without Amurath making any attempt against his life or liberty; but after the overthrow of the pretender, Mustapha, his supposed uncle, he listened to the suggestions and promises of the emissaries whom the Greek Emperor now sent to him; and being supported with some troops by the Princes of Caramania and Kermian, he suddenly invaded his brother's dominions, made himself master of several places of importance, and laid siege to Brusa. The rapidity with which Amurath marched a veteran and well-appointed army to the rescue, disconcerted all young Mustapha's projects. The Ottomans who had joined him after his first successes deserted him; his Greek allies were far too feeble to encounter Amurath's forces; and the unfortunate prince fled for his life, but was pursued, overtaken, and captured by some of his brother's officers, who instantly hanged their prisoner on the nearest tree, without giving an opportunity to their master either to exercise a perilous clemency, or to become an actual participator in taking away his brother's life.

The civil war was thus promptly extinguished; and in 1424 Amurath returned to Europe, having re-established perfect order in his Asiatic provinces, and chastised the neighbouring sovereigns who had promoted the late hostilities against him. Amurath did not renew the siege of Constantinople, but accepted a treaty by which the Greek Emperor bound himself to pay an annual tribute of 30,000 ducats to the Sultan, and surrendered the city of Zeitoun (Lysimachia) and all the other remaining Greek cities on the river Strania (Strymon) and the Black Sea, except Selymbria and Derkos.

In 1430 Amurath besieged and captured the important city of Thessalonica, which had thrown off its allegiance to the Emperor, and placed itself under the protection of the Venetians, who were at that time in enmity with the Sultan. Other accessions of power in the same quarter, and successful hostilities with various Asiatic princes, are recorded in the detailed narratives of the acts of Amurath; but the main feature of the reign of this great Sultan is his long contest with the warlike nations on the northern and western frontiers of his European dominions; a struggle marked by many vicissitudes, and which called forth into energetic action the high qualities of Amurath himself, and also of his renowned opponents, Hunyades, the hero of Hungary, and Scanderbeg, the champion of Albania.

We have seen how valuable to the Turkish Empire, in its season of disaster, after the overthrow of Sultan Bajazet, was the steady fidelity and friendship with which the Lord of Servia, Stephen Lasarevitch, adhered to his engagements with the house of Othman. That prince died in 1427; and his successor, George

Brankovich, who was bound by no personal ties, like those of his predecessor, to the interest of the Ottomans, resolved to check their further progress.   The Hungarians also, whom the recollection of dreadful defeat at Nicopolis had kept inactive during the temporary dismemberment and feebleness of the power which had smitten them, now felt their martial confidence in their own prowess revive ; and their jealousy of the growth of the Turkish dominion was reawakened.   Moreover, the Bosnians, who saw their country gradually overrun from the military frontier on which the Ottomans had established themselves at Scupi, and the Albanians, who beheld their strong places, Argyro-castrum and Croia, in Amurath's possession, were conscious that their national independence was in danger, and were favourably disposed for action against the common foe.[1]   Wallachia was eager for liberation ; and the un-sleeping hatred of the Caramanians to the Ottomans made it easy for the Christian antagonists of the Sultan in Europe to distract his arms by raising war and insurrection against him in Asia.   Yet there was for several years no general and vigorous confederation against the Sultan ; and a chequered series of partial hostilities and negotiations filled nearly twenty years, during which the different Christian neighbours of the Sultan were sometimes his antagonists and sometimes his allies against each other.   At last the accession of Ladislaus, the third King of Lithuania and Poland, to the crown of Hungary, brought fresh strength and enterprise to the Sultan's foes; and a severe struggle followed, which after threatening the utter expulsion of the house of Othman from Europe, confirmed for centuries its dominion in that continent, and wrought the heavier subjugation of those who were then seeking to release themselves from its superiority.

In 1442 Amurath was repulsed from Belgrade ; and his generals, who were besieging Hermanstadt, in Transylvania, met with a still more disastrous reverse.   It was at Hermanstadt that the renowned Hunyades first appeared in the wars between the Hungarians and the Turks.   He was the illegitimate son of Sigismond, King of Hungary, and the fair Elizabeth Morsiney.   In his early youth he gained distinction in the wars of Italy ; and Comines, in his memoirs, celebrates him under the name of the White Knight of Wallachia.   After some campaigns in Western Christendom, Hunyades returned to protect his native country against the Ottomans ; and in 1442 he led a small but chosen force to the relief of Hermanstadt.   He planned his movements ably ; and aided by an

---

[1] Ranke's " Servia," p. 27.

opportune sally of the garrison, he completely defeated Mezid Bey, the Turkish general, killing 20,000 of his troops, and taking prisoner Mezid Bey himself, his son, and many more. Hunyades was no whit inferior to the fiercest Turkish generals in cruelty. Mezid Bey and his son were hewn to pieces in his presence; and one of the chief entertainments at the triumphal feast of the victorious Hungarians was to see captive Turks slaughtered during the banquet.

Amurath sent Schehadeddin Pacha with an army of 80,000 men against Hunyades to avenge this disgrace. But the "White Knight," as the Christians called Hunyades, from the colour of his armour, met Schehadeddin at Vasag, and, though his numbers were far inferior, utterly routed the Turks with even heavier loss than they had sustained before Hermanstadt. The next year, 1443, is the most illustrious in the career of Hunyades, and brought the Ottoman power to the very brink of ruin. The Servian, the Bosnian, and the Wallachian princes were now actively co-operating with King Ladislaus against the Sultan; and an attack of the Caramanians on the Ottoman dominions in Asia compelled Amurath to pass over to that continent and carry on the war there in person, while he left to his generals the defence of his empire in Europe against the Hungarians and their allies.

The Christian army that invaded European Turkey in the remarkable campaign of this year, was the most splendid that had been assembled since the French chivalry and the Hungarians advanced against Bajazet at Nicopolis; and it was guided by the ablest general that Christendom had yet produced against the house of Othman. The fame of Hunyades had brought volunteers from all the nations of the West to serve under him in the holy war against the Mahometans; and the most energetic efforts of Pope Eugenius and his legate, Cardinal Julian, had been devoted to give to these champions of their faith the enthusiasm as well as the name of crusaders. The main body of the confederates, consisting chiefly of Hungarian, Servian, Wallachian, and German troops, crossed the Danube near Semendra. Hunyades, at the head of 12,000 chosen cavalry, then pushed forward nearly to the walls of Nissa. King Ladislaus and the Cardinal Julian followed him with the Polish, and part of the Hungarian troops, and with the crusaders from Italy. On the 3rd of November Hunyades won the first battle of the campaign on the banks of the Morava, near Nissa. The grand army of the Turks was beaten, and fled beyond the Balkan, with the loss of nine standards, 4000 prisoners, and many thousand slain. Hunyades followed close upon the foe, captured the city of Sophia, and then prepared to cross the Balkan, and advance upon Philippopolis.

The passage of the Balkan is an exploit almost as rare in military history as those passages of the Alps that have conferred so much lustre on Hannibal, Charlemagne, and Napoleon.[1] Alexander forced the barrier of the Balkan in 335 B.C., probably through the same pass which Hunyades penetrated from the opposite direction, in A.D. 1443. Amurath I. crossed the Balkan in 1390; and the Russian general, Diebitsch, forced this renowned mountain chain near its eastern extremity in 1827. Hunyades and Diebitsch are the only two commanders who have crossed it from north to south, in spite of armed opposition; and the fact of their accomplishing that exploit against the same enemy (though with an interval of nearly four centuries), and the splendour of the success which each thereby obtained over the Ottoman power, make the similitude between their achievements more remarkable. If the Balkan campaign of Hunyades presents nothing equal to the noble audacity, with which Diebitsch threw a numerically feeble army across the mountain to Adrianople, trusting to the moral effect of such a blow at the crisis when it was dealt, the actual passage which the Hungarian leader effected in the December of 1443 was a more brilliant scene of mountain-warfare, than that of the Russian marshal in 1829, both on account of the enormous increase in the natural difficulties of the transit, caused by the difference of season, and by reason of the superior preparation on the part of the Turks, which Hunyades encountered and overcame.

Two defiles, the openings of which on the northern side are near each other, one to the west named the defile of Soulourderbend, the other to the east that of Isladi, or Slatiza, lead through the Balkan on the road from Sophia to Philippopolis. The Turks, who defended the passage against Hunyades, had barricaded both these defiles with heaps of rocks; and when they found the Hungarian vanguard approach, they poured water throughout the night down the mountain slope, which froze as it fell, and formed at morning a wall of ice against the Christians. Undaunted by these obstacles and the weapons of the enemy, Hunyades encouraged his men by voice and example to clamber onward and through the western defile, until they reached a part where the old Roman works of Trajan completely barred the way. The Hungarians

---

[1] The operations of the Persian Darius Hystaspis (B.C. 506), and of the Russian Svatoslaus (A.D. 907), in the regions of the Hæmus, cannot be satisfactorily traced or verified.

retreated ; but it was only to advance up the eastern defile, which was less perfectly fortified.

There, through the rest of the winter's day, Hunyades and his chivalry fought their gallant upward battle against Turkish arrow and scimetar, amid the still more formidable perils of the precipice, the avalanche, the whelming snowdrift, and the bitter paralysing cold. They triumphed over all; and the Christmas-day of 1443 was celebrated by the exulting Hungarians on the snow-plains of the southern slopes of the conquered Balkan.

The Turks, who had rallied and received reinforcements at the foot of Mount Cunobizza, again fought with Hunyades and were again defeated. It surprises us to read that after this last victory, the Christian army, instead of pushing forward to Adrianople, returned to Buda, where Hunyades displayed his trophies and his prisoners before his rejoicing fellow-countrymen. There is little sign here of such high spirit as afterwards animated Diebitsch, or even of common generalship or policy. But we may be acting unjustly if we throw on the hero of mediæval Hungary the blame of this infirmity of purpose. Such an army, as he led, was very different in subordination and discipline to the regular troops of modern times, or even to the Turkish troops who were its contemporaries and opponents.

Amurath had been personally successful in Asia; but the defeats which his forces had sustained in Europe, and the strength of the confederacy there formed against him filled him with grave alarm. He sought by the sacrifice of the more remote conquests of his House to secure for the rest of his European dominions the same tranquillity which he had re-established in the Asiatic. After a long negotiation a treaty of peace for ten years was concluded at Szegeddin on the 12th of July, 1444, by which the Sultan resigned all claims upon Servia, and recognised George Brankovich as its independent sovereign. Wallachia was given up to Hungary; and the Sultan paid 60,000 ducats for the ransom of Mahmoud Tchelebi, his son-in-law, who had commanded against Hunyades, and had been taken prisoner in the late campaign. The treaty was written both in the Hungarian and in the Turkish languages; King Ladislaus swore upon the Gospels, and the Sultan swore upon the Koran, that it should be truly and religiously observed.

Amurath now thought that his realm was at peace, and that he himself, after so many years of anxiety and toil, might hope to taste the blessings of repose. We have watched him hitherto as a man of action, and we have found ample reason to admire his capacity and vigour in council and in the field. But Amurath had

also other virtues of a softer order, which are not often to be found
in the occupant of an Oriental throne.   He was gentle and affec-
tionate in all the relations of domestic life.   Instead of seeking to
assure his safety by the death of the two younger brothers, for
whose fate their father had been so anxious, Amurath treated them
with kindness and honour while they lived, and bitterly lamented
their loss when they died of the plague in their palace at Brusa.
The other brother, who took up arms against him, was killed without his orders.   He forgave, for the sake of a sister who was
married to the Prince of Kermian, the treasonable hostility with
which that vassal of the House of Othman assailed him ; and the
tears of another sister for the captivity of her husband Mahmoud
Tchelebi, and her entreaties that he might be rescued from the
power of the terrible Hunyades, were believed to have prevailed
much in causing Amurath to seek the pacification of Szegeddin.
When that treaty was concluded, Amurath passed over to Asia,
where he met the deep affliction of learning the death of his eldest
son Prince Alaeddin, who had shared with him the command of
the Ottoman forces in Asia during the operations of the preceding
year.   The bitterness of this bereavement increased the distaste
which Amurath had already acquired for the pomp and turmoil of
sovereignty.   He determined to abdicate the throne in favour of
his second son, Prince Mahomet, and to pass the rest of his life in
retirement at Magnesia.   But it was not in austere privation, or in
the fanatic exercises of Mahometan monasticism, that Amurath
designed his private life to be wasted.   He was no contemner of
the pleasures of sense; and the scene of his retreat was amply
furnished with all the ministry of every delight.

The tidings of warfare renewed by the Christian powers soon
roused the bold Paynim, like Spenser's Cymochles, from his Bower
of Bliss.   The King of Hungary and his confederates had recommenced hostilities in a spirit of treachery that quickly received its
just reward.   Within a month from the signature of the treaty of
Szegeddin the Pope and the Greek Emperor had persuaded the
King of Hungary and his councillors to take an oath to break the
oath which had been pledged to the Sultan.   They represented
that the confessed weakness of the Ottomans, and the retirement
of Amurath to Asia, gave an opportunity for eradicating the Turks
from Europe, which ought to be fully employed.   The Cardinal
Julian pacified the conscientious misgivings, which young King
Ladislaus expressed, by his spiritual authority in giving dispensation and absolution in the Pope's name, and by his eloquence in
maintaining the infamously celebrated thesis, that no faith is to be

5—2

kept with misbelievers. Hunyades long resisted such persuasions to break the treaty ; but his conscience was appeased by the promise that he should be made independent King of Bulgaria, when that province was conquered from the Turks. He only stipulated that the breach of the treaty should be delayed till the 1st of September ; not out of any lingering reluctance to violate it, but in order that the confederates might first reap all possible benefit from it by securely establishing their forces in the strongholds of Servia, which the Ottomans were then evacuating in honest compliance with their engagements. On the 1st of September the King, the legate, and Hunyades, marched against the surprised and unprepared Turks with an army of 10,000 Poles and Hungarians. The temerity which made them expect to destroy the Turkish power in Europe with so slight a force was equal to the dishonesty of their enterprise. They advanced into Wallachia, where Drakul, the prince of that country, joined them with his levies. That sagacious chieftain saw the inadequacy of King Ladislaus's means for the task which he had undertaken, and remonstrated against advancing farther. This brought on a personal difference between him and Hunyades, in the course of which Drakul drew his sabre against the Hungarian general, and was punished by an imprisonment, from which he was only released on promising fresh supplies of troops, and a large contribution of money. The Christian army, in full confidence of success, crossed the Danube, and marched through Bulgaria to the Black Sea. They then moved southward along the coast, destroying a Turkish flotilla at Kaundjik, receiving the surrender of many fortresses, and storming the strongholds of Sunnium and Pezech. The Turkish garrisons of these places were put to the sword, or thrown over precipices. Kavarna was next attacked and taken, and finally the Christians formed the siege of the celebrated city of Varna.

The possession of Varna was then, as now, considered essential for the further advance of an invading army against the Turkish European Empire. Hunyades was still successful ; Varna surrendered to his arms : the triumphant Christians were encamped near it, when they suddenly received the startling tidings, that it was no longer the boy Mahomet that was their adversary, but that Sultan Amurath was himself again. They heard that the best warriors of Asiatic Turkey had thronged together at the summons of their veteran sovereign—that the false Genoese had been bribed to carry Amurath and his army, 40,000 strong, across the Bosphorus, by a ducat for each soldier's freight, thus baffling the papal fleet that cruised idly in the Hellespont. Other messengers

soon hurried into the Christian camp, who announced that the
unresting Sultan had come on against them by forced marches,
and that the imperial Turkish army was posted within four miles
of Varna.

A battle was inevitable ; but the mode, in which Hunyades prepared for it, showed that his confidence was unabated. He rejected
the advice which some gave in a council of war to form intrench-
ments and barricades round their camp, and there await the
Sultan's attack. He was for an advance against the advancing
foe, and for a fair stricken field. The young King caught the
enthusiastic daring of his favourite general, and the Christian
army broke up from their lines, and marched down into the level
ground northward[1] of the city, to attack the Sultan, who had
carefully strengthened his encampment there by a deep ditch and
palisades.

On the eve of the feast of St. Mathurin, the 10th of November,
1444, the two armies were arrayed for battle. The left wing of
the Christian army consisted chiefly of Wallachian troops. The
best part of the Hungarian soldiery was in the right wing, where
also stood the Frankish crusaders under the Cardinal Julian. The
King was in the centre with the royal guard and the young
nobility of his realms. The rear-guard of Polish troops was under
the Bishop of Peterwaradin. Hunyades acted as commander-in-
chief of the whole army. On the Turkish side the two first lines
were composed of cavalry and irregular infantry, the Beyler-Bey of
Roumelia commanding on the right, and the Beyler-Bey of Anatolia
on the left. In the centre, behind their lines, the Sultan took his
post with his Janissaries and the regular cavalry of his body-
guard. A copy of the violated treaty was placed on a lance-
head, and raised on high among the Turkish ranks as a standard
in the battle, and as a visible appeal to the God of Truth, who
punishes perjury among mankind. At the very instant when the
armies were about to encounter, an evil omen troubled the Christians. A strong and sudden blast of wind swept through their
ranks, and blew all their banners to the ground, save only that of
the King.

Yet, the commencement of the battle seemed to promise them
a complete and glorious victory. Hunyades placed himself at the
head of the right wing, and charged the Asiatic troops with such
vigour that he broke them and chased them from the field. On

[1] Amurath had probably crossed the Balkan by the pass that leads from
Aidos to Pravadi, and had then marched eastward upon Varna. This would
bring him to the rear of Hunyades.

the other wing, the Wallachians were equally successful against the cavalry and Azabs of Roumelia. King Ladislaus advanced boldly with the Christian centre; and Amurath seeing the rout of his two first lines, and the disorder that was spreading itself in the ranks round him, despaired of the fate of the day, and turned his horse for flight. Fortunately for the House of Othman, Karadja, the Beyler-Bey of Anatolia, who had fallen back on the centre with the remnant of his defeated wing, was near the Sultan at this critical moment. He seized his master's bridle, and implored him to fight the battle out. The commandant of the Janissaries, Yazidzi-Toghan, indignant at such a breach of etiquette, raised his sword to smite the unceremonious Beyler-Bey, when he was himself cut down by an Hungarian sabre. Amurath's presence of mind had failed him only for a moment; and he now encouraged his Janissaries to stand firm against the Christian charge. Young King Ladislaus, on the other side, fought gallantly in the thickest of the strife; but his horse was killed under him, and he was then surrounded and overpowered. He wished to yield himself up prisoner, but the Ottomans, indignant at the breach of the treaty, had sworn to give no quarter. An old Janissary, Khodja Khiri, cut off the Christian King's head, and placed it on a pike, a fearful companion to the lance, on which the violated treaty was still reared on high. The Hungarian nobles were appalled at the sight, and their centre fled in utter dismay from the field. Hunyades, on returning with his victorious right wing, vainly charged the Janissaries, and strove at least to rescue from them the ghastly trophy of their victory. At last he fled in despair with the wreck of the troops that he had personally commanded, and with the Wallachians who collected round him. The Hungarian rearguard, abandoned by their commanders, was attacked by the Turks the next morning and massacred almost to a man. Besides the Hungarian King, Cardinal Julian, the author of the breach of the treaty and the cause of this calamitous campaign, perished at Varna beneath the Turkish scimetar, together with Stephen Bahory, and the Bishops of Eilau and Grosswardein. This overthrow did not bring immediate ruin upon Hungary, but it was fatal to the Sclavonic neighbours of the Ottomans, who had joined the Hungarian King against them. Servia and Bosnia were thoroughly reconquered by the Mahometans; and the ruin of these Christian nations, which adhered to the Greek Church, was accelerated by the religious intolerance with which they were treated by their fellow Christians of Hungary and Poland, who obeyed the Pope, and hated the Greek Church as heretical. A

Servian tradition relates that George Brankovich once inquired of Hunyades what he intended to do with respect to religion, if he proved victorious. Hunyades answered that he would compel the country to become Roman Catholic. Brankovich thereupon asked the same question of the Sultan, who replied that he would build a church near every mosque, and leave the people at liberty to bow in the mosques or to cross themselves in the churches, according to their respective creeds. The Servians, who heard this, thought it better to submit to the Turks and retain their ancient faith, than to accept the Latin rites.[1] The tradition expresses a fact, for which ample historical evidence might be cited. So also in Bosnia, the bigotry of the Church of Rome in preaching up a crusade against the sect of the Patarenes, which was extensively spread in that country, caused the speedy and complete annexation of an important frontier province to the Ottoman Empire. Seventy Bosnian fortresses are said to have opened their gates to the Turks within eight days. The royal House of Bosnia was annihilated, and many of her chief nobles embraced Mahometanism to avoid a similar doom.[2]

Amurath's projects for retirement had been disappointed by the necessity of his resuming the sovereign power to save the Ottoman Empire from the Hungarians and their confederates. After the decisive blow which he had dealt at Varna to the enemies of his race, the Sultan again sought to obtain the calm of private life, and was again compelled to resume the cares of state. Early in 1445 he abdicated a second time in favour of his son, and went back to his Epicurean retreat at Magnesia. But the young hand of Mahomet was too feeble to curb the fierce Turkish soldiery; and the Janissaries showed their insubordinate violence in acts of pillage and murder, and in arrogant demands for increased pay, which threatened open mutiny and civil war. The veteran statesmen, whom Amurath had placed as councillors round his son, saw the necessity of recalling their old master to the helm of the empire. Amurath yielded to their entreaties, and hastened to Adrianople, where he showed himself once more to the people and the army as their sovereign. He was rapturously welcomed. The ringleaders in the late disorders were promptly punished, and the masses were judiciously pardoned. Order was thoroughly restored

---

[1] Ranke's "Servia," p. 80.
[2] The complete degradation of Servia and Bosnia was not effected until the reign of Mahomet II., Amurath's successor. But Ranke ("History of Servia," p. 78) rightly treats this as the result of the battle of Varna.

in court and camp. Young Prince Mahomet, who had twice
during twelve months tasted supreme power, and twice been compelled to resign it, was sent to Magnesia, to remain there till more
advanced age should make him more capable of reigning. Amurath did not venture a third time on the experiment of abdication.
He has been highly eulogised as the only sovereign who had ever
abdicated *twice*, and descended into private life after having learned
by experience the contrast between it and the possession of a
throne.

The remaining six years of Amurath's life and reign were signalised by successful enterprises against the Peloponnesus, the
petty despots of which became tributary vassals of the Ottomans,
and by a great defeat which he gave his old antagonist, Hunyades, at
Kossova, after a three days' battle in October, 1448. In Albania
his arms were less fortunate ; and during the latter part of Amurath's reign his power was defied, and his pride repeatedly humbled
by the celebrated George Castriot, called by the Turks Scanderbeg, or Lord Alexander, the name by which he is best known in
history.

The father of this champion, John Castriot, Lord of Emalthia
(the modern district of Moghlene), had submitted, like the other
petty despots of those regions, to Amurath early in his reign, and
had placed his four sons in the Sultan's hands as hostages for his
fidelity. Three of them died young. The fourth, whose name was
George, pleased the Sultan by his beauty, strength, and intelligence.
Amurath caused him to be brought up in the Mahometan creed ;
and, when he was only eighteen, conferred on him the government
of one of the Sanjaks of the empire. The young Albanian
proved his courage and skill in many exploits under Amurath's eye,
and received from him the name of Iskanderbeg, the Lord Alexander.
When John Castriot died, Amurath took possession of his principalities, and kept the son constantly employed in distant wars.
Scanderbeg brooded over this injury; and when the Turkish
armies were routed by Hunyades in the campaign of 1443, Scanderbeg determined to escape from their side, and assume forcible
possession of his patrimony. He suddenly entered the tent of the
Sultan's chief-secretary, and forced that functionary, with the
poniard at his throat, to write and seal a formal order to the
Turkish commander of the strong city of Croia, in Albania, to
deliver that place and the adjacent territory to Scanderbeg, as the
Sultan's viceroy. He then stabbed the secretary, and hastened to
Croia, where his stratagem gained him instant admittance and
submission. He now publicly abjured the Mahometan faith, and

declared his intention of defending the creed of his forefathers, and restoring the independence of his native land. The Christian population flocked readily to his banner, and the Turks were massacred without mercy. For nearly twenty-five years Scander- beg contended against all the power of the Ottomans, though directed by the skill of Amurath and his successor Mahomet, the conqueror of Constantinople. The difficult nature of the wild and mountainous country, which he occupied, aided Scanderbeg mate- rially in the long resistance which he thus opposed to the else- where triumphant Turks. But his military genius must have been high : and without crediting all the legends of his personal prowess, we may well believe that the favourite chief of the Albanian mountaineers, in the guerilla warfare by which he chiefly baffled the Turks, must have displayed no ordinary skill and daring, and may have possessed strength and activity such as rarely fall to the lot of man.[1] The strongest proof of his valour is the superstitious homage which they paid to him when they occupied Lissa in the Venetian territories, whither Scanderbeg had at last retired from Albania, and where he died in 1567. The Turkish soldiers forced open his tomb, and eagerly sought portions of his bones to wear as amulets, thinking that they would communicate a spirit of valour similar to that of the hero to whose mortal fabric they had once belonged.

The Sultan, under whom Scanderbeg fought in youth, died long before the bold Albanian, who once had been his favourite pupil in the art of war, and afterwards his most obstinate adversary. Amurath expired at Adrianople in 1451, after having governed his people with justice and in honour for thirty years. His noble qualities are attested by the Greek as well as by Turkish historians. He was buried at Brusa. Our own old historian, Knolles, who wrote in 1610, says of his sepulchre : "Here he now lieth in a

---

[1] According to the authorities that were used and decorated by Knolles, Scanderbeg "ever fought against the Turks with his arm bare, and that with such fierceness, that the blood did oftentimes burst out of his lips. It is written that he, with his own hand, slew three thousand Turks in the time of his wars against them." One of the best of the numerous harangues which Knolles introduces in his history, is the speech which, at p. 198 of his first volume, he puts in the mouth of a Turkish soldier, "a rough, bold- spirited fellow," at Sfetigrade, in defiance of the threats of Scanderbeg. The Turk bids Scanderbeg's messengers tell their master, that "If he seeks to impose those conditions on us, *let him once more bare that arm of his which men of courage fear not so much as he thinketh.*" Byron, when a boy, was (like Johnson) fond of reading Knolles, and he must have had this picture of Scanderbeg in his mind when he described Alp in the "Siege of Corinth."

chapel without any roof, his grave nothing differing from that of the common Turks, which they say he commanded to be done in his last will, that the mercy and blessing of God might come unto him by the shining of the sun and moon, and the falling of the rain and dew of heaven upon his grave."

CHAPTER V.

REIGN AND CHARACTER OF MAHOMET II.—SIEGE AND CONQUEST
OF CONSTANTINOPLE—FURTHER CONQUESTS IN EUROPE AND
ASIA—REPULSE BEFORE BELGRADE—CONQUEST OF THE CRIMEA
—UNSUCCESSFUL ATTACK ON RHODES—CAPTURE OF OTRANTO
—DEATH OF MAHOMET.[1]

MAHOMET II., surnamed by his countrymen "the Conqueror," was
aged twenty-one years when his father died.   He heard of that event
at Magnesia, whither the Grand Vizier had despatched a courier
to him from Adrianople.   He instantly sprang on an Arab horse,
and exclaiming, "Let those who love me, follow me," galloped off
towards the shore of the Hellespont.   In a few days he was
solemnly enthroned.   His first act of sovereign authority showed
that a different spirit to that of the generous Amurath would now
wield the Ottoman power.   Amurath had left a little son, a babe
still at the breast, by his second wife, a princess of Servia.   Mahomet ordered his infant brother to be drowned in a bath; and
the merciless command was executed at the very time when the
unhappy mother, in ignorance of her child's doom, was offering
her congratulations to the murderer on his accession.   Mahomet
perceived the horror which the atrocity of this deed caused among
his subjects; and he sought to avert it from himself by asserting
that the officer who had drowned the infant prince had acted
without orders, and by putting him to death for the pretended
treason.   But Mahomet himself, when in after years he declared
the practice of royal fratricide to be a necessary law of the state,
confessed clearly his own share in this the first murder of his
deeply-purpled reign.

He had now fully outgrown the boyish feebleness of mind, which
had unfitted him for the throne when twice placed on it by his
father six years before.   For craft, capacity, and courage, he ranks
among the highest of the Ottoman Sultans.   His merits also as a
far-sighted statesman, and his power of mind as a legislator, are as

[1] See Von Hammer, books 12 to 18.

undeniable as are his military talents. He was also keenly sensible to all intellectual gratifications, and he was himself possessed of unusually high literary abilities and attainments. Yet with all these qualities we find combined in him an amount of cruelty, perfidy, and revolting sensuality, such as seldom stain human nature in the same individual.

Three years before Mahomet II. was girt with the scimetar of Othman, Constantine XI. was crowned Emperor of Constantinople —a prince whose heroism throws a sunset glory on the close of the long-clouded series of the Byzantine annals. The Roman Empire of the East was now shrunk to a few towns and a scanty district beyond the walls of the capital city; but that city was itself a prize of sufficient splendour to tempt the ambition and excite the hostility of a less aspiring and unscrupulous spirit than that of the son of Amurath. The Ottomans felt that Constantinople was the true natural capital of their empire. While it was in the hands of others, the communication between their European and their Asiatic provinces could never be secure. Its acquisition by themselves would consolidate their power, and invest them with the majesty that still lingered round those walls, which had encircled the chosen seat of Roman Empire for nearly eleven hundred years.

The imprudence of Constantine, who seems to have judged the character of Mahomet from the inability to reign which he had shown at the premature age of fourteen, hastened the hostility of the young Sultan. Constantine sent an embassy, demanding the augmentation of a stipend which was paid to the Byzantine Court for the maintenance of a descendant of Solyman, Sultan Bajazet's eldest son. This personage, who was named Orkhan, had long been in apparent retirement, but real custody at Constantinople, and the ambassadors hinted that if their demands were not complied with, the Greek Emperor would immediately set him loose, to compete with Mahomet for the Turkish throne. Mahomet, who at this time was engaged in quelling some disturbances in Asia Minor, answered with simulated courtesy; but the old Grand Vizier, Khalil, warned the Byzantines, with indignant vehemence, of the folly of their conduct, and of the difference which they would soon experience between the fierce ambition of the young Sultan and the mild forbearance of his predecessor. Mahomet had indeed bent all his energies on effecting the conquest of the Greek capital, and he resolved to secure himself against any interruption or division of his forces while engaged in that great enterprise. He provided for the full security of his territories in Asia; he made a truce of three years with Hunyades, which

guaranteed him from all attack from the north in Europe; and
he then contemptuously drove away the imperial agents who received the revenues of the lands allotted for the maintenance of
Orkhan, and began to construct a fortress on the European side of
the Bosphorus, about five miles above Constantinople, at a place
where the channel is narrowest, and immediately opposite one
that had been built by Bajazet Yilderim on the Asiatic shore.
Constantine remonstrated in vain against these evident preparations for the blockade of his city; and the Ottomans employed in
the work were encouraged to commit acts of violence against the
Greek peasantry, which soon led to conflicts between armed bands
on either side. Constantine closed the gates of his city in alarm,
and sent another embassy of remonstrance to the Sultan, who
replied by a declaration of war, and it was evident that the death-
struggle of the Greek Empire was now fast approaching.

Each party employed the autumn and winter of 1452 in earnest
preparations for the siege, which was to be urged by the one and
resisted by the other in the coming spring. Mahomet collected
the best troops of his empire at Adrianople; but much more than
mere numbers of soldiery, however well disciplined and armed for
the skirmish or the battle-field, was requisite for the capture of
the great and strong city of Constantinople. Artillery had for
some time previously been employed both by Turkish and Christian
armies; but Mahomet now prepared a more numerous and formidable park of cannon than had ever before been seen in warfare.
A Hungarian engineer, named Urban, had abandoned the thankless service and scanty pay of the Greeks for the rich rewards and
honours with which the Sultan rewarded all who aided him in
his conquest. Urban cast a monster cannon for the Turks, which
was the object both of their admiration and terror. Other guns
of less imposing magnitude, but probably of greater efficiency,
were prepared; and ammunition and military stores of every
description, and the means of transport, were collected on an
equally ample scale. But Mahomet did not merely heap together
the materials of war with the ostentatious profusion so common
in Oriental rulers. He arranged all, he provided for the right use
of all, in the keen spirit of skilful combination, which we admire
in the campaigns of Cæsar and Napoleon. He was almost incessantly occupied in tracing and discussing with his officers plans of
the city, of his intended lines, of the best positions for his batteries
and magazines, of the spots where mines might be driven with
most effect, and of the posts which each division of his troops
should occupy.

In the devoted city, the Emperor, with equal ability, but far different feelings, collected the poor resources of his own remnant of empire, and the scanty succours of the Western nations for the defence. The efforts which he had made to bring the Greek Church into communion with the Church of Rome, as the price of cordial and effectual support against the Mahometans, had alienated his own subjects from him ; and the bigoted priests of Byzantium, when called on by the Emperor to contribute their treasures, and to arm in the defence of their national independence, replied by reviling him as a heretic. The lay leader of the orthodox Greeks, the Grand Duke Notaras, openly avowed that he would rather see the turban of the Sultan than the tiara of the Pope in Constantinople.[1] Only six thousand Greeks, out of a population of one hundred thousand,[2] took any part in the defence of the city; and the Emperor was obliged to leave even these under the command of the factious Notaras, whose ecclesiastical zeal showed itself in violent dissensions, instead of cordial military co-operation with the chiefs of the Latin auxiliaries.

These auxiliaries were partly contributed by the Pope, who sent Cardinal Isidore with a small body of veteran troops, and some pecuniary aid, to the Greek Emperor. The Italian and Spanish commercial cities that traded with Constantinople, showed their interest in her fate, by sending contingents to her defence. Bands of Aragonese, of Catalans, and of Venetians, gave assistance to Constantine, which their skill and bravery made of great value, though their numbers were but small. His most important auxiliary was the Genoese commander, John Giustiniani, who arrived with two galleys and three hundred chosen men, a little before the commencement of the siege. Altogether, Constantine had a garrison of about 9000 troops to defend walls of fourteen miles in extent, the whole landward part of which, for a space of five miles, was certain to be attacked by the Turkish troops. The fortifications, built in ancient times, and for other systems of warfare, were ill adapted to have heavy cannon placed and worked on them ; and many places had been suffered to become dilapidated. Still, amid all this difficulty and distress, Constantine did his duty to his country and his creed. No means of restoring or improving the defences were neglected, which his own military skill and that of his Latin allies could suggest, and which his ill-supplied treasury, and his disloyal subjects, would enable him to supply.

[1] Ducas, 148. Finlay, vol. ii. 627.
[2] Finlay, 646.

But the patriotism, and even the genius, of a single ruler are vain to save the people that will not save themselves. The Greeks had long been ripe for slavery, nor could their fall be further delayed.

In the spring of 1453, the Turks were for the last time before the city, so often besieged by them and others, and so often besieged in vain.[1] Mahomet formed his lines, as Amurath had done, from the harbour to the sea, and they were strengthened with a similar embankment. Fourteen batteries were formed opposite those parts of the landward wall of the city that appeared to be the feeblest. The chief attack was directed against the gate of St. Romanus, near the centre of the wall. Besides the Turkish cannon, balistas were planted along the lines, which hurled large stones upon the battlements. The Turkish archers kept up a shower of arrows on any part of the walls where the defenders showed themselves; and a body of miners, whom the Sultan had brought from the mines of Novoberda, in Servia, carried on their subterranean works as far as the city wall, and forced large openings in the outer of the two walls. The aggregate of the Turkish troops is variously estimated at from 70,000 to 250,000. The smaller number must have been sufficient for all the military operations of the siege; nor is it probable that Mahomet would have increased the difficulty of finding sufficient provisions for his army by uselessly crowding its ranks. Besides the land forces, the

---

[1] Von Hammer enumerates twenty-nine sieges of the city since its foundation by the Megarians, 658 B.C., under the name of Byzantium. It was besieged, 477 B.C., by Pausanias, Generalissimo of the Greeks, after the campaign of Platæa; in 410 B.C., by Alcibiades; in 347 B.C., by Leon, General of Philip of Macedon; in 197 A.D., by the Emperor Severus; in 313, by the Cæsar Maximius; in 315, by Constantine the Great; in 616, by Khosroes, King of Persia; in 626, by the Chagan of the Avars; in 654, by the Arabs under Moawya; in 667, by Yezid, the Arab; in 672, by Sofien Ben Aouf, the Arab; in 715, by Moslema and Omar Abdul-Aziz, the Arabs; in 739, by Solyman, son of the Caliph Abdul Melek; in 764, by Paganos, Kral of the Bulgarians; in 780, by Haroun-al-Rashid: in 798, by Abdul-Melek, Haroun's general; in 811, by Kramus, Despot of the Sclavi; in 820, by the Sclavian Thomas; in 866, by the Russians, under Oswald and Dir; in 914, by Simeon, Kral of the Bulgarians; in 1048, by the rebel Thornicius; in 1081, by Alexius Comnenus; in 1204, by the Crusaders; in 1261, by Michael Palæologus; in 1356, by Bajazet Yilderim, for the first time; in 1402, by the same, for the second time; in 1414, by Musa, Bajazet's son; in 1422, by Amurath II.; and in 1453, by Mahomet II. Since then it has been unbesieged for four centuries. Of the numerous commanders who have attacked the city, eight only have captured it:— Pausanias, Alcibiades, Severus, Constantine, Alexius Comnenus, Dandolo, Michael Palæologus, and Mahomet.

Sultan had collected a fleet of 320 vessels, of various sizes, but all inferior to the large galleons of the Greeks and their allies. But the Christian ships were only fourteen in number. These were moored in the Golden Horn, or Great Harbour, the entrance of which was secured by a strong chain. The siege commenced on the 6th of April, and was prolonged by the bravery and skill of Constantine, Giustiniani, and their Latin troops until the 29th of May. Many gallant deeds were performed during this time. The ability with which Giustiniani taught the defenders to work their artillery, and to use the important arm of war which they still exclusively possessed in the Greek fire, excited the regretful eulogies of the Sultan himself. A general assault, which the Turks hazarded before the walls were completely breached, and in which they employed the old machinery of movable towers, was repulsed ; and the besiegers' engines were destroyed. A squadron of four Genoese ships, and one Greek ship from Chios, forced their way through the Turkish flotilla, and brought seasonable supplies of corn and ammunition to the city. This action, which took place in the middle of April, was the most brilliant episode of the siege. Mahomet had ordered out a division of his galleys, 150 strong, to intercept the five ships of the Christians, that were seen running swiftly and steadily through the Propontis, before a full and favourable wind. The Greeks thronged the walls, and the Turks crowded down to the beach to watch the issue of this encounter. The Sultan himself rode down to the water's edge, in full expectation of witnessing a triumph of his marine force, and the destruction or capture of his enemies. On came the Christian ships, well-armed, well-manned, and well-manœuvred. They crashed through the foremost of their brave but unpractised assailants. Their superior height made it impossible for their enemies to grapple or board them, and the very number and eagerness of the Turks increased the disorder in which their vessels soon were heaped confusedly together. Shouts of joy rose from the city walls ; while Mahomet, furious at the sight, spurred his horse into the very surf, as if with his own hand he would tear the victory from the Greeks. Still onward came the exulting Christian seamen. From their tall decks, they hurled large stones, and poured incessant volleys of the inextinguishable Greek fire upon the Turkish barks beneath and around them. Onward they came to the harbour's mouth ; the guard-chain was lowered to receive them ; and the welcome reinforcement rode securely in the Golden Horn, while the shattered remnant of the Turkish squadron crept back to the shore, where their sorrowing comrades of the land force, and their indignant Sultan awaited them. Mahomet, in his wrath at the loss, and still more at the humiliation which he had sustained, ordered his defeated admiral, Baltaoghli, to be impaled on the spot. The murmurs and entreaties of the Janissaries made him recall the atrocious command; but he partly wreaked his wrath by inflicting personal chastisement on his brave but unsuccessful officer. Four slaves stretched the admiral prostrate on the ground, and Mahomet dealt him one hundred blows with his heavy battle-mace. This reverse of the first Turkish admiral is said to have given rise to a national opinion among the Ottomans, that God had given them the empire of the earth, but had reserved that of the sea for the unbelievers. If such an opinion did really exist among the Turks before their late centuries of defeat and disaster, it must have been largely modified by the exploits of Barbarossa, Dragut, Pialé, Piri Reis, Sidi-Ali, Kilig-Ali, and their other naval commanders, who have shed such splendour over the history of the Turkish navy.

The victory which the five relieving galleys obtained, did more even than the material succour which they conveyed, to re-animate the defenders of Constantinople. But it was a solitary reinforcement. Constantine and Giustiniani never again "saw the horizon whiten with sails" that bore hope and succour on their wings. And Mahomet was no Xerxes,[1] to be disheartened by a single defeat, or to turn back from an enterprise because its difficulties surpassed expectation. Unable to gain the entrance of the harbour, he determined by a bold engineering manœuvre to transport part of his fleet across the land, and launch it at the upper part of the Golden Horn, where in the narrow smooth water, and with aid ready from either shore, his galleys would have the mastery over the far less numerous though larger vessels of the Greeks. A smooth road of planks was accordingly made along the five miles of land which intervene between the Bosphorus and the Golden Horn; and a large division of the Turkish galleys was hauled along it, and safely launched in the harbour. As it was necessary to overcome a considerable inclination of the ground, this engineering achievement reflects great credit on Sultan Mahomet; though the transport of war-galleys over broad spaces of land was no novelty either in classical or mediæval warfare; and a remarkable instance had lately occurred in Italy, where the Venetians, in 1437, had moved a fleet overland from the Adige to the Lake of Garda.

Thus master of the upper part of the port, Mahomet formed a

[1] See Herodotus, Urania, xc., and Æschylus, Persæ, 471, for the description of Xerxes witnessing the defeat of his armament at Salamis.

6

pontoon bridge across it, the western end of which was so near to the angle of the landward and the harbour walls, that cannon placed on the pontoon bridge could play upon the harbour side of the city. Giustiniani in vain attempted, with the Genoese and Greek galleys, to destroy this bridge and burn the Turkish flotilla. The Venetians renewed the attempt with equally bad success. Although no serious effect was produced on the fortifications from the additional line of attack along which the Ottomans now established their cannonade, the labours of the scanty garrison were made more severe; and it became necessary to weaken the defence on the landward side, by detaching men and guns to the wall along the harbour. Meanwhile, the exertions of the besiegers on the original and chief line of the siege were unremitting. The fire of their batteries, though slow and feeble in comparison with the artillery practice of modern times, was kept up for seven weeks, and its effects were at last visible in the overthrow of four large towers, and the yawning of a broad chasm in the city walls, near the gate of St. Romanus. The ditch was nearly filled up by the ruins of the defences, and the path into Constantinople was at last open. Mahomet now sent a last summons to surrender, to which Constantine nobly replied, that if the Sultan would grant him peace he would accept it, with thanks to Heaven, that he would pay the Sultan tribute if demanded, but that he would not surrender the city which he had sworn to defend to the last moment of his life.

The capitulation was demanded and refused on the 24th May, and the Sultan gave orders for a general assault on the 29th. He announced to his army that all the plunder of the city should be theirs; and that he only reserved the land and the buildings. The Ottoman soldiery received the announcement with shouts of joy. The chiefs of the Janissaries pledged themselves that victory was certain, and a general illumination of the Turkish camp and fleet at night showed to the besieged the number, the purpose, and the exulting confidence of their foes.

Within the city, the Greek population passed alternately from terror at the coming storm to turbulent confidence in certain superstitious legends, which promised the help of saints and angels to men who would not help themselves. Only a small proportion of his subjects listened to the expostulations and entreaties, by which their noble-minded Emperor urged them to deserve the further favour of Heaven by using to the utmost those resources which Heaven had already placed in their hands. Even among those who bore arms as part of the garrison, the meanest jealousy

of their Latin auxiliaries prevailed.   On the very eve of the final
assault, when Giustiniani, who was charged with the defence of
the great breach, required some additional guns, the Grand Duke
Notaras, who had the general control of the ordnance, refused the
supply, saying that it was unnecessary.   The Latins did their duty
nobly.   Of the twelve chief posts in the defence, ten were held
by them.   Giustiniani in particular distinguished himself by his
valour and skill.   He formed new works in rear of the demolished
towers and gate of St. Romanus ; and extorted the admiration of
the Sultan, who watched his preparations, and exclaimed, " What
would I not give to gain that man to my service !"   But the chief
hero of the defence was Constantine himself.   He knew that his
hour was come ; and prepared to die in the discharge of duty
with the earnest piety of a true Christian and the calm courage of
a brave soldier.   On the night before the assault, he received the
Holy Sacrament in the church of St. Sophia.   He then proceeded
to the great palace, and lingered for a short time in the halls
where his predecessors had reigned for so many centuries, but
which neither he nor any prince sprung from his race was ever to
see again.   When he had passed forth from the palace to take his
station at the great breach, and there await his martyrdom, all
thoughts of earthly grandeur were forgotten ; and turning to those
around him, many of whom had been his companions from youth,
Constantine asked of them, as fellow-Christians, their forgiveness
for any offence that he had ever committed towards them.   Amid
the tears and prayers of all who beheld him, the last of the Cæsars
then went forth to die.

In the Ottoman camp all was ready for the work of death.
Each column had its specified point of attack ; and the Sultan had
so arranged the vast masses of men at his command, that he was
prepared to send fresh troops successively forward against the
city, even if its defenders were to hold their ground against him
from daybreak to noon.   At sunrise, on the 29th May, 1453, the
Turkish drums and trumpets sounded for the assault, and the
leading divisions of the Sultan's army rushed forward.   Prodigal
of lives, and reckoning upon wearing down the resistance of the
garrison by sending wave upon wave of stormers against them,
Mahomet placed his least valued soldiers in the van, to receive
the first steady volleys of the Greek guns, and dull the edge of
the Christian sword.   The better troops were to follow.   The
main body of the Janissaries, under the Sultan's own eye, was to
assault the principal breach.   Detachments of those chosen warriors
were also directed against other weakened points of the defence.

6—2

At the same time that the attack commenced from the camp, the Turkish flotilla moved against the fortifications along the harbour; and the assault soon raged by sea and by land along two sides of the Greek city. For two hours the Christians resisted skilfully and steadily; and though the Sultan in person, by promises, by threats, and by blows, urged his columns forward to the great breach, neither there nor elsewhere along the line could they bear back the stubborn courage of the defenders; nor could a living Mahometan come into Constantinople. At last Giustiniani, who, side by side with the Emperor, conducted the defence of the great breach, received a severe wound, and left his post to die on board his galley in the harbour. The garrison was dispirited at the loss; and the chiefs of the assailing Janissaries observing that the resistance had slackened, redoubled their efforts to force a passage. One of them, named Hassan of Ulubad, conspicuous by his stature and daring, rushed with thirty comrades up the barricaded ruins of one of the overthrown towers that flanked the breach. They gained the summit; and though Hassan and eighteen of his forlorn hope were struck down, others rapidly followed, and carried the Greek defences by the overwhelming weight of their numbers. Nearly at the same time, another Ottoman corps effected an entrance at a slightly-protected part of the long line of walls, and wheeling round, took the garrison in the rear. Constantine saw now that all was lost, save honour, and exclaiming, "I would rather die than live!" the last of the Romans rushed amid the advancing foe, and fell stretched by two sabre wounds among the undistinguished dead.

Torrent after torrent of the conquerors now raged through the captured city. At first they slew all whom they met or overtook; but when they found that all resistance had ceased, the love of plunder predominated over the thirst for blood, and they strove to secure the fairest and strongest of the helpless thousands that cowered before them, for service or for sale as slaves. About the hour of noon, Sultan Mahomet, surrounded by his viziers, his pachas, and his guards, rode through the breach at the gate of St. Romanus into the city which he had conquered. He alighted at the church of St. Sophia, and entering the splendid edifice, he ordered one of the muezzins who accompanied him to summon the true believers to prayer. He then himself mounted the high altar, and prayed. Having thus solemnly established the creed of the Prophet in the shrine where his fallen adversary had on the preceding eve celebrated the holiest Christian rite, and where so many generations of Christians had worshipped, Mahomet ordered search to be made for Constantine's body. It was found under a heap of slain in the great breach, and was identified, beyond all possibility of dispute, by the golden eagles that were embroidered upon the Emperor's buskins. The head was cut off, and exhibited for a time between the feet of the bronze horse of the equestrian statue of Justinian in the place called the Augustan. The ghastly trophy of Mahomet's conquest was subsequently embalmed, and sent round to the chief cities of Asia. The greater number of the Emperor's Latin auxiliaries had shared his noble death. Some few had made their way to the harbour, and escaped through the Ottoman fleet. Others came as captives into Mahomet's power, and were either put to death or required to pay heavy ransoms. The Genoese inhabitants of the suburb of Galata obtained terms of capitulation, by which they were protected from pillage. The Grand Duke Notaras was brought prisoner before Mahomet, who made a show of treating him with favour, and obtained from him a list of the principal Greek dignitaries and officers of state. The Sultan instantly proclaimed their names to his soldiers, and offered 1000 sequins for each of their heads.[1]

On the day after the capture of the city, Mahomet continued his survey of his conquest, and took possession of the imperial palace. Struck by the solitude of its spacious halls, and the image of desolation which it presented, Mahomet repeated two lines of the Persian poet Firdousi:—"The spider's web is the royal curtain in the palace of Cæsar; the owl is the sentinel on the watch-tower of Afrasiab."[2] The quotation showed the well-read and elegant scholar, and the subsequent deeds of the Sultan on that day exemplified the truth that intellectual eminence is no sure guarantee against the co-existence of the vilest depravity.[3] On leaving the palace, Mahomet repaired to a sumptuous banquet which had been prepared for him in the vicinity. He there drank deeply of wine; and he ordered the chief of his eunuchs to bring to him the youngest child of the Grand Duke Notaras, a boy aged fourteen years of age. Notaras during the siege had only dis-

---

[1] The general accuracy of Gibbon's splendid description of the taking of Constantinople is not impeached by the minute diligence of Von Hammer or Finlay, though they supply us with some not unimportant connections and additions. I think that Mr. Finlay's vindication of the Genoese commander Giustiniani from the heavy censures of Gibbon is successful, and have gladly followed it.

[2] The full meaning of this couplet, with reference to the customs of Eastern Courts, is explained in a note to Thornton's "Turkey," p. 10.

[3] See Arnold's remarks (p. 255, vol. i., " History of the later Roman Commonwealth ") on the character of Sylla.

played the qualities of a factious bigot; but he now acted as became a Christian, a father, and a man. He told the messenger that his child should never minister to the Sultan's brutality, and that he would rather see him under the executioner's axe. Furious at hearing this reply, Mahomet ordered Notaras and his whole family to be seized and put to death. Notaras met his fate with dignity, and exhorted his children to die as fitted Christians. He saw their heads fall one by one before him; and then, after having asked a few moments for prayer, he gave himself up to the executioner, acknowledging with his last breath the justice of God. The bloody heads were brought to Mahomet, and placed by his order in a row before him on the banquet table. Many more executions of noble Christians followed on that day, to please the tyrant's savage mood; and it was said that the natural ferocity of Mahomet was goaded on by the malevolent suggestions of a French renegade, whose daughter was in the Sultan's harem, and was at that time the object of his passionate fondness.

But though thus merciless in his lust and wrath, Mahomet knew well that for Constantinople to become such a seat of empire as his ambition desired, it was necessary that the mass of the Greek population which had escaped death and captivity during the sack of the city, should be encouraged to remain there, and to be orderly and industrious subjects of their new master. The measures taken by him with this design attest the clear-sighted statesmanship which he possessed. Constantine had alienated his subjects from him by conforming to the Latin Church. Mahomet now gratified the Greeks, who loved their orthodoxy far more than their liberty, by installing a new patriarch at the head of the Greek Church, and proclaiming himself its protector. This was on the 1st of June, only ten days after the storm. He then by solemn proclamation invited all the fugitives to return to their homes, assuring them of safety, and encouraging them to resume their former occupations. A formal charter was afterwards granted by him, which declared the person of the Greek patriarch inviolable, and exempted him and the other dignitáries of his Church from all public burdens. The same document assured to the Greeks the use of their churches, and the free exercise of their religious rites according to their own usages.[1] But the Greek population of Constantinople had been long declining, and even before its sufferings in the fatal siege, had been far inadequate

---

[1] The contents of this charter (which had been destroyed in a fire) were solemnly proved in the reign of Selim I. by an old Janissary, who had been at the taking of Constantinople.—Von Hammer.

for the vast space occupied by the buildings. Mahomet therefore sought other modes of replenishing the city. Thousands
of families were transplanted to the capital from various parts of
his empire; and throughout his reign, at every accession of
territory that he made, he colonised his capital with portions of
his new subjects. Before the close of his reign, Constantinople
was again teeming with life and activity; but the Greek character
of the city was merged amid the motley crowds of Turkomans,
Albanians, Bulgarians, Servians, and others, who had repaired
thither at the Sultan's bidding.

The vision of Othman was now accomplished, and Constantinople had become the centre jewel in the ring of Turkish Empire.
The capture of that city closes the first of the seven periods into
which Von Hammer divides the Ottoman history.[1] The first
period consists of 150 years of rapid growth, from the assumption of independent sovereignty by Othman to the consolidation
of the European and Asiatic conquests of his house by the taking
of Constantinople. The second is the period of its further growth
by conquest until the accession of Solyman I. in 1520. The third
is its period of meridian ascendency under Solyman and Selim II.,
(from 1520 to 1574). The fourth is the commencement of its
decline under Amurath III. (1574) to the epoch when the sanguinary vigour of Amurath IV. (from 1623 to 1640) restored for a
time its former splendour. The fifth is the period of anarchy and
insurrection, between the death of Amurath IV. (1640) and the
ministry of the first Kiuprili (1656). The sixth is the period of
new energy given to the empire by men of the family of Kiuprili,
from 1656 to the calamitous war with Austria, which was closed
by the treaty of Carlowitz in 1688. Then comes the seventh
period, one of accelerated disaster and downfall, to 1763, when the
treaty of Kainardji with Russia confirmed its humiliation.

Mahomet II. was but twenty-three years of age when he took
Constantinople; being one year older than Alexander was when
he fought the battle of the Granicus, and three years less than the
age of Napoleon when he commanded at Lodi. The succession
of wars and victories which filled the thirty years of Mahomet's
reign might perhaps bear comparison with the exploits of the other
two imperial conquerors whom we have mentioned. The fragments
of the Greek Empire, which had lingered for a while unconnected
with the central power of the Emperor, were speedily subdued by
the new ruler of Constantinople. The Peloponnesus was con-

---

[1] Von Hammer. Supplement.

quered in 1454, and Trebizond in the following year.   Servia and Bosnia were completely reduced into Turkish provinces.   The last Bosnian King and his sons surrendered to Mahomet on a capitulation which guaranteed their lives, and which the Sultan swore to observe.   Mahomet obtained a decision from the Mufti Ali-Bestami, which declared that the Sultan's treaty and oath were not binding on him, as being made with unbelievers, and that he was at liberty to put his prisoners to death.   The Mufti begged as a favour that he might carry his own opinion into effect by acting as executioner.   The captive Bosnian King was ordered into the Sultan's presence, and came with the treaty of capitulation in his hand.   The Mufti exclaimed, " It is a good deed to slay such infidels," and cut the King down with his own sabre.   The princes were put to death in the interior of the tent.   The elder and better spirited of the Ottomans, who witnessed this treacherous murder, must have thought with shame how completely Mahometan and Christian had changed characters since the days of Amurath and of Cardinal Julian.

In Albania, Scanderbeg held out gallantly against the power of the Sultan, who, in 1461, was even forced to accede to a temporary treaty which acknowledged Scanderbeg as Lord of Albania and Epirus.   Hostilities were soon renewed, and the Turks gradually gained ground by the lavish sacrifice of life and treasure, and by the continued pressure of superior numbers.   But the breakwater which Scanderbeg long formed against the flood of Mahometan conquest, and the glorious resistance which Hunyades accomplished at Belgrade, were invaluable to Western Christendom. They delayed for many years the cherished projects of Mahomet against Italy; and the victory of Hunyades barred the principal path into the German states.   It was in 1456 that the Sultan besieged Belgrade, then regarded as the key of Hungary.   Hunyades exerted in its defence all the fiery valour that had marked him from his youth up, and the skill and caution which he had acquired during maturer years.   He was powerfully aided by the bands of Crusaders, whom the efforts of Pope Calixtus II., and the celebrated preacher, St. John Capistran, brought to his assistance. The tidings of the fall of Constantinople had filled Western Christendom with shame, indignation, and alarm.   Formal vows of warfare for the rescue of the fallen city from the Infidel were made by many of the chief princes, but evaporated in idle pageants and unexecuted decrees.   But when another great Christian city was assailed, and when it was evident that, if Belgrade fell, Vienna, and other Western capitals would soon be in jeopardy, religious zeal and patriotic caution were for a time active; and a large and efficient auxiliary force was led by Capistran in person to fight under the banner of Hunyades. Mahomet had been made over-confident by his success at Constantinople, and boasted that Belgrade would be an easy prize. His powerful artillery soon shattered the walls; and in a general assault on the 21st July, 1456, the Janissaries carried the trenches, and forced their way into the lower part of the town. But the Christians at Belgrade were numerous, were brave, and ably commanded. Capistran rallied the garrison ; the Turks were repulsed from the upper town ; and after six hours' hard fighting they were driven out of the portion which they had occupied. At this critical moment the martial saint, with the discernment of a great general, and the fiery energy of a devotee, sallied with a thousand Crusaders upon the enemy's batteries. Calling on the name of Jesus, while their panic-stricken enemies fled with cries of " Allah," the Christians fought their way into the Ottoman camp, and captured the whole of the besiegers' artillery. Mahomet, indignant at the flight of his troops, strove in vain to stem the tide, and fought desperately in person against the advancing foes. With a blow of his sabre he struck off the head of one of the leading Crusaders, but received at the same instant a wound in the thigh, and was obliged to be carried off by his attendants. Furious at his defeat and disgrace, he saw, as they bore him away, Hassan, the general of the Janissaries, and overwhelmed him with reproaches and threats. Hassan replied that many of his men were slain, and that the rest would no longer obey the word of command. He then, before his sovereign's eyes, threw himself among the advancing Hungarians, and met a soldier's death. The Sultan's horseguards checked the further pursuit of the Christians, and secured the retreat of their wounded master. But three hundred cannons, and the whole of the Turkish military stores, were captured ; and 25,000 of Mahomet's best troops had fallen. Hunyades did not long survive this crowning triumph of his gallant though chequered career. He died at Belgrade twenty days after the flight of Mahomet from before the walls ; and the other hero of the defence, to whom even more than to Hunyades the Christian victory was due, died also in the October following. John Capistran was canonised by the Pope ; and there are few saints in the long Romish calendar whose names Christendom has worthier cause to venerate.

In Asia Mahomet's arms were more uniformly successful. He conquered and annexed to his empire Sinope and Trebizond, and he finally subdued the princes of Caramania, those long and rancorous enemies of the House of Othman. The most important of all his conquests, after that of Constantinople, was the subjugation of the Crimea in 1475, by one of the most celebrated of the Turkish captains, Ahmed, surnamed Kedük, or Broken-mouth, who was Mahomet's Grand Vizier from 1473 to 1477. The immediate causes of the expedition to the Crimea were the Sultan's hostility with the Genoese, who possessed the strong city of Kaffa in that country, and the entreaties which the deposed Khan of the Crim Tartars addressed to Mahomet for aid against his revolted brothers. But it cannot be doubted that a prince of Mahomet's genius discerned the immense value of the Crimea to the occupiers of Constantinople, and the necessity of securing his dominions by its annexation. Ahmed Kedük attacked Kaffa with a powerful fleet, and an army of 40,000 men. That city, then called Little Constantinople from its wealth and strength, surrendered in four days. The booty which the conqueror seized there was immense ; 40,000 of the inhabitants were transplanted to Constantinople ; and 1500 young Genoese nobles were compelled to enter into the corps of Janissaries. The whole of the Peninsula was speedily occupied by the Turkish troops ; and the Crimean Khans were thenceforth for three centuries the vassals of the Ottoman Sultans.

Mahomet was frequently engaged in hostilities with the Venetians as well as with the Genoese. The Archipelago and the coasts of Greece were generally the scenes of these wars ; in the course of which the Sultan obtained possession of Eubœa, Lesbos, Lemnos, Cephalonia, and other islands. The conquest of the Eubœa was marked by base treachery and cruelty on the part of the Sultan, and signalised by the pure courage of a Christian heroine. The Venetian commander, Paul Erizzo, after a long and brave defence, surrendered the citadel on condition of the Sultan pledging his word for the safety of all within it. Mahomet signed the capitulation ; and when the garrison had marched out, and laid down their arms, he put all of them, except the Greeks, to death with the cruellest tortures. Paul Erizzo was sawn in two by his orders. The daughter of the Venetian general, the young and fair Anne Erizzo, was dragged to the Sultan's tent : but the Christian maiden preferred death to dishonour ; and, unmoved by either promise or threat, she was killed by the slaves of the angry tyrant.

Towards the end of Mahomet's reign, Scanderbeg was completely overpowered by the Ottoman forces ; and Albania and the district of Herzegovinia were united with the Sultan's dominions. These conquests brought the Turkish arms into more extensive contact

with the possessions of Venice along the eastern coasts of the
Adriatic. In 1477, a powerful Turkish army marched into the
territory of Friuli at the northern extremity of that sea, and
menaced Venice itself. The Venetians formed fortified camps at
Gradina and Fogliania, and carried a line of entrenchments from
the mouth of the Isonzo to Gærz. But the Turks in the October
of that year passed their lines, and defeated their army. Omar
Pacha, the Ottoman general, next passed the Tagliamento, a stream
destined to become illustrious in after warfare. The Turkish
troops spread themselves without resistance over all the rich level
country as far as the banks of the Piave; and the trembling
senators of Venice saw from their palace-roofs the northern horizon
glow with the light of burning towns and villages. The Turks
retired in November, loaded with booty. Venice eagerly concluded a treaty of peace with the Sultan, which (according to one
Italian historian) contained a stipulation, by which the republic
was to aid the Sultan, if attacked, with a fleet of 100 galleys, and
the Sultan was, in case of like necessity, to send 100,000 Turkish
cavalry against the enemies of Venice.

The subjugation of Italy was a project which Mahomet, though
often obliged to delay, had never abandoned. In 1480 he prepared to carry it into execution on a scale of military and naval
preparation equal to the grandeur of the enterprise; and at the
same time he resolved to quell the sole formidable enemy that yet
remained near the heart of his dominions. The strong island of
Rhodes was still in the possession of the Knights of St. John of
Jerusalem, who had established themselves there in 1311, and
gallantly maintained their sovereignty of the island as an independent power for upwards of a century and a half. Three renegades from the order had incited the Sultan to attack Rhodes, by
giving him plans of its fortifications, and promising that it would
be easily captured by forces which the Turks could employ
against it. Mesih Pacha was sent to capture Rhodes in the April
of 1480, with a fleet of 160 galleys, a powerful army, and a large
park of the heaviest artillery. The Ottoman Pacha effected a
landing on the island; and after capturing some inferior posts, he
formed his lines of siege against the city itself, which is built on
the northern extremity of the isle. The Grand Master of the
Knights, Peter d'Aubusson, defended the city with indomitable
fortitude and consummate skill; but it must have fallen, had it
not been for the ill-timed avarice or military rigour of the Turkish
commander. After a long siege and many severe encounters, the
Turks made a general assault on the 28th July, 1480. Their

artillery had opened a wide rent in the walls; their numbers were ample; their zeal was never more conspicuous. In spite of the gallantry of the Christian knights, the attacking columns had gained the crest of the breach; and the Ottoman standard was actually planted on the walls, when Mesih Pacha ordered a proclamation to be made that pillage was forbidden, and that all the plunder of the place must be reserved for the Sultan. This announcement filled the Turkish army with disgust and disaffection. The soldiery yet outside the town refused to march in to support their comrades who had won the breach, and these were borne back and driven in disorder from the city by a last desperate charge of the chevaliers, who had marked the sudden wavering of their assailants. The siege was raised, and Rhodes rescued for half a century.

On the same day that the Turks advanced to their unsuccessful assault on Rhodes, the leader of their other great expedition, Ahmed Kedük, the conqueror of the Crimea, effected his disembarkation on the southern coast of Italy, where no Ottoman before him had placed his foot. He landed on the Apulian shore, and marched against Otranto, which was then considered the key of Italy. His fleet cast anchor in the roads; and the city was promptly and fiercely assailed both by sea and by land. The resistance of Otranto, though spirited, was brief. The place was stormed on the 11th August, 1480. Out of a population of 22,000, the greater number were massacred without mercy, and the wretched survivors subjected to the worst atrocities of Turkish warfare.

Mahomet was now master of a strong city and harbour, which secured an entrance for his armies into Italy. His arms had met reverses at Rhodes when he was absent; but he resolved to conduct the next enterprise in person. Early in the spring of 1481 the horsetails were planted on the Asiatic shore of the Bosphorus, as signals for a new campaign; but no one, save the Sultan himself, knew against which quarter the power of Turkey was now to be directed. His maxim was that secrecy in design and celerity in execution are the great elements of success in war. Once, when at the commencement of a campaign one of his chief officers asked him what were the main objects of his operations, Mahomet answered sharply, "If a hair of my beard knew them, I would pluck it out and cast it into the fire." No one could tell what throne was menaced by the host that now gathered at the Sultan's bidding; but while the musters were yet incomplete, the expedition was arrested by the death of the Sultan, who expired suddenly in the midst of his army on the 3rd May, 1481.

CHAPTER VI.

INSTITUTES OF MAHOMET II.—TURKISH GOVERNMENT—ARMIES—
TENURES OF LAND—INSTITUTIONS—EDUCATION—THE ULEMA—
THE RAYAS—SLAVERY—RENEGADES—TURKISH CHARACTER—
TURKISH WARFARE.[1]

THE personal character of Mahomet II. has been already discussed;
nor would we willingly turn again to a repulsive subject. What
he accomplished as a conqueror for the advancement of the Ottoman power has been made apparent in the narrative of his reign,
but it would be injustice to pass over his political institutions;
and we may conveniently take this occasion of surveying generally
the internal organisation of the Turkish Empire.

From the time when Othman first killed his uncle in full council
for contradicting his schemes, to the self-imposed limitations of the
Sultans during the last few years, there is no trace in Turkish history of any civil constitutional restraint upon the will of the ruling
sovereign. There is indeed a popular tradition among the Turks
that the Sultan has a right to put to death seven men, and no
more, in each day without any cause, save that it is his pleasure
so to do.[2] But even the limitation of arbitrary homicide which
this tradition imports, has never been real; and abundant instances
may be found in the reigns of Selim I., of Amurath IV., Mahomet IV., and of Mahomet the Conqueror himself, where far
greater numbers have been sacrificed without form of trial, at the

[1] See Von Hammer, books 18, 34, and Supplement; D'Ohsson, "Tableau
Général de l'Empire Ottoman;" Thornton; Urquhart's "Turkey and her
Resources;" and Ubicini, "Lettres sur la Turquie."

[2] See Von Hammer, book 53, ad. fin. In Thornton, "Account of the
Turkish Empire" (p. 69), the number that the Sultan is privileged to slay
is fifteen. Rycaut (cited by Thornton), in his "State of the Ottoman
Empire," written at the close of the 17th century, says: "The Grand
Signior can never be deposed or made accountable to any for his crimes,
while he destroys causelessly of his subjects under the number of *a thousand* a day." The same writer states that death by the Sultan's hand, or
by his order, was, if submitted to without resistance or murmur, considered
to give a title to eternal felicity.

royal command. The title of "Hunkiar," the "Manslayer," is (or till lately has been) one most commonly used by the subjects of the Sultan in speaking of their sovereign, not as conveying any censure or imputation of tyranny, but in simple acknowledgment of his absolute power of life or death. Only the person of the mufti, the chief of the men of law, has been supposed to be inviolable; an exception doubtful even in theory, and unimportant in practice, as the Sultan could depose a refractory mufti whenever he pleased, and the inviolability of the individual must cease with the loss of office. The sovereign's power is absolute over property as well as over person; but the Sultans have ever refrained from seizing property that has been consecrated to pious uses. Such an act would have been regarded as sacrilegious by zealous Mahometans, and have been probably followed by an insurrection. Nor, in practice, has private property suffered in Turkey from royal rapacity, except in the case of officers in the service of the government, whose wealth has always been subject to confiscation. All honours, commands, and dignities have been in the Sultan's absolute disposal to give or to take away as he pleases; and all his Mahometan subjects are equal before him, none having any privilege of birth, either from family or from place of nativity, one over the other.

But though free from the barriers of civil law, and unchecked by the existence of any privileged aristocracy, no Turkish Sultan could openly disregard with impunity the obligations and restraints of the religious law of the Mahometans. He combines legislative with executive power; but his khatti-cherifs, or imperial edicts, are regarded as subordinate to the three primary sources of law, which are, the Koran itself the written word of God, the Sounna or traditional sayings of the Prophet, and the sentences or decisions of the four first great Imams, or Patriarchs, of the Mahometan religion. The edicts of princes are called Ourfi, which means supplemental. The collection of the edicts, which successive Sultans pronounce on each ecclesiastical or temporal emergency not provided for in the first three sources of Mahometan law, is called Kanounnamé (the book or the code of canons) from the Greek word Kanon, which has been applied by the Turkish jurists to political as well as to ecclesiastical legislation.

By ancient and long-continued custom, the Sultan, before the execution of any important political act, obtains its sanction by a solemn declaration, or Fetva, of the chief mufti in its favour. Instances occur in Turkish history, where the refusal of the mufti has caused the sovereign to abandon his project; and some writers have represented this officer as exercising an effective constitutional check on the royal prerogative, and possessing a veto like that of the old Roman tribunes, or the Polish nobles. But the fact of the mufti being removable from office at the royal will (like our judges before 1714) shows how erroneous are such theories.[1] When a resolute and not unpopular Sultan is on the throne, the mufti is a mere passive instrument in his hands; though sagacious rulers in Turkey, as elsewhere, have understood the policy of sometimes showing a seeming deference to judicial rebuke; and the deep devotion of most of the Sultans to their religion must have made them to some extent really value the solemn opinions of the highest interpreters of their law, which is based upon their religion. When indeed the reigning sovereign is feeble and unsuccessful, the opposition of the mufti, seconded by "the hoarse voice of insurrection" round the palace walls, may be truly formidable; and his declaration that the Sultan is a breaker of the divine law, a tyrant, and unfit to govern, forms a sentence of deposition which popular violence has often carried into effect.

In truth, with a martial and high-spirited people, earnestly attached to the national religion, and keenly sensitive as to their national honour, such as the Ottoman Turks have ever been, the worst practices of despotic sovereignty are, and ever must be, curbed by the practice of armed resistance and popular vengeance. As we proceed in this history, we shall often see the heads of the sovereigns' ministers fall at the people's bidding, and we shall become familiar with scenes of dethronement and regicide. These wild and terrible remedies of the evils of absolute monarchy have often in Turkey, as elsewhere, been cruelly misapplied. They have often degenerated into mere military mutinies, or into the sordid and anarchical riotings of a city rabble. But they have preserved the Ottoman race from utter prostration; and they are less odious than the series of domestic and oligarchical assassinations, by which despotism has been tempered in the rival empire of the Czar.

The implicit and religious loyalty of the Ottoman nation to the House of Othman (however roughly they may have dealt with individual members of it) has been uniform and undiminished. It is from that family alone that the Padishah (the Emperor), the Zil-Ullah (the shadow of God as the Sultan is styled), can be supplied. Governors of provinces have frequently revolted against the sovereign authority. They have made themselves locally in-

---

[1] See **Thornton**, p. 94, and note.

dependent, and carried on wars on their own account, even against the sovereign himself. But they have always professed titular allegiance to the royal house ; nor has any adventurous seraskier or pacha ever attempted to seat a new dynasty on the throne of Constantinople. The certain continuity with which Sultans of the race of Othman, in lineal male descent from their great founder, have for four centuries held that throne, offers a marked contrast to the rapid vicissitudes with which imperial families rose and fell during the ages of the Greek Empire. Nor can the annals of any of the royal houses of Western Christendom show us, like the Turkish, an unbroken succession of thirty sovereigns, without the sceptre ever lapsing to the spindle, and without the accession of a collateral branch.

The will of the Sultan has been, from the earliest period of Turkish history, to the reign of Abdul Medjid, the mainspring of the Ottoman Government; and in demonstrating its plenary importance, we have been led far beyond the times of the conqueror of Constantinople. In continuing our examination of the Turkish institutions as organised by the legislation of that prince, there will be less need to deviate from chronological regularity.

The figurative language of the institutes of Mahomet II., still employed by his successors, describes the state under the martial metaphor of a tent.[1] The Lofty Gate of the Royal Tent (where Oriental rulers of old sate to administer justice) denotes the chief seat of government. The Italian translation of the phrase, " La Porta Sublima," has been adopted by Western nations with slight modifications to suit their respective languages ; and by " The Sublime Porte " we commonly mean the Imperial Ottoman Government. The Turkish legists and historians depict the details of their government by imagery drawn from the same metaphor of a royal tent. The dome of the state is supported by four pillars. These are formed by, 1st, the Viziers ; 2nd, the Kadiaskers (judges); 3rd, the Defterdars (treasurers); and 4th, the Nischandyis (the secretaries of state). Besides these, there are the Outer Agas, that is to say, the military rulers; and the Inner Agas, that is to say, the rulers employed in the court. There is also the order of the Ulema, or men learned in the law.

The Viziers[2] were regarded as constituting the most important pillar that upheld the fabric of the state. In Mahomet II.'s time the Viziers were four in number. Their chief, the Grand Vizier,

---

[1] See Othman's dream, pp. 6, 7, *suprà.*
[2] See p. 12, *suprà.*

is the highest of all officers, both of the dignitaries of the sword and of the pen. The legal order supplied the second pillar of the state. The chiefs of the legal order were, in the time of Mahomet II., the two Kadiaskers, who respectively presided over the judicial establishments of Europe and Asia. The other high legal dignitaries (who were at that time next in rank to the Kadiaskers) were, 1st, the Kho-dya, who was the tutor of the Sultan and the Princes Royal; 2nd, the Mufti, the authoritative expounder of the law; and, 3rdly, the Judge of Constantinople. As has been mentioned, the third and fourth state pillars consisted of the officers of the Exchequer, who were called Defterdars, and of the secretaries, who were termed Nis-chandyis.

The great council of state was named the Divan; and, in the absence of the Sultan, the Grand Vizier was its president. The other Viziers and the Kadiaskers took their stations on his right; the Defterdars and the Nis-chandyis on his left. The Teskeredyis (or officers charged to present reports on the condition of each department of the state) stood in front of the Grand Vizier. The Divan was also attended by the Reis-Effendi, a general secretary, whose power afterwards became more important than that of the Nis-chandyis; by the Grand Chamberlain, and the Grand Marshal, and a train of other officers of the court. The Grand Vizier had the power of convoking a special divan at his own palace when he judged it necessary; and to him was intrusted the custody of the imperial seal.

Besides the military Agas, who were very numerous, many officers in the civil departments held the rank of Aga, which means ruler. The administration of the provinces was in the time of Mahomet II. principally intrusted to the Beys and Beylerbeys. These were the natural chiefs of the class of feudatories, whom their tenure of office obliged to serve on horseback in time of war. They mustered under the Sanjak, the banner of the chief of their district, and the districts themselves were thence called Sanjaks, and their rulers Sanjak-beys. The title of Pasha, so familiar to us when speaking of a Turkish provincial ruler, is not strictly a term implying territorial jurisdiction, or even military authority. It is a title of honour, meaning literally the Shah's or Sovereign's foot, and implying that the person to whom that title was given was one whom the sovereign employed. The classical reader will remember that among the ancient Persians the King's officers were called the King's eyes and the King's hands.[1] The

---

[1] Xenophon, Cyrop., lib. viii. c. 2; see also Aristoph. Acharn., 234.

title of Pacha was not at first applied among the Ottomans exclusively to those officers who commanded armies, or ruled provinces or cities. Of the five first Pachas, that are mentioned by Ottoman writers, three were literary men.[1] By degrees this honorary title was appropriated to those whom the Sultan employed in war, and set over districts and important towns; so that the word "Pacha" became almost synonymous with the word governor. The title "Padischah," which the Sultan himself bears, and which the Turkish diplomatists have been very jealous in allowing to Christian sovereigns, is an entirely different word, and means the great, the imperial Schah or Sovereign.[2]

In the time of Mahomet II. the Ottoman Empire contained in Europe alone thirty-six Sanjaks or banners, round each of which assembled about 400 cavaliers. The entire military horse and foot of the empire in both continents was more than 100,000, without reckoning the irregular bands of the Akindji and Azabs. The ordinary revenues of the state amounted to more than 2,000,000 ducats.

The Janissaries were still the main strength of the Turkish armies. Mahomet increased their number, yet he had never more than 12,000 under arms. But when we remember to how great a degree the other nations of that age relied on their cavalry, and neglected the composition and equipment of their infantry, we can well understand the advantage which the presence of a chosen body of perfectly trained foot soldiers in the Turkish armies must have given them in pitched battles, and still more in sieges and other elaborate operations of warfare. The English and the Swiss were the only two Christian nations of that period which sent into the field a well-armed infantry, not raised from the mere rabble, but from the valuable classes of the population ; and the Turkish sabre never clashed with the English bills and bows, or with the heavy halberds of Helvetia.

The pay and the privileges of the Janissaries were largely

---

[1] See Von Hammer, vol. i. p. 141.

[2] "Le titre de *Padichah*, du persan *pad* (protecteur) et *chah* (roi), est le titre exclusif des souverains Ottomans en Orient. François 1er fut le premier et longtemps le seul monarque chrétien qui fut qualifié de padichah par les Turcs. L'Empereur d'Allemagne n'avait à la Porte que le titre de *Nemtchè tchaçari* (César d'Allemagne) ; les czars de Russie, celui de *Mosgovtchari* et ensuite de *Rouciatchari*. Ce ne fut qu'en 1774, dans le traité de Kaïnardji, que l'Impératrice Catherine II. obtint l'addition à son titre des mots *vè padichahi*, En décembre 1805, Napoléon fut reconnu avec la double qualité de *Imperathor vè padichah*. Depuis, le titre de Padichah a été étendu à la plupart des souverains de l'Europe, alliés de la Porte."—Ubicini, vol. i. p. 34.

augmented by the conqueror of Constantinople : and, as the
Turkish power was extended in Europe, care was taken to recruit
that chosen corps from children who were natives of that continent rather than among the Asiatics. The levies for that purpose
were generally made in Albania, Bosnia, and Bulgaria. It is said
that there was seldom need to employ force in collecting the
requisite number of suitable children, and that the parents were
eager to obtain the enrolment of their boys in the list of Janissary
recruits.[1] This, if true, is rather a proof of the moral depravity
of the Christian population, which the Ottomans subdued, than of
any mildness of the Ottomans in enforcing the institutions of
Khalil Tchendereli. It is also stated that no compulsion was used
to induce the young recruits to leave the Christian and adopt the
Mahometan faith : but this was a mere pretext of forbearance ; as,
from the early age at which the children were selected, it would
be absurd to suppose that they were free agents in following the
new religious rites, and repeating the new prayers, which were
taught them as soon as they entered the training schools of the
Janissaries. It is certain that the compulsory enrolment and
conversion of youths taken in war was often practised ; as in the
instance of the young Genoese nobles, who became the captives
of Mahomet at the conquest of Kaffa.

The attention which the Ottomans paid to their artillery, and
to the adoption of every improvement in military engineering,
must have been another great cause of their superiority to the
nations, whose brave but tumultuous and ill-provided armies they
encountered. Nor is the care, which their Sultans and Pachas
bestowed upon what in modern military language would be termed
the ordnance and commissariat departments, less remarkable. The
Greek Chalcondylas, the contemporary of Amurath II., in his account of the Ottoman armies, after describing their number, the
excellence of their organisation, and the strictness of their discipline, mentions the corps that were especially employed in keeping the roads on the line of march in available condition ; he
speaks of the abundant supply of provisions that was always to
be found in their well-arranged and symmetrical camps ; and he
notices the large number of beasts of burden which always accompanied a Turkish army, and the employment of a special corps to
ensure the proper transport of provisions and military stores.[2]
There was certainly no state of Christendom during the fifteenth

[1] D'Ohsson, Constitution et Administration de l'Empire Ottoman,
vol. viii.
[2] Lib. v. p. 122, cited by Von Hammer in book v.

or sixteenth century, which cared for the well-being of its soldiers, on such seemingly generous but truly economical principles. The campaigns of Mahomet himself, especially that against Constantinople, and those of his grandson Sultan Selim, furnish many instances of the enlightened liberality and forethought, with which the mediæval Turks provided their soldiery with those material instruments and adjuncts of warfare, the importance of which, in order to enable an army "to go anywhere and do anything," our own great captain of the present age has so fully taught us.

In examining the political and military institutions of the Ottomans, we have been repeatedly led to notice the Ziamets and Timars, the lands granted to individual subjects of the Sultan on condition of military service. The phraseology of the feudalism of mediæval Christendom has generally been adopted by writers who have treated of these parts of the Turkish system ; and the real resemblance between these institutions of the East and of the West is in many respects so remarkable, that the historical inquirer may at first feel surprised at feudalism failing to produce in Turkey those important effects on the progress of civilisation[1] and constitutional development, which he knows to have been wrought by it in the west and centre of Christian Europe. The problem offered by this variance between the results of apparently like causes, is complicated and difficult. It cannot be dealt with so fully in these pages as it deserves ; but even the partial investigation of it, which can be undertaken here, may be of service towards acquiring a clearer discernment of many important points in the Turkish laws and usages, and in the national character of the Turks themselves. The tenures of land in Turkey will first require consideration.[2]

When the Ottomans conquered a country, the territory was divided into three portions. Part became ecclesiastical property, and was devoted to pious and charitable purposes, to the maintenance of the mosques, the public schools, the hospitals, and other institutions of a similar character. The lands appropriated to these purposes were called Vaks or Vakoufs. A second part became full private property, resembling the allodial lands in mediæval Christendom. This property was subject to different liabilities, according to the creed of its owner. If held by a

---

[1] See Guizot's " Lectures on European Civilisation."
[2] The account in the text of the Turkish tenures is taken almost entirely from Ubicini, vol. i. p. 263, *et seq.*

Mussulman, it was called Aschriie, that is to say, tithable, and the holder was obliged to pay a tithe of its produce to the state. This was the only burden attached to it. If left in the possession of a Christian, its holder paid tribute (kharadj) to the state, which consisted of a capitation tax, and also of a tax levied on the estate, which was sometimes a fixed sum according to its extent, and was sometimes an impost on its proceeds varying from an eighth to one half. The remaining part of the conquered country became domain-land, including, 1st, those of which the revenues were appropriated to the state treasury or *miri ;* 2nd, unoccupied and waste lands (of which the amount is large in Turkey); 3rd, the private domain of the Sultan ; 4th, escheated and forfeited lands ; 5th, the appanages of the Sultan's mother, and other members of the blood royal; 6th, lands assigned to the offices filled by Viziers; 7th, lands assigned to Pachas of the second rank; 8th, lands assigned to the ministers and officers of the palace ; and, 9th, the military fiefs, the Ziamets and Timars. These last formed the largest class of the domain-lands, and are the objects of most interest to the student of comparative history.

The smallest fief or portion of conquered land granted out to a distinguished soldier was called a Timar, and generally contained from three to five hundred acres.[1] Each fief was to furnish in time of war an armed horseman for each 3000 aspres of its revenue ; like the knight's fee, which was the integer of our own feudal array. The larger fiefs or Ziamets comprehended upwards of five hundred acres ;[2] and there was a still higher class of fiefs, called Beyliks or lordships. The general name for the holders of military fiefs was Spahi, a Cavalier, a title which exactly answers to those which we find in the feudal countries of Christian Europe. The Ziamets and Timars appear to have been generally hereditary in the male line. When any became vacant by failure of heirs or by forfeiture for misconduct, the Beylerbey of the district filled up the vacancy, his nomination being subject to approval by the Porte.[3] The higher rank of Bey, and the still higher rank of Beylerbey, were not at first hereditary, but were conferred by the Sultan on individuals selected by him. It was, however, usual to let the rank and estate of a Bey pass from father to son, and in later times the custom of hereditary descent grew often into a right; there being a considerable difference in this respect among the various provinces of the empire.

[1] Thornton's "Turkey," 164.
[2] Ibid.
[3] Report presented to Sultan Ahmed III., cited by Ubicini, vol. i. p. 540.

We seem to have here before us the essential elements of feudalism ; and we might naturally expect to find a feudal aristocracy developing itself in Turkey, and aggrandising itself, as in mediæval Christendom, at the expense both of the monarchy and commonalty.   We shall, in fact, find such an aristocracy growing up in the Ottoman Empire ; but not until we come to the recent century and a half of decline and corruption, which preceded the reforms of Sultan Mahmoud II. and of the late Sultan Abdul Medjid.   Such an aristocracy did not exist during the ages of Ottoman progress and splendour.   The causes of its non-existence during that period are, I believe, to be principally found, 1st, in the high personal energies and abilities of the Sultans, under whom the Turkish conquests were effected, and the Turkish Empire consolidated ; 2ndly, in the existence of the Janissary force ; 3rdly, in the effects of the religion of the Turks, both in elevating the authority of the sovereign, and in maintaining a feeling of equality among all his Mahometan subjects ; [1] and, 4thly, in the absence of that habitual aptitude for public assemblies, which is the characteristic of nations that contain a considerable element of Germanic or Scandinavian race.

It is to be remembered that the feudal system of mediæval Europe was principally fashioned and matured during the reign of feeble and unsuccessful princes, who were engaged in repeated and calamitous contests not only with barbarous invaders and domestic temporal rebels, but with the bishops and the Popes of their church.   But let us suppose a succession of princes, such as Charlemagne and his father, to have continued among the Franks, and we shall readily understand that the haughty peers and insubordinate noblesse of the eleventh and twelfth centuries, with their rights of private warfare, of subinfeudation, and territorial jurisdiction, would never have arisen in France.   We shall still more fully realise to our minds the difference ; if we suppose the Frankish sovereigns to have been, like the Turkish Sultans, the heads both of the church and state, and to have combined in their own persons the claims of both Pope and Emperor.   And if we look to the history of our own country, we shall clearly see that a feudal system of baronial reforms, as well as of baronial aggrandisements, never could have grown up under successive rulers of the stamp of our Henry VIII.

The fact is indisputable (to whatever cause we assign it), that the Ottoman Empire employed the military spirit of feudalism for

[1] See Ubicini, vol. i. p. 512-516 ; and pp. 62-69.

national defence and for conquest; but kept clear (during its flourishing ages) of the social and political influences both for good and for bad, which feudalism produced in the west of Europe. No feudal nobility existed among the Turks until the period of the decline of the empire, when the Dereh Beys, or lords of the valleys, as the mutinous feudatories termed themselves, made themselves hereditary chiefs; and, fortified in their strongholds and surrounded by their armed vassals, defied their sovereign, and oppressed their dependents. But except this period (which the new reforms have terminated), the Ottomans have never had a nobility or noblesse, or a caste or class of any kind, that was privileged by reason of birth. All the Mahometan subjects of the Sultan (who are not in a state of domestic slavery) are on a level beneath him. Equality in the eye of the law among the Turks themselves is a social fact, as well as a legal theory.[1] Neither law nor popular opinion ever recognised in Turkey any superior claim of one part of the nation to the enjoyment of civil or military offices, such as the noblesse of France possessed over the roturiers. No surprise or indignation was ever felt if the Sultan elevated the poorest Osmanli from the toils of a common artisan or labourer to the highest dignity; and, on the other hand, the deposed Vizier or Seraskier descends to an inferior employment, or into the mass of the Moslem population, without loss of caste, or any change in his future civil rights and capabilities. With a few exceptions (such as that of the remarkable House of the Kiuprilis), family names are unknown in Turkey. There could not be a stronger proof of the entire absence of aristocracy from her institutions.

There is another element of European civilisation, the analogue of which appears among the Ottomans. This is the municipal, or the principle of local self-government in local matters. Each trade or craft has its guild (esnaf)[2] and every village has its municipality. The inhabitants choose their own elders or head-men, who assess and collect the amount of public contributions imposed upon the community, manage the municipal funds, which are in some cases considerable, act as arbitrators in minor disputes, attest important contracts, and are the customary organs of remonstrance against official oppression. This excellent system is not confined to the Ottomans themselves, but it flourishes among the Greeks, the Armenians, and the Christian Bulgarians under their sway.

---

[1] See Ubicini, vol. i. p. 57.
[2] Ibid. vol. i. p. 519.

It is believed[1] that these nations acquired it from the Turkish conquest, and the boon may be thought to outbalance much of the misery that has fallen upon the Rayas from the same quarter.

The Ulema, the order of men learned in the law, has been mentioned as supplying, according to the institutes of Mahomet II., one of the four pillars of the Turkish state. The predecessors of Mahomet II., especially Orkhan, had been zealous in the foundation of schools and colleges ; but Mahomet surpassed them all, and it was by him that the "Chain of Ulema" was organised, and the regular line of education and promotion for the legists and judges of the state was determined. The conqueror of Constantinople knew well that something beyond mere animal courage and military skill was requisite in order to maintain as well as to create a great empire. Eminent himself for learning and in the acquirements of general science, Mahomet provided liberally for the encouragement of learning and science among his people. He knew also well that to secure the due administration of justice it is necessary that the ministers of justice should be respected ; and that in order for them to be respected, it is necessary that they should not only have learning and integrity, but rank and honour in the state ; and that they should be raised above the temptations and anxieties of indigence. Mahomet established and endowed numerous public schools of the higher order, or colleges, called Medresses, in addition to the elementary schools, the Mektebs, that are to be found in every quarter of every town, and in almost every large village in Turkey.[2] The students at the Medresses went through ten regular courses of grammar, syntax, logic, metaphysics, philology, the science of tropes, the science of style, rhetoric, geometry, and astronomy. This is a curriculum which will certainly bear comparison with those of Paris and Oxford in the middle of the fifteenth century. The Turkish collegian, who had mastered these ten subjects, received the title of Danis-chmend (gifted with knowledge), and in that capacity, like the Western masters of arts, instructed the younger students. A Danis-chmend might claim the headship of one of the minor public schools, without further study ; but in that case he renounced the prospect of becoming a member of the Ulema, and of all the higher educational appointments. To become a member of the Ulema, it was necessary to commence and complete an elaborate course of study of the law, to pass repeated examinations, and to take several successive

[1] See Mr. Urquhart's work on "Turkey and its Resources," and Ubicini.
[2] Von Hammer, book xviii. ; Ubicini, vol. i. pp. 200, 201.

degrees. While care was thus taken to make the Ulema consist of men of the highest learning and abilities, great outward honour, liberal endowments, and many important privileges were conferred on those who attained that rank. The Ulema supplies all the professors in the high schools, who are called Muderris; and from this order also are chosen all the ministers of justice, including the Cadis, or judges of the smaller towns and rural districts; the Mollas, or judges of the principal cities; the Istambol Effendi, the judge and inspector-general over the city of Constantinople; the Cadiaskers, or supreme judges of Roumelia and Anatolia; and the Mufti, the importance of whose office has been already considered.[1] It is to be carefully remembered that the Ulema is not an ecclesiastical body, except so far as law in Mahometan countries is based on the Koran. The actual ministers of public worship, such as the Imans, who pronounce the public prayers, the Scheiks or preachers, and others, form a very subordinate part of the Ulema. There is no country in which the clergy,[2] properly so called, have less authority than in Turkey, or where the legal profession has more. It ought also to be recorded to the honour of the Ottomans, that more respect is shown among them than in any Christian nation to the schoolmaster, and to all who are eminent for possessing intellectual endowments themselves, or for their skill in guiding others to acquire them.[3]

Hitherto we have been examining the institutions of the Turkish Empire with reference chiefly to the dominant Mahometans. They are yet to be regarded with reference to the conquered but unconverted races, the Rayas, who have always formed the large majority of the population in European Turkey, and a very considerable proportion of the inhabitants of the Asiatic provinces. We must also consider the position of the slaves.

The Koran, while it enjoins war against unbelievers, requires the Mahometan to spare the peoples of the Books (a term including the Christians and the Jews), on their submission to pay tribute. "The bended head is not to be stricken off;" such is the maxim of the Turkish law. It was once asked of the Mufti, "If eleven Mussulmans without just cause kill an infidel, who is a subject of

---

[1] See Von Hammer, book xviii. and Supplement; D'Ohsson, vol. iv.; Ubicini, vol. i. pp. 81, 202; Thornton, p. 111.

[2] The influence exercised over the multitude by the fanatic dervishes, who are the monks and friars of Mahometanism, is quite unconnected with any state authority. See, on this subject, the fifth letter in Ubicini's first volume.

[3] Ubicini and Von Hammer.

the Padischah and pays tribute, what is to be done ?"   The judicial
reply was, "Though the Mussulmans should be a thousand and
one, let them all die."   The Rayas (as the tributary Christians are
called in Turkey) were entitled to protection for property as well
as for person, and to the free exercise of their religion.[1]   It is
written in the Koran, "My mission," saith the prophet, "is to
combat the unbelievers until they say 'there is no God but God.'
When they have uttered these words, they have preserved their
blood and their goods from all attack from me.   Of their own
belief, they must give account to God."[2]   The earliest capitulation
between Mussulmans and Christians, being the capitulation granted
by the Caliph Omar to the Christians of Jerusalem in 637, A.D.,
and the charter given by Mahomet II. to the Greeks of Constantinople, were alike framed in the spirit of this text.   The Christian
subjects of Mahometan power were bound to pay tribute; they
were forbidden the use of arms and horses; they were required to
wear a particular costume to distinguish them from the true
believers, and to obey other social and political regulations, all
tending to mark their inferior position.   In Turkey, the terrible
tribute of children was an additional impost on the Rayas.   This
last most cruel liability (which was discontinued two centuries
ago) must be remembered; and so must the sufferings and the
shames caused by the horrible practices, which we have been compelled to notice, when speaking of the reign and character of
Bajazet Yilderim.   Otherwise, it is correctly said that the lot of
the Christian subjects of the Ottomans was less severe than that
of the Jews in the various states of mediæval Christendom.   During
the later ages of corruption and anarchy in the Turkish Empire,
the Rayas were unquestionably made the victims of numberless
acts of lawless cruelty and brutal oppression; but these were the
results of the decay of the Ottoman government, and not the
effects of its institutions as ordained in the ages of its vigour.[3]

Domestic slavery has always existed among the Turks, as among
other Oriental nations, but in a milder form, and with brighter
hopes for those who undergo it, than the history of servitude
among the various races and in the various ages of the world
usually exhibits.[4]   The Turkish law protects the slave from arbitrary cruelty and brutal or excessive chastisement; and the general

---

[1] Thornton, p. 63; Ubicini, vol. ii. p. 17.
[2] See Ubicini, vol. ii.
[3] "It is not the Turkish laws, but a corrupt administration of them, that
brings opprobrium on the Empire."—Sir James Porter.
[4] See Ubicini, vol. i. pp. 153-159.

kindness of the Turkish character (when not excited by war or religious fanaticism), has been a still more effectual safeguard. The Koran inculcates the duty of treating a faithful servant with generosity; and teaches that the man, who sets free his fellow-creature from slavery, does much to set himself free from the infirmities of human nature and from the torments of hell fire. The emancipated slave, if a true believer, becomes at once the equal in civil rights of all the other Mahometan subjects of the Sultan. Many of the ablest officers, both in war and in peace, of the Sublime Porte, have been originally slaves: and a wide field has thus ever been open to her rulers for choosing men of tried ability and devotion, for the highest and most confidential employments.

Another important source, whence the Ottoman ranks have been recruited, has been the long stream of voluntary deserters from the Cross. The Turkish court and camp, where no heed was taken of a man's pedigree or birth-place, but where distinction, wealth, and power were open to all the bold and brave, who would profess the creed of the Prophet, presented irresistible attractions to many of the Rayas, and also to those strong and daring spirits from abroad, for whom, either through their own faults, or the fault of their fellow-countrymen, all similar careers in Christendom were closed. We may observe the working of this attraction even in the recent times of Turkish adversity. It was far more effective when the Crescent was the symbol of victory and conquest. If we look to the period when the Turkish power was at its height, the period of the reign of Solyman I. and Selim II.,[1] we shall find that out of ten Grand Viziers of this epoch eight were renegades. Of the other high dignitaries of the Porte during the same period, we shall find that at least twelve of her best generals, and four of the most renowned admirals, were supplied to her by Christian Croatia, Albania, Bosnia, Greece, Hungary, Calabria, and Russia. There was no fear of these apostates from the Christian faith ever halting in zeal for their new masters. Their sincerity as to their adopted creed might be doubtful, but not so their animosity against that faith which they had deserted; and Christendom for ages supplied her foes with the ablest, the most unscrupulous, and the most deadly leaders against herself.

All the circumstances of the settlement of the Turks in Europe tended to keep up in them the spirit of war and the capacity as well as the zeal for future victories. By enrolling the flower of

[1] See the list in Von Hammer, book xxxvi.

the children of the subjugated European provinces as Janissaries, by the impost of tribute money, by the sale of captives, and the acquisition of other plunder, by parcelling out the conquered lands into fiefs, wherein the best soldiers of the victorious army were planted as military colonists—each conquest was made to supply the means for further conquests, and Turkish war grew by what it fed on.   The Moslem occupants of the rich and beautiful lands east of the Adriatic felt their pride in their own prowess daily confirmed, and their fervour for the faith of the Prophet daily rekindled by the sight of the Christian Rayas around them, on whom fell the chief burdens of taxation and manual toil, " a weaponless herd, whose duty was obedience and subjection."[1]

This long-continued position of unquestionable and unquestioned superiority, " with nothing to provoke the strong to needless cruelty," may have conduced to develop in the Turkish character that dignity of manner, that honourable self-respect, that truthfulness, honesty, and sense of justice, that gentleness and humanity even towards the brute creation, which the bitterest enemies of the Ottomans confess, and which is the theme of uniform admiration with foreigners who have been dwellers in the Ottoman Empire.[2]   Lying and theft are the vices of weakness; and a morbid fondness for practising petty tyranny over creatures weaker than themselves is the special sin of those who have been subject to oppression.   But it would be eminently unjust to attribute the characteristic virtues of the Turks solely to the circumstance of their having long been a conquering people settled among a subject population, though such a fact must have had its

---

[1] Ranke's " Servia," p. 52.   " The Turks in the country—not only those of distinction, but others of lower rank who had gradually assembled around them—considered themselves the masters of the Raya.   Not only did the Turks reserve for themselves the exercise of arms, but also the right of carrying on such trades as were in any way connected with war.   Like our northern ancestors, or their own Oriental forefathers, amongst whom the son of a smith once founded a dynasty, many a Turk has been seen to turn back his silken sleeve, and shoe a horse ; still he regarded himself as a kind of gentleman.   Other occupations the Mussulmans left with contempt to Christian mechanics : for instance, no Turk would have condescended to be a furrier.   Everything that they thought suitable and becoming—beautiful arms, rich dresses, magnificent houses—they claimed exclusively for themselves"—*Ibid.*   In Constantinople and other large cities the proportionate number of Moslems engaged in trade and labour, and the variety of their occupations, was far greater than in the country.

[2] D'Ohsson, vol. iv. p. 25 ; Thornton, 288, n., citing Busbequius and other older writers.   More modern evidence will be found in Ubicini, and the preface to Murray's " Handbook."

influence. Those virtues are found among the Ottoman Turks of Asia, where the number of Rayas is far less than westward of the Dardanelles, as well as among the sparse Moslems of European Turkey: nor have those virtues been found to decay with the declining fortunes of their empire. Much is due to the moral precepts of their creed, which ensures sobriety and cleanliness, as well as benevolence, integrity, and charity, among its true disciples. But the Turks are also distinguished above other Mahometan nations for their high personal qualities, though these are alloyed with many evil traits, which, however, are to a great extent the peculiar vices of their men in power. Among no people are the injurious effects of court intrigue, and of elevation to high authority and wealth upon individual character, so marked as among the Ottomans. Modern observers have been repeatedly struck by the metamorphosis of the high-minded and generous country gentleman of Anatolia or Roumelia, exemplary in all the relations of domestic life, into a sordid grasping tyrant and a selfish voluptuary of the worst description, when invested with the power and exposed to the temptations of a Pacha. And it must be confessed that the renegades from Christendom, of whom so large a portion of the Turkish officials has been composed, have generally set the worst example in all respects to the rulers of native origin. The ferocious cruelty, which has too often marked the Turks in warfare, and their ruthless fanaticism, when roused by the cry that their religion is in danger, are seeming contradictions to the general benevolence and gentleness of character, which have been ascribed to them as a people ; but they are seeming contradictions only. The Turk is, in ordinary life, calm, mild, and indulgent, not because he is void of the fiercer passions, but because he is self-trained to control them. When the occasions come, on which it seems to him to be a duty to withdraw that strong curb of self-control, all those passions— Wrath, Revenge, and

> " The blind wild beast of force,
> Whose home is in the sinews of a man,"[1]

stir in him to strike, with a wild unchained delirium such as is unknown in bosoms, where no similar restraint has been practised. It is like what we often witness in private life, when the man, who habitually rules his temper the best, is, if it once gets the mastery of him, hurried into excesses, from which others, more frequently prone to anger, would have been able to stop short.

[1] Tennyson.

The Sultan's summons to war still meets a ready response from the inherent bravery of every Turk: and Europe has of late years justly admired the gallantry with which the Ottomans have risen to defend their land and their faith from almost overv helming enemies, and amid every circumstance of difficulty and d'scourage-ment. If such is the martial spirit of the people, now that they advance to the campaign " with no fear and little hope," what must it have been in the olden time, when almost unvarying victory crowned their arms, and when honour and wealth were the prompt rewards of distinguished valour ? We may imagine the excitement and the exultation, which the announcement of a new war and the summons to a fresh enterprise, must have created throughout the Moslem world on either side of the Dar-danelles. from the Euphrates to the Danube, from the Crimea to the Peloponnesus, in the days of Mahomet the Conqueror, or Solyman the Magnificent. The feudal chivalry left their Ziamets and Timars, and mustered beneath the banner of the neighbouring Bey or Pacha, each vying with the other in the condition and mag-nificence of his horse and accoutrements, and in the display of his band of armed and mounted retainers. The Ziam, who signalised his prowess, might hope for elevation to the rank of Bey; and the Timariot, who brought in ten prisoners, or ten enemies' heads, was entitled to have his minor fief enlarged into a Ziamet.[1] The Moslem, who did not yet possess either Ziamet or Timar, and was not enrolled in the regular paid troops, still served as a zealous volunteer on horse or foot according to his means ; and, besides the prospect of enriching himself by the plunder of the province that was to be invaded, or the city that was to be besieged, he looked forward to win by daring deeds performed among the Akindji or Azabs one of the Timars, that at the end of the war would be formed out of the newly-conquered territory, or which the casualties of the campaign would leave vacant. The regular troops, the Janissaries, and the royal horseguards, who fought immediately under the Sultan's eye, and whose trade was war, were even more eager for the opportunities of booty and promotion. Above all, religious enthusiasm roused the Moslem of every class to share in the Holy War against the misbelievers. The Koran teaches, indeed, that war is in itself an evil, and pro-nounces that " Man is the work of God. Cursed be he who dares to destroy God's workmanship."[2] But it teaches also that, when there is war between the true believers and the enemies of Islam,

---

[1] See the Report to Sultan Achmet III., already cited from Ubicini.
[2] D'Ohsson, vol. ii.

it is the duty of every Mussulman to devote to such a war his property, his person, and his life. The Koran divides the world into two portions, the House of Islam, *Dar-ul-Islam*, and the House of War, *Dar-ul-harb*.

It has generally been represented by Western writers on the institutes of Mahometanism, and on the habits of Mahometan nations, that the *Dar-ul-harb*, the House of War, comprises all lands of the misbelievers; so that there is, or ought to be, perpetual hostility on the part of the true believers against the dwellers in *Dar-ul-harb*, although actual warfare may be suspended by treaty.[1]

There is even a widely-spread idea among superficial talkers and writers that the holy hostility, the "Jehad"[2] of Mussulmans against non-Mussulmans is not limited to warfare between nation and nation; but that "it is a part of the religion of every Mahometan to kill as many Christians as possible, and that by counting up a certain number killed, they think themselves secure of heaven." But careful historical investigators, and statesmen long practically conversant with Mahometan populations have exposed the fallacy of such charges against those who hold the creed of Islam.[3]

"The craving of the Mahometans, as such, for Christian blood is purely a myth."[4] Their Prophet was certainly a stern iconoclast, and taught the duty of unremitting warfare against idolaters. In the Koran he bids his disciples "Fight on till there be no temptation to idolatry, and the religion becomes God's alone." But the Prophet also taught them with regard to Jews and Christians, "Dispute not except with gentleness; but say unto them, We believe in the revelation which has been sent down to us, and also in that which hath been sent down to you, and our God and your God are one."[5] A country which is under Christian rulers, but in which Mahometans are allowed free profession of their faith, and peaceable exercise of their ritual, is not portion of the House of War, of the *Dar-ul-harb*; and there is no religious duty of warfare, no "*Jehad*," on the part of true Mussulmans against such a state. This has been of late years formally determined by the chief authorities in Mahometan law with respect to British India, and

[1] See the introduction to Ubicini's second volume, and D'Ohsson.
[2] Sometimes written "Dhihad."
[3] See particularly Sir George Campbell's "Handy Book on the Eastern Question," and Bosworth Smith's "Mohammed and Mohammedanism."
[4] Sir G. Campbell, p. 33.
[5] Bosworth Smith, p. 261.

the principle is practically acknowledged by our sovereign being publicly prayed for in every mosque throughout her Indian dominions, which contain a population of not less than 40,000,000 of Mahometans.[1]

But, unquestionably, Mahometans of all ages have believed and have acted on the belief that when there is actual warfare between a state that holds the faith of Islam, and enemies who are of a different creed, it is a holy war on the part of the Moslems. Certain pacific texts of the Koran may be cited, that appear to some extent to qualify the fierce spirit of others, but the general tone of the Mahometan Sacred Book is eminently warlike, and must in the palmy days of Islam have stirred the bold blood of the Turks, like the sound of a trumpet, to wrest fresh cities and provinces for Allah from the Giaour. The Turkish military code breathes the full inspiration of the words of the Prophet, "In the shade of the crossing scimetars, there is Paradise." Every Mahometan is required to be a soldier.[2] Every soldier killed in battle, for the defence of the faith, is styled *schedid* or martyr.[3] And the Moslem who deserts his post, or flies before the foe, is held to sin against both God and man : his punishment is death in this world, and

---

[1] "Not long ago, in India, a question was raised and discussed by various Moslem lawyers, which might have had a tremendous result for ourselves. It was nothing less than the question whether Hindustan was a *Dar-ul-harb* or enemies' country, that is, whether the Jehad was in active or potential existence there, and consequently whether or no Moslems could, consistently with their faith, preserve their allegiance to their Christian rulers. The decision was given almost unanimously in favour of peace and submission to the existing rulers : and the chief argument adduced in support of this view is a convincing proof of the truth of Mr. Bosworth Smith's theory that not only is the spirit of Islam favourable to peace and progress, but that such spirit really actuates its professors now. The practice of Mohammed himself was adduced, namely, that when he laid siege to a town, or declared war against a tribe or people, he invariably delayed his operations till sunset, that he might ascertain whether the 'izan' or call to prayers was heard amongst them. If it were, he refrained from the attack, maintaining that where the practice of his religion was allowed by the rulers of the place he had no grievance against them. This one argument, and the fact that the name of our most gracious sovereign is now inserted in the 'Khotbah' or Friday 'bidding-prayer' in all mosques throughout India, is a sufficient proof that Islam is not antagonistic either to religious or political toleration, and that the doctrine of Jehad, a holy war, is not so dangerous or barbarous as is generally imagined."—*Quarterly Review,* January, 1877, p. 230.

[2] D'Ohsson, 202.

[3] D'Ohsson, 208. By a somewhat strange limitation the crown of martyrdom is denied to those who die *off* the field of battle by the effects of their wounds received on it.

hell-fire in the next. No enemy with arms in his hands is entitled to quarter; and war is held to make all modes of destruction lawful. Captives, women, and children, and all that can do Mahometans no harm, are ordered to be spared; but those among the enemy, who from their abilities, station, or other causes, may hereafter become dangerous to the true believers, may be slain, though they have ceased to resist. All cruelty and mutilation are forbidden, and all breach of faith. Capitulations must be observed, and promises to an enemy kept by whomsoever they were given. If the sovereign disapprove of the terms, he must punish his Mahometan officer who made them. The Turk is never to make a disadvantageous treaty unless when every mode of warfare has been tried, and under pressure of the direst necessity. But such a treaty, if once made, is to be kept strictly.[1]

In the general view which we have been taking of the Turkish institutions, we have lost sight of the individual Mahomet the Conqueror. But our attention is forcibly recalled to him when we cite one of the canons of the Turkish system of government, without notice of which our survey would be incomplete. It is the legislation of imperial fratricide. Mahomet II. ordained it by the following part of his institutes : " The majority of my jurists have pronounced, that those of my illustrious descendants who ascend the throne, may put their brothers to death, in order to secure the repose of the world. It will be their duty to act accordingly."[2]

---

[1] D'Ohsson, vol. ii. p. 49, *et seq.* D'Ohsson collected the Turkish military (and other) laws from the great Ottoman Code, that was compiled and published by the celebrated Turkish jurist Ibrahim Halebey, who died in 1549. See D'Ohsson's Introduction, p. 23. But now that Turkey is formally admitted to the public law and system of Europe (see Treaty of Paris, article vii.) she must be considered, even more decidedly than before, bound to observe the laws of war as generally recognised by civilised nations. I have discussed these laws in chapter xi. of the "First Platform of International Law."

[2] Von Hammer, book xviii.

CHAPTER VII.

BAJAZET II.—PRINCE DJEM—CIVIL WAR—ADVENTURES AND
DEATH OF DJEM IN CHRISTENDOM—FIRST WAR WITH EGYPT
—BAJAZET DETHRONED BY HIS SON, SELIM.[1]

ON the death of Sultan Mahomet II., a struggle for the sovereignty
ensued between his two sons, Prince Bajazet and Prince Djem, in
which success rested with the eldest but not the bravest or ablest
of the brothers.   Both the princes were absent from Constantinople at the time of their father's decease.   Prince Bajazet, then
aged thirty-five, was at Amassia, the capital of the province which
he ruled ; and Prince Djem, who was twenty-two years old, was
in Caramania, of which his father had made him governor.
Bajazet was of a contemplative, melancholy disposition, simple in
his habits, austere in his devotions, fond of poetry and speculative
philosophy ; whence came the surname of Sofi (the Mystic), which
is given to him by many of the Ottoman historians.   Djem had
the energy, the ambition, the love of pomp and the voluptuousness,
which had marked his father the Conqueror ; and, without sharing
his brother's fondness for metaphysics and abstruse learning, Djem
was more eminent even than the other members of his highly-
gifted family for his love of poetry ; and his own poems are ranked
among the most beautiful in Turkish literature.   On the death of
Sultan Mahomet being known in the camp and capital, the Janissaries rose in open anarchy, plundered the houses of the rich Jews
and other wealthy inhabitants, and put to death the Grand Vizier,
who had vainly endeavoured to disguise from them the fact of the
Sultan's death.   As this minister was known to be a supporter of
the interests of Prince Djem, the Janissaries were easily led by the
adherents of the elder brother to pronounce in favour of Prince
Bajazet ; and the rest of the army followed their example.   Messengers had been despatched to each prince by their respective
partisans in the capital ; but the bearer of the important tidings
to Prince Djem was waylaid and slain on the road ; and Bajazet

[1] Von Hammer, books xix., xx , xxi.

obtained the inestimable advantage over his competitor of first learning that the throne was vacant, and first reaching Constantinople to claim it. The Janissaries appeared before him on his arrival at the capital, and asked forgiveness for their late acts of violence; but these formidable suppliants asked it in battle array, and accompanied their petition by a demand for an increase of pay, and for a donative on their new sovereign's accession. Bajazet obeyed all their requests; and thenceforth the distribution of large sums of money at the commencement of each reign among these Mahometan prætorians became a regular custom in Turkey, alike burdensome to the treasury and disgraceful to the Sultan, until it was abolished by the Sultan Abdul-Hamid, during the war with Russia, 300 years after the time of the second Bajazet.

Djem was not of a disposition to resign the sovereignty to his brother without a struggle; and, remembering the bloody law by which their father had made imperial fratricide a state maxim, the young Ottoman prince may be said to have armed as much for life as for empire. A civil war followed, in which the abilities of the veteran Ahmed-Kedük, the conqueror of Kaffa and Otranto, and the treachery of some of Djem's principal followers gave the victory to Bajazet. A proposition had been made before the battle by Djem to his brother to divide the empire, Bajazet taking the European and Djem the Asiatic provinces. Bajazet refused to listen to such a scheme; and when the aged Sultana, Seldjoukatoun, who was the daughter of Mahomet I., and the great aunt of the two rivals, came to his camp and endeavoured to move his fraternal feelings in Djem's favour, Bajazet answered with stern brevity, by citing the Arab proverb, "There is no relationship among princes." Nevertheless, the Mystic Sultan, though resolute to maintain his rights, and to suffer no dismemberment of the Ottoman Empire, showed no remorseless eagerness for his brother's death, till after Djem had proved that, so long as life was in him, he would strive for a kingly crown at Bajazet's expense. After his first defeat (20th June, 1481), and the dispersion of his army, Djem fled to the dominions of the Sultan of Egypt and Syria, where he was favourably received and sheltered for a year, during which time he visited the holy cities of Medina and Mecca. He and a daughter of Mahomet I. are the only members of the Turkish royal family that have made that pilgrimage. In 1482, Djem, assisted by the Egyptian sovereign, and some of the malcontent Ottoman commanders in Asia Minor, renewed the war, but was again defeated and forced to seek safety in foreign lands. He did not return to his former protector, but

8—2

sought the means of passing to the Ottoman dominions in Europe, in the hopes of reviving the civil war with effect in that continent, though unsuccessful in the Asiatic, as Prince Musa had done during the interregnum after the defeat of the first Bajazet. With this view, he requested the Grand Master of Rhodes to grant him a temporary shelter, and the means of passing into Europe.

The Knights of St. John assembled in solemn chapter to discuss Prince Djem's requisition ; and it was finally resolved that it was consonant with the dignity and policy of the Order to receive the Ottoman prince.[1] Accordingly on the 23rd of July, 1482, Djem, with thirty attendants, landed at Rhodes, and entered on a long period of captivity most discreditable to the Christian potentates by whom he was nominally protected, but who in reality made him the subject of barter and sale, of long imprisonment, and ultimately of treacherous murder. He was received at Rhodes by the Grand Master and his Knights with ostentatious pomp, and every semblance of hospitable generosity. But it was soon thought desirable to remove him from Rhodes to one of the commanderies which the Order possessed in France. It was considered by D'Aubusson and his comrades that by removing the Ottoman prince from their island they would be better able to evade the demands which Sultan Bajazet was sure to make for the surrender of his brother to him, and that there would be less risk of losing their prisoner by assassination. Before Djem left Rhodes, D'Aubusson took the precaution of obtaining his signature to a treaty, by which Djem bound himself, in the event of his ever becoming Sultan, to conditions highly favourable to the Order.

D'Aubusson, whose skill as an unscrupulous diplomatist was at least equal to his gallantry as a soldier (which we have had occasion to admire while tracing the times of Mahomet II.), next sent an embassy to the reigning Sultan, in order to secure all possible advantages from having the Pretender in the power of the Knights. It was agreed that there should be peace and free trade between the Order and the Porte, and that the Sultan should pay a yearly sum of 45,000 ducats, ostensibly for the maintenance of his brother, but in reality as the price of his compulsory detention in some of the possessions of the Knights.

Before Djem had thrown himself into the hands of the Christians, Bajazet had offered him the revenues of the province which

---

[1] Senatus - consultum, *"Regem excipiendum, alendum, fovendum."* — Caoursin, cited in Von Hammer.

he had formerly governed, on condition of his living quietly at Jerusalem. Djem refused this offer, and demanded the cession of certain provinces to him in full sovereignty. Bajazet replied, that "Empire is a bride whose favours cannot be shared." On Djem's persisting in his resolution to seek through Christian help the means of renewing the civil war, Bajazet endeavoured unremittingly to compass his death, or at least to purchase his imprisonment.

The high-spirited but unhappy prince (whose adventures and poetical talents have made him a favourite character in Frankish as well as Turkish history) was landed by a galley of the Knights at Nice in November, 1482. Djem expressed his gratification with the beautiful scenery of the Frankish city, but was urgent to commence his journey to Hungary, whence he designed to pass into Roumelia. His conductors informed him that as he was on French territory, he ought not to depart without the formal permission of the king of the country. Djem accordingly sent one of his suite to Paris, and was assured by the chevaliers that his messenger might easily travel thither, and return in twelve days. But care was taken to arrest the Turkish envoy on the road ; and Djem lingered for many months at Nice, closely watched, though treated with apparent respect, and in vain expectation of a messenger from the French court. At last the plague broke out in that city, which gave the Knights a plausible excuse for conveying their prisoner to a commandery in the interior of the kingdom. The greater number of the Ottoman prince's native followers were now forcibly removed from him ; and Djem was confined, first at Roussillon, then at Puy, and afterwards at Sassenage, where he inspired the fair Phillippine Helena, the daughter of the lord of the castle, with an ardent passion, which was not unreturned ; and love for a time lightened the weary hours of the captive prince. At last the Knights took Prince Djem to a tower which they had caused to be built expressly for his safe custody. It was seven stories high. The kitchens were on the first story ; the chambers of the domestics on the second and third. The fourth and fifth were for the apartments of the prince ; and his jailors, the Knights, themselves occupied the two highest. For seven years the Ottoman prince was detained in France. The remonstrances against such treatment which he addressed to the Knights, and to the Christian princes and chiefs by whom he was visited, and his repeated attempts to escape, were fruitless ; though he was an object of interest to all Christendom ; and many kings negotiated with the Grand Master D'Aubusson, for the purpose of obtaining possession of the claimant to the Ottoman throne. D'Aubusson purposely protracted the discussion of terms, and was unwilling to put an end to a custody, which although little creditable, was eminently lucrative to the Knights of St. John. Djem's family, consisting of his mother, his wife, and his infant children, were at Cairo. D'Aubusson had the unknightly craft to obtain 20,000 ducats from the wife and mother of his victim, under pretence that the prince was immediately to be set at liberty, and that the money was necessary for the expenses of his voyage. This was in addition to the 45,000 ducats, which Sultan Bajazet paid annually as the price of his brother's captivity.

At last Charles VIII. of France interposed, not to set Prince Djem free, but to transfer him from the hands of the Knights of Rhodes, to the custody of the Pope. A guard of fifty French knights was appointed to attend the Turkish prince ; and it was agreed that in the event of the Pope giving him up to any other Christian sovereign without leave from the French court, a sum of 10,000 ducats should be paid as forfeit money to Charles. The court of Rome undertook to indemnify the Knights of Rhodes ; and a variety of privileges were accordingly granted to them by the sovereign Pontiff ; and D'Aubusson himself received the honour of being made a Cardinal.

In 1489, Prince Djem made his entry into Rome, with the empty pageantry of honours like those amid which he had eight years previously been conducted into Rhodes. He was lodged in the Vatican, and formerly presented to Pope Innocent VIII., by the Grand Prior of Auvergne and the ambassador of France. It was in vain that the chamberlains and other Papal officers urged on Djem the necessity of paying the accustomed homage to the spritual head of the Church and temporal sovereign of Rome. The son of Mahomet the Conqueror would neither vail the turban, nor bend the knee ; but walking straight up to the Pope, Djem saluted him as the Cardinals do, by a kiss on the shoulder. Then in a few words, full of manly feeling and princely spirit, Djem asked the Pontiff's protection, and requested a private interview. It was granted ; and Djem then narrated the hopes deferred, the deceits and the hardships, which he had undergone during his captivity. He spoke of the cruelty of his separation from his mother, his wife, and his children, and of his earnest desire to behold them again, and to sail to Egypt for that purpose. The tears flowed fast down the cheeks of the unhappy Turkish prince, while he told his wrongs ; and even the Pope was moved and wept as he listened. But Innocent said that for Djem to sail for Egypt was incompatible with his project for winning his father's throne ; that the King of Hungary required his presence on the frontiers of that kingdom ; and that, above all, he ought to think seriously of embracing the Christian faith. Djem replied that such an act of apostasy would irretrievably ruin him in the opinion of his fellow-countrymen ; and he proudly stated that he would not be false to his religion for the sake of the Ottoman Empire, or for the sake of the empire of the world. Innocent did not press the work of conversion further, and closed the interview with hollow words of consolation and encouragement.

At this time there happened to be at Rome an ambassador from the Sultan of Egypt ; and soon afterwards there arrived an ambassador from Sultan Bajazet. The Egyptian ambassador sought out Prince Djem, and prostrated himself before him as before the lawful sovereign of Turkey. Djem learned from him that the Rhodian Grand Master had extorted the 20,000 ducats from Djem's mother and sister, under the false pretence of their being required for the voyage from France. Djem and the Egyptian envoy complained loudly at the Papal court against the Rhodian Knights for this fraud, and demanded the restitution of the money. The Pope and Sultan Bajazet's ambassador interceded in favour of the Knights, and by their means the Order was discharged from the debt for 5000 ducats paid down immediately. The ambassador from the Turkish court was charged with the ostensible mission of presenting to the Pope certain holy relics of the Crucifixion, but he was also commissioned to arrange the price for which Innocent VIII. would pledge himself to keep Djem within the Papal States. 40,000 ducats a year was the sum agreed on between the rulers of Rome and Constantinople for this purpose ; and Djem was accordingly detained at the court of Innocent for three years ; and on the death of that Pontiff, the Turkish prince was safely guarded in the Vatican until the successor to Innocent was elected. The new Pope was the infamous Alexander Borgia. He forthwith sent an ambassador to Bajazet, and bargained for the continuation of the payment of the 40,000 ducats for continuing the detention of Djem. But Borgia also stipulated that he was to have the option of receiving 300,000 ducats paid down at once, if he took the shortest and most effectual means of securing Djem from invading Turkey, by putting him to death. Borgia is said to have been the only Pope that sent an ambassador to an Ottoman Sultan. His envoy was George Bocciardo, his Master of the Ceremonies. Bajazet was so pleased with the ambassador, and thought so much of the assurances which were conveyed to him of the Pope's high esteem and friendly regard for him, that he requested the Pope, as a personal favour to himself, to make Bocciardo a Cardinal.[1]

While the Sultan and the Pope's ambassador at Constantinople were trafficking for Djem's bondage and blood, Charles VIII. invaded Italy, and on the last day of 1495 entered Rome. Pope Alexander sought refuge in the Castle of St. Angelo, taking Djem with him as one of the most valuable of the Papal treasures. Eleven days after the entry of the French army, there was an interview between Pope Alexander and King Charles for the purpose of arranging a treaty of peace. One of the chief conditions was the transfer of Prince Djem into Charles's hands. A meeting of the Pope, the King and Djem, subsequently took place, in which the Pope gave Djem for the first time the title of Prince, and asked him if he was willing to follow the King of France, who desired his presence. Djem answered with dignity, "I am not treated as a prince, but as a prisoner; and it matters little whether the King takes me with him, or whether I remain here in captivity." Djem was transferred to the French King, who intrusted him to his Grand Mareschal. He accompanied the French army from Rome to Naples, and witnessed the slaughters of Monte Fortino and Monte San Giovanni. The Pope had now given up all chance of making any profit by the custody of Djem; but there yet remained the still more lucrative venture of procuring his assassination. This was accordingly done; though the Italian and Turkish historians differ as to the mode in which Borgia effected the crime. According to the first, Djem was poisoned by a bribed attendant, who mixed in the sugar, of which the Turkish prince ordinarily partook, some of the white powder, by means of which the Pope was wont to rid himself of obnoxious or over-wealthy cardinals, and with which he at last accidentally poisoned himself. According to the Oriental writers, Djem's barber, a Greek renegade, named Mustafa, inoculated his master with deadly venom, by slightly wounding him with a poisoned razor.

[1] Von Hammer, in his note, says, that about the middle of the last century, a Dalmatian monk relied on this precedent of Mahometan interest with the Holy See, and begged the then reigning Sultan to aid him in obtaining a Cardinal's hat. But, in order to save the officers of the Porte the trouble of sending a formal letter of recommendation, he framed himself a laconic note, which he addressed in duplicate to both the Sultan and the Pope. It was as follows: "Most Holy Father,—The poor friar, N. W., is to be made a Cardinal, or all the friars in Jerusalem are to be impaled."

They add, that Mustafa, though it was for the sake of the Pope's money that he did the deed, acquired favour afterwards with Bajazet for this service, and was raised by degrees to the dignity of Grand Vizier. All agree that Djem was murdered by the Pope, and that he died by a slowly wasting poison. A letter, which his mother had written from Egypt, reached Naples before his death, but the unhappy prince was too weak to be able to read it. His last prayer was—" Oh, my God, if the enemies of the true faith are to make use of me to further their destructive projects against the followers of Islam, let me not outlive this day, but take at once my soul unto Thyself." Djem died in the thirty-sixth year of his age, after thirteen years of captivity. Sultan Bajazet sent a formal embassy to reclaim his remains from Christendom, and Prince Djem was buried with royal pomp at Brusa.

Sultan Bajazet, though victorious in civil war, gained little glory in the encounters of the Ottoman power with foreign enemies during his reign. Immediately on his accession, the veteran conqueror Ahmed Kedük was recalled from Otranto to aid Bajazet against domestic foes; and Ahmed's successor, Khaireddin, unsupported from Turkey, was obliged to capitulate to the Duke of Calabria, after a long and gallant defence. Thus, Italy was relieved from the grasp which the dreaded Ottomans had laid on her; nor was any lodgement of the Turks within her peninsula again effected. Bajazet was engaged in frequent wars against the Venetians and the Hungarians, and also against the Poles, which brought little increase to the empire, except the acquisition of the cities of Lepanto, Modon, and Coron. There is small interest in tracing the details of the campaigns of the Ottoman troops in Europe during this reign, marked, as they are, by a degree of ferocity and cruelty on the Christian as well as on the Turkish side, which is repulsively striking, even in the history of mediæval warfare.[1] The epoch of Bajazet II. is brighter in the history of the Turkish navy than in that of the Ottoman armies. Kemal-Reis, the first great admiral of the Turks, signalised himself under this prince, and became the terror of the Christian fleets. He was originally a slave, and had been presented to the Sultan by the

---

[1] One specimen may suffice. The Hungarian commander, Demetrius Yaxich (a Servian by birth), had taken prisoner the Turkish general, Ghazi Mustafa, and his brother. Yaxich broke all Mustafa's teeth in his head, and then forced him to turn the spit on which his own brother was roasted alive at a slow fire. It is not surprising to read that Mustafa, some years afterwards, when Yaxich was sent on an embassy to Constantinople, waylaid him and slew him.

Capitan-Pacha Sinan. His remarkable beauty caused Bajazet to name him " Kemal," which means " Perfection," and he was in youth one of the royal pages. The first mention of him as a sea-captain is in 1483, where he was placed in command of the fleet which Bajazet sent to ravage the coasts of Spain, in consequence of an earnest entreaty which the Moors of Granada had sent to the Sultan of Constantinople, as " lord of the two seas and the two continents," for succour against the overwhelming power of the Spanish Christians. Kemal-Reis afterwards, in 1499, won a desperate battle over the Venetians off the island of Sapienza, and materially assisted in the reduction of the city of Lepanto. We find him also, in 1500, contending skilfully and boldly against the far superior fleets of the Pope, of Spain, and of Venice. The Ottoman marine had not yet acquired such an ascendency in the Mediterranean as it afterwards held under Bajazet's grandson, Sultan Solyman.

Bajazet's melancholy and dreamy disposition made him indifferent to the excitements of strife and conquest; and though, as a zealous devotee, he looked on warfare against the infidels as meritorious; and though sometimes, as an act of religious duty, he shared in the campaigns of his troops, his general policy was to seek peace at almost any sacrifice. As is usually the case with over-pacific princes, he was unfortunate enough to be entangled against his will in many wars, from which his empire acquired little advantage, and he himself less credit. Besides his hostilities with Christian powers, he was obliged to oppose by armed force the encroachments which the Mameluke Sultan of Egypt and Syria continually made on the Ottoman territory on the south-eastern confines of Asia Minor. The first war between the Ottoman sovereigns of Constantinople and the rulers of Egypt began in 1485, and was eminently disastrous for the Turks. Their armies were repeatedly beaten by the Mamelukes; and the spirit of revolt which had so long smouldered in Caramania, broke out and menaced open war. The Ottoman generals succeeded in reducing the Caramanians to subjection; but Bajazet, after five years of defeats by the Egyptians, concluded a peace with them, which left in their hands three fortresses which they had conquered. The wounded pride of the Sublime Porte was soothed by the pretext that the three fortresses were to be considered as given to endow the holy cities of Mecca and Medina, of which the Egyptian Sultan was protector.

As Bajazet advanced in years, the empire was again troubled with domestic dissension and civil war. He had made his sons and grandsons governors over provinces; and as the Sultan's infirmities increased, his three surviving sons, Korkoud, Ahmed, and Selim, began to intrigue against each other with a view to secure the succession. Selim was the youngest of the three, but the ablest, and the least likely to be deterred by any scruples of remorse from cutting his way to the throne by the readiest path. He was governor of Trebisond. His martial habits and bold readiness with tongue and hand had made him the favourite of the troops; and he sought to aggrandise his influence by making incursions into the Circassian territory on his own account. When the old and pacific Sultan remonstrated against these proceedings, Selim replied by demanding a Sanjak in Europe, so as to place him nearer to the central seat of government. He next asked permission to visit his father at Adrianople, to pay his filial respects; and, on this being refused, he crossed the Black Sea, and advanced to Adrianople with a retinue so numerous and well appointed, that it deserved the name of an army. The old Sultan, who was suffering under severe illness, joined the forces which some of his faithful followers had collected for his defence; but he wept bitterly on seeing the standards of Selim's troops, and at the prospect of encountering his own child in battle. In this mood, he was easily persuaded to negotiate by the Beyler-bey of Roumelia, who strove to avert the unnatural conflict, and acted as mediator between father and son. Selim received the European government of Semendra; and the Sultan promised not to abdicate in favour of his brother Ahmed, who was known to be the old man's favourite child. While these events were passing in Europe, Asia Minor was troubled by the machinations of the other two princes, Korkoud and Ahmed, and still more by the hordes of brigands who, under the feeble sovereignty of Bajazet, long infested the kingdom, and at last formed a regular army in conjunction with the numerous devotees of the Shia sect, who at that time abounded in Asia Minor. They professed unbounded veneration for the great Shia Prince, the Persian ruler, Shah Ismail: and the leader of this mixed force of ruffians and fanatics, took the name of Schah-Kouli, which means "Slave of the Schah;" but the Ottomans called him Scheytan-Kouli, which means "Slave of the Devil." He defeated several detachments of the Sultan's troops; and at last it was thought necessary to send the Grand Vizier against him. The Devil's Slave resisted skilfully and desperately, and both he and the Vizier at last perished in an obstinate battle which was fought near Sarimschaklik in August, 1511.

Selim took advantage of these disturbances as pretexts for his keeping an army together, to be ready for any emergencies of the State. At last he forcibly entered Adrianople, and assumed the rights of an independent sovereign. Some, however, of the Ottoman soldiery were yet averse to the dethronement of their old sovereign, and Bajazet marched upon Adrianople with a true though small army. Selim came out with his troops to meet him; and the old Sultan was with difficulty persuaded to give the order to engage his rebellious son. At length Bajazet raised himself on the cushions of his litter, and called out to his army, " My slaves, you who eat my bread, attack those traitors." Ten thousand loyal soldiers at once raised the battle-cry of " God is great," and rushed upon the rebel ranks. Selim's troops were broken by the charge, and fled in disorder; and Selim was indebted for his safety to the fleetness of his horse, called Karaboulut (the Black Cloud), and to the devotion of his friend Ferhad, who threw himself in a narrow pass between the flying prince and the foremost cavaliers of the pursuers. Selim fled to Akhioli on the Black Sea, where he embarked for the Crimea. The Khan of that peninsula was his father-in-law, and Selim was soon at the head of a new army of Tartar allies and Turkish malcontents, and in readiness to strike another blow for the throne.

Bajazet anxiously wished to make his second son, Ahmed, his successor; but neither this prince nor his elder brother Prince Korkoud, was popular with the Janissaries, who looked on Selim as the fit Padischah of the warlike House of Othman, and who considered the impiety of his attacks upon his own father to be far outweighed by the warlike energy and relentless vigour which he displayed. Bajazet had secretly encouraged some warlike preparations of Ahmed in Asia; but the indignation of the soldiery of the capital against that prince compelled the old Sultan to disown his acts, and even to send a messenger to the Crimea to Selim, requiring him to march to the protection of the capital from Ahmed. It was winter when Selim received the welcome summons; but he instantly assembled 3000 horsemen, half of whom were Tartars, and hastened round the north-western coast of the Euxine. Many of his followers perished by the severity of the cold, and the length and rapidity of their marches; but the indomitable Selim still pressed forward. He crossed the Dniester on the ice near Akerman, and, disregarding an injunction which the terrified Bajazet sent him to repair to his government at Semendra, he continued his progress towards the capital. When he was yet thirty miles from Constantinople, the Aga of

the Janissaries came to meet him ; and he made his entry into the
capital in almost royal state, with the viziers and other dignitaries
of state in his train. The old Sultan had amassed a large
treasure during his reign ; and he now sought to bribe his rebellious son back to obedience by an immediate donation of 300,000
ducats, and the promise of a yearly payment of 200,000 more.
Selim regarded the offered treasure as an additional inducement
to seize the throne, and refused all terms of compromise. Bajazet
still occupied the royal palace, the Serail ; but on the 25th of
April, 1512, the Janissaries, the Spahis, and the turbulent population of Constantinople assembled before the palace-gates, and demanded to see the Sultan. The gates of the Serail were thrown
open ; and Bajazet received them, seated on his throne. He
asked them what it was they desired, and the populace cried with
one voice, " Our Padischah is old and sickly, and we will that
Selim shall be the Sultan." Twelve thousand Janissaries followed
up the popular demand by shouting their formidable battle-cry ;
and the old Sultan, seeing the people and the army against him,
yielded, and uttered the words, " I abdicate in favour of my son
Selim. May God grant him a prosperous reign !" Shouts of joy
pealed round the palace and through the city at this announcement. Selim now came forward and kissed his father's hand with
every semblance of respect. The old Sultan laid aside the
emblems of sovereignty with the calm indifference of a philosopher, and asked his successor the favour of being allowed to retire
to the city of Demotika, where he had been born. Selim escorted
him to the gate of the capital, walking on foot by his father's
litter, and listening with apparent deference to the counsels which
the old man gave him. But the dethroned Sultan never reached
Demotika : he died at a little village on the road on the third day
of his journey. His age, and his sufferings both of mind and
body, sufficiently accounted for his death ; but a rumour was
widely spread that he had been poisoned by an emissary of his
son. The savage character of Selim may be thought justly to
have exposed him to suspicion ; but there seems to have been no
clear evidence of the horrible charge.

Bajazet's feeble and inglorious reign was clouded by insurrection and military mutiny at its commencement and at its close.
Nor were these the only scenes in which the insolent power of the
soldiery, and the infirmity of Bajazet's government were displayed. At one period during his reign the vice of drunkenness
had become so common in Constantinople, that Bajazet published
an edict threatening the punishment of death to all who were

detected in using wine, and orderi g all the public places, at which it had been sold, to be closed. But the Janissaries assembled, and breaking the taverns nd wine stores open, forced their proprietors to resume their trade ; and Bajazet, alarmed at the anger and threats of these peri ous guardians of his throne, withdrew the obnoxious edict four days after it had been pronounced. Had Bajazet been succeeded on the Turkish throne by princes of a character like his own, there seems little doubt that the decline of the Ottoman power would have been accelerated by many years. But the stern energy of Selim I., and the imperial genius of the great Solyman, not only gave to the Turkish Empire half a century of further conquest and augmented glory, but reinvigorated the whole system of government, so as long to delay the workings of corruption.

It is in the reign of Bajazet II. that the ominous name of Russia first appears in Turkish history. In 1492 the Czar, Ivan III., wrote a letter to Bajazet on the subject of certain exactions which had recently been practised on Russian merchants in Turkey, and proposing a diplomati intercourse between the two empires. Three years afterwards, Michael Plettscheieff, the first Russian ambassador, appeared at Constantinople. He was strictly enjoined by his master not to bow the knee to the Sultan, and not to allow precedence to any other ambassador at the Ottoman court. Plettscheieff appears to have displayed such arrogance as justly to offend the Sultan. Bajazet stated in a letter on the subject to the Khan of the Crimea (who had exerted himself to promote friendship between the empires), "that he was accustomed to receive respect from the powers of the East and the West, and blushed at the thought of submitting to such rudeness." Had Bajazet's father or son been on the Turkish throne, the haughty Muscovite would probably have received a sharper chastisement than the mild mark of offended dignity which Bajazet displayed by sending no ambassador to Russia in return. No one at Bajazet's court could foresee that in the rude power of the far North, whose emissaries then excited the contemptuous indignation of the proud and polished Osmanlis, was reared the deadliest foe that the House of Othman was ever to encounter.

CHAPTER VIII.

SELIM I.—HIS CHARACTER—MASSACRE OF THE SHIIS — WAR
WITH PERSIA—CONQUESTS IN UPPER ASIA—WAR WITH THE
MAMELUKES—CONQUEST OF SYRIA AND OF EGYPT—NAVAL
PREPARATIONS—DEATH OF SELIM—THE MUFTI DJEMALE'S
INFLUENCE OVER HIM.[1]

SULTAN SELIM I. was forty-seven years of age when he dethroned
his father. He reigned only eight years, and in that brief period
he nearly doubled the extent of the Ottoman Empire. The
splendour of his conquests, the high abilities which he displayed
in literature and in politics, as well as in war, and the imperious
vigour of his character, have found panegyrists among European
as well as Asiatic writers ; but his unsparing cruelty to those who
served, as well as to those who opposed him, has justly brought
down on his memory the indignant reprobation of mankind, as
expressed by the general sentence of the great majority both of
Oriental and Western historians. In his own reign the wish
" Mayst thou be the vizier of Sultan Selim," had become a
common formula of cursing among the Ottomans. Selim's viziers
seldom survived their promotion more than a month. They
whom he raised to this perilous post, knew that they were
destined for the executioner's sabre, and carried their last wills
and testaments with them, whenever they entered the Sultan's
presence. One of these officers, the Grand Vizier Piri Pacha,
ventured to say to Selim, in a tone half in earnest and half
sportive, " My Padischah, I know that sooner or later thou wilt
find some pretext for putting me, thy faithful slave, to death ;
vouchsafe me, therefore, a short interval, during which I may
arrange my affairs in this world, and make ready for being sent
by thee to the next." Selim laughed loud in savage glee at the
frank request, and answered, " I have been thinking for some
time of having thee killed ; but I have at present no one fit to
take thy place ; otherwise I would willingly oblige thee."

[1] See Von Hammer, books xxii., xxiii., xxiv.

Unsparing of the blood of his relations, his subjects, and his ablest servants, Selim was certain to be fond of war; and his reign was one of almost ceaseless carnage. Vigorous in body and mind, and indifferent to sensual pleasures, he pursued with keenness the martial pastime of the chase. He devoted all his days to military duties or to hunting. He slept but little; and employed the greater part of the night in literary studies. His favourite volumes were books of history, or of Persian poetry. He left a collection of odes written by himself in that language, for which he showed a marked preference. An Italian writer has asserted that Selim, like his grandfather, Mahomet II., loved to study the exploits of Cæsar and Alexander; but the classical histories of those conquerors were unknown in the East, and the Turkish Sultan only possessed the Oriental romances on their exploits, which are of the same character with the chivalrous legends current in the West respecting Charlemagne and the Knights of the Round Table. Selim showed especial favour and honour to men of learning, and promoted many of them to posts of high dignity and importance. He intrusted to the historian Idris the task of organising the newly-conquered province of Kurdistan; and the jurist Kemel Paschazadé accompanied him on his Egyptian expedition as historiographer. Selim was tall in stature, with long body though short limbs. Contrary to the example of his predecessors he kept his chin close shaved, but he wore enormously large black moustachios, which, with his dense and dark eyebrows, contributed to give him the fierce aspect which impressed with awe all who beheld him. His eyes were large and fiery; and his red complexion showed (according to the report of the Venetian ambassador Foscolo) a sanguinary disposition. His pride met with a sharp trial on the very first day of his reign. The Janissaries resolved to force from their new Sultan a donative, and drew up in double lines along the street through which he was expected to pass. They were to clash their arms together when he arrived, as an impressive hint of the means which had given him the throne, and of the means which might force him from it. Selim was apprised of their gathering; and, indignant at the prospect of thus passing publicly under the yoke of his own soldiers on the first day of his reign, he avoided the humiliation by riding round in another direction. He dared not however refuse the donative; and a distribution larger than had been made on any similar occasion, nearly exhausted the treasury. Emboldened by this concession, one of the governors of the smaller departments, a Sanjak-bey, approached the Sultan, and asked for an increase of revenue. Selim answered by drawing his sabre and striking the bold petitioner's head off on the spot.

Selim had acquired the throne by successful rebellion against his father; and he had good reason to dread the jealousy of his brothers, who were in command of some of the best provinces of the empire, and were little likely to give up the imperial heritage without a struggle. Five of the eight sons of Bajazet had died in their father's lifetime, Abdallah, Mahomet, Schehinshah, Alem-shah, and Mahmoud. Schehinshah left a son named Mahomet; and Alemshah, one named Osman. Mahmoud left three, Musa, Orchan, and Emin. Of the two surviving brothers of Selim, the eldest, Prince Korkoud was childless; the second, Prince Ahmed, had four sons. Selim himself had but a single son, Prince Soly-man. Thus there were twelve princes of the blood of Bajazet alive.

At first, Selim's brothers appeared willing to acknowledge him as Sultan, and accepted the confirmation in their respective govern-ments which he offered. But Prince Ahmed, who ruled at Amassia, soon showed his design of striving for the throne, by occupying the great city of Brusa, and levying heavy taxes on the inhabitants. Selim marched instantly into Asia Minor at the head of a powerful army, and sent a fleet to cruise along the coasts. Ahmed fled before him, and despatched two of his sons to implore assistance from the Persian prince, Shah Ismail. Selim took possession of Brusa, and sent the greater part of his army into winter quarters. Encouraged by some of Selim's officers, whom he had gained over, Ahmed renewed the war, and gained several slight advantages. Selim instantly caused his Grand Vizier, who was one of the traitors against him, to be strangled; and proceeded to further executions of a more atrocious character. Five of the young princes, his nephews, were in honourable deten-tion in the houses of some of the chief men of Brusa. The eldest of them, Osman, son of Prince Alemshah, was twenty years old; the youngest, Mahomet, son of Prince Schehinshah, was only seven. Selim sent Janissaries to apprehend them, and they were shut up by his orders in one apartment of the palace. On the next morning the Sultan's mutes entered to put them to death. A fearful scene ensued, which Selim witnessed from an adjoining chamber. The youngest of the captive princes fell on their knees before the grim executioners, and with tears and childish prayers and promises begged hard for mercy. The little Prince Mahomet implored that his uncle would spare him, and offered to serve him all the days of his life for an aspre (the

9

lowest of all coins) a day. The elder of the victims, Prince Osman, who knew that there was no hope of mercy, rushed fiercely upon the murderers, and fought hard for a time against them. One of the mutes was struck dead, and another had his arm broken. Selim ordered his personal attendants to run in and assist in the execution ; and at length the unhappy princes were overpowered by numbers, and strangled. Their bodies were deposited with all display of royal pomp near the sepulchre of Amurath II.

At the tidings of this massacre, Prince Korkoud, who had hitherto been quiet in his government of Saroukhan, saw clearly what doom was designed for himself. He endeavoured to win over the Janissaries, and prepared for a struggle for life or death with Selim. Selim detected his brother's plans ; and without giving any intimation of his discovery or his purpose, he left Brusa, under pretence of a great hunting ; and then suddenly advanced with 10,000 cavalry into Korkoud's province. Korkoud fled with a single attendant of the name of Pialé. They were pursued and captured. Selim sent an officer named Sinan to announce to his brother that he must die. Sinan arrived in the night at the place where the royal captive was detained ; and, waking Prince Korkoud from sleep, he bade him come forth to death. Korkoud demanded a respite of an hour, and employed it in writing a letter in verse to his brother, in which he reproached him with his cruelty. He then gave up his neck to the fatal bowstring. Selim wept abundantly when he read his brother's elegy. He carried his real or pretended grief so far as to order a general mourning for three days ; and he put to death some Turkomans who had guided the pursuers of Korkoud to his hiding-place, and who came to Brusa to ask a reward for that service.

In the meanwhile, Prince Ahmed had collected a considerable force ; and had gained further advantages over Selim's forces, which, if vigorously followed up, might have given him the throne. But Ahmed, though personally brave, was far inferior to his brother in energy and perseverance. Selim reinforced his army, and on the 24th of April, 1513, a pitched battle was fought, in which Ahmed was completely defeated and taken prisoner. His doom was the same as that of Korkoud, and was executed by the same officer, Sinan. Before death, Ahmed had begged to see the Sultan ; but the request was refused ; and Selim remarked that he would give his brother such a domain as fitted an Ottoman prince. Ahmed understood the words ; and when Sinan entered, gave himself up to death without resistance.

Before he was bowstrung, he drew from his finger a jewel said to equal in value a year's revenue of Roumelia, and charged Sinan to convey it to Selim as his brother's parting gift, with a hope that the Sultan would excuse the smallness of its worth. Ahmed was buried with the five murdered young princes at Brusa.

Selim now thought himself secure on the throne; and prepared for foreign warfare. Fortunately for Christendom, it was against other Mahometan powers that his energies were directed; and he willingly arranged or renewed a series of treaties with the different states of Europe, which secured tranquillity along the western frontiers of the Ottoman Empire. Selim had not fallen off from his ancestors in zeal for the faith of Islam. He was indeed the most bigoted of all the Turkish Sultans, But it was the very vehemence of his bigotry, that made him hate the heretics of Islam even more than the Giaours of Christendom.

The schism of the Sunnites and the Schiis (the first of whom acknowledge, and the last of whom repudiate the three immediate successors of the Prophet, the Caliphs Abubeker, Omar, and Othman) had distracted the Mahometan world from the earliest times. The Ottoman Turks have been Sunnites. The contrary tenets have prevailed in Persia : and the great founder of the Saffide dynasty in that country, Shah Ishmail, was as eminent for his zeal for the Schii tenets, as for his ability in the council, and his valour in the field.

The doctrine of the Schiis had begun to spread among the subjects of the Sublime Porte before Selim came to the throne ; and, though the Sultan, the Ulema, and by far the larger portion of the Ottomans, held strictly to the orthodoxy of Sunnism, the Schiis were numerous in every province, and they seemed to be rapidly gaining proselytes. Selim determined to crush heresy at home before he went forth to combat it abroad ; and in a deliberate spirit of fanatic cruelty he planned and executed a general slaughter of all his subjects, who were supposed to have fallen away from what their sovereign considered to be the only true faith. This is a deed to which the massacre of St. Bartholomew in the same century offers too sad a parallel ; and indeed the treachery, by which that crime of Christendom was accomplished, makes it the more detestable of the two.

Selim did not allure his victims by false professions of esteem, or by profaning the rights of hospitality, but he organised a system of secret police throughout his dominions, which contemporary writers term admirable; and he thus obtained a complete list of all the Mahometans in European and in Asiatic Turkey, who were suspected of belonging to the sect of the Schiis. The number of the proscribed, including men, women, and children, amounted to 70,000. Selim distributed troops throughout the empire, and stationed them in each city and district, in strength proportioned to the number of Schiis that it contained. He then suddenly sent forth the messengers of death, and the whole of those unhappy beings were arrested. 40,000 of them were slain; the rest were condemned to perpetual imprisonment. The contemporaneous Ottoman historians give Selim the title of " The Just," for this act of atrocity. The modern German historian well remarks that it is still more revolting to read that the Christian ambassadors at the Sultan's court adopted the surname, and that it is found applied to Selim in the reports of the massacre which they sent to their respective countries. Indeed, at a later time, and when Selim had shown by many more ferocious deeds, how deeply his soul was incarnadined with cruelty, the Venetian Mocenigo, who had been accredited to his court, and had known him well, declared that he never met a man who was Sultan Selim's equal in virtue, justice, *humanity*, and greatness of mind.[1]

The slaughter of his co-religionists increased the animosity with which Shah Ismail already regarded Selim; and the two sovereigns prepared for an encounter with equal rancour and resolution. Many grounds of quarrel, besides that of religious difference, existed between them. Shah Ismail had humbled the Ottoman arms in some encounters with the troops of the governors of the Turkish provinces near his frontier in Bajazet's reign; he had also sheltered the fugitive Prince Amurath, son of Selim's brother Ahmed; and he now assembled his troops, with the avowed intention of deposing and punishing Selim, and of placing young Amurath on the Turkish throne. Selim, on his part, made his preparations for an aggressive campaign with his accustomed vigour and determination. The renown of the Persian arms, and of the skill and good fortune of Shah Ismail, was widely spread throughout the East; and when Selim announced his intention of attacking Persia, the members of his council were ominously mute. Thrice the Sultan told them that he would lead them to

---

[1] Giovio, in a letter written to Charles V., in 1541, says : " Mi diceva il clarissimo Messa Luigi Mocenigo quel fù uno dei ambasciadori di Venetia appresso V. M. in Bologna, che essendo lui al Cairo ambasciadore appresso a Sultan Selim e se havendo molto ben pratticato, nullo huomo era par ed esso in virtu, justizia, *humanita*, e grandezza d' animo." It is difficult to imagine among what human creatures humanity existed in that age.

war, and thrice they spake not, till at last a common Janissary, named Abdullah, who stood by on guard, broke the silence, and throwing himself on his knees before the Sultan, told him that he and his comrades would rejoice in marching under him to fight the Shah of Persia. Selim made him Bey of the Sanjak of Selnik on the spot.

The Turkish army mustered in the plain of Yenischeer. Selim began his march on the 20th of April, 1514, on a Thursday, a day of the week thought fortunate by the Ottomans. On the 27th a Persian spy was seized in the camp, and Selim sent him to Ismail with a letter containing a declaration of war. Von Hammer cites this remarkable document from the contemporary Oriental writers;[1] and as he truly states, it admirably represents the general spirit of the age, and the especial character of Selim himself. It is as follows:

"The Supreme Being, who is at the same time the Sovereign of the destiny of man, and the source of all light and all knowledge, announces in His holy scripture that the true religion is the religion of the Mussulmans; and that he who professes another religion, far from being heard and saved, will be cast out among the reprobates at the great day of the last judgment. Again He saith, the God of truth, that His designs and His decrees are immutable, and all the actions of man ought to have regard to Him, and that he who abandons the good path shall be condemned to hell fire and eternal punishment. Place us, Lord, in the number of the true Believers, of those who walk in the path of salvation, and take heed to turn away from vice and unbelief! May the purest and most holy blessings be upon Mohammed-oul-Mustapha, the master of two worlds, the prince of prophets; and blessed also be his descendants and those who follow his law!

"I, chief and sovereign of the Ottomans;—I, the master of the heroes of the age;—I, who combine the force and power of Feridoon, the majesty of Alexander the Great, the justice and the clemency of Keikhosrew;—I, the exterminator of the idolators, the destroyer of the enemies of the true faith, the terror of the tyrants, and of the Pharaohs of the age;—I, before whom proud and imperious kings are abased, and the strongest sceptres shattered;—I, the glorious Sultan Selim Khan, son of the Sultan Bajazet Khan, who was the son of the Sultan Mohammed Khan, who was the son of the Sultan Murad Khan;—I graciously address my words to thee, Emir Ismail, chief of the

---

[1] It is also cited at length by D'Ohsson.

Persian troops, who art like in tyranny to Zohak and Afrasiab, and art destined to perish like the last Dara [Darius], to make thee know that the words of the Most High are not the frail productions of caprice or foolishness, but that they contain an infinity of mysteries impenetrable by the spirit of man. The Lord Himself hath said in His holy book, 'We have not created the heaven and earth that they should be a sport.' Man, who is the noblest of the creatures, and a compendium of the marvels of God, is consequently the living image of the Creator on earth. It is He that hath made ye, oh men, the Caliphs of the earth, because man, who unites the faculties of the soul with perfection of body, is the only being, that can comprehend the attributes of the Divinity, and adore His sublime beauties. But man does not possess that rare intelligence, nor does he arrive at that divine knowledge except in our religion, and by keeping the commandments of the prince of prophets, the caliph of caliphs, the right arm of the God of mercy. It is therefore only by the practice of the true religion that a man will prosper in this world, and deserve eternal life in the world to come. As for thee, Emir Ismail, such a reward will never be thy lot; for thou hast deserted the path of salvation, and of the holy commandment; thou hast defiled the purity of the doctrine of Islam; thou hast dishonoured and cast down the altars of the Lord; thou hast by unlawful and tyrannical devices usurped a sceptre in the East; thou hast by base stratagem alone raised thyself—thou sprung from the dust—to a seat of splendour and glory; thou hast opened to Mussulmans the gate of tyranny and oppression; thou hast joined iniquity, perjury, and blasphemy to impiety, heresy, and schism; thou hast under the cloak of hypocrisy sown in all parts the seeds of trouble and sedition; thou hast raised the standard of ungodliness; thou hast given way to thy shameful passions, and abandoning thyself without restraint to the most disgraceful excesses; thou hast untied the band of Mussulman laws, and thou hast permitted licentiousness and rape, the massacre of the most virtuous and honourable of men, the destruction of shrines and temples, the profanation of tombs, the contempt of the Ulema, of teachers of the law, and of descendants of the Prophet, and the degradation of the Koran, and the cursing of the true and lawful Caliphs [Abubeker, Omar, and Othman.] Therefore, as the first duty of a Mussulman, and above all of a pious prince, is to obey the commandment, 'Oh ye faithful, who believe, perform ye the decrees of God,' the Ulema and our teachers of the law have pronounced death upon thee, perjurer and blasphemer as thou art, and have laid upon every good Mussulman the sacred duty of taking arms for the defence of religion, and for the destruction of heresy and impiety in thy person and the persons of those who follow thee.

"Animated by the spirit of that Fetva, in conformity with the Koran, the code of the divine laws, and wishing both to strengthen Islam and to deliver the countries and the peoples who are groaning under thy yoke, we have resolved to lay aside our royal robes of state, to put on the cuirass and the coat of mail, to unfurl our ever-victorious banner, to assemble our invincible armies, to draw the avenging sword from the scabbard of our wrath and indignation, to march with our soldiers, whose swords deal mortal blows, and whose arrows fly to pierce a foe even in the constellation of the Sagittary. In fulfilment of that noble resolution we have taken the field ; we have passed the channel of Constantinople, and, guided by the hand of the Most High, we trust soon to put down thy arm of tyranny, to dispel those fumes of glory and grandeur that now confuse thy head and cause thee deadly wanderings ; to rescue from thy despotism thy trembling subjects ; and finally to smother thee in those same fiery whirlwinds which thy infernal spirit raises wherever it passes. So shall we fulfil upon thee the saying, 'He who sows discord must reap affliction and woe.' Nevertheless, jealous in our obedience to the spirit of the law of the Prophet, we propose, before we begin war, to place before thee the Koran, instead of the sword, and to exhort thee to embrace the true religion : therefore do we address to thee this letter.

"We differ in our dispositions, one man from another ; and the human race is like mines of gold and silver. Among some vice is deeply rooted ; they are incorrigible ; and it is as impossible to lead them back to virtue as to make a negro white. With others vice has not yet become a second nature ; they may return from their wanderings of the will, by seriously retiring into themselves, mortifying their senses, and repressing their passions. The surest mode to cure evil is for a man to search deeply his conscience, to open his eyes to his own faults, and to ask pardon from the God of mercy with a true repentance and a bitter sorrow. We therefore invite thee to retire into thyself, to renounce thy errors, and walk towards that which is good, with a firm and resolute step. We further require of thee that thou give up the lands wrongfully detached from our dominions, and that thou replace our lieutenants and our officers in possession of them. If thou valuest thy safety and thy repose, thou wilt resolve to do this without delay.

"But if, for thy misfortune, thou persist in conduct like thy past; if, drunk with the thoughts of thy power and foolish bravery, thou wilt pursue the course of thy iniquities, thou shalt in a few days see thy plains covered with our tents and flooded with our battalions. Then shall be performed prodigies of valour; and then shall the world witness the decrees of the Most High, who is the God of battles and the Sovereign Judge of the deeds of men. For the rest, may he fare well, who walks well in the true faith."

Much as Selim prided himself on his piety and his literary skill, he neglected no means of bringing more substantial weapons to bear upon his heretical opponent. In a general review of his army at Sivas, Selim ascertained that his available forces amounted to 140,000 well-armed men; and 5000 more were employed in the commissariat department, which also was provided with 60,000 camels. He had a reserve force of 40,000 men placed in echelon, between Kaissyraia and Sivas. The great difficulty of the campaign was to keep up his line of communications and to ensure a supply of provisions; as the Persians, instead of encountering him on the frontier, retired before him, laying waste the whole country, and leaving nothing that could shelter or feed a foe. Selim's chief magazines were at Trebizond, whither his fleets brought large supplies, and whence they were carried on mules to the army. Selim endeavoured to provoke Ismail to change his judicious tactics and risk a battle, by sending him more letters, written partly in verse and partly in prose, in which he taunted the Persian sovereign with cowardice in not playing out the royal part which he had usurped. "They, who by perjuries seize sceptres," said Selim, "ought not to skulk from danger, but their breast ought, like the shield, to be held out to encounter peril; they ought, like the helm, to affront the foeman's blow. Dominion is a bride to be wooed and won by him only, whose lip blenches not at the biting kiss of the sabre's edge." Ismail replied to the homilies and rhapsodies of the Sultan by a calm and dignified letter, in which he denied the existence of any reason why Selim should make war on him, and expressed his willingness to resume peaceful relations. Ismail then regretted that the Sultan should have assumed in his correspondence a style so unnatural and so unfitting the dignity of the nominal writer; but with polished irony Ismail asserted his firm belief that the letters must have been the hasty productions of some secretary who had taken an overdose of opium. Ismail added, "that, without doubt, the will of God would soon be manifested; but it would be too late

to repent when that manifestation had commenced.   For his part,
he left the Sultan at liberty to do what he pleased, and was fully
prepared for war if his amicable letter was ill received." This
letter was accompanied by the present of a box of opium, ostensibly for the supposed secretary who had written the letter in
Selim's name ; but, as Selim himself was addicted to the use of
that drug, the satiric stroke was sure to be keenly felt.   Enraged
at the dignified scorn of his adversary, Selim vented his wrath by
an outrage on the law of nations, and ordered the Persian envoy
to be torn to pieces.   His nephew Amurath, the refugee prince at
Ismail's court, had, with Ismail's sanction, set the example of such
atrocity, by mutilating and putting to death a Turkish ambassador,
who had been sent to the Persian court to demand that Amurath
should be given up to Selim.

The Ottoman army continued to advance through the north of
Diarbekir, Kourdistan, and Azerbijan, upon Tabriz, which was
then the capital of Persia, and the usual royal residence of Shah
Ismail.   The prudent system of operations, which the Persian
prince continued to follow, inflicted great hardships upon the advancing Turks, as wherever they moved they found the country
entirely desolate, and the difficulty of forwarding supplies increased with each march.   The Janissaries murmured ; but Selim
only redoubled his vigilance in preserving strict order, and his
exertions in providing as far as possible the means of reaching
Tabriz.   One of his generals, Hemdar Pacha, who had been
brought up with Selim from infancy, was persuaded by the other
officers to remonstrate with the Sultan against marching farther
through those desert countries.   Selim beheaded him for his
interference, and still marched on.   At Sogma, Selim received an
embassy from the Prince of Georgia, and a welcome supply of
provisions.   After a short halt he gave orders to resume the march
upon Tabriz, and the Janissaries broke out into open tumult, and
loudly demanded to be led back to their homes.   Selim had pretended not to observe their murmurs on former occasions during
the march, but he now rode boldly into the midst of them.   " Is
this," he cried, " your service to your Sultan ?   Does your loyalty
consist of mere boast and lip-worship ?   Let those among you who
wish to go home, stand out from the ranks, and depart.   As for
me, I have not advanced thus far merely to double on my track.
Let the cowards instantly stand aloof from the brave, who have
devoted themselves with sword and quiver, soul and hand, to our
enterprise."   He ended by quoting a passage from a Persian
poem :

" I never flinch, or turn back from the purpose
Which once has gained dominion o'er my soul."

He then gave the word of command to form column and march,
and not a Janissary dared leave his banner.

At length the pride of Ismail overcame his prudence ; and, exasperated at the devastation which the war caused to his subjects,
and at the near approach of his insulting enemy to his capital, the
Persian prince determined to give battle, and arrayed his forces in
the valley of Calderan.   Selim's joy was extreme when, on mounting the heights to the westward of that valley, on the 23rd of
August, 1514, he saw the Persian army before him.   He gave
command for an immediate engagement, and drew up his troops
in order of battle on the heights, before marching to action in the
valley.   He had about 120,000 troops, of whom 80,000 were
cavalry.   But both men and horses were worn by the fatigues and
privations of the march, and seemed to be ill-fitted to encounter
the magnificent cavalry of the Persians, which was perfectly fresh
and in admirable spirit and equipment.   The Persian cavalry was
equal in numbers to the Turkish horse, but it constituted the
whole of Shah Ismail's army.   He had neither infantry nor
cannons ; while Selim brought a powerful train of artillery into
action, and a large portion of his Janissaries bore firearms.

Selim drew up the feudal cavalry of Anatolia on his right wing
under Sinan Pacha, and the feudal cavalry of Roumelia on the
left, under Hassan Pacha.   He placed his batteries at the extremity of each wing, masking them by the light troops of his
army, the Azabs, who were designed to fly at the enemy's first
charge, and lure the best Persian troops under the muzzles of the
Turkish guns.   The Janissaries were a little in the rear, in the
centre, protected by a barricade of baggage-waggons.   Behind
them were the Sultan's horse-guards, and there Selim took his
own station.   On the other side Ismail drew up two chosen
brigades of cavalry, one on each side of his line, one of which he
led himself, and the other was intrusted to the command of a
favourite general, Oustadluogli.   Ismail designed to turn his
enemy's wings with these two brigades, and, avoiding the Ottoman
batteries, to take the Janissaries in the rear.   He anticipated that
Selim's light troops, the Azabs, would, when charged, wheel away
to the extreme right and left of the Ottoman line, so as to unmask
the cannons ; and he therefore ordered that his two brigades
should not endeavour to break through the Azabs, but should
wheel as they wheeled, so as to keep the Azabs between them and

the artillery, until they were clear of the guns, and then ride in
on the flanks and rear of the Ottoman army. This manœuvre
seemed the more practicable as Selim's cannons in each wing were
chained together, so that it was almost impossible to change their
position when the battle had once commenced. Full of confidence,
the Persian cavaliers galloped forward with loud cries of "The
Shah! the Shah!" and the Turks raised the cry of "Allah!" and
stood firm to meet them. The wing which Ismail led in person
was completely successful. He outflanked the wheeling Azabs,
and then, bursting in on the left of the Ottomans, he drove them
in confusion upon their rear-guard. But, on the other side of the
field, Sinan Pacha, the commander of the Turkish right wing, out-
generalled his opponent Oustadluogli. Instead of wheeling his
retreating Azabs away from the front of the batteries, Sinan called
them straight back, let them pass over the chains by which the guns
were fastened together, and then poured in a deadly discharge
upon the dense column of Persian horse that was galloping forward in close pursuit. Oustadluogli was one of the first that fell,
and the whole left of the Persians was thrown into disorder, which
a charge of Sinan's Spahis soon turned into utter rout. Victorious
in this part of the battle, Selim was able to bring succour to his
defeated troops, who had been broken by Shah Ismail. He led
his Janissaries into action, and the Shah's cavalry, already somewhat exhausted and dismayed by their previous efforts, were
unable to break this veteran infantry, or long to endure their
fusillade. The Persians had begun to waver, when Shah Ismail
himself fell from his horse, wounded in the arm and the foot.
The Turks closed upon him; and he was only saved by the
devoted gallantry of one of his followers, Mirza Sultan Ali, who
rushed upon the Ottomans, exclaiming, "I am the Shah." While
the enemy mastered Mirza Ali and examined his person, Ismail
was raised from the ground. Another of his attendants named
Khizer, gave up his own horse, on which Ismail was mounted by
those around him, and hurried from the field.

The victory of Selim was complete, but it had been dearly purchased. No less than fourteen Ottoman Sanjak Beys ("Lords
of Standards") lay dead on the field of battle; and an equal
number of Khans who had fought on the Persian side had also
perished.

Selim took possession of his enemy's camp, in which were his
treasures and his harem, including the favourite wife of the Shah.
Selim put all his prisoners, except the women and children, to

death; and then marched upon Tabriz, and entered the Persian capital in triumph.

Selim levied on the conquered city a contribution of 1000 of its most skilful artisans. These were sent by him to Constantinople, and received houses and the means of carrying on their respective manufactures in the Ottoman capital. After a halt of only eight days at Tabriz, the Sultan marched northwards towards Karabagh, meaning to fix his winter quarters in the plains of Azerbijan, and resume his career of conquest in the spring. But the discontent of the troops at this prolongation of their hardships, and their desire to revisit their homes, broke out into such general and formidable murmurings, that Selim was, like Alexander, compelled to give way, and return with his victorious, but refractory veterans towards Europe. His expedition, however, was not barren of important augmentation to his empire. The provinces of Diarbekir and Kurdistan, through which he had marched against Ismail, were thoroughly conquered and annexed to his dominions by the military skill of the generals whom he detached for that purpose, and still more by the high administrative ability of the historian Idris, to whom Selim confided the important duty of organising the government of the large and populous territories which had been thus acquired. The pacific overtures of Shah Ismail were haughtily rejected by the Sultan; and throughout Selim's reign there was war between the two great Mahometan sovereigns, in which the Persian arms were generally unsuccessful against the Turkish, though Shah Ismail maintained the contest with spirit, and preserved the greater part of his territories under his sway.

Selim's hatred against the Schii heretics and his warlike energy were unchecked throughout his life; but after the campaign of Calderan he did not again bring the whole weight of the Ottoman power to bear upon Persia, nor did he himself again lead his invading armies against her. Syria and Egypt proved more tempting objects to his ambition; and the aggressive strength of the Mameluke rulers of those countries made a decisive contest between them and the Ottomans almost inevitable. The dominion of the Mamelukes is one of the most remarkable phenomena in history, especially in the history of slavery. The word Mameluke, or Memlook, means slave; and this body of Oriental chivalry, which, for nearly six centuries, maintained itself in lordly pride in Egypt, which encountered Selim and Napoleon with such valour as to extort the admiration of those two great conquerors, and which, though often partially broken, was only destroyed by the

darkest treachery in our own age ;—this military aristocracy of the
East consisted of men, who had been bought and sold and bred as
slaves, and who recruited their own ranks, not from among the
natives of the land which became their country, but from the
slave markets of far distant regions.   Malek Salech, of the Eyoub
dynasty of the Sultans of Egypt, formed in the beginning of the
thirteenth century (a hundred years before the institution of the
Janissaries), an armed corps of twelve thousand slaves, chiefly
natives of the Caucasian countries.   These, from their servile condition, were called Memlooks.   Their discipline and military spirit
soon made them formidable to their masters, and in 1264 they
killed Touroon Shah, the last prince of the Eyoub dynasty, and
placed one of their own body on the throne of Egypt.   The first
Mameluke sovereigns of Egypt were called Baharites.   They
conquered Syria; a country which the Pharaohs, the Ptolemies,
and all the various rulers of Egypt, down to the times of Napoleon
and Mehemet Ali, have ever regarded as a necessary rampart for
their dominions along the banks of the Nile.   In 1382 Berkouk, a
Mameluke of Circassian race, overthrew the Baharite sovereign,
and founded the dynasty of the Circassian Mamelukes, which continued to reign till the time of Selim's invasion.   At this period
the military force of the Mamelukes consisted of three classes of
warriors ; all cavalry superbly mounted and armed, but differing
materially in rank.   First, there were the Mamelukes themselves
—properly so called—all of whom were of pure Circassian blood,
and who had all been originally slaves.   The second corps was
called the Djelbans, and was formed principally of slaves brought
from Abyssinia.   The third, and lowest in rank, was called the
Korsans, and was an assemblage of mercenaries of all nations.
There were twenty-four Beys or heads of the Mamelukes, and they
elected from among themselves a sultan, who was called also
Emirol-Kebir, or Chief of Princes.   He reigned over Egypt and
Syria, and was also recognised as supreme sovereign over that
part of Arabia in which the holy cities of Mecca and Medina are
situate.

The first war between the Mamelukes and the Ottoman Turks
broke out, as we have seen, during the weak reign of Bajazet II.
at Constantinople, and terminated to the disadvantage of the
Sublime Porte.   The Mameluke princes saw clearly that under
Sultan Selim the vast resources of the Turkish Empire would be
wielded in a far different spirit from that of his father, and they
watched with anxious attention the conquests of the provinces of
Diarbekir and Kurdistan, which Selim made from the Persians,

and which brought the Ottoman frontiers more extensively in contact with those of the Egyptian possessions in Syria. The Sultan
of Egypt, Kanssou-Ghawri, assembled a strong army of observation
in the north of Syria, in 1516. Sinan Pacha, the commander of
the Ottoman forces in the south-east of Asia Minor, reported this
to Selim, and stated that he could not with safety obey the
Sultan's orders to march towards the Euphrates, while menaced
by the Mamelukes on flank and rear. Selim assembled his divan
at Constantinople, and the question of war with Egypt was
earnestly deliberated. The Secretary Mohammed (who was ·dis-
tinguished for his scientific attainments, and whom Selim had
raised to office as a mark of his regard for science) spoke strongly
in favour of war, and urged that it ought to be a point of honour
with the Sultan of the Ottomans to acquire by conquest the protectorate of the Holy Cities. Selim was so delighted with the
warlike speech of his favourite philosopher, that he gave him the
rank of Vizier on the spot. Mohammed at first declined the promotion, but Selim took a summary method of curing his scruples.
With his own royal hands he applied the bastinado to the man
whom he delighted to honour, till the diffident follower of science
accepted the proffered dignity. It was resolved to wage war in
Egypt, but messengers requiring submission were first to be sent
in obedience to the precepts of the Koran. Selim, however, did
not delay his preparations for warfare until the result of the message was ascertained. He left Constantinople at the same time
with his ambassadors, and placed himself at the head of the
intended army of Egypt.

Kanssou-Ghawri was at Aleppo when Selim's ambassadors
reached him. He committed the folly as well as the crime of
treating them with insult and personal violence, though on the
approach of the Turkish army he set them at liberty, and vainly
endeavoured to open negotiations. The first battle, which determined the fate of Syria, was fought on the 24th August, 1516,
not far from Aleppo, in a plain where, according to Mahometan
tradition, is the tomb of David. The effect of the Turkish
artillery, and the dissensions among the Mamelukes themselves,
gave Selim an easy victory ; and the aged Sultan Ghawri died
while endeavouring to escape. The Mamelukes chose as their
new Sultan, Touman Bey, a chief eminent for his valour and the
nobility and generosity of his disposition. Their defeat had not
damped the spirits of the Mamelukes, who remembered their
victories in the former war, and considered themselves far superior
to the Ottomans in military skill and personal prowess. During

the confusion caused by the defeat and death of the Sultan, and the retreat of the principal surviving Beys to Cairo for the purpose of electing his successor, Selim had been suffered to occupy Aleppo, Damascus, Jerusalem, and the other Syrian cities, without resistance ; but it was resolved to defend the passage of the Desert against him ; and an advanced force of Mamelukes was sent to Gaza, while Touman Bey concentrated the mass of the Egyptian forces in the vicinity of Cairo.

Selim prepared for the difficult march from the inhabited portion of Syria to the Egyptian frontier with his customary forethought and energy. He purchased many thousand camels, which were laden with water for the use of his army while crossing the Desert, and he distributed a liberal donative of money among his men. His Grand Vizier, Sinan Pacha, defeated the advanced force of the Mamelukes near Gaza, after an obstinate fight, which was determined in favour of the Turks by their artillery. The Turkish army then crossed the Desert in ten days, and marched upon the Egyptian capital, Cairo. Touman Bey's army was at Ridania, a little village on the road leading towards that city ; and it was there that the decisive battle was fought on the 22nd January, 1517. Two of the Egyptian Sultan's chief officers, Ghazali and Khair Bey, had betrayed him, and baffled the skilful tactics by which he hoped to take the Ottoman army in flank while on the march. Though compelled to fight at disadvantage, the Mameluke chivalry never signalised their valour more than on the fatal day of Ridania. At the very commencement of the action, a band of horsemen, armed from head to foot in steel, galloped from the Egyptian left in upon the Turkish centre, to where the Sultan's own banner was displayed. Touman Bey himself, and two of his best captains, Alan Bey, and Kourt Bey, led this daring charge. They had sworn to take the Ottoman Sultan dead or alive ; and Selim was only saved by their mistaking for him Sinan Pacha, the Grand Vizier, who was at that moment in the centre of a group of the principal officers of the Turkish army. Touman Bey speared Sinan through and through : Alan Bey, and Kourt Bey, killed each a pacha ; and then rapidly wheeling their ready chargers, the bold Mamelukes rode back to their own army, though Alan Bey received a severe wound from a bullet. The other Mamelukes (save those whom treachery kept back) charged with valour worthy of such chiefs ; but the efforts of this splendid cavalry were as vain against the batteries of Selim's artillery, as were in aftertime the charges of their successors against the rolling fire of Napoleon's squares.

Touman Bey and a relic of his best cavaliers escaped to Adviyé, but 25,000 Mamelukes lay heaped on the plain of Ridania.

Selim sent a detachment of his army to occupy Cairo. They entered it without resistance, seven days after the battle ; but the indomitable Touman Bey suddenly came upon the intrusive garrison, and slew them to a man. Selim sent his best troops to retake the city, which had no regular fortifications, but in which the Turks now found every street barricaded, and every house a fortress. A desperate street battle now ensued, and for three days the Mamelukes held Cairo against the assaulting columns of the Sultan. At the suggestion of the traitor Khair Bey, Selim now proclaimed an amnesty to such Mamelukes as would surrender. On the faith of this promise the warfare ceased, and 800 of the chief Mamelukes voluntarily became Selim's prisoners, or were given up to him by the citizens. Selim had them all beheaded, and then ordered a general massacre of the wretched inhabitants of Cairo, 50,000 human beings are said to have perished in this atrocious butchery. Kourt Bey, who was reputed the most valiant of the Mamelukes, was for a time concealed in Cairo ; but Selim, by promises of safety, induced the champion of the Circassian race to present himself before him. Selim received him, seated on his throne, and with all the dignitaries of his camp around him. Selim, looking on him, said, " Thou wast a hero on horseback—where is now thy valour ?" " It is always with me," answered Kourt Bey, laconically. " Knowest thou what thou hast done to my army ?" " Right well." Selim then expressed his astonishment at the attack on his person, which Kourt Bey had, in concert with Touman Bey and Alan Bey, dared to make at Ridania, and which had proved so fatal to Sinan Pacha. Upon this, Kourt Bey, who was as renowned for his eloquence as for his courage, poured forth a brilliant eulogy on the valour of the Mamelukes, and spoke with contempt and abhorrence of guns, which, he said, killed so cowardly and so like an assassin.[1] He

[1] The reader will remember Hotspur. Old Knolles, in relating the victory of Selim over the Persians, breathes the same spirit. He says that the Persian cavalry "had been of the Turks invincible, if it had not been overwhelmed by the *cruel, cowardly,* and murdering artillery, and wonderful multitude of men." See also Byron's "Island," canto 3, and note.

With respect to the speech of Kourt Bey in the text, it is to be observed that it ought not to be considered a mere imaginary composition, like the speeches in many of the classical historians, and in many of their modern imitators. Von Hammer gives this dialogue between Kourt Bey and Selim, on the authority of, among others, the Scheik Seinel, who had held an appointment at Touman Bey's court, and who must have been an eye and

told Selim that the first time that Venetian[1] bullets (so the Mamelukes call cannon and musket-balls) were brought into Egypt,
was in the reign of Eschref-Kanssou, when a Mauritanian offered
to arm the Mamelukes with them; but the Sultan and the Beys
of the army rejected that innovation in warfare as unworthy of
true valour, and as a departure from the example of the Prophet,
who had consecrated the sabre and the bow as the fit weapons for
his followers. Kourt Bey said that the Mauritanian had, on this
refusal, cried out, "Some of you shall live to see this empire
perish by these bullets." "Alas!" added Kourt Bey, "that prediction is accomplished: but all power is in the hands of God the
Most High." "How comes it," said Selim, "if ye place all your
strength in the word of God, that we have beaten you, and driven
you from your strong places, and thou thyself standest here a
prisoner before me?" "By Allah," answered Kourt Bey, "we
were not overthrown because ye were braver in battle or better
horsemen than we; but because it was our destiny. For, all that
has a beginning must have an end, and the duration of empires is
limited. Where are the Caliphs, those champions of Islam?
Where are the mightiest empires of the world? And your time
also, ye Ottomans, will come; and your dominion shall in turn be
brought to nothing. As for myself, I am not thy prisoner, Sultan
Selim, but I stand here free and secure by reason of thy promises
and pledges." Kourt Bey then turned to the traitor Khair Bey,
who stood by Selim during this interview, and after heaping the
most withering invectives on him, he counselled Selim to strike
the betrayer's head off, lest he should drag him down to hell.
Then said Selim, full of wrath, "I had thought to set thee free,
and even to make thee one of my Beys. But thou hast loosened
thy tongue in an unseemly course, and not set respect of my
presence before thine eyes. He who stands before princes without reverence, is driven from them with shame." Kourt Bey
answered with spirit: "God preserve me from ever being officer
of thine." At these words Selim's rage overflowed, and he called
for executioners. A hundred swords were ready at his command.
"What good will my single head do thee," continued the fearless
Mameluke, "when so many brave men are on the watch for thine;
and Touman Bey still trusts in God?" Selim signed to one of his
headsmen to strike. While the sabre was swung round to slay,

ear-witness of much related in his narrative of the conquest of Egypt. See
the list of Oriental authorities prefixed to Von Hammer, book xiii.

[1] Bindikia, *i.e.* Venetian. Von Hammer says that bullets are still called
so in Egypt.

the doomed hero turned to Khair Bey, "Take my bloody head, traitor, and place it in thy wife's lap, and may 'God make the betrayer betrayed.'" Such were the last words of Kourt Bey, the bravest of the brave Mamelukes.

Touman Bey, after the final loss of Cairo, had sought to strengthen himself by employing Arabs in his army, contrary to the former practice of the Mamelukes. He gained some advantages over detachments of Selim's army: and Selim offered him peace on condition of his acknowledging himself to be vassal of the Ottoman Sultan. But the treacherous massacre at Cairo, and the execution of Kourt Bey, had exasperated the Mamelukes; and they put Selim's messenger and the whole of his attendants to death. Selim retorted by the slaughter of 3000 prisoners. The war continued a little longer; but the Arabs and the Mamelukes under Touman Bey quarrelled with each other, and fought in the very presence of the Ottoman army, which poured its cannonade upon the combatants with impartial destructiveness. At length, Touman Bey's forces were entirely dispersed; and he himself was betrayed into the hands of the Turks. When Selim was informed of his capture, he exclaimed, "God be praised; Egypt is now conquered." He at first treated his brave prisoner with merited respect; but the traitors Ghazali and Khair Bey were determined that their former sovereign should perish, and they raised Selim's suspicions that there was a plot to liberate the royal prisoner and restore him to power. Selim, on this, ordered him to be put to death; and the last Mameluke Sultan, the brave, the chivalrous, the just Touman Bey perished on the 17th of April, 1517.

Egypt was now completely subdued by the Turks; but Selim remained there some months, engaged in settling the future government of the new empire which he had acquired, and in visiting the public buildings of its capital. The mysterious monuments of the Pharaohs and the relics of the splendours of the Ptolemies had no interest for the Ottoman Sultan. He did not even visit the Pyramids; but all his attention was concentrated on the mosques and other religious foundations of the early Mahometan sovereigns of Egypt. He attended divine worship in the chief mosques of Cairo on the first Friday after his conquest, and gave to the assembled people an impressive example of religious humility and contrition, by causing the rich carpets which had been spread for him to be removed, and by prostrating himself with his bare forehead on the bare pavement, which he visibly moistened with his tears.

It is throwing no slur on the Mahometan religion to believe in the sincerity of Selim's devotion; though at this very time the most cruel exactions were practised on the people of Egypt by his orders. Christendom could, during that century, show many a crowned tyrant, as earnest in bigotry, and as barbarous and unprincipled towards his fellow-creatures as Sultan Selim. Some of his principal followers imitated their master in oppression and rapacity; but there were also nobler and more generous spirits among the Ottoman chiefs. The historian Idris has been already mentioned with honour for the justice and skill, with which he organised the administrative system of Diarbekir and Kurdistan, when set over those newly-conquered countries by Selim. He had subsequently attended the Sultan during the Egyptian campaign; and he now risked his life by interceding with his savage master in behalf of the oppressed natives. He had been commissioned by Selim to translate from the Arabic the work of Demiri on natural history; and he added to his translation a short poem, which he wrote in Persian, and in which he gave the Sultan severe and salutary advice about the administration of Egypt. The Ottoman Viziers in whose hands he placed his book (according to the court ceremonial) for presentation to the Sultan, dreaded his wrath on receiving such free-spoken counsel; and they offered Idris 1000 ducats if he would take his poem of advice back, and suffer the "Treatise on Natural History" to be laid before their royal master without it. Idris refused the money, and insisted on his treatise and poem being presented to the Sultan, threatening the Viziers that unless they did their duty he would himself bring his writings to Selim's notice, and inform him of the negligence of his court officers. Thus threatened, the Viziers were obliged to comply, and Idris had the noble daring to subjoin to his poem a letter, in which he requested the Sultan's permission to leave Egypt, unless the misery and misgovernment, which he saw in all directions there, were remedied.

The heads of Selim's best generals would have fallen for half this boldness; but Selim's admiration for literary merit was strong and sincere, and he only showed the mortification which he experienced from Idris's rebuke, by sending the high-minded historian to Constantinople by the Turkish fleet, which at Selim's orders had sailed to the harbour of Alexandria, and which, on its return, menaced, but did not attack, the island of Rhodes.

Another literary favourite of Selim, Kemal Paschazadé, who held the high legal station of Cadiasker of Anatolia, ventured with impunity, about the same time, to bring to the knowledge of the

Sultan the discontent that was gathering among the ranks of the army at their prolonged detention in Egypt. Thus cautioned, Selim abandoned the projects which, like Cambyses, he had formed of conquering the countries beyond the cataracts of the Nile, and prepared for his march back to Europe. He had respected the persons of his literary reprovers, and he abstained, as was his custom, from punishing the common soldiery for their opposition to his wishes; but he vented his wrath on his Viziers and other high officers at every opportunity. The Grand Vizier, Younis-Pacha, was one of his victims. As he rode with Selim on the march back to Syria, Selim said to him, "Well, our backs are now turned on Egypt, and we shall soon see Gaza." Younis-Pacha (who had always opposed the Egyptian expedition) answered hastily, "And what has been the result of all our trouble and anxiety, except that we have left half our army on the battle-field, or in the sands of the Desert, and have set up a gang of traitors as chiefs of Egypt?" Selim instantly bade his guards put Younis to death, and the Grand Vizier's head was struck off as he sate on horseback by the Sultan's side.

The mode of administering the government of Egypt was a subject of deep anxiety to Selim, as it had been to all former conquerors of that wealthy and powerful country. The Persian Kings, the Roman Emperors,[1] and the Syrian Caliphs, had ever

---

[1] "He would not sow in a foreign soil the seeds of independence, which he was intent upon crushing nearer home. Egypt, with the sea in its front, and a desert on either hand, was difficult of access to the Roman armies; its overflowing stores of grain might give it the command of the Italian markets, and its accumulated treasures might buy the swords of mercenary legions. Octavius made it his own. He appointed a favourite officer, Cornelius Gallus, whose humble rank as a knight, as well as his tried services, seemed to ensure his fidelity, to govern it. In due time he persuaded the senate and people to establish it as a principle, that Egypt should never be placed under the administration of any man of superior rank to the equestrian, and that no senator should be allowed even to visit it, without express permission from the supreme authority. For the defence of this cherished province Octavius allotted three legions, besides some squadrons of cavalry, and a body of nine cohorts of pure Roman extraction. One legion was quartered in Alexandria, the inhabitants of which, though turbulent, were incapable of steady resistance; a division of three cohorts garrisoned Syene on the Nubian frontier, and others were stationed in various localities. Under the military commander was a revenue officer, whose accounts were delivered to Octavius himself, by whom he was directly appointed." — Merivale's "History of the Romans under the Empire," vol. iii. pp. 356, 357. See also the observations of Napoleon on Egypt, vol. iv.; Montholon's Memoirs, pp. 210-277. Though not always accurate in his historical details, Napoleon is the best writer on the subject

found good cause to dread that their Egyptian province would assert its independence. An ambitious Pacha, if of daring genius and favoured by circumstances, might have raised up against the Ottomans the Arabian nation, of which Egypt (according to its last great conqueror, Napoleon) is the natural metropolis. Selim even feared that the division of Egypt into several pachalics would not be a sufficient guarantee for its subjection to the Porte; and he, therefore, resolved to divide authority among the variety of races in the country, and so to secure his imperial sovereignty. He did not extirpate the Mamelukes; nor did he provide for their gradual extinction by forbidding the Beys to recruit their households with new slaves from Circassia. Twenty-four Beys of the Mamelukes, chosen from those who had acted with the invaders, continued to preside over the departments of the province, and their chief, the arch-traitor Khair Bey, was styled governor of Egypt. Selim, however, sent Khair Bey's wives and children to Europe, as securities for his good behaviour. He formed a more effectual and lasting safeguard for the Turkish supremacy, by placing a permanent force of 5000 Spahis and 500 Janissaries in the capital, under the command of the Ottoman Aga Khaireddin, who had orders never to leave the fortifications. This force was recruited from among the inhabitants of Egypt, and formed gradually a provincial militia with high privileges and importance. Selim placed the greater part of the administrative functions of law and religion in the hands of the Arab Scheiks, who possessed the greatest influence over the mass of the population, which, like themselves, was of Arabic origin. The Scheiks naturally attached themselves, through religious spirit and inclination, to Constantinople rather than to the Mamelukes, and drew the feelings of the other Arab inhabitants with them. Selim took no heed of the Copts, the aboriginal natives of Egypt; but it was from among this despised class and the Jews, that the Mameluke Beys generally selected their agents and tax-gatherers, and the villages were commonly under the immediate government of Coptic local officers.[1]

The Mameluke Sultans of Egypt, whose dynasty Selim cut short, had been the recognised suzerains, and protectors of the holy cities of Arabia; and Selim now acquired the same titles and

---

of Egypt that a general or a statesman can consult. He seems to have almost prophesied the rising of Mehemet Ali against the Porte.

There is a sketch of the history of Egypt under the Mamelukes and under the Porte, in the first volume of Hope's " Anastasius," which is worth consulting for other purposes than those of mere amusement.

[1] See Von Hammer, Napoleon, and Hope, *ut suprà.*

rights, which were of infinite worth in the eyes of that imperial devotee, and which were, and are, of real practical value to an Ottoman Sultan, from the influence which they give him over the whole Mahometan world.

Another important dignity, which the Sultan Selim and his successors obtained from the conquest of Egypt, was the succession to the Caliphate, and to the spiritual power and pre-eminence of the immediate Vicars of Mahomet himself. After the deaths of the four first Caliphs, who had been personal companions of the Prophet, the spiritual sovereignty of Islam passed successively to the Ommiade Caliphs and to the Abbassides, whose temporal power was overthrown by Houlogou Khan, a grandson of Zenghis Khan, in 1258. But though the substantial authority of the Caliphs as independent princes was then shattered, the name was perpetuated three centuries longer in eighteen descendants of the House of Abbas, who dwelt in Egypt with titular pomp, but no real power, in the capital of the Mameluke rulers, like the descendants of the Great Mogul in British India. They gave their names to the edicts of the Mameluke Sultans when required; and we have seen in the case of the Ottoman Bajazet I., that Mahometan princes in other countries still regarded the Egyptian Caliph as the fountain of honour, and sought from him the stamp and sanction of sovereignty. When Selim conquered Egypt, he found there Mohammed, the twelfth Caliph of the family of Abbas, and he induced him solemnly to transfer the Caliphate to the Ottoman Sultan and his successors. At the same time Selim took possession of the visible insignia of that high office, which the Abbassides had retained—the sacred standard, the sword, and the mantle of the Prophet.

In a preceding chapter of this volume, attention has been drawn to the importance of the Turkish Sultan being at once the spiritual and the temporal chief of his Mahometan subjects—of his being both Pope and Emperor. It will readily be imagined how much the Sultan's authority must have been augmented by his acquiring the sacred position of Caliph, Vicar of the Prophet of God, Commander of the Faithful, and Supreme Imam of Islam. It gives the Turkish Sultan dignity and authority (and may possibly give him practical influence), not only over his own Mahometan subjects, but over all who profess the creed of Islam, whatever be their race, and whatever be their country—except the Persians, and the few others who hold the Schiite tenets.[1]

[1] Sir George Campbell (p. 40) speaks contemptuously of the idea of the Turkish Sultan having any influence beyond the Turkish dominions over

In September, 1517, Sultan Selim led back his victorious army from Egypt to Syria. A thousand camels, laden with gold and silver, carried part of the rich spoils of the war; and a more valuable portion had been sent by Selim on board the Ottoman fleet to Constantinople. This consisted of the most skilful artisans of Cairo, whom Selim selected, as he had done at Tabriz, and removed to the capital city of his empire. Selim halted his army for some months, first at Damascus and afterwards at Aleppo. During this time he received the submission of several Arabian tribes, and arranged the division of Syria into governments, and the financial and judicial administration of that province. He returned to Constantinople in August, 1518. He had been absent but little more than two years, and in that time had conquered three nations, the Syrian, the Egyptian, and the Arabian.

Selim's attention was now earnestly directed to the development of the maritime resources of his empire. In 1519 he built 150 new ships of various dimensions, some of 700 tons; at the same time 100 new galleys, that lay ready for launching, were ordered to be rigged and fully equipped for sea. A powerful army of 60,000 men, with a large train of artillery, was collected and kept on foot in Asia Minor, ready to enter on a campaign at the first word of command. It was supposed by some that Selim designed a great attack upon Persia; but it was generally believed that the Turkish preparation would make for Rhodes. But Selim was resolved not to strike until the blow was sure to be effective; and

---

Sunnite Mahometans, because he is Caliph. I do not presume to compare my opportunities for observing Mahometan populations with those long possessed by Sir George Campbell, nor do I cavil at his ability in using such opportunities. But I have had practical occasion to learn much of the habits and feelings of the Moormen of Ceylon, a country never under Turkish rule, and I have conversed much with those who have long been familiar with Mahometans in other parts of the Far East. I know as a fact that on one occasion of deep interest to the Mahometan population of Ceylon, when their principal mosque at Barberyn had been polluted by some Sinhalese, who laid a dead pig in it, on the desk of the reader of the Koran, and when there was great difficulty felt among the Moormen as to the lawfulness of their religious rites and liturgy being resumed there, a deputation was sent to Mecca to seek the advice of the chief doctors of the law in the Holy City, and that such advice was obtained and followed. I believe that the teachers of the law at Mecca are generally consulted on questions of religious duty by Sunnite Mahometans; and certainly the authority of the Sultan, as Caliph, is fully recognised at Mecca. I may add that there is full proof in Eastern newspapers at present, that very deep interest in the fate of Turkey is felt and expressed by Mahometans far beyond the limits of Turkish temporal power.

the armaments in the Turkish seaports, and the building of fresh dockyards and arsenals, were continued with unremitting industry in the succeeding year. From the immense naval force which was thus created, it could no longer be doubted that Rhodes was the object of attack. Selim had not forgotten the humiliating repulse from that stronghold of the Christians, which his grandfather had sustained ; and he would not open the campaign until everything that could be required during the expedition had been amply provided and arranged, even in the minutest details. His Viziers were more eager to commence the enterprise, and drew down on themselves the rebuke of their stern and thoughtful master. One day when the Sultan, in company with Hasandschan, the father of the historian Seadeddin, was leaving the mosque of Eyoub, he saw one of the new first-class galleys, which he had ordered to be fitted out and kept ready for launching, sailing along the port of Constantinople. Transported with fury, he demanded by whose order the galley had left the stocks ; and it was with great difficulty that the Grand Vizier, Piri Pacha, saved the admiral's head, by representing to the Sultan that it had long been usual to launch vessels when they were completely ready. Selim called his Viziers round him, and said to them, "You try to hurry me to the conquest of Rhodes; but do you know what such an expedition requires ? Can you tell me what quantity of gunpowder you have in store ?" The Viziers, taken by surprise, were unable to answer; but the next day they came to the Sultan, and said that they had ammunition sufficient for a siege of four months. Selim answered, angrily, "What is the use of ammunition for four months, when double the amount would not be enough ? Do you wish me to repeat the shame of Mahomet II. ? I will not begin the war, nor will I make the voyage to Rhodes, with such scant preparations. Besides, I believe that the only voyage, which I have to make, is the voyage to the other world."

These words were uttered with a true presentiment of approaching death. He left his capital with the intention of going to Adrianople ; and though symptoms of acute disease had already appeared, he rode on horseback, notwithstanding the remonstrance and entreaties of his physicians: nor could they prevail on him to discontinue the use of opium. When he reached the little village, on the road to Adrianople, where he had formerly given battle to his father, and where, according to the Venetian narrative of his death, he had received his father's curse, the agony of his disease became so violent that he was compelled to stop. On the seventh night after he had left Constantinople, Hasand-

schan, who was his inseparable companion, was sitting by the
dying monarch, and reading to him from the Koran. The movement of Selim's lips seemed to show that he followed the words
of the reader; but, suddenly, at the verse "The word of the
Almighty is salvation," Selim clenched his hand convulsively, and
ceased to live (22nd September, 1520).

This prince died in the fifty-fourth year of his age, and the ninth
of his reign. The maxim which, in our great dramatist, the evil
spirit gives to the northern usurper, "Be bloody, bold, and resolute,"
might seem to have been the ruling principle of Sultan Selim's life.
But no one can deny his high administrative and military abilities;
and in religion, though a bigot of the darkest order, he was unquestionably sincere. His personal eminence in literature, and his
enlightened and liberal patronage of intellectual merit in others
are matters of just eulogy with the Oriental writers. One of the
most remarkable legal characters of this reign is the Mufti Djemali.
If he disgraced himself by the fetva with which he sanctioned, on
the most frivolous pretexts, the war with Egypt, the honesty and
the courage with which he often opposed the cruelty of Selim are
highly honourable to his memory ; nor can we refuse our praise
to the monarch, who repeatedly curbed his haughty will, and abstained from the coveted bloodshedding at his subject's rebuke.
On one occasion Selim had, for some slight cause of wrath, ordered
150 of the persons employed in his treasury to be put to death.
Djemali stood before the Sultan, and said to him, "It is the duty
of the Mufti to have a care for the weal of the Sultan of Islam in
the life to come. I therefore ask of thee the lives of the 150 men
unrighteously sentenced by thee to death." Selim answered,
"The Ulema have nothing to do with affairs of state. Besides,
the masses are only to be kept in order by severity."[1] Djemali replied,
"It is not a question of policy of this world, but of the next,
where mercy meets with everlasting reward, but unjust severity
with everlasting punishment." Selim gave way to the Mufti ; and
not only spared those whom he had sentenced, but restored them
to their functions.

At another period in Selim's reign he had issued an ordinance
prohibiting the trade in silk with Persia, and he had seized the
goods of the merchants engaged in the traffic, and ordered the
merchants themselves, to the number of 400, to be put to death.
Djemali interceded in their favour as he rode by the Sultan's side

---

[1] The German of Von Hammer gives this more pithily :
"Man beherrſcht die menge nur mit Strenge."

on the Adrianople road. Selim cried out, in indignation, "Is it not lawful to slay two-thirds of the inhabitants of the earth for the good of the other third?" "Yes," answered the Mufti, "if those two-thirds threaten to bring great wickedness upon earth." "And can there be greater wickedness," said Selim, "than disobedience to a sovereign's command? Every country that renounces obedience to its rulers goes headlong to destruction." "The disobedience is not proved here," rejoined the intrepid Djemali. "The trade in silk was not previously prohibited." "Keep yourself from meddling with state affairs," exclaimed Selim in fury; and the Mufti, not seeking to conceal his indignation, left the Sultan without the customary reverence. Selim's surprise equalled his wrath. He checked his horse, and sate for some time absorbed in reflection. But at last he gained the victory over himself, and on his return to Constantinople he set the condemned merchants at liberty, and restored their merchandise. He then sent a letter to Djemali, in which he announced his royal pleasure to confer on him the united highest dignities of the law, those of Judge of Roumelia and Judge of Anatolia. Djemali declined the proffered rank, but continued to retain the Sultan's esteem and friendship. The most memorable exercise of his salutary influence was in preserving the whole Greek population of the Ottoman Empire from the destruction with which they were menaced by Selim's bigotry. After the massacre of the heretical Schiis, Selim formed the idea of extirpating unbelief and misbelief of every kind from his dominions; and he resolved to put all the Christians to death, and turn their churches into Mahometan mosques. Without avowing his precise purpose, he laid before his Mufti Djemali the general question, "Which is the most meritorious—to conquer the whole world, or to convert the nations to Islam?" The Mufti gave an answer that the conversion of the infidels was incontestably the more meritorious work, and the one most pleasing to God. Having obtained this fetva, Selim ordered his Grand Vizier forthwith to change all the churches into mosques, to forbid the practice of the Christian religion, and to put to death all who refused to become Mahometans. The Grand Vizier, alarmed at the sanguinary edict, consulted Djemali, who had unconsciously given the fetva, which the Sultan used to justify the massacre of this Christians. By Djemali's recommendation the Greek patriarch sought an audience of the Sultan; and although with much difficulty, was heard before the Divan at Adrianople. He appealed to the pledges given by Mahomet II. in favour of the Christians when Constantinople was conquered ; and he eloquently invoked the passages of the Koran, which forbid compulsory conversion, and enjoin the Mussulmans to practise religious toleration to all the people of the Books, who submit to pay tribute. Selim yielded to the remonstrances and entreaties of the menaced Greeks, and to the urgent advice of his best counsellors, so far as to abstain from the slaughter of the Rayas which he had intended. Still he refused to suffer the finest churches of Constantinople to be used any longer by the Christians :—they were changed into mosques ; but inferior structures of wood were built in their stead, and the ruinous churches were repaired by Selim's orders, so that apparent respect might be paid to the grant of liberties from his great ancestor to the Greeks.

CHAPTER IX.

IMPORTANCE OF THE EPOCH OF SOLYMAN'S REIGN—HIS CHA-
RACTER—JOY AT HIS ACCESSION—CONQUEST OF BELGRADE A`ID
RHODES—BATTLE OF MOHACZ—SIEGE OF VIENNA—CRITICAL
REPULSE OF THE TURKS.[1]

THE period comprised within the reign of Solyman I. (1520-1566),
is one of the most important, not only in Ottoman history, but in
the history of the world. The great monarchies of Western
Christendom had now emerged from the feudal chaos. They had
consolidated their resources, and matured their strength. They
stood prepared for contests on a grander scale, for the exhibition
of more sustained energy, and for the realisation of more sys-
tematic schemes of aggrandisement, than had been witnessed
during the centuries which we term the ages of mediæval history.
At the commencement of this epoch (1520), nearly forty years
had passed away since the Ottomans had been engaged in earnest
conflict with the chief powers of central and western Europe.
The European wars of the feeble Bajazet II. had been coldly
waged, and were directed against the minor states of Christendom;
and the fierce energies of his son Selim the Inflexible had been
devoted to the conquest of Mahometan nations. During these
two reigns, the great kingdoms of modern Europe had started
from childhood into manhood. Spain had swept the last relics
of her old Moorish conquerors from her soil, and had united the
sceptres of her various Christian kingdoms under the sway of a
single dynasty. France, under three warlike kings, Charles VIII.,
Louis XII., and Francis I., had learned to employ in brilliant
schemes of foreign conquest those long-discordant energies and
long-divided resources, which Louis XI. had brought beneath the
sole authority of the crown. In England, and in the dominions
of the House of Austria, similar developments of matured and
concentrated power had taken place. Moreover, while the arts,
which enrich and adorn nations, had received in Christendom,

---

[1] See Von Hammer, books xxv., xxvi.

towards the close of the fifteenth century, an almost unprecedented
and unequalled impulse, the art of war had been improved there
even in a higher degree. Permanent armies, comprising large
bodies of well-armed and well-trained infantry, were now employed. The manufacture and the use of firearms, especially of
artillery, were better understood, and more generally practised ;
and a school of skilful as well as daring commanders had arisen,
trained in the wars and on the model of the Great Captain Gon-
salvo of Cordova. Besides the commencement of the struggle
between France and Austria for the possession of Italy, many
great events signalised the transition period from mediæval to
modern history, at the end of the fifteenth and the commencement of the sixteenth centuries : and those events, though not all
strictly connected with warfare, were all of a nature calculated
to waken a more far-reaching, and a more enduring heroism among
the Christian nations, and to make them more formidable to their
Mahometan rivals. The great maritime discoveries and the conquests effected by the Portuguese and the Spaniards in the East
Indies and in the New World ; the revival of classical learning ;
the splendid dawnings of new literatures ; the impulse given
by the art of printing to enlightenment, discussion, and free
inquiry ; all tended to multiply and to elevate the leading spirits
of Christendom, to render them daring in aspiration, and patient
of difficulty and of suffering in performance. There was also
reason to expect that these new energies of the Franks would find
their field of action in conquests over Islam ; for, religious zeal
had again become fervent in that age ; and the advancement of
the Cross was the ultimate purpose of the toils of the mariner,
the philosopher, and the student, as well as of the statesman and
the soldier. The hope that the treasures to be derived from his
voyages would serve to rescue the Holy Land from the infidels,
was ever present to the mind of Columbus amid his labours and
his sufferings, and amid the perils of the unknown deep ; even as
Charles VIII., amid his marches and battle-fields between the
Alps and Naples, still cherished the thought of proceeding from
conquered Italy to the rescue of Constantinople from the
Turks.

The probability of a marked change in the balance of power
between Christendom and Islamism before the middle of the
sixteenth century, may seem to have been materially increased by
the fact that one Christian sovereign combined many of the most
powerful states under his single rule. The Emperor Charles V.
reigned over an empire equal to that of Charlemagne in space,

14

and immeasurably surpassing it in wealth and strength. He had inherited the Netherlands, the Austrian states, and the united Spanish monarchy, with the fair kingdoms of Naples and Sicily. He obtained by election the imperial throne of Germany; and Cortés and Pizarro gave him the additional transatlantic empires of Mexico and Peru, with their almost countless supplies of silver and gold. It might perhaps have been foreseen that the possessor of this immense power would be trammelled when employing it against the Ottomans, by the ambitious rivalry of France, and by the religious dissensions of Germany; but, on the other hand, the Ottoman Empire was at least in an equal degree impeded from full action against Christendom by the imperial rivalry of Persia, by the hatred of Schiite against Sunnite, and by the risk of revolt in Syria and Egypt.

Yet, the House of Othman not only survived this period of peril, but was lord of the ascendant throughout the century, and saw numerous and fair provinces torn from the Christians, and heaped together to increase its already ample dominions. Much, unquestionably, of this success was due to the yet unimpaired vigour of the Turkish military institutions, to the high national spirit of the people, and to the advantageous position of their territory. But the principal cause of the Ottoman greatness throughout this epoch was the fact that the empire was ruled by a great man—great, not merely through his being called on to act amid combinations of favouring circumstances—not merely by tact in discerning and energy in carrying out the spirit of his age—but a man great in himself, an intelligent ordainer of the present, and a self-inspired moulder of the future.

Sultan Solyman I., termed by European writers "Solyman the Great," and "Solyman the Magnificent," bears in the histories written by his own countrymen the titles of "Solyman Kanouni" (Solyman the Lawgiver), and "Solyman Sahibi Kiran" (Solyman the Lord of his Age). That age was remarkably fertile in sovereigns of high ability. The Emperor Charles V., King Francis I., Pope Leo X., our Henry VIII., Vasili Ivanovitch, who laid the foundations of the future greatness of Russia, Sigismond I. of Poland, Andreas Gritti, the sage Doge of Venice, Shah Ismail, the restorer and legislator of Persia, and the Indian Akbar, the most illustrious of the dynasty of the Great Moguls,[1] shone in the drama of the world at the same time that Solyman appeared

---

[1] Von Hammer, vol. ii. p. 14.

there.[1] Not one of these great historical characters is clothed with superior lustre to that of the Ottoman Sultan.

Solyman had, while very young, in the time of Bajazet II., been intrusted with the command of provinces; and in his father's reign he had, at the age of twenty, been left at Constantinople as viceroy of the empire, when Selim marched to attack Persia. He governed at Adrianople during the Egyptian war; and during the last two years of Selim's reign he administered the province of Saroukhan. Thus, when at the age of twenty-six he became Sultan of the Ottoman Empire, he had already gained experience as a ruler; and he had displayed not only high abilities, but also a noble generosity of disposition, which won for him both affection and respect. The people, weary of the ferocity of Selim the Inflexible, rapturously welcomed the accession of a new ruler in the prime of youthful manhood, conspicuous by dignity and grace of person, and whose prowess, justice, clemency, and wisdom were painted by fame and hope in the brightest colours.

The first acts of Sultan Solyman announced that an earnest love of justice and generous magnanimity would be the leading principles of his reign. Six hundred Egyptians, whom Selim had forcibly transplanted to Constantinople, received permission to return to their homes. A large sum of money was distributed to merchants who had suffered by Selim's arbitrary confiscation of their property for trafficking with Persia. Several officers, high in rank, including the admiral of the fleet, who were accused of cruelty and malversa-

---

[1] Körner, in his tragedy of "Zriny," well makes Solyman say of himself:

> "Jch hab' gelebt, ich fühl's, für alle Zeiten,
> Und an die Sterne knüpft ich meinen Ruhm.
> Die Welt, die flammende hätt ich bezwungen,
> War' ich der einzge Held in meiner Zeit.
> Doch große Männer lebten mein Jahrhundert,
> Und große Helden standen wider mich.
> Jch darf mich nicht des Glückes Liebling schelten,
> Jch hab's mit Kraft dem Schicksal abgetroßt,
> Was es dem Bittenden verweigen wollte."

> "I have lived for all time;—of that I'm conscious—
> And on the immortal stars have knit my fame.
> I had subdued the world, had I been born
> Sole hero of my age.   My toil was harder.
> My century was rich in mighty spirits,
> And many and strong were they who strove with me.
> I scorn the name of Fortune's favourite.
> With resolute force I wrung from destiny
> What had to fond entreaties been denied."

tion, were brought to trial, convicted and executed. The report of these and similar deeds of the new Sultan spread rapidly through the empire; and Solyman's commands to his viceroys to repress every kind of disorder among rich and poor, among Moslems and Rayas, and to make the impartial dispensation of justice the great object of their lives, received universal applause and general obedience. The people felt that they were under a strong as well as a merciful government; and the Sultan was better loved for being also feared. It was only in Syria that any troubles followed the death of Sultan Selim. There, the double traitor, Ghazali, the Mameluke Bey, who had betrayed the Mameluke cause to the Turks, and had received the Syrian government as his reward, attempted to make himself independent; but Solyman sent an army against him without delay; and the defeat and death of the rebel not only restored tranquillity to Syria, but checked the hostile designs of Shah Ismail, who had assembled his forces on the frontier, and stood in readiness to avail himself of Ottoman weakness as Persia's opportunity.

It was not, however, long before Solyman was called on to display his military abilities in foreign warfare; and it was over the Hungarians that his first conquests were achieved. There had been disturbances and collisions on the frontiers of Hungary and Turkey in the last part of Selim's reign; and the weak prince, who filled the Magyar throne, Louis II., now imprudently drew the full weight of the Ottoman power against his dominions, by insulting and putting to death the ambassador of Solyman. The young Sultan instantly placed himself at the head of a powerful army, which was provided with a large train of heavy artillery; and arrangements were made for the transport and regular delivery of stores and supplies, which showed that Solyman possessed the forethought and skill, as well as the courage of his father. The Ottoman soldiery followed him to battle with peculiar alacrity; and their military enthusiasm was augmented by their belief in his auspicious destiny, on account of his name, on account of the prosperous commencement of his reign, and still more on account of the fortunate recurrence of the mystical number Ten in all that related to him. The Orientals have ever attached great importance to numbers, and they esteem the number Ten the most fortunate of all. Solyman was the Tenth Sultan of the House of Othman; he opened the Tenth century of the Hegira; and for these and other decimal attributes he was styled by his countrymen "the Perfecter of the Perfect Number." The firm conviction which his soldiers felt that their young Sultan was the favourite of Heaven,

made them march at his bidding as to certain victory in the cause
of God.   They commonly quoted, as prophetic of the fate which
awaited the enemies of their soverèign, the words of the epistle
from Solyman (or Solomon) to Balkis, Queen of Sheba, in the
xxviith chapter of the Koran : "Thus saith Solyman, 'In the
name of the Most Merciful God, dare not to rise up against me, but
come and submit yourselves to me, and confess the true faith.'"[1]

Such military prophecies do much to work out their own fulfilment.   The first campaign of Sultan Solyman against the Giaours
was eminently successful.   Sabacz and other places of minor importance in Hungary were besieged and taken by his generals ; but
Solyman led his main force in person against Belgrade, which long
had been a bulwark of Christendom against the Turks, and before
which Mahomet, the captor of Constantinople, had so signally
failed.   Belgrade was now captured (29th of August, 1521), and
Solyman, after having turned the principal church into a mosque,
repaired the fortifications, and provided for the maintenance of the
city as a Turkish stronghold, marched back in triumph to Constantinople, after his first victorious campaign.

Under his active and skilful superintendence new buildings for
ornament and use in peace and in war rose rapidly in the principal
cities of the Empire.   The arsenal at Constantinople was enlarged ;
and thousands of workmen were daily employed in framing and
fitting out new squadrons, and in the preparation of naval and
military stores on an unprecedented scale of grandeur.   In taking
Belgrade, Solyman had surmounted one of the two shoals, by
which the victorious career of Mahomet II. had been checked.   He
now resolved to efface the shame of the other reverse ; which his
renowned ancestor had sustained, and to make himself master of
the Isle of Rhodes, where the Christian knights of St. John of
Jerusalem had so long maintained themselves near the heart of the
Turkish power.   Indeed, the possession of Rhodes by the Ottomans was indispensable for free communication between Constantinople and her new conquests along the Syrian coasts and in Egypt,
and for the establishment of that supremacy of the Ottoman navy
in the east of the Mediterranean, which Solyman was determined
to effect.   On the 18th of June, 1522, the Ottoman fleet of 300
sail quitted Constantinople for Rhodes.   Besides its regular crews
and immense cargoes of military stores, it carried 8000 chosen
soldiers and 2000 pioneers.   At the same time Solyman led an
army of 100,000 men along the western coast of Asia Minor.   The
place of rendezvous for fleet and army was the Bay of Marmarice,

[1] Hulme.

11

where, long afterwards, in 1801, the English fleet and army, under Sir Ralph Abercromby, were mustered as allies of the Turks for the re-conquest of Egypt from the French.

The Grand Master of Rhodes at the time of Solyman's attack was Villiers De Lisle Adam, a French knight of proved worth and valour. The garrison consisted of 5000 regular troops, 600 of whom were knights. Besides these, the seafaring men of the port were formed into an effective corps; the citizens were enrolled and armed; the peasantry, who crowded from the rest of the island into the city to escape the Turkish marauders, were disciplined as pioneers, and the slaves were made to work on the fortifications. The defences of the city had been much increased and improved, since the siege by Mahomet II.'s troops; and even if the outer walls were breached and carried, there were now inner lines of strong walls prepared to check the assailants; and several quarters of the city had their own distinct fortifications, so as to be tenable (like the quarters of ancient Syracuse) even after other parts of the city were in possession of the besiegers.

Solyman landed in the island of Rhodes on the 28th of July, 1522, and the siege began on the 1st of August. It was prolonged for nearly five months by the valour of De Lisle Adam and his garrison, and by the skill of his engineer, Martinego. The war was waged almost incessantly underground by mines and countermines, as well as above ground by cannonade and bombardment, desperate sallies, and still more furious assaults. A breach was effected, and some of the bastions of the city were shattered early in September; and four murderous attempts at storming were made and repulsed during that month. Three more assaults, one on the 12th of October, one on the 23rd, and one on the 30th of November, were fiercely given and heroically withstood, though the effect of the cannonade on the fortifications was more and more visible. The Turkish commanders at length resolved to lavish no more lives in attempts to storm the city, but to trust to their mines and artillery for its gradual destruction. Advancing along trenches according to the plan of gradual approach which since has been habitually employed, but which was previously unknown, or, at least, never used so systematically,[1] the Turks brought their batteries to bear closer and closer upon the city;

---

[1] " Achmet Bascha delibère de ne donner plus d'assault mais suyvre ces tranchées."—Ramazan dans Tercier Mémoires, xxii. p. 755, cited in Von Hammer. " It appears that the first regular approaches against a fortress were introduced by this people."—Col. Chesney's " Turkey," p. 367. The Turks also used shells for the first time in this siege.—Von Hammer, ii. 33

and at length established themselves within the first defences. Solyman now offered terms of capitulation, and the besieged reluctantly treated for a surrender. There were yet the means of prolonging the defence ; but there were no hopes of succour, and the ultimate fall of the city was certain. Honourable terms might now be obtained, the Order might be preserved, though forced to seek a home elsewhere, and the Rhodians might gain protection from the conqueror for person and property. To continue their resistance until the exasperated enemy overpowered them, would be not only to sacrifice themselves, but to expose the citizens to massacre, and their wives and daughters to the worst horrors of war. These reasons weighed with De Lisle Adam and his knights, as with truly brave men, and they laid down their good swords which they had so honourably wielded. That they did their duty to Christendom in their surrender, as well as in their previous resistance, was proved afterwards by the effectual check which their Order gave to Solyman at Malta. How much heroism would the world have lost, if the Knights of St. John had obstinately sought in Rhodes the fate of Leonidas ![1]

By the terms of capitulation (Dec. 25, 1522) which Solyman granted to the Knights, he did honour to unsuccessful valour ; and such honour is reflected with double lustre on the generous victor. The Knights were to be at liberty to quit the island with their arms and property within twelve days in their own galleys, and they were to be supplied with transports by the Turks if they required them : the Rhodian citizens, on becoming the Sultan's subjects, were to be allowed the free exercise of their religion ; their churches were not to be profaned ; no children were to be taken from their parents ; and no tribute was to be required from the island for five years. The insubordinate violence of the Janissaries caused some infraction of these terms ; but the main provisions of the treaty were fairly carried into effect. By Solyman's request, an interview took place between him and the Grand Master before the knights left the island. Solyman addressed, through his interpreter, words of respectful consolation to the Christian veteran ; and, turning to the attendant Vizier, the Sultan observed: "It is not without regret that I force this brave man from

---

[1] I have been guided in these remarks on the surrender of Rhodes by the criticisms made by Marshal Marmont on this siege (Marmont's "State of the Turkish Empire, &c.," translated by Sir F. Smith, p. 208, 2nd ed.). While giving conclusive military reasons for thinking that the defence might have been prolonged, the marshal justly terms it "honourable, and even glorious."

his home in his old age." Such indeed was the esteem with which the valour of the Knights had inspired the Turks, that they refrained from defacing their armorial bearings and inscriptions on the buildings. For more than three hundred years the Ottomans have treated the memory of their brave foemen with the same respect; and the escutcheons of the Knights of St. John, who fought against Sultan Solyman for Rhodes, still decorate the long-captured city.[1]

Solyman had experienced the turbulence of the Janissaries at Rhodes; and he received three years afterwards a more serious proof of the necessity of keeping that formidable body constantly engaged in warfare, and under strict, but judicious discipline. The years 1523 and 1524 had not been signalised by any foreign war. The necessity of quelling a revolt of Ahmed Pacha, who had succeeded Khair Bey in the government of Egypt, had occupied part of the Ottoman forces; and after the traitor had been defeated and killed, Solyman sent his favourite Grand Vizier Ibrahim, a Greek renegade, into that important province to re-settle its administration, and assure its future tranquillity. Solyman's personal attention for the first eighteen months after the campaign of Rhodes was earnestly directed to improving the internal government of his empire; but, in the autumn of 1525, he relaxed in his devotion to the toils of state; and, quitting his capital, he repaired, for the first time, to Adrianople, and followed there with ardour the amusement of the chase. The Janissaries began to murmur at their Sultan's forgetfulness of war, and at last they broke out into open brigandage, and pillaged the houses of the principal ministers. Solyman returned to Constantinople, and strove to quell the storm by his presence. He boldly confronted the mutinous troops, and cut down two of their ringleaders with his own hand; but he was obliged to pacify them by a donative, though he afterwards partly avenged himself by putting to death many of their officers, whom he suspected of having instigated or of having neglected to check the disorder. He then recalled his Vizier Ibrahim from Egypt; and, by his advice, determined to lead his armies into Hungary, with

[1] "Three hundred and fifteen years have now elapsed since this illustrious order was obliged to abandon its conquests, after a possession of two hundred and twelve years. The street of the knights is uninjured, and the door of each house is still ornamented with the escutcheon of the last inhabitant. The buildings have been spared, but are unoccupied; and we could almost fancy ourselves surrounded by the shades of departed heroes. The arms of France, the noble fleur-de-lis, are seen in all directions. I observed those of the Clermont-Tonnerres, and of other ancient and illustrious families."—Marshal Marmont, 205.

which country he was still at war, though no important operations had taken place since the campaign of Belgrade. Solyman was at this time vehemently urged to invade Hungary by Francis I. of France, who wished to distract the arms of his rival Charles V. ;[1] and, on the other hand, an ambassador had been sent from Persia, the natural foe of Turkey, to the courts of Charles and the King of Hungary, to form a defensive and offensive league against the Ottomans.[2]

In 1526, the Sultan invaded Hungary with an army more than 100,000 strong, and 300 pieces of artillery. Like his predecessors Selim and Mahomet II., he paid extreme attention to this important arm of war ; and, throughout his reign, the artillery of the Ottomans was far superior in number, in weight of metal, in equipment, and in the skill of the gunners, to that possessed by any other nation. King Louis of Hungary rashly gave battle, with a far inferior force, to the invaders. The Hungarian chivalry charged with their wonted gallantry ; and a chosen band forced their way to where Solyman had taken his station at the head of his Janissaries. The Sultan owed his life to his cuirass, against which the lance of a Magyar knight was shivered. But the fiery valour of the "furious Hun" was vain against superior numbers, arms, and discipline. In less than two hours the fate of Hungary was decided. King Louis, eight of his bishops, the greater number of the Magyar nobles, and 24,000 Hungarians of lower rank had perished. Search was made by the victors for the body of King Louis, which was found in a stream near the field of battle. Louis had been wounded in the head, and was endeavouring to escape, but his horse was forced from the bank by the throng of the fliers, and the weight of his armour bore him down in the deep water. The Sultan felt a generous sorrow on learning the fate of his rival sovereign, who was nearly his equal in years. Solyman exclaimed, "May Allah be merciful to him, and punish those who misled his inexperience. I came indeed in arms against him ; but it was not my wish that he should thus be cut off, while he had scarcely tasted the sweets of life and royalty." This battle was fought at Mohacz, on the 28th August, 1526, and is still known by the terribly expressive name of "the Destruction of Mohacz."

After this decisive victory, Solyman marched along the Danube to the twin cities of Buda (or Ofen) and Pesth, on the opposite banks of that river, and the capital of Hungary at once submitted to him. The Akindji swept the whole country with fire and desolation ; and it seemed as if it was the object of the Ottomans to

[1] Von Hammer, vol. ii. p. 45. [2] Ibid.

make a desert rather than a province of Hungary. At last, at the end of September, Solyman began his homeward march. His soldiers were laden with the richest plunder; and they drove before them a miserable herd of 100,000 Christians, men, women, and little children, destined for sale in the Turkish slave-markets.

Disturbances in Asia Minor had hastened Solyman's departure from Hungary, but he returned in the third year, still more menacing and more formidable. The struggle was now to be with Austria; and the next campaign of Solyman, the campaign of the first siege of Vienna, is one of the most important in German and in Ottoman history.

Solyman entered Hungary in 1529 under the pretext of placing on the throne the rightful successor to King Louis, who fell at Mohacz. That prince died without issue; and the Archduke Ferdinand of Austria, brother of Charles V., claimed the crown as Louis's brother-in-law, and by virtue of an old treaty. But there was an ancient law of Hungary, by which none but a native prince could occupy the throne; and a powerful noble, named Zapolya, appealed to this in opposition to Ferdinand, and procured some of the surviving magnates of the land to elect him as king. A civil war ensued, in which the adherents of Ferdinand and his Austrian forces defeated Zapolya's troops, and drove him from the kingdom. Zapolya then took the desperate step of applying for aid to the Sultan. Ferdinand, alarmed on hearing of this proceeding of his rival, sent an embassy to Constantinople to negotiate for a peace with Solyman, or at least to obtain a truce. His envoys had the ill-timed boldness to require, at the same time, the restoration of Belgrade and of the chief places which the Turks had captured in Hungary. Nothing could exceed the arrogance shown by the Ottoman ministers to the rival claimants of the Hungarian throne. The Grand Vizier told the Polish Palatine Lasczky, who acted as ambassador for Zapolya, that every place where the hoof of the Sultan's horse once trod, became at once, and for ever, part of the Sultan's dominions. "We have slain King Louis of Hungary," said the Vizier; "his kingdom is now ours, to hold, or to give to whom we list. Thy master is no king of Hungary till we make him so. It is not the crown that makes the king—it is the sword. It is the sword that brings men into subjection; and what the sword has won, the sword must keep." He promised, however, that Zapolya should be king, and that the Sultan should protect him against Ferdinand of Austria and all his other enemies. Solyman himself confirmed his Vizier's promise; and added, "I will be a true friend to thy master. I will march in person to aid him. I swear it, by our Prophet Mahomet, the beloved of God, and by my sabre." Ferdinand's ambassadors were dismissed with indignant scorn. They were ordered to say from Solyman to Ferdinand, that hitherto there had been little acquaintance or neighbourhood between them; but that they soon should be intimate enough. He would speedily visit Ferdinand, and drive him from the kingdom he had stolen. "Tell him," said Solyman, " that I will look for him on the field of Mohacz, or even in Pesth; and if he fail to meet me there, I will offer him battle beneath the walls of Vienna itself." These were no idle menaces from the Lord of the Age; and the forces of the Ottoman Empire were speedily mustered for the march from Constantinople to Vienna.

Solyman left Constantinople on the 10th May, 1529, with an army of 250,000 men and 300 cannons. A season of almost incessant rain made their march to the Danube laborious and slow; and it was the 3rd of September before the Sultan reached Ofen, which had been occupied by the troops of Ferdinand during the preceding year. Ofen was taken in six days, and Zapolya was solemnly installed by the Turkish victors on the ancient throne of the dynasty of Arpad. The Sultan then continued his advance to Vienna, taking with him his vassal king, and a corps of the Hungarians who recognised Zapolya as their sovereign.

With the storms of the autumnal equinox, the first squadrons of the terrible irregular cavalry of the Turks swept round the walls of Vienna. These Akindji, 30,000 strong, called by the French " Faucheurs" and " Ecorcheurs"—"mowers" and " flayers"—by the Germans " Sackmen," were led by Michael Oglou, the descendant of Michael of the Peaked Beard, who had been the friend of the first Othman.[1] These ferocious marauders, who received no pay, and whose cruelty exceeded even their rapacity, spread devastation and slaughter throughout all Austria, as far as the river Ems. On the eve of the feast of St. Wenceslaus (27th September), Solyman himself arrived with the main Turkish army beneath Vienna, and fixed the imperial headquarters on the high ground to the west of the village of Simmering. 12,000 Janissaries were posted round the Sultan's tent. Seven encampments were raised by the various divisions of the army, forming nearly a circle round Vienna: and the whole country west of the Danube, far as the eye could range from the highest steeple in the city, was white with the Moslem tents. The water-meadows and islands of the Danube, and its branches near the city, were

[1] See *supra*, p. 5.

also strongly occupied ; and a flotilla of 400 Turkish barks, well-manned and commanded, watched the city by water, and kept up the communication between the besieging troops.

The force that defended Vienna amounted to only 16,000 men ; and, when the campaign began, the fortifications of the city consisted of little more than a continuous wall, about six feet thick, without bastions ; the artillery amounted to only seventy-two guns.   King Ferdinand had exerted himself earnestly to induce the other German princes to aid him ; but his brother, the Emperor Charles, was occupied with his own ambitious schemes in Italy ; and the princes of the empire, to whom Ferdinand had appealed at the Diet of Spires, thought more of their religious differences with each other than of the common danger of their fatherland, though warned by Ferdinand that Sultan Solyman had declared his determination to carry his arms to the Rhine. The Diet voted aid ; but it was inadequate and tardy ; and, while the princes deliberated, the Turk was in Austria.   Ferdinand himself dreaded Solyman's threats, and kept aloof from Vienna. But some brave Christian leaders succeeded in forcing their way into the city before it was entirely beleaguered ; and a body of Spanish and German veterans, under the Palgrave Philip, proved an invaluable reinforcement to the garrison.   But, though the Christian defenders of Vienna were few, they were brave and well commanded.   The Palgrave Philip was the nominal superior, but the veteran Count of Salm was the real director of the defence. All possible preparations were made while the Turks were yet approaching.   The suburbs were destroyed.   A new earthen rampart was raised within the city ; the river bank was palisadoed ; provisions and stores were collected ; and the women and children, and all the other inhabitants who were unable to do service as combatants or as labourers, were compelled to leave the city. Providentially for Vienna, the incessant rains, and the consequent badness of the roads, had caused the Turks to leave part of their heaviest artillery in Hungary.   They were obliged to rely chiefly on the effect of mines for breaching the walls ; but the numbers, and the zeal of the besiegers, made the fall of the city apparently inevitable.

Many sallies and partial assaults took place, in which great gallantry was displayed on both sides ; and infinite skill and devotion were shown by the defenders in counteracting the mining operations of their enemies.   But the Ottoman engineers succeeded in springing several mines, which tore open large gaps in the defences ; and on three consecutive days, the 10th, 11th, and 12th of October, the Turks assaulted the city with desperation, but were repelled with heavy carnage by the steady valour of the besieged. The Ottoman forces now began to suffer severely by scarcity of provisions, and by the inclemency of the season; and the slaughter which had fallen on their best troops filled the army with discouragement. But it was resolved to make one more attempt to carry Vienna; and, on the 14th of October, the Turkish infantry, in three huge columns, charged up to the breach, which their miners and cannoneers had rent for their road to victory and plunder. Solyman had endeavoured to stimulate their courage and emulation by a liberal distribution of money, and by the promise of high rank and wealth to the Moslem who should be first on the crest of the breach. The Grand Vizier and the highest officers of the army accompanied the stormers: and when the Christian cannons and musketry roared forth their deadly welcome, and the dispirited Mahometans reeled back from the blood-stained ruins, the Turkish chiefs were seen amid the confusion, striving, after the old Oriental custom, to force their men on again to the assault by blows with stick and whip and sword.[1] But even the best veterans now sullenly refused obedience, and said that they had rather be killed by the sabres of their own officers than by the long muskets of the Spaniards and the German spits, as they called the long swords of the lanzknechts.[2] About three in the afternoon, the Turkish engineers sprung two new mines, which threw down much more of the wall; and under cover of a fire from all their batteries, the Sultan's troops were again formed into columns, and brought forward once more up to the breach. It was only to heap it again with Turkish dead. The hero of the defence, Count Salm, received a wound on the last day of the siege that proved ultimately fatal: but though other chiefs had fallen;—though the Ottoman shot and shell had told severely among the Christian ranks;—though many brave men had perished in sorties, and in hand-to-hand conflict in the breaches;—and though many had been swept away by the bursting of the Turkish mines, the courage of the garrison grew higher and higher at each encounter with their lately boastful, but now despairing foes. Solyman himself felt at last compelled to

---

[1] See the account in Herodotus (Polymnia, 223), of the last Persian attack on Thermopylæ. Ὄπισθεν οἱ ἡγεμόνες τῶν τελέων ἔχοντες μάστιγας ἐρράπιζον πάντα ἄνδρα αἰεὶ ἐς τὸ πρόσω ἐποτρύνοντες. One of the Assyrian bas-reliefs discovered by Mr. Layard represents an officer with a whip in his hand, directing the passage of a river by the troops.

[2] "Two Sieges of Vienna by the Turks," p. 38.

abandon the favourite project of his heart, and drew his troops finally back from the much-coveted city. The 14th of October, the day on which Vienna was saved from the greatest of the Sultans, is marked by the German historian as being made memorable in his country's history by many great events. It is the day of the fall of Brisach (1639), of the peace of Westphalia (1648), of the battle of Hochkirken (1758), of the surrender of Ulm (1805), of the battle of Jena (1806), and of the overthrow of Napoleon at the Battle of the Nations at Leipsic in 1813.[1]

It was near midnight, after the repulse of Solyman's last assault upon Vienna that its full effect appeared. The Janissaries then, by the Sultan's order, struck their tents; and all the spoil which had been swept into the Turkish camp, and which could not be carried away, was given to the flames. At the same time, the disappointed and savage soldiery commenced a general massacre of thousands of Christian captives, whom the deadly activity of the Akindji had brought in during the three weeks of the siege. The fairest girls and boys were preserved to be led into slavery, but the rest were put to the sword, or thrown yet alive into the flames without mercy. After this last act of barbarous but impotent malignity, the Turkish army retreated from Vienna. Solyman's courtiers pretended to congratulate him as victorious; and he himself assumed the tone of a conqueror, whom the fugitive Ferdinand had not dared to meet, and who had magnanimously retired after chastising, though not destroying his foes. But the reverse, which he had sustained, was felt deeply by him throughout his life; and it was said that he laid a curse upon any of his descendants who should renew the enterprise against Vienna. There is no foundation for the charge which later writers have brought against the Grand Vizier Ibrahim, of having been bribed to betray his master, and to baffle the operations of the besiegers.[2] The city was saved by the heroism of her defenders, aided, unquestionably, by the severity of the season, which the Asiatic troops in the Ottoman army could ill endure, and by the insubordination of the impatient Janissaries. But, whatever be the cause assigned to it, the repulse of Solyman from Vienna is an epoch in the history of the world.

The tide of Turkish conquest in central Europe had now set its mark. The wave once again dashed as far; but only to be again broken, and then to recede for ever.

[1] Von Hammer, vol. ii. p. 73.   [2] Ibid. p. 76.

CHAPTER X.

WARS AND TREATIES WITH AUSTRIA—CONQUESTS OVER PERSIA
—AUSTRIA TRIBUTARY TO THE PORTE—EXPLOITS OF THE
TURKISH ADMIRALS—BARBAROSSA—PIRI REIS—SIDI ALI—
DRAGUT—PIALÉ—SOLYMAN'S DOMESTIC TRAGEDIES—DEATHS
OF PRINCE MUSTAPHA AND PRINCE BAJAZET—SIEGE OF MALTA
—SIEGE OF SIGETH—DEATH OF SOLYMAN—EXTENT OF THE
EMPIRE UNDER HIM—ARMY—NAVY—INTERNAL ADMINISTRA-
TION—LAWS—COMMERCE—BUILDINGS—LITERATURE.[1]

A PEACE was concluded between the Sultan and Ferdinand in 1533,
by which Hungary was divided between Ferdinand and Zapolya.
Solyman had, in the interval, again invaded Germany with forces
even stronger than those which he led against Vienna; and as
Charles V., on this occasion (1532), put himself at the head of the
armies of the empire, which gathered zealously around him, a decisive conflict between the two great potentates of Christendom
and Islam was anxiously expected. But Solyman was checked
in his advance by the obstinate defence of the little town of Güns;
and after honourable terms had been granted to the brave garrison
of that place (29th August, 1532), Solyman finding that Charles
did not come forward to meet him, but remained posted near
Vienna, turned aside from the line of march against that city;
and, after desolating Styria, returned to his own dominions.
Each, probably, of these two great sovereigns was unwilling to
risk life, and empire, and the glorious fruits of so many years of
toil and care, on the event of a single day; and neither was sorry
that his adversary's lukewarmness for battle furnished a creditable
excuse for his own. The warlike energies of the Ottomans were
now for some time chiefly employed in the East, where the unremitted enmity of Persia to Turkey, and the consequent wars between these two great Mahometan powers, were a cause of relief
to Christendom, which her diplomatists of that age freely acknowledged.[2] Solyman led his armies against the Persians in several

[1] Von Hammer, books xxvii. to xxxv.
[2] Busbequius, Ferdinand's ambassador at Solyman's court, says : " 'Tis

campaigns (1533, 1534, 1535, 1548, 1553, 1554), during which the Turks often suffered severely through the difficult nature of the countries through which they traversed, as well as through the bravery and activity of the enemy. But the Sultan effected many important conquests. He added to the Ottoman Empire large territories in Armenia and Mesopotamia, and the strong cities of Erivan, Van, Mosul, and, above all, of Bagdad, which the Orientals call "The Mansion of Victory."

The modern Turk, who seeks consolation in remembering the glories of the Great Solyman, must dwell with peculiar satisfaction on the tokens of respectful fear, which his nation then received from the most powerful as well as from the weaker states of Christendom. And the year 1547 is made a peculiarly proud one in the annals of the House of Othman, by the humble concession which its rival, the Austrian House of Hapsburg, was then compelled to make to its superior strength and fortune. The war in Hungary had been renewed in consequence of the death of John Zapolya, in 1539; upon which event Ferdinand claimed the whole of Hungary, while the widow of Zapolya implored the assistance of the Sultan in behalf of her infant son. Solyman poured his armies into that country, and in 1541, and the following years, he again commanded in person on the banks of the Danube. He professed the intention of placing the young Prince Zapolya on the throne of Hungary and Transylvania, when he should have attained the age of manhood; but Ofen and the other chief cities were now garrisoned with Turkish troops; the country was allotted into Sanjaks, over which Turkish governors were appointed: and the Ottoman provincial system was generally established. The strong cities of Gran, Stuhlweissenburg, and many others, were taken by the Turks in this war; and though their success was not unvaried, the general advantage was so far on the side of the Sultan, that as early as 1544 Charles V. and Ferdinand made overtures for peace; and in 1547 a truce for five years was concluded, which left the Sultan in possession of nearly the whole of Hungary and Transylvania, and which bound Ferdinand to pay to the Sublime Porte 30,000 ducats a year—a payment which the Austrians called a present, but the Ottoman historians more correctly term a tribute.

---

only the Persian stands between us and ruin. The Turk would fain be upon us, but he keeps him back. This war with him affords us only a respite, not a deliverance." See also the letters of Sir John Masone, our ambassador at the French court, given by Mr. Tytler in his "Reigns of Edward VI. and Mary," vol. i. p. 360, vol. ii. p. 352.

This treaty, to which the Emperor Charles, the Pope, the King of France, and the Republic of Venice were parties, may be considered as a recognition by Christendom of the truth of Solyman's title, "Sahibi Kiran," "Lord of his Age." Austrian pride, indeed, had previously stooped so low before the Sultan, that King Ferdinand, when seeking peace in 1533, consented to style himself the brother of Ibrahim, Solyman's favourite minister, and thus to place himself on the level of a Turkish Vizier. Francis I. had repeatedly sought the aid of Solyman in the most deferential and submissive terms. That aid was more than once effectively given by the Turkish invasions of Hungary and Germany, which compelled the Emperor to draw the weight of his arms from off France; and, still more directly, by the Turkish fleets which were sent into the Mediterranean to attack the enemies of the French King.[1] England, during the reign of Solyman, had no need of foreign help; but we shall see her in the reign of Solyman's grandson, when menaced by the power of Spain, have recourse to the Sublime Porte for aid and protection, as respectfully and earnestly as the proudest Follower of the Prophet could desire.

We have hitherto directed our chief attention to the military history of Solyman's reign; but the awe which the Ottoman Empire inspired in this age, was due not only to the successes gained by the Turkish armies, but also to the achievements of the Turkish navy, which extended the power and the renown of Sultan Solyman along all the coast of the Mediterranean, and in the more remote waters of the Red Sea and the Indian Ocean. His predecessors had devoted much care and treasure to the maritime force of their empire, but they were all surpassed in this respect by Solyman; and the skill and valour of his Admirals made the Ottoman flag almost as formidable by sea as it was by land. The most celebrated of the Turkish naval commanders in

---

[1] As early as 1525, while Francis was a prisoner at Madrid, the aid of the young Sultan Solyman had been implored and promised in his behalf. Hellert, the French translator of Von Hammer, gives in his notes to the fifth volume of his translation (p. 150), a translation of a remarkable letter of Solyman to Francis, promising him assistance, which has been discovered in the French archives. The letter is couched in the loftiest strain of haughty generosity, and bids the French monarch, now that he has laid his petition before the throne which is the refuge of the world, fear no longer the enemy who has threatened and ravaged his dominions, and made him captive. M. Hellert gives another letter of Sultan Solyman's to Francis, written in 1528, in answer to requests made by the French King in favour of the Christians of the Latin Church at Jerusalem. M. Hellert truly says that the Sultan's letter shows a spirit of justice, and religious toleration, as honourable as it was rare, especially in the age in which it was written.

this reign was Khaireddin Pacha, better known in Europe by the surname of Barbarossa. It was principally by, his means that the piratical states of North Africa placed themselves under the sovereignty of the Sultan; and that the naval resources of the Sublime Porte were augmented by the commodious havens, the strong forts and cities, the well-built and well-found squadrons, and the daring and skilful corsairs of Algiers, Tripoli, and Tunis.[1]

[1] A description of the system of Mediterranean warfare of this age, and of the character of the vessels employed in it, may be found useful; and I subjoin one, which I have partly drawn from Fincham's "Naval History," but chiefly from an admirable paper by Mr. Hulme in his "Chapters on Turkish History."

The names commonly given to vessels of war in the Mediterranean during this century, were galley, galleon, and galleas. The two last are names familiar to the student of the history of the Spanish Armada. They both were applied to vessels of considerable size, and some galleons and galleases are said to have been of from 1500 to 2000 tons burthen. They had more than one deck, and heavy cannon were used by means of portholes on the lower decks, as well as the upper. They were very lofty at both stem and stern. Guns were mounted on the elevated poop; and also on the fore-castle, a term which then was strictly accurate. These large vessels, which were also called carracks, had one or more tiers of long oars, each worked by several rowers, but they depended principally on their masts and sails for locomotion. But though large ships of this description were used in war, it was not in them but in the long, low, light galleys, that the principal force of contending navies consisted. In order to understand this, we must bear in mind the difference between the naval gunnery of those times and our own; and how much less the peril was, which small and light craft then incurred by exposing themselves to the broadside of those of far superior tonnage.

The galleys with which the sea-captains of Venice, Genoa, Barcelona, Carthagena, Malta, Algiers, and Constantinople performed their chief ex-ploits, during the fifteenth and sixteenth centuries, were essentially row-boats; and the oars were usually pulled by slaves or prisoners of war.

The hull lay very low and close to the water, extremely sharp built and straight in the run, and of such extraordinary length in proportion to the beam or width, that the Venetian galleys of the largest class, which measured 165 feet from stem to stern, were only thirty-two feet in total breadth. The prow was furnished, as of old, with a long and sharp beak: and from this, as well as from the usually black colour of the hull, the epithet of *grab* (literally *raven*) was popularly applied to these vessels by the Moors. The after-part was occupied by an extensive poop or quarter-deck, which was the station of the captain and the soldiers, and which was defended on the quarter by galleries and boarding-nettings. From this a descent of two or three steps led to a long narrow platform (called in French *coursier*, and in Spanish *cruxia*, running the whole length of the vessel from the forecastle to the poop, and serving both for a gangway and a flush deck; on this the guns were mounted, usually a single long heavy piece pointed forwards in a groove near the bow, and two or four others of smaller calibre amidships. The rowing benches (to which the galley-slaves were usually chained by one foot) were arranged

Barbarossa was born in the island of Mitylene.   His father, a Spahi of Roumelia, had settled there when the island was conquered by Mahomet II.   Of four sons, the eldest, Ishak, traded as a merchant in Mitylene; the other three, Elias, Urudsch, and Khizr (afterwards called Khaireddin), practised commerce and piracy conjointly during the reign of Bajazet II. and Selim. Elias fell in a sea-fight with the Knights of Rhodes.   Urudsch was taken prisoner, but was released through the influence of Prince Korkoud, then governor of Caramania.   Urudsch and Khaireddin next practised as bold and fortunate sea-rovers, under Mohammed the Sultan of Tunis.   They saw, however, the feebleness of the Mahometan Princes of the North African seaports, and they knew the strength of the Ottoman Empire, especially under such a ruler as Selim.   They paid court therefore to the Sublime Porte, by sending one of their richest prizes to Constantinople, and received in return two galleys and robes of honour.

---

on a sort of sloping gallery or wide gunwale (in French *pont*), which projected over the ship's side, so that those who rowed in the highest rank were immediately below the *coursier*, and under the eye of their taskmasters, who quickened their exertions by the unsparing use of the lash. The galley was pulled with twenty-six oars on a side—a number which seems to have been nearly invariable in all rates ; but the smaller classes *galères subtiles*, or *legères*, called *fergata* or frigate, and *khirlangitsch* by the Turks, and by the Moors *jafan* and *thelthi*) had only one or two men to each oar ; the largest (*galeazza* of the Venetians, and *maona* of the Turks) had sometimes even as many as five or six ; those of the ordinary rate (*galères bâtardes*, whence the Turkish *bashtarda*), which were almost exclusively employed by the Turks, had three.

The galley was provided with a main and foremast, which might be raised or struck as required, and which carried large lateen sails ; but a craft of the construction just described could only have been trusted under sail in light winds and smooth seas, as her want of heel, and deficiency in beam, must have made her at all times a bad sea-boat ; while her great length must have exposed her to *break her back* and founder in a rough sea.   But these disadvantages were compensated by the swiftness with which vessels so navigated could be impelled, like the steamboats of modern days, over the smooth summer seas of the Mediterranean, and by the facility with which they penetrated into creeks, rivers, and inlets, which the intricacy or shallowness of their waters rendered impervious to vessels of draught, and depending only on sails.   With their masts lowered, and their long, low hulls undiscernible on the surface of the sea by the sentinels on shore, the corsair galleys lay during the day unsuspected in the offing, opposite to a town which they had marked for plunder ; at midnight the inhabitants were roused by the flames of their dwellings, and the fierce cry of the *tecbir*, and daybreak saw the marauders again far at sea, bearing with them their booty, and such of their captives as had been spared from the slaughter, long ere the ineffectual aid of the neighbouring garrisons could reach the scene of devastation.

They now made themselves masters of some small towns on the African coast; and being joined by their brother, Ishak, the merchant of Mitylene, they increased their squadron, and succeeded in taking possession by force or by stratagem of Tennes and Telmessan, and also of the strong city of Algiers. Ishak and Urudsch soon after this fell in battle with the Spaniards, and Khaireddin was left sole master of their conquests. He formally recognised the sovereignty of the Turkish Sultan, and received from Selim the regular insignia of office, a sabre, a horse, and a banner, as Beyler Bey of Algiers. Khaireddin carried on active war against the Spaniards, and the independent Arab tribes of North Africa. He took from the Spaniards the little island in front of the port of Algiers, which had for fourteen years been in their occupation; and he defeated and captured a Spanish squadron which was sent to succour the garrison. Acting steadily up to his policy of professing allegiance to the Sublime Porte, Barbarossa sent regular reports of his operations to Constantinople, and desisted, in obedience to orders received thence, from attacking the ships or coasts of France, when that country became connected by treaty with Turkey. The red-bearded Sea-King of Algiers was now required by Sultan Solyman to measure himself with a formidable opponent in the Genoese Doria, Charles V.'s favourite admiral. Barbarossa repulsed Doria's attack on the island of Djerbel; and then joining his galleys with those of the corsair, Sinan, he sailed in triumph along the Genoese coast, which he swept with fire and devastation. He next conveyed 70,000 of the persecuted Moors of Spain from Andalusia to strengthen his own Algerine dominions. In the meanwhile, Doria had captured from the Turks the city of Koron, in the Morea; and Solyman, who recognised in Barbarossa the only Mahometan admiral that could compete with the Genoese hero, sent for Khaireddin to Constantinople to consult with him as to the best mode of carrying on the war by sea against the Spaniards. Khaireddin set sail from Algiers (1533) in obedience to his Padischah's commands, with eighteen vessels, five of which belonged to pirates, who had volunteered into the Sultan's service; and he captured on the voyage two of Doria's galleys. He was received by the Sublime Porte with the highest honours; and under his personal direction the arsenals of Constantinople were busy throughout that winter with the equipment of a powerful fleet of eighty-four vessels (including the Algerine squadron), with which Barbarossa sailed for Italy in the spring of 1534, while Solyman was commencing his campaign against Persia. Barbarossa (now Khaireddin Pacha), sacked Reggio, Citraro, Sperlonga, and Fondi. His attack on the last-mentioned place was made principally in the hope of surprising and carrying off the celebrated beauty of the age, Giulia Gonzaga, the wife of Vespasian Gonzaga. Barbarossa wished to present her as a courtly offering to Solyman, and he designed that the flower of the fair of Christendom should shine in his Sultan's harem. Barbarossa's crews landed stealthily in the night, and assailed Fondi so vigorously, that the beautiful Giulia was only roused from sleep by the alarm that the Turks were in her palace. Evading their hot pursuit with the greatest difficulty and danger, she was set on horseback in her night-dress by an Italian cavalier, who rescued and rode off with her alone to a place of safety. The sensitive beauty afterwards caused her preserver and companion to be assassinated, whether it was, says the German historian, that he had dared too much on that night, or that he had only seen too much.[1]

After plundering the Neapolitan coasts, Barbarossa stood across to Africa, and captured Tunis, which had long been the object of his ambition. He did not, however, retain this prize more than five months. The Moorish prince, whom he expelled, implored the assistance of Charles V.; and the Emperor led to Tunis an army and fleet of such strength, that Barbarossa, after a brave and skilful defence, was obliged to abandon the city. The cold-blooded and unsparing cruelty with which, after Barbarossa's retreat, the unresisting and unoffending city was sacked by the Christian forces which had come thither as the nominal allies of its rightful King, equalled the worst atrocities that have ever been imputed to the Turks.

Though driven from Tunis, Khaireddin was still strong at Algiers, and, sailing from that port with seventeen galleys, he took revenge on Spain by plundering Minorca, and he then repaired to Constantinople, where the Sultan conferred on him the highest naval dignity, that of Capitan Pacha. In 1537, he again desolated the shores of Italy; and when Venice took part in the war against the Sublime Porte, Barbarossa captured from her nearly all the islands that she had possessed in the Archipelago, and the cities of Napoli di Romania, and Castel Nuovo. He recovered Koron from the Spaniards; and on the 28th September, 1538, he engaged the combined fleets of the Pope, Venice, and the Emperor in a great battle off Prevesa. Barbarossa on this

---

[1] Von Hammer, vol. ii. p. 129. Giulia was the sister of "the divine" Joanna of Aragon, whose portraits are to be seen at Rome, Paris, and Warwick Castle.

occasion practised the bold manœuvre of cutting the line, which Rodney, St. Vincent, and Nelson made afterwards so celebrated in the English navy. The Turkish admiral's force was inferior to the enemy in number and size of vessels and in weight of metal; but by seamanship and daring, Barbarossa gained a complete and glorious victory, though the coming on of night enabled the defeated Christians to escape without very heavy loss.

The disastrous reverse which Charles V. sustained when he attacked Algiers in 1541, was chiefly the work of the elements. Barbarossa commanded the Turkish fleet sent by Solyman to protect Algiers, but he was detained in harbour by the same tempest that shattered the ships of Spain. The last great service in which Khaireddin was employed by the Sultan, was in 1543, when he was sent with the Turkish fleet to assist Francis I., and acted in conjunction with the French squadron in the Mediterranean. He captured the city of Nice, though the castle held out against him; and he is said to have roughly reproved the French officers for their negligence, and for the defective state of their ships as to equipment and necessary stores. The allies, whom he came to protect, were obliged to listen submissively to his rebukes; and it was only by the earnest entreaties and apologies of the French admiral, the Duc d'Enghien, that the choler of the old Turkish veteran was appeased.

During the latter years of Barbarossa's life, he was, when not employed at sea, a regular attendant, as Capitan Pacha, at the Divan of the Sublime Porte, where the counsels of the old admiral were always listened to with respect. He died in 1546; and his tomb on the side of the Bosphorus near Beschiktasch still invites attention by the romantic beauty of its site, and by the recollection of the bold corsair, who sleeps there by the side of the sounding sea, which so long he ruled. His wealth had been principally devoted by him to the foundation of a college: a striking tribute to the general respect for literature and science which prevailed in Solyman's court, and which exercised its influence over even the rugged temper of Barbarossa, who, from the circumstances of his early life, could not possibly have been a Turkish Ralegh.[1]

Some, however, of the Ottoman admirals were themselves

---

[1] The true biography of Barbarossa has been little known in western Europe before the German Von Hammer narrated it from the full and indisputable authorities which are found in the Ottoman literature. Barbarossa himself had, by Sultan Solyman's order, dictated an account of his life and adventures to a writer named Sinan, which is still extant; and it is also epitomised and embodied in the "History of the Naval Wars of the Turks," written by Hadji Khalssa.

eminent for their scientific attainments, and for their contributions
to the literature of the country. Such were Piri Reis, and Sidi
Ali, two of the commanders of the squadrons which by Solyman's
orders were equipped in the ports of the Red Sea, and which,
issuing thence, conquered for the Sultan of Constantinople the
port of Aden, which England now possesses, and justly values for
its important position in the line of European commerce with
India by the Red Sea and Egypt.[1] Many other cities and districts
on the coasts of Arabia, Persia, and the north-west of India were
added to the Ottoman Empire ; and many gallant contests were
sustained with the Portuguese, as well as with the native rulers,
by the Turkish admirals, the octogenarian Solyman Pacha and
Mourad, and the two whose names have been already mentioned.
Piri Reis was the author of two geographical works, one on the
Ægean, and one on the Mediterranean Sea, in which their currents,
their soundings, their harbours, and their best landing-places were
described from personal surveys. Sidi Ali was a poet as well as
a sailor ; and besides his productions in verse, he wrote a description of his travel overland to Constantinople from Goojerat, where
his fleet had been damaged by tempests so as to be no longer able
to cope with the Portuguese. Sidi Ali was also the author of
several mathematical and nautical treatises, and of a work called
"Mouhit," on the navigation of the Indian Sea, which he drew
from the best Arabian and Persian authorities of his time on the
subject of India.[2]

Two other Turkish admirals of this reign must not be omitted,
Dragut (more correctly called Torghoud) and Pialé. Pialé was a
Croatian by birth, Dragut was born a subject of the Sultan, but
of Christian parentage. He, early in life, joined the crew of a
Turkish galley, and was chosen captain of a band of thirty sea
rovers. He collected a force of thirty vessels, and attacked the
Island of Corsica, but was defeated by Doria, who took him
prisoner, and chained him to the bench of his galley, where

[1] I had the advantage in 1868 of going over the lines round Aden in company with a distinguished engineer officer in the Indian Military Service.
The traces and remnants of the old Turkish fortifications were clearly discernible ; and my companion eulogised highly the scientific skill with which
they had been designed, and the judicious labour bestowed on them, as well
as upon the vast reservoirs of water, which have been restored and improved
since Aden has been a British possession.

[2] Von Hammer states that copies of the work of Piri Reis on the Archipelago and Mediterranean are to be found in the Royal Libraries at Berlin
and Dresden, in the Vatican, and at Bologna. The only known copy of
Sidi Ali's " Mouhit " is at Naples.

Dragut toiled at the victor's oar for many a weary month. At last Barbarossa rescued him by threatening to lay Genoa waste if Dragut was not set free ; and under the patronage of Khaireddin, Dragut soon reappeared on the waves, chief of a squadron of twenty galleys, that spread terror along the coasts of Italy and Spain.   He made himself master of Mehdijé and Tripoli ; and, following the example of Barbarossa, he acknowledged himself to be the Sultan's vassal, and received in return high rank and substantial aid from Constantinople.   The Spaniards took Mehdijé from him ; but Dragut had more than once the advantage of Doria in their encounters, and was almost as much dreaded in the Mediterranean as Barbarossa himself.   His boldness of spirit was shown even towards the Sultan.   He had on one occasion been tempted by the sight of a rich fleet of Venetian argosies, and had captured them, though there was peace at that time between the Republic of St. Mark and the Porte.   Dragut was ordered to Constantinople to answer for this outrage, and, as the Grand Vizier Roostem was his enemy, his head was in serious peril. But Dragut, instead of obeying the order of recall, sailed out of the Straits of Gibraltar, and took service under the Emperor of Morocco, until Solyman, after Barbarossa's death, recalled him by pledge of pardon and ample promises of promotion.   We shall soon have occasion to notice his final services and death at the siege of Malta.

Pialé Pacha was chiefly signalised during the reign of Solyman by the capture of Oran, and by the great defeat which he gave in 1560 to the combined Christian fleets that were destined for Tripoli and the isle of Djerbé.   Two hundred vessels were prepared for this expedition by the Pope, and by the rulers of Genoa, Florence, Malta, Sicily, and Naples.   Doria was high admiral of the fleet, and Don Alvaro de Sandi commanded the army which it conveyed.   The fleet effected the passage to Djerbé in safety ; the troops were landed , the island nearly subdued, and a fortress erected.   But before the Christian galleys left the waters of Djerbé, Pialé had heard of the attack, and had left the Dardanelles with a fleet which was reinforced at Modon by the squadrons of the governors of Rhodes and Mitylene.   On the 14th May, 1560, he attacked Doria's fleet, and completely defeated it.   Twenty galleys and twenty-seven transports of the Christians were destroyed ; seven galleys ran for shelter up the channel of Djerbé, where they were subsequently captured ; the rest fled to Italy, leaving their comrades of the land forces to be besieged and captured in their new fortress by the troops, whom the active

Pialé soon brought together against them. On the 27th of September Pialé re-entered the harbour of Constantinople in triumph. He had previously sent a vessel to announce his victory, which appeared in the Golden Horn with the captured high standard of Spain trailing in the sea behind her stem. On the day of the arrival of Pialé, Solyman went to the kiosk of his palace, at the water's edge, to honour with his presence the triumphal procession of his Capitan Pacha. Don Alvaro and other Christian prisoners of high rank were placed conspicuous on the poop of the Ottoman admiral's galley, and the captured vessels were towed along rudderless and dismasted. Those who were near Sultan Solyman observed that his aspect on this proud day of triumph bore the same grave and severely calm expression, which was its usual characteristic. The ambassador of King Ferdinand, who was present, attributed this stoical composure to magnanimity, and admired "the great heart of that old sire," which received unmoved anything that fortune could bring.[1] The modern German historian of the House of Othman points out that this unexulting austerity of the great Sultan may have been caused by the domestic affliction, which by this time he had sustained, and which may have steeled while it saddened his heart.[2]

Glorious, indeed, and prosperous as had been the reign of Solyman the Magnificent, he had, as a man, drunken deeply of sorrow and remorse ; and the Erinnys of family bloodshed, that for so many centuries has haunted the House of Othman, was fatally active in his generation. To be friendless is the common penalty of despotic power ; and Solyman must have felt it the more severely, inasmuch as he appears naturally to have had a capacity for friendship, and to have sought earnestly for it in the early part of his reign. His celebrated Grand Vizier, Ibrahim, was for many years not only his most trusted councillor and general, but the companion of his pleasures and his studies. Yet his suspicions were at last raised against the overpowerful and incautious

[1] "Eadem erat frontis severitas et tristitia, ac si nihil ad eum hæc victoria pertineret, nihil novum aut inexpectatum contigisset. Tam capax in illo sene quantævis fortunæ pectus, tam confidens animus, ut tantam gratulationem velut immotus acciperet."—Busbequius. Old Knolles translates this nobly : "I myself saw him with the same countenance that he had always ; with the same severity and gravity ; as if the victory had nothing concerned him, nor anything chanced strange or unexpected ; so capable was the great heart of that old sire of any fortune, were it never so great, and his mind so settled as to receive so great applause and rejoicing without moving."

[2] Von Hammer, vol. ii. p. 382.

favourite ; and a Vizier, whom a Sultan begins to dread, has not long to live. Ibrahim was married to Solyman's sister, but not even this close affinity could save him. Ibrahim came to the palace at Constantinople on the 5th March, 1536, to dine with the Sultan, as was his custom ; and when on the next morning messengers from his home came to seek him, they found him strangled. The state of his body showed that he had struggled hard for life ; and, a hundred years afterwards, the traces of his blood on the palace walls were pointed out ; fearful warnings of the lot that awaited those who sought to win their entrance there as royal favourites. Von Hammer gives a long list of other high officers whom Solyman once honoured and trusted, but whom he ultimately gave to the fatal bowstring.[1] But these acts of severity seem slight, compared with the deaths of the princes of his own race, who perished by his orders. Having been an only son, Solyman was spared the guilt of fratricide on his accession to the throne ; but he showed repeatedly in the course of his reign, that when state necessity called for blood, the holiest feelings of humanity interposed in vain. His cousin, the descendant of the unfortunate Prince Djem, who came into his power when Rhodes was taken, was put to death with all his family by Solyman's command, and there was still nearer and dearer blood upon his hands.

While Solyman was still young, a Russian girl in his harem, named Khourrem[2] (which means "the joyous one"), had gained an almost unbounded influence over him by her beauty and liveliness ; and such was the fascination of her manners—so attractive and soothing to the weary spirit of royalty were the animated graces of her conversation ; her skill was so subtle in reading the thoughts of her lord, and in selecting the most favourable times

[1] Von Hammer remarks as an occurrence without parallel in Turkish history, the suicide of one of Solyman's officers, Khosrew Pacha, who starved himself to death, on being deprived of the government of Bosnia. The profound feeling of submission to the Divine Will, which characterises the Mussulmans, makes suicide almost unknown in Mahometan countries. Another high officer of Solyman's, Loutfi Pacha, who was cashiered by the Sultan about the same time, acted much more wisely than Khosrew. He employed his involuntary leisure in writing a history of the Ottoman Empire down to his own times,

[2] The French writers erroneously claim Solyman's favourite Sultana as a Frenchwoman. Von Hammer says that Khourrem was frequently spoken of by the contemporaneous Imperial and Venetian ambassadors as "La Rossa," *i.e.*, "The Russian woman." This was subsequently euphonised into Roxalana, and supposed to have been the personal name of the French fair one. The Italians also laid claim to Roxalana.

for the exercise of her power in guiding them, that she preserved
her ascendancy in his affections long after they both had outlived
the season of youth, and until the day of her death, in 1558. She
had persuaded Solyman to enfranchise her, and to make her his
wife, according to the Mahometan ritual.   And the honours paid
by him to her memory proved the constancy and fervour of his
passion even after death.   Her domed mausoleum was raised by
him close to the magnificent mosque, the Suliemaniye, which he
had constructed, and which he appointed as his own place of sepul-
ture.   The tomb of the Sultana Khourrem still attests the fatal
fondness which the Russian beauty inspired in the greatest of the
Turkish Sultans, and which transferred the succession to the
throne of Othman from a martial and accomplished hero to a
ferocious but imbecile drunkard.   Solyman had a son, Prince
Mustapha, born to him by a Circassian, who had been the favourite
Sultana before the Muscovite slave Khourrem enslaved her master.
Khourrem also bore children to Solyman ; and all her address was
employed to secure the succession to the throne for her son Prince
Selim.   As a necessary step towards that object, she sought the
destruction of Prince Mustapha, who, as the elder born, was
regarded as the natural heir.   A daughter of the Sultana Khourrem was married to Roostem Pacha, who, by her influence, was
raised successively to the dignities of Beyler Bey of Diarbekir,
and of Second Vizier ; and, finally, to the highest station in the
empire below the throne, to the office of Grand Vizier.   Roostem
Pacha employed all his power and influence as his mother-in-law
directed him ; and she thus acquired a ready and efficient instrument for the ruin of the devoted Mustapha.   This unhappy
Prince was distinguished for personal grace and activity, and for
high spirit and intelligence.   In the various governments which
were intrusted to him by Solyman, as he advanced towards manhood, he gave proof of such abilities, both civil and military, that
he was looked on as likely to surpass his father in glory, and to
become the most eminent of all the House of Othman.   The
malignant artifices of Khourrem and Roostem awakened in Solyman's mind, first jealousy, and then dread of his over-popular and
over-praised son.   As Solyman advanced in years, the poisonous
whisperings of the step-mother grew more and more effective.
The old Sultan was studiously reminded how his own father,
Selim, had dethroned Bajazet II. ; and the vision was kept before
him of a renewal of that scene ; of a young and vigorous Prince,
the favourite of the soldiery, seizing the reins of empire, and of an
aged father retiring to Demotika and death.   It was at last, in

1553, when Solyman was preparing for the second war with Persia, that he was fully wrought up to the conviction that Prince Mustapha was plotting against him, and that it was necessary, before he marched against the foreign enemy, to crush the germs of treason at home.   In the autumn of that year, Solyman placed himself at the head of the troops which had been collected in Asia Minor, and with which it was designed to invade Persia.   The season was then too far advanced for such military operations, and the army was to winter at Aleppo, and to open the campaign in the following spring.   But Solyman had been persuaded that it was not safe for him to tarry at Constantinople.   He was told by his Grand Vizier that the soldiers in Asia Minor were murmuring, and plotting among themselves in favour of Prince Mustapha, and that the Prince encouraged their preparations for a military revolution against the old Padischah Solyman.   He repaired, therefore, to the army ; and Khourrem's son, Prince Selim, at his mother's instigation, sought, and obtained, the Sultan's permission to accompany him.   When the army reached Eregli (the ancient Archelais), Prince Mustapha arrived at head-quarters, and his tents were pitched with great pomp in the vicinity of those of the Sultan.   On the next day, the Viziers paid their visits of compliment to the Prince, and received presents of sumptuous robes of honour.   On the following morning, Prince Mustapha mounted a stately and richly-caparisoned charger, and was conducted by the Viziers and Janissaries, amid the loud acclamations of the soldiery, to the royal tent, where he dismounted in expectation of having an audience of his father.   His attendants remained at the entrance of the tent ; Prince Mustapha passed into the interior ; but he found there, not the Sultan, not any of the officers of the Court, but the seven Mutes, the well-known grim ministers of the blood-orders of the Imperial Man-Slayer.   They sprang upon him, and fastened the fatal bow-string round his throat, while he vainly called for mercy to his father, who was in an inner apartment of the tent.   According to some accounts, Solyman, impatient at the long-continued struggle between the Mutes and his victim, looked in upon the horrible scene, and with threatening arm and angry brow urged his executioners to complete the work of death.   While the Prince thus perished within the tent, his master of the horse, and a favourite Aga, who had accompanied him to the entrance, were cut down on the outside.   The tidings of this execution soon spread through the camp ; and the troops, especially the Janissaries, gathered together in tumultuous indignation, and called for the punishment of the Grand Vizier, to whose intrigues they imputed the death of their favourite Prince. To appease their fury, the obnoxious Roostem was deprived of his office, and Ahmed Pacha, who had distinguished himself in the Hungarian wars, was made Grand Vizier in his stead. But after the lapse of two years, the son-in-law of the all-powerful Sultana was restored to his former dignity, and Ahmed Pacha was put to death on frivolous charges of misconduct and disloyalty.[1]

The tragedy of the death of Prince Bajazet, another son, whom Solyman, at a later period of his reign, caused to be put to death, was attended with even more melancholy circumstances. After the death of the Sultana Khourrem, but while her son-in-law, the Vizier Roostem, yet lived, a deadly rivalry arose between her two sons, Selim and Bajazet. The tutor of the princes, Lala Mustapha Pacha, had originally favoured Prince Bajazet; but, finding that his prospects of promotion would be greater if he sided with Prince Selim, he made himself the unscrupulous partisan of the latter, and, by a series of the darkest intrigues,[2] by suggesting false hopes, and unreal dangers, by intercepting and suppressing some letters, and procuring others to be written and read, he drove Bajazet into rebellion against his father, the result of which was the overthrow and death of the unhappy Prince. Solyman believed that Prince Bajazet was an unnatural son, towards whom his fatherly remonstrances and warnings had been vainly employed; and Bajazet was led by the arts of the tutor to regard his father as a morose tyrant, who rejected his child's filial submission and

[1] Von Hammer (vol. ii. p. 231) disputes the accuracy of many of the pathetic details with which Robertson and others, after Busbequius, have narrated the death of Prince Mustapha. But he states that all the Ottoman historians agree with the Christian writers, in representing Roostem as having caused the Prince's death, at the instigation of the Sultana, his step-mother. In a letter written 23rd Dec., 1553, by Dr. Wotton, our English envoy at Paris, he says : " The Great Turk, going towards Aleppo, sent for his eldest son to come to him ; who, trusting to be well received of his father, was most cruelly murdered in his father's presence, and by his commandment. Men, that have seen the said son, say that of all the Ottoman's posterity, there was never none so like to attempt great enterprises, and to achieve them with honour, as he was. The cause hereof is taken to be the favour and love which the Turk beareth to the children he hath by another woman, not mother to him that is slain. But his other sons are nothing of that towardness and activity that this man was of."— (Tytler's "Reigns of Edward VI. and Mary," vol. ii. p. 275.) When the close intimacy which was maintained between the Turkish and French courts at this period is remembered, this testimony as to the high expectations that were formed of Prince Mustapha, and also as to the manner of his death, is remarkably strong.

[2] Von Hammer, vol. ii. p. 264, relates them at length, on the authority of the Ottoman writer, Ali, who had been Lala Mustapha's secretary.

entreaties for pardon, and who was resolved to exercise again the
same cruel severity which he had shown towards Prince Mustapha.
Bajazet was far more popular with the soldiery and people than
Prince Selim, whose drunken and dissolute habits made him an
object of general contempt, and whose unpopularity was increased
by his personal resemblance to his hated mother, the Sultana
Khourrem.   Bajazet's features and demeanour resembled those of
his father ; his habits of life were blameless ; his intellectual powers
and literary accomplishments were high ; and his capacity for civil
government and military command, though not equal to those of
the lamented Mustapha, were such as to gain favour and command
respect.   Thus, even after his defeat at Koniah (8th May, 1559)
by his father's Third Vizier, Sokolli, a considerable force adhered
to Prince Bajazet in his fallen fortunes, and followed him into
Persia, where he took refuge, together with his four infant sons, at
the court of Shah Tahmasp.   He was at first treated there with
princely honours, and the Shah pledged a solemn oath never to
give the royal refugee up to his father.   But Solyman sternly and
imperatively required the extradition or the execution of the rebel
and the rebel's children.   Prince Selim also sent letters and messengers to Persia, to procure the death of his brother and nephews,
and he gave liberal quotations of misapplied verses of the Koran,
and copied passages from eminent writers,[1] to overcome the conscientious scruples of the Shah, who long hesitated at the treacherous breach of hospitality which he was urged to commit.   Fear at
last prevailed over honour.   Persia's " cicatrice yet looked too raw
and red after the Turkish sword," for the " sovereign process " of
the Sultan to be disregarded ; and the present death of Bajazet
and his children was resolved on.   Tahmasp thought that he evaded
the obligation of his oath by giving up his guests, not to the immediate officers of Solyman, but to emissaries sent specially by
Selim to receive and slay them.   It was the period of the solemn
fast which the Schii Mahometans kept annually, in memory of
Hossein, when the Turkish princes were delivered up to the
executioners.   Such was the sympathy which their fate inspired
among the Persians, that they interrupted their lamentations for
the murdered son of Ali, to sorrow over the royal victims then
perishing before them ; and instead of the curses on the slayers of
Hossein which the Schiis are then accustomed to pour forth,[2] impre-

---

[1] One of these was a sentence from Saadi, worthy to be paralleled with
the famous epigraph from Publius Syrus, " Judex damnatur," &c.   It is
this : " Kindness to the Undeserving is injury to the Good."

[2] The English reader will remember the vivid description which Lord

cations resounded throughout Tabreez against the executioners of
the innocent grandchildren of Sultan Solyman. A short elegiac
poem, written by Prince Bajazet a little before his death, is preserved in the work of the Turkish historian, Solakzade, and proves
to how great an extent that unhappy prince inherited the poetical
talent which has so remarkably characterised the Ottoman royal
family.[1]

Besides the domestic sorrows which clouded the last years of
Solyman, his military glory and imperial ambition sustained, in the
year 1565 (the year before his death), the heaviest blow and most
humiliating disappointment, that had befallen them since the
memorable retreat from Vienna. This second great check was
caused by the complete failure of the expedition against Malta,
which was led by the admirals Mustapha and Pialé, and nobly and
victoriously encountered by the Knights of St. John of Jerusalem,
under their heroic Grand Master, La Valette. After the Knights
had been driven from Rhodes, on Solyman's conquest of that island
in the beginning of his reign, they had established their Order at
Malta, which, together with the neighbouring island of Goza, was
given to them by the Emperor Charles V., who compassionated
their misfortunes, admired their valour, and appreciated the im-

---

Macaulay, in his Essay on Clive, gives of the effect produced on the Schii
Mahometans by this annual commemoration of the death of Hossein.

[1] Von Hammer's version of this poem is as follows :

> Soll Lebenshoffnung mir verlängern noch die Stunden?
> Aus meinem Herzen ist der Lebens Luft verschwunden.
> Nun heisst es fort, hinunter zu des Nichtseyns Reichen;
> Die Karawanen-glocke tönt das Aufbruch-zeichen.
> Geduld, o Seelen-vogel! dass dein Flug sich hebe,
> Zerbrochen sind bereits des Kaffich's Gitterstabe.
> An Seel und Leibe krank, ist Schatzi voll von Sünden.
> Er wird bey dir, o Freund, O Gott, die Hülfe finden.

Which may be thus paraphrased in English :

> Why cling to hopes of life with fond misgiving?
> Why lengthen out thine hours, my weary heart?
> For thee is withered all the joy of living :
> To the void realms below thou summoned art.
> The caravan-bell sounds the sign to part.
> Bird of my soul, the cage that round thee prest,
> Is shattered now :—hence on free pinion dart.
> In mind and body sick, with sin distrest,
> To thee, my Friend, my God, I come for healing rest.

Sultan Solyman was himself a poet ; but, according to Von Hammer, his
compositions, though dignified and elegant, are not of the highest rank in
Turkish poetry.

portance of the services which they rendered to Christendom, as a barrier against the advancing power of the Ottomans. When the Knights took possession of Malta, it was little more than a shelter-less rock ; but they discerned the natural advantages of the place, and immediately commenced fortifying the remarkable system of harbours on the south-eastern side of the island, where the city of Malta now rears its grim ranges of batteries and bastions beneath the British flag. The squadrons of the Knights, issuing from the Maltese havens, co-operated actively with the fleets of Spain, and of every foe of the Crescent ; and an incessant warfare was carried on under the Maltese Cross against the Turks, in which deeds of chivalrous enterprise were often performed, but in which a piratical love of plunder and a brutal spirit of cruelty too often disgraced the Christian as well as the Mahometan belligerents. The atten-tion of Solyman was soon fixed on Malta, as the new nest of the revived hornets, who intercepted the commerce and assailed the coasts of his empire ; and at last the capture by five Maltese galleys of a rich Turkish galleon, belonging partly to some of the ladies of the seraglio, exasperated the Sultan, who regarded it as an insult to his household. He was further urged to an attack upon the Order by the Mufti, who represented to him how sacred a duty it was to rescue the numerous Moslem slaves who were held in cruel bondage by the Knights. Nor can we suppose him to have been indifferent to the military and political importance of the possession of Malta. If the Ottoman arms had once been securely established in that island, it would have served as a basis for operations against Sicily and South Italy, which hardly could have failed of success.

Accordingly, a mighty armament was prepared in the port of Constantinople, during the winter of 1564. The troops amounted to upwards of 30,000, including 4500 Janissaries, and the fleet comprised 181 vessels. The Fifth Vizier, Mustapha Pacha, was appointed Seraskier, or commander-in-chief of the expedition, and under him was the renowned Pialé, the hero of Djerbé. The equally celebrated Dragut was to join them at Malta, with the naval and military forces of Tripoli ; and all the stores and muni-tions of war that the skilful engineers and well-stocked arsenals of Constantinople could supply, were shipped in liberal provision for a difficult siege and long campaign. The fleet sailed from the Golden Horn on the 1st of April, 1565. The Grand Vizier, Ali, accompanied the Seraskier and Capitan Pacha to the place of embarcation ; and it was long remembered that, at parting, he said laughingly, "There go two brisk companions, of an exquisite

relish for coffee and opium, on a voyage of pleasure among the
islands.   Their fleet must be all laden with the Arabian bean and
essence of henbane."   Von Hammer recounts this pleasantry, not
for its humour, but on account of the characteristic comments made
on it by the principal Ottoman historians.   They blame it as unworthy of the Grand Vizier's dignity, and say that such levity from
such a personage was a bad omen at the commencement of a serious
and important enterprise.   The remarks which they add, that the
Grand Vizier was on bad terms with the two officers at whom he
thus jested, and that the Seraskier and admiral were unfriendly towards each other, and both jealous of Dragut, with whom they were
to co-operate, show better causes for the failure of the expedition,
than the ill-timed jest which they gravely criticise.

The Knights knew well what a storm was about to break upon
Malta, and they exerted themselves to the utmost to improve the
defences of their island home.   The old city, as it then existed,
occupied the central of the three spits of land which project into
the Great Harbour on the eastern side.   The innermost of these
projecting peninsulas, called Isle de la Sangle, was also occupied
and fortified.   Mount Sceberras, the ridge of land which runs out
to the open sea, dividing the great eastern harbour from the
western harbour, called Port Muscet, and on which the modern
city of La Valletta stands, was not at this time built upon; except at the extremity, where an important castle, called the Fort
of St. Elmo, had been raised to command the entrances of both
harbours.   On a muster of the forces of the defenders of Malta,
they were found to consist of 700 Knights, besides serving
brothers, and about 8500 soldiers, comprising the crews of the
galleys, hired troops, and the militia of the island.   Spain sent a
small auxiliary force, and promised that her Viceroy of Sicily
should bring ample succour.   The Pope gave a sum of 10,000
crowns; but from no other Christian power did the Knights receive aid.   Their means of safety consisted in their strong and
well-armed walls, their own skill and courage, and, above all, the
genius and heroism of their Grand Master, John de la Vallette,
who had been elected, providentially for Malta, about seven years
before its memorable siege.   When the approach of the Ottoman
armament was announced, La Vallette assembled his Knights and
addressed them :—" A formidable enemy is coming like a thunder-
storm upon us ; and, if the banner of the Cross must sink before
the misbelievers, let us see in this a signal that Heaven demands
from us those lives which we have solemnly devoted to its service.
He who dies in this cause, dies a happy death ; and, to render

ourselves worthy to meet it, let us renew at the altar those vows, which ought to make us not only fearless, but invincible in the fight." The brotherhood devoutly obeyed their Master's exhortation. They renewed the vows of their religious knighthood; and after this solemn ceremonial, and after partaking together of the Holy Sacrament, they swore to give up all feuds among themselves, to renounce all temporal objects and pleasures until their deliverance should be effected, and to stand between the Cross and profanation to the last drop of their blood.

The Ottoman fleet appeared off Malta on the 19th May, 1565. Pialé wished to wait for the arrival of Dragut before they commenced operations; but the Seraskier on the next day disembarked the troops and began the attack upon St. Elmo. The rocky nature of the ground on Mount Sceberras made it impossible for the Turkish engineers to work trenches; and, as substitutes, they pushed forward movable breastworks of timber, which were thickly coated on the outside with clay and rushes kneaded together. Five days after the commencement of the siege, the Turkish Sea-Captain Ouloudj Ali (called by the Christians Ochiale), who was destined to acquire such celebrity in the next reign, arrived with six galleys from Alexandria; and at last, on the 2nd June, Dragut appeared with the squadron of Tripoli. The old admiral disapproved of the attack on St. Elmo, saying that the fort must have fallen of itself when the city was taken; but he declared that as the operation had been commenced, it ought to be persevered with. Fresh batteries were placed by his directions against the fort; and in particular he established one upon the opposite or western side of Port Muscet—on the cape that still bears his name. The Turkish ships plied the seaward defences of the fort with their artillery; on the land side thirty-six heavy guns battered it in breach, and the balls of Dragut's battery from across Port Muscet swept the ravelin with a raking fire. The little garrison did their duty nobly; and aided by occasional reinforcements from the main body of their comrades who held the Bourg and the Isle de La Sangle, they repulsed repeated attempts made by the Turks to escalade their walls; and they impeded the advance of the enemy's works by bold and frequent sorties. The Viceroy of Sicily had promised La Vallette to send a relieving force to the island by the middle of June; and every day that the defence of St. Elmo could be prolonged, was considered by the Knights to be of vital importance for the safety of the island. When some of the Knights posted in the fort represented to La Vallette the ruined state of its defences, and the rapidly increasing

destructiveness of the Ottoman fire, he told them that they must
die in discharge of their duty; and the noble band of martyrs
remained in St. Elmo to die accordingly.   Dragut ordered a
general assault on the fort on the 16th of June.   The landward
walls had now been shattered and rent, and the Turkish stormers
advanced without difficulty through the yawning breaches; but
behind these the Knights, arrayed in steady phalanx, and armed
with long pikes, formed a living wall, against which the bravest
Turks rushed with their scimetars in vain.   Meanwhile, the
Christian cannon from St. Angelo and St. Michael, the forts at
the extremities of the Bourg and the Isle de la Sangle, played
with terrible effect on the flanks of the huge columns of the assailants.   After six hours' conflict the Ottomans retreated, leaving
two thousand of their comrades slain.   Dragut himself received
his death-wound during the assault.   A cannon-ball from the
Castle of St. Angelo splintered a rock near which he was standing,
and the fragments of stone struck the old seaman's head.   The
Seraskier, with whom he had been conversing respecting the construction of a new battery to reply to St. Angelo, ordered a cloak
to be flung over the corpse, and remained calmly on the spot
while he completed the requisite instructions to the engineers.
Seven days afterwards, the death of Dragut was avenged by the
fall of St. Elmo, after a furious and long-continued assault, in
which every man of the defenders "was slain in valiant fight."[1]
In the siege of this outwork, 300 Knights and 1300 soldiers of
the Order, and 8000 of the Turks, perished.   Mustapha Pacha,
when he looked from the ruins of this small castle across to the
massive towers of the Bourg, which was now to be attacked, could
not help exclaiming, "If the child has cost us so much, what shall
we have to pay for the father?"   He sent a Christian slave to
summon the Grand Master to surrender.   La Vallette led the
messenger round the lofty ramparts, and pointing down to the
deep ditches beneath them, he said, "Tell the Seraskier that this
is the only land I can give him.   Let him and his Janissaries come
and take possession."   Mustapha commenced the attack with
ardour, and both the Bourg and the Isle de la Sangle were closely
invested and cannonaded from the mainland; while also a row of
formidable Turkish batteries thundered on them from St. Elmo
and Mount Sceberras.   This great siege was prolonged until the
11th of September, by the obstinate vehemence of the besiegers,
and the truly chivalrous gallantry of the besieged.   During the continuance of the operations, the Turks were reinforced by a flotilla

[1] Knolles.

from Algiers, commanded by the Beyler Bey Hassan, the son of the great Barbarossa, and son-in-law of Dragut.   Hassan demanded leave to sustain the honour of these illustrious names by leading an assault upon the Isle de la Sangle.   The Seraskier placed 5000 men at his disposal, and with these Hassan attacked the works from the mainland, while Candelissa, a Greek renegade, who had grown grey in piracy and war, led the Algerine galleys to an attack on the inner part of the harbour.   Hassan brought back only 500 men out of his 5000 ; nor was Candelissa more successful.   No less than ten general assaults were made and repulsed before the siege was raised ; and innumerable minor engagements took place, in which each side showed such valour as to earn its enemy's praise, and each side also unhappily too often stained its glory by the exhibition of ferocious cruelty.   In one of these encounters, the Seraskier had sent a band of able swimmers across part of the harbour with axes to destroy a stockade which the Knights had erected.   La Vallette opposed these assailants by calling for volunteer swimmers from among the Maltese.   The islanders came forward readily for this service ; and stripping themselves naked, and armed only with short swords, a band of them swam to the stockade, and after a short but desperate struggle in the water, they completely routed the Turkish hatchet-men, and saved the works.[1]   The long repetition of defeat and bootless carnage by degrees wore out the energies of the Turks.   And at last, at the beginning of September, the news arrived that the long-expected fleet of the Sicilian Viceroy was on the sea.   The succours thus tardily sent to La Vallette and his brave comrades amounted to less than 8000 men ; but rumour magnified their numbers, and the weary and dispirited besiegers on the 11th of September abandoned their heavy ordnance, and left the island, which had been crimsoned with so much slaughter, and had been made the theatre of such unrivalled heroism.   This memorable siege is said to have cost the lives of 25,000 Turks, and of 5000 of the brave defenders.   So reduced, indeed, was the garrison at the time of its rescue, that when they marched out to take possession of the guns which the Turks had abandoned, La Vallette could only muster six hundred men fit for service.[2]

---

[1] Constable's "History of the Knights of Malta," vol. ii. p. 200.
[2] Ibid., vol. ii. p. 227.   The writer well quotes Knolles's eulogy on the defenders : "If a man do well consider the difficulties and dangers the besieged passed through in this five months' siege, the manifold labours and perils they endured in so many and terrible assaults, the small relief to them sent in so great distress, with the desperate obstinacy of so

At the time when the tidings that the siege of Malta was raised, reached Constantinople, Solyman was preparing for a new struggle with Austria. The disputes between the rival parties in Hungary had again brought on hostilities. Maximilian II. (who had succeeded Ferdinand) had in person attacked and captured Tokay and Serencz, and the Turkish Pacha, Mustapha Sokolli, had invaded Croatia. Solyman determined to conduct the campaign against the young German Emperor in person ; and there can be little doubt that this Austrian war saved the Knights of Malta from a renewed attack in 1566, which must, in all human probability, have been fatal. Solyman was now seventy-six years old, and so enfeebled by age and illness, that he was no longer able to sit on horseback, but was borne in a litter at the head of his army, which commenced its march from Constantinople to Hungary on the 1st of May, 1566. Before he left his capital for the last time, Solyman had the satisfaction of seeing the great aqueducts completed, which had been built by his orders for the supply of the city. The Sultan arrived at Semlin, in Hungary, the 27th of June, and received the solemn homage of young Sigismund Zapolya, the titular King of Hungary and Transylvania under Ottoman protection. Solyman especially desired to capture in this campaign the two strong places of Erlau and Szigeth, which had on former occasions baffled the attacks of the Turks. A bold exploit of Count Zriny, the Governor of Szigeth, who surprised and cut off a detachment of Bosnian troops while on their march to reinforce the Sultan's army, determined Solyman to make Szigeth the first object of his arms ; and on the 5th of August the Ottoman forces encamped round that city. It was destined to be the death-place both of the Turkish sovereign and the Christian chief. Zriny himself burnt the lower, or new town, as indefensible ; but great reliance was placed on the strength of the citadel, which was protected by a deep fen, that lay between it and the old or upper town. The Turks carried the town in five days, though not without severe fighting and heavy loss ; and Zriny and his garrison of 3200 men then retired to the citadel, where they hoisted the black flag, and took an oath never to surrender, but to fight to the last man and the last gasp. The Turkish engineers formed causeways across the marsh ; and they established breastworks near the walls, where the Janissaries were posted, who kept down the fire of the artillery of the besieged by

puissant an enemy, he shall hardly find any place these many years more mightily impugned, or with greater valour and resolution defended."

an incessant discharge of musketry upon the embrasures, and at every living object that appeared above the parapet.[1] The heavy cannons of the Ottomans were placed in battery, and the walls began to crumble beneath their salvoes. Solyman was impatient of the delay which the resistance of so small a place as this citadel now caused him, and he summoned Zriny to surrender, and sought to win him over to the Ottoman service by offering to make him ruler of all Croatia. Zriny, whom his countrymen have not unworthily named the Leonidas of Hungary, was resolute to die in defence of his post, and he inspired all his men with his own spirit of unflinching courage. Three assaults were given by the Turks in August and September, all of which Zriny repelled with great loss to the besiegers. The Turkish engineers now ran a mine under the principal bastion, and the attacking columns were kept back until the effect of the explosion could be ascertained. The mine was fired early in the morning of the 5th of September, and the bright streak of fire, that shot up into the sky from the shattered bastion, might have been thought to be the death-light of the great Sultan, who had died in his tent during the preceding night. A few hours before his death, he had written to his Grand Vizier complaining that "the drum of victory had not yet beat." He was not destined to witness Szigeth's fall; though his army continued the siege as if by his command, and all except his Grand Vizier, Sokolli, believed that he still lived and reigned. Sokolli is said to have killed the Sultan's physicians lest the important secret should transpire, and to have issued orders in Solyman's name, while the messengers conveyed the despatches to Prince Selim which summoned him to the throne. The fire of the Turkish batteries upon Szigeth was continued for four days after the explosion of the great mine, until all the exterior defences of the citadel were destroyed, and of the inner works only a single tower was left standing. In that tower were Zriny and 600 of his men; the rest of the garrison had perished. On the 8th of September the Janissaries advanced in a dense column along a narrow bridge, that led to this last shelter of the defenders;

[1] Knolles describes these works with his usual graphic, though quaint vigour. "Then might a man have seen all the fields full of camels, horses, and of the Turks themselves, like emmets, carrying wood, earth, stone, or one thing or another, to fill up the marsh; so was there with wonderful labour two plain ways made through the deep fen from the town to the castle, where the Janissaries, defended from the great shot with sacks of wool and such like things, did with the multitude of their small shot so overwhelm the defenders, that they could not against those places, without most manifest danger, show themselves upon the walls."

and Zriny, feeling that his hour was come, resolved to anticipate
the charge. The gallant Magyar prepared himself for death as
for a marriage feast. He wore his most splendid apparel, and a
diamond of high price glittered in the clasp of his crest of the
heron's plumes. He fastened to his girdle a purse containing the
keys of the tower, and a hundred ducats carefully chosen of Hungarian coinage. "The man who lays me out," he said, "shall not
complain that he found nothing on me for his trouble. These
keys I keep while this arm can move. When it is stiff, let him
who pleases take both keys and ducats. But I have sworn never
to be the living finger-post of Turkish scorn." Then from among
four richly-ornamented sabres, which had been presented to him
at some of the most brilliant epochs of his military career, he
chose the oldest one. "With this good sword," he exclaimed,
"gained I my first honours, and with this will I pass forth to hear
my doom before the judgment-seat of God." He then, with the
banner of the empire borne before him by his standard-bearer,
went down into the court of the tower, where his 600 were drawn
up in readiness to die with him. He addressed them in a few
words of encouragement, which he ended by thrice invoking the
name of Jesus. The Turks were now close to the tower gate.
Zriny had caused a large mortar to be brought down and placed
in the doorway, and trained point-blank against the entrance. He
had loaded this with broken iron and musket balls. At the
instant when the foremost Janissary raised his axe to break in the
door, it was thrown open. Zriny fired the mortar; the deadly
shower poured through the mass of the assailants, destroying
hundreds of them in an instant; and amid the smoke, the din, and
the terror of this unexpected carnage, Zriny sprang forth sword
in hand against the Turks, followed by his devoted troop. There
was not one of those 600 Magyar sabres but drank its fill on that
day of self-immolation, before the gallant men who wielded them
were overpowered.[1] Zriny met the death he sought, from two
musket-balls through the body, and an arrow wound in the head.
The Ottomans thrice raised the shout of "Allah" when they saw
him fall, and they then poured into the citadel, which they fired
and began to plunder; but Zriny, even after death, smote his
foes. He had caused all his remaining stores of powder to be
placed beneath the tower, and, according to some accounts, a slow
match was applied to it by his orders immediately before the

[1] "It is said that some were spared in the conflict by the Janissaries, who,
admiring their courage, placed their own caps on their heads, for the purpose of saving them."—"Two Sieges of Vienna," p. 64.

Magyars made their sally.   Either from this, or from the flames which the Turks had themselves kindled, the magazine exploded while the tower was filled with Ottoman soldiery; and together with the last battlements of Szigeth, 3000 of its destroyers were destroyed.

Solyman the Conqueror lay stark in his tent before the reeking and smouldering ruins.   The drum of victory beat unheeded by him who had so longed for its sound.   He was insensible to all the roar of the assault, and to the "deadly earthshock" of the fired magazine of Szigeth.   Nor could the tidings which now reached the camp of the surrender of the city of Gyula to Pertaw Pacha "soothe the dull cold ear of death."   The secret of the decease of the Sultan was long well guarded.   For more than seven weeks the great Turkish army of 150,000 soldiers, went, and came, and fought, and took towns and cities in the name of the dead man. The Vizier Sokolli had caused the body to be partly embalmed before the royal tent was removed from before Szigeth; and, when the camp was struck, the corpse was placed in the covered litter in which Solyman had travelled during the campaign, and which was now borne along among the troops, surrounded by the customary guards, and with all the ceremonies and homage which had been shown to the living monarch.   Sokolli and the other high officers, who knew the truth, after the siege and capture of Babocsa, and some other operations which employed the attention of the troops, gradually drew them towards the Turkish frontier.   Solyman's signature was adroitly counterfeited; written orders were issued in his name, and the report was sedulously spread among the soldiers, that a severe attack of gout prevented the Sultan from appearing in public.   At last Sokolli received intelligence that Prince Selim had been enthroned at Constantinople; and he then took measures for revealing to the soldiery the death of the great Padischah.   The army was now (24th of October, 1566) four marches distant from Belgrade, and had halted for the night in the outskirts of a forest.   Sokolli sent for the readers of the Koran, who accompanied the troops, and ordered them to assemble round the Sultan's litter in the night, and at the fourth hour before day-break (the hour at which Solyman had expired forty-eight days before), to read the appointed service for the dead from the Koran, and call upon the name of God.   At the chosen time, amid the stillness of the night, the army was roused from sleep by the loud clear voices of the Muezzins, that rose in solemn chant from around the royal tent, and were echoed back from the sepulchral gloom of the forest.   Those who stood on the right of the corpse called aloud, " All dominion perishes, and the last hour awaits all mankind !" Those on the left answered, " The everliving God alone is untouched by time or death." The soldiers, who heard the well-known announcement of death, gathered together in tumultuous groups, with wild cries of lamentation. When the day began to break, the Grand Vizier went through the camp addressing the assemblages of troops, and exhorting them to resume their ranks and march. He told them how much the Padischah, who was now at rest and in the bosom of God, had done for Islam, and how he had been the soldier's friend ; and he exhorted them to show their respect for his memory not by lamentations, which should be left to the priests, but by loyal obedience to his son, the glorious Sultan Selim Khan, who now was reigning in his stead. Soothed by these addresses, and the promise of a liberal donative from the new Sultan, the army returned to military order, and escorted the remains of their monarch and general back to Belgrade. Solyman's body was finally deposited in the great mosque at Constantinople, the Soleimaniye, which is the architectural glory of his reign.

Sultan Solyman I. left to his successors an empire, to the extent of which few important permanent additions were ever made, except the islands of Cyprus and Candia ; and which under no subsequent Sultan maintained or recovered the wealth, power, and prosperity which it enjoyed under the great lawgiver of the House of Othman. The Turkish dominions in his time comprised all the most celebrated cities of biblical and classical history, except Rome, Syracuse, and Persepolis. The sites of Carthage, Memphis, Tyre, Nineveh, Babylon, and Palmyra were Ottoman ground ; and the cities of Alexandria, Jerusalem, Damascus, Smyrna, Nice, Prusa, Athens, Philippi, and Adrianople, besides many of later but scarcely inferior celebrity, such as Algiers, Cairo, Mecca, Medina, Bassorah, Bagdad, and Belgrade, obeyed the Sultan of Constantinople. The Nile, the Jordan, the Orontes, the Euphrates, the Tigris, the Tanais, the Borysthenes, the Danube, the Hebrus, and the Ilyssus, rolled their waters " within the shadow of the Horsetails." The eastern recess of the Mediterranean, the Propontis, the Palus Mæotis, the Euxine, and the Red Sea, were Turkish lakes. The Ottoman Crescent touched the Atlas and the Caucasus ; it was supreme over Athos, Sinai, Ararat, Mount Carmel, Mount Taurus, Ida, Olympus, Pelion, Hœmus, the Carpathian and the Acroceraunian heights. An empire of more than forty thousand square miles, embracing many of the richest and most beautiful regions of the world, had been acquired by the descendants of Ertoghrul, in three centuries from the time when their forefather wandered a homeless adventurer at the head of less than five hundred fighting men.

Solyman divided this empire into twenty-one governments, which were again subdivided into 250 Sanjaks.[1] The governments were, 1st, Roumelia, under which term were then comprised all the Ottoman continental possessions in Europe south of the Danube : these included Ancient Greece, Macedonia, Thrace, Epirus, Illyria, Dalmatia, and Mœsia; 2. The islands of the Archipelago : this government was vested in the Capitan Pacha; 3. Algiers and its territory ; 4. Tripoli in Africa; 5. Ofen, comprising the conquered portions of Western Hungary ; 6. Temeswar, combining the Bannat, Transylvania, and the eastern part of Hungary ; 7. Anatolia, a title commonly given to the whole of Asia Minor, but here applied to the north-western part of the Peninsula, which includes the ancient Paphlagonia, Bithynia, Mysia, Lydia, Caria, Lycia, Pisidia, and the greater part of Phrygia and Galatia; 8. Caramania, which contains the residue of the last-mentioned ancient countries, and also Lycaonia, Cilicia, and the larger part of Cappadocia; 9. Roum, called also the government of Siwas, and sometimes the government of Amasia : it comprehended part of Cappadocia, and nearly the whole of the ancient Pontus that lay in Asia Minor ; 10. Soulkadr : this embraced the cities of Malatea, Samosata, Elbostan, and the neighbouring districts, and the important passes of the eastern ridges of Mount Taurus ; 11. Trebizond : the governor of this city commanded the coasts round the south-eastern extremity of the Black Sea ; 12. Diarbekir, 13. Van : these two governments included the greater part of Armenia and Kourdistan ; 14. Aleppo, 15. Damascus : these two embraced Syria and Palestine ; 16. Egypt ; 17. Mecca and Medina, and the country of Arabia Petræa ; 18. Yemen and Aden : this government extended over Arabia Felix and a considerable tract along the coast of the Persian Gulf and North-western India ; 19. Bagdad ; 20. Mosul ; 21. Bassorah : these three last contained the conquests which Selim and Solyman had made from the Persians in Mesopotamia and the adjacent southern regions : the Tigris and the Euphrates (after its confluence with the other river) formed their eastern limit, and at the same time

---

[1] The reader may find it useful to compare this list of the divisions of the Turkish empire in Solyman's time, with that given by D'Ohsson, whose "Constitution et Administration de l'empire Ottoman" was published in 1788, and the list of them given by Ubicini, vol. i., Lettre Première.

were the boundaries between the Turkish and the Persian dominions.

Besides the countries that were portioned out in these twenty-one governments, the Sultan was also sovereign over the vassal states of Wallachia, Moldavia, Ragusa, and Crim Tartary. They paid him tribute, which in the cases of the two former were considerable; and the last-named feudatories of the Porte, the Crim Tartars, furnished large and valuable contingents to the Turkish armies. It is not easy to define the territory then belonging to the vassal khans of the Crimea beyond that peninsula. They and their kinsman, the Tartar khans of Astrakhan, were chiefs of numerous and martial tribes that roved amid the steppes to the north of the Euxine, and round the Sea of Azof; but the fluctuation of their almost perpetual wars with the Cossacks, the Muscovites, and each other, prevents the fixing of any territorial boundaries in those regions for any specified epoch.

At least twenty different races of mankind inhabited the vast realms ruled by the great Solyman. The Ottomans themselves, who are now calculated to amount to about thirteen millions,[1] are believed to have declined in number during the last three centuries; and we may take fifteen millions as an approximate enumeration of them in the 16th century, distributed then, as now, very unequally over the empire; Asia containing four-fifths of them, and Asia Minor being especially their chosen home. Three millions of Greeks (the name and the language continue, whatever we may think as to the predominance of the Sclavonic over the Hellenic element in the modern Greek nation), dwelt in the southern portion of European Turkey; a million more were in Asia Minor. The Armenian race, little extended in Europe, was numerous in Asia; and may have formerly amounted, as now, to between two and three millions. The Sclavonic part of the population was the largest. Bulgaria, Servia, Bosnia, Montenegro, the Herzegovine, were chiefly peopled by Sclaves; who were also numerous in Moldavia and Wallachia, and there were many thousands of them in Transylvania and Albania. They may be estimated at six millions and a half at the epoch which we are particularly examining. The race called Rumanys, and supposed to have sprung from the Roman conquerors of the Dacians, and from the conquered Dacians themselves, dwelt principally in Wallachia and Moldavia; their number may then, as now, have been four millions. The Albanians, who term themselves Skipe-tars, and are termed by the Turks Arnauts, were and are a nation

[1] See Ubicini, vol. i. p. 22.

of mountaineers—bold, hardy, and unscrupulous; fond of robbery at home, and warfare abroad. Their number is now estimated at one million and a half, and is likely to have varied but little. The Tartar race formed the population of the Dobruska and of the Crimea, and the countries round the coast of the continent connected with it, Judging from the amount of soldiery supplied by the Crim Tartars to the Ottoman armies, and other circumstances, I should reckon a million and a half as their probable number in the reign of Solyman. The Arabic race was extensively spread through Syria, Arabia, Egypt, and the whole North African coast; and the Arabian subjects of Solyman must have been nearly six millions. The Maronites, the Chaldeans, and the Druses of Syria were together under a million. The Kurds, a race of close affinity to the Persians, can be only guessed to have numbered the like amount; and the Turkomans of Diarbekir and the neighbourhood cannot be numbered at more than 100,000. We have yet to add the Magyars of that part of Hungary which obeyed the Sultan; the Germans of Transylvania, the Berbers of Algeria and the other African provinces, the Copts of Egypt, the Jews, the Tsiganés (who were and are numerous in Moldavia), and the remnants of the Mamelukes. In speaking of an age and of nations in which the numbering of the people was not practised, it is vain to take a retrospective census with any pretensions to minute accuracy; but probably our calculation would not be very erroneous if we considered that from forty-five to fifty millions of subjects obeyed the commands and were guided by the laws of Solyman Kanounni.[1]

[1] In making this estimate, I have used the calculations of Ubicini and others, as to the present state of the population of the Turkish empire. I have added the probable amounts of those provinces which the Porte has lost since Solyman's time; and I have generally set off against the natural tendency to increase, the checks which war, revolt, and other depopulating causes are known to have exercised in the empire during its decline. It is certain that the progress of depopulation in the beginning of the seventeenth century was very rapid. Sir Thomas Roe, who was ambassador at Constantinople for James I., in a letter written by him in 1622, says, "I will tell you a wonder. About sixteen years past, there was a view made of all the villages inhabited in the dominion of the Grand Signior, and the lists were 553,000, and odd; and now this last year before the war of Poland, another being made, they are found to be decreased to 75,000 in all, which is a strange depopulation."—(Sir Thomas Roe's Embassy, p. 66). The first enumeration mentioned by Sir T. Roe would have included the provinces conquered from Persia in the reign of Amurath III., but lost again before 1622. And the smaller number would exclude all those, and also many other former Turkish possessions in Asia, which the Persians then occupied. Probably also every "Esnaf," and rural commune, was

Of the various races which we have enumerated, the Ottomans, the Tartars, the Arabs, the Kurds, the Turkomans, the Mamelukes, and the Berbers held the Mahometan creed, which had been adopted also by large numbers of the Bosnians, Bulgarians, and Albanians. The rest, except the Jews and the Tsiganés, belonged to different branches of the Christian religion, the adherents of the Greek Church being by far the most numerous.

The regular military force of the empire, in the year of the capture of Szigeth, the sunset glory of Solyman's reign, was double that which he found at his accession. He raised the number of the Janissaries to 20,000; and the whole paid and permanent army, including the Royal horseguards and other troops, amounted under him to 48,000 men. Solyman bestowed the greatest attention upon his Janissaries. He formed from among them a corps of invalids, into which only veteran soldiers of high merit, who had grown grey in the service, or had been disabled by wounds, were admitted. Solyman also complimented these formidable troops (and his successors continued the custom) by being himself nominally enrolled in their first regiment, and coming among them at the pay day, and receiving a soldier's pay from the colonel. He honoured another distinguished regiment of the Janissaries by accepting a cup of sherbet from their commander, when he inspected the barrack. This incident also gave rise to a custom for each Sultan, on his accession, to receive a cup of sherbet from the aga or commander-in-chief of the Janissaries, which he returned to that warlike functionary with the words, (significant of Ottoman pride and ambition) "We shall see each other again at the Red Apple," the name which the Turks commonly give to the city of Rome. The number of the feudatory troops, and the irregular levies, at the time of the campaign of Szigeth, exceeded 200,000. The park of artillery contained 300 cannons, and the fleet amounted to 300 sail.

Notwithstanding the improvement in the armies of Western Christendom, to which we have referred when speaking of the epoch of the accession of Solyman, the Ottoman troops were still far superior to them in discipline, and in general equipment. We

---

reckoned separately (see p. 103, *suprà*). Still, after all allowances, I cannot help suspecting the accuracy of the figures of either Sir Thomas or his printers. If we take the first figures to be correct, they would indicate (after allowing for the provinces acquired subsequently to Solyman's death) an aggregate of about five millions of guilds and communes in Solyman's time; and we must then rate the population at more than double the number which I have assigned to it.

have already mentioned the pre-eminence of the Turks of that age in the numerical force and efficiency of their artillery; and the same remark applies to their skill in fortification, and in all the branches of military engineering. The difference between the care that was paid to the physical and moral well-being of Solyman's troops, and the neglect of "the miserable fate of the poor soldier" in his rivals' camps, is still more striking. There are some well-known passages in the writings of Busbequius, the Austrian ambassador at the Ottoman court, who accompanied the Turkish forces in some of their expeditions, in which he contrasts the cleanliness, and the good order of a Turkish camp, the absence of all gambling, and the sobriety and temperance of the men, with the tumult, the drunkenness, the licence, the brawling, and the offensive pollution that reeked in and around Christian tents in that age. It were difficult, even for the most experienced commissary-general of modern times, to suggest improvements on the arrangements and preparations for the good condition and comfort of the Ottoman soldiers, that may be read of in the narratives of Solyman's campaigns. We may mention as one of many beneficial regulations, the establishment of a corps of *Sakkas*, or water-carriers, who attended in the field and on the march to supply water to the weary and wounded soldiers.[1] Compare this with the condition of the Black Bands who followed Bourbon under the banner of the Emperor Charles.

An ample revenue judiciously collected, and prudently though liberally employed, was one decisive advantage which Solyman possessed over his contemporary monarchs. The crown lands of the Sultan at that time produced the large sum of 5,000,000 of ducats. The tithe or land-tax, the capitation tax on the rayas, the customs, and the other regular taxes raised this to between 7,000,000 and 8,000,000. The burden of taxation on the subject was light, and it was only twice in his reign that Solyman levied an additional impost. The necessity caused by the sieges of Belgrade and Rhodes, in the beginning of his reign, and the cost of armaments in the year of the battle of Mohacz, compelled him to impose a poll-tax on all his subjects, without distinction of creed or fortune. But the amount was small on each occasion; and never was a similar measure again necessary. The victorious campaigns of the Sultan were soon made to reimburse their outlays, and still further to enrich the Porte. Large contributions were drawn from Hungary and Transylvania; and Ragusa, Mol-

[1] See Thornton, p. 185.

davia, and Wallachia poured tribute into the treasury of the
Porte. Another less glorious source of revenue was found in the
confiscated goods of the numerous high officers of state, who were
executed during this reign. By invariable usage the property of
those who die thus, is forfeited to the Crown; and the riches of
the Grand Vizier Ibrahim, and other unhappy statesmen of this
age were no unimportant accessions to the ways and means of the
years in which they perished.

We examined the general principles of the Ottoman government when reviewing the institutes of Mahomet the Conqueror.
Every branch of the administration of the empire received improvement from Solyman Kanouni; and, like another great
conqueror and ruler, he has come down to posterity with his
legislative works in his hand. He organised with especial care
the Turkish feudal system of the Ziamets and Timars, reforming
the abuses which had then already begun to prevail. He ordained
that no Timar (small fief) should be allowed to exist if below a
certain value. A number of the smaller fiefs might be united so
as to form a Ziamet (a grand fief), but it was never lawful to
subdivide a Ziamet into Timars, except in the case of a feudatory
who was killed in battle and left more than one son. By permission of the supreme government several persons might hold a
fief as joint tenants; but it was still reckoned a single fief; and
any partition and subdivision not especially authorised by the
Sublime Porte itself was severely punished. The reader who
is familiar with the workings of the feudal system in Western
Europe will perceive how admirably these provisions were adapted
to check the growth of evils, like those, which the practice of
subinfeudation produced in mediæval Christendom. The Turkish
fiefs descended from father to son, like our fees in tail male.
There was no power of devise or alienation : and in default of
male issue of the deceased holder, the Timar or Ziamet reverted
to the Crown. It had been usual before Solyman's time to allow
the Viziers and governors of provinces to make grants of the
lapsed fiefs within their jurisdiction, but Solyman restricted
this to the case of the minor fiefs. None but the Sultan could
make a new grant of a lapsed Ziamet, and in no instance did the
feudatory who received the investiture of a Timar from a subject
pay any homage, or enter into any relation of feudal duty to
the person who invested him. There was no mesne lordship.
The Spahi was the feudal vassal of his Sultan and of his Sultan
alone.

The number of the larger fiefs, or Ziamets, in Solyman's time was 3192 ; that of the smaller fiefs, or Timars, was 50,160.[1] It will be remembered, that each Spahi (or holder of a military fief) was not only bound to render military service himself in person, but, if the value of his fief exceeded a certain specified amount, he was required to furnish and maintain an armed horseman for every multiple of that sum ; or (to adopt the phraseology of our own early institutions), the estate was bound to supply the Crown in time of war with a man-at-arms for each knight's fee. The total feudal array of the empire in the reign of Solyman amounted to 150,000 cavalry, who, when summoned by the Beyler Beys, and Sanjak Beys, joined the army at the appointed place of muster, and served throughout the campaign without pay. We must not only add this number to the 48,000 regularly paid and permanent troops, when we estimate the military force of the Turkish empire in its meridian, but we must also bear in mind the numerous squadrons of Tartar cavalry, which the vassal Khans of the Crimea sent to swell the Turkish armies ; and we must remember the swarms of irregular troops, both horse and foot, the Akindji and the Azabs, which the Sultan's own dominions poured forth to every campaign.[2]

There is no surer proof of the true greatness of Solyman as a ruler, than the care, which, at the same time that he reformed the Turkish feudal system, so as to make it more efficient as an instrument of military force, he bestowed on the condition of those Rayas, who, like the serfs of mediæval Europe, cultivated the lands assigned to the Spahis. The "Kanouni Raya," or "Code of the Rayas," of Solyman, limited and defined the rents and services which the Raya who occupied the ground was to pay to his feudal lord. It is impossible to give any description of this part of the Turkish law which shall apply with uniform correctness to all parts of the Sultan's dominions. But the general effect of Solyman's legislation may be stated to have been that of recognising in the Raya rights of property in the land which he tilled, subject to the payment of certain rents and dues, and the performance of certain services for his feudal superior.[3] The Englishman, who

---

[1] See Thornton, p. 164, and the authorities cited in his notes. See also D'Ohsson and Porter.

[2] See p. 110, *suprà*.

[3] The reader should consult the third chapter of Ranke's "History of Servia," which gives the "Outlines of the Turkish institutions in Servia." That learned writer informs us that in Servia, "the Spahis received a tithe of all that the field, vineyard, or beehive produced ; and also a small tax on each head of cattle. Moreover, they had a right to demand for themselves a tax, called Glawnitza, of two piastres from every married couple.

understands the difference between the position of a modern copy-holder and that of a mediæval villain towards the lord of his manor, will well understand the important boon which the enlightened wisdom of the Turkish lawgiver secured, if he did not originate.   And when the difference of creed between the lawgiver and the Rayas[1] is remembered, and we also bear in mind the fact that Solyman, though not a persecutor like his father, was a very sincere and devout Mahometan, we cannot help feeling that the great Turkish Sultan of the sixteenth century deserves a degree of admiration, which we can accord to none of his crowned contem-

---

To avoid unpleasant inquiries into the extent of their income, many persons added a portion of the tithe to the Glawnitza. In some parts of the country the people agreed to pay the Spahis for each married couple, whether rich or poor, ten piastres a year in full of all dues. This was at once accepted, as it enabled the Spahis to ascertain the amount on which they might annually reckon. But the Spahis cannot properly be considered as a class of nobles. In the villages they had neither estates nor dwellings of their own : they had no right to jurisdiction ; they were not allowed to eject the tenantry by force, nor could they even forbid them from moving and settling elsewhere. What they had to demand, was what might be termed a hereditary stipend, in return for which the duty of serving in war remained unaltered. No real rights of property were ever bestowed on them : for a specific service a certain revenue was granted to them."

There would, however, be need of caution in applying this description to other parts of the Ottoman Empire ; for instance, to Asia Minor, where the number of the Rayas was far less than in Europe, and where the Spahis seem to have generally occupied some part, at least, of their fiefs. Probably the analogy suggested in the text, of our lords of manor and copyhold tenants, will give the clearest and least deceptive idea of the relative positions of the Turkish Spahi and his Raya ; especially as it involves the supposition of a great variety of local customs.

In Egypt, the Ottoman conquerors retained the system which they found established there by the Mameluke sovereigns ; that of granting, or rather of farming out lands to military tenants, who took possession of the lands, and paid the State a certain fixed rent for them ; and then they, and their sub-tenants, the Fellahs, who tilled the ground, took the residue of the profits, in such proportion as the military lords thought fit. Of course, the position of an Egyptian Fellah was far worse than that of the Raya of an Anatolian or Roumelian Spahi.

[1] There might be Mussulman tenants under the Spahis, but in the immense majority of cases, the tillers of Turkish feudal lands were Christians. The name of Solyman's Code on the subject, "Kanouni *Raya*," itself proves this. And it is observable that the number and value of the fiefs in Turkish Europe, where the number of the Ottoman population has always been very small in comparison with that of the Christian, exceeded the number and value of the fiefs in Asia, where the numerical proportion of the followers of the two religions is reversed. See the authorities cited in the note to Thornton, p. 165 ; and see D'Ohsson and Porter.

poraries in that age of melancholy injustice and persecution between Roman Catholic and Protestant throughout the Christian world.

The difference between the lot of the Rayas under their Turkish masters and that of the serfs of Christendom, under their fellow-Christians and fellow-countrymen, who were their lords, was practically shown by the anxiety which the inhabitants of the countries near the Turkish frontier showed to escape from their homes, and live under that Turkish yoke which is frequently represented as having always been so tyrannical. "I have seen," says a writer, who was Solyman's contemporary, "multitudes of Hungarian rustics set fire to their cottages, and fly with their wives and children, their cattle and instruments of labour, to the Turkish territories, where they knew that, besides the payment of the tenths, they would be subject to no imposts or vexations."[1]

Besides the important branches of law and government that have been mentioned, the ceremonial law (a far more serious subject in the East than in Western Europe), the regulations of police, and the criminal law, received the personal attention of the great Sultan, and were modified and remodelled by his edicts. Every subject-matter of legislation is comprised in the great code of Ottoman law, compiled by Solyman's Molla, Ibrahim of Aleppo, which has been in authority down to the present age in the Turkish Empire.[2] Solyman mitigated the severity of the punishments which had previously been appointed for many offences. The extreme slightness of the penalties with which crimes of sensuality were visited by him, is justly blamed as a concession to the favourite vices of the Turkish nation;[3] but, in general, his diminution of the frequency with which the punishments of death and mutilation were inflicted, entitles him to the praise of the modern jurist. The minuteness of the laws, by which he strove to regulate rates of prices and wages, and to prescribe the mode in which articles of food should be prepared and sold, may raise a smile in our more enlightened age; but we should remember how

[1] Leunclavius, apud Elzevir, cited in Thornton and other writers. At a later period, the beginning of the seventeenth century, we learn from Sandys that the inhabitants of the Morea sought eagerly to return to the Turkish from the Venetian rule. Dr. Clarke's Travels inform us how bitterly the natives of the Crimea regretted the change of masters when the Russians succeeded the Turks in the dominion of that country.

[2] Its author fancifully named it "Multeka-ul-ubhur, the Confluence of the Seas," from its oceanic comprehensiveness of the contents of multitudinous libraries.

Von Hammer, vol. ii. p. 357.

full our own statute book is of similar enactments, and how far
our own excise laws still maintain the spirit of vexatious and mis-
chievous interference. Some of the more noticeable laws of Sultan
Solyman are those by which slanderers and tale-bearers are required to make compensation for the mischief caused by their evil-
speaking; false witnesses, forgers, and passers of bad money are
to have the right hand struck off; interest is not to be taken at a
higher rate than eleven per cent.; a fine is imposed for three consecutive omissions of a Mussulman's daily prayer, or a breach of
the solemn fasts; kindness to beasts of burden is enjoined.

Whatever the political economists of the present time may think
of the legislation of Solyman Kanouni as to wages, manufactures,
and retail trade, their highest praises are due to the enlightened
liberality with which the foreign merchant was welcomed in his
empire. The earliest of the contracts, called capitulations, which
guarantee to the foreign merchant in Turkey full protection for
person and property, the free exercise of his religion, and the safeguard of his own laws administered by functionaries of his own
nation, was granted by Solyman to France in 1535.[1] An ex-

---

[1] There is a remarkable State paper published by the Ottoman government, 1832, in the *Moniteur Ottoman*, justly claiming credit for their nation
on this important subject. Mr. Urquhart cites, in his "Turkey and her
Resources," the following passages from this official declaration of Turkish
commercial principles:

"It has often been repeated, that the Turks are encamped in Europe; it
is certainly not their treatment of strangers that has given rise to this idea
of precarious occupancy; the hospitality they offer their guest is not that of
the tent, nor is it that of the Turkish laws; for the Mussulman code, in its
double civil and religious character, is inapplicable to those professing
another religion; but they have done more, they have granted to the
stranger the safeguard of his own laws, exercised by functionaries of his
own nation. In this privilege, so vast in benefits and in consequences,
shines forth the admirable spirit of true and lofty hospitality.

"In Turkey, and there alone, does hospitality present itself, great, noble,
and worthy of its honourable name; not the shelter of a stormy day, but
that hospitality which, elevating itself from a simple movement of humanity
to the dignity of a political reception, combines the future with the present.
When the stranger has placed his foot on the land of the Sultan, he is
saluted guest (*mussafir /*). To the children of the West who have confided
themselves to the care of the Mussulman, hospitality has been granted, with
those two companions, civil liberty according to the laws, commercial
liberty according to the laws of nature and of reason.

"Good sense, tolerance, and hospitality, have long ago done for the Ottoman Empire what the other states of Europe are endeavouring to effect by
more or less happy political combinations. Since the throne of the Sultans
has been elevated at Constantinople, commercial prohibitions have been unknown; they opened all the ports of their empire to the commerce, to the
manufactures, to the territorial produce of the occident, or, to say better

tremely moderate custom duty was the only impost on foreign
merchandise; and the costly and vexatious system of prohibitive
and protective duties has been utterly unknown among the Ottomans.   No stipulation for reciprocity ever clogged the wise
liberality of Turkey in her treatment of the foreign merchant who
became her resident, or in her admission of his ships and his
goods.

We have already observed, in referring to the institutes of
Mahomet II.,[1] the authority which the Ulema, or educators and
men learned in the law, possess in Turkey, and the liberal provisions made there for national education.   Solyman was a munifi-
cent founder of schools and colleges; and he introduced many improvements into the educational discipline and rank of the Ulema.
But the great boon conferred by him on this order, and the peculiar homage paid by him to the dignity of learning, consisted in
establishing, as rules of the Ottoman government, the exemption
of all the Ulema from taxation, and the secure descent of their
estates from father to son; the property of a member of this body
being in all cases privileged from confiscation.   Hence it has
arisen, that the only class among the Turks in which hereditary

---

of the whole world.   Liberty of commerce has reigned here without limits,
as large, as extended, as it was possible to be.   Never has the Divan
dreamed, under any pretext of national interest, or even of reciprocity, of
restricting that facility, which has been exercised, and is to this day in the
most unlimited sense, by all the nations who wish to furnish a portion of
the consumption of this vast empire, and to share in the produce of its
territory.

"Here every object of exchange is admitted and circulates without meeting other obstacle than the payment of an infinitely small portion of the
value to the Custom-house.

"The extreme moderation of the duties is the complement of this régime
of commercial liberty; and in no portion of the globe are the officers charged
with the collection of more confiding facility for the valuations, and of so
decidedly conciliatory a spirit in every transaction regarding commerce.

"Away with the supposition that these facilities granted to strangers are
concessions extorted from weakness!   The dates of the contracts termed
capitulations, which establish the rights actually enjoyed by foreign merchants, recall periods at which the Mussulman power was altogether predominant in Europe.   The first capitulation which France obtained was in
1535, from Solyman the Canonist (the Magnificent).

"The dispositions of these contracts have become antiquated, the fundamental principles remain.   Thus, three hundred years ago, the Sultans, by
an act of munificence and of reason, anticipated the most ardent desires of
civilised Europe, and proclaimed unlimited freedom of commerce."

The remarks of Ubicini (vol. i. p. 393) on this subject, are also well worth
consulting.

[1] See p. 104, *suprà.*

wealth is accumulated in families, is furnished by the educational and legal professions; and the only aristocracy that can be said to exist there, is an aristocracy of the brain.

The splendour of the buildings, with which Solyman adorned Constantinople, suggests a point of comparison between the great Turkish legislator and the Roman Emperor who ruled ten centuries before him, in addition to that which their codes naturally bring before the mind. It would be dishonouring to Solyman to carry the parallel between him and Justinian further than as regards architecture and legislation; nor can there be any balancing of the courage and magnanimity of the victor of Mohacz, with the cowardice and meanness of the unworthy master of Belisarius and personal ringleader of the factions of the Circus. But the long list, in which the Oriental historians enumerate the sumptuous edifices raised by Solyman in the seven-hilled city of the Bosphorus, recalls the similar enumeration which Procopius has made of the architectural splendours of Justinian. And it was not only in the capital, but at Bagdad, Koniah, Kaffa, Damascus, and other cities that the taste and grandeur of Solyman were displayed. Besides the numerous mosques which were founded or restored by his private liberality, he decorated his empire and provided for the temporal welfare of his subjects by numerous works of practical utility. Among them the great aqueduct of Constantinople, the bridge of Tschekmedji, and the restored aqueducts of Mecca are mentioned as the most beneficial and magnificent.

The names of the poets, the historians, the legal and scientific writers who flourished under Solyman, would fill an ample page; but it would be one of little interest to us, while Turkish literature remains so generally unknown in Western Europe, even through the medium of translations.[1] But, because unknown, it must not be assumed to be unreal; and Solyman was as generous and discerning a patron of literary merit, as any of those sovereigns of Western Europe who have acquired for their ages and courts the much-coveted epithet of "Augustan."

Solyman's own writings are considered to hold an honourable station, though not among the highest in his nation's literature. His poems are said to be dignified in sentiment and correct in expression; and his journals, in which he noted the chief events of each day during his campaigns, are highly serviceable to the investigator of history. They prove the Sultan's possession of

[1] Von Hammer's work on Ottoman literature is an honourable exception; and a series of very valuable letters, on the same subject, by Von Hammer, appeared in the English "Athenæum" some years ago.

14

qualities, which are of far more value in a sovereign than are the accomplishments of a successful author. They show his sense of duty, his industry, and his orderly and unremitting personal attention to the civil as well as the military affairs of the vast empire that had been committed to his charge. Faults, deplorable faults, are unquestionably to be traced in his reign. The excessive influence which he allowed his favourite Sultana to acquire; the cruel deaths of his children, and of so many statesmen, whom he gave over to the executioner, are heavy stains on his memory. His own countrymen have pointed out the defects in his government. Kotchi Bey, who wrote in the reign of Amurath IV. (1623), and who is termed by Von Hammer the Turkish Montesquieu, assigns in his work on the "Decline of the Ottoman Empire," which he traces up to the reign of the first Solyman, among the causes of that decline—1st, the cessation in Solyman's time of the regular attendance of the Sultan at the meetings of the Divan; 2nd, the habit then introduced of appointing men to high stations who had not previously passed through a gradation of lower offices; 3rd, the venality and corruption first practised by Solyman's son-in-law and Grand Vizier, Roostem, who sold to people of the lowest character and capacity the very highest civil offices, though the appointment to all military ranks, high or low, was still untainted by bribery or other dishonest influence. The fourth censure passed by Kotchi Bey on Solyman is for his evil example in exceeding the limits of wise liberality by heaping wealth upon the same favourite Vizier, and allowing him not only to acquire enormous riches, but to make them, by an abuse of the Turkish mortmain law, inalienable in his family. This was done by transforming his estates into Vaks or Vakoufs; that is to say, by settling his property on some mosque or other religious foundation, which took from it a small quit-rent, and held the rest in trust for the donor and his family. While admitting the justice of these charges of the Oriental historian, Von Hammer exposes the groundlessness of the censure, which European writers have passed upon Solyman, when accusing him of having introduced the custom of shutting up the young princes of the House of Othman in the seraglio, instead of training them to lead armies and govern provinces. He points out that all the sons of Solyman, who grew up to manhood, administered pachalics under him, and that one of his last acts before his death was to appoint Amurath, his grandson, to the government of Magnesia.

In the same spirit in which Arrian sums up the character of Alexander the Great,[1] the German historian rightly warns us, when

[1] Arrian, Vit. Al., lib. vii. 28.

estimating that of Solyman the Great, not to fix our attention exclusively on the blamable actions of his life, but to remember also the bright and noble qualities which adorned him. As a man, he was warm-hearted and sincere, and honourably pure from the depraved sensuality which has disgraced too many of his nation. We must remember his princely courage, his military genius, his high and enterprising spirit, his strict observance of the laws of his religion without any taint of bigoted persecution, the order and economy which he combined with so much grandeur and munificence, his liberal encouragement of art and literature, his zeal for the diffusion of education, the conquests by which he extended his empire, and the wise and comprehensive legislation with which he provided for the good government of all his subjects; let him be thus taken for all in all, and we shall feel his incontestable right to the title of a great sovereign, which now for three centuries he has maintained.

CHAPTER XI.

SELIM II. — HIS DEGENERACY — PEACE WITH AUSTRIA — FIRST
CONFLICT BETWEEN TURKS AND RUSSIANS — CONQUEST OF
CYPRUS — BATTLE OF LEPANTO — OULOUDJ ALI'S ENERGY —
DEATH OF SELIM.[1]

SOLYMAN the Great, the Magnificent, the Lawgiver, the Lord of
his Age, was succeeded by a prince to whom his own national
historians give the epithet of "Selim the Sot." The ignoble vices
of this prince (to secure whose accession so much and such dear
blood had been shed) had attracted the sorrowful notice and drawn
down the indignant reprimand of the old Sultan in his latter
years; but there was now no brother to compete for the throne
with Selim; and on the 25th of September, 1566, the sabre of
Othman was girt for the first time on a sovereign, who shrank
from leading in person the armies of Islam, and wasted in low
debauchery the hours which his predecessors had consecrated to
the duties of the state. The effects of this fatal degeneracy were
not immediately visible. The perfect organisation, civil and military, in which Solyman had left the empire, cohered for a time
after the strong hand, which had fashioned and knit it together
for nearly half a century, was withdrawn. There was a numerous
body of statesmen and generals who had been trained under the
great Sultan: and thus somewhat of his spirit was preserved in
the realm, until they had passed away, and another generation
arisen, which knew not Solyman. Foremost of these was the
Grand Vizier Mohammed Sokolli, who had victoriously concluded
the campaign of Szigeth after Solyman's death; and who, fortunately for Selim and his kingdom, acquired and maintained an
ascendency over the weak mind of the young Sultan, which was
not indeed always strong enough to prevent the adoption of evil
measures, or to curb the personal excesses of Selim's private life,
but which checked the progress of anarchy, and maintained the
air of grandeur in enterprise and of vigour in execution, by which
the Sublime Porte had hitherto been distinguished.

[1] See Von Hammer, books 35, 36.

An armistice was concluded with the Emperor Maximilian in 1568, on the terms that each party should retain possession of what it then occupied; and there was now for many years an unusual pause in the war between the Houses of Hapsburg and Othman.   The great foreign events of Selim's reign are the attempts to conquer Astrakhan, and unite the Don and the Volga; the conquest of Cyprus; and the naval war of the battle of Lepanto.   The first of these is peculiarly interesting, because the Turks were then for the first time brought into armed collision with the Russians.

In the middle of the sixteenth century, while the Ottoman Empire, then at the meridian of its glory, was the terror and admiration of the world; the Russian was slowly and painfully struggling out of the degradation and ruin, with which it had been afflicted by two centuries and a half of Tartar conquest.   The craft and courage of Ivan III. and Vasili Ivanovich had, between 1480 and 1533, emancipated Moscow from paying tribute to the Khans of Kipchakh; and, by annexing other Russian principalities to that of Muscovy, these princes had formed an united Russia, which extended from Kief to Kasan, and as far as Siberia and Norwegian Lapland.   Even thus early the Grand Dukes, or, as they began to style themselves, the Czars[1] of Muscovy, seem to have cherished ambitious projects of reigning at Constantinople.   Ivan III. sought out and married Sophia, the last princess of the Greek Imperial family, from which the conquering Ottomans had wrested Byzantium.   From that time forth, the two-headed eagle, which had been the imperial cognisance of the Emperors of Constantinople, has been assumed by the Russian sovereigns as their symbol of dominion.[2]   During the minority of Ivan the Terrible (who succeeded in 1533) a period of anarchy ensued in Russia, but on that Prince assuming the government, the vigour of the state was

[1] "This title is not a corruption of the word *Cæsar*, as many have supposed, but is an old Oriental word which the Russians acquired through the Slavonic translation of the Bible, and which they bestowed at first on the Greek Emperors, and afterwards on the Tartar Khans.   In Persia it signifies *throne, supreme authority*; and we find it in the termination of the names of the kings of Assyria and Babylon, such as Phalas*sar*, Nabonas*sar*," &c.— Kelly, "Hist. Russia," p. 125 *n.*, citing Karamsin.   Von Hammer, in his last note to his 31st book, says, "The title *Czar* or *Tzar*, is an ancient title of Asiatic sovereigns.   We find an instance of it in the title 'The Schar,' of the sovereign of Gurdistan; and in that of Tzarina (Ζαρίνη) of the Scythians."

[2] "Until after the marriage of Ivan III. with Sophia, the cognisance of the grand princes of Moscow had always been a figure of St. George killing the dragon."—Kelly's "Hist. Russia," p. 125 *n.*

restored ; the Khanates of Astrakhan and Kasan were conquered
and finally annexed to Russia ; the Don Cossacks were united with
the empire, and Yermak, one of their chiefs, invaded and acquired
for Ivan the vast regions of Şiberia. The extent of Russia at Ivan's
accession, was 37,000 German square miles : at his death, it was
144,000. But so little was Russia then heeded or known in Western
Europe, that the charter given by Philip and Mary to the first
company of English merchants trading thither purports to be
granted "upon the discovery of the said country;" likening it to
some region of savages which civilised man might then tread for
the first time amid the American wilderness. Yet even at that
period, those who watched the immense extent of the crude
materials for warlike power, which the Czar of Muscovy possessed,
the numbers, the rugged hardihood of his people, their implicit
obedience to their autocrat, their endurance of privations, and the
nature of the country so difficult for an invader, expressed their
forebodings of the peril to which the independence of other states
might be exposed by Muscovite ambition, if once those rude masses
acquired the arms and the discipline of civilised war.[1] It is melancholy to recognise in the fate of Poland and so many other countries
the truth of the words used by the Polish King, Sigismund, nearly
three centuries ago, when, in remonstrating with England for supplying the Czar with military engineers and stores, he called him
"the Muscovite, the hereditary enemy of all free nations."[2]

[1] Richard Chancellor, who sailed with Sir Hugh Willoughby in search
of a North-East Passage, and who travelled from Archangel up to Moscow,
and afterwards resided at Ivan's court, in his curious account of the
Russians (published in "Hakluyt's Voyages," vol. i. p. 239), after mentioning
the immense number of troops which the Muscovite Duke raised for war,
and their endurance of hard fare and cold, graphically describes their want
of discipline. He says : "They are men without all order in the field, for
they run hurling on heaps." He afterwards says : "Now, what might be
made of these men, if they were broken to order, and knowledge of civil
warres ? If this prince had within his country such men as could make
them understand the thing aforesaid, I do believe that two of the best or
greatest princes in Christendom were not well able to match with him, considering the greatness of his power, and the hardiness of his people, and
straite living both of man and horse, and the small charges which his warres
stand him in." In another page (240), Chancellor says of the Russians : "If
they knew their strength, no man were able to make match with them ; nor
they that dwell near them should have any rest of them. But I think it is
not God's will. For I may compare them to a horse, that knoweth not his
strength, whom a little child ruleth and guideth with a bridle, for all
his great strength ; that if he did [know it] neither man nor child
could rule him."

[2] "Hostem non modo regni nostri temporarium sed etiam omnium natio-
num liberarum hæreditarium Moscum."   The letter of Sigismund to Queen

The Russians, at the time of Selim's accession, had been in-volved in fierce and frequent wars with the Sultan's vassals, the Crim Tartars ; but the Porte had taken no part in these contests. But the bold genius of the Vizier Sokolli now attempted the reali-sation of a project, which, if successful, would have barred the southern progress of Russia, by firmly planting the Ottoman power on the banks of the Don and the Volga, and along the shores of the Caspian Sea. The Turkish armies, in their invasions of Persia, had always suffered severely during their marches along the sterile and mountainous regions of Upper Armenia and Mazer-bijan. Some disputes with Persia had arisen soon after Selim's accession, which made a war with that kingdom seem probable; and Sokolli proposed to unite the rivers Don and Volga by a canal, and then send a Turkish armament up the sea of Azoph and the Don, thence across by the intended channel to the Volga, and then down the latter river into the Caspian; from the southern shores of which sea the Ottomans might strike at Tabriz and the heart of the Persian power. Those two mighty rivers, the Don and the Volga, run towards each other, the one from the north-west, the other from the north-east, for many hundred leagues, until they are within thirty miles of junction. They then diverge; and the Don (the "extremus Tanais" of the ancients), pours its waters into the sea of Azoph, near the city of that name ; the Volga blends with the Caspian, at a little distance from the city of Astrakhan, which is built on the principal branch of the Delta of that river. The project of uniting them by a canal is said to have been one entertained by Seleucus Nicator, one of the ablest of the successors of Alexander the Great. It was now revived by the Grand Vizier of Selim II.; and though the cloud of hostility with Persia passed over, Sokolli determined to persevere with the scheme : the immense commercial and poli-tical advantages of which, if completed, to the Ottoman Empire, were evident to the old statesman of Solyman the Great. Azoph already belonged to the Turks, but in order to realise the great project entertained, it was necessary to occupy Astrakhan also.

Elizabeth is cited in the recent work of the Russian Dr. Hamel on "England and Russia." In another letter of Sigismund's, translated by Hakluyt (see Hamel, p. 185), the Polish King says of the Czar : "We seemed hitherto to vanquish him only in this, that he was rude of arts and ignorant of policies. If so be that this navigation to the Narva continue, what shall be unknowen to him ? The Moscovite, made more perfect in warlike affaires with engines of warre and shippes, will slay or make bound all that shall withstand him, which God defend."

Accordingly, 3000 Janissaries and 20,000 horse were sent to besiege Astrakhan, and a co-operative force of 30,000 Tartars was ordered to join them, and to aid in making the canal. 5000 Janissaries and 3000 pioneers were at the same time sent to Azoph to commence and secure the great work at its western extremity. But the generals of Ivan the Terrible did their duty to their stern master ably in this emergency. The Russian garrison of Astrakhan sallied on its besiegers, and repulsed them with considerable loss. And a Russian army, 15,000 strong, under Prince Serebinoff, came suddenly on the workmen and Janissaries near Azoph, and put them to headlong flight. It was upon this occasion that the first trophies won from the Turks came into Russian hands. An army of Tartars, which marched to succour the Turks, was also entirely defeated by Ivan's forces; and the Ottomans, dispirited by their losses and reverses, withdrew altogether from the enterprise. Their Tartar allies, who knew that the close neighbourhood of the Turks would ensure their own entire subjection to the Sultan, eagerly promoted the distaste, which the Ottomans had acquired for Sokolli's project, by enlarging on the horrors of the climate of Muscovy, and especially on the peril, in which the short summer nights of those northern regions placed either the soul or the body of the true believer. As the Mahometan law requires the evening prayer to be said two hours after sunset, and the morning prayer to be repeated at the dawn of day, it was necessary that a Moslem should, in a night of only three hours long (according to the Tartars), either lose his natural rest, or violate the commands of his Prophet. The Turks gladly re-embarked, and left the unpropitious soil; but a tempest assailed their flotilla on its homeward voyage, and only 7000 of their whole force ever returned to Constantinople.

Russia was yet far too weak to enter on a war of retaliation with the Turks. She had subdued the Tartar Khanates of K san and Astrakhan; but their kinsmen of the Crimea were still formidable enemies to the Russians, even without Turkish aid. It was only two years after the Ottoman expedition to the Don and Volga, that the Khan of the Crimea made a victorious inroad into Russia, took Moscow by storm, and sacked the city (1571). The Czar Ivan had, in 1570, sent an ambassador, named Nossolitof, to Constantinople, to complain of the Turkish attack on Astrakhan, and to propose that there should be peace, friendship, and alliance between the two empires. Nossolitof, in addressing the Viziers, dwelt much on the toleration which his master showed to Mahometans in his dominions, as a proof that the Czar was no

enemy to the faith of Islam. The Russian ambassador was favourably received at the Sublime Porte, and no further hostilities
between the Turks and Russians took place for nearly a century.
But the Ottoman pride and contempt for Russia were shown by
the Sultan omitting to make the customary inquiry of Nossolitof
respecting his royal master's health, and by the Czar's representative not receiving the invitation to a dinner before audience,
which was usually sent to ambassadors.

Besides his project for uniting the Volga and the Don, the
Grand Vizier Sokolli had revived the oft-formed project of opening a communication between the Red Sea and the Mediterranean.
Sokolli grandly designed to make such a channel through the
Isthmus of Suez, as would enable the Ottoman fleets to sail from
sea to sea. His schemes in this quarter were delayed by a revolt
which broke out in Arabia, and was not quelled without a difficult and sanguinary war. And when that important province was
brought back to submission, the self-willed cupidity and violence
of Sultan Selim himself involved the Porte in a war with Venice
and other Christian states, for the sake of acquiring the island of
Cyprus, which he had coveted while he was governor of Kutahia
in his father's lifetime.[1]   There was a treaty of peace between
Venice and the Porte; but Selim obtained from his Mufti
Ebousououd a Fetva authorising him to attack Cyprus, in open
violation of the treaty.   Cyprus had at one time been under
Mahometan rulers; and the Turkish authorities now proclaimed
and acted on the principle, that the sovereign of Islam may at any
time break a treaty, for the sake of reconquering from the misbelievers a country, which has formerly belonged to the territory
of Islam.[2]

The Grand Vizier Sokolli earnestly, but vainly, opposed the
war with Venice. His influence was counteracted by that of the
infamous Lala Mustapha, who had in Solyman's reign been Selim's
instrument in the foul practices by which Prince Bajazet and his
family were destroyed. Lala Mustapha obtained the command of
the expedition against Cyprus; and the island was subdued by
the Turks (1570-71), though fifty thousand of them perished to

---

[1] It seems that Selim, like Cassio, found the attraction of Cyprus wine
irresistible.   A Jew, named Joseph Nassy, had been Selim's boon companion, and persuaded him that he ought to be master of the isle in which the
juice of the grape was so delicious. See Von Hammer, vol. ii. p. 400.

[2] The case laid by Selim before the Mufti, and the answer of that functionary, are given at length by Von Hammer, vol. ii. p. 402. The reader
will observe how utterly opposed this principle is to the doctrine laid down
in the Turkish military code, cited page 113, *suprà*.

effect its conquest. The conduct of the war of Cyprus was as disgracefully treacherous and cruel on the part of the Turks, as its inception had been flagrantly unjust. The Venetian commandant, Bragadino, who had defended Famagosta, the chief stronghold of the island, with heroic valour and constancy, was subjected to the grossest indignities, and at last flayed alive, though he had surrendered on the faith of a capitulation, by which the garrison were to march out with all their arms and property, and to be transported in Turkish vessels to Candia. The charges which Lala Mustapha made against the Venetian general of personal insolence to himself in an interview after the capitulation, of cruelty to the Turkish prisoners during the siege, and of having formerly put Mahometan pilgrims to death, could, even if true, be no justification for the treacherous and inhuman treatment, of which Bragadino was made the victim. But the modern German historian, who narrates with just horror and indignation the crime of the Turkish commander, observes that such an act was too much in the spirit of the age. Selim II. was the contemporary of Charles IX. and Ivan the Cruel. The massacre of St. Bartholomew took place not a year before the murder of Bragadino ; and scarcely another year had passed away when, at the capture of the fortress of Wittenstein, in Finland, the garrison was cut in pieces by the Russians, and the commandant tied to a spear and roasted alive. If this took place in France and Finland, what was to be expected in Turkey under the government of a young prince who had been the murderer of his own brother, and who, in direct violation of the law of Mahomet, was an open drunkard, and gave free scope to every vice ? We might (if crimes could excuse each other), in addition to the instances of contemporaneous cruelty cited by Von Hammer, refer to the horrors practised by the Spaniards under Don Ferdinand of Toledo, at Naarden, in 1572, in insolent defiance of the terms of a treaty of surrender.[1] But it is both unprofitable and revolting to enter at length on a retrospective study of comparative cruelty. Such deeds bring shame, not only upon particular nations of mankind, but upon human nature in general.

The fall of Cyprus, the unscrupulous violence with which it had been attacked, and the immense preparations in the Turkish seaports and arsenals, now raised anxious alarm, not only at Venice, but all along the Christian shores of the Mediterranean. The Pope Pius V. succeeded in forming a maritime league, of which the Spaniards, the Venetians, and the Knights of Malta were the

---

[1] See vol. i. p. 195, of Mrs. Davies's admirable "History of Holland."

principal members ; and at the head of it was placed Don John of
Austria, the natural son of Charles V., and one of the most renowned commanders of the age.

The confederate fleets mustered at Messina early in the autumn
of 1571. The force led thither by Don John consisted of seventy
Spanish galleys, six Maltese, and three of Savoy. The Papal squadron, under Marc Colonna, added twelve galleys. The Venetian
Admiral Veniero brought 108 galleys, and six huge galeasses, or
mahons, of a larger size and carrying a heavier weight of metal
than had yet been known in Mediterranean warfare. Great care
had been paid by all the confederates to the proper selection of
their crews and the equipment of their vessels. Nobly born
volunteers from all parts of Roman Catholic Christendom had
flocked together to serve under so celebrated a chief as Don John,
and in such an honourable enterprise : and the Christian fleet
sailed across to seek its enemies eastward of the Ionian Gulf, in
the highest state of efficiency.

The Turkish naval forces were assembled in the Gulf of Corinth.
The Capitan Pacha, Mouezinzade Ali, was commander-in-chief ;
and under him were the well-known Ouloudj Ali, Beyler Bey of
Algiers ; Djaffer Pacha, Beyler Bey of Tripoli ; Hassan Pacha, the
son of Khaireddin Barbarossa, and fifteen other Beys of maritime
Sanjaks, each of whom was entitled to hoist his banner on his
galley, as a Prince of the Sea. The troops embarked on board
the fleet were commanded by Pertew Pacha. The fleet amounted
to 240 galleys, and sixty vessels of smaller size. Ouloudj Ali and
Pertew Pacha represented to the commander-in-chief that the fleet
was hastily and imperfectly manned, and that it was imprudent to
fight a general battle until it was in a better state of equipment.
But Mouezinzade's courage prevailed over his discretion, and the
destruction of his fleet was the result.

On the 7th October, 1571, a little after noon, the Christian
fleet appeared near the entrance of the Gulf of Patras, off the
little islands of Curzolari (the ancient Echinades), which lie at the
mouth of the Aspro Potamo (the Achelous), on the Albanian
shore. The Ottoman fleet sailed out of the Gulf of Lepanto to
encounter them, and formed in line of battle, Ouloudj Ali commanding the left wing ; Mohammed Schaoulah, Bey of Negropont,
heading the right wing ; and the Capitan Pacha, aided by Pertew
Pacha, being in the centre. Don John drew up his chief force in
the centre in the form of a crescent. The Prince of Parma (afterwards so well known in Holland, and the intended conqueror of
England), the Admiral of Savoy, Caraccioli, the Neapolitan

admiral, and other illustrious leaders were in command of it.
The Marquis of Santa Croce commanded a squadron that was
stationed in the rear of the main line as a reserve. A division of
fifty-three galleys, under the Venetian proveditor, Barbarigo,
formed the right wing ; and the left wing consisted of fifty-four
galleys, under Jean André Doria, nephew of the great admiral of
the Emperor Charles. Don John took his own station in advance
of the centre line, and the other two admirals of the fleet, Colonna
and Veniero, were at his sides. The Turkish Capitan Pacha
seeing this, brought forward his own galley and those of Pertew
Pacha and his treasurer, to answer the challenge of the three
admiral galleys of the Christians, that thus stood forward between
the battles, like the Promachi in the conflicts of the Homeric
heroes.

Don John showed his gallantry by thus taking the post of
danger ; but he also showed his skill by placing the six great
Venetian galeasses like redoubts at intervals in front of the confederate fleet. The Turks had less fear of these huge vessels than
might have been justified by the event of the day ; but there was
a pause before they began the attack, and each fleet lay motionless
for a time, regarding with admiration and secret awe the strength
and the splendour of its adversary's array. At length the Turkish
admiral fired a gun, charged with powder only, as a challenge to
begin the action. A ball from one of Don John's heaviest cannon
whistled through the Ottoman rigging in answer ; the Turks
rowed forward with loud shouts amid the clangour of their drums
and fifes to the attack ; and the action, commencing on the
Christian left, soon became general along the line. The large
Venetian galeasses now proved of the utmost service to the
Christian fleet. The Turkish galleys in passing them were
obliged to break their order ; and the fire kept up by the Venetian
artillerymen from the heavy ordnance of the galeasses was more
destructive than ever yet had been witnessed in naval gunnery.
Still the Turks pressed forward and engaged the Christian left and
centre with obstinate courage. The two high admirals of the
conflicting fleets, Don John and Mouezinzade Ali, encountered
each other with equal gallantry. Their vessels clashed together,
and then lay closely locked for upwards of two hours, during which
time the 300 Janissaries and 100 arquebusiers of the Turk, and the
400 chosen arquebusiers who served on board Don John's ship,
fought with the most determined bravery. The two other admiral
galleys of the Christians had come to the support of Don John, and
the Capitan Pacha's galley was similarly aided by her consorts ; so

that these six ships formed a compact mass in the midst of the
battle, like that which was grouped round Nelson in the *Victory,*
by the *Temeraire,* the *Redoubtable,* and the *Neptune* at the battle of
Trafalgar. The death of Mouezinzade, who fell, shot dead by a
musket ball, decided the memorable contest. The Turkish
admiral galley was carried by boarding; and when Santa Croce
came on to support the first line with the reserve, the whole
Ottoman centre was broken, and the defeat soon extended to the
right wing. In their left Ouloudj Ali was more successful. He
outmanœuvred Doria; turned his wing; and, attacking his ships
when disordered and separated one from another, Ouloudj Ali
captured fifteen Maltese and Venetian galleys, and with his own
hand struck off the head of the commandant of Messina. But
seeing that the day was irreparably lost for Turkey, Ouloudj
collected forty of his best galleys, pushed with them through the
Christian vessels that tried to intercept him, and stood safely out
to sea. They were the only Turkish vessels that escaped. The
Ottomans lost in this great battle 260 ships; of which ninety-four
were sunk, burnt, or run aground and destroyed upon the coast,
the rest were captured and divided among the allies. Thirty
thousand Turks were slain; and 15,000 Christians, who had served
as galley slaves in the Ottoman fleet, were rescued from captivity.

The confederates lost fifteen galleys and 8000 men. Many
princely and noble names are recorded in the lists of the killed
and wounded of that day; but there is none which we read with
more interest than that of Cervantes. The author of "Don
Quixote" served at Lepanto, as a volunteer in the regiment of
Moncada, which was distributed among part of the fleet. On the
day of the battle Cervantes was stationed on board the galley
Marquesa, and though suffering severely with illness, he distinguished himself greatly in the action, during which he received
two arquebuss wounds, one of which maimed his left hand for
life. He often referred with just pride to the loss of his hand,
and ever rejoiced at having been present at the glorious action at
Lepanto; "on that day so fortunate to Christendom, when" (in his
own words) "all nations were undeceived of their error in believing
that the Turks were invincible at sea."[1]

The glories of the "Fight of Lepanto" thrilled Christendom
with rapture; and they have for centuries been the favourite
themes of literature and art. But the modern German historian
well observes, that we ought to think with sadness of the nullity
of the results of such a battle. After occupying three weeks in

[1] "Don Quixote," book iv. c. 12.

dividing the spoils of Lepanto, and nearly coming to blows over them, the Christian squadrons returned to their respective ports, to be thanked, lauded, and dismissed. Meanwhile, the indefatigable Ouloudj Ali, with the squadron which he had saved from Lepanto, gleaned together the Turkish galleys that lay in the different ports of the Archipelago ; and, at the end of December, sailed proudly into the port of Constantinople at the head of a fleet of eighty-seven sail. In recompense of his zeal, he received the rank of Capitan Pacha ; and the Sultan changed his name of Ouloudj into Kilidj, which means "The Sword." The veteran Admiral, Pialé, the hero of Djerbé, was yet alive ; and under his and Kilidj Ali's vigorous and skilful directions, a new fleet was constructed and launched before the winter was past. While the rejoicing Christians built churches, the resolute Turks built docks. The effect was, that before June, a Turkish fleet of 250 sail, comprising eight galeasses or mahons of the largest size, sailed forth to assert the dominion of the seas. The confederate Christian powers, after long delays, collected a force numerically superior to the Ottoman ; but, though two indecisive encounters took place, they were unable to chase Kilidj Ali from the western coasts of Greece, nor could the Duke of Parma undertake the siege of Modon, which had been designed as the chief operation for that year. It was evident, that though the Christian confederates could win a battle, the Turk was still their superior in a war.[1] The Venetians sought peace in 1573, and in order to obtain it, consented not only that the Sultan should retain Cyprus, but that Venice should pay him his expenses of the conquest. It was not unnaturally remarked by those, who heard the terms of the treaty, that it sounded as if the Turks had gained the battle of Lepanto.

After Venice had made peace with the Porte, Don John undertook an expedition with the Spanish fleet against Tunis, which Ouloudj Ali had conquered during the year in which Cyprus was attacked. Don John succeeded in capturing the city, which was the more easy, inasmuch as the citadel had continued in the power of the Spaniards. Don John built a new fortress and left a powerful garrison in Tunis ; but, eighteen months after his departure, his old enemy Kilidj Ali reappeared there ; and after a

---

[1] The Venetian envoy, Barbaro, endeavoured to open negotiations at Constantinople in the winter after the battle of Lepanto. The Vizier, in reference to the loss of the Turkish fleet, and the conquest of Cyprus, said to him : "There is a great difference between our loss and yours. You have shaved our chin ; but our beard is growing again. We have lopped off your arm ; and you can never replace it."

sharp siege, made the Sultan again master of the city and citadel, and stormed Don John's new castle. Tunis now, like Algiers and Tripoli, became an Ottoman government. The effectual authority which the Porte exercised over these piratical states of North Africa (which are often called the Barbaresque Regencies) grew weaker in course of time; but the tie of allegiance was not entirely broken: and though the French have in our own time seized Algiers, the Sultan is still sovereign of Tripoli and Tunis, the scenes of the successful valour of Dragut and Kilidj Ali.

Selim the Sot died not long after the recovery of Tunis; and the manner of his death befitted the manner of his life. He had drunk off a bottle of Cyprus wine at a draught, and on entering the bath-room with the fumes of his favourite beverage in his head, he slipped and fell on the marble floor, receiving an injury of the skull which brought on a fatal fever (1574). He showed once a spark of the true Othman, by the zeal with which he aided his officers in restoring the Turkish navy after Lepanto. He then contributed his private treasures liberally, and gave up part of the pleasure-gardens of the Serail for the site of the new docks. Except this brief flash of patriotism or pride, his whole career, both as Prince and Sultan, is unrelieved by a single merit; and it is blackened by mean treachery, by gross injustice and cruelty, and by grovelling servitude to the coarsest appetites of our nature.

CHAPTER XII.

AMURATH III.—RAPID DECLINE OF THE EMPIRE—CONQUESTS FROM
PERSIA—PROGRESS OF CORRUPTION AND MILITARY INSUBOR-
DINATION—WAR WITH AUSTRIA—MAHOMET III.—BATTLE OF
CERESTES—ACHMET I.—PEACE OF SITVATOROK—UNSUCCESSFUL
WARS WITH PERSIA—REVOLTS—MUSTAPHA I. DEPOSED—OTH-
MAN I.—VIOLENCE OF THE TROOPS—OTHMAN MURDERED—
MUSTAPHA RESTORED AND AGAIN DEPOSED—WRETCHED STATE
OF THE EMPIRE.[1]

THERE is an Eastern Legend, that when the great King and
Prophet Solomon died, he was sitting on his lion-throne, clad in
the royal robes, and with all the insignia of dominion round him.
The lifeless form remained in the monarch's usual attitude; and
the races of men and beasts, of genii and demons, who watched
at respectful distance, knew not of the change, but long with accustomed awe, paid homage, and made obeisance before the form
that sat upon the throne; until the staff on which Solomon had
leaned, holding it in both hands towards the mouth, and on which
the body had continued propped, was gnawed by worms and gave
way, letting the corpse fall to the ground. Then and not till then
the truth was known; and the world was filled with sorrow and
alarm.

This fable well images the manner in which the empire of Sultan Solyman remained propped on the staff of the Vizierate, and
retained its majesty after his death and during the reign of Selim,
so long as the power of Solyman's Grand Vizier Sokolli remained
unimpaired. When Sokolli's authority was weakened and broken
by the corrupt influence of favourites and women at the court of
Selim's successor, Amurath III., the shock of falling empire was
felt throughout the Ottoman world;[2] spreading from the court to
the capital, from the capital to the provinces, and at last becoming sensible even to foreign powers.

Amurath III. was summoned at the age of twenty-eight from

---

[1] Von Hammer, books 37-39.   [2] Ibid., vol. ii. p. 439.

his government at Magnesia to succeed his father at Constantinople. He arrived at the capital on the night of the 21st of December, 1574, and his first act was to order the execution of his five brothers. In the morning the high officers of state were assembled to greet their master, and the first words of the new Sultan were anxiously watched for, as ominous of the coming events of his reign. Amurath, who had retired to rest fatigued with his voyage, and literally fasting from all but sin, turned to the Aga of the Eunuchs and said, "I am hungry; bring me something to eat." These words were considered to be prophetic of scarcity during his reign; and the actual occurrence of a famine at Constantinople in the following year did much to confirm the popular superstition.

Sokolli retained the Grand Vizierate until his death in 1578, but the effeminate heart of Amurath was ruled by courtiers, who amused his listless melancholy; and by four women, one of whom was his mother, the dowager Sultana, or (as the Turks term her) the Sultana Validé, Nour Banou: the next was Amurath's first favourite Sultana, a Venetian lady of the noble House of Baffo, who had been captured by a Turkish corsair in her early years. The fair Venetian so enchanted Amurath, that he was long strictly constant to her, slighting the other varied attractions of his harem, and neglecting the polygamous privileges of his creed. The Sultana Validé, alarmed at the ascendency which the Sultana Safiye (as the Venetian lady was termed) was acquiring over Amurath, succeeded in placing such temptation in her son's way, as induced him to make his Venetian love no longer his only love; and he thenceforth rushed into the opposite extreme of licentious indulgence even for a Mahometan prince. Such was the demand created for the supply of the imperial harem, that it is said to have raised the price of beautiful girls in the slave-market of Constantinople. One of this multitude of favoured fair, a Hungarian by birth, obtained considerable influence over her lord; but his first love, Safiye, though no longer able to monopolise Amurath's affections, never lost her hold on them; and it was her will that chiefly directed the Ottoman fleets and armies during his reign; fortunately for her native country Venice, which she prevented Turkey from attacking, even under circumstances of great provocation, caused by the outrages and insolence of some of the cruisers of the Republic of St. Mark. The fourth lady who had sway in Amurath's councils, did not owe it to her own charms, but to the adroitness with which she placed before him the charms of others. This was Djanfeda, who was Kiaya (or grand mistress) of the

15

harem. These were the chief ladies who interposed and debated on all questions how the power bequeathed by the great Solyman should be wielded, and with whom the House of Othman should have peace or war.

Generals and admirals trained in the camps and fleets of Solyman still survived; and the hostilities, in which the Turkish Empire was engaged during the reign of Amurath III., were marked by more than one victory, and were productive of several valuable acquisitions of territory. War between Turkey and Persia broke out again soon after Amurath's accession, and was continued for several years. The death of the Shah Tahmasp, and the tyranny and misgovernment of his successors had thrown Persia into a state of anarchy and weakness, which greatly favoured the progress of the Ottoman arms; though the fortune of the war was often chequered, and the losses of the Turks by the sword, and by fatigue and privation were numerous and severe. In this war the Turkish armies attacked and conquered Georgia, which had been in alliance with Persia, and they penetrated as far as Daghestan and the shores of the Caspian Sea. The Turkish troops from the Crimea and their Tartar auxiliaries took an important part in those campaigns in the regions of the Caucasus. The Bey of Azoph was, in 1578, rewarded for the alacrity with which he had led the vanguard of an army round the north of the Euxine, with the sounding title of Capitan Pacha of the Caspian Sea. The most remarkable episode in the war was the march in 1583 of Osman Pacha, surnamed Ozdemir or Osman of the Iron Nerves, the commander of the Turkish forces in Georgia, who led an army in the depth of winter through the defiles of the Caucasus, through Circassia, and across the frozen plains of the Kuban to Azoph, and thence to the Crimea, where his unexpected appearance crushed an incipient revolt against the Sultan. Osman carried the head of the rebel Khan from the Crimea to Constantinople, where he was received with rapturous honours by the Sultan, who took the jewels from his own turban, and the richly adorned yataghan from his own belt to deck the veteran hero, the recital of whose exploits and sufferings had excited interest and animated attention in the jaded spirit of the imperial voluptuary. A peace was at last made between Turkey and Persia in 1590, by which the Ottomans obtained Georgia, the city of Tabriz, and also Azerbijan, Schirwan, Loristan, and Scherhezol. A clause was inserted in the treaty, which required the Persians not to curse any longer the three first Caliphs. As this implied the conversion of the Persian nation from Schiism to Sunnism, which was impracticable the stipulation could only be regarded as a mere form to gratify the religious pride of the Sultan, or as designed to furnish pretexts for renewing the war, when the Porte might judge it convenient.

Except the collisions, that from time to time took place near the boundary line in Hungary between the Turkish Pachas and Christian commandants of the respective border countries, the Ottoman Empire preserved peace with the powers of Christian Europe during the reign of Amurath III. until two years before his death, when war was declared against Austria. Commercial and diplomatic relations were established under Amurath with the greater part of Western Europe; the Ottomans ever showing the same wise liberality in all that relates to international traffic, that has been already mentioned. England, which, until the time of Amurath III., had been a stranger to Turkey, sent in 1579 three merchants, William Harebone, Edward Ellis, and Richard Stapel, to Constantinople, who sought and obtained from the Porte the same favour to English commerce, and the same privileges for English commercial residents in Turkey, that other foreign nations enjoyed. In 1583, William Harebone was accredited to Constantinople as the ambassador of our Queen Elizabeth, who was then the especial object of the hatred of Philip II. of Spain, and sought anxiously to induce the Sultan to make common cause with her against the Spanish King, and his great confederate the Pope of Rome. In her state papers to the Ottoman court, the Protestant Queen takes advantage of the well-known horror with which the Mahometans regard anything approaching to image-worship, and styles herself " The unconquered and most puissant defender of the true faith against the idolaters who falsely profess the name of Christ;" and there is a letter addressed by her agent at the Porte to the Sultan in November, 1587, at the time when Spain was threatening England with the Great Armada, in which the Sultan is implored to send, if not the whole tremendous force of his empire, at least sixty or eighty galleys, "against that idolater, the King of Spain, who, relying on the help of the Pope and all idolatrous princes, designs to crush the Queen of England, and then to turn his whole power to the destruction of the Sultan, and make himself universal monarch." The English advocate urges on the Ottoman sovereign, that if he and Elizabeth join promptly and vigorously in maritime warfare against Spain, the "proud Spaniard and the lying Pope with all their followers will be struck down;" that God will protect His own, and punish the idolaters of the earth by the arms of England and Turkey.[1]

[1] The letters are given at length by Von Hammer, in his notes to his

The evils, which the general prevalence of venality and the force of feminine intrigue at the Sultan's court had brought upon the Ottoman Empire, were not yet apparent to foreigners, who only saw its numerous fleets and armies, and only heard of its far-extended conquests; but before the close of Amurath's reign, the inevitable fruits of corruption and favouritism were unmistakeably manifest. Every appointment, civil, military, judicial, or administrative, was now determined by court influence or money. The Sultan, who squandered large sums on the musicians, the parasites, and buffoons, by whom he loved to be surrounded, was often personally in need of money, and at last stooped to the degradation of taking part of the bribes, which petitioners for office gave to his courtiers. One of his principal favourites was Schemsi Pacha, who traced his pedigree up to a branch of those Seljukian princes, whom the House of Othman had superseded in the sovereignty of the East. The historian Ali, who afterwards wrote Schemsi Pacha's biography, relates, that one day he himself was in that favourite's apartments, when Schemsi came thither from the Sultan's presence, and said with a joyous air to one of his domestics, " At last I have avenged my house on the House of Othman. For, if the Ottoman

---

39th book. They are in Latin. The first is from Elizabeth to the Vizier Mohammed dated at Windsor, November 15, 1582. The second letter, laid by Elizabeth's ambassador before the Sultan, is dated November 9, 1587. There are two more : one, in 1587, requesting the release of some English subjects from Algiers ; the other, which is dated on the last day of November, 1588, announces the victory of the English, and still urges the Sultan to attack Spain. Henry III. of France had sent an envoy to Constantinople, in April, 1588, for the same purpose ; and to warn the Sultan that if Philip conquered England he would soon overpower Turkey. (See Mignet's "Mary Queen of Scots," vol. ii. p. 392.) The Turks seem to have met these applications with fair promises ; but they certainly did no more. The English are said to have given considerable sums to the Turkish historian, Seadeddin, to employ in their favour the influence which that learned writer possessed, or was supposed to possess with the Sultan, who inherited the family fondness for literature. Some of the Ottoman grandees were much impressed by the distinction between the Roman Catholic image-worshippers and the Protestant English. Sinan Pacha is reported to have told the Austrian Ambassador Pezzen, " That there was nothing needed to make the English into genuine Mussulmans, save a lifting of the finger and a recital of the Eschdad" (the formula of confession of faith). But Seadeddin does not seem to have been worth his pay. Perhaps, if Sultana Safiye, or the matron Djanfeda, had been well bribed by our Virgin Queen, the result might have been different. A Turkish squadron in the Channel, co-operating with Drake and Raleigh, would have formed a curious episode in the great epic of the Spanish Armada. I may add that Professor Ranke also, in his recent "History of England" (vol. i. p. 433. *Eng. Trans.*), speaks of "the advances made by the English Government to the Turks in the time of Elizabeth."

dynasty caused our downfall, I have now made it prepare its own."
"How has that been done?" cried the old domestic gravely. "I
have done it," said Schemsi, "by persuading the Sultan to share
in the sale of his own favours. It is true I placed a tempting bait
before him; 40,000 ducats make no trifling sum. Henceforth the
Sultan will himself set the example of corruption; and corruption
will destroy the empire."

The armies and military organisation of the Porte now began to
show the workings of this taint, not only through the effect of
incompetent men receiving rank as generals and as officers, but
through the abuses with which its feudal system was overrun, and
the sale of Ziamets and Timars to traffickers of every description:
even to Jews and Jewesses, who either sold them again to the best
bidders, or received the profits of the feudal lands, in defiance
both of the spirit and letter of the law. An alarming relaxation
of discipline among the troops, and increasing turbulence and insubordination accompanied those scandals; and at last, in 1589,
the Janissaries openly attacked the Serail of the Sultan where the
Divan was assembled, and demanded the head of Mohammed Pacha,
Beyler Bey of Roumelia, surnamed "the Falcon" for his rapacity.
Their anger against this royal favourite was not causeless, for it
was at his instigation that the pay of the troops had been given
in grossly debased coinage. They now attacked the palace, and
cried, "Give us up the Beyler Bey, or we shall know how to find
our way even to the Sultan." Amurath ordered that the soldiery
should receive satisfaction; and accordingly the heads of the guilty
Pacha, and of an innocent treasurer whom they had involved in
their angry accusations, were laid before these military sovereigns
of the sovereign.

It has been truly said that the government which once has
bowed the knee to force, must expect that force will thenceforth
be its master. Within four years the Janissaries revolted twice
again, and on each occasion compelled the Sultan to depose and
change his Vizier. In 1591 these haughty Prætorians coerced
their sovereign into placing on the vassal throne of Moldavia the
competitor who had obtained their favour by bribes. While these,
and many other tumults, in some of which the Spahis and
Janissaries waged a civil war against each other in the streets,
convulsed the capital, the provinces were afflicted by the rapacious tyranny of their governors and the other officers of state,
and by its natural results. The garrisons of Pesth and Tabriz
mutinied on account of their pay being kept back. The warlike
tribes of the Druses in Lebanon took arms against their provincial

20

oppressors. The revolt of Transylvania, Moldavia, and Wallachia was a still more formidable symptom of the wretched condition of the empire. The risings in these provinces were encouraged by the war with Austria, which broke out in 1693. And in 1694 the war with Persia was renewed, and marked by little success on the Turkish side.

While his realm was in this distracted state, Sultan Amurath sickened and died (16th January, 1595). Weak both in mind and body, he had long been perplexed by dreams and signs, which he believed to be forebodings of death. On the morning of the last day of his life he had gone to a magnificent kiosk lately built by Sinan Pacha on the shore of the Bosphorus, which commanded an extensive prospect; and he lay there watching the ships that sailed to and from the Propontis and the Euxine. His musicians, as usual, were in attendance, and they played an air which recalled to Amurath's memory the melancholy words of the song to which it belonged. He murmured to himself the first line :

"Come and keep watch by me to-night, O Death !"

And it chanced that at that very time two Egyptian galleys saluted the Porte, and the concussion caused by the guns' fire shattered the glazed dome of the kiosk. As the fragments fell around the Sultan, he exclaimed, " At another time the salute of a whole fleet would not have broken that glass ; and now it is shivered by the noise of the cannon of these galleys. I see the fate of the kiosk of my life." Saying so he wept bitterly, and was led by his attendants back to his palace, where he expired that very night.

The multitudinous seraglio of Amurath III. had produced to him 103 children, of whom twenty sons, and twenty-seven daughters, were living at the time of his decease. The eldest son, Prince Mahomet, whom his mother, the Venetian Sultana Safiye, promptly summoned from his government in Asia Minor, instantly put his nineteen brothers to death—the largest sacrifice to the Cain-spirit of Mahomet, the Conqueror's law, that the Ottoman histories record. Seven female slaves, who were in a condition from which heirs to the empire might be expected, were at the same time sewn in sacks and thrown into the sea. Safiye had kept the death of Amurath secret until the successor arrived to secure the throne. This was the last time that this precautionary measure was needed on a Turkish sovereign's death ; for Mahomet III., who now succeeded to Amurath, was the last hereditary prince who was trusted with liberty and the government of provinces during his predecessor's lifetime. Thenceforth the Ottoman princes of the blood royal were kept secluded and immured in a particular part of the palace called the Kaweh (cage), from which they passed to die or to reign, without any of the minor employments of the state being placed in their hands. The fear lest they should head revolts was the cause of this new system; the effect of which on the character and capacity of the rulers of Turkey was inevitably debasing and pernicious.

Mahomet III. was twenty-three years of age when he came to the throne, On the eighth day after his accession, he went in state to public prayer at the mosque of St. Sophia, a ceremony that had not taken place for two years, on account of Amurath's fear of being insulted by the troops as he passed along the streets. A donative of unprecedented extravagance was now lavished on the soldiery, in order to buy their favour to the new Sultan; and anxious exertions were then made to send reinforcements to the armies in Hungary, where the war went hard with the Turks. While these preparations were being made, two regiments that were dissatisfied with the share which they had received of the imperial bounty, surrounded the Grand Vizier, Ferhad Pacha, and with angry cries demanded that more should be paid to them. Ferhad replied by bidding them march to the frontiers, where they should receive their due. They redoubled their murmurs and menaces at this, and Ferhad then said to them, " Know you not that the men who refuse obedience to their chiefs are infidels, and that their wives are barren?" Indignant at this taunt, the mutineers repaired to the Mufti, and repeating to him Ferhad's words, asked him to issue a Fetva condemning the Grand Vizier : but the Mufti's answer to their reply was, " My friends, let the Grand Vizier say all he can, he cannot make you infidels, and he cannot make your wives barren." Being but indifferently satisfied with this legal opinion, the mutineers sought their comrades' aid in getting up an insurrection, saying that the Mufti would only give his Fetvas for money, and not for justice. The Spahis (the horseguards of the capital) took up the supposed grievance of the malcontents, and clamoured for the head of Ferhad. A tumult ensued, in which several of the high officers of state, who vainly endeavoured to pacify the rioters, were wounded; but the Janissaries were prevailed on to charge their rivals the Spahis, and the mutiny was thus suppressed.

Safiye, now Sultana Valide, ruled generally in the court and councils of her son Mahomet, with even more predominant sway than she had exercised in the time of the late Sultan. Mahomet was a weak-minded prince, but capable of occasional outbursts of energy, or rather of violence. The disasters which the Turkish arms were now experiencing in Wallachia and Hungary, made the Sultan's best statesmen anxious that the sovereign should, after the manner of his great ancestors, head his troops in person, and endeavour to give an auspicious change to the fortune of the war. Safiye, who feared that her son when absent from Constantinople would be less submissive to her influence, opposed this project; and for a long time detained the Sultan· among the inglorious pleasures of his seraglio, while the Imperialists, under the Arch-duke Maximilian and the Hungarian Count Pfalfy, aided by the revolted princes of the Danubian Principalities, dealt defeat and discouragement among the Ottoman ranks, and wrung. numerous fortresses and districts from the empire. The cities of Gran, Wissgrad, and Babocsa, had fallen; and messengers in speedy succession announced the loss of Ibrail, Varna, Kilic, Ismail, Silistria, Rustchuk, Bucharest, and Akerman. These tidings at last roused the monarch in his harem; and he sent for the Mufti, who, fortunately for Turkey, was a man of sense and patriotic spirit. Adopting a characteristic mode of advising an Ottoman Prince, the Mufti took an opportunity of placing in Mahomet's hands a poem of Ali-Tchelabi, one of the most eminent writers of the time, in whose verses the misfortunes of the empire, and the calamitous progress of the Hungarian war, were painted in the strongest colours. The Sultan was sensibly affected by its perusal, and ordered that the solemn service of prayer and of humiliation should be read, which requires the Mussulman to pray and weep, and do acts of contrition and penitence for three days. The Sultan and all his officers of state, and all the Mahometan popula-tion of the city, attended, and humbled themselves at these prayers, which were read by the Scheik Mohizedden in the place of the Okmeidan, behind the arsenal. Eight days afterwards, an earthquake shook Constantinople, and overthrew many towns and villages in Anatolia. The consternation and excitement of the Ottomans now were excessive. All classes called on the Padischah to go forth to the holy war against the unbelievers; and the formidable Janissaries refused to march to the frontier unless the Sultan marched with them. The historian Seadeddin, who held the high dignity of Khodja, or tutor to Mahomet, the Mufti, and the Grand Vizier, urged on their sovereign that the only hope of retrieving the prosperity and even of assuring the safety, of the empire, lay in his appearing at the head of his armies. Their exhortations, aided by the pressure from without, prevailed over the influence of the Sultana Validé. In her anger and irritation at this decision, and hoping perhaps to cause a tumult during which the current of popular opinion might be changed, or the ministers who opposed her might be killed, the daughter of Venice forgot all the ties which had once bound her to Christendom, and proposed that there should be a massacre of all the Giaours in Constantinople. The fanatics in the Divan approved of this proposal of a most atrocious and most useless crime; but the authority of wiser statesmen prevailed, and a banishment of all unmarried Greeks in the capital was the only result of the infuriated Sultana's design.

Mahomet III. left his capital for the frontier in the June of 1596, with pomp and state which recalled to some spectators the campaigns of the great Solyman. The Sultan's resolution to head his armies had revived the martial spirit of the Ottomans; and the display of the sacred standard of the Prophet, which now for the first time was unfurled over a Turkish army, excited still more the zeal of the True Believers to combat the enemies of Islam. This holy relic had been left at Damascus by Sultan Selim I. after he obtained it from the last titular Caliph of the Abassides, on his conquest of Egypt.[1] During the reign of Amurath III. it was conveyed from Damascus to Constantinople; and it has since that time been preserved by the Sultans as a treasure for extreme need, to be displayed only on great emergencies, when it has become necessary to employ some extraordinary means to rouse the military spirit of the Ottomans, or to recall them to their religious allegiance to their Sultan, as the Caliph, and the successor of the Prophet Mahomet, whose holy hands once bore that standard in battle.

The historian Seadeddin accompanied his imperial pupil in this campaign; and his presence proved of value for the purpose of gaining victories, as well as for that of recording them. The Grand Vizier, Ibrahim Pacha, Hassan Sokolli Pacha, and Cicala Pacha, were the principal commanders under the Sultan. The biography of the last-mentioned Pacha (whom the Oriental writers call Dzigalizadé) furnishes so striking an example of the career of a renegade of that age, that it may claim a short space in these pages. Cicala was, as his name denotes, an Italian by birth. His father, the Vicomte di Cicala, head of a noble Genoese family that had settled in Sicily, commanded a force of privateers (or, as the Turks would have termed them, pirates), and he cruised against the Mahometan coasts and commerce with as little heed to truce

[1] See p. 150, *supra*.

or treaty as any Algerine Reis ever showed in his enterprises against Christians. The Knights of Malta sought the co-operation of this daring maritime partisan in many of their adventures; and his galleys joined those of the Order when they attacked Modon in the Morea, in 1531. Though unable to storm the citadel, the chevaliers sacked the town, and showed the most savage and sordid rapacity for plunder of every description. Among other spoils, they carried off 800 Turkish ladies, one of whom, a girl of remarkable beauty, fell to the share of Count Cicala; who was so enraptured with his prize, that on his return to Sicily he married her, having first had her baptised under the name of Lucretia. There were several sons of this marriage. The youngest of them, Scipio, at the age of eighteen, accompanied his father in the expedition against Djerbé, which terminated so disastrously for the Christian confederates.[1] Both the Cicalas were among the captives whom the victorious Turkish Admiral, Pialé, led in triumph to Constantinople. The elder one died in prison; but the youth and beauty of young Scipio Cicala attracted the pitying notice of Sultan Solyman. The boyish sea-rover was half a Turk by birth, and he had little scruple about becoming one entirely in religion. Sinan Pacha, an old officer high in rank and influence, took the juvenile Mahometan under his especial patronage; and Cicala entered eagerly on the field of distinction and promotion which was opened to him in the Sultan's service. He rose to the high office of Aga of the Janissaries; and though his extreme oppression of the Christians of Constantinople caused him to be removed from that dignity, he obtained an important command in the Persian war, where he greatly signalised himself in several engagements, especially in a nocturnal victory gained by the Turks in 1583, called the "Battle of the Torches." He had married the granddaughter of Sultan Solyman, and thus obtained influence in the seraglio, which even more than his victories and abilities favoured his promotion during the reign of Amurath III., and protected him from the effects of prejudice caused by his occasional defeats, and the unpopularity into which he brought himself by his excessive severity to his own men, and by his cruelty to the Rayas of Turkey as well as to the natives of the foreign countries where he commanded. He more than once held the rank of Capitan Pacha, and twice he availed himself of his command of the Turkish navy for the purpose of sailing to Messina, and demanding an interview with his mother and sister, who resided there. On the first of these occasions the Spanish Viceroy of

[1] See p. 180, *suprà.*

Sicily refused his request, and Cicala revenged himself by ravaging the whole coast of the island. This had its effect. Cicala returned in a subsequent year and sent a flag of truce to the Viceroy, urging that he should at least be allowed to have an interview with his mother, whom he had not seen since he was first carried to Constantinople. The Viceroy now thought it prudent to send the Countess Cicala to her son's galley, covenanting that she should be sent back at sunset. Strange reminiscences must have been awakened at that interview between the mother, who in her youth had been torn from a Turkish home, and forcibly converted into a Christian matron, and the son, who had begun his life and career in a Christian court and under the flag of the Cross, but now had so long been one of the most dreaded champions of the Crescent. Cicala kept his word, and sent his mother back on shore at the stipulated time; he then sailed away, leaving for once a Christian shore unvisited by fire or slaughter. The conclusion of Cicala's career after many vicissitudes of fortune was disastrous. He was routed by Shah Abbas in Persia, and died during the hurried retreat of his discontented and mutinous troops, of a fever brought on by anxiety and fatigue. But in 1596, when Mahomet III. marched into Hungary, Cicala, though disliked by the Sultana Validé, was high in favour with the Sultan, and his most brilliant exploit was performed during this campaign.

The Archduke Maximilian, who commanded the Imperialists, retired at first before the superior numbers of the great Ottoman army; and the Sultan besieged and captured Erlau. The Imperialists now having effected a junction with the Transylvanian troops under Prince Sigismund, advanced again, though too late to save Erlau; and on October 23rd, 1596, the two armies were in presence of each other on the marshy plain of Cerestes, through which the waters of the Cincia ooze towards the river Theiss.

There were three days of battle at Cerestes. On the first day part of the Turkish force under Djaffer Pacha passed the Cincia, and after fighting bravely against superior numbers, was obliged to retreat with the loss of 1000 Janissaries, 100 Spahis, and forty-three cannon. The Sultan now wished for a general retreat of the army, or at least that he should himself retire. A council of war was summoned in the Ottoman camp, at which the historian Seadeddin was present, and advocated vigorously a more manly policy. " It has never been seen or heard of," said he, " that a Padischah of the Ottomans turned his back upon the enemy without the direst necessity." Some of those present recommended that the Pacha Hassan Sokolli should lead the troops against the enemy. Seadeddin answered, "This is no affair for Pachas : the personal presence of the Padischah is absolutely indispensable here." It was finally resolved to fight ; and the Sultan was with difficulty persuaded to stay with the troops. On the 24th there was another action ; and the Turks secured some passages through the marsh. Each side now concentrated its strength, and on the 26th October, the decisive encounter took place. At first the Christians seemed completely victorious. They drove back the leading divisions of the Turks and Tartars ; attacked the Ottoman batteries in flank, captured the whole of the guns, forced the Janissaries to give way, and drove the Asiatic feudal cavalry in headlong rout from the field. The Sultan, who beheld the engagement from an elevated seat on a camel's back, wished to fly, but Seadeddin exhorted him to be firm, and quoted the verse of the Koran that says, "It is patience that brings victory, and joy succeeds to sorrow." Mahomet clasped the sacred standard, and kept his station, protected by his bodyguard and his pages from the victorious Imperialists, who now broke their ranks, and rushed to plunder the Ottoman camp. At this critical moment, Cicala, who had hitherto sate inactive in command of a large body of irregular Turkish cavalry, gave the word to his men, and the spur to his steed, and down came the wild horsemen galloping over friend and foe, and sweeping the panic-stricken Christians by thousands into the swamps of the Cincia. Terror and flight spread through every division of the Imperialists ; and in less than half an hour from the time when Cicala began his charge, Maximilian and Sigismund were flying for their lives, without a single Christian regiment keeping their ranks, or making an endeavour to rally and cover the retreat. 50,000 Germans and Transylvanians perished in the marshes or beneath the Ottoman sabre. Ninety-five cannons, of very beautiful workmanship, were captured by the Turks, who, at the beginning of the battle, had lost all their own ; and the whole camp, and treasure of the Archduke, and all his material of war were among the fruits of this victory, one of the most remarkable that the Ottomans ever obtained.

The principal credit of the day was fairly ascribed to Seadeddin[1] and Cicala. Cicala was promoted after the battle to the rank of Grand Vizier ; but was speedily deprived of it by the jealous interference of the Sultana Validé. He held it, however, long

---

[1] It is but just to the Turkish historian to remark that his reputation for these military services does not rest merely on his own testimony. Naima and other writers are his witnesses.

enough to be the cause of infinite evil to the empire, by his ill-judged and excessive severity to the troops, that had given way at the beginning of the battle.   It was found that 30,000 Ottoman soldiers, principally belonging to the Asiatic feudal force, had fled before the Giaours.   Cicala stigmatised them as Firaris, or runaways.   He ordered that their pay should be stopped, and their fiefs forfeited.   He publicly beheaded many of these unfortunate soldiers who came into his power; but by far the greater number, when they heard of the new Vizier's severity, dispersed, and returned to their homes.   The attempts made to apprehend and punish them there, naturally caused armed resistance; and the Firaris of Cerestes were among the foremost and most formidable supporters of the rebellion, which soon afterwards broke out in Asia Minor, and desolated that country for many years.

Mahomet III. eagerly returned after the battle to Constantinople, to receive felicitations and adulation for his victory, and to resume his usual life of voluptuous indolence.   The war in Hungary was prolonged for several years, until the peace of Sitvatorok in the reign of Mahomet's successor.   But neither the Imperialists nor the Turks carried on operations with any vigour in the intermediate campaigns; and the chiefs of the revolted principalities of Moldavia, Wallachia, and Transylvania, after disputes with each other, sought and obtained terms of reconciliation with the Porte.

During the inglorious remainder of Mahomet III.'s reign, the evils of military insubordination, and the tyranny of the provincial rulers, continued to increase.   In 1599 a chief of the military feudatories in Asia Minor, named Abdoulhamid, but better known by the title of Karazaridji, which means "The Black Scribe," availed himself of the universal disorder and discontent to organise a wide-spread revolt against the Porte, and to assume the rank of an independent prince.   He formed an army of Koords, Turcomans, and the fugitive Spahis of Cerestes; and, aided by his brother, Delhi Housin, the Governor of Bagdad, he gave repeated defeats to the Ottoman armies sent against him.   In 1601, the Persian monarch, Shah Abbas, took advantage of the weakness of the ancient enemy of his nation, to make war upon Turkey; and began rapidly to recover the provinces which Persia had lost in the last reign.   In the June of 1603 Sultan Mahomet put to death his eldest son, Mahmoud, a prince of high abilities and courage, and of whose reign great expectation had been formed. Mahmoud had requested his father to give him the command of the armies employed against the rebels in Asia Minor.   This show of spirit alarmed the weak and jealous mind of Mahomet; and on being informed that a holy man had predicted to the prince that a new Sultan would soon ascend the throne, he ordered his son to be seized and strangled. The Sultana who had borne the prince to him, and all Mahmoud's favourite companions, were at the same time thrown into prison, and at the end of a month were all put to death. Mahomet III. did not long survive this act of cruelty. On the 27th of October a Dervise met him in the palace-gate, and prophesied to him that in fifty-five days he would meet with some great calamity. The prediction weighed heavily on the superstitious mind of the sickly voluptuary; and, like many other predictions of the same kind, tended powerfully to work its own fulfilment. On the fifty-fifth day (22nd December, 1603), Mahomet III. died, and was succeeded by Sultan Achmet I., the elder of his two surviving sons.

Achmet I. was fourteen years of age when he commenced his reign. By his humanity, or the humanity of his councillors, his brother, Prince Mustapha, was spared from being put to death according to established usage. The mental imbecility of Prince Mustapha may also have been a reason for saving his life, partly out of contempt, and partly out of the superstitious reverence with which all lunatics are regarded in the East. In the beginning of young Achmet's reign he showed some flashes of imperious decision, which might have been thought to be the dawnings of a vigorous and successful reign. His Grand Vizier, who was to lead a fresh army into Hungary, made some exorbitant demands on the treasury, and threatened not to march unless they were complied with. Achmet sent him the laconic and effective answer, "If thou valuest thy head thou wilt march at once." But the promise of Achmet's boyhood was belied by weakness and selfishness as he approached maturer years. The Turkish historian, Naima, relates a scene which took place in Achmet's Divan in 1606, when the Sultan had attained the age of seventeen, which illustrates his character as compared with that of the great sovereign who had ruled Turkey only forty years before, and which shows the influence for good or for bad which the personal example of the monarch must exercise. It was May. The horsetails had been planted on the Asiatic side of the Bosphorus, announcing a campaign in that continent, and an army was now being assembled at Scutari, which the young Sultan was expected to lead to the Persian war. The Divan was assembled at the Grand Vizier's palace, and the Sultan presided there in person. Achmet addressed his councillors: "It is now too late for a campaign.

Provisions are scarce and dear. Is it not better to put off the
expedition till next year ?" The astonished assembly was silent,
until the Mufti, who vainly wished that Achmet would follow the
example of the great Solyman, said, " Would it, then, be fitting
to carry back the horsetails, that have been planted in the sight of
so many foreign ambassadors ? Let the troops at least be marched
to Aleppo, to winter there, and to collect stores of provisions." The
Sultan interposed, " What is the use of a march to Aleppo ?"
" It is of use," answered the Mufti, firmly, " to save the honour of
our tents that have been pitched. Even so Sultan Solyman in
the campaign against Nachdshivan wintered at Aleppo, and then
attacked the enemy at the opening of the following spring."
Then said the Sultan, " Let Ferhad Pacha go forward with part
of the army, so that the camp be not brought back." " Will
he receive the money necessary for the purchase of provisions ?"
asked the Mufti. The Sultan replied, " The public treasury is
empty. Whence am I to draw the money ?" " From the treasury
of Egypt." " That," said the Sultan, " belongs to my private
purse." " Sire," was the rejoinder, " your great ancestor, Sultan
Solyman, before the campaign of Szigeth, sent all his own treasures of gold and silver to the public mint." Sultan Achmet knit
his brows, and said, " Effendi, thou understandest not. Times
are changed. What was fitting then is not convenient now." So
saying, he dismissed the council. The result was, that Ferhad
Pacha, who seems to have been rightly called Delhi Ferhad, or
Ferhad the Foolhardy, did set forth with a part of the army
without pay or supplies. The troops mutinied on their march,
and were routed by the first bands of rebels whom they encountered in Asia Minor.

Negotiations for a peace between Austria and the Porte had
long been pending, and a treaty was finally concluded on the 11th
November, 1606, at Sitvatorok. No change of importance was
made in the territorial possessions of either party, except that the
Prince of Transylvania was admitted as party to the treaty, and
that province became to some extent, though not entirely independent of the Ottoman Empire. But the peace of Sitvatorok is
important as marking an era in the diplomatic relations of Turkey
with the states of Christendom. Hitherto the Ottoman Sultans,
in their pacifications with Christian princes, had affected to grant
short truces as favours from a superior to inferiors. They
generally exacted annual contributions of money, which Oriental
pride considered to be tributes ; and they displayed, both in the
style of their state papers, and by the low rank of the persons

employed by them to conduct the negotiations, the most haughty and offensive arrogance. But at Sitvatorok the Turks acknowledged and observed the general principles and courtesies of international law. Their commissioners had full powers signed by the Sultan and the Grand Vizier ; and they gave the Austrian sovereign the title of Padischah, or Emperor, instead of terming him, as had been usual with their predecessors, merely "the King of Vienna." The peace was to be a permanent one; the annual payment of the 30,000 ducats by Austria to the Porte was abolished; presents were to be made by the Turks to the Imperialists, as well as by the Imperialists to the Turks; and in future, all ambassadors sent by the Sultan to Vienna were not to be as formerly, chosen from among the menial officers of his court or camp, but were to be at least of the rank of Sanjak Bey.

It was fortunate for the Ottoman power that the religious dissensions in Germany soon after this period caused the outbreak of the great war which devastated that country for thirty years, and kept the House of Austria fully occupied in struggling for empire and safety against Bohemians, Saxons, Danes, Swedes, and French, instead of availing itself of the weakness of the Turks, and entering upon a career of conquest along the Saave and the Danube. The Spanish monarchy, the other great enemy of the Porte, after the death of Philip II. decayed even more rapidly and uniformly than the Turkish Empire after the death of Solyman. France and England were friendly towards the Turks ; and even if they had been hostile, were too much engaged each with its own domestic dissensions during the first half of the seventeenth century for any formidable projects of conquest in the East. Russia had declined during the last years of the reign of Ivan the Terrible ; and she was, long after his death, rent by revolts and civil wars, which were terminated by the accession of the House of Romanoff (1613) ; but the reign of the first Czar of that dynasty (1613-1645) was fully occupied with endeavours to restore the Russian nation from the misery and anarchy into which it had fallen, and in recovering provinces which had been seized by the Swedes and Poles. No first-class European power was in a condition to attack Turkey during that crisis of her extreme misery and feebleness, which lasted through the first thirty years of the seventeenth century, which was checked by the stern hand of Amurath IV. during the last seven years of his reign, but was renewed under the reigns of his imbecile successors, until the ministry of the first Kiuprili in 1656. The Poles and the Venetians were the chief European foes of Turkey throughout this time. Poland was too much torn by domestic faction to accomplish aught worthy of the chivalrous valour of her armies ; and Venice, never a sufficient adversary to cope single-handed with a great empire, was in a state of skilfully disguised, but incurable, and increasing decrepitude. Persia was the most dangerous foreign enemy of Turkey during the first half of the seventeenth century ; but though the Asiatic possessions of the Porte beyond the Taurus were often in imminent peril, there was little risk of Persian armies advancing so far westward as to strike at the vital parts of the Ottoman dominions.

Achmet I. reigned for eleven years after the peace of Sitvatorok. During this time, his Grand Vizier, Mourad, gained advantages over the rebels in Asia Minor, which partially suppressed the spirit of revolt in that quarter. The war with Persia was continued, but almost uniformly to the disadvantage of the Turks ; and the weakness of the empire was signally proved by the ravages which the fleets of the Cossacks perpetrated with impunity along the southern coasts of the Black Sea. In 1613, a flotilla of these marauders surprised the city of Sinope, which is described as having been then one of the richest and best fortified ports of Asia Minor. The Cossacks of the seventeeth century subjected Sinope to the same rapacious and cruel devastation, which it was to experience from their descendants under Russian guidance in 1853. In both cases the city was taken by surprise ; and in both cases, the fleets, which should have encountered the attacking squadron, or at least have taken vengeance on it while retiring with its plunder, were absent from the proper scene of operations.

Sultan Achmet died 22nd November, 1617.[1] He left seven sons, three of whom, in course of time, ascended the throne, but his immediate successor was his brother Mustapha. Hitherto there had been an uninterrupted transmission of the empire from father to son for fourteen generations. According to Von Hammer, the law of succession, which gives the throne to the elder surviving

---

[1] The second year of the reign of Achmet I. is marked by the Turkish writers as the date of the introduction of tobacco into the empire. The Ottomans became such enthusiastic and inveterate smokers that within fifty years a pipe was looked on as the national emblem of a Turk. The use of coffee had been introduced into Constantinople in the reign of the great Solyman. The severer expounders of the Mahometan law censure the use of these luxuries. On the other hand the Oriental poets say, that coffee, tobacco, opium, and wine are "the four cushions of the sofa of pleasure," and "the four elements of the world of enjoyment." But the strict legists call them "the four pillars of the tent of debauchery," and "the four ministers of the devil."

16

male relation of the deceased sovereign, had been adopted by the
House of Othman from the House of Zenghis Khan; but so long
as the practice of royal fratricide continued, it was impossible for
any dispute to arise between the son of a Sultan and that son's
uncle. In consequence of the life of his brother Mustapha having
been spared by Achmet I., that prince now became Sultan, to the
temporary exclusion of his young nephew Prince Othman. But
the idiocy of Mustapha, as soon as he was drawn from his place of
confinement and enthroned, was so apparent, that in less than
three months the high officers of state concurred in deposing him,
and summoning Prince Othman, then aged fourteen, to reign in
his stead (26th February, 1618). The soldiery acquiesced in this
measure the more willingly, that it brought them a new donative.
The public treasury was drained of 6,000,000 ducats by this
renewed claim of the military within a quarter of a year.

The short and unhappy reign of Othman II. was marked by the
signature of a peace with Persia, on conditions agreed to during
the preceding reign, and rendered necessary by the repeated
defeats of the Turks. The Ottomans restored all the conquests
that had been made during the reigns of Amurath III. and Mahomet III., and the eastern boundary of the empire receded to its
line in the reign of Selim II. Relieved from the burden of the
Persian war, Othman devoted all his thoughts to the overthrow of
his domestic enemies, the Janissaries and Spahis, whom he not
unjustly regarded as the chief curses of the empire, of which they
had formerly been the chief support. The Janissaries, in particular, were now regarded as the tyrants over both sovereign and
people; and the long feud between the throne and the barrack of
the troops of Hadji Bektasch now commenced, which was only
terminated in our own century by the ruthless energy of Mahmoud II. Othman II. had sufficient hardness of heart for the task
which he undertook. A prince, who kept himself in practice as
an archer by using prisoners of war as his marks, or, if they were
not at hand, by putting one of his own pages up as a living target,
was not likely to be deterred by the scruples of humanity from
using the most efficacious measures against military malignants.
Othman made war on Poland in 1621, chiefly with the view of
weakening the Janissary regiments by loss in battle and the hardships of the campaign. The losses which the whole army sustained in that war, and the calamitous retreat with which the
operations of the Sultan (though partially victorious) were concluded, made Othman unpopular with all ranks. And by ill-
considered changes in laws and customs, by personal affronts to

leading statesmen, and by the exercise of vexatious severity in trifling regulations of police he alienated all classes of his subjects from his throne. In the spring of 1622, he announced an intention of performing the pilgrimage to Mecca. It was well known that his real design was to proceed to Damascus, and place himself at the head of an army of Koords and other troops, which his favourite Grand Vizier, Dilawer Pacha, was to collect near that city. With this army, when disciplined on a new model, the Sultan was to march upon Constantinople, destroy the Janissaries and Spahis, and completely re-organise the government. Sir Thomas Roe, our ambassador, then resident at the Turkish capital, whose letters graphically describe the tragical career of Othman, says of this scheme, that, "Certainly this was a brave and well-grounded design, and of great consequence for the recovery of this decayed empire, languishing under the insolence of lazy slaves, if God had not destroyed it." But, in truth, Othman utterly lacked the secrecy and the vigour, with which alone actions of such depth and danger can be performed. When the Janissaries rose in furious tumult (May, 1622) to forbid the pilgrimage to Mecca, and to demand the heads of Othman's ministers, the Sultan had neither troops ready to defend him, nor was there any party in his favour among the people, to which he could appeal. Instigated by the traitor Daoud Pacha, who hated Othman for having raised a rival to the Grand Vizierate, and by the mother of Sultan Mustapha, who knew that, if this revolt were quelled, Othman would seek to secure himself by putting all his kin to death, the insurgent soldiery proceeded from violence against the ministers to an attack upon the person of the Sultan, which had hitherto been held sacred amidst the wildest commotions. Othman was dragged off to the Seven Towers, while the lunatic Mustapha was a second time carried from his cell, and installed on the throne. Daoud Pacha, now Grand Vizier, was determined not to leave his traitorous enterprise incomplete; and with three comrades he proceeded to Othman's prison, and strangled him, with circumstances of gross and insolent cruelty.[1]

The atrocity of this murder before long caused remorse among the Janissaries themselves. Among the few glimmerings of intellect which Sultan Mustapha showed during his second reign, were an expression of grief for the death of Othman, and a hatti-scherif, commanding that his murderers should be punished.

---

[1] Von Hammer, vol. ii. p. 808, gives a painfully curious parallel between the death of Othman and that of Andronicus, who built the grand reservoir "Pyrgus" or "Burgas" at Constantinople, which Othman restored.

Generally, Mustapha continued to be as incapable of governing an empire, or of common self-government, as he had been found at his first accession. His mother, the Sultana Validé, exercised the principal power in his name; and the high offices of state were intrigued, or fought for, by competitors, who relied on the bought swords of the Janissaries and Spahis, as their best means of promotion. So fearful at length became the anarchy and misery at Constantinople, that even the very soldiers were touched by it. Some instinctive spirit of military discipline still survived among them; and their proud attachment to the Ottoman Empire, which the valour of their predecessors had raised to such power and splendour, had not become wholly inoperative. They assented to the urgent entreaties of the chief ministers that they would forego their customary donative if a new Sultan was invested with power; and in August, 1623, the lunatic Mustapha was a second time deposed; and Prince Amurath, the elder surviving brother of Sultan Othman, a child of only eleven years of age, was placed on the throne. Mustapha's second reign had lasted little more than a year, but it had been productive of infinite misery to the empire. The Persian war had been renewed. Bagdad and Bassorah fell into the hands of enemies. All Asia Minor was desolated by the revolt of Abaza, who had been governor of Merasch, and who was said to have aided the Sultan Othman in concerting that sovereign's project for destroying the Janissaries. It is certain, that after Othman's murder, Abaza proclaimed himself as that Prince's avenger, and the sworn foe of the Janissaries, whom he pursued with implacable ferocity. In the general dissolution of all bonds of government, and in the absence of all protection to industry or property, the empire seemed to be sinking into the mere state of a wilderness of beasts of prey. Nothing can exceed the strength of the expressions which an eye-witness, Sir Thomas Roe, employs in his correspondence with our King James I. and other persons in England, respecting the misery of the inhabitants of the Turkish dominions, and the symptoms of decay and ruin which he witnessed all around him.[1] And it is to be remembered, that there was no wish among Englishmen for the downfall of Turkey. This country sympathised strongly with James's son-in-law, the Prince Palatine, and the other Protestant antagonists of the House of Austria in Germany; and any prospect of the arms of Austria being disturbed by a Turkish war, would have been gladly hailed by our statesmen. But the graphic despatches of Roe describe vividly and repeatedly a state of fallen grandeur,

[1] "Sir Thomas Roe's Embassy," p. 22.

which he regarded as irretrievable. He employs almost the same metaphor which, in our time, has been applied to the Turkish power by one "whose wish was father to the thought," and who has spoken of it "as a sick man about to die upon one's hands," Roe says : "It has become, like an old body, crazed through many vices, which remain when the youth and strength is decayed." He gives in a letter, written in the year of Sultan Othman's death, some calculations as to the extent to which depopulation had lately taken place, which may possibly be exaggerated ;[1] but his testimony as to the general nature of what he actually beheld, is unimpeachable. He says: "The ruined houses in many places remain ; but the injustice and cruelty of the government hath made all the people abandon them. All the territory of the Grand Seignior is dispeopled for want of justice, or rather, by reason of violent oppression ; so much so, that in his best parts of Greece and Natolia, a man may ride three, four, and sometimes six days, and not find a village able to feed him and his horse ; whereby the revenue is so lessened, that there is not wherewithal to pay the soldiers, and to maintain the court. It may be patched up for a while out of the treasury, and by exactions, which now are grievous upon the merchant and labouring man, to satisfy the harpies ; but when those means fail, which cannot long endure, either the soldiery must want their pay, or the number must be reduced ; neither of which will they suffer : and whosoever shall attempt either remedy, shall follow Othman to his grave. This is the true estate of this so much feared greatness ; and the wisest men in the country foresee it, and retyre their estates as fast as they can, fearing that no haste can prevent their danger."[2]

These seemingly well-founded prognostications of the speedy dissolution of the Ottoman Empire were written in 1622. Since then, that empire has endured already for two centuries and a half. Our attention will now be directed to one of those rulers, who have been mainly instrumental in falsifying these and similar predictions.

[1] See note, *suprà* at p. 200. n.
[2] "Sir T. Roe's Embassy," pp. 66, 67.

CHAPTER XIII.

MISERY OF THE EMPIRE AT THE ACCESSION OF AMURATH IV.—
MILITARY REVOLTS—AMURATH TAKES POWER INTO HIS OWN
HANDS AND RESTORES ORDER—HIS SEVERITY AND CRUELTY
—RECONQUERS BAGDAD—HIS DEATH.[1]

AMURATH IV., at the time of his accession (10th September, 1623),
was under twelve years of age. But even thus early, he gave in-
dications of a resolute and vengeful character, and showed that a
prince, animated by the spirit of the first Selim, was once more
on the Ottoman throne. The Turkish historian, Evliya, relates
of him : " When Sultan Amurath entered the treasury after his
accession, my father, Dervish Mohammed, was with him. There
were no gold or silver vessels remaining—only 30,000 piastres in
money, and some coral and porcelain in chests. 'Inshallah'
(please God), said the Sultan, after prostrating himself in prayer,
'I will replenish this treasury fifty-fold with the property of those
who have plundered it.' "[2]

The young Sultan, during the first year of his reign, acted principally under the directions of his mother, the Sultana Mahpeiker,
who, providentially for the Ottoman Empire, was a woman of
remarkable talent and energy, which were taxed to the uttermost
to meet the dangers and disasters that clouded round the dawn of
her child's sovereignty. From every part of the empire messengers arrived with evil tidings. The Persians were victorious on
the frontier. The rebel Abaza was lord and tyrant over Asia
Minor. The tribes of the Lebanon were in open insurrection.
The governors of Egypt and other provinces were wavering in
their allegiance. The Barbaresque regencies assumed the station
of independent powers, and made treaties with European nations
on their own account. The fleets of the Cossack marauders not
only continued their depredations along the Black Sea, but even
appeared in the Bosphorus, and plundered the immediate vicinity
of the capital. In Constantinople itself there was an empty treasury, a dismantled arsenal, a debased coinage, exhausted maga-

---

[1] See Von Hammer, books 46—52.   [2] Hulme.

zines, a starving population, and a licentious soldiery. Yet the semblance of authority was preserved, and by degrees some of its substance was recovered by those who ruled in the young prince's name ; and, though amid tumult and bloodshed, and daily peril to both throne and life, young Amurath, observing all things, forgetting nothing, and forgiving nothing, grew up towards man's estate.

There is a wearisome monotony in the oft-repeated tale of military insurrections ; but the formidable mutiny of the Spahis, which convulsed Constantinople in the ninth year of Amurath's reign, deserves notice on account of the traits of the Turkish character, which its chief hero and victim remarkably displayed ; and also because it explains and partly palliates the hard-heartedness which grew upon Amurath, and the almost wolfish appetite for bloodshed, which was shown by him in the remainder of his reign. In the beginning of that year, a large number of mutinous Spahis, who had disgraced themselves by gross misconduct in the late unsuccessful campaign against Bagdad, had straggled to Constantinople, and joined the European Spahis, already collected in that capital. They were secretly instigated by Redjib Pacha, who wished by their means to effect the ruin of the Grand Vizier Hafiz, a gallant though not fortunate general, to whom the young Sultan was much attached, and who had interchanged poetical communications[1] with his sovereign, when employed against the Persians. The Spahis gathered together in the hippodrome, on three successive days (February, 1632) and called for the heads of the Grand Vizier Hafiz, the Mufti Jahia, the Defterdar Mustapha, and other favourites of the Sultan, seventeen in all. The shops were closed, and the city and the Serail were in terror. On the second day the mutineers came to the gate of the Palace, but withdrew on being promised that they should have redress on the morrow. On the third day, when the morning broke, the outer court of the Seraglio was filled with raging rebels. As the Grand Vizier Hafiz was on his way thither to attend the divan, he received a message from a friend, who warned him to conceal himself until the crowd had dispersed. Hafiz answered with a smile, " I have already this day seen my fate in a dream: I am not afraid to die." As he rode into the Seraglio, the multitude made a lane for him, as if out of respect, but as he passed along they cast stones at him: he was struck from his horse, and borne by his attendants into the inner

---

[1] The poems or Gazelles of the Sultan and Vizier are given in German by Von Hammer in his note to his 47th book. They are full of fanciful imagery drawn from the game of chess.

part of the Palace. One of his followers was murdered, and one grievously wounded by the Spahis. The Sultan ordered Hafiz to make his escape, and the Grand Vizier took a boat at the water-gate of the Serail, and crossed over to Scutari. Meanwhile the rebels forced their way into the second court of the Seraglio, which was the usual hall of the divan, and they clamoured for the Sultan to come forth and hold a divan among them. The Sultan appeared and held a divan standing. He spoke to the mutineers, "What is your will, my servants?" Loudly and insolently they answered, "Give us the seventeen heads. Give these men up to us, that we may tear them in pieces, or it shall fare worse with thee." They pressed close upon the Sultan, and were near upon laying hands on him. "You give no hearing to my words; why have you called me hither?" said Amurath. He drew back, surrounded by his pages, into the inner court. The rebels came after him like a raging flood. Fortunately the pages barred the gate. But the alarm and the outcry became the greater. They shouted aloud, "The seventeen heads, or abdicate."

Redjïb Pacha, the secret promoter of the whole tumult, now approached the young Sultan, and urged on him that it was necessary to still the tumult by granting what was demanded. He said that it had become a custom for the chiefs to be given up to the soldiery. "The Unchained Slave must take what he pleases; better the head of the Vizier than that of the Sultan." Amurath sorrowfully gave way, and sent a summons to Hafiz to return and die. The Vizier hesitated not; and, as he came back, the Sultan met him at the water-gate. The gate of the inner court was then opened. The Sultan ascended the throne of state; and four deputies from the insurgents, two Spahis and two Janissaries, came before him. He implored them not to profane the honour of the Caliphate; but he pleaded in vain; the cry was still "The Seventeen Heads." Meanwhile Hafiz Pacha had made the ablution preparatory to death, which the Mahometan law requires, and he now stood forth and addressed Amurath. "My Padischah," said he, "let a thousand slaves, such as Hafiz, perish for thy sake. I only entreat that thou do not thyself put me to death, but give me up to these men, that I may die a martyr, and that my innocent blood may come upon their heads. Let my body be buried at Scutari." He then kissed the earth, and exclaimed, "In the name of God, the All-merciful, the All-good. There is no power or might save with God, the most High, the Almighty. His we are, and unto Him we return." Hafiz then strode forth a hero into the fatal court. The Sultan sobbed aloud, the pages wept bitterly, the Viziers gazed with tearful eyes. The rebels rushed to meet him as he advanced. To sell his life as a martyr, he struck the foremost to the ground with a well-aimed buffet, on which the rest sprang on him with their daggers, and pierced him with seventeen mortal wounds. A Janissary knelt on his breast, and struck off his head. The pages of the Seraglio came forward and spread a robe over the corpse. Then said the Sultan, "God's will be done ! But in His appointed time ye shall meet with vengeance, ye men of blood, who have neither the fear of God before your eyes, nor respect for the law of the Prophet." The threat was little heeded at the time, but it was uttered by one who never menaced in vain.

Within two months after this scene fresh victims had fallen before the bloodthirsty rabble that now disgraced the name of Turkish troops. The deposition of Amurath was openly discussed in their barracks ; and the young Sultan saw that the terrible alternative, " Kill, or be killed," was no longer to be evaded. Some better spirits in the army, shamed and heart-sick at the spirit of brigandage that was so insolently dominant over court and camp, placed their swords at their sovereign's disposal ; and a small but brave force, that could be relied on in the hour of need, was gradually and quietly organised. The dissensions also among the mutinous troops themselves, and especially the ancient jealousy between the Spahis and the Janissaries, offered means for repressing them all, of which Amurath availed himself with boldness and skill. His first act was to put the archtraitor, Redjib Pacha, suddenly and secretly to death. He then proceeded to the more difficult one of reducing the army to submission. This was done on the 29th day of May, 1632, the day on which the Sultan emancipated himself from his m litary tyrants, and commenced also his own reign of terror. Amurath held a public divan on the shore of the sea near the Kiosch of Sinan. The Mufti, the Viziers, the chief members of the Ulema were there, and the two military chiefs, who had devoted themsel es to the cause of the Sultan against the mutinous troops, Kœsè Mohammed and Roum Mohammed. Six squadrons of horseguards, whose loyalty could be trusted, were also in attendance, and ready for immediate action. Amurath seated himself on the throne, and sent a message to the Spahis, who were assembled in the hippodrome, requiring the attendance of a de utation of their officers. Amurath then summoned the Janissaries before him and addressed them as faithful troops who were enemies to the r bels in the other corps. The Janissaries shouted out that the adischah's enemies were their enemies also, and took with zealous readiness an oath of implicit obedience, which was suggested at the moment. Copies of the Koran were ready, and were handed through the ranks. The Janissaries swore on the sacred book, "By God, with God, and through God." Their oath was formally registered; and Amurath then turned to the deputies of the Spahis, who had by this time arrived, and had witnessed the loyal fervour of the Janissaries. The Sultan reproached them for the rapacity and lawlessness of their body. They answered humbly that the Sultan's charges were true, but that they were personally loyal, though unable to make their men obey them. "If ye are loyal," said Amurath, "take the oath which your brethren the Janissaries have taken, and deliver up to me the ringleaders of rebellion from your ranks." Surrounded by the royal horseguards and Janissaries, the Spahi officers obeyed in fear and trembling. Amurath then ordered the judges to stand forward. He said to them, "Ye are accused of selling your judgments for gold, and of destroying my people. What answer have you to give?" "God is our witness," said they, "that we seek not to make a traffic of justice, or to oppress the poor; but we have no freedom or independence; and if we protect thy subjects against the violence of the Spahis and the taxgatherers, we are accused of corruption, our tribunals are assailed by armed men, and our houses are pillaged." "I have heard of these things," said the Sultan. Then arose in the Divan a valiant judge of Asia, an Arab by birth, and he drew his sabre, and cried "My Padischah, the only cure for all these things is the edge of the sword." At these words the Sultan and the whole assembly fixed their eyes on the Arabian judge, who stood before them with flashing eyes and weapon, but said no more. The declaration of the judge was registered; and then all present, the Sultan, the Viziers, the Mufti, and the chief officers, signed a written manifesto, by which they bound themselves to suppress abuses and maintain public order, under the penalty of bringing on their heads the curses of God, of the Prophet, of all angels, and of all true believers.

Amurath had need of acts as well as of words; and the work of death speedily began. Energetic and trusty emissaries were sent through Constantinople, who slew the leaders of the late insurrection, and all whom Amurath marked for destruction. The troops, deprived of their chiefs, and suspicious of each other, trembled and obeyed. The same measures were taken in the provinces, and for many months the sword and the bowstring were incessantly active. But it was in the capital, and under Amurath's own eye, that the revenge of royalty for its long humiliation reaped the bloodiest harvest. Every morning the Bosphorus threw up on its shores the corpses of those who had been executed during the preceding night; and in them the anxious spectators recognised Janissaries and Spahis, whom they had lately seen parading the streets in all the haughtiness of military licence. The personal appearance and courage of Amurath, his bold and martial demeanour, confirmed the respect and awe which this strenuous ferocity inspired. He was in the twentieth year of his age; and though but little above the middle stature, his bodily frame united strength and activity in a remarkable degree. His features were regular and handsome. His aquiline nose, and the jet-black beard which had begun to grace his chin, gave dignity to his aspect: but the imperious lustre of his full dark eyes was marred by an habitual frown; which, however, suited well the sternness of his character. Every day he displayed his horsemanship in the hippodrome; and he won the involuntary admiration of the soldiery by his strength and skill as a cavalier and swordsman, and by his unrivalled force and dexterity in the use of the bow. He patrolled the streets in disguise at night; and often, with his own hand, struck dead the offenders against his numerous edicts in matters of police. If any menacing assemblage began to form in any of the streets, the Sultan received speedy tidings from his numerous spies; and, before revolt could be matured, Amurath was on the spot, well armed, and with a trusty guard of choice troops. He rode fearlessly in among the groups of Spahis or Janissaries, who slunk in savage silence from before their Sultan, each dreading lest that keen eye should recognise and mark him, and that unforgiving lip pronounce his doom.

The insurrection in Asia Minor had been quelled in 1630, by the defeat and submission of Abaza, whom Amurath had spared, principally out of sympathy with his hatred towards the Janissaries, and had made Pacha of Bosnia. He now employed that able and ruthless chief in Constantinople, and appointed him Aga of his old enemies the Janissaries. Abaza served his stern master well in that perilous station; but he at last incurred the displeasure of Amurath, and was executed in 1634. The habit of bloodshedding had now grown into a second nature with the Sultan. All faults, small or great, were visited by him with the same short, sharp, and final sentence; and the least shade of suspicion that crossed his restless mind was sufficient to ensure its victim's doom. He struck before he censured: and, at last, the terror with which he was regarded was so general and profound, that men who were summoned to the Sultan's presence, commonly made the death-ablution before they entered the palace. The career of Amurath is a memorable proof of how perilously the possession of unlimited power tempts, first to excessive severity for real wrongs—next to ruthless haste in punishing for imaginary offences—and, finally, to the practice of inhuman cruelty on the slightest suspicion or vexation. The earliest executions which Amurath ordered, when he assumed independent power, were those of traitors and mutineers, whose guilt was as heinous as it was unquestionable. His slaughters grew more sweeping; but still, for a long time, his cruelty was seldom or never awakened out of mere wantonness or caprice. It was against real or suspected state offenders that the Imperial Manslayer exercised his terrible prerogative during the first two years of his actual sovereignty. But by degrees his temper grew more moody, and human life became as nothing in his eyes. When he rode forth, any unfortunate wretch who displeased him by crossing or impeding the road, was instantly put to death, and frequently fell pierced by an arrow from the gloomy despot's own bow. He once caused a party of women, whom he saw dancing in a meadow, to be seized and drowned, because their noisy merriment disturbed him. At another time, a boat, with many females on board, passed along the Bosphorus nearer to the walls of the Seraglio than he thought proper. He ordered the batteries to open on them, and they were sent to the bottom before his eyes. He beheaded his chief musician for singing a Persian air, which he said was doing honour to the enemies of the empire. Many other acts of equal atrocity are recorded of him; and the number of those who died by his command is reckoned at 100,000. Among them were three of his brothers, and, as was generally believed, his deposed uncle Mustapha. One of his sayings is preserved by an Italian writer, who asserts that Amurath's favourite book was "The Prince" of Machiavelli, which had been translated into Turkish. The Sultan's own maxim is certainly worthy of such inspiration. It is this: "Vengeance never grows decrepit, though she may grow grey." In the last years of Amurath's life, his ferocity of temper was fearfully aggravated by the habits of intoxication which he acquired. In one of his nocturnal perambulations of the capital, he met a drunkard, named Mustapha Bekir, who entered into conversation with him, and boasted that he possessed that which would purchase all Constantinople, and "the son of a slave" himself. ("The son of a slave" is a term by which the Turkish people often speak of the Sultan.)

In the morning, Amurath sent for the man, and reminded him of his words. Nothing daunted, Bekir drew a flask of wine from his robe, and held it out to the Sultan, saying, "Here is the liquid gold, which outweighs all the treasures of the universe, which makes a beggar more glorious than a king, and turns the mendicant Fakir into a horned Alexander."[1] Struck with the confidence and joyous spirit of the bold bacchanal, Amurath drained the flask, and thenceforth Mustapha Bekir and the Sultan were boon companions. When the plague was in 1637 carrying off 500 victims daily at Constantinople Amurath often passed his nights in revels with his favourite. "This summer," he said, "God is punishing the rogues. Perhaps by winter He will come to the honest men."

Never, however, did Amurath wholly lose in habits of indulgence the vigour of either mind or body. When civil or military duty required his vigilance, none could surpass him in austere abstemiousness, or in the capacity for labour. And, with all his misdeeds, he saved his country. He tolerated no crimes but his own. The worst of evils, the sway of petty local tyrants, ceased under his dominion. He was unremittingly and unrelentingly watchful in visiting the offences of all who were in authority under him, as well as those of the mass of his subjects; and the worst tyranny of the single despot was a far less grievous curse to the empire than had been the military anarchy which he quelled. Order and subordination were restored under his iron sway. There was discipline in the camps; there was pure justice on the tribunals. The revenues were fairly raised, and honestly administered. The abuses of the feudal system of the Ziamets and Timars were extirpated; and, if Amurath was dreaded at home, he made himself still more feared by the foe abroad.

It was at first highly perilous for him to leave the central seat of empire. He commenced an expedition into the troubled parts of his Asiatic dominions in the end of the year 1633; but when he had marched a little beyond Nicomedia, he hanged the chief judge of that city, because he found the roads in bad repair. This excited great indignation among the Ulema, and the leaders of that formidable body in the capital began to hold language little favourable to the Sultan's authority. Warned by his mother, the Sultana Validé, of these discontents, Amurath returned suddenly to Constantinople, and put the chief Mufti to death. This is said to be a solitary instance of the death of a Mufti by a Sultan's

---

[1] So Horace says to the wine-flask :
    "Addis cornua pauperi."

order. It effectually curbed the tongues and pens of the men of
the law during the remainder of Amurath's reign. In the spring
of 1635, he again marched forth from his capital with the avowed
intention of not only inspecting his Asiatic provinces, but of
expelling the Persian heretics from the cities within the ancient
limits of the Ottoman Empire, which they still occupied. In the
campaign of this year he conquered the city of Eriwan, and
showed the true spirit of the ancient Ottoman Sultans in the care
with which his troops were provided for, as well as in the strict
discipline which he maintained, and the personal valour and
generalship which he displayed. When it was necessary to
undergo privations, the Sultan shared them with his men; and
the English writer, Rycaut, says of him, that "for several months
he made use of no other pillow for his head than his saddle, no
other blanket or quilt than the covering or foot-cloth of his horse."
The recovery of the city and territory of Eriwan was an important
exploit; but the march of Amurath through Asia Minor and back,
was also a royal visitation of terrible severity to all the provincial
governors, whom he convicted or suspected of the slightest disaffection or neglect. In 1638 he made his final and greatest
expedition against the Persians, to re-annex to the Ottoman
Empire the great city of Bagdad, which had been in the power of
those enemies of the House of Othman and of the Sunnite creed
for fifteen years, and had been repeatedly besieged in vain by
Turkish armies. There is a tradition in the East that Bagdad,
the ancient city of the Caliphate, can only be taken by a
sovereign in person. The Great Solyman had first won it for
Turkey; and now, at the end of a century after that conquest,
Amurath IV. prepared his armies for its recovery. The imperial
standard of the Seven Horsetails was planted on the heights of
Scutari on the 9th March, 1638, and a week afterwards Amurath
joined the army. A proclamation was made by which the march
from Scutari to Bagdad was divided into 110 days' journey,
with fixed periods for halts; and on the 8th of May the vast
host moved steadily forward in unmurmuring obedience to its
leader's will. Throughout this second progress of Amurath (the
last ever made by an Ottoman sovereign in person through any of
the Asiatic provinces not immediately adjacent to Constantinople)[1] he showed the same inquisitorial strictness and merciless severity in examining the conduct of all the provincial
authorities, that had been felt on his former march to Eriwan.
Pashas, judges, Imams, and tax-collectors thronged to kiss the

[1] Hulme.

Sultan's stirrup; and, if there was the slightest taint of suspicion on the character of any functionary for probity, activity, or loyalty, the head of the unhappy homager rolled in the dust beneath the imperial charger's hoofs.

On the 15th November, 1638, after the pre-appointed 110 days of march, and eighty-six days of halt, the Ottoman standards appeared before Bagdad, and the last siege of this great city commenced. The fortifications were strong; the garrison amounted to 30,000 men, 1200 of whom were regularly trained musketeers; and the Persian Governor, Bektish Khan, was an officer of proved ability and bravery. A desperate resistance was expected, and was encountered by the Turks: but their numbers, their discipline, and the resolute skill of their Sultan, prevailed over all. Amurath gave his men an example of patient toil, as well as active courage. He laboured in the trenches, and pointed the cannon with his own hands. And, when in one of the numerous sorties made by the garrison, a Persian soldier, of gigantic size and strength, challenged the best and boldest Turk to single combat, Amurath stood forth in person, and after a long and doubtful conflict clove his foe from skull to chin with a sabre stroke. On the 22nd December, the Turkish artillery had made a breach of 80 yards, along which the defences were so completely levelled, that, in the words of an Ottoman writer, "a blind man might have galloped over them with loose bridle without his horse stumbling."[1] The ditch had been heaped up with fascines; and the Turks rushed forward to an assault, which was for two days baffled by the number and valour of the besieged. On the evening of the second day Amurath bitterly reproached his Grand Vizier, Tayar Mohammed Pacha, for the repulse of the troops, and accused him of want of courage. The Vizier replied, "Would to God, my Padischah, that it were half as easy to ensure for thee the winning of Bagdad, as it will be for me to lay down my life in the breach to-morrow in thy service." On the third day (Christmas Eve, 1638) Tayar Mohammed led the forlorn hope in person, and was shot dead through the throat by a volley from the Persian musketeers. But the Turks poured on with unremitted impetuosity, and at length the city was carried. Part of the garrison, which had retired to some inner defences, asked for quarter, which was at first granted; but a conflict having accidentally recommenced in the streets between some Persian musketeers and a Turkish detachment, Amurath ordered a general slaughter of the Persians, and after a whole day of butchery,

[1] Cited by Hulme.

scarcely 300 out of the garrison, which had originally consisted of 30,000 men, were left alive. A few days afterwards, Amurath was exasperated by the accidental or designed explosion of a powder magazine, by which 800 Janissaries were killed and wounded; and he ·commanded a massacre of the inhabitants of the city, in which 30,000 are computed by the Ottoman historian to have perished. In February Amurath commenced his homeward march, after having repaired the city walls, and left one of his best generals with 12,000 troops to occupy Bagdad, which has never since been wrested from the Turks. The Sultan reached Constantinople on the 10th June, 1638, and made a triumphal entry into his capital; which is memorable, not only on account of its splendour, and of the importance of the conquest which it celebrated, but because it was then that Constantinople beheld for the last time the once familiar spectacle of the return of her monarch victorious from a campaign, which he had conducted in person. The Ottoman writer,[1] who witnessed and described the scene, says that the Sultan "repaired to his palace with splendour aud magnificence which no tongue can tell, and no pen adequately illustrate. The balconies and roofs of the houses were everywhere thronged with people, who exclaimed with enthusiasm, 'The blessing of God be on thee, O Conqueror! Welcome, Amurath! May thy victories be fortunate!' The Sultan was sheathed in resplendent armour of polished steel, with a leopard-skin over his shoulders, and wore in his turban a triple aigrette, placed obliquely, in the Persian mode. He rode a Nogai charger, and was followed by seven led Arab horses with jewelled caparisons, while trumpets and cymbals resounded before him, and twenty-two Persian Khans were led captives at the imperial stirrups. As he passed along he looked proudly on each side, like a lion who has seized his prey, and saluted the people, who shouted '*Barik-Allah!*' and threw themselves on the ground. All the vessels of war fired constant salutes, so that the sea seemed in a blaze; and seven days and nights were devoted to constant rejoicings."

A peace with Persia, on the basis of that which Solyman the Great had granted in 1555, was the speedy result of Amurath's victories (15th September, 1639). Eriwan was restored by the Porte; but the possession of Bagdad, and the adjacent territory by the Ottomans, was solemnly sanctioned and confirmed. Eighty years passed away before Turkey was again obliged to struggle against her old and obstinate enemy on the line of the Euphrates. For this long cessation of exhausting hostilities, and this enduring

[1] Cited by Hulme.

acknowledgment of superiority by Persia, Turkey owes a deep debt
of gratitude to the memory of Amurath IV.

Amurath died at the age of twenty-eight, on the 9th of February, 1640.   In the interval between his return from Bagdad and
his last illness, he had endeavoured to restore the fallen naval power
of his empire, he had quelled the spirit of insurrection that had
been rife in Albania and the neighbouring districts during his
absence in Asia, and he was believed to be preparing for a war
with Venice.   A fever, aggravated by his habits of intemperance,
and by his superstitious alarm at an eclipse of the sun, proved
fatal to him after an illness of fifteen days.   One of his last acts
was to command the execution of his sole surviving brother
Ibrahim.   It may be doubted whether this mark of " the ruling
spirit strong in death " was caused by the delirium of fever, or
from a desire that his favourite the Silihdar Pacha should succeed
to the throne on the extinction of the race of Othman, or
whether Amurath IV. wished for the gloomy satisfaction of
knowing that his House and Dynasty would descend to the grave
with him.   The Sultana Validé preserved Ibrahim's life, and used
the pious fraud of a false message to the Sultan that his command
had been fulfilled.   Amurath, then almost in the pangs of death,
" grinned horrible a ghastly smile " in the belief that his brother
was slain, and tried to rise from his bed to behold the supposed
dead body.   His attendants, who trembled for their own lives
should the deception be detected, forcibly held him back on the
couch.   The Iman, who had been waiting in an adjoining room, but
had hitherto feared to approach the terrible dying man, was now
brought forward by the pages ; and, while the priest commenced
his words of prayer, the " effera vis animi " of Amurath IV. departed from the world.

CHAPTER XIV.

CHARACTER OF THE LATTER PORTION OF TURKISH HISTORY—
ACCESSION OF SULTAN IBRAHIM—FOLLY AND WICKEDNESS OF
HIS GOVERNMENT—REVOLUTION—IBRAHIM DEPOSED AND PUT
TO DEATH—FOREIGN EVENTS DURING IBRAHIM'S REIGN—WAR
WITH THE COSSACKS—BEGINNING OF THE WAR OF CANDIA—
MAHOMET IV., AT THE AGE OF SEVEN, RAISED TO THE THRONE—
CONTINUED TUMULT AND MISERY—THE FIRST KIUPRILI MADE
VIZIER.[1]

WE have now traced the fortunes of the House of Othman during
a period of nearly four hundred years. A further space of rather
more than two centuries remains to be examined, which comprises the reigns of fifteen princes. But, with the exception of
the great though unsuccessful Mahmoud II., perhaps with the
exceptions also of Mustapha II. and Selim III., the Turkish
princes whom we are proceeding to contemplate form figures of
but languid interest on the historic page. The decay of the State
accords with the degeneracy of its rulers ; and minute descriptions
of the troubles and calamities of declining empire are generally
monotonous and unattractive. We shall indeed still have our
attention drawn to fierce and eventful wars ; and we shall still
meet with names, that must ever live high in martial renown ;
but they are wars in which the Crescent has generally, though
not invariably, gone back ; they are principally the names of commanders, who have grown great, not in the advancement, but at
the expense of the House of Othman : such names as Montecuculi,
Sobieski, Eugene, and Suwarrow. Yet gleams of glory and
success on the Turkish side will not be found altogether wanting,
and there have been truly great men in the councils and the armies
of Turkey. She has had her Kiuprilis, and others, whose names
have long deserved and commanded more than merely Oriental
celebrity. We may remark, also, that these last two centuries of
Ottoman history, though less picturesque and spirit-stirring than
its earlier periods, are more practically instructive and valuable

[1] See Von Hammer, books 49-51.

for us to study, with reference to the great problems which the states of Central and Western Europe are now called on to solve.

When Sultan Amurath IV. expired, his brother Ibrahim, whom he had vainly doomed with his own dying breath to die, was the sole surviving representative in male descent of the House of Othman. Ibrahim had during Amurath's reign been a prisoner in the royal palace; and for the last eight years had trembled in the daily expectation of death. When the grandees of the empire hastened to his apartment with the tidings that Sultan Amurath was no more, and with congratulations to their new sovereign, Ibrahim in his terror thought that the executioners were approaching, and barred the door against them. He long refused to believe their assurances of Amurath's decease; and was only convinced when the Sultana-mother ordered the body of her dead son to be carried within sight of the living one. Then Ibrahim came forth, and mounted the Turkish throne, which received in him a selfish voluptuary, in whom long imprisonment and protracted terror had debased whatever spirit nature might have originally bestowed, and who was as rapacious and blood-thirsty, as he was cowardly and mean. Under Ibrahim the worst evils that had prevailed in the time of Amurath's weakest predecessors were speedily revived; while the spirit of cruelty, in which Amurath had governed, continued to rage with even greater enormity.

For a short period Ibrahim's first Grand Vizier, Kara-Moustafa, laboured to check the excesses and supply the deficiencies of his sovereign. The Christian subjects of the Porte received from Kara-Moustafa impartial justice; and he attempted with some degree of temporary success to keep down the growth of abuses in the financial administration of the empire. He had the perilous honesty to speak with frankness to the dissolute tyrant whom he served, to oppose Ibrahim's mad caprices, and to strive against the pernicious influence of the favourite sultanas and buffoons, who trafficked in the sale of posts and dignities. The offence which the Vizier thus gave, and the reputation of having amassed much wealth, were sure causes of ruin to one who served a moody and avaricious master like Ibrahim. At the same time the Vizier's character was far from faultless; and his errors and his merits co-operated to effect his destruction. Moustafa was violent and implacable in his enmity towards all who rivalled or seeemed likely to rival him in power; and he was unscrupulous as to the means which he employed in order to overthrow an adversary. But his deadliest foes were those whose inferiority of sex and station screened them from reprisals; and the immediate cause of the Grand Vizier's fall was an affront which he gave to the lady who held the office of governess of the harem.   This female functionary of Ibrahim's State, the Kiaya-Khatoum, had sent a requisition to the Grand Vizier for an instant supply of 500 carts of wood for the use of the harem.   At this very time grave tidings of troubles in the provinces and on the frontiers had reached Constantinople.   Intent on these matters, Kara-Moustafa neglected to send the faggots for the ladies.   A few days after-wards, while he was presiding in the Divan, he received, two hours before the usual time of the council's rising, a message from Ibrahim commanding him immediately to dismiss the Divan and appear before the Sultan.   The Vizier obeyed, and hastened before his royal master.   Ibrahim instantly demanded of him, "Why have not the 500 loads of wood for the harem been supplied?"   "They shall be sent," replied the Vizier.   Then, with more courage than prudence, he added, "My Padischah, is it wise or proper for thee to call on me to break up the Divan, and to confuse and delay the weightiest affairs of State, for the sake of attending to 500 loads of wood, the whole value of which does not amount to 500 aspres?   Why, when I am before thee, dost thou question me about firewood, but sayest not a word about the petitions of thy subjects, the state of the frontier, and of the finances?"   The Mufti Yahya, who was informed of this conversation by Husein Effendi, who was present, advised the Grand Vizier to be more guarded in his words, and to treat nothing as of trifling importance in which the Sultan took an interest.   Kara-Moustafa replied, "Is it not doing the Sultan good service to tell him the truth?   Am I to turn flatterer?   I had rather speak freely and die, than live in servile falsehood."[1]

Resolved, however, not to die without an effort to overthrow his enemies, Kara-Moustafa formed a device to ruin Youssouf Pacha, who had lately risen rapidly in favour with the Sultan, and who was the Vizier's mortal foe.   Kara-Moustafa caused money to be distributed among the Janissaries of the capital, to induce them to refuse their rations, and to allege the undue in-fluence of Youssouf Pacha as the cause of their discontent.   But the scheme was soon disclosed to the Sultan, who summoned Kara-Moustafa before him, and ordered his instant execution.   Kara-Moustafa escaped from the royal presence to his own house; and, when pursued thither by the executioners, instead of exhibiting the

[1] The Turkish historian, Naima, who narrates this speech, states that he heard it related by Husein Effendi.   Von Hammer, vol. iii. p. 234, n.

passive submission, which Oriental statesmen have generally shown
in such circumstances, he drew his sabre and fought desperately,
till he was overpowered by numbers, disarmed, and strangled.[1]

The successor of Kara-Moustafa in the Grand Vizierate was
Sultanzadé Pacha. He was determined not to incur his predecessor's fate by uncourtly frankness towards his sovereign. He
flattered every caprice, and was the ready instrument of every
passion of the Sultan, whose immoderate appetite for sensual
pleasures, and savage fondness of ordering and of witnessing acts
of cruelty now raged without stint or shame. Ibrahim, who remembered the check which Kara-Moustafa used to impose on him,
could not help feeling some degree of surprise at the universal
obsequiousness of his new Grand Vizier; and asked one day of
Sultanzadé, "How is it that thou art able always to approve of
my actions, whether good or evil?" "My Padischah," replied the
shameless minister of despotism, "thou art Caliph; thou art God's
shadow upon earth. Every idea, which thy spirit entertains, is a
revelation from Heaven. Thy orders, even when they appear un-
reasonable, have an innate reasonableness, which thy slave ever
reveres, though he may not always understand." Ibrahim accepted
these assurances of infallibility and impeccability; and thenceforth
spoke of himself as a divinely inspired agent in the midst of the
most disgraceful scenes of folly, vice, and crime. So gross were
these, that the very inmates of his harem sometimes murmured;
and the Sultan's mother remonstrated with him against the corruption and frivolity of his conduct; but in vain. Ibrahim replied
by quoting the words of his Grand Vizier; and let loose his
absolute power in the gratification of every frivolous vanity and
caprice, of every depraved appetite, of every feverish fit of irritable
passion, and every gloomy desire of suspicious malignity.

The treasures, which the stern prudence of Amurath had accumulated, were soon squandered by the effeminate prodigality of
his successor. In order to obtain fresh supplies of gold for his

---

[1] When Kara-Moustafa's palace was searched by the Sultan's officers, five
pictures, being portraits of Kara-Moustafa and four other ministers of state,
were found in a place of concealment. It was supposed that the late Vizier
had used them in magical rites; and a Moor, who was said to have been his
tutor in sorcery, was burnt alive. Von Hammer remarks that probably
Kara-Moustafa was fond of paintings, but kept them as forbidden treasures
in a secret part of his house. The strict followers of the Mahometan law
consider all representations of the human form, either in statuary or paint-
ing, to be impious : both as encouragements to idolatry and as profanations
of God's chief workmanship. They say, that at the Last Day pictures and
statues will rise round the artists who produced them, and call on the unhappy makers to supply their creatures with souls.

worthless favourites, and for the realisation of his wild fancies, Ibrahim sold every office of state, and every step in the honours both of Pen and Sword, to the highest bidder. The burdens of the old taxes were inordinately increased, and new imposts were added ; the very names of which showed the frivolous causes for which the Sultan drained the resources of his subjects, thus adding the sense of insult to that of oppression. One of Ibrahim's passions was a morbid craving for perfumes, especially for amber. Another was an excessive fondness, not only of wearing, but of seeing around him, furs of the most rare and costly description. To meet these desires, Ibrahim created two new taxes ; one called the Fur Tax, and the other called the Amber Tax. The madness of the Sultan's love for furs was worked up to the utmost by hearing a legend told by an old woman, who used to amuse the ladies of the harem by narrating stories to them at night. This legend described a certain king of the olden time, who was dressed in sable-skins, whose sofas and couches were covered, and whose palace was carpeted and tapestried also with the fur of the sable. Ibrahim instantly set his heart on being similarly arrayed, and on decking the Serail in like manner. He dreamed all night of sables ; and in the morning he commanded in the Divan that letters should be sent to all the governors and great men of the empire, enjoining each of them to collect and forward to Constantinople a certain number of sable-skins. A similar requisition was made on all the Ulema, and all the civil and military officers in the capital. Some of them were driven to desperation by this mad tyranny, and openly gave vent to the indignation which it inspired. Mohammed Tchelibi, the judge of Galata, appeared before the Grand Vizier clad in the gown of a common dervise, and reproached him bitterly for the folly and wickedness of the government. He demanded an audience of the Sultan, and added, " There can but happen to me one of three things. You may kill me ; and, in that case, I shall think myself fortunate in being made a martyr. Or, you may banish me from Constantinople ; which will not be unpleasant, as there have been several shocks of earthquake here lately. Or, perhaps, you will deprive me of my employments. But in that I have saved you the trouble. I have appointed my deputy, and have changed my judge's robe and turban for the dervise's gown and cap." The Vizier, alarmed at such boldness, heard him in silence, and concealed his resentment. A colonel of the Janissaries, named Black Mourad, to whom the 500 men of his regiment were devotedly attached, at this time returned from the Candian wars, and was met on landing by a treasury officer, who, in conformity with the resolution of the Divan, demanded of him so many sable-skins, so many ounces of amber, and a certain sum of money.   Rolling his eyes, bloodshot with wrath, on the tax-gatherer, Black Mourad growled out, " I have brought nothing back from Candia but gunpowder and lead.   Sables and amber are things that I know only by name.   Money I have none; and, if I am to give it you, I must first beg or borrow it."   Not satisfied with the produce of these exactions, the Sultan arbitrarily confiscated and sold a large mass of heritable property.   The capricious fancies of his favourite ladies were as costly to the empire as his own.   Ibrahim permitted them to take what they pleased from the shops and bazaars without payment.   One of these fair plunderers complained to the sovereign that she disliked shopping by daylight; and forthwith appeared a mandate from the Sultan requiring all the merchants and shop-keepers of the capital to keep their establishments open all night, and to provide sufficient torchlight for their wares to be seen clearly.   Another lady told Ibrahim that she wished to see him with his beard adorned with jewels.   Ibrahim decked himself accordingly, and appeared in public thus bedizened.   The Turks looked on this as an evil omen; because, according to Oriental traditions, the only sovereign who had adopted such embellishment was King Pharaoh of the Red Sea.   Enormous treasures were squandered on the construction of a chariot, incrusted with precious stones, for the use of another Celœno of the harem; and 25,000 piastres were expended, that an equally splendid skiff should bear the Sultan along the Bosphorus.   The disasters of the Venetian wars during the year 1648 irritated more and more the Ottoman nation against their imbecile but oppressive ruler; and a formidable conspiracy was organised to deprive him of the power which he abused.

Foremost among the conspirators were the chief officers of the Janissaries; and the most active of these was Black Mourad, the colonel who had spoken with such rough frankness of the royal requisition for amber and sable.   He knew that his head was in hourly peril; and it was indeed only by a timely warning from a private friend in the seraglio that he escaped death.   The Sultan and his Vizier celebrated with great splendour on the 6th of August, 1648, the marriage of one of Ibrahim's daughters, a child of eight years old, with the Vizier's son.   Mourad and three other Janissary colonels, named Moussliheddin, Begtasch, and Kara-Tschaoush, were bidden to the royal marriage feast, at which it was intended to secure and slay them.   But the doomed men avoided their sovereign's snare, and summoned, the same night, their comrades to the mosque of the Janissaries. It was there resolved to depose the Grand Vizier. This was the first avowed object of the conspirators, but they were fully prepared to strike further. The birth of several princes since Ibrahim's accession, the eldest of whom, named Mahomet, was now seven years old, had deprived the Sultan of the protection, which, in the early part of his reign, he derived from being the sole representative of the House of Othman. The whole body of the Ulema co-operated with the soldiery; and no one was more active or determined in promoting the revolution than the chief Mufti, whose deadly enmity Ibrahim had earned by a gross insult offered to his daughter. Ibrahim heard the demand of the insurgents respecting his Vizier, and took away from him the seals of office; but with a gleam of friendship and humanity, feelings of which at other times he seemed destitute, he strove to protect his fallen favourite's life. The soldiery and the Ulema made Sofi Mohammed Grand Vizier, and sent him to the Sultan to make known their will that the evil minister should be given up to them for punishment. Ibrahim had the imprudence to strike the chosen Vizier of the army and the people, and to threaten him that his own turn for punishment should soon arrive. The insurgents now surrounded the palace, and their words grew more and more menacing. The Sultan sent his master of the horse to bid them disperse. The veteran Moussliheddin harangued him in the hearing of the Janissaries, the Spahis, and the civil officers, who were now all joined in the revolt, saying, " The Padischah has ruined the Ottoman world by pillage and tyranny. Women wield the sovereignty. The treasury cannot satiate their caprices. The subjects are ruined. The armies of the infidels are winning towns on the frontiers : their fleets blockade the Dardanelles. Hast thou not been an eye-witness of the state of affairs? and why hast thou not told the Padischah the truth?" " The Padischah," answered the envoy, "knows nought of this. The guilt is mine : for I feared to speak the truth to the Padischah in the presence of the late Vizier. But now tell me what ye desire, and I will faithfully repeat your words before the throne." Moussliheddin, in the name of the assembly, demanded three things : first, the abolition of the sale of offices ; secondly, the banishment of the favourite Sultanas from the court ; thirdly, the death of the Grand Vizier. The master of the horse took back this message to the Sultan, who made feeble preparations for resistance by arming the gardeners and pages of the palace. It was now night, and the chiefs of the Ulema among the insurgents wished to retire to their homes. But the men of the sword were wiser than the men of the law; and the colonels of the Janissaries said to their judicial comrades, "If we separate to-night, we may be unable to assemble again in the morning. Let us keep together till we have re-established order in the world; and let us in a mass pass this night in the mosque." The Ulema obeyed, and in the morning the united revolutionists began their work of vengeance. The obnoxious Vizier was discovered in his hiding-place and slain, as was the grand judge of Roumelia, who was hated by the people for his debauchery and venality. A message was now sent into the Serail, requiring the Sultan to come forth to the troops. As Ibrahim complied not with this desire, two of the chief Ulema were commissioned to wait upon Ibrahim's mother, the Sultana Validé, and to inform her that it was resolved to depose the Sultan, and to enthrone her grandson Mahomet in his stead. It has been mentioned that this princess had vainly expostulated with Ibrahim respecting his career of insane profligacy and tyranny. The only effect of her remonstrances had been to draw on her the Sultan's hatred; and Ibrahim had treated her and the princesses, his sisters, with gross indignity, and was justly suspected of meditating their destruction. But the aged Sultana now strove hard to avert the wrath of the people from her unworthy son. It was known that the force of armed attendants in the Serail was utterly inadequate to protect Ibrahim against an assault by the insurgents; and this slight guard was evidently indisposed to peril their lives for an odious and despised master. The Sultana Validé consented to receive a deputation from the army and people, consisting of the Mufti, the Cadiaskers, and of Moussliheddin, Begtasch, and Black Mourad, the Janissary colonels. They found her apparelled in the deepest mourning, and only a negro eunuch attended to fan her. They stood before her in respectful silence, and she said to them, "Is it a just thing thus to raise revolts? Are ye not all slaves, whom the bounty of this House has fed?" The old veteran, Moussliheddin, moved to tears by these words, replied, "Gracious mistress, thou art right. We have all known the benefactions of this House; no one more than myself for these eighty years. It is because we are not thankless men, that we can no longer stand idly by, and witness the ruin of this illustrious House and of this realm. Oh, would that I had not lived on to see these days! What is there that I can covet further for myself? Neither gold nor rank could profit me. But oh, most gracious lady, the foolishness and the wicked-

23

ness of the Padischah are bringing irreparable ruin upon the land. The unbelievers have captured forty strong places on the Bosnian frontier, and eighty of their ships cruise before the Dardanelles, while the Padischah thinks of nothing but of his lusts and his sports, of squandering and of corruption. Your wise men, learned in the law, have met together, and have issued a Fetva for a change in the occupation of the throne. Until this be accomplished, ruin cannot be averted. Be gracious, oh lady! oppose this not. You would not strive against us, but against the holy law." The Sultana begged hard that they would leave her son in possession of the sovereignty, under the guardianship of the Ulema and the Grand Vizier. Some of the deputies seemed disposed to yield; but the aged grand judge of Anatolia, Hanefizadé, took up the discourse, and said: " Oh, royal lady, we have come hither, fully relying on your grace, and on your compassionate solicitude for the servants of God. You are not only the mother of the Sultan; you are the mother also of all true believers. Put an end to this state of trouble; the sooner the better. The enemy has the upper hand in battle. At home, the traffic in places and ranks has no bounds. The Padischah, absorbed in satisfying his passions, removes himself farther and farther from the path of the laws. The call to prayers from the minarets of the Mosque of Aya Sofia is drowned in the noise of fifes, and flutes, and cymbals from the palace. No one can speak counsel without peril to the speaker: you have yourself proved it. The markets are plundered. The innocent are put to death. Favourite slaves govern the world."

The Validé made one more effort, and said, " All this is the doing of wicked ministers. They shall be removed; and only good and wise men shall be set in their stead." " What will that avail?" replied Hanefizadé. " Has not the Sultan put to death good and gallant men who served him, such as were Kara-Moustafa Pacha, and Youssouf Pacha, the conqueror of Canea?" " But how," urged the Sultana, " is it possible to place a child of seven years upon the throne?" Hanefizadé answered: " In the opinion of our wise men of the law a madman ought not to reign, whatever be his age; but rather let a child, that is gifted with reason be upon the throne. If the sovereign be a rational being, though an infant, a wise Vizier may restore order to the world; but a grown-up Sultan, who is without sense, ruins all things by murder, by abomination, by corruption, and prodigality." " So be it, then," said the Sultana; " I will fetch my grandson, Mahomet, and place the turban on his head." The little prince was led forth amid the enthusiastic acclamations of the military and legal chiefs. All the attendants of Ibrahim had now abandoned him. A throne was raised near the Gate of Happiness of the Serail; and three hours before sunset, on the 8th of August, 1648, the principal dignitaries of the empire paid homage to Sultan Mahomet IV. Only a few were admitted at a time, lest a crowd should frighten the child. The Sultana Validé placed her grandson in charge of a trusty guard; and the Viziers and the Ulema proceeded to announce to Ibrahim the sentence of deposition. "My Padischah," said Abdul-aziz-Effendi, "according to the judgment of the Ulema, and the chief dignitaries of the empire, you must retire from the throne." "Traitor," cried Ibrahim, "Am I not your Padischah? What means this?" "No," answered Abdul-aziz-Effendi, "thou art not Padischah, for as much as thou hast set justice and holiness at nought, and hast ruined the world. Thou hast squandered thy years in folly and debauchery; the treasures of the realm in vanities: and corruption and cruelty have governed the world in thy place." Ibrahim still remonstrated with the Mufti, saying repeatedly, "Am I not Padischah? What means all this?" A Janissary colonel said to him, "Yes, you are Padischah; you are only required to repose yourself for a few days." "But why then," said Ibrahim, "must I descend from the throne?" "Because," answered Aziz Effendi, "you have made yourself unworthy of it, by leaving the path in which your ancestors walked." Ibrahim reviled them bitterly as traitors; and then, lowering his hand towards the ground, he said, "Is it a child so high, that you are going to make Padischah? How can such a child reign? And is it not my child, my own son?" At last the fallen Sultan yielded to his destiny, and suffered them to lead him to prison, repeating, as he went, "This was written on my forehead; God has ordered it." He was kept in sure, but not rigorous captivity for ten days, when a tumult among the Spahis—some of whom raised a cry in his favour, decided his fate. The chiefs of the late revolution resolved to secure themselves against a reaction in behalf of Ibrahim, by putting him to death. They laid a formal case before the Mufti, and demanded his opinion on the following question: "Is it lawful to depose and put to death a sovereign, who confers the dignities of the pen and of the sword not on those who are worthy of them, but on those who buy them for money?" The laconic answer of the Mufti was, "Yes." The ministers of death were accordingly sent to Ibrahim's prison, whither the Mufti, the new Grand Vizier Sofi Mohammed, and their principal colleagues also repaired, to witness and to ensure the fulfilment of the sentence. Ibrahim was reading the Koran when they entered. Seeing them accompanied by the executioners, whom he himself had so often employed to do their deadly work in his presence, he knew his hour was come; and he exclaimed, " Is there no one of all those who have eaten my bread, that will pity and protect me ? These men of blood have come to kill me ! Oh, mercy ! mercy !" The trembling executioners were sternly commanded by the Mufti and the Vizier to do their duty. Seized in their fatal grasp, the wretched Ibrahim broke out into blasphemies and curses; and died, invoking the vengeance of God upon the Turkish nation for their disloyalty to their sovereigns.

The Mufti justified his regicidal Fetva by the authority of the sentence in the law, which says : " If there are two caliphs, let one of them be put to death." A sentence which Von Hammer terms " a proposition to shudder at in the law of Islam. A proposition, which, arbitrarily applied and extended, sanctions the execution not only of all deposed sovereigns, but also of all princes whose existence seems to menace the master of the throne with rivalry. It is the bloody authorisation of the state-maxim of the Ottomans for the murder of kings' brothers, sons, and fathers."[1]

The principal foreign events of the reign of Ibrahim, were the siege of Azoph, and the commencement of the long war with the Venetians, called the war of Candia. The important city of Azoph, which commands the navigation of the sea of that name, and gives to its occupiers great advantages for warlike operations in the Crimea, and along all the coasts of the Euxine, had, at the time of Ibrahim's accession, been for four years in the possession of the Cossacks of the vicinity, who were nominal subjects of the Russian Czar. Ibrahim's first Vizier, Kara-Moustafa, was well aware of the necessity of maintaining the Turkish power northward of the Black Sea ; and in 1641, a strong army and fleet left Constantinople for the recovery of Azoph. This expedition was aided by a Tartar force, under the Khan of the Crimea. The Cossacks defended the place bravely ; and after a siege of three months, the Turks were obliged to retire with a loss of 7000 Janissaries, and of a multitude of auxiliary Wallachians, Moldavians, and Tartars, whom the Ottoman historians do not enumerate. A fresh expedition was sent in the next year ; and on this occasion Mohammed Ghirai, the Crimean Khan, led no less than 100,000 Tartars to Azoph, to co-operate with the regular Turkish troops. The Cossacks found themselves unable to resist such a force. The Czar

[1] Von Hammer, vol. iii. p. 321.

refused to aid them; and sent an embassy from Moscow to Ibrahim, renouncing all concern with Azoph, and desiring to renew the old amity between Russia and the Porte.[1] In this emergency the Cossack garrison, with the same ferocious energy which their race has often displayed, set fire to the city which they could no longer defend, and left a heap of ruins for the Turks and Tartars to occupy. The Ottoman general rebuilt the city and fortified it anew with care commensurate with the importance of the post. A garrison of 26,000 men, including twenty companies of Janissaries, with a numerous train of artillery, was left under Islam Pacha, to protect the Turkish interest in these regions.

The incessant attacks of the Cossacks on the Turkish, and of the Tartars on the Russian territories, were the subjects of frequent complaints between the courts of Moscow and Constantinople during Ibrahim's reign. Each sovereign required the other to keep his lawless vassals in check. The Czar Alexis Michaelowicz protested against being held responsible for the acts of the Cossacks, whom, in a letter to the Sultan, he termed "a horde of malefactors who had withdrawn as far as possible from the reach of their sovereign's power, in order to escape the punishment due to their crimes."[2] The Sultan and the Vizier,[3] on the other hand, required that no one on the side of Russia should do the least damage to aught that belonged to a subject of the Sublime Porte, either on the Sea of Azoph or the Black Sea. The pretext of shifting the blame on the Cossacks, and, in general, all excuses were to be inadmissible. On condition of this being done, and of the Czar paying the ancient tribute to the Khan of the Crimea, the Sultan promised not to aid the Tartars against Moscow. But, whatever the sovereigns might write or desire, still the system of border war between Cossack and Tartar was carried on; and the Turkish and Russian troops more than once came into collision north of the Euxine in Ibrahim's time, while protecting their irregular confederates, or seeking redress for themselves. In 1646 the Tartars pursued the Cossacks into the southern provinces of Russia; and brought away thence 3000 prisoners, whom they sold for slaves at Perekop. A Russian army advanced against Azoph, to avenge that affront, but was beaten in several actions by Mousa Pacha and the Turkish garrison, who sent 400 prisoners, and 800 Muscovites' heads to Constantinople, as trophies of their success.

[1] Rycaut, book ii. p. 52.
[2] See his letter in the Appendix to Von Hammer's 48th book. Pesth Edition.
[3] See their letters, ibid.

The Crimean Khan, Islam Ghirai, was more bitter against the Russians than was his master the Sultan; and boldly refused to obey orders from Constantinople not to molest those whom he regarded as the natural enemies of the Turkish Empire. He had early in 1648 made an incursion into Poland and Russia, and carried off 40,000 subjects of those realms into slavery. The Polish and Russian sovereigns sent ambassadors to the Sublime Porte to ask redress: and Ibrahim despatched two of his officers to the Crimea with a letter to the Khan, in which he was commanded to collect the Christian prisoners whom he had seized in violation of all treaties, and to send them to Constantinople, that they might be given up to the representatives of their governments. Khan Ghirai read the letter, and coldly replied—" I and all here are the Sultan's servants. But the Russians only desire peace in appearance; they only ask for it while they feel the weight of our victorious arms. If we give them breathing time, they ravage the coasts of Anatolia with their squadrons. I have more than once represented to the Divan that there were two neglected strong places in this neighbourhood, which it would be prudent for us to occupy. Now, the Russians have made themselves masters of them; and they have raised more than twenty little fortified posts. If we are to remain inactive this year, they will seize Akkermann, and conquer all Moldavia." With this answer the Sultan's messengers were obliged to return to Constantinople.

The immediate occasion of the war of Candia was the offence given in 1644 to the Sultan by the capture of a rich fleet of merchant vessels, which was voyaging from Constantinople to Egypt. The captors were Maltese, not Venetian galleys: but they anchored with their prizes in the roads of Kalisméne on the south coast of Candia, which had now been in the possession of the Venetians since the time of the fourth crusade, when, on partitioning the conquered Greek Empire, they purchased that important island from their fellow-crusader the Marquis of Montserrat, to whom it had first been allotted as his portion of the sacred spoil. Sultan Ibrahim was maddened with rage, when he heard of the capture of the Turkish ships, some of which were the property of one of the chief eunuchs of the imperial household. He threatened destruction to the whole Christian name, and ordered armaments to be instantly despatched against the Maltese knights; but his officers persuaded him not to renew the enterprise, in which the great Solyman had failed so signally, against the barren and strongly fortified rock of Malta; and rather to turn his arms to the acquisition of the rich and valuable Isle of Candia. They

pointed out to him that Candia was most advantageously situated
for incorporation with the Ottoman dominions, and that it might
be easily wrested by surprise from its Venetian masters, who had
given just cause for hostilities by allowing the piratical Maltese to
secure their booty on the Cretan coasts. It was resolved accordingly by the Porte to attack Candia. There was at that time
peace between Turkey and Venice. Ibrahim and his ministers
determined to aid force by fraud; and they pretended to receive
most graciously the excuses which the republic of St. Mark offered
for the accidental reception of the Maltese galleys at Kalisméne.
A large fleet and army left the Dardanelles, on the 30th April, 1645,
with the declared object of assailing Malta; but, after the expedition had paused for a time on the south coast of the Morea, the
generalissimo Youssouf Pacha put to sea again, read to his assembled captains the Sultan's orders, which had previously been kept
secret; and instead of sailing westward for Malta, stood to the
south with a favourable wind, which brought the Turkish
squadron to Canea, at the western extremity of the Isle of
Candia, on the 24th of June. The suspicions of the Venetian
government as to the real object of the expedition, had not been
wholly quieted by the protestations of the Sultan's ministers.
Orders had been sent from Venice to put the fortresses of the
island in a state of defence, and to collect the militia; and reinforcements had been sent to the garrison. But the native population hated the rule of the Venetian oligarchy; and the troops and
galleys under the governor's command were inadequate for the
defence of so long a line of sea-board as Crete presents to an
invader. The Turks landed without opposition; and Canea, the
principal city of the western part of the island, was besieged and
captured by them before the end of August. In the following
year they took Retino, and in the spring of 1648 they began the
siege of Candia, the capital of the island. This memorable siege
was prolonged for twenty years by the desperate exertions of the
Venetians, who strained their utmost resources to rescue Candia.
They frequently inflicted severe and humiliating defeats on the
Turkish squadrons; they even captured the islands of Lemnos and
Tenedos from the Ottomans, and more than once ravaged the
coasts near Constantinople; but they were never able to drive
away the besieging army from before Candia; though the operations of the Turks were retarded and often paralysed by the imbecility and corruption of the Sublime Porte throughout the reign
of Ibrahim, and the first part of that of his son Mahomet IV.,
whose elevation to the throne at the age of seven years, when his

father was deposed and murdered, has been already narrated. It would be useless to dwell on the internal history of Turkey during Mahomet IV.'s minority, and to recapitulate the ever-recurring incidents of court intrigue, military insubordination and violence, judicial venality, local oppression and provincial revolt. The strife of factions was aggravated by the deadly rivalry that sprang up between the old Sultana Validé, the Sultan's grandmother, and his mother the young Sultana Validé, whose name was Tarkhan—a rivalry which led to the murder of the elder princess. As no stronger foe than Venice attacked the Ottoman Empire, it lingered on through this period of renewed misery and weakness, until at length, in 1656, through the influence of the Sultana Tarkhan, the Grand Vizierate was given to an aged statesman named Mohammed Kiuprili, who deserves to be honoured as the founder of a dynasty of ministers that raised Turkey, in spite of the deficiency of her princes, once more to comparative power, and prosperity, and glory, and who long retarded, if they could not avert, the ultimate decline of the Ottoman Empire.

CHAPTER XV.

MOHAMMED KIUPRILI—RIGOUR AND SUCCESS OF HIS MINISTRY—
HIS SON AHMED KIUPRILI SUCCEEDS HIM IN THE VIZIERATE
—GREAT QUALITIES OF AHMED KIUPRILI—WEAKNESS OF SUL-
TAN MAHOMET IV.—WAR WITH AUSTRIA—GREAT DEFEAT OF
THE TURKS BY MONTECUCULI AT ST. GOTHARD—TRUCE WITH
AUSTRIA—AHMED KIUPRILI TAKES CANDIA—WAR WITH RUSSIA
AND POLAND—SOBIESKI DEFEATS THE TURKS AT KHOCZIM AND
LEMBERG—PEACE OF ZURAUNA—DEATH AND CHARACTER OF
AHMED KIUPRILI.[1]

THE court astronomer at Constantinople, on September 15th, 1656,
determined that the most favourable time for the investiture of
Mohammed Kiuprili with the Grand Vizierate, was the hour of the
midday prayer, at the instant when the cry of "God is Great"
resounds from the heights of the minarets.

According to a prescribed rule of Islam, the noontide prayer is
repeated, not at the exact moment when the sun is on the meridian,
but a few seconds afterwards ; because the tradition of the prophets
teaches that at the astronomical noon the devil is wont to take
the sun between his two horns, so that he may wear it as the crown
of the world's dominion ; and the fiend then rears himself as Lord of
the Earth, but he lets the sun go directly he hears the words,
"God is Great," repeated on high in the summons of the true
believers to prayer. "Thus," says the Turkish historian, "the
demons of cruelty, debauchery, and sedition, who had reached the
meridian in the reigns of Amurath and Ibrahim, and during the
minority of Mahomet, were obliged to yield up their crown of
domination, when the voice was heard, that proclaimed Kiuprili
Grand Vizier of the empire."[2]

Mohammed Kiuprili was the grandson of an Albanian, who had
migrated to Asia Minor, and settled in the town of Kiupri, near
the mouth of the river Halys. The ruler of the councils of the

[1] See Von Hammer, books 52-56.
[2] Ibid., vol. iii. p. 462.

Ottoman Empire had been, in early youth, a kitchen-boy, from which situation he rose to that of a cook. After twenty-five years of service he became the steward of the Grand Vizier Khosrew; and under Khosrew's successor he was made Master of the Horse. That successor favoured Kiuprili, as being a native of the same province as himself; and by his influence Kiuprili was made Governor of Damascus, Tripoli, and Jerusalem, and one of the Viziers of state. Afterwards he accepted the inferior post of Sanjak Bey of Giuztendil in Albania, where he led an armed force against some of the numerous insurgents of that region, but was defeated and taken prisoner. After he was redeemed from captivity, he retired to his native town; but was persuaded by a Pacha, called Mohammed with the Wry Neck, to follow him to Constantinople. His new patron became Grand Vizier, but soon began to regard Kiuprili as a dangerous rival for court favour. It does not, however, appear that Kiuprili used any unfair intrigues to obtain the Grand Vizierate. Friends, who knew the firmness of his character, his activity, and his keen common sense, recommended him to the Sultana Validé, as a man who might possibly restore some degree of tranquillity to the suffering empire; and the Grand Vizierate was offered to Kiuprili, then in the seventieth year of his age. He refused to accept it, save upon certain conditions. He required that all his measures should be ratified without examination or discussion; that he should have free hands in the distribution of all offices and preferments, and in dealing out rewards and punishments, without attending to recommendations from any quarter, and without any responsibility; that he should have authority superior to all influence of great men or favourites; that exclusive confidence should be placed in him, and all accusations and insinuations against him should be instantly rejected. The Sultana Validé, in behalf of her son, swore solemnly that all these conditions should be fulfilled, and Mohammed Kiuprili became Grand Vizier of the Ottoman Empire.

His former patron, Mohammed the Wry-Necked, had been dismissed to make room for him; and the court had ordered that the deposed minister should be put to death, and that his goods should be confiscated in the usual manner. Kiuprili interceded, and saved his life, and gave him the revenues of the government of Kanischa. This was the first, and it was almost the last act of humanity that marked Kiuprili's administration. A stern correction of abuses was required; and Kiuprili applied it, not indeed with the ostentatious cruelty of Sultan Amurath IV., but with the same searching and unsparing severity, which had marked that monarch's rule. Kiuprili took the precaution of compelling the Mufti to sign a Fetva, sanctioning by anticipation all the Grand Vizier's measures; and he then employed the most efficacious means for ridding the empire of all who disturbed or threatened public order. A number of fanatical Scheiks and Dervishes, who troubled Constantinople by their tumults, and their lawless violence against all who did not comply with their dogmas, were seized and banished. One of them, who murmured against the Vizier, and who had great influence with the populace, was strangled, and thrown into the Bosphorus. Kiuprili intercepted a letter from the Greek Patriarch to the Vaivode of Wallachia, containing a prediction very similar to those which are frequent in our own time. The Patriarch said, " The power of Islam is drawing to an end. The Christian faith will soon be supreme. All their lands will speedily be in the possession of the Christians; and the Lords of the Cross and the Church-bell will be the Lords of the empire." Kiuprili read in this an encouragement to revolt, and hanged the Greek Patriarch over one of the city gates. No delinquency past or present, no preparation for plot or mutiny, escaped the Vizier's vigilance. He planted his spies in every province and town, and secured the agency of trusty and unquestioning executioners of his commands. The impress of a resolute will was felt throughout the empire; and men obeyed without hesitation the man, whom they perceived never to hesitate himself, never to neglect or abandon those who served him, and never to forgive those who thwarted or disobeyed him. Kiuprili dealt his blows against every race, class, profession, and station, where he saw or suspected offence. He never vented his wrath in threats. " His blows outsped his words;" and, while he was biding his time to strike, he was of unrivalled skill in disguising his preparations. The Turkish historian Naima relates, on the authority of Medschibi, who had been one of the Grand Vizier's confidential servants, that Mohammed Kiuprili had a maxim, that wrath and reproach are always superfluous, and frequently dangerous for the possessor of power; that it is silly for a statesman to fly out into a passion; and that lulling a victim to sleep is the safest way of killing him.

Thirty-six thousand persons are said to have been put to death by Mohammed Kiuprili's command, during the five years of his Grand Vizierate. The chief executioner of Constantinople, Soulfikar, confessed afterwards that he himself had strangled more than 4000, and thrown them into the Bosphorus. Von Hammer, who repeats and accredits these numbers, states that the aged despot, who thus marked every month of his ministry by the sacrifice of more than 500 lives, had acquired a reputation for mildness and humanity when he was a provincial governor. It is fair to suppose that he lavished human life when Grand Vizier, not out of any natural cruelty in his disposition, but from the belief that he could not otherwise suppress revolt and anarchy, and maintain complete obedience to his authority.[1] The price at which the restoration of order was bought under Mohammed Kiuprili, was indeed fearful; but, though excessive, it was not paid in vain. The revolts which had raged in Transylvania and Asia Minor were quelled; the naval strength of the empire was revived; the Dardanelles were fortified; the Ottoman power beyond the Black Sea was strengthened by the erection of castles on the Dnieper and the Don; and, though the war in Candia still lingered, the islands of Lemnos and Tenedos were recovered from the Venetians. His own authority in the empire was unshaken until the last hour of his life; and he obtained for his still more celebrated son, Ahmed Kiuprili, the succession to the Grand Vizierate. It is said that old Kiuprili, when on his death-bed (31st October, 1661), after recommending his son as the future Vizier, gave the young Sultan four especial rules to follow. One was, never to listen to the advice of women : another was, never to let a subject grow over-rich : the

---

[1] Our English traveller, Wheeler, who visited Turkey a few years after Mohammed Kiuprili's death, relates a legend which he heard respecting him, which proves how terrible his severities must have been, and the impression left by them on the public mind.   Wheeler, in describing one of the streets of Constantinople, says of it : "This street is adorned with several of the monuments of the Viziers and Bashas, who have highly merited of the Emperor either in the wars or government.   Among which we observed one with the Cuppalo covered only with a grate of wire ; of which we had this account, 'That it was the monument of Mahomet Cupriuli, father to the present Vizier, who settled the government, which during the minority of the present Emperor was very near destruction through the discontents and faction of the principal Hagaes, and the mutinies of the Janissaries.   Concerning whom, after his decease, being buried here and having this stately monument of white marble covered with lead erected over his body, the Grand Signior and the Grand Vizier had this dream both in the same night ; to wit that Cupriuli came to them and earnestly begged a little water to refresh him, being in a burning heat.   Of this the Grand Signior and the Vizier told each other in the morning, and thereupon thought fit to consult the Mufti what to do concerning it : who, according to their gross superstition, advised that he should have the roof of his Sepulchre uncovered that the rain might descend on his body, thereby to quench the flames tormenting his soul.   And this remedy, the people who smarted under his oppression, think he had great need of, supposing him to be tormented in the other world for his tyrannies and cruelties committed by him in this." Wheeler's Travels, p. 133 : see also *suprà*, Knolles's account of the Sepulchre of Sultan Amurath I.

third was, to keep the public treasury full by all possible means :
and the last, to be continually on horseback, and keep his armies
in constant action.

Sultan Mahomet IV. was now advancing towards manhood ;
but he was of far too weak a character to govern for himself.
His great delight was the chase ; and to this he devoted all his
energies and all his time. Fortunately for his empire, he placed
the most implicit confidence in Ahmed Kiuprili, the new Vizier,
and maintained his favourite minister in power against all the
numerous intrigues that were directed against him. Ahmed
Kiuprili was the real ruler of Turkey from 1661 to his death in
1676 ; and he is justly eulogised both by Ottoman and Christian
historians as the greatest statesman of his country. He was only
twenty-six years of age when he was called on to govern the
empire ; but his naturally high abilities had been improved by the
best education that the Muderris of Constantinople could supply ;
and he had learned practical statesmanship as a provincial governor
and general, during the ministry of his father. Ahmed Kiuprili
could be as stern as his sire, when duty to the state required
severity ; and he was equally tenacious in not permitting the least
encroachment on his authority. But he was usually humane and
generous ; and his most earnest endeavours were directed to
mitigate the burdens of imperial taxation, and to protect the
people from the feudal exactions of the Spahis, and from the
arbitrary violence of the Pachas and other local functionaries.

Like his father, Ahmed Kiuprili commenced his administration
by securing himself against any cabals of the Ulema ; and he gave
at the same time a noble rebuke to the chief of that order, who
spoke in the divan against the memory of the late Grand Vizier.
Ahmed Kiuprili said to him, " Mufti, if my father sentenced men
to death, he did so by the sanction of thy Fetva." The Mufti
answered, " If I gave him my Fetva, it was because I feared lest
I should myself suffer under his cruelty." " Effendi," rejoined the
Grand Vizier, " is it for thee, who art a teacher of the law of the
Prophet, to fear God less than His creature ?" The Mufti was
silent. In a few days afterwards he was deposed and banished to
Rhodes ; and his important station given to Sanizadé, a friend on
whom Ahmed Kiuprili could rely.

It was in the civil administration of the Turkish Empire that
the genius of Ahmed Kiuprili found its best field of exercise ; but
he was soon called on to fulfil the military duties of the Grand
Vizierate, and to head the Ottoman armies in the war with
Austria, which broke out in 1663. This, like most of the other

24

wars between the two empires, originated in the troubles and dissensions which were chronic for a century and a half in Hungary and Transylvania. After several conflicts of minor importance during 1661 and 1662, between the respective partisans of Austria and the Porte in these provinces, who were aided against each other by the neighbouring Pachas and commandants, an Ottoman army was collected by the Grand Vizier on a scale of grandeur worthy of the victorious days of Solyman Kanouni : and Kiuprili resolved not only to complete the ascendency of the Turks in Hungary and Transylvania, but to crush entirely and finally the power of Austria. Mahomet IV. marched with his troops from Constantinople to Adrianople ; but there he remained behind to resume his favourite hunting while his Grand Vizier led the army against the enemy. The Sultan placed the sacred standard of the Prophet in Kiuprili's hands at parting ; and on the 8th June, 1663, that formidable ensign of Turkish war was displayed at Belgrade. Kiuprili had under his command 121,000 men, 123 field-pieces, 12 heavy battering cannon, 60,000 camels, and 10,000 mules. With this imposing force, he overran the open country of Hungary and Transylvania, almost without opposition ; and besieged and captured the strong city of Neuhausel in the September of that year, which was the most brilliant achievement that the Turks had effected in Europe, since the battle of Cerestes, more than fifty years before. The Vizier, after this siege, did not recommence active operations with his main army until the spring of the following year, but his light troops spread devastation far and wide through Austria.[1] In May, 1664, Kiuprili advanced and crossed the river Mur ; and he besieged and captured the fortress of Serivar, which the Turks dismantled and set fire to, on the 7th July, as a mark of contempt for the reigning Emperor of Austria, by whom it had been founded. From the ruins of Serivar the Ottoman army marched northward, passing by the western extremity of Lake Balaton. They captured Egervar, Kipornak, and other strong places ; and on the 26th July, the Turks reached the right bank of the river Raab, near to the town of Kærmend. Could they cross that river the remainder of the march against Vienna seemed easy ; the Imperialist army which opposed them in this campaign was inferior to them in numbers ; but happily

---

[1] Sir Paul Rycaut says, "The Tartars, every one after the manner of his country leading one or more spare horses, made inroads witnm five miles of Vienna ; destroying and laying waste all places before them. Things there resembling Doomsday, covered with fire ; and not as much left as made an appearance of habitation."

for Austria, that army was commanded by one of the ablest generals of the age, who was destined to gain the first great victory of Christendom in a pitched battle in open field against the full force of the Turkish arms.

Count Raymond de Montecuculi was, like many other of the greatest generals known in modern history, an Italian. He was born at Modena, of a noble family of that duchy, in 1608. He entered into the Austrian service; and acquired distinction in the latter part of the Thirty Years' War; and afterwards in hostilities against Poland. In 1664 he was named generalissimo of the Imperial forces, and sent to check the menacing progress of the Turks. The Austrian and Hungarian army, which was placed under Montecuculi's command, was weak in numbers; and at the opening of the campaign he was unable to prevent the Vizier Kiuprili from crossing the Mur, and reducing the Christian cities that lay between that river and the Raab. But, while the Turks were engaged in these operations, Montecuculi effected a junction with the auxiliary troops of the states of the empire, and also with a valuable force of French troops, which had voluntarily marched under the Count of Coligny and other noblemen, to serve in the Hungarian war. With his army thus strengthened, Montecuculi took up a position near Kærmend on the Raab, covering the road to Vienna; and, from the breadth and rapidity of the river in that place, the attempts made by the Ottoman vanguard to force a passage were easily repulsed. Kiuprili now marched up the Raab, along the right bank towards Styria, closely followed along the left bank by Montecuculi, who thus turned the enemy farther away from the Austrian capital, and also from the Turkish reserves which were concentrating at Ofen and Stuhweissenburg. Several efforts of the Turks to cross the river were checked by the Imperialists; but at last the armies marched past the point where the Laufritz flows into the Raab, in the vicinity of the village of St. Gothard; and then, the single stream of the Raab wanted depth and breadth sufficient to present a serious obstacle to the Turks. Both armies, therefore, halted and prepared for the battle, which appeared to be inevitable. Some overtures for negotiation first took place, in which the Turkish officers behaved with the utmost arrogance. When Reningen, the Austrian envoy, spoke of the restoration of Neuhausel to the Emperor, the Vizier and his Pachas laughed at him, and asked whether any one had ever heard of the Ottomans voluntarily giving up a conquest to the Christians. They refused to admit the terms of the old treaty of Sitvatorok as a basis for a peace; and said that peace must be granted, if at all, on principles created by the recent successes of the Sublime Porte. Montecuculi continued his preparations for battle : he issued careful directions to his troops, particularising the order of their array, the relative positions of each corps, the depth of the lines, and the disposal of the baggage and stores. The 1st of August, 1664, saw the result of Montecuculi's sage dispositions, and the first great proof that the balance of supe-riority between the Ottoman and Christian arms had at last been changed.

The convent of St. Gothard, which has given name to this memorable battle, is on the right bank of the Raab, at a little distance above its confluence with the Laufritz. A space of level ground extends along the right bank of the Raab westward from the convent and village of St. Gothard to the village of Windisch-dorf, also on the right bank of the river. These two villages formed the extreme wings of the Turkish position before the battle. Along the left bank of the river there is an extent of level ground of equal length with that on the right side, but of much greater breadth ; and it was here, on the left side, that the conflict took place. In the centre of the plain, on the left side (that is to say in the centre of the Imperialist position), stands the village of Moggersdorf ; and immèdiately opposite to Moggers-dorf the river bends in and describes an arc towards the southern or Turkish side. This greatly facilitated the passage of the river by the Vizier, as he was enabled to place guns in battery on each side of the convex of the stream, and sweep away any troops that disputed the landing-place on the other bank, in the centre of the bend of the river. Montecuculi placed the auxiliary German troops of the empire in the centre of his line, in and near to the village of Moggersdorf. The Austrians and Hungarians were in his right wing ; the French auxiliaries formed his left. The Turks had a large superiority in numbers, and in personal courage they were inferior to no possible antagonists. But the military discipline of the Turkish soldiers had become lamentably impaired since the days of Solyman, when it commanded the envious admiration of its Christian foes. It had even declined rapidly since the time when the last great battle between Turk and German was fought at Cerestes (1596). The deterioration in the intelligence and skill of the Ottoman officers was still more con-spicuous. On the opposite side, the German and the other armies of Western Christendom, had acquired many improvements in their weapons, their tactics, and their general military organisa-tion, during the Thirty Years' War, which had called into action

the genius of such commanders as Tilly, Wallenstein, Gustavus Adolphus, Bernhard, Torstenston, Turenne, and Montecuculi himself. The Turkish artillery, though numerous, was now cumbrous and ill-served, compared with the German. The Janissaries had given up the use of the pike (which seems to have been one of their weapons in Solyman's time[1]), and the Ottoman army was entirely deficient in foot brigades of steady spearmen, and also in heavily-armed regular cavalry. The German infantry was now formed of pikemen and of musqueteers ; and part of their horse consisted of heavy cuirassier regiments, which, in Montecuculi's judgment, were sure, if a fair opportunity of charging were given them, to ride down Turkish infantry or cavalry, without it being possible for any serious resistance to be offered to them. In that great general's opinion, the want of the pike, which he calls "the queen of weapons,"[2] was the fatal defect in the Turkish military system. We shall find the Chevalier Folard, half a century afterwards, expressing a similar judgment with reference to the negligence of the Turks in not adopting the invention of the bayonet.

Montecuculi's criticisms on the defects in the Turkish armies were written by him after the battle of St. Gothard ; but his military sagacity must have divined them, as soon as he observed the Vizier's troops, and made trial of their tactics and prowess in the early operations of the campaign. But the Turks themselves, before they fought at St. Gothard, knew not their own deficiencies ; they were flushed with triumph at the advantages which they had hitherto gained under Ahmed Kiuprili ; and with full confidence in their chief and themselves, they advanced, about nine in the morning of the 1st of August, 1664, to the Raab, and began the passage of the eventful stream. Kiuprili had placed his batteries along the sides of the arc of the stream, which has already been described ; and his Janissaries, who were drawn up in the Turkish centre, crossed the river without much loss, and attacked and carried the village of Moggersdorf. The centre of the Christians was thus completely broken, and the Ottomans appeared to be certain of victory, when Montecuculi brought succour from the right wing. Prince Charles of Lorraine, who in this battle gave the prelude of his long and brilliant career, led his regiment of Austrian heavy cavalry to the charge in person, and killed with his own hand the commander of the Grand Vizier's guards. The advanced troops of the Turkish centre, thus taken in flank by the

[1] See Von Hammer, vol. ii. p. 185.
[2] "Al Turco manca la picca, che è la regina delle armi a piedi."—Montecuculi Opere, vol. ii. p. 124.

Austrian cavalry, were driven back to the Raab; Moggersdorf was then attacked by the Imperialists, and set on fire; but the Janissaries, who had intrenched themselves in the village, refused to retreat or surrender, and kept their post till they perished in the flames, with obstinacy (says Montecuculi) worthy to be reflected on and admired. Kiuprili brought large reinforcements over from the right bank, and Montecuculi now sent word to the Count of Coligny and the French in his left wing, that it was time for them to aid him with all their might. Coligny sent him instantly 1000 infantry and two squadrons of cavalry, under the Duc de la Feuillade and Beauvezé. When Kiuprili saw the French coming forward with their shaven chins and cheeks, and powdered perruques, he asked scornfully of one of his attendants, "Who are these young girls ?" But the young girls, as he termed them, without regarding the formidable Turkish battle-cry of "Allah !" rushed upon the Turks and cut them down, shouting out on their part, "Allons ! Allons ! Tue ! Tue !" Those Janissaries who escaped that carnage remembered long afterwards the French cry of "Allons ! Tue !" and the Duc de la Feuillade was for many years talked of in their barracks as "Fouladi," which means "The man of steel."

Kiuprili's first attack had failed, though he still retained some ground on the left bank of the Raab. He now (towards noon) prepared for a combined attack (such as he ought to have made in the first instance) upon both the Christian wings, while he, at the same time, assailed their centre with greater forces. Four large masses of irregular Ottoman cavalry dashed across the Raab at Montecuculi's right wing: three similar bodies attacked the French on the left; Kiuprili led a force of cavalry and infantry upon the centre; and, at the same time, detached squadrons were ordered to pass the river at points a little distant from the field of battle, and gain the flanks and rear of the Imperialists. An obstinate conflict now took place all along the line. Some parts of the Christian army gave ground, and several of its generals advised a retreat; but Montecuculi told them that their only chance of safety, as well as of victory, was to take the offensive with a mass of the best troops, and make a desperate charge on the Ottoman centre. A strong force of the Christian cavalry was now concentrated for this purpose; and the word was passed along the ranks that they must break the Turks or perish. John Spork, the Imperialist general of cavalry, who was called the Austrian Ajax, prostrated himself bareheaded on the ground in front of his men, and prayed aloud : "Oh, mighty Generalissimo, who art on high, if thou wilt not this day help thy children the Christians, at least do not help these dogs the Turks, and thou shalt soon see something that will please thee."[1]

Having arranged his lines for the decisive charge, Montecuculi gave the word, and the Imperialists rushed forward with a loud shout, which disconcerted the Turks, who, accustomed themselves to terrify their enemy by their battle-cry, and to give the attack, recoiled before the unexpected assault of their opponents. Thrown into utter confusion by the irresistible shock of Montecuculi's cuirassiers, which was supported vigorously by the Christian musketeers and pikemen, the Ottomans were driven into the Raab; Janissary, Spahi, Albanian, Tartar, going down alike beneath the impetuous rush of the Christian centre, or flying in panic rout before it. The Ottoman cavalry in the wings lost courage at seeing the defeat of their centre, where the Vizier and all their best troops were stationed, and they rode off the field without an effort to retrieve the fortune of the day. More than 10,000 Turks perished in the battle; and the triumph of Montecuculi was graced by the capture of fifteen pieces of cannon and forty standards. On the morrow, the victor caused a solemn service of thanksgiving to be celebrated on the field of battle. A chapel was founded there, and still attests the scene of this memorable battle, which commenced the compensation for the 300 years of defeat which European Christendom had sustained from Turkey, ever since the day when the confederate forces of Servia and Hungary were crushed by Sultan Amurath I. at Kossova.

It is because the battle of St. Gothard presents thus to our notice a turning point in the military history of Turkey, that it has been described with a particularity of detail, such as can be given to none of the long list of battles, which yet will come before our notice, while tracing the declining fortunes of the Ottoman Empire. The advantage also of possessing the com-

---

[1] This may remind some readers of the wish of Miltiades before Marathon, not for favour, but merely for fair play, from the gods. Θεῶν τὰ ἴσα νεμόντων, οἷοι τέ εἶμεν περιγενέσθαι τῇ συμβολῇ. Herodotus, lib. vi. sect. 116. The well-known prayer of the American backwoodsman when about to attack the bear, is still more like Spork's devotions. This Austrian Ajax could ill have comprehended the sublime spirit in which his assumed prototype the Homeric Ajax prayed in battle (Iliad, book xvii. verse 645). Most probably he had never heard of it. Spork was made a Count by the Austrian Emperor in reward for his services, but he always wrote his name (which he did with great difficulty) "Spork, Count," and not "Count Spork." He said he was a Spork, before he was a Count.

ments of Montecuculi himself on this campaign, and on Turkish warfare generally, has been an additional reason for giving prominence to his victory at St. Gothard. The defects which he points out in the Turkish military system, have continued to exist, or rather have existed with aggravation, until the reign of the late Sultan Mahmoud. They may be summed up as consisting in the neglect of the Turks to keep pace with the improvements made by other nations in the weapons and in the art of war; and in the appointment of incompetent officers through bribery and other corrupt influences. The pernicious effects of these vices of the Ottoman war department have been partly counteracted by the remarkable personal valour of the common soldiers among the Turks, their sobriety, and the vigour of their constitutions; and also by the care taken to provide them with good and sufficient provisions both when in barracks and when employed on active duty. These are favourable points in the Ottoman service, which every military critic from Count Montecuculi down to Marshal Marmont has observed; and the more important of them, those which regard the natural soldierly qualities of the Ottoman population, show that Turkey has never lost that element of military greatness, which no artificial means can create or revive, but to which the skill of great statesmen and great generals (if the Sultan's empire should be blessed with them) may superadd all that has for nearly two centuries been deficient.

The immediate result of the battle of St. Gothard was a truce for twenty years on the footing of the treaty of Sitvatorok, which the Turks before their defeat had so arrogantly refused. But Neuhausel remained in the possession of the Ottomans; so that Ahmed Kiuprili, notwithstanding his great overthrow by Montecuculi, was able to re-enter Constantinople as a conqueror. His influence over the Sultan was undiminished; and the next great military enterprise, that Kiuprili undertook, was one of unchequered success and glory. This was the reduction of the city of Candia, which had now for nearly twenty years been vainly besieged or blockaded by the Turks. Mahomet IV. at first proposed to lead in person the great armament which Kiuprili collected at Adrianople for this expedition. The imperial tent was raised in the camp; and the Sultan caused those parts of the Turkish historians to be read before him, which narrate the capture of Constantinople by Mahomet II., the battle of Calderan under Selim I., and the sieges of Rhodes and Belgrade by Solyman. But Mahomet IV. appeased the martial ardour,

which those recitals produced in him by hunting with redoubled
energy.   It was only in the chase that he was enterprising and
bold : he shrank from the battle-field ; and he was not even a
hero in his harem, where a Greek slave-girl of Retino tyrannised
with capricious violence over the over fond and over-constant
Padischah.   This favourite Sultana was zealously devoted to the
interests of Kiuprili, who was thereby rendered so secure in his
authority, that he ventured to remain in the island of Candia
from the time of his landing there in 1666 to the surrender of
the long-besieged capital in 1669.   During these three last years
of the siege, every possible effort of bravery and all the then
available resources of the military art were employed both by
assailants and defenders.   Morosini (afterwards renowned as the
conqueror of the Morea, and surnamed the Peloponnesian) commanded in the city ; ably seconded by the Duc de la Feuillade,
the hero of St. Gothard, and many other high-born and high-
spirited volunteers, who flocked from every country of Christendom to Candia, as the great theatre of military glory   On the
Turkish side, Kiuprili and his generals and admirals urged on the
operations of the besiegers by sea and by land with indomitable
obstinacy, and with a degree of engineering skill, from which the
Turks of more recent times have far degenerated.[1]   It is computed that during the final thirty-four months of the siege, during
which Kiuprili commanded, 30,000 Turks and 12,000 Venetians
were killed.   There were fifty-six assaults, and ninety-six sorties ;
and the number of mines exploded on both sides was 1364.
Several attempts were made by the Venetians to purchase peace
without ceding Candia.   But to their offers of large sums of
money, Kiuprili replied : " We are not money-dealers ; we make
war to win Candia, and at no price will we abandon it."   The
Ottomans persevered in their enterprise, until Morosini, on the
6th September, 1669, surrendered on honourable terms the city
which the incessant mining had converted into a confused mass
of gigantic mole-heaps.   A peace was made between Venice and
the Porte, by which the city and island of Candia became the
property of the Sultan.   Kiuprili remained there several months
after the conquest was completed, during which time he was well

---

[1] Juchereau says of the Turks of this century, "It is only since the establishment of the school for engineers at Sulitzi, that they have learned under
Frank officers, in consulting their military archives and the plans of their
ancient engineers, those ways and parallels of trenches, of which they were
the inventors, and which so distinguished the siege of Candia."

and wisely employed in organising the local government of Crete under its new sovereign.

The next scene of warlike operations, on which Ahmed Kiuprili entered, deserves especial attention, because it brings us to the rival claims of Poland, Russia, and Turkey to dominion over the Cossacks, and is intimately connected with the long and still enduring chain of hostilities between the Russian and Turkish Empires. The Cossacks of the Don had become subjects of Ivan the Terrible, Czar of Muscovy, in 1549; but the Cossacks of the Dnieper and the Ukraine were long independent; and their first connection was with Poland. The Poles affected to consider them as vassals, but the wisest Polish rulers were cautious in the amount of authority which they attempted to exercise over these bold and hardy tribes. The imperious tyranny of other less prudent sovereigns of Poland was met by fierce opposition on the part of the Cossacks, who called in their former constant enemies, the Tartars, to aid them against their new Polish oppressors. Deserted, after some years of warfare, by the Tartars, the Cossacks of the Ukraine appealed to the Russian Czar Alexis. Many years of chequered and sanguinary hostilities followed, and at last the Cossack territory was nominally divided between Russia and Poland at the truce of Androssan, in 1667. But the Cossacks who dwelt near the mouths of the rivers Boug and Dnieper, and who were called the Zaporofskian Cossacks, refused to be included in the Polish dominions by virtue of that arrangement, and placed themselves under the protection of the Czar. In 1670, the Cossacks of that part of the Ukraine which had been left under Poland, petitioned the Polish Diet for certain privileges, which were refused; and a Polish army under Sobieski was sent into the Ukraine to coerce the Cossack malcontents. The Cossacks, under their Hetman Dorescensko, resisted bravely; but at last they determined to seek the protection of the Sublime Porte; and Dorescensko, in 1672, presented himself at Constantinople, and received a banner with two horse-tails,[1] as Sanjak Bey of the Ukraine, which was immediately enrolled among the Ottoman provinces. At the same time, the Khan of the Crimea was ordered to support the Cossacks, and 6000 Turkish troops were marched to the Ukraine. The Poles protested loudly against

---

[1] Since the time of Amurath III. the governors of the large provinces, or Eyalets, received the rank of Vizier, and were Pachas with three horse-tails. The Sanjak Beys, or governors of the smaller districts, were Pachas with two horse-tails.

these measures. The Czar added his remonstrances, and threatened to join Poland in a war against Turkey. The Grand Vizier haughtily replied that such threats were empty words and out of place, and that the Porte would preserve its determination with regard to Poland. A short time previously, another Turkish minister had answered similar warnings by boasting, "God be praised, such is the strength of Islam, that the union of Russians and Poles matters not to us. Our empire has increased in might since its origin; nor have all the Christian kings, that have leagued against us, been able to pluck a hair from our beard. With God's grace it shall ever be so, and our empire shall endure to the day of judgment." Kiuprili himself, when the Polish ambassador reproached the Turks with injustice in aiding the revolted subjects of Poland, replied in a remarkable letter, written with his own hand; in which he states that "the Cossacks, a free people, placed themselves under the Poles, but being unable to endure Polish oppression any longer, they have sought protection elsewhere, and they are now under the Turkish banner and the horse-tails. If the inhabitants of an oppressed country, in order to obtain deliverance, implore the aid of a mighty emperor, is it prudent to pursue them in such an asylum? When the most mighty and most glorious of all emperors is seen to deliver and succour from their enemies those who are oppressed, and who ask him for protection, a wise man will know on which side the blame of breaking peace ought to rest. If, in order to quench the fire of discord, negotiation is wished for, so let it be. But if the solution of differences is referred to that keen and decisive judge, called 'The Sword,' the issue of the strife must be pronounced by the God, who hath poised upon nothing heaven and earth, and by whose aid Islam has for 1000 years triumphed over its foes." This avowal of the principle of intervention in behalf of an oppressed people was a bold measure for the prime minister of a nation, like the Turkish, which kept so many other nations in severe bondage; it was especially bold in Kiuprili, who at that very time was directing the construction of fortresses in the Morea to curb the reviving spirit of independence, of which the Greeks had given some signs during the recent Venetian war.

In the Polish campaign of 1672, Sultan Mahomet IV. was persuaded to accompany the powerful army which Kiuprili led to the siege of the important city of Kaminiec, in Podolia. Kaminiec fell after nine days' siege (26th August, 1672), and Lemberg shared its fate on the 9th of September. The imbecile King of Poland, Michael, then made the peace of Bucsacs with the Turks,

by which Poland was to cede Podolia and the Ukraine, and pay
an annual tribute to the Porte of 220,000 ducats. The Sultan
returned in triumph to Adrianople; but the congratulations which
were lavished on him as conqueror of the Poles were premature.
Sobieski and the other chiefs of the Polish nobility determined to
break the treaty which their King had made. They refused to pay
the stipulated tribute; and, in 1673, the Grand Vizier made preparations for renewing the war upon the Poles, and also for attacking
the Czar of Russia, from whom they had received assistance. The
Turks marched again into Podolia; but, on the 11th of November,
1673, Sobieski, who now led the Poles, surprised the Turkish
camp near Khoczim, and routed Kiuprili with immense slaughter.
The Princes of Wallachia and Moldavia had deserted from the
Turkish to the Polish side with all their contingents; a transfer
of strength which aided materially in obtaining Sobieski's victory.
But Kiuprili's administrative skill had so re-invigorated the resources of Turkey, that she readily sent fresh forces into the
Ukraine in the following year. Sobieski with his Poles and the
Russians (who now took an active part in the war) had the advan-
tage in the campaign of 1674; and, in 1675, Sobieski gained one
of the most brilliant victories of the age over the Turks at Lemberg. But the superior strength and steadiness of the Porte and
Kiuprili in maintaining the war against the discordant government of Poland, were felt year after year; and, in 1676, the
Turkish commander in Podolia, Ibrahim, surnamed Scheitan, that
is, "Ibrahim the Devil," made himself completely master of
Podolia, and attacked Galicia. Sobieski (who was now King of
Poland) fought gallantly with far inferior forces against Ibrahim
at Zurawna; but was glad to conclude a peace (27th October,
1676), by which the Turks were to retain Kaminiec and Podolia;
and by which the Ukraine, with the exception of a few specified
places, was to be under the sovereignty of the Sultan.

Three days after the peace of Zurawna, Ahmed Kiuprili died.
Though his defeats at St. Gothard and Khoczim had fairly given
rise to an opinion among the Ottoman ranks that their Vizier was
not born to be a general, his military services to the empire, for
which he won Candia, Neuhausel, and Kaminiec, were considerable; and no minister ever did more than he accomplished in repressing insurrection and disorder, in maintaining justice and good
government, and in restoring the financial and military strength
of his country. He did all this without oppression or cruelty. He
protected all ranks of the Sultan's subjects; he was a liberal
patron of literature and art; he was a warm friend, and a not im-

placable enemy; he was honourably true to his plighted word towards friend or foe, towards small or great: and there is far less than the usual amount of Oriental exaggeration in the praises, which the Turkish historians bestow upon him, as "The light and splendour of the nation; the conservator and governor of good laws; the vicar of the shadow of God; the thrice learned and all-accomplished Grand Vizier."

CHAPTER XVI.

KARA MUSTAPHA VIZIER—UNSUCCESSFUL WAR WITH RUSSIA—
WAR WITH AUSTRIA—SIEGE OF VIENNA—RESCUE OF THE CITY
AND COMPLETE OVERTHROW OF THE TURKS BY SOBIESKI—
HEAVY LOSSES OF THE OTTOMANS—MAHOMET IV. DEPOSED—
HIS CHARACTER—CHANGE OF THE JANISSARY FORCE—THE
BARBARESQUE REGENCIES—THE PRETENDED MESSIAH SAB-
BATHAI—MAHOMET IV.'S PATRONAGE OF LITERATURE.[1]

THE value of such a minister as Ahmed Kiuprili to Turkey was
soon proved by the rapid deterioration in her fortunes under his
successor in the Vizierate, Kara Mustapha, or Black Mustapha: a
man whose character was in every respect the opposite of Kiuprili's;
and who to slender abilities united the wildest ambition and
almost boundless presumption.   He was son-in-law to the Sultan;
and by the influence which that marriage gave him, he obtained
the high office, which he abused to the ruin of his master, and the
deep disaster of his country.   Kara Mustapha's favourite project
was a new war against Austria, in which he hoped to capture
Vienna, and to make himself the nominal viceroy, but real sovereign of ample provinces between the Danube and the Rhine.
But the first years of his Vizierate were occupied in an inglorious
war with Russia.   That empire had been no party to the late
peace of Zurawna; and it supported Dorescensko against the Porte,
when that fickle Cossack grew discontented with the Sultan's
authority.   Kara Mustapha led a large army into the Ukraine,
and besieged Cehzrym, but was beaten by the Russians, and fled
with ignominy across the Danube.   In the following year he resumed the war with fresh forces; and after several alternatives of
fortune, he stormed Cehzrym on the 21st of August, 1678.   But
the losses which the Turks sustained both from the Russian sword
and the climate, were severe; and it is said, that even at this
early period of the wars between the two nations, the Turks
entertained an instinctive apprehension of the power of the Mus-

[1] Von Hammer, books 57-58.

covites.[1] A peace was made in 1681, by which the Porte gave up the disputed territory to Russia ; and it was stipulated that neither power should raise fortifications between the rivers Boug and Dniester. Five years afterwards, a territorial arrangement was concluded between Poland and Russia, which recognised the sovereignty of the Czar over the whole of the Ukraine.

In 1682, Kara Mustapha commenced his fatal enterprise against Vienna. A revolt of the Hungarians under Count Tekeli, against Austria, which had been caused by the bigoted tyranny of the Emperor Leopold, now laid the heart of that empire open to attack ; and a force was collected by the Grand Vizier, which, if ably handled, might have given the House of Hapsburg its death-blow. Throughout the autumn of 1682 and the spring of 1683, regular and irregular troops, both horse, foot, artillery, and all kinds of munitions of war, were collected in the camp at Adrianople on a scale of grandeur that attested and almost exhausted the copiousness, which the administration of Kiuprili had given to the Turkish resources. The strength of the regular forces, which Kara Mustapha led to Vienna, is known from the muster-roll which was found in his tent after the siege. It amounted to 275,000 men. The attendants and camp-followers cannot be reckoned ; nor can any but an approximate speculation be made as to the number of the Tartar and other irregular troops that joined the Vizier. It is probable that not less than half a million of men were set in motion in this last great aggressive effort of the Ottomans against Christendom. The Emperor Leopold had neither men nor money sufficient to enable him to confront such a deluge of invasion ; and, after many abject entreaties, he obtained a promise of help from King Sobieski of Poland, whom he had previously treated with contumely and neglect. Poland was at peace with Turkey, nor had the Porte in any way failed in observance of the recent treaty. But neither Sobieski nor other Christian adversaries of the Turks were very scrupulous as to such obligations ; and the Polish King promised to aid the Austrian Emperor with 58,000 men. The Turkish army proceeded along the western side of the Danube from Belgrade, and reached Vienna without experiencing any serious check, though a gallant resistance was made by some of the strong places which it besieged during its advance. The city of Vienna was garrisoned by 11,000 men under Count Stahremberg, who proved himself a worthy successor

---

[1] Thornton, p. 73, citing Spon, whose travels were published in 1678. " Spon says, ' Of all the princes of Christendom, there was none whom the Turks so much feared as the Czar of Muscovy.' "

of the Count Salm, who had fulfilled the same duty when the city was besieged by Sultan Solyman. The second siege of Vienna lasted from the 15th July to the 12th September, 1683, during which the most devoted heroism was displayed by both the garrison and the inhabitants. The numerous artillery of the Turks shattered the walls and bastions, and the indefatigable labours of their miners were still more effective. The garrison was gradually wasted by the numerous assaults which it was called on to repulse, and in the frequent sorties, by which the Austrian commander sought to impede the progress of the besiegers. Kara Mustapha, at the end of August, had it in his power to carry the city by storm, if he had thought fit to employ his vast forces in a general assault, and to continue it from day to day, as Amurath IV. had done when Bagdad fell. But the Vizier kept the Turkish troops back out of avarice, in the hope that the city would come into his power by capitulation ; in which case he would himself be enriched by the wealth of Vienna, which, if the city were taken by storm, would become the booty of the soldiery. The Turkish army murmured loudly at the incompetency, the selfishness, and the vain confidence of their chief, who took no measures for checking the approach of the relieving army that was known to be on its march ; though the passage of the Danube might easily have been guarded against Sobieski by a detachment from the immense forces which were at the Grand Vizier's command.

Sobieski had been unable to assemble his troops before the end of August ; and, even then, they only amounted to 20,000 men. But he was joined by the Duke of Lorraine and some of the German commanders, who were at the head of a considerable army, and the Polish King crossed the Danube at Tulm, above Vienna, with about 70,000 men. He then wheeled round behind the Kalemberg Mountains to the north-west of Vienna, with the design of taking the besiegers in the rear. The Vizier took no heed of him ; nor was any opposition made to the progress of the relieving army through the difficult country which it was obliged to traverse. On the 11th of September the Poles were on the summit of the Mount Kalemberg ; and "from this hill," says the biographer of Sobieski, "the Christians were presented with one of the finest and most dreadful prospects of the greatness of human power; an immense plain and all the islands of the Danube covered with pavilions, whose magnificence seemed rather calculated for an encampment of pleasure than the hardships of war ; an innumerable multitude of horses, camels, and buffaloes ; 2,000,000 men all in motion, swarms of Tartars dispersed along the foot of the mountain in their usual confusion; the fire of the besiegers incessant and terrible, and that of the besieged such as they could contrive to make; in fine, a great city, distinguishable only by the tops of the steeples and the fire and smoke that covered it."[1]

But Sobieski was well accustomed to the menacing aspect of Turkish armies; his eagle glance saw instantly the Vizier's want of military skill, and the exposure of the long lines of the Ottoman camp to a sudden and fatal attack. "This man," said he, "is badly encamped: he knows nothing of war; we shall certainly beat him." And in a letter, sent by him to the Queen of Poland on the night before the battle, he wrote these words: "We can easily see that the general of an army, who has neither thought of intrenching himself nor concentrating his forces, but lies encamped as if we were 100 miles from him, is predestined to be beaten."

The ground through which Sobieski had to move down from the Kalemberg, was broken by ravines; and was so difficult for the passage of the troops, that Kara Mustapha might, by an able disposition of part of his forces, have long kept the Poles in check, especially as Sobieski, in his hasty march, had brought but a small part of his artillery to the scene of action. But the Vizier displayed the same infatuation and imbecility that had marked his conduct throughout the campaign. He at first refused to believe that Sobieski and any considerable number of Polish troops were on the Kalemberg; and, when at last convinced that an attack would be made upon his lines, he long delayed the necessary order for the occupation of the hollow ways, through which alone the Poles could debouch from the slopes of the high ground which they had gained. Unwilling to resign Vienna, Mustapha left the chief part of his Janissary force in the trenches before the city, and led the rest of his army towards the hills, down which Sobieski and his troops were advancing. In some parts of the field, where the Turks had partially intrenched the roads, their resistance to the Christians was obstinate; but Sobieski led on his best troops in person in a direct line for the Ottoman centre, where the Vizier's tent was conspicuous; and the terrible presence of the victor of Khoczim was soon recognised. "By Allah! the King is really among us," exclaimed the Khan of the Crimea, Selim Ghirai; and turned his horse's head for flight. The mass of the Ottoman army broke and fled in hopeless rout, hurrying Kara Mustapha with them from the field. The Janissaries, who had been left in the trenches before the city, were now attacked both by the garrison and the

[1] Coyer, "Memoir of Sobieski."

Poles, and were cut to pieces. The camp, the whole artillery, and the military stores of the Ottomans became the spoil of the conquerors; and never was there a victory more complete, or signalised by more splendid trophies. The Turks continued their panic flight as far as Raab. There Kara Mustapha collected round him some of the wrecks of the magnificent army which had followed him to Vienna. He sought to vent his fury by executing some of the best Turkish officers, who had differed from him during the campaign. His own fate, when he was executed by the Sultan's orders a few weeks afterwards at Belgrade, excited neither surprise nor pity.

The great destruction of the Turks before Vienna was rapturously hailed throughout Christendom as the announcement of the approaching downfall of the Mahometan Empire in Europe. The Russians and the Venetians declared war against the Porte; and Turkey was now assailed on almost every point of her European frontiers. The new Grand Vizier Ibrahim strove hard to recruit the armies, and supply the deficiency in the magazines, which the fatal campaign of his predecessor had occasioned. But city after city was now rent rapidly away from Islam by the exulting and advancing Christians. The Imperialist armies, led by the Duke of Lorraine, captured Gran, Neuhausel, Ofen, Szegedin, and nearly all the strong places which the Turks had held in Hungary. The Venetians were almost equally successful on the Dalmatian frontier; and the Republic of St. Mark now landed its troops in Greece, under Morosini, who rapidly made himself master of Coron, Navarino, Nauplia, Corinth, Athens, and other chief cities of that important part of the Turkish Empire. In Poland the war was waged less vigorously; nor did the Turks yet relinquish their hold on Kaminiec. But a great defeat which the main Ottoman army sustained on the 12th August, 1687, at Mohacz (on the very scene of Solyman's ancient glory), excited the discontents of the soldiery into insurrection against the Sultan, and on the 8th of November, in that year, Mahomet IV. was deposed, in the forty-sixth year of his age, and thirty-eighth of his reign.

It had been the good fortune of this prince to have able Grand Viziers during a considerable part of his reign; but he chose his ministers from female influence or personal favouritism, not from discernment of merit, as was proved when he intrusted power to Kara Mustapha, who did more to ruin the Ottoman Empire than any other individual that is mentioned in its history. Mahomet IV. reigned without ruling. His mind was entirely absorbed by his infatuation for the chase; and the common people believed

that he was under a curse, laid on him by his father, Sultan
Ibrahim, who had been put to death when Mahomet was placed
on the throne, and who was said to have prayed in his last
moments that his son might lead the wandering life of a beast of
prey. Though not personally cruel, Mahomet IV. as soon as
heirs were born to him, sought anxiously to secure himself on the
throne by the customary murder of his brothers. They were
saved from him by the exertions of the Sultana Validé and his
ministers; but he often resumed the unnatural design. His
mother, the Sultana Validé Tarkhan, was determined at even the
risk of her own life to shelter her two younger sons from being
slaughtered for the further security of the elder; and she took at
last the precaution of placing the two young princes in an inner
room of the palace, which could only be reached by passing
through her own apartments. Even there one night the Sultan
himself entered with a dagger in his hand, and was gliding through
to the chamber where his brothers lay. Two pages watched near
the Sultana Validé; they dared not speak in the presence of the
imperial man-slayer, but one of them touched her and awakened
her. The mother sprang from sleep, and, clinging round the
Sultan, implored him to strike her dead before he raised his hand
to shed his brothers' blood. Mahomet, accustomed to yield to
the superior spirit of the Validé, renounced for the time his
scheme of fratricide, and retired to his apartment; but on the
morrow he put to death the two slaves who had hindered him
from effecting the murderous project which he wished to have
accomplished, but which he wanted nerve to renew. Timidly
vindictive, and selfishly rather than constitutionally cruel, Mahomet continued to long for the death of his brothers, though he
hesitated to strike. And when he was at last deposed to make
room for his brother Solyman on the throne, he may have regretted that his infirmity of purpose had spared the fated rival,
whom an adherence to the old fratricidal canon of the House of
Othman would have removed for ever from his path.

In the reign of Mahomet IV. another innovation on the ancient
stern institutions of the empire was completed, which also was
probably caused as much by weakness as by humanity. It was in
1675, in the last year of the Vizierate of Ahmed Kiuprili, that the
final levy of 3000 boys for the recruiting of the Turkish army
was made on the Christian population of the Ottoman Empire in
Europe. The old system of filling the ranks of the Janissaries
exclusively with compulsory conscripts and converts from among
the children of the Rayas, had been less and less rigidly enforced

since the time of Amurath IV.[1] Admission into the corps of Janissaries now conferred many civil as well as military advantages ; so that it was eagerly sought by men who were of Turkish origin, and born to the Mahometan faith. The first measure of relaxation of the old rule was to treat those, who were the children of Janissaries, as eligible candidates for enrolment. Other Mussulman volunteers were soon received ; and the levies of the tribute of children from the Christians grew less frequent and less severe ; though they were still occasionally resorted to in order to supply the thousands of pages, who were required to people the vast chambers of the Serail, and who were in case of emergency drafted into the army of the state. But ever since the year 1675, the Rayas of the empire have been entirely free from the terrible tax of flesh and blood, by which the Ottoman military force was sustained during its early centuries of conquest. With this change in the constitution of the corps of Janissaries, the numbers of that force were greatly increased : large bodies of them were now settled with their families in the chief cities of the empire, where they engaged in different trades and occupations.

Though still able to contend at sea with such an enemy as Venice, the Sublime Porte had seen a still greater decline take place in its naval power than in its military, compared with the state of its fleets and armies in the days of the great Solyman. This was principally caused by the progress of carelessness and corruption in the navy-boards and arsenals at Constantinople ; but much of it was due to the Sultan's losing that firm hold on the resources of the Mahometan powers of North Africa, which his great ancestor possessed, when Barbarossa and Dragut executed his bidding with the fleets of Tripoli, Tunis, and Algiers.

The Barbaresque Regencies had in the middle of the seventeenth century become practically independent states. They sometimes sent naval succour to the Porte in its wars ; but this was done rather in a spirit of voluntary goodwill and recognition of community of creed and origin, similar to that which formerly made Carthage give occasional aid to Tyre, than out of the obedient subordination of provincial governments to central authority. The strength and audacity of these piratical states, especially of Algiers, had so increased, that not only did their squadrons ravage the Christian coasts of the Mediterranean, but their cruisers

---

[1] There is some difficulty in reconciling the various dates assigned to the discontinuance of the recruiting the Janissaries by enrolments of Christian children. The change was most probably gradual. See Von Hammer, vol. i. p. 88 ; vol. iii. pp. 668, 680.

carried on their depredations beyond the Straits of Gibraltar, both northward and southward in the Atlantic. They pillaged the island of Madeira; they infested the western parts of the English Channel and the Irish Sea for many years; and the Algerine rovers more than once landed in Ireland, and sacked towns and villages, and carried off captives into slavery.[1] They even ventured as far as Iceland and Scandinavia, as if in retaliation for the exploits of the old Norse Sea-Kings in the Mediterranean seven centuries before. Algiers had a marine force comprising, besides light galleys, more than forty well-built and well-equipped ships, each manned by from 300 to 400 corsairs, and mounting from forty to fifty guns. The number of Christians who toiled in slavery in the dockyards and arsenals at Algiers or at the oar in her fleets, fluctuated from between 10,000 to 20,000. Tunis and Tripoli had their fleets and their slaves, though on a smaller scale. Our Admiral Blake tamed the savage pride of these barbarians in 1655. He awed the Dey of Algiers into the surrender of all his English prisoners; and when the Dey of Tunis refused to do the same, Blake burnt the pirate fleet under the guns of the town, destroyed the forts, and compelled obedience to his demands. The Dutch admiral De Ruyter, and the French admiral De Beaufort also at different times punished the insolence of the Barbary corsairs; but their outrages and cruelties were never entirely quelled till Lord Exmouth's bombardment of Algiers in the present century. In 1663 England concluded a treaty with Algiers and the Porte, by which she was to be at liberty to chastise the Algerines when they broke their engagements, without its being considered a breach of amity between England and Turkey. The rulers of the Barbaresque States styled themselves Dahis or Deys. According to some authorities, the Algerine chiefs termed themselves Deys as delegates of the Sultan. According to others, the title came from the old Asiatic word Dahi, which signified a superior, even at the time of the ancient republic of Mecca, and afterwards among the Ishmaelites. They were elected by the military body, consisting of the descendants of the Janissaries and others of Turkish race. They used to apply to the Sultan for his firman appointing them Pachas, and confirming their election; but this soon became a mere formality.

The contests between the Greeks and the Christians of the

---

[1] See the Autobiographical Memoir of Robert Boyle; and see Sir John Eliot's letters cited in Forster's "Life of Eliot," vol. i. p. 317. A tradition of these scenes was versified in the fine ballad in the "Songs of the Nation," of "Hackett of Dungarvan who steered the Algerine."

Latin Church in Jerusalem raged furiously during Mahomet IV.'s reign. But the Ottomans of that age watched with far stronger interest the agitation caused among the Jewish nation by the celebrated Sabbathai Levi, who in 1666 came forward at Jerusalem, and asserted that he was the Messiah. Under that title he sent circular letters to all the Jewish synagogues of the Ottoman Empire; and such was his dexterous audacity in imposition, so eagerly were the legends respecting his miraculous powers received, that thousands of his countrymen flocked together at his bidding, not only from Constantinople, Smyrna, and other Turkish cities, but from Germany, Leghorn, Venice, and Amsterdam. Some of the Rabbis opposed him; and the most violent tumults were raised at Jerusalem, Cairo, Smyrna, and other cities of the East, where Sabbathai proclaimed his pretended mission. The Ottomans observed his progress with religious anxiety; not from any belief in his alleged character, but on the contrary, from the fear that he was the Dedjal or Antichrist, who, according to the Mahometan creed, is to appear among mankind in the last days of the world. They believe also that the speedy advent of the Day of Judgment is to be announced by the reappearance on earth of the prophet Mehdi. And, as at the same time at which Sabbathai came forward in Palestine, another religious impostor arose in Kurdistan, who called himself the prophet Mehdi, and excited thousands of Kurds to follow him, the alarm of many orthodox Moslems at these combined signs of the end of the world was extreme. The Vizier Ahmed Kiuprili, in order to check the troubles caused by Sabbathai, seized and imprisoned him: but his fanatic followers only saw in this the certain prelude to their Messiah's triumph. They said that according to an ancient prophecy Messiah was to disappear for nine months, and was then to return mounted on a lioness, which he was to guide with a bridle made of seven-headed serpents; and then he was to be lord of the world. But one of Sabbathai's countrymen, who was jealous of his influence, denounced him before the Sultan's ministers as endeavouring to raise a revolt among the people. Sabbathai was brought before the Sultan for examination; and Mahomet then made him the characteristic offer of an opportunity of proving by a miracle his right to be acknowledged the Messiah. One of the Sultan's best archers was called forward, and Sabbathai was invited to stand steady as a mark for the arrows, which of course could do no harm to a personage gifted with miraculous powers; only the Sultan wished to see them bound back from off his body. At these words, and the sight of the bended bow, Sabbathai's

courage failed him. He fell prostrate, and owned that he was
nothing but a poor Rabbi, and no whit different from other men.
The Sultan then offered to allow him to embrace the Mahometan
faith, and so make some amends for the scandal which he had caused,
and for the crime of high treason which he had committed by
assuming the title of Messiah of Palestine, which was one of the Sanjaks of the Sublime Porte. Sabbathai eagerly accepted the proposal. He became a Moslem; and instead of being worshipped as
Messiah or dreaded as Antichrist, he filled for ten years the
respectable but prosaic station of a doorkeeper in the Sultan's
palace. He, however, still made himself conspicuous by his religious zeal; but that zeal was now directed to winning converts
from Judaism to Mahometanism, in which he was singularly successful. He was ultimately banished to the Morea, where he died.[1]
The Kurdish spiritual pretender, the self-styled Mehdi, was captured by the Governor of Moussul and sent before the Sultan, a
few months after Sabbathai had owned his imposture in the royal
presence. The young Kurd abandoned the character of Precursor
of the Last Judgment, as soon as he was led before his sovereign.
He answered his interrogators with sense and spirit; and his life
also was spared. The Jewish Antichrist was serving the Sultan
as a doorkeeper, and the Kurdish Mehdi was made his fellow-
servant, in the capacity of one of the pages of the treasure-
chamber of the palace.

Although his immoderate fondness for hunting made Mahomet IV. habitually neglect the duties of government, he was
never indifferent to literary pursuits; and he showed an hereditary fondness for the society of learned men. His patronage of
the chase and his patronage of letters were sometimes strangely
blended. He was liberal in his encouragement of historical
writers, especially of such as professed to record the current
history of his own reign. He loved to see them at his court; he
corrected their works with his own pen; but he expected that
each royal hunting should be chronicled by them with sportsman-
like minuteness, and that the death of each wild beast, which was
slain by the Sultan's hand, should be portrayed with poetic
fervour. A despotic patron is dangerous to the life of the author,
as well as to the vitality of his works. The Turkish historian
Abdi was one whom Sultan Mahomet IV. delighted to honour.

---

[1] According to the graphic sketch of the career of Sabbathai by the late
Dean of St. Paul's, some of the Jews continued to believe in him notwith-
standing his apostasy and death, and "Sabbathaism still exists as a sect of
Judaism."—Milman's "History of the Jews," vol. iii. p. 395.

The Sultan kept him always near his person, and charged him with the special duty of writing the annals of his reign. One evening Mahomet asked of him, "What hast thou written to-day?" Abdi incautiously answered that nothing sufficiently remarkable to write about had happened that day. The Sultan darted a hunting-spear at the unobservant companion of royalty, wounded him sharply, and exclaimed, "*Now* thou hast something to write about."[1]

[1] Von Hammer, vol. iii. p. 571, cites this from Abdi's own book.

CHAPTER XVII.

SOLYMAN II.—INSURRECTIONS AND DEFEATS—SUCCESSES AGAINST
RUSSIA—KIUPRILI-ZADE MUSTAPHA MADE GRAND VIZIER—HIS
CHARACTER AND MEASURES—WISE POLICY TO THE RAYAS—
SUCCESSFUL CAMPAIGN—DEATH OF SOLYMAN II.—AHMED II.
SULTAN—KIUPRILI DEFEATED AND KILLED AT SALANKEMAN
—DISASTROUS REIGN OF AHMED II.—MUSTAPHA II. SUCCEEDS,
AND HEADS THE ARMIES—VICTORIOUS AT FIRST, BUT DE-
FEATED BY EUGENE AT ZENTA—HUSEIN KIUPRILI GRAND
VIZIER—CONQUESTS OF PETER THE GREAT OF RUSSIA OVER
THE TURKS—AZOPH TAKEN—NEGOTIATIONS FOR PEACE—TREATY
OF CARLOWITZ.[1]

SOLYMAN II. when raised to the throne of the Ottoman Empire in
1687, had lived for forty-five years in compulsory seclusion, and in
almost daily peril of death. Yet, as sovereign, he showed more
capacity and courage than the brother whom he succeeded ; and,
perhaps, if he had been made Sultan at an earlier period, Turkey
might have escaped that shipwreck of her state, which came on
her after the death of her great minister Ahmed Kiuprili, through
the weakness of Sultan Mahomet IV. and the misconduct of his
favourite Vizier Kara Mustapha, the originator of the fatal march
upon Vienna. Solyman despised the idle sports and debasing
sensuality of his predecessors, and earnestly devoted himself to
the task of re-organising the military power of his empire, and of
stemming, if possible, the progress of defeat and disaster. But
he was unable to control the excesses of the mutinous Janissaries,
who, throughout the winter which followed Solyman's accession,
filled Constantinople with riot and slaughter, and compelled the
appointment and displacement of ministers according to their
lawless will. At length this savage soldiery resolved to pillage
the palaces of the Grand Vizier and the other chief dignitaries.
The Vizier, Siavoush Pacha, defended his house bravely against
the brigands, who were joined by the worst rabble of the capital,

[1] See Von Hammer, books 58, *et se*ĵ.

Jewish and Christian, as well as Mahometan.   On the second day of the insurrection they forced the gate of the house, and rushed in, slaying and spoiling all that they met with.   Siavoush Pacha, with a few of his surviving servants round him, made a last attempt to defend the entrance to the harem, that sanctuary of Moslems, which the rebels now assailed, regardless alike of every restraint of law, of creed, of national and of private honour. More than a hundred of the wretches were slain before the resistance of the brave man of the house was overcome, and Siavoush fell dead on the threshold of his harem, fighting bravely to the last gasp.   The worst outrages and abominations were now practised by the rebels ; and the sister of the slain Vizier, and his wife (the daughter of Mohammed Kiuprili), were cruelly mutilated and dragged naked through the streets of Constantinople. The horror and indignation which these atrocities inspired, and the instinct of self-preservation, roused the mass of the inhabitants to resist the brigands, who were proceeding to the sack of other mansions, and to the plunder of the shops and bazaars. The chief Preacher of the Mosque of the Great Solyman, and other members of the Ulema, exerted themselves with energy and success to animate the well-affected citizens, and to raise a feeling of shame among the ranks of the Janissaries ; many of whom had been led away by temporary excitement and the evil example of the ruffians, who had joined them from out of the very dregs of the populace.   The Sacred Standard of the Prophet was displayed over the centre gate of the Sultan's palace, and the true believers hastened to rally round the holy symbol of loyalty to their Prophet's Vicar on earth.   The chief pillagers and assassins in the late riot were seized and executed.   The Mufti and three other principal Ulema, who had shown a disposition to obey the mutinous Janissaries, were deposed ; and men of more integrity and spirit were appointed in their places.   Some degree of order was thus restored to the capital ; but the spirit of insubordination and violence was ever ready to break out ; and the provinces were convulsed with revolt and tumult.   It was not until the end of June, 1688, that the Sultan was able to complete the equipment of an army, which then marched towards the Hungarian frontier.

The Austrians and their allies had profited vigorously by the disorders of the Turkish state, and had continued to deal blow after blow with fatal effect.   Three generals of the highest military renown, Charles of Lorraine, Louis of Baden, and Prince Eugene, now directed the Imperialist armies against the discouraged and discordant Ottomans. The important city of Erlau in Hungary surrendered on the 14th of December, 1687, and came again into the dominion of its ancient rulers, after having been for a century under Mahometan sway. Gradiska, on the Bosnian frontier, was captured by Prince Louis of Baden. Stuhweissenberg was invested ; and, as the Turks had abandoned Illock and Peterwaradin, the route to Belgrade lay open to the Austrian armies. A Turkish general named Yegen Osman was ordered to protect Belgrade ; but he was cowardly or treacherous ; and, as the Imperialists advanced, he retreated from Belgrade, after setting fire to the city. The Austrian troops, following close upon the retiring Turks, extinguished the flames, and laid siege to the citadel, which surrendered after a bombardment of twenty-one days, on the 20th of August, 1688. Stuhweissenberg was stormed on the 6th of September ; and Yegen Osman fired Semendra, and abandoned it to the advancing Christians. Prince Louis destroyed a Turkish army in Bosnia ; and city after city yielded to the various Austrian generals who commanded in that province and in Transylvania, and to the Venetian leaders in Dalmatia. The campaign of the next year in these regions was almost equally disastrous to Turkey. The Sultan announced his intention of leading the Ottoman armies in person ; and proceeded as far as the city of Sofia. Part of the Turkish forces were posted in advance at the city of Nissa, and were attacked there and utterly defeated by the Imperialists under Prince Louis of Baden. Nissa, evacuated by the Turks, was occupied by the conquerors. On the tidings of this defeat reaching the Turkish head-quarters at Sofia, the Sultan, in alarm, retreated within the mountain range of the Balkan to the city of Philippopolis. Florentin, Fethislam, and Widdin, next fell into the power of the Imperialists ; and before the close of the year 1689, Great Waradein and Temeswar were all that the Ottomans retained of their late extensive provinces north of the Danube ; while even to the south of that river the best portions of Bosnia and Servia were occupied by the victorious Austrians.

In the southern parts of European Turkey, the fortune of the war was equally unfavourable to Sultan Solyman. Morosini, one of the greatest generals that the Republic of St. Mark ever produced, completed the conquest of the Morea, which he divided into four Venetian provinces. It was only against the Poles and the Russians that the Turks and their Tartar allies obtained any advantages. A large Tartar force from the Crimea, led by Azmet Ghirai, overran part of Poland in 1688 ; reinforced the Tartar garrison in Kaminiec, and defeated the Poles on the Sireth. The Russian general Galitzin attempted to invade the Crimea. He obtained some advantages over part of the Tartar forces, but when he advanced towards the Isthmus of Perekop, in the autumn of 1688, he found that the retreating Tartars had set fire to the dry grass of the steppes, and reduced the country to a desert, from which he was obliged to retire. And, in 1689, when the Russians again advanced to the Isthmus, they were completely defeated by the Ottoman troops, that had taken post there to guard the Crimea. But these gleams of success could not dissipate the terror which the disasters in Hungary and Greece had spread among the Turkish nation. Only seven years had passed away since their magnificent host, under the fatal guidance of Kara Mustapha, had marched forth across the then far-extended north-western frontier, with the proud boast that it would sack Vienna and blot out Austria from among the kingdoms of the earth. Now, the Austrians, and their confederates the lately despised Venetians, the conquered of Candia, held victorious possession of half the European Empire of the House of Othman. For the first time since the days of Hunyades, the Balkan was menaced by Christian invaders; and at sea the Turkish flag, the flag of Khaireddin, Pialé, and Kilidj Ali, was now swept from the Mediterranean. Seldom had there been a war, in which the effect that can be produced on the destinies of nations by the appearance or the absence of individual great men, was more signally proved. On the Christian side, Sobieski, Eugene, Louis of Baden, the Prince of Lorraine, and Morosini had commanded fortune; while among the Turks, no single man of mark had either headed armies, or directed councils. Yet the Ottoman nation was not exhausted of brave and able spirits: and at length adversity cleared the path of dignity for merit.

In the November of 1689, the Sultan convened an extraordinary Divan at Adrianople, and besought his councillors to advise him as to what hands he should intrust with the management of the state. In the hour of extreme peril the jealous spirit of intrigue and self-advancement was silent; and all around Solyman II. advised him to send for Kiuprili-Zadé-Mustapha, brother of the great Ahmed Kiuprili, and to give the seals of office to him as Grand Vizier of the Empire.

Kiuprili-Zadé-Mustapha, at the time when he assumed this high dignity, was fifty-two years of age. He had been trained in statesmanship during the vizierates of his father and brother, Mohammed and Ahmed Kiuprili: and it was expected and hoped, on the death of Ahmed in 1676, that Sultan Mahomet IV. would place the seals in the hands of Kiuprili-Zadé. Unhappily for the Ottoman nation, that Sultan's partiality for his own son-in-law prevailed; nor was it until after thirteen years of misgovernment and calamity had nearly destroyed the empire, that the third Kiuprili succeeded his father and brother, as director of the councils, and leader of the armies of Turkey.

His authority was greatly increased by the deserved reputation which he enjoyed of being a strict observer of the Mahometan law, and an uncompromising enemy to profligacy and corruption. After having paid homage to the Sultan on his appointment, he summoned to the Divan all the great dignitaries of the empire, and addressed them on the state of the country. He reminded them in severe terms of their duties as Moslems, of their sins; and he told them that they were now undergoing the deserved chastisement of God. He described to them the extreme peril in which the empire was placed. "If we go on thus," said he, "another campaign will see the enemy encamped beneath the walls of Constantinople." He then pointed out to them how they ought to act as true believers; and bade them take heart, and be courageous in the defence of their country, however hardly they might find themselves pressed. Kiuprili abolished some imposts introduced by his predecessor, which produced little to the state, while they were peculiarly vexatious to the subject; but he sought to fill the exhausted treasury by exacting heavy contributions from all the late officials who had enriched themselves at the public expense. All the superfluous gold and silver vessels of the palace were sent to the mint to be coined into money for the military chest. And Kiuprili set the example to the other chief men of the state of aiding the public cause by similar contributions. He gave up the whole of his plate; and the Grand Vizier's table was served thenceforth with vessels of copper. Funds for the immediate prosecution of the war were thus obtained; and the belief of the Turks in the ability and in the holiness of the new Vizier brought recruits rapidly to the army, which was collected near the capital. Kiuprili called out all the veterans who had been discharged and pensioned, and he distributed them among the new levies. He placed governors, on whom he could rely, in the most important pachalics. He sought also fit men and measures for the revival of the Turkish marine. Mizirli-Zadé-Ibrahim, who had distinguished himself in the defence of Negropont against the Venetians, was raised to the chief naval command in the Mediterranean; and

20

another bold and skilful officer, Mezzomorto, was commissioned to form and lead a flotilla on the Danube.

But the highest merit of Kiuprili-Zadé-Mustapha is, that he had the wisdom to recognise the necessity of the Sublime Porte strengthening itself by winning the loyal affections of its Christian subjects. Although he was so earnest a believer in Islam, and so exemplary in his obedience to its precepts, that he was venerated by his contemporaries as a saint, he did not suffer bigotry to blind him to the fact, that cruelty to the Rayas must hasten the downfall of the Ottoman Empire. He saw that the Christian invaders of Turkey found everywhere sympathy and recruits among the populations of the land. The Christian Albanians were enrolling themselves ·under the banner of Venice ; the Servians were rising to aid the Emperor of Austria ; and in Greece the victorious progress of Morosini had been aided by the readiness with which the village municipalities and the mountain tribes placed themselves under his authority, and by the strenuous support which bands of Christian volunteers gave him, in beleaguering the fortresses held by the Turks.[1] Kiuprili-Zadé was not content with judging correctly : he took prompt practical measures to check the evils which he was swift to discern. One of the first acts of his vizierate was to despatch the most explicit and imperative orders to all the Pachas, that no Turkish officer should exercise or permit any kind of oppression towards the Rayas ; and that no payment should be required of them except the Capitation Tax. For the purposes of this tax, Kiuprili divided the Rayas into three classes, according to their incomes. The first or wealthiest paid four ducats, the middle class two ducats, and the lowest one ducat a head. This institution was called the Nizami Djidid, the New Order. Kiuprili also took the bold and sagacious step of making a Mainote Greek Bey of Maina. This was Liberius Geratschari, who had passed seven years as a Turkish galley-slave. He was now set at liberty, and sent to the Morea to support the Turkish interest among his countrymen against that of the Venetians, who had begun to alienate the Greek Rayas from their side by impolitic government. Von Hammer remarks that Kiuprili-Zadé showed himself in this measure to be superior as a politician, both to his brother Ahmed, who had sought, in the former Venetian war, to curb the rising disaffection in the Morea by fortified posts and garrisons ; and also to the subsequent Grand Viziers, who, when it was proposed to make the Morea a principality like Moldavia

[1] Von Hammer, vol. iii. p. 841. Emerson Tennant's "Greece," vol. i. p. 218 et seq.

and Wallachia, and govern it by native Christians, rejected the
scheme as derogatory to the dignity of the Sublime Porte.[1]   Kiuprili had even the enlightened spirit to despise the old dogmas of
Turkish Muftis and judges, according to which the Rayas were
allowed only such churches as they already possessed, but were
strictly forbidden to enlarge them, or to build new places of worship.   Kiuprili sanctioned the foundation of a Greek Church
wherever it was desired; and thereby became the founder of
thriving villages, which sprang up in districts where there had
been previously only scanty bands of suffering and disaffected out-
casts.   Once, in passing through part of Servia, Kiuprili halted
for the night in a wretched hamlet of Rayas, who had neither
edifice nor minister of religion.   Kiuprili ordered that a church
should be built there, and that a Christian priest should be sent
for to serve it.   In return for this boon, which filled the poor
peasants with rapturous gratitude, Kiuprili required of them, that
each head of a family should bring him a fowl, whenever he passed
through the village.   Fifty-three fowls were immediately brought
to him; that being the number of families.   In the next (and,
unhappily for the Rayas, the last) year of his vizierate, Kiuprili
passed through the same place.   He received a hundred and
twenty-five fowls from the heads of the happy population, which
flocked together with their Greek priest at their head to welcome
the benevolent Vizier.   " Look," said Kiuprili to the staff of
Turkish officers round him, " Look at the fruits of toleration.   I
have increased the Sultan's power; and I have brought blessings
on his government from those who were wont to curse it."[2]   The
Greeks of the empire used to say that Kiuprili founded more
churches than Justinian.   Had subsequent Turkish ministers
imitated Kiuprili-Zadé Mustafa in their policy towards the Christian population of Turkey, the Ottoman Empire would now command far ampler resources, than it can derive from the unaided
valour and loyalty of its Moslem inhabitants; and the most
serious sources of its internal weakness would long ago have been
removed.

Besides the glory of having, while sincerely religious, practised
religious toleration, the third Kiuprili deserves honourable mention
for his recognition of the great principle of political economy, **that**
(with very few and very peculiar exceptions) trade between man
and man ought to be free from all state interference.   When
pressed by one of his advisers to frame regulations **for purchases**

---

[1] Von Hammer, vol. iii. p. 841.
[2] Ubicini, vol. ii. p. 55, citing Cantemir.

and sales, Kiuprili-Zadé replied, "The Koran prescribes nothing on the subject. Purchase and sale ought to be left to the free will of the contracting parties."[1]

Kiuprili-Zadé Mustapha is termed by Ottoman historians Kiuprili Fazyl, which means "Kiuprili the Virtuous." They say of him, as his highest praise, that he never committed a crime, and that he never used an unnecessary word. They record as an instance of his eminence in taciturnity, that once, while Grand Vizier, he received a ceremonial visit from three of the Ulema, who had formerly held the offices of army judges. Kiuprili let them depart without having addressed a syllable to them. His old Master of Requests, Nigahi Effendi, said to him, "My gracious lord, you should have spoken something to them." "I am not a hypocrite," answered Kiuprili. He was austerely simple in all his habits. In his campaigns he generally marched on foot, like the rank and file of the infantry. He disliked military music. He seldom moved his quarters before sunset. Amid the pomp and splendour of the Turkish court and camp the Grand Vizier was distinguishable by the plainness of his dress. He was an indefatigable student, and read diligently in his tent, when on active service, as well as in his palace when at Constantinople.

Such are some of the praises by which his country's historians signalise Kiuprili-Zadé Mustapha. The renown for statesmanship acquired by him, and which Christian writers have concurred with Mahometan in bestowing, is the more remarkable, by reason of the shortness of the period permitted to him for the display of his administrative genius. He was killed in battle within two years from the time when the seals of office were placed in his hands. His contemporaries judged of him, as of his brother Ahmed, that he shone more in the council than in the field. But the military career of Kiuprili-Zadé was highly honourable to his abilities as well as to his courage; and, though ultimately defeated, he gained a respite of infinite importance for the Ottoman Empire, by the successes which he at first obtained. When he was made Grand Vizier, one of the invading armies of the enemy had advanced as far as Ouskoup, in northern Macedonia, where it was actively aided by the Christian Albanians and their Patriarch. A chieftain of those regions, named Karpos, had accepted a diploma of investiture from the Austrian Emperor, and, assuming the old title of Kral, had fortified himself in Egri-Palanka. It was indispensable to relieve Turkey at once from the foes, who thus struck at the very heart of her power in Europe. Kiuprili held a council

[1] Von Hammer, vol. iii. p. 849.

of war at Adrianople, at which Selim Ghirai, the Khan of the Crimea, and Tekeli, the Hungarian refugee, were present. Khodja Khalid Pacha, the Seraskier of the Morea, a native of Ouskoup, was sent with all the regular Turkish troops that could be collected, against that place. The Crimean Khan, at the head of a large Tartar force, co-operated with him. They gained two victories over the combined bodies of Germans, Hungarians, and Albanians, who had assumed the old mediæval badge of the cross. The chieftain Karpos was seized by the Tartars and executed on the bridge of Ouskoup. Nearly all the important posts which the invaders and their insurgent confederates had occupied in those districts, were recovered by the Sultan's troops, and the pressure on this vital part of the empire was almost entirely removed. Encouraged by these successes, Kiuprili pushed forward with the greatest vigour his armaments for the next campaign. Louis XIV., who was at war with the German Empire, sent in the winter of 1680 a new ambassador, the Marquis de Chateunef, to Constantinople, to encourage the Turks to persevere in hostilities against Austria. Chateunef was also ordered to negotiate, if possible, a peace between Turkey and Poland, to prevent the recognition of William of Orange as King of England by the Sublime Porte, and to regain for the Catholics in Palestine the custody of the Holy Sepulchre, which the Greek Patriarch had lately won from them. Chateunef obtained the last object, and he found in the new Vizier a zealous ally against Austria. But the Turks refused to suspend hostilities with Poland ; and with regard to the Prince of Orange and the English crown, Kiuprili answered that he should recognise the king whom the English people had proclaimed. He added that it would ill become the Turks, who had so often dethroned their own sovereigns, to dispute the rights of other nations to change their masters.

In August, 1690, Kiuprili-Zadé Mustapha took in person the command of the Ottoman armies that advanced from Bulgaria and Upper Albania through Servia, against the Imperialists. After a murderous fight of two days, Kiuprili drove the Austrian general, Schenkendorf, from his lines at Dragoman, between the cities of Sofia and Nissa. The Vizier then formed the siege of Nissa, which capitulated in three weeks. The Austrian generals were prevented from concentrating their forces for its relief, by a well-planned irruption into Transylvania, by the Hungarian refugee Tekeli at the head of a Turkish army. Tekeli defeated the Imperialists in that province, and proclaimed the Sultan as sovereign lord, and himself as Prince of Transylvania. After the capture of Nissa, the Grand Vizier marched upon Semendra, which was stormed after resisting desperately for four days. Widdin was also regained; and Kiuprili then undertook the recovery of Belgrade. On the twelfth day of the siege a shell from the Turkish batteries pierced the roof of the principal powder magazine of the city; and a destructive explosion ensued, which gave the Turks an easy conquest. Having placed a strong garrison in this important city, and completed the expulsion of the Austrians from Servia, Kiuprili returned to Constantinople. He was received there with deserved honours after his short, but brilliant campaign, in which he had compelled the invading Giaours to recede from the banks of the Morava and the Nissa to those of the Danube and the Saave.

On the 10th of May, 1691, Kiuprili the Virtuous received a second time the Sacred Standard from the hands of his sovereign, Sultan Solyman, who died before the campaign was opened. Solyman II. was succeeded by his brother Achmet II., who was girt with the sabre of Othman on the 13th July, 1691. The new Sultan confirmed Kiuprili in his dignity; and the Vizier proceeded to concentrate his forces at Belgrade, and to throw a bridge over the Saave. He then marched up the right bank of the Danube to encounter the Imperialists, who, under the command of Louis of Baden, descended from Peterwaradin. The two hosts approached each other on the 19th of August, near Salankemen. At the same time, the Christian and Mussulman flotillas, which accompanied their respective armies along the Danube, encountered on the river. The Turkish flotilla was victorious; but, on the land, the day proved a disastrous one for the House of Kiuprili and for the House of Othman. Contrary to the advice of the oldest Pachas in the army, the Vizier refused to await behind the lines the attack of the Imperialists. The veteran warrior Khodja Khalid censured this impetuosity. Kiuprili said to him, " I invited thee to follow me that thou mightest figure as a man, and not as a phantom." Khalid, touching the thin hairs of his grey beard, replied, " I have but a few days to live. It matters little whether I die to-day, or to-morrow; but I would fain not have been present at a scene in which the empire can meet with nought but calamity and shame." " Advance the cannon !" cried Kiuprili; and himself formed the Spahis for the fight. Kemankesh Pacha began the battle by rushing, with 6000 Kurdish and Turcoman irregular cavalry, upon the Christian lines. " Courage, my heroes," cried Kemankesh, " the Houris are waiting for you !" They galloped forward with shouts of " Allah !" but were received by the Christians with a steady fire, which drove them back in discomfited and diminished masses. Again they charged impetuously; again they broke, fell or fled. The Austrians now pressed forward to where the Sacred Standard was reared in the Mahometan ranks. Ismael, the Pacha of Caramania, dashed against them with the troops of Asia. His squadrons were entangled in an abattis of felled trees, by which the Prince of Baden had protected his right wing. The Asiatics wavered and were repulsed. Kiuprili saw his best men shot down round him by the superior musketry of the Imperialists. "What is to be done?" he cried to the officers of his guards. They answered, "Let us close, and fight sword in hand." Kiuprili, arrayed in a black vest, invoked the name of God, and threw himself, with drawn sabre, against the enemy. His guards rushed onward with him. An obstinate and sanguinary struggle followed, which was decided against Turkey by the bullet that struck Kiuprili, while cleaving his way desperately through the Austrian ranks. His guards lost courage when they saw him fall; and the fatal tidings that their great Vizier was slain, soon spread disorder and panic throughout the Ottoman army. The Prince of Baden's triumph was complete; and the Turkish camp with 150 cannon fell into the conqueror's power. But the victory was dearly purchased, and the Austrian loss in men and officers was almost equal to that of the Turks. The battle of Salankemen drove the Ottomans again from Hungary; Tekeli was defeated by the Imperialists and expelled from Transylvania; and throughout the four years of the disastrous reign of Achmet II. the current of defeat was unabated. Besides the curse of the victorious sword of the foreigners, and the usual miseries of domestic insurrection, the fearful visitations of pestilence and famine came upon the devoted empire. A great earthquake threw down part of Smyrna; and a still more destructive conflagration ravaged Constantinople in September, 1693. Heartbroken at the sufferings and shame of the State, and worn by disease, Achmet II. expired on the 6th February, 1695.

Mustapha II., the son of the deposed Mahomet IV., now came to the throne, and showed himself worthy of having reigned in happier times. On the third day after his accession, he issued a Hatti-Scherif, in which he threw the blame of the recent misfortunes upon the Sultans, and announced his intention of restoring the ancient usages, and of heading his armies in person. As the German historian observes,[1] this document is too remarkable not

---

[1] Von Hammer, vol. iii.

to deserve citation. Sultan Mustapha II. thus announced his royal will.

"God, the supreme distributor of all good, has granted unto us, miserable sinner, the Caliphate of the entire world. Under monarchs, who are the slaves of pleasure, or who resign themselves to indolent slumber, never do the servants of God enjoy peace or repose. Henceforth, voluptuousness, idle pastime, and sloth are banished from this court. While the Padischas, who have ruled since the death of our sublime father Mahomet, have heeded nought but their fondness for pleasure and for ease, the Unbelievers, the unclean beings, have invaded with their armies the four frontiers of Islam. They have subdued our provinces. They have pillaged the goods of the people of Mahomet. They have dragged away into slavery the faithful, with their wives and little ones. This is known to all, as it is known to us. I therefore have resolved, with the help of the Lord, to take a signal revenge upon the Unbelievers, that brood of Hell; and I will myself begin the holy war against them. Our noble ancestor the Sultan Solyman (May his tomb exhale unceasingly the odour of incense!) during the forty-eight years of his reign, not only sent his Viziers against the unclean Christians, but placed himself at the head of the Champions of the Holy War, and so took upon the infidels the vengeance which God commands. I also, I, have resolved to combat them in person. Do thou, my Grand Vizier, and ye others, my Viziers, my Ulema, my Lieutenants and Agas of my armies, do ye all of you assemble round my person, and meditate well on this my imperial Hatti-Scherif. Take counsel; and inform me if I ought to open hostilities in person against the Emperor, or to remain at Adrianople. Of these two measures choose that which will be most profitable to the Faith, to the empire, and to the servants of God. Let your answer be the truth; and let it be submitted to me before the imperial stirrup. I wish you Health."

The deliberation of the Divan on this summons lasted for three days. Many thought that the presence of the Sultan in the camp was undesirable. Others feared that he had only addressed them with a view of learning their thoughts. Finally, they all resolved that the departure of the Padischah to assume the command-in-chief of the army, would not only expose the sacred person to too much risk and fatigue, but would involve excessive expense. Consequently, the Divan represented to the Sultan that his Majesty ought not to commit his imperial person to the chances of a campaign, but ought to leave the care of war to the Grand Vizier.

To this address the Sultan returned a laconic Hatti-Scherif, "I persist in marching." The most active measures then were taken to hasten the preparations for the campaign ; and the gallantry of the young Sultan was at first rewarded by important success. He advanced in the summer of 1695, from Belgrade to Temesvar, and recaptured the important fortresses of Karansebes, Lipna, and Lugos. On the 22nd of September, he encountered near Lugos the Austrian army under general Veterani. Sultan Mustapha gained a complete victory, and Veterani and half his troops were left dead on the field.

During the winter, which followed this victory, Mustapha and his councillors toiled unremittingly to repair the finances of the empire, and to increase the number and improve the discipline of the troops. Heavy taxes were laid on tobacco, on black eunuchs, and other articles of luxury. Many of the chief men of the empire seconded their sovereign's zeal, and raised bodies of troops at their own expense, of which they took the command. Mustapha had formed a corps of 3000 infantry from the royal gardeners, or Bostandjis, of Adrianople and Constantinople. He now divided those into three regiments, which were equipped in peculiar uniform, and trained with especial care. The Sultan opened the campaign of 1696 at the head of a numerous and well-appointed army. He defeated the Austrians under the Duke de Saxe near Temesvar, and raised the siege of that place. Mustapha strengthened the garrisons of the fortresses which the Turks still held in Hungary, and then returned to Adrianople, not unjustly proud of his achievements ; though the great Solyman, whom he chose as his model, would probably have pushed his advantages further. The hopes and pride of Turkey now began to revive ; but in 1697, Prince Eugene took the command of the Imperialist armies in Hungary ; and the Crescent soon went down before him. Sultan Mustapha collected his army for this fatal campaign at Sofia, and marched thence to Belgrade, where he halted and held repeated councils of war. Some enterprises of minor importance, the sending forward a detachment to reinforce the garrison of Temesvar, and the occupation of several posts along the Danube were successfully attempted ; but there was discord among the Ottoman officers, and there was oscillation in the Sultan's will as to the main line of operations that ought to be followed. The Grand Vizier, Elwas Mohammed, was unpopular with the other Pachas, who leagued together to oppose his projects, and thwart his tactics. The Vizier himself was depressed by a dream, which he saddened his equally credulous comrades

27

also by narrating. He dreamed that the late Grand Vizier, Kiu-prili-Zadé Mustapha, the martyr of Salankeman, had entered his tent and given him a cup of sherbet, which the Apparition had first tasted. "God knows," cried the Grand Vizier, when he told his dream, "that this was the cup of martyrdom, which I, too, am destined to drink in this campaign." He wished to keep the army on the right bank of the Danube, and crossing the Saave to march upon Peterwaradin, and attempt the recovery of that important fortress. The other officers proposed to cross the Danube and the Theiss, and to endeavour to surprise Eugene's army, which was camped on the banks of the Bacska. After much angry discussion this last project was adopted. The army crossed the Danube and the Theiss; but it was found that all hope of surprising Eugene was idle, and the Austrians and Turks both endeavoured to gain the fort of Zitel, which is situate at the junction of the Theiss with the Danube. The Ottomans obtained some advantage over a detachment of Eugene's army, and sacked Zitel. They then reverted to the scheme of besieging Peterwara-din, and marched to Valova; where they began to construct bridges to enable them to pass to the right bank of the Danube and attack Peterwaradin; the old bridges having been occupied or destroyed by the Austrians. Finding that Eugene had secured Peterwaradin against attack, they held another council of war, and resolved to march northwards up the right or eastern bank of the Theiss and attack Szegedin. The activity of Eugene discon-certed this project also. He threw a strong division into Szege-din; and with the rest of his army followed the Turks, watching for a favourable opportunity of attacking them. This was soon obtained. The Austrian hussars captured one of the Pachas, named Djafer; who, finding his life threatened, confessed to the Austrians that the Sultan had given up his project of attacking Szegedin, and now designed to cross the Theiss near Zenta, with the intention of marching upon upper Hungary and Transylvania. Eugene instantly moved with all possible speed towards Zenta, in the hopes of assailing the Ottoman army while in the act of passing the river.

It was on the 11th of September, about two in the afternoon, that the Sultan saw his great enemy approach. The Turks had formed a temporary bridge across the river; and the Sultan, the cavalry, and the greater part of the artillery of his army, had passed over to the left or eastern bank; but the infantry was still on the western side. The Sultan and his officers had taken the precaution of forming a strong entrenchment to protect their rear during the passage of the bridge, and seventy guns had been kept in position on the right bank for that purpose. Undaunted by these preparations, Eugene formed his columns, as they came up, into line for the attack; and although at this critical time a courier arrived from Vienna with peremptory orders to Eugene not to risk a battle, he determined to disobey his Emperor's orders, and continued his preparations for a decisive engagement.[1] If the Ottomans had anticipated him by a resolute advance against the Austrian centre, before Eugene's troops had all arrived, and before his artillery had been brought into position, it is probable that they would have crushed the Imperialists. But discord and disorder were rife in the Sultan's camp. The Grand Vizier summoned the Pachas and Spahis, most of whom had passed over to the eastern bank, back to the menaced side; but he did not move beyond his entrenchments, and the Sultan himself did not recross the river to share in and conduct the conflict. Only two hours of daylight were left when Eugene had completed his dispositions for action. He formed his army into a half-moon, so as to assail the whole semicircle of the Turkish entrenchments, and he posted his cannon where they commanded the bridge. He then made a simultaneous attack on every part of the Turkish lines, which was everywhere successful. The Turks fought without concert or confidence; and a large body of Janissaries mutinied, and began to massacre their own officers in the very heat of the action. The Christians gave no quarter; more than 20,000 Turks were slain, including the Grand Vizier and a large number of Pachas; and more than 10,000 were drowned in endeavouring to pass the river. The battle was lost and won before the close of the day; and in the words of Eugene in his despatch to Vienna: "The sun seemed to linger on the horizon to gild with his last rays the victorious standards of Austria."

The Sultan, from the eastern bank of the Theiss, witnessed the destruction of his host, and fled with the remnants of his cavalry in dismay to Temesvar. Thence he retired to Constantinople, and never appeared again at the head of an army. In the extreme distress to which the defeat at Zenta had once more reduced the Ottoman Empire, resort was again had to the House of Kiuprili, and again that illustrious family supplied a minister who could prop, if he could not restore, the falling state.

Housein Kiuprili had in the time of the vizierate of Ahmed

---

[1] Coxe's "History of the House of Austria," vol. ii. p. 456.

Kiuprili, received the name of Amoud-schah-zadé, which means "Son of the Uncle." He was so called because he was the son of Hassan, who was the younger brother of Mohammed Kiuprili, and the uncle of Ahmed Kiuprili. Amoud-schah-zadé Housein Kiuprili had in early life been an idle voluptuary; but the disasters which befell Turkey after the expedition against Vienna roused him to a sense of what he owed to the honour of his House and to his country. He filled many important offices with zeal and ability; and when raised to the Grand Vizierate in 1697, he gave proofs of his possessing in ample degree that genius for finance and for administrative reform, which was the eminent characteristic of his family. Every possible effort was made by him to collect the means of opposing further resistance to the enemies of the empire. A tax was laid upon coffee : a contribution in the nature of an income tax was required from all the principal officers of the state : and Housein Kiuprili even ventured to appropriate to the urgent necessities of the country a large sum from the revenues of the religious foundations. He succeeded in collecting and equipping an army of 50,000 foot and 48,000 horse for the defence of the European provinces. A Turkish fleet was sent into the Black Sea, and another into the Mediterranean.[1] But while the Vizier thus prepared war, it was with the wish for peace. He knew too well the exhaustion of the empire, and felt the impossibility of preventing further disasters if hostilities were continued. It was not only in the Danubian provinces that the war went hard with Turkey. The Venetians were making further progress in Dalmatia; and in Greece they were advancing beyond the isthmus of Corinth; though Negropont had been bravely and successfully defended against them, and seasonable relief had been obtained for the Ottoman forces that were employed along the coasts and in the islands of the Archipelago, through the gallantry of the Turkish Admiral Mezzomorto, who gained two victories over the Venetian fleets. Poland was an inactive antagonist; but Russia had become a truly formidable enemy. Peter the Great was now sovereign of that vast empire, and was teaching the lately rude and barbarous Muscovy to know her own gigantic strength, and also to use it like a giant. He had already drawn around him skilful officers and engineers from Western Europe; and he had formed a body of troops on the models of the Imperialist and

---

[1] Von Hammer cites, in a note to his 60th book, an official list, which a Turkish writer gives of the Ottoman forces on land and sea, as augmented by Housein Kiuprili. It specifies the number of troops supplied by each province, and their character.

French armies. But ships, harbours, and maritime power were the dearest objects of his heart; and one of the earliest marks of his ambition (never lost sight of by himself or any of his successors) was to obtain the mastery of the Black Sea. With this view he prosecuted the war against Turkey with a vigour and skill very different from the conduct of Galitzin and other former Russian commanders. Peter resolved first to conquer the strong city of Azoph, which, as has been mentioned, had been fortified by the Turks with peculiar care, and was justly regarded as a position of the greatest importance. He led an army of 60,000 men (including his new-modelled regiments) against Azoph, in 1695. He also formed a large flotilla of vessels, drawing but little water, which co-operated with his army in the siege. His first attempt was unsuccessful; and he sustained a repulse, which was severe enough to discourage a spirit of ordinary firmness. The Russians were driven back from Azoph, in 1695, with a loss of 30,000 men. But in the following spring the Czar renewed the siege with fresh forces. His flotilla defeated a squadron of light Turkish vessels, that attempted to relieve the city; and he kept in check the Ottoman Pachas, who advanced from the Crimea with troops along the coast as far as the village of Akkoumin. Azoph surrendered to the Czar on the 28th July, 1696; and he immediately began to improve the fortifications and harbour, and to fit out vessels of war, on a scale, which showed for what important ulterior projects the possession of Azoph had been sought by Russia.

Thus menaced from many quarters, the Ottoman court listened willingly to the English ambassador, Lord Paget, who urged on the Turkish statesmen the necessity of peace, and offered the mediation of England to obtain it. Similar proposals had been made by the representatives of Holland and England at earlier periods of the war, and negotiations had once been opened at Vienna, but no salutary result had followed. But now both Turkey and her chief antagonist Austria were sincerely desirous of peace. The Emperor Leopold had indeed seen his armies obtain triumphs, which might have filled many monarchs with ambitious visions of ampler conquests, and might have led to a march upon Constantinople, as the fit retribution for the repeated siege of Vienna. But Leopold was of a wiser or a colder spirit. He was anxious for sure and peaceful possession of the valuable provinces that had already been re-conquered from the Turks in the war; and, though Austria had been generally victorious, she had suffered severely in men and in treasure. Above all, the prospect that the succession to the Spanish throne would soon become vacant, made the German Emperor anxious to terminate hostilities in Eastern Europe, and prepare for the great struggle in the West, which was already foreseen as inevitable.

Lord Paget proposed to the Porte that England should intervene to effect a pacification on the footing of the "Uti Possidetis;" that is to say, on the principle that each of the contending parties should keep what it possessed at the time of commencing negotiations. Sultan Mustapha could ill brook the cession of such broad and fair territories, as a treaty, framed on this rule, would assign to his adversaries; and he endeavoured to introduce some important modifications. He placed before Lord Paget a counter-project, written in his own hand (an unprecedented act for a Turkish Sultan), and which was accompanied by a letter from the Grand Vizier to the King of England. The mediation of England was requested, in order that a peace might be concluded generally on the foundation of the "Uti Possidetis," but with stipulations that the Austrians should abandon Transylvania, that the city of Peterwaradin should be razed, that the Austrians should evacuate all the fortified places on the Turkish side of the river Unna, and with other exceptions of a similar nature. Lord Paget's secretary was sent by him with the Grand Vizier's letter to Vienna; and the Austrian Government was informed of the readiness of England to mediate between the belligerents. In reply to this, a communication was made to the Porte that the Emperor Leopold was willing to treat for peace, but on condition that each party was to keep all that it then possessed, and on condition also that Russia was comprised in the treaty. Venice and Poland were added; and Holland co-operated with England as a mediating power. The Czar Peter, though not desirous of continuing the war, single-handed, against Turkey, was disinclined for peace, and dissatisfied with the proposed principle for negotiation. He passed through Vienna in 1698; and, while in that capital, he had an interview with the Emperor Leopold on the subject of the treaty with the Ottoman. Peter questioned the Austrian sovereign about the causes of his desire for peace with Turkey. Leopold replied that he had not sought for peace, but that England had, in the first instance, offered her mediation; and that each of the allied Christian sovereigns was to keep the conquests which he had made. But the Russian was anxious, not only to secure Azoph, but to obtain the important city of Kertch in the Crimea; and he insisted that the cession of this place should be made a term of the treaty, and that in the event of Turkey declining to give it up, Russia and Austria should form a fresh league against her. He was answered by a promise to

endeavour to obtain Kertch for him ; but he was told that it was
not fit to renew an offensive alliance on the eve of assembling a
congress for pacification. In another conversation, which Peter
had with the Austrian minister, Count Kinsky, he asked what
power it was that insisted on a peace. The Austrian replied,
"Our Holy Roman Empire insists on it ; Spain insists on it ; it is
required by England and Holland ; and, in a word, by all Christendom." "Beware !" replied the Czar, "how you trust to what the
Dutch and the English say. They are looking only to the benefit
of their commerce ; they care nothing about the interests of their
allies." The Polish sovereign also objected to recognise the " Uti
Possidetis" principle. He complained that a treaty on this footing
would leave the Ottomans in possession of Kaminiec, which was
the key to Poland. At length, after many difficulties and delays,
the five belligerent, and the two mediating powers sent their
plenipotentiaries to the place appointed for that congress, which
was the town of Carlowitz, on the right bank of the Danube, a
little below Peterwaradin (24th October, 1698).

The German historian, Von Hammer, says truly of the Peace of
Carlowitz,[1] that it is one of those treaties which ought to be considered with particular care, even as there are certain battles which
demand and receive the special attention of the historical student.
The treaty of Carlowitz is memorable, not only on account of the
magnitude of the territorial change which it ratified ; not only
because it marks the period when men ceased to dread the Ottoman Empire as an aggressive power ; but, also, because it was
then that the Porte and Russia took part, for the first time, in a
general European Congress ; and because, by admitting to that
congress the representatives of England and Holland, neither of
which states was a party to the war, both the Sultan and the
Czar thus admitted the principle of intervention of the European
powers, one with another, for the sake of the general good.

The negotiations at Carlowitz were long ; and the representatives of the mediating powers had, more than once, great difficulty
in preventing an angry rupture. Besides disputes as to ceremonials
and titles, the congress was required to arrange many serious
claims and objections, and each of the belligerents, except Austria
and Venice, desired some deviations in its own favour from the
general principle of "Uti Possidetis." The Russian envoy long
and fiercely insisted on the cession of Kertch. The Ottomans
wished Austria to give up Transylvania, or to pay an annual sum

[1] Vol. iii. p. 913.

for retaining it. They also desired Venice to restore many of her conquests beyond the Morea, and that the Russians should evacuate Azoph. The Poles asked for the restoration of Kaminiec; and the Imperialists, though generally loyal to the fundamental principle of the congress, introduced new matters of dissension, by demanding that the custody of the Holy Sepulchre should be restored to the Franciscans, that the Jesuits should be confirmed in their possessions in the Isle of Chios, and that the Porte should grant certain privileges to the Trinitarians, a society instituted for the purpose of ransoming Christian captives from slavery. The Greek Mavrocordato, who was the principal diplomatist on behalf of the Sultan at the congress, replied to these claims of Austria, that the Sublime Porte knew nothing of Trinitarians, of Franciscans, or of Jesuits. It was, however, agreed that certain articles should be drawn up, by which the Sultan promised to continue his protection to the Christians according to the ancient capitulations and Hatti-Scherifs. On another point the Ottomans were characteristically and honourably firm. Austria required that Count Tekeli, the Hungarian chief, who had taken shelter in Turkey, should be given up as a rebel to the Emperor. This was refused; and nothing could be exacted, beyond a promise on the Sultan's part, that Tekeli and his partisans should be kept at such a distance from the frontier, as not to be able to foment disturbances in any part of the Emperor's dominions. Austria, on the other hand, consented that the confiscated dowry of Helen Zriny, Tekeli's wife, should be restored to her, and that she should be allowed to join her husband.[1]

At length, after many weeks of arguments, bickerings, threats and intrigues, the terms of pacification were arranged. Austria and Turkey concluded a treaty for twenty-five years; by which

[1] In a former negotiation in 1689 between the Turkish and Imperialist envoys, under the mediation of the Dutch ambassador at Vienna (which proved abortive), the Austrians had peremptorily insisted on Tekeli being given up to them to be punished for his treasons. The Turkish envoy, Soulfikar, observed that he himself looked on Tekeli as an enemy to the Porte, and the author of the war. He said that Tekeli was no more than the Sultan's dog, and that it mattered little to the Padischah whether such a creature lived or died, but that he himself had not travelled so far on that embassy to become Tekeli's assassin. The Dutch ambassador observed on this, that the Turks could not make a serious matter about giving up Tekeli, now that they had themselves treated him as a mere dog. Soulfikar replied, "Ay, Tekeli is indeed a dog; a dog that lies down or rises, that barks or is quiet, according to the Sultan's bidding. But this dog is the dog of th Padischah of the Ottomans; and at a sign from him the dog may be metamorphosed into a terrible lion."

the Emperor was acknowledged sovereign of Transylvania, all Hungary north of the Marosch and west of the Theiss, and of Sclavonia, except a small part between the Danube and the Saave. With Venice and Poland treaties without limitation of time were effected. Poland recovered Podolia and Kaminiec. Venice retained her conquests in Dalmatia and the Morea; but restored to the Turks those which she had made to the north of the Isthmus of Corinth. Russia refused to consent to anything more than an armistice for two years, which was afterwards enlarged into a peace for thirty years; as the Czar's attention was, in the commencement of the eighteenth century, principally directed to schemes of aggrandisement at the expense of Sweden. By this armistice the Russians kept possession of Azoph, and of the districts which they had conquered to the north of the sea of that name.

It was on the 26th of January, 1699, that the pacification of Carlowitz was completed. It left the two feebler Christian powers, Venice and Poland, restored to temporary importance; the one by the acquisition of the Morea, the other by the recovery of Kaminiec. But it was in the altered state of the three greater belligerents, compared with what they had been in 1682, that men recognised the momentous effects of the seventeen years' war, which was terminated at Carlowitz. Russia had now stretched her arms southward, and grasped the coasts of the Mæotis and the Euxine. At the beginning of the war Austria trembled for the fate of her capital, and saw her very national existence seriously menaced: at the end of the conflict the empire of the House of Hapsburg was left not merely in security, but enlarged: not merely enlarged, but permanently strengthened and consolidated: while the House of Othman saw many of its fairest dominions rent away, and was indebted for the preservation of the remainder from conquest by the invading Christians, to the intervention of two other Christian states. From that time forth all serious dread of the military power of Turkey has ceased in Europe. " Her importance has become diplomatic. Other nations have from time to time sought to use her as a political machine against Austria, or the growing power of Russia; and this diplomatic importance of Turkey has grown proportionably greater as the sovereigns of Russia became desirous of possessing the Black Sea for the carrying out of their plans."[1] Another, and that a more general and enduring cause why the affairs of Turkey have con-

---

[1] See Schlosser's Introduction to the "History of the Eighteenth Century." I have modified some of his expressions.

tinued to inspire interest and anxiety, has been the consideration. of the formidable increase of aggressive power which must be acquired by the conquering state that makes the Ottoman territories integral portions of its own dominions. The empire, which, while possessed by the Turks, is effete for purposes of attack, might, under the lordship of others, supply the means for crushing the liberties of the world.

CHAPTER XVIII.

DEATH OF KIUPRILI HOUSEIN—ABDICATION OF MUSTAPHA II.—
ACCESSION OF ACHMET III.—CHARLES XII. IN TURKEY—WAR
WITH RUSSIA—SUCCESS OF THE TURKS AND TREATY OF THE
PRUTH—WAR WITH VENICE—THE MOREA RECOVERED—WAR
WITH AUSTRIA—DISASTERS OF THE TURKS—PEACE OF PAS-
SAROWITZ—LEAGUE WITH RUSSIA AGAINST PERSIA—DEPO-
SITION OF ACHMET III.—THE HOSPODARS—THE FANARIOTS.[1]

THE Grand Vizier Kiuprili Housein availed himself of the return
of peace to check the disorders which had arisen in many parts of
the empire, especially in Egypt and the Crimea, during the last
calamitous years of the war. He also endeavoured to effect a
general reform in the administrative departments of the army and
navy, in the finances, in the public schools and colleges, in the
laws respecting religious and charitable foundations, and in the
treatment of the Christian subjects of the Porte. It was particularly in this last respect—in his humane and wise mitigation
of the burdens of the Rayas, that Amoud-schah-zadé Housein
showed himself a worthy successor of his relative Kiuprili the
Virtuous. Unhappily for the empire, the influence of Kiuprili
Housein was thwarted by that of other favourites of Sultan Mustapha; and the fourth great minister of the House of Kiuprili
retired from office, worn out in body and in mind, within three
years after the peace of Carlowitz. Kiuprili the Wise, as Kiuprili
Housein was justly surnamed, died in the autumn of 1702. The
Sultan did not retain the throne long after the loss of his able
minister. Mustapha II. appears to have been spirit-broken by the
disastrous close of his military career; and the latter part of his
reign shows no trace of the vigour, or of the conscientious zeal in
the discharge of duty, which signalised him in the commencement
of his sovereignty. The once resolute leader of his own armies
sank into an effeminate sensualist, who forgot the boasted example
of Solyman the Lawgiver, and appeared rather to follow that of

[1] See Von Hammer, books 61-65.

Ibrahim. The general discontent of the nation produced the usual result. An insurrection broke out in Constantinople, in 1703, which raged for several weeks ; until Mustapha, who showed no spark of his former courage, abdicated in favour of his brother Achmet III., who became Sultan at thirty years of age.

The position, which the successes of Russia in the late war had given her on the shores of the Sea of Azoph and the Euxine, continued to fill the Ottoman councils with anxiety. Although the armistice, which alone the Russians would agree to at Carlowitz, was not broken, there were six months of earnest and often angry negotiations between the Czar and the Porte in 1700, before the final terms of peace between them were arranged. Eventually a treaty was signed, which purported to assure amity between Russia and Turkey for thirty years. By the second article of that treaty, the fortifications of four of the places conquered by the Russians—Toghan, Ghazi-kerman, Schahim-kerman, and Nassret-kerman—were to be demolished. The fifth article directed that in order to form a border land for the two empires, there should be a desert-space for twelve leagues between Perekop[1] and Azoph. By the sixth article the Tartars and the Russians were to have equal rights of fishery, hunting, taking hives, cutting wood, and collecting salt in the district between Perekop and the fortress of Meyusch. The seventh assigned to the Russians, as appurtenant to the city of Azoph, which they possessed, a territory of seven leagues in the direction of the river Kuban ; and ordained that the Nogai Tartars and Circassians should give the Russians and Cossacks no annoyance in that domain. The eighth required that the Tartars of the Crimea should make no more incursions into the Russian territories. The ninth related to the exchange of prisoners ; the tenth to the freedom of commerce ; the twelfth stipulated protection for pilgrims to Jerusalem ; the thirteenth concerned the privileges of agents and interpreters ; and the fourteenth directed that each party should within two months send an embassy to ratify the articles.

A little time after the conclusion of the treaty with Russia, the Sublime Porte gave a public proof of how highly it valued the friendship of England, and of its sense of the gratitude due from Turkey to this country for the mediation which terminated the late war. When Lord Paget was succeeded as ambassador at Constantinople by Sir Robert Sutton, the Sultan personally addressed the English envoy at his audience of reception, in these words : " The English are old and good friends to us ; and we shall

[1] Called "Or" in the treaty.

show, when there is an opportunity, that we are the same to them. Especially do we desire to prove to your king our remembrance of his friendly intervention at Carlowitz, and our confidence in his kindly feeling towards us."

This high esteem for the friendship of England was probably due in part to the troubled state of the Turkish relations with Russia, which did not cease when the treaty of 1700 was formally ratified. About the same time that the new English ambassador reached Constantinople, there was imminent risk of a collision between the Turkish and Russian forces north of the Euxine. The Crimean Khan, and other Moslem dignitaries wished for a renewal of the war ; and sent exaggerated representations to Constantinople, respecting the naval preparations of the Russians in the Sea of Azoph, and the strength of the new fortresses, which it was alleged they were building. These reports were contradicted by the Russian ambassador ; and the Crimean Khan was deposed by the Sultan for his false intelligence. But the Turks laboured hard to strengthen the defences of their empire against Russia. In order to confine the Czar's fleet to the Sea of Azoph, they built a strong fortress at the eastern extremity of the Crimea, with which to command the northern entrance of the straits of Kertch. This fortress was called Yenikale. It was finished in 1703 ; and its batteries were arranged on a level with the water, so that the bullets could sweep away any vessel that attempted to force the passage. On the other hand the Russians continued to strengthen Azoph ; and they built a new fortress at Taighan, since known as Taganrok. They also repaired the old works of Kamienska, on the banks of the Dnieper.

One of the first acts of Sultan Achmet III., on his accession to the Turkish throne, was to write a letter to Peter, in which he complained of the menacing preparations in the Czar's southern provinces, and declared that he could place no reliance on the Russian protestations of friendship. But Achmet was not of a warlike disposition ; and the intestine commotions, by which his realm was troubled in the beginning of his reign, made him anxious to avoid hostilities with his powerful neighbour. Russia also was too much occupied at this time by her contest with Sweden, to make her desire a new war with Turkey ; and another temporary settlement of the disputes between the two empires was effected in 1705. Still, the Porte watched every movement of the Czar with jealous care. A fleet of Turkish galleys was sent every year to cruise in the Black Sea, and observe the new fortifications which the Russians formed on its coast. Kertch and

Yenikale were strongly garrisoned with regular Ottoman troops, and a Turkish castle was built near Taman, on the Asiatic side of the straits of Kertch.

The gallant conflict which Charles XII. maintained with Russia was the object of the admiring attention of all Europe during the first decade of the eighteenth century; and by none was the romantic career of that heroic king watched more earnestly than by the Ottomans, who felt deeply the value of the Swedish arms in averting from Turkey the ambitious attacks of the Muscovite sovereign. The Czar Peter was called by the Ottoman historians "White Moustache," while they speak of King Charles by the appropriate title of "Iron Head." It is known from these writers that the Turkish governor of Oczakow sent an envoy to Charles's camp at Thorn, to negotiate an alliance against Russia. And, when the Swedish King was in the Ukraine, he received assurances from the same quarter, that the Khan of the Crimea should lead an army of Tartars to his aid. But these communications were without the sanction of Sultan Achmet; and when Charles, after his disastrous overthrow at Pultowa[1] (8th July, 1709), took refuge in Turkey, he was received with dignified hospitality; but Achmet showed no desire to break the peace with Russia for the purpose of restoring the King of Sweden to power. But the Porte returned a noble refusal to the demands of the triumphant Czar, when he required that Charles should not be permitted to remain in the Ottoman dominions, and sought by every possible threat and promise to obtain the extradition of the Hetman Mazeppa, who had accompanied Charles into Turkey, and whom the Russian claimed for punishment as a traitor to their sovereign.

Charles XII. at first took shelter at Oczakow, but soon removed to Bender, where the Porte assembled a little army for his protection. The necessity of such a precaution had been shown by an attack which the Russians made on a body of Swedes, who were collected in Moldavia. The Czar's forces suddenly crossed the frontier; surprised the Swedes near Czarnowicz, and carried nearly all of them away into Russia as prisoners. This violation of the Ottoman territory caused the greatest indignation at Constantinople; and it was with extreme difficulty that the Russian ambassador Tolskoi prevented an immediate declaration of war. The Grand Vizier, Tschuli Ali, was in favour of maintaining peace with the Czar, and opposed vehemently the demands of Charles, who wished the Sultan to furnish him with 30,000 Spahis

[1] See chapter xii. of the "Fifteen Decisive Battles of the World."

and 20,000 Janissaries to escort him across Poland towards his own dominions. To have sent such an army as this with Charles, would have necessarily involved the Porte in hostilities with both Poland and Russia; and Tschuli Ali bade the Divan remember the sufferings of Turkey in the last war, as decisive arguments against such a measure. On the other hand, the Sultana Validé, who admired the chivalrous courage of Charles, pleaded his cause warmly with the Sultan, and asked often of her son, "When would he aid her lion against the bear?" At the end of 1709, the pacific party in the Divan prevailed; and the treaty which had been signed between Russia and Turkey in the reign of Mustapha II., was renewed, but with an additional article, which stipulated that the King of Sweden should be at liberty to return to his states by such road as he should judge fitting. The Sultan sent a letter to the King, informing him that by virtue of this clause he could return to his kingdom in full security; and the letter was accompanied by 10,000 ducats for the expense of the journey, and by presents of horses from the Sultan and the Vizier. Charles accepted the Sultan's gifts, but made no preparations for leaving Turkey; and the Sultan, irritated at the failure of the Vizier's plans for relieving him of the burden of Charles's presence in the empire, deprived Tschuli Ali of the seals of office, and made Nououman Kiuprili Grand Vizier, in June, 1710.

Nououman Kiuprili was the son of Kiuprili the Virtuous, the Grand Vizier who fell in battle at Salankaman. The accession to power of a fifth Grand Vizier of this illustrious family was hailed with joy by all the inhabitants of the Ottoman Empire; and Nououman began his ministry amid the highest expectations of all ranks of his countrymen. These expectations were not fulfilled. Nououman Kiuprili showed the same toleration, the same wisdom and justice, which had marked his father in his treatment both of Rayas and Moslems. But he was one of those statesmen, who, partly out of vanity, partly out of nervousness, take upon themselves the personal discharge of more duties than they are equal to; and who give disgust and annoyance to their colleagues and subordinate officials, by needlessly and unseasonably interfering with the petty details of departmental business. Hence there speedily arose confusion and discord in the government, of which he was the chief: and the disappointment, which men felt at the failure of their exaggerated hopes and predictions respecting him, brought on the last Kiuprili by a natural reaction an equally excessive amount of unpopularity. He was dismissed from the Grand Vizierate within fourteen months from the time when he had received that high office, and retired to his former subordinate, but honourable station of governor of the important island of Eubœa.

One measure of foreign policy, that marked Nououman Kiu prili's brief administration, was singularly unfortunate with regard to the effect which its author wished it to produce. Nououman Kiuprili was as desirous of maintaining peace as his predecessors in office had been; and he endeavoured earnestly, but in vain, to persuade the King of Sweden to retire quietly from the Sultan's dominions. But he thought that it would be politic at the same time to create a general impression that the resources and warlike spirit of the Turkish Empire were undiminished; and he accordingly issued orders for the assembling a large army, and caused a resolution of the Divan to be circulated, that the Sublime Porte intended to conduct the Swedish King back to his own country with a host equal to that which Kara Moustafa had led against Vienna. The effect of this boast, and of the military display with which it was accompanied, was to excite to an irrepressible ardour the warlike spirit of the Ottoman troops, who were generally zealous in behalf of the King of Sweden against Russia, and who were also eager for an opportunity of effacing the dishonours of the last war.

The numerous aggressions of the Russians on the Turkish territory caused frequent petitions for protection and redress to be sent to the Sultan by the inhabitants of his frontier provinces; and the agents of Charles XII. at the Turkish Court used all possible means to make these and similar inducements to war produce their full effect upon Sultan Achmet. The Khan of the Crimea, Dewlet Ghirai, was as anxious as the Swedish King for immediate hostilities between Turkey and Russia. No part of the Ottoman dominions was so seriously menaced by the ambitious preparations of the Czar, as the Crimean peninsula and the adjacent districts, which Dewlet Ghirai ruled as vassal to the Sublime Porte. The Russians had built fortified posts near Kamienska, at a short distance from Perekop; they had also erected a castle at Samandjik, at the point of the confluence of the Samara and the Dnieper. Another fortress had been built by them at Taighan; and the care with which Azoph and the new port of Taganrok were fortified, and the strength of the flotilla which the Czar had formed there, were also causes of alarm to the Khan, which he succeeded in communicating to the Sultan. Poniatowski, Charles's chief agent in the Turkish Court, pointed out these preparations of the Czar, as proofs that he designed, now that he was master of Azoph and the coasts of the Mæotis, to assail and conquer the Crimea, whence the victorious Russians would soon attack Constantinople.[1] Besides these causes of complaint against Russia, the partisans of Charles in the Divan referred to the growing ascendency of that power in Poland, where the troops of the Czar had now seized and garrisoned the important fortress of Kaminiec. Other causes why Turkey should suspect Russia were also mentioned; such as the Czar's subjugation of the Cossacks Potkal and Bersbasch, and the Russian occupation of Stanileschti, a fortress over against Jassy. Moved by these representations of the anti-Russian party, the Sultan summoned the Crimean Khan to Constantinople, and in a solemn audience, which Achmet gave him, Dewlet Ghirai urged with vehemence the necessity of an immediate rupture with Russia. He warned the Porte that the Czar's agents were secretly intriguing with the Rayas of the empire; and that, if time were allowed for the completion of their machinations, the Russians would by these means win all the European dominions of the Porte. His reasonings finally prevailed with Sultan Achmet. The Khan was dismissed with rich presents of honour; and the Mufti was consulted as to the lawfulness of war with Russia, and returned a Fetva, which pronounced the war to be not only justifiable but necessary. Orders were issued to enrol 30,000 Janissaries, and large numbers of other troops; and a circular was sent to all the governors of the coasts, enjoining them to prepare and place at the disposition of the Capitan Pacha (whose fleet was ready for sea) a certain number of vessels, drawing but little water, and therefore fit for operations in the Sea of Azoph. According to a barbarous usage which the Ottomans have only lately discontinued, the declaration of war with Russia (November 28, 1710) was marked by the imprisonment of the Russian Ambassador Tolskoi, in the Castle of the Seven Towers.[2]

It is probable that the Russian sovereign would willingly have deferred hostilities with Turkey. It was not till near the close of the year 1710, that Peter completed his conquest of Livonia and

---

[1] Levesque, "Histoire de Russie," vol. iv. p. 393.

[2] The state-answer of the ancient Sultans, when requested to receive an embassy, was, "The Sublime Porte is open to all." This, according to the Turkish interpretation, implied a safe conduct in coming, but gave no guarantee about departing. "Vestigia nulla retrorsum." Levesque in his "History of Russia" (vol. iv. p. 394), fairly remarks on this Turkish custom of imprisoning ambassadors when a war broke out: "On leur a justement reproché cet usage barbare. Mais Charles XII. retenait encore et laissa mourir dans la captivité le prince Khilkof, ambassadeur de Russie; et aucun historien ne lui a reproché cet attentat contre le droit des gens."

was at liberty to draw troops from the scene of his operations against the Swedes, and against the party among the Poles that was opposed to him, towards the Ottoman frontier. Had the war been delayed for another year, it is probable that the Russians would have entered upon the contest with much greater advantages than they possessed in 1711. But finding it impossible by negotiations to induce the Sultan to desist from his preparations for an immediate conflict, the Czar, on the 25th of February, 1711, directed war against the Turks to be solemnly proclaimed in the principal church of Moscow. In order to rouse the fanaticism, and increase the zeal of the Russian soldiery (and probably also with a view of inducing the Christian populations of Turkey to join him), Peter endeavoured to give the war all the appearances of a war of religion. Instead of the usual ensigns of the Russian troops they bore red standards, which on one side were inscribed with these words, "In the name of God, and for the cause of Christianity;" and on the other side was a cross, and the well-known inscription of the Labarum of the former Greek Emperors of Constantinople, Ἐν τούτῳ νίκα.

The rapid development of the vast power of Græco-Christian and Slavonic Russia, and the approaching conflict between her and the House of Othman, excited in the highest degree the Greek and Slavonic nations that were subject to the Turkish yoke. They looked upon the Czar as their coming liberator, and their enthusiasm was augmented by a rumour that an ancient prophecy had been discovered in the tomb of Constantine, which pointed to the Russians as the nation destined to chase the Turks from Constantinople.[1] Even the small and remote tribes of the Montenegrins sent messengers to Peter, offering to attack their Turkish rulers, and make a diversion in his favour. The Czar thanked them by a letter and by presents : but the primary aim of his negotiations with the Christian subjects of the Sultan, was to secure the co-operation of the Hospodars of Wallachia and Moldavia. It was into these principalities that he designed first to lead his army; and he wished to make them a secure basis for his further operations in invading Turkey. Brancovan, the Hospodar of Wallachia, had for a long time established an intelligence with Russia, which the Porte at last suspected, and directed Prince Cantemir, the Hospodar of Moldavia, to attack him and deprive him of his

----

[1] Levesque, "Histoire de Russie," vol. iv. p. 400. This rumour has often been revived, especially in the time of the victories of the Empress Catherine II. See the remarks of Gibbon as to its antiquity, vol. vi. p. 88 (Dr. Smith's edition), and notes.

government. But Cantemir himself determined to aid the Russians, and obtained such favour with the Czar as raised the jealousy of Brancovan, who, by a double treachery, began to intrigue with the Turks, for the purpose of misleading Peter and bringing him and his army into a position, where the Turks could assail them with advantage.

The new Grand Vizier, Baltadji Mehemet Pacha (who had originally been a wood-cutter in the Serail), began his march from the neighbourhood of Constantinople towards the Moldavian frontier, in May, 1711, at the head of a large and admirably equipped army. The Czar collected his forces in the south of Poland, and in June advanced into Moldavia. His troops suffered severely on their line of march; and great numbers perished by privations and disease before they reached Jassy, and before any actual hostilities had commenced. Peter halted at Jassy for a short time, and endeavoured to gain stores of provisions in that city; but the supplies which Cantemir obtained for him were but scanty, and the Wallachian Hospodar, Brancovan, was now acting in the interest of the Turks. In this emergency the Czar was advised to march southward towards some extensive magazines of provisions, which the Turks were said to have collected near the lower part of the river Sereth, and which he was assured that he might seize without difficulty. At the same time he was misled by false reports that the Vizier's army had not yet passed the Danube. The Czar accordingly marched the main body of his army down the right (or western) bank of the river Pruth, which runs nearly southward from the vicinity of Jassy to the Danube, falling into that river near Galatz, a little below the confluence of the Sereth. But while the Russians were at Jassy, the Grand Vizier had crossed the Danube at Isakdji, below the junction of the Pruth, and had been joined in Bessarabia by the Khan of the Crimea, at the head of a large force of Tartar cavalry. The Ottoman commanders were informed of the march of the Czar down the western bank of the Pruth, and they forthwith led their combined troops to the eastern bank of the river, that they might cross it and attack the Russians in Moldavia. The Russian General Scheremitoff was posted with a detachment from the Czar's army near the part of the river which the Turks and Tartars approached. He endeavoured to prevent them from passing; but 10,000 Tartar horsemen swam the river, and four bridges were thrown over by night, which enabled the Vizier to place an overwhelming force on the western or Moldavian side. Scheremitoff fell back and rejoined the main Russian army near Faltasch. The intelligence which he brought was in the highest degree alarming to the Czar : whose force, weakened by disease and famine, was far inferior to that of the Ottomans, and was at this time still further reduced, in consequence of two large detachments, under Generals Renne and Jonas, having been sent into the interior districts of Moldavia and Wallachia. The Czar retreated a little distance up the right bank of the river in the vicinity of the village of Kousch, and he then entrenched himself in a seemingly strong position between the Pruth and a marsh, in imitation of the tactics of Sobieski at Zurawna. But the low ground, on which the Russians were encamped, was commanded by hills at a little distance, which the superior numbers of the Vizier's army enabled him to occupy. The Russians were thus completely blockaded in their camp : they were almost destitute of provisions, and suffered severely from thirst, as the Turks had planted batteries on the left bank of the Pruth, which swept the river and made it almost certain death for the Russians to approach the water. The Vizier prudently abstained from attacking them ; and all the efforts which the Russians made in two days of severe fighting to force the Turkish lines were completely repulsed. In this emergency the Czar and his men must either have perished with famine and thirst, or have surrendered at discretion, if it had not been for the dexterity of Catherine, the Czar's wife, who had accompanied Peter in this expedition, and was truly the saving angel of Russia. Catherine collected her own jewels and trinkets, and all the gold that was in the possession of the chief Russian officers in the camp. She sent these by the Chancellor Schaffiroff, to the quarters of the Turkish Vizier ; and together with the presents of Catherine, the Chancellor carried a letter written by the General Scheremitoff, in the name of the Czar, asking for peace. The Kiaya of the Grand Vizier had great influence with Mehemet Baltadji, and to him Catherine's envoy addressed himself. The Kiaya received the presents, and advised the Vizier to be favourable to the Russian petitioners. Mehemet Baltadji assented ; and negotiations for a treaty were accordingly commenced. The agent of the King of Sweden, Count Poniatowski, who was in the Vizier's camp, protested against any terms being granted to the Russians ; and the Khan of the Crimea joined warmly in Poniatowski's remonstrance. But the Grand Vizier paid no regard to their opposition ; and his secretary, Omar Effendi, drew up the celebrated treaty which liberated the Czar and his army from their extreme peril on the 21st July, 1711.

The treaty commenced with a recital that By the grace of God, the victorious Mussulman army had closely hemmed in the

Czar of Muscovy with all his troops in the neighbourhood of the river Pruth, and that the Czar had asked for peace, and that it was at his request that the following articles were drawn up and granted :

By the first article the Czar was to surrender the fortress of Azoph and its territories, and dependencies, in the same condition as they were in when the Czar took possession of them.

By the second article the Czar consented that his new city of Taganrok, in the Sea of Azoph, his fortifications at Kamienski, and his new castle on the river Taman should be destroyed, and that they should never be rebuilt. The cannon and all the military stores of the Czar at Kamienski were to be given up to the Sublime Porte.

The third article stipulated that the Czar should no longer interfere in the affairs of the Poles, or of the Cossacks, who were dependent either on the Poles or on the Khan of the Crimea : and all the Russian forces in their territories were to be withdrawn.

The fourth provided for freedom of commerce ; but directed that in future, no Russian ambassador should reside at Constantinople. It is probable that the Russian intrigues with the Greeks and other Rayas may have caused this stipulation.

The fifth article required that the Russians should set at liberty all the Moslems whom they had taken prisoners, or made slaves of, either before or during the war.

The sixth declared that, inasmuch as the King of Sweden had placed himself beneath the wings of the mighty protection of the Sublime Porte, he should have a free and safe passage to his own kingdom without any hindrance from the Muscovites : and it was recommended that Russia and Sweden should make peace with each other, if they could come to an understanding.

The seventh ordained that in future the Porte should do no harm to the Muscovites, and that they should do none to the subjects and dependents of the Sublime Porte.

The treaty concluded with a declaration of the Grand Vizier, that the royal and infinite goodness of his thrice powerful and gracious Lord and Padischah was entreated to ratify those articles, and to overlook the previous evil conduct of the Czar. It averred that the Vizier made the peace by virtue of full powers vested in him It directed that hostages should be given by the Czar for the fulfilment of the articles, and that the army of the Czar might then return forthwith by the nearest road to their own country, without being molested by the victorious forces, by the Tartars, or by any other persons whatever. The Chancellor Baron Schaffiroff, and General Scheremitoff, were given up to the Ottomans, as hostages; and then the Czar and his surviving troops, glad at this escape from destruction, but shame and sorrow-stricken at their losses and humiliations, marched back from the fatal banks of the Pruth to the Russian territories.

It has been said by an able investigator of Turkish history and institutions,[1] that " The genius of the Ottoman Empire slumbered when the treaty of the Pruth was signed :" and it might be interesting to speculate on the probable complexion that would have been given to the subsequent history of the world if Baltadji Mehemet had availed himself to the utmost of the advantages which the Turkish arms possessed when the Russians supplicated for peace ; if the Czar and his troops had then perished, and Charles had been sent with strong supplies back to Sweden, to seek his revenge for Pultowa. Many of the reforms which Russia owes to Peter the Great, were scarcely commenced in 1711. None were mature. It is quite possible, that by his death or captivity at that period, Russia might have been remanded into barbarism ; and also that Sweden might have recovered and retained the international rank which Gustavus Adolphus formerly gave her, that of a first-class European power, and the dominant state of the north.

With regard to the personal conduct of the chief actors in the campaign and pacification of the Pruth, the Czar more than compensated for any want of generalship which he may have shown, by the magnanimity which he displayed as a patriot and a sovereign, when encompassed by his enemies, and reduced to the apparent extremity of adverse fortune. His body was at this time prostrated by an attack of a fearful malady, to which he was subject, but his spirit was unshaken ; and a letter, written by him from his tent at the Pruth to the Russian Senate at Moscow on the evening before Catherine made her happy attempt at negotiation, " ensures to Peter a place among the heroes of antiquity, for he thereby sacrifices himself and his family for the well-being of the empire."[2] Fortunately for the fame of the great Czar, the bearer of that letter passed the Turkish lines in safety, and conveyed it to the Russian Senate, while the pacification was yet unknown. That document is preserved in the Imperial palace at St. Petersburg ; nor is there the least reason to question its authenticity, or to doubt that it represents the genuine feelings of Peter on the occasion when it was written. It is as follows :—" I announce to you, that deceived by false intelligence, and without blame on my

[1] Thornton.   [2] Schlosser.

part, I find myself here shut up in my camp by a Turkish army four times stronger than mine. Our supplies are cut off; and we momentarily expect to be destroyed or taken prisoners, unless Heaven come to our aid in some unexpected manner. Should it happen to me to be taken captive by the Turks, you will no longer consider me your Czar and Sovereign, nor will you pay attention to any order that may be brought to you from me ; not even if you recognise my own handwriting : but you will wait for my coming in person. If I am to perish here, and you receive well confirmed intelligence of my death, you will then proceed to choose as my successor him who is the most worthy among you."[1] Codrus or Leonidas could not have surpassed the unselfish heroism that was shown here. Francis I. and Charles XII. were far beneath it.

The debt of Russia to Catherine, who united all woman's wit to all man's firmness at the Pruth, was worthily acknowledged by Russia's sovereign in 1724, when Peter caused her to be solemnly crowned as Empress, and proclaimed to his subjects and the world, how Catherine had aided him at the battle of the river Pruth against the Turks, where " our [the Russian] army was reduced to 22,000 men, and that of the Turks consisted of 270,000. It was in this desperate exigency that she especially signalised her zeal with courage superior to her sex, and to this all the army and the whole empire can bear witness." Historians of all nations have vied with each other in repeating these praises of the heroine of the Pruth ; but with respect to the third chief actor in that memorable scene, the Turkish commander, a far different tone has prevailed both among his contemporaries, and among those who in subsequent times have discussed that crisis in the affairs of the Muscovite and the Ottoman nations. The current charge against the Vizier is that he was bribed by the gifts of Catherine, and consented to the escape of the deadly enemies of his country. It has been replied to this, on behalf of Mehemet Baltadji, that all the presents which Catherine had in her power in the Russian camp at the Pruth to offer to him and his Kiaya, even if all that she could collect from the officers and soldiers were added to her own jewels and furs, must have been quite insignificant as bribes for one in the station of Grand Vizier. It may also be thought that the Turkish commander, if avaricious, could have gratified his avarice better by compelling an unconditional surrender of the Russian army, and all that it possessed ; in which case he would also have had a prospect of obtaining rich gifts from the friends of the chief captives in order to secure his influence for

[1] Levesque, "Histoire de Russie," vol. iv. p. 410, n.

their release. By some it has been thought that the Vizier favoured the Czar, out of dislike to his rival the King of Sweden, who had treated Mehemet Baltadji with injudicious rudeness and contempt. But so many other methods of punishing the ill-manners of Charles were open to the Vizier, if he chose to do so, that it is difficult to suppose such a motive to have been the primary principle of his conduct in signing the armistice with the Muscovite commanders. It is impossible to suppose that the Vizier feared the effect of a desperate attack by the enemy, whom he spared, or to adopt the opinion expressed by one historian of Russia,[1] that the Russians at the Pruth would probably have defeated the Turkish force if they had boldly attacked it. They had already been worsted in several engagements; and the spirit and discipline of Mehemet Baltadji's army were far superior to those of the oft-defeated Ottoman troops whom Romanzoff afterwards broke through in a similar situation. The Czar's confession of his extreme distress (made by him both at the time in his letter to the Senate, and in the armistice, and also afterwards in the treaty of 1713, and in the proclamation calling Catherine to the throne), is decisive evidence that the condition of the Russian army was forlorn, when the Vizier consented to treat. It was probably on no one fixed principle, or from any one definite motive that the Turkish commander acted, when he took the half-measure of releasing his prey on conditions which humiliated and injured, without incapacitating for revenge. Mehemet Baltadji deserves credit as a military man for his conduct of the war; but, though we may acquit him of corruption, the pacification by which he concluded the campaign, must be censured as grievously unstatesmanlike. If it was his desire to disarm the hostility of Russia by generous moderation, he exacted too much; if he wished to crush her power, he did too little. The advice of the old Samnite, Herennius Pontius, to his son, when he held the Roman legions in his power at Caudium, even as Mehemet Baltadji held the Russians at the Pruth, was sound and true. "Frank generosity may, in such cases, win a friend; or stern severity may destroy an enemy. To halt between the two is pernicious imbecility."[2] Turkey had as deep cause as Samnium to rue the middle course that was taken by her

---

[1] Levesque, vol. iv. p. 415.

[2] "Ista quidem sententia ea est, quæ neque amicos parat, neque inimicos tollit. Servate modo quos ignominiâ irritaveritis, et ea est Romana gens quæ victa quiescere nesciat. Vivet semper in pectoribus illorum quicquid istuc præsens necessitas inusserit; neque eos ante multiplices pœnas expetitas a vobis quiescere sinet."—Livy, lib. ix. c. 3.

general. Though the war between Russia and the Ottoman Porte
did not actually break out again during the lifetime of Peter, it
is well known that he designed its renewal, and made immense
preparation for that purpose, of which the leaders of the Russian
armies availed themselves in the campaign against the Crimea in
1736.[1] The heritage of hatred and revenge passed undiminished
to Peter's successors; and Russia taught Turkey in 1774, when
the anniversary of the treaty of the Pruth was carefully selected
for the signature of the treaty of Kainardji, that the ignominy
which Mehemet Baltadji had inflicted on the great Czar, was
neither forgiven nor forgotten.

The indignation of Charles XII. at the pacification of the Pruth,
his refusal to leave the Turkish dominions, and his obstinate conflict at Bender with the Spahis and Janissaries sent to remove
him, are well-known passages of the biography of that adventurous prince. It was not only by the partisans of the Swedish
King at the Sultan's court that the Grand Vizier was assailed
with reproaches for his suspicious lenity to the Russians. The
general discontent of the Turks was such that Achmet deposed
Mehemet Baltadji from the vizierate; and the two officers who
were believed to have been most active at the Pruth in forwarding the peace, the Kiaya Osman Aga, and the Reis Effendi, were
put to death at Constantinople by the public executioner. The
delay of the Russians in fulfilling the treaty increased the irritation of the Porte against the Czar; and it was with considerable
difficulty that the English ambassador, Sir Robert Sutton, and the
Dutch ambassador, Collyer, prevented a new declaration of war
on the part of the Turks. By their mediation a treaty was signed
on the 16th of April, 1712, which substantially re-enacted the
stipulations agreed on at the Pruth, and explicitely provided that
the Czar should withdraw his troops from Poland within thirty
days. But the Russian sovereign showed no disposition to cease
from his armed interference in the affairs of that unhappy country;
and, in the East, though some of the smaller fortifications which
had been raised by him near the Sea of Azoph and the Black Sea,
were demolished by his orders, the important new city of Taganrok
was maintained by him, nor was Azoph itself surrendered to the
Turks. The Sultan again prepared for war; but again the intervention of the English and Dutch ministers was successful. A
treaty was finally arranged in 1713, between Russia and Turkey;
of which the first six and the eleventh articles corresponded with
the seven articles dictated by Mehemet Baltadji at the Pruth.

[1] See Manstein's "Memoirs of Marshal Münnich," p. 117.

22

The eleventh article determined the respective frontiers of the two empires between the rivers Samara and Orel in such a manner that the territory near the banks of the Samara was thenceforth to belong to the Turks, and that washed by the Orel to the Russians. Eastward of those rivers to the Don and to Azoph the boundary was to be the same that it had been before the first Russian occupation of Azoph. It was stipulated that on the one part the Cossacks and the Calmucks, and on the other, the Tartars of the Crimea, the Noghai Tartars, and the Circassians, who were subject to the Porte, should cease from molesting each other. Five commissioners were appointed to mark out the frontier line in accordance with those terms. This was effected in the course of the year 1714. Azoph was then restored to the Turks, and Taganrok demolished; and the great strife between Turkey and Russia now ceased for an unusually long period; though the Czar never forgot his purposes of ambition and revenge, and the collection of magazines and military stores at the river Don was continued throughout his reign.[1]

The Grand Vizierate was at this time held by Sultan Achmet's favourite son-in-law, Damad Ali, called by some writers Ali Coumourgi, the name by which he is immortalised in English poetry.[2] He was a statesman of considerable administrative ability, an eloquent speaker, and distinguished for his literary acquirements. The character of wild and bigoted ferocity, which has sometimes been ascribed to him, is erroneous. He was an earnest advocate of the peace with Russia; but he willingly promoted the scheme of a war of retaliation and recovery against Venice, a design which the Porte had never ceased to cherish since the peace of Carlowitz. At the very time of that treaty the Turks seem to have been well aware of the weakness of the Venetian Republic, if unsupported by the great powers of Christendom; and, when they ceded the Morea, it was with the knowledge that they were powerful enough to regain it, whenever they could compel Venice to fight single-handed against them.[3]

---

[1] See Manstein's "Memoirs of Marshal Münnich," *ut suprà.*

[2] See Byron's "Siege of Corinth."

[3] "A consciousness of the real weakness of Venice, and of their own ability at some more opportune period to reclaim their possessions, was, no doubt, one powerful cause of the facility with which the Porte acceded to the treaty of Carlowitz; and Cantemir relates an anecdote of the Reis Effendi, which amply supports the assumption. During the Conference of the Plenipotentiaries, previous to the accommodation of the articles, the ambassador of Venice had conducted himself rather haughtily towards the ministers of Turkey, when the officer I have alluded to gave him a cutting

The feebleness shown by Venice during the great war among the Christian states, which was closed by the treaties of Utrecht and Rastadt; her timorous inaction, which she vainly strove to hide under the pretext of dignified neutrality; and the contemptuous infringements of her territory by the belligerent parties all tended to excite the Ottomans to attack her. Her great Captain Morosini, to whose individual genius her victories in the last war were mainly due, was now dead; and it was known that so far from having strengthened her hold on the Morea by winning the affections of the Greeks, and binding them to her cause by a feeling of community of creed and of interest against the Turks, she was as bitterly hated in her new province, as she had formerly been hated by her subjects in Cyprus and Candia; and that the Moreotes would rather be under the rule of the Mahometans than under that of the schismatics of the Latin Church. The Turks had made great military preparations in 1712 and 1713, in consequence of the expectation then prevalent of a renewal of hostilities with Russia: and, when the risk of war in that quarter had ceased, it was resolved to employ the forces of the empire in a sudden and overwhelming attack upon Venice. The Grand Vizier, Damad Ali, led this enterprise the more readily, because he was a firm believer in astrology, and the language of the stars announced to him in 1715 that he was to be the conqueror of the Morea. Some collisions that had taken place between the Turkish and Venetian galleys, and the aid which Venice had given, or was said to have given, to the insurgents of Montenegro, served as pretexts for the war. The Grand Vizier led an army of 100,000 men, supported by a fleet of 100 sail, against the weak Venetian force in the Morea, in the summer of 1715. The siege of Corinth was terminated by the fall of that city on the 25th of June; Palamidi, Napoli di Romania, Modon, and Koron, were captured by the triumphant Vizier, with almost equal celerity. The operations of the Turkish fleet were no less successful; and, by the end of November, 1715, Venice had lost the whole of the Morea, and had been driven from all the islands of the Archipelago.

The Ottomans designed to follow up their success by attacking

---

reproof, by relating a proverb of a pickpocket having slily crept in and stolen away the garments of two athletic wrestlers, which they had for a moment doffed for the sake of convenience; but, he added, that a period was fast approaching when the thief should be obliged to surrender his booty, and, in all probability, be obliged to yield up his *skin* along with his borrowed habiliments."—Emerson Tennant's "Modern Greece," vol. i. p. 240.

Corfu and then proceeding to assail the Venetian possessions along the coasts of the Adriatic. But the Emperor Charles VI., who at first only offered his mediation between the belligerents, had now decided on taking a more active part; ostensibly for the sake of protecting the Venetians, but it is probable that hopes of aggrandising himself by further conquests from the Turks principally led him to form an offensive and defensive alliance with Venice, in the beginning of the year 1716.[1] The greater number of the Turkish statesmen and generals were anxious to avoid a war with the Germans; but the Grand Vizier was eager to attack them. He had again had recourse to his favourite astrological science; and the stars appeared to promise him victory over Austria, as clearly as in the preceding year. They had assured him of triumph over Venice. His self-conceit also was inflated by success; and, in the words of his Turkish biographer Raschid, "his pride had spread the veil of negligence before the eye of his sagacity." War was declared against Austria in a council held at Adrianople; and the Fetva of the Mufti sanctioning the war was solemnly read before the assembled dignitaries of the Sword and Pen. The Grand Vizier had shown in previous Divans that he would brook no opposition to his martial policy, and he now addressed them thus: "We are not met here to waste idle words about the necessity of a war, which we have already resolved on, but to excite ourselves to conduct it in a fitting manner, and in accordance with the word of the Prophet, 'Fight against the unbelievers, and be wrathful with them.' Ye, Sirs, who are learned in the law, what say ye?" Some of the Ulema, whom the Grand Vizier thus addressed, replied, "God speed you and give you success." Others referred to the generals present, as the fit persons to answer. The Grand Vizier glanced at the military members of the Divan, and they all protested in loud and strong words that they were the Padischah's slaves, and that they were ready to offer themselves, body and soul, in the service of the Faith and the Empire. The Grand Vizier then said, "Beyond doubt, God will give us the victory, if we obey the precept, 'Exult not, and despond not, so shall ye prevail.'" The Sheikh of the Imperial Camp closed the proceedings of the council by

[1] "Austria was now roused, in which at that time Prince Eugene had fortunately the greatest influence. He found the circumstances very favourable; and besides, a war with the Turks would serve as an excellent pretext for keeping the army on foot, without raising the suspicion of the Christian power, instead of disbanding it after the close of the war with France, as was the custom; and this was the more desirable as Spain still continued threatening."—Schlosser, "Hist. Eighteenth Century," vol. iii. p. 285.

reciting other verses of the chapter of the Koran, which the Grand Vizier had partly quoted, and which forms the noblest of the war hymns of the Mahometans.[1]

Damad Ali took, in person, the command of the forces that were to act against the Austrians. This army was assembled at Belgrade in July; and a council of war was held there, in which (as at the opening of the campaign under Sultan Mustapha, in 1696) it was debated whether Temeswar or Peterwaradin should be the point on which the troops should march. Housein, the Aga of the Janissaries, advised a movement towards Temeswar. The Khan of the Crimea (who, as usual, had joined the army at the Danube with his contingent of Tartar cavalry) proposed that an incursion should be made into Transylvania. The Beylerbey of Roumelia replied that they ought to remember the disaster of the Zenta, and not risk another army in the presence of Prince Eugene, along the difficult line of march to Temeswar. With regard to the scheme of an inroad into Transylvania, he remarked that the Tartar cavalry, if once let loose on such an enterprise, would cumber themselves with plunder, and would thereafter be no more fit for warfare than so many pregnant women. Consequently, his voice was for the march on Peterwaradin, either to fight the enemy if he would give them battle, or to form the siege of that city. The Grand Vizier heard the discussion without giving his own opinion, but he determined to march upon Peterwaradin, which he believed to be protected only by 1500 Austrians under Count Pfalfy, the main body of the army being encamped at Futaks, under Prince Eugene. A bridge was accordingly formed across the river Saave, and the Turkish army moved along the south bank of the Danube towards Peterwaradin. It was remarked, and remembered by the Ottoman soldiery, as an evil omen, that their commander, though he might have chosen one of the lucky days of the week for the passage of the Saave, such as Saturday, Monday, or Thursday, yet thought fit to cross the river on a Tuesday, and not in the fortunate hour of morning, but in the afternoon.

The first encounter with the Austrians took place near Carlowitz. The Turks found a body of the enemy's troops posted there, under Count Pfalfy, amounting to 8000 men, according to the Ottoman historians; to 3000, according to the reports of the German generals. Kourd Pacha, who commanded the Turkish vanguard, demanded of the Grand Vizier, and obtained permission to charge them; and thus the first act of hostilities, by which the

[1] See chapter iii. of the Koran, and Sale's notes.

peace of Carlowitz between the Houses of Hapsburg and Othman was formally broken, took place in the immediate vicinity of the spot where the treaty had been signed.   The Turks were victorious in the action, and took 700 prisoners, among whom was General Count Brenner.   On the following day, Damad Ali continued his advance upon Peterwaradin, which is only two leagues from Carlowitz.   But Prince Eugene had already taken up a position across the intended Turkish line of march.   He encamped in the very entrenchments which Surmeli Pacha had formed in the last war.   Damad Ali halted his army in presence of the Austrians, and kept his men under arms for three hours, in the expectation that Eugene would sally from his lines and attack him.   But the Austrians moved not, and the Vizier hesitated to assail them in their fortified camp.   He ordered his men to break ground, and form trenches as if for a siege ; and the Turks laboured so zealously during the night that before morning they had pushed the approaches within a hundred feet of the Austrian camp.

On the following day (13th August, 1716), Eugene drew out his forces for a regular battle, which Damad Ali had no wish to avoid.   Eugene had 187 squadrons of horse and 62 battalions of infantry.   He arranged them so that the left wing was protected by a marsh, and his right by some rising ground.   The Turkish army numbered 150,000, of whom 40,000 were Janissaries, and 30,000 Spahis ; the rest consisted of Tartars, Wallachians, Arnaouts, and Egyptians.   Ali drew up his cavalry on the right wing to oppose that of the Austrians; his infantry was ranged in the centre and on the left.   The battle began at seven in the morning. The German cavalry proved their superiority to the Asiatic in regular charges, and the victory of the Christians seemed secure, when the Janissaries on the Turkish left broke the Austrian infantry, routed the wing opposed to them, and pressed hard upon the centre.   Eugene immediately brought up a reserve of horse, with which he charged the Janissaries, and retrieved the fortunes of the day.   The Grand Vizier, during the beginning of the action, took his station near the Sacred Standard of the Prophet, which was displayed in front of his tent; he remained there till Turk Ahmed, the commander of his right wing, was slain, and till the flying Spahis from that part of the battle began to sweep by him, heedless of the reproaches and sabre strokes by which he strove to check their panic rout.   Damad Ali then put himself at the head of a body of officers, and galloped forward into the thick of the fight.   A bullet pierced his forehead, and he fell mortally wounded. His followers placed him on a horse, and removed him to Carlowitz, where he soon expired. Two of the Turkish generals, and the historian Raschid formed a guard round the Sacred Standard, and bore it safely away to Belgrade. As soon as their flight and the Grand Vizier's fall were known in the left wing, where Sari Ahmed, the Beylerbey of Anatolia commanded, the Janissaries who had hitherto combated valiantly, gave way, and retreated towards Belgrade. The battle was over at noon. 3000 Germans and twice that number of Turks had fallen. Eugene took possession of his enemy's camp, and 140 cannon; 150 banners, five horse-tails, and an immense amount of booty and military stores were the trophies of the prince's victory. But the joy of the Austrians was troubled by the sight of the body of the unfortunate General Brenner, which was found barbarously mutilated.

The chief surviving Turkish officers, who re-assembled their defeated forces at Belgrade, after paying the last honours to the corpse of Damad Ali, met together in the tent of the Sacred Standard to draw up a report of the disastrous campaign to be sent to Constantinople, and to elect a provisional commander of the army. Sari Ahmed Pacha, the Beylerbey of Roumelia, was next in rank to the slain Grand Vizier, and was entitled to assume the chief anthority; but he declined the office, from fear of exposing himself to the envious intrigues of the Kiaya, who was with the troops, and who was the object of universal hatred and fear. The other generals felt a similar reluctance. But they all concurred in resolving that the Kiaya should not take the command of the forces; and the remark made by one of the council, that it could not be the Sultan's wish for that functionary to lead the army, inasmuch as he had not received the horse-tails, was admitted to be conclusive. At last, a deputation of the troops prevailed on Sari Ahmed to take the command-in-chief; but he was soon afterwards put to death in a mutiny of the garrison of Belgrade, whom he had irritated by a severe reprimand.

A feeble attempt was made by the Turks to relieve the important city of Temeswar, the last bulwark of Islam in Hungary, the siege of which had been commenced by Prince Eugene twenty days after his victory at Peterwaradin. Eugene defeated Kourd Pacha, who led a division of the Ottoman army against him, and Temeswar capitulated on the 28th of November, 1716. At the beginning of the war, Eugene had endeavoured to rouse the Servians and their kindred tribes beyond the Saave to co-operate with the Austrians, and had promised them the aid of the Emperor's armies to shake off the yoke of Turkish oppression. The Servian youth flocked zealously under Eugene's banners; and after the fall of Temeswar a corps of 1200 Servians, under the command of the Imperial General Dettin, made an inroad into Wallachia, and penetrated as far as Bucharest.

The great object of the Austrian operations in the year 1717 was the capture of Belgrade. Eugene invested that city in June with a magnificent army of 80,000 men, which comprised great numbers of the princes and nobles of Germany and France, who sought distinction by serving under so renowned a commander as Eugene, and in so brilliant an enterprise. Belgrade was garrisoned by 30,000 Turks, who resisted their besiegers bravely, and endured with patience a blockade of two months. In the beginning of August, an Ottoman army, 150,000 strong, under a new Grand Vizier, advanced to attempt the rescue of Belgrade. Eugene's troops had suffered severely during the siege; and, if the Turks had attacked him promptly on their arrival, their superiority of numbers and condition, and the panic caused by their appearance, would, in all probability, have assured their victory. But the Grand Vizier hesitated, and held councils of war, and formed earthworks and redoubts round the lines of the Austrian army, which was now besieged in its turn, but which rapidly regained its former confidence in itself and its commander, on finding that the foes, notwithstanding their numbers, delayed the expected attack. The greater part of the Imperialist forces was posted round Belgrade, between the Danube and the Saave, but there were strong detachments on the opposite banks of these rivers, which were required to keep the garrison in check and complete the investment of the city. The Vizier's army was ranged round the rear of Eugene's main force, in a large semicircle, from the south bank of the Danube to the east bank of the Saave. For fifteen days the Vizier kept up a heavy cannonade upon the Austrian lines; which Eugene replied to with all the artillery that he could safely withdraw from the batteries against the city; but the sufferings of the Austrian troops from fatigue, disease, and want of provisions were so severe, that the liberation of Belgrade and the capture or destruction of the besiegers seemed inevitable. The Vizier now drew his works nearer to those of the Austrian entrenchment; the cannonade grew fiercer, and the Turks were evidently making preparations to storm the Imperialists' lines of defence. In this emergency, Eugene resolved on the daring measure of anticipating the enemy's assault, and of leading his enfeebled and scanty army against the strong fortifications and

immense numbers of the Vizier s host. He made the attack at
two in the morning of the 16th of August, with complete success.
The Turkish outposts were negligent; the discipline of their
whole army was lax; they had slept in careless confidence; they
woke to panic confusion: and when once the Christian columns
were within their works, the greater part of them fled without
even attempting resistance. 10,000 Ottomans were slain or
trampled to death in flight. Their camp, their artillery, and the
whole of their military stores were captured. Belgrade surrendered on the second day after the battle. Eugene had the prudence to grant favourable terms of capitulation to its numerous
garrison; and a campaign which had seemed likely to be marked
with his utter ruin and the destruction of the Austrian army, was
thus terminated by him with a splendid triumph and a most important conquest.

The Porte now sought earnestly for peace with Austria; and
the proffered mediation of England and Holland was again gladly
accepted. The Court of Vienna was at this time alarmed at the
prospects of a new general war in the west of Europe, which had
been created by the restless genius of Cardinal Alberoni. The
victorious career of Eugene in the East was therefore checked;
and the Emperor determined to secure the conquests which had
been already won, by treating with Turkey on the basis of the
" Uti Possidetis;" though a negotiation on this principle was a
flagrant sacrifice of the interests of Venice, the ally for whose sake
Austria had pretended to embark in the war. The operations of
the Venetian and Turkish forces against each other during 1716
and 1717 had been unimportant, in comparison with the great
events of the war on the Danube and the Saave. Corfu had been
ably defended for Venice against the Turks by Count Stahremberg
and a German force; and several sea-fights had taken place, in
which the Republic of St. Mark had generally the advantage.
But it was obvious that Turkey, if once liberated from an Austrian
war, was far too powerful for Venice to cope with; and the
humbled Queen of the Adriatic was obliged to consent to a pacification, in which she was the chief sufferer, and Austria the chief
gainer; while their common enemy, the Porte, might be thought
to indemnify herself for the cessions made by her to the latter
power, by the acquisition which she obtained at the expense of
the former.

The negotiations for peace were opened at a small town in
Servia, called Passarowitz, in June, 1718. The representatives of
the mediating states, England and Holland, were present, as had

been the case at Carlowitz. The articles of peace were solemnly signed on the 21st of July. Venice gave up the Morea to the Porte ; and though she retained a few fortresses, which she had acquired in Dalmatia or Albania, she was obliged to make over to the Sultan the unconquered districts of Zarine, Ottovo, and Zubzi in order to keep open the Turkish communications with Ragusa. Her cession of the Morea showed that the power and glory of Venice had departed from her with the last of her heroes, Morosini. After the peace of Passarowitz, Venice possessed no part of Greece except the Ionian Islands ; and, on the Albanian coast, she had nothing but the cities and districts of Butrinto, Parga, and Prevesa, a little strip of territory two leagues broad, and twenty in length. Like Spain, Venice had been illustrious as a defender of Christendom against the Ottomans, when the power of Turkey was at its height ; and, like Spain, Venice sank into corruption and imbecility, even more rapidly than their fast-declining antagonist.

Austria, by the treaty of Passarowitz, not only obtained the city of Temeswar and its territory, and thus completed the recovery of Hungary from the Turkish power ; but she then extended her dominion over large portions of Wallachia and Servia—aggrandisements of her empire, which she failed to retain long, but which were long remembered by her rulers with ambitious regret and desire. The treaty of 1718 assigned to Austria the cities of Belgrade, Semendra, Rimnik, Krasova, and many more. It made the river Aluta, in Wallachia, the boundary of the two empires, thus assigning to Austria the whole of the country termed Little Wallachia. Six other rivers, the Danube, the Timok, the little Morava, the Dwina, the Saave, and the Unna then formed the frontier line : so that nearly all Servia and some valuable territories in Bosnia, were transferred from the Sultan to the House of Hapsburg. The Austrians had not indeed realised the threat expressed by some of their generals in the first year of the war, when they boasted that they would go on conquering until the Austrian Empire touched the Black Sea and the Ægean ; but Eugene gave to the Emperor Charles VI. a dominant position in Eastern Europe, such as the most renowned of his predecessors had never acquired, and which that Emperor himself lost soon after the death of the great commander, to whom its temporary possession was due.

It is difficult to read without a melancholy smile that Russia and Turkey, in 1720, made a solemn treaty of eternal peace with each other. At that time the Czar was menaced by a league which was formed against him by many of his late allies, and which the Porte was vainly solicited to join by the ambassadors of Austria and England. This made Peter desirous to secure tranquillity, at least for a time, on his Turkish frontier: though he never abandoned his schemes for aggrandising his empire at the expense of its Mahometan neighbours. The next war in which Turkey and Russia took part, found them arrayed not as antagonists, but as confederates. The extreme weakness into which the Persian Empire had been reduced by misgovernment, insurrection, and the attacks of the Affghans, tempted both Muscovite and Ottoman cupidity; and the armies of the Czar and the Sultan invaded the north-western provinces of Persia with the design of dismembering her, and of appropriating at least those portions of her empire. A partition treaty was signed by the Russian and Turkish ministers in 1723, by which the Czar was to take the Persian provinces that lie near the Caspian Sea, from the country of the Turcomans, round to the confluence of the Araxes and the Kur, and thence to Derbend. This assigned to Russia the districts of Asterabad, Mazanderad, Ghilan, part of Schirvan, and Daghistan. The acquisitions of the Porte were to be traced out by a line drawn from the junction of the Araxes and the Kur, and passing along by Erdebil, Tabriz, and Hamadan, and thence to Kermanschai. The Persian Shah Tahmasp was to retain the rest of his paternal kingdom on condition of his recognising the treaty. Both Russia and Turkey had already attacked parts of Persia before that treaty was signed; and the Porte had manifested considerable jealousy of the extension of the power of the Czar along the shores of the Caspian. But the Russian diplomatists were too skilful for the Turkish, and prevailed on them to assent to terms, which (besides the original injustice of the whole transaction with regard to Persia) were very unequal, and very disadvantageous for the Ottomans: inasmuch as the Czar had already led his troops down from Astrakhan between the Caucasus and the Caspian, and secured the greater part of the countries assigned to him by the treaty; while nearly all the territories, which Turkey was to gain, remained yet to be conquered. The Ottomans however subdued a large part of Georgia; and they strengthened their positions in Mingrelia, Imeritia, Gouriel, and other Caucasian districts, eastward of the Black Sea, which had long acknowledged the supremacy of the Porte, or of the Porte's vassal, the Khan of the Crimea, but where little effective authority of the Sultan had been practically exercised. The Turkish Court sought to palliate to itself the moral iniquity of the war upon Persia by procuring a Fetva from the Mufti, which sanctioned all hostilities against the Schiis, and expressly required the orthodox Mahometans to put the men of an heretical nation to the edge of the sword, and to reduce their wives and children to slavery. The polemical adage that a heretic is worse than an infidel, has nowhere been more frequently verified than in the Divans of Sunnite Turkey.

The abilities of Sultan Achmet's Grand Vizier Ibrahim, who directed the government from 1718 to 1730, preserved an unusual degree of internal peace in the empire, though the frontier provinces were often the scenes of disorder and revolt. This was repeatedly the case in Egypt and Arabia; and still more frequently in the districts northward and eastward of the Euxine, especially among the fierce Noghai tribes of the Kuban. The state of the countries between the Black Sea and the Caspian was rendered still more unsettled by the rival claims of Russia and the Porte; for it was difficult to define a boundary between the two empires in pursuance of the partition treaty of 1723; and a serious dispute arose early in the reign of Achmet's successor, in 1731, as to the right of dominion over the Circassians of the Kabartas, a region about half way between the Euxine and the Caspian, near the course of the river Terek. The Russians claimed the Kabartas as lands of Russian subjects. They asserted that the Circassians were originally Cossacks of the Ukraine, who migrated thence to the neighbourhood of a city of Russia called Terki, from which they took their name of Tchercassians, or Circassians. Thence (according to the memorial drawn up by the Czar's ministers) the Circassians removed to the neighbourhood of Kuban : still, however, retaining their Christian creed and their allegiance to the Czar. The continuation of the story told that the tyranny of the Crim Tartars forced the Circassians to become Mahometans, and to migrate farther eastward to the Kabartas; but it was insisted on that the Circassians were still to be regarded as genuine subjects of their original earthly sovereign, and that the land which they occupied became the Czar's territory.[1] This strange political ethnology had but little influence upon the Turks, especially as the Czar had in a letter, written nine years previously, acknowledged the sovereignty of the Sultan over the Circassians.

The course of the Persian war, in which the Turks had at first made successive conquests with little check from the Shah's armies, though often impeded by the nature of the country and the fierce spirit of the native tribes, became after a few years less

[1] See Von Hammer, book lxvi. note 1.

favourable to Ottoman ambition. The celebrated Nadir Kouli Khan (who afterwards reconquered and conquered states for himself), gained his first renown by exploits against the enemies of Shah Tahmasp. A report reached Constantinople that the lately despised Persians were victorious, and were invading the Ottoman Empire. This speedily caused excitement and tumult. Sultan Achmet had become unpopular by reason of the excessive pomp and costly luxury in which he and his principal officers indulged; and on the 20th of September, 1730, a mutinous riot of seventeen Janissaries, led by the Albanian Patrona Khalil, was encouraged by the citizens as well as the soldiery, till it swelled into an insurrection, before which the Sultan quailed, and gave up the throne. Achmet voluntarily led his nephew Mahmoud to the seat of sovereignty, and made obeisance to him as Padischah of the empire. He then retired to the apartments in the palace from whence his successor had been conducted, and died after a few years of confinement.

The reign of Achmet III., which had lasted for twenty-seven years, though marked by the deep disasters of the Austrian war, was, on the whole, neither inglorious nor unprosperous. The recovery of Azoph and the Morea, and the conquest of part of Persia, more than counterbalanced the territory which had been given up to the Austrian Emperor at the peace of Passarowitz. Achmet left the finances of the Ottoman Empire in a flourishing condition, which had been obtained without excessive taxation or extortionate rapacity. He was a liberal and discerning patron of literature and art; and it was in his time that the first printing press was set up in Constantinople. It was in this reign that an important change in the government of the Danubian Principalities was introduced. Hitherto, the Porte had employed Voivodes, or native Moldavian and Wallachian nobles, to administer those provinces. But after the war with Peter the Great in 1711, in which Prince Cantemir betrayed the Turkish and aided the Russian interests, the Porte established the custom of deputing Greeks from Constantinople as Hospodars, or viceroys, of Moldavia and Wallachia. These were generally selected from among the wealthy Greek families that inhabited the quarter of Constantinople called the Fanar, and constituted a kind of Raya Noblesse, which supplied the Porte with functionaries in many important departments of the state. The Moldo-Wallachians called the period of their history, during which they were under Greek viceroys (and which lasted till 1821), the Fanariote period.[1]

[1] Ubicini, vol. ii. p. 66.

CHAPTER XIX.

MAHMOUD I.—TOPAL OSMAN—PEACE WITH PERSIA—RUSSIA AND
AUSTRIA ATTACK TURKEY—RUSSIAN INVASIONS OF THE CRIMEA
—SUCCESSES OF THE TURKS AGAINST THE AUSTRIANS—BEL-
GRADE RECOVERED—TREATY OF BELGRADE—PACIFIC POLICY
OF TURKEY—DEATH OF SULTAN MAHMOUD—SHORT PACIFIC
REIGN OF OTHMAN III.[1]

SULTAN MAHMOUD was recognised by the mutineers, as well as by
the court officials; but for some weeks after his accession the
empire was in the hands of the insurgents. Their chief, Patrona
Khalil, rode with the new Sultan to the Mosque of Eyoub, when
the ceremony of girding Mahmoud with the sword of Othman was
performed; and many of the chief officers were deposed, and
successors to them were appointed at the dictation of the bold
rebel, who had served in the ranks of the Janissaries, and who
appeared before the Sultan bare-legged, and in his old uniform of
a common soldier. A Greek butcher, named Yanaki, had formerly
given credit to Patrona, and had lent him money during the three
days of the late insurrection. Patrona showed his gratitude by
compelling the Divan to make Yanaki Hospodar of Moldavia.
The insolence of the rebel chiefs became at length insupportable.
The Khan of the Crimea, whom they threatened to depose, was in
Constantinople; and with his assistance the Grand Vizier, the
Mufti, and the Aga of the Janissaries, succeeded in freeing the
government from its ignominious servitude. Patrona was killed
in the Sultan's presence, after a Divan in which he had required
that war should be declared against Russia. His Greek friend,
Yanaki, and 7000 of those who had supported him, were also put
to death. The jealousy which the officers of the Janissaries felt
towards Patrona, and their readiness to aid in his destruction,
facilitated greatly the exertions of the Sultan's supporters in
putting an end to the reign of rebellion, after it had lasted for
nearly two months.

The conduct of the war in Persia against the Turks was resumed

[1] Von Hammer, books 66-70.

in 1733, by Nadir Kouli Khan (during whose absence the Otto-mans had obtained considerable advantages), and that chieftain gave the Sultan's forces several defeats, and laid siege to the city of Bagdad. But that important bulwark of the Ottoman Empire was rescued from him by the Grand Vizier, Topal Osman.

This is a name justly celebrated by Christian as well as Maho-metan writers; and it is gratifying to turn from the scenes of selfish intrigue, and of violence and oppression, which the careers of Grand Viziers generally exhibit, and to pause on the character of a Turk of the last century, who was not only skilful, sage, and valiant, but who gave proofs of a noble spirit of generosity and gratitude, such as does honour to human nature. The English traveller, Hanway, has given a biography of Topal Osman, which he introduces by saying that "the design of it is to instruct us by example, which is confessedly the great use of history; and I am persuaded this relation will give pleasure to every one who does not think gratitude a pious frenzy, or that it is a virtue fit only for little minds, whose weakness betrays them into a passion, which clashes with self-love, so much the idol of mankind."[1]

Osman was born in the Morea: he was educated in the Serail, at Constantinople, where native Turks were now frequently brought up, since the practice of levying Christian children for the Sultan's service had been discontinued. At the age of twenty-six he had attained the rank of Beylerbey; and was sent on a mission from the Porte to the Governor of Egypt. On the voyage his ship encountered a Spanish corsair, and was captured after a brave defence, in the course of which Osman received a wound, which lamed him for life, whence he obtained his name of Topal or lame Osman. The Spanish pirates carried their prize into Malta, where a Frenchman of Marseilles, named Vincent Arnaud, was then harbour-master. Arnaud came on board the prize, and was scru-tinising the prisoners, when Osman addressed him, and said, "Can you do a generous and gallant action? Ransom me, and take my word you shall lose nothing by it." Struck by Osman's appearance and manner the Frenchman turned to the captain of the vessel, and asked the amount of the ransom. The answer was a thousand sequins, a sum nearly equal to £500. Arnaud then said to the Turk, "I know nothing of you, and would you have me risk a thousand sequins on your bare word?" Osman replied that Arnaud could not be blamed for not trusting to the word of a stranger; "but," he added, "I have nothing at present but my word of honour to give to you, nor do I pretend to assign any

[1] Hanway, vol. iii. p. 100.

reason why you should trust to it. However, I tell you if you *do* trust to it, you shall have no occasion to repent." The Oriental proverb says well that " there are paths which lead straight from heart to heart." Arnaud was so wrought upon by Osman's frank and manly manner, that he prevailed on the Spaniards to set him at liberty for 600 sequins, which sum the generous Frenchman immediately paid. He provided Osman with a home and medical assistance until his wounds were healed ; and then gave him the means of proceeding on his voyage to Egypt. As soon as Osman reached Cairo, he sent back 1000 sequins as payment to Arnaud, with a present of 500 crowns, and of rich furs, which are considered the most honourable of all gifts in the East. A few years afterwards, Osman signalised himself greatly in the Turkish reconquest of the Morea, and in 1722 he was appointed Seraskier, and commanded all the Turkish troops in that country. He immediately invited Arnaud's son to visit him in the Morea, and conferred mercantile privileges on the young man, and placed opportunities for lucrative commerce within his reach, which enabled him to accumulate large wealth, with which he returned to his father. In 1728 Osman was Governor of Roumelia, and he then invited his French benefactor and his son to visit him at Nissa, his seat of government, where he treated them with distinction and honour, such as no Ottoman Turk had ever before been seen to accord to a Christian. On taking leave of him at Nissa, Arnaud said, as a compliment, that he trusted to live to visit Osman as Grand Vizier, at Constantinople. When Topal Osman attained that rank in 1731, he again invited Arnaud and his son to become his guests ; and, receiving them in his palace, in the presence of the highest dignitaries of the state, Osman pointed out the elder Arnaud, and said, " Behold ˙this Frenchman : I was once a slave loaded with chains, streaming with blood, and covered with wounds : this is the man who redeemed and saved me ; this is my master and benefactor ; to him I am indebted for life, liberty, fortune, and everything I enjoy. Without knowing me, he paid for me a large ransom ; sent me away upon my bare word, and gave me a ship to carry me where I pleased. Where is there even a Mussulman capable of such generosity ?" He then took both the Arnauds by the hand, and questioned them earnestly and kindly concerning their fortune and prospects, ending with an Asiatic sentence, " God's goodness is without bounds." He afterwards gave them many receptions in private, when they met without ceremony as friends, and he sent them back to their country loaded with the richest presents. Hanway well remarks on this

exhibition of gratitude by the Vizier, that "his behaviour was
truly great and noble, since every action of his life demonstrates
a mind superior to affectation. This conduct appears the more
generous, when it is considered what contempt and aversion the
prejudices of education often create in a Turk against the Christian; and, if we reflect further that this confession was made
before his whole court, the action will appear in all its lustre."[1]

Topal Osman was superseded in the Grand Vizierate in 1732.
His friends and dependents lamented bitterly over his downfall,
but Osman bore it with a nobler feeling than the ordinary stoicism
of a Turk under misfortune. According to his English biographer,
he summoned his friends and family round him, and addressed
them thus : " What is the reason of your affliction ?   Have I not
always said that the office of Grand Vizier is of all the most likely
to be short ?   All my concern was I should get out of it with
honour; and, thanks to God, I have done nothing with which I
reproach myself.   My master, the Sultan, approves of my services,
and I resign with perfect satisfaction."   He then gave orders for
rendering thanks to Heaven, as if it had been one of the most
happy events of his life.[2]

Before Topal Osman had been long in retirement, the alarming
progress of the Persian armies made the Porte again require
his services; and he was sent into Asia as generalissimo of
the Turkish armies in that continent, and was invested with
almost unlimited powers.   He marched to encounter the dreaded
Nadir; and on the 19th July, 1733, gave him a complete overthrow in a pitched battle, near the banks of the Tigris, about
twelve leagues from Bagdad.   There is a narrative of this battle,
written by Jean Nicodeme (who attended Topal Osman as his
physician) to the Marquis of Villeneuve, which exhibits the
manners and spirit of Osman in the same amiable and noble light
in which they are presented to us by Hanway.   He is represented
as free from all pride and arrogance; he treated his soldiers as if
they were his brothers; and all who served under his command
regarded him with the strongest feelings of personal attachment.
The movements of his troops were ably directed, and in the actual
conflict his forces were handled by him with great judgment and
decision.   The French writer thus describes Topal Osman's own
conduct and demeanour on the day of battle.   " After he had

---

[1] Hanway's "Travels," part iii. p. 106.   Hanway travelled in the East
between 1743 and 1750.   Von Hammer praises his works, and states that
they were eulogised by Arago.
[2] Hanway, part iii. p. 106.

prayed, he mounted on horseback, which he had not done before throughout the campaign, having been carried in a litter on account of the infirmity of his health, and the pain of his old wounds. I could not attribute the strength which he now showed to aught but his martial spirit, and the fire that glowed within him. I saw before me on horseback, a man, who had been bowed down by weakness, and by the numerous sword and gunshot wounds which he had received in war, and several of which had been injudiciously treated by his surgeons. I saw him riding along like a young man, sword in hand, with animated countenance and sparkling eyes. He rode from rank to rank, examined all with his own eyes, and gave his orders with admirable readiness and presence of mind."[1]

The victory thus gained by Topal Osman on the Tigris, rescued Bagdad; and he again defeated the Persians, near Leitan, in the same year. But in a third battle with Nadir, near Kerkoud, the Turks were routed; and Topal Osman himself died the death of a gallant soldier, fighting sword in hand to the last, rather than disgrace himself by flight. His body was borne off the field by some of his attendants, and was afterwards brought for burial to Constantinople.

Nadir gained repeated victories over the Ottoman generals who succeeded Topal Osman, and in 1736 the Porte gladly made a treaty of peace with its formidable enemy, which fixed the same boundary between Turkey and Persia that had been determined by the old treaty made with Amurath IV. In the preceding year the Russians had made a compact of peace and amity with Nadir, by which they abandoned those Persian provinces which they had appropriated by the partition treaty made between Peter the Great and Achmet III. The Court of St. Petersburg thought it more profitable to begin a war of conquest against Turkey, now weakened by the sword of Nadir Shah, than to strive for the retention of districts round the Caspian Sea, which were then far distant from any strong parts of the Russian Empire.

It was with reluctance and alarm that the Porte found itself again involved in hostilities with the powers of Christendom. The war with Persia had been zealously undertaken; and, though unsuccessful, was not unpopular. In combating the Persians, the Turks fought against heretics, whom they hated a hundredfold worse than the unbelievers, and they hoped also to achieve new

[1] The report of Nicodeme is cited in the note to Von Hammer's 66th book.

conquests, or to recover ancient dominions. But the prospect of
collision with either of the great neighbouring Christian empires
caused far different feelings. Neither Ottoman pride nor Mahometan fanaticism could now expect to see the Crescent reassert
in the battle-field that superiority over the Cross, which it had
held in the days of Mahomet the Conqueror, and in those of
Solyman the Lord of his Age. The last dreams of such a reaction
had vanished when Damad Ali, the conqueror of the Morea, fell
before Eugene at Peterwaradin. The Turkish ministers who
succeeded that "dauntless Vizier,"[1] knew the superiority which
the military system of Austria and Russia had acquired over the
Turkish. They watched carefully the political movements of
Christendom, and made it their chief study to preserve peace.
It was in vain that the French ambassadors at Constantinople
strove to excite the Porte to war with Austria, and that the
Swedish envoys urged it to recommence the struggle against
Russia. The Turkish statesmen sought and followed the pacific
advice of the representatives of England and Holland, the two
maritime powers whose intervention had obtained the treaties of
Carlowitz and Passarowitz, and who had no selfish interest in
plunging Turkey into the perils of new wars. In general the
Ottoman Empire was then regarded by the Christian powers much
as it has been in our own times. The decay of its military force
was considered to be irretrievable ; and the speedy expulsion of
the Turks from Europe, and the dismemberment of their dominions were confidently and covetously expected. Some sagacious
observers judged differently. The celebrated French military
writer, the Chevalier Folard, attributed the defeats of the Turkish
armies in the early part of the eighteenth century almost entirely
to their neglect in not availing themselves of the improvements
that had been made in the weapons of war. In his opinion
it was the bayonet that had given the Christians their victories
over the Moslems. He thought the Turks inferior in courage to
no nation living, and far superior in all soldierly qualities to the
Muscovites, whom Peter the Great had then recently made formidable to Europe. Folard believed that there needed but the
appearance of some military reformer, some enlightened Vizier
among the Ottomans, to restore them to their old renown, and
change the face of the affairs of the whole world.[2] Montesquieu

---

[1] "Thus uttered Coumourgi, the dauntless Vizier."—Byron.
[2] "Les Turcs ne sont battus que par le seul desavantage de leurs armes.
Ils ne sçavent ce que c'est que baionette au bout du fusil: car, depuis l'invention de cette arme ils n'ont pû rien gagner contre les Chrétiens, &c.

also, the highest political genius of the first half of the eighteenth century, pointed out to his contemporaries, that their anticipations of witnessing the fall of the Ottoman Empire were premature. He foresaw with marvellous sagacity, that Turkey, if her independence were ever seriously menaced by either of the great military monarchies in her neighbourhood, would find protection from the maritime powers of Western Europe, who knew their own interests too well to permit Constantinople to become the prize of either Austrian or Russian invaders.[1]

This caution was in 1734, as in after years, unknown or unheeded at the Court of St. Petersburg. Russia had at this time ready for action a veteran army, which had gained reputation in the war in Poland ; and she possessed a general of no ordinary military genius in Count Münnich, who had brought her troops into a high state of efficiency, and was eager for opportunities of further distinction. The Russian army was excellently officered, chiefly by foreigners from Western Europe ; and the artillery (that important arm of modern warfare to which the Russians have owed so many advantages) was unusually numerous and well-appointed. The Czarina Anne and her advisers thought that the time had come for avenging upon the Turks the disgrace which had been sustained in 1711, on the banks of the Pruth ; and Austria, which was then governed by the infirm Charles VI., was persuaded to join Russia in her schemes of aggression. There had been numerous disputes between the Czarina and the Porte, arising out of their unsettled claims to Daghestan, and the Kabartas, and

---

Nous méprisons les Turcs : ils sont certainement peu à craindre par le seul desavantage de leurs armes et non pas autrement.

" A l'égard du courage, les Turcs ne le cédent à aucune nation du monde. Il viendra quelque Vizir un jour plus habile et plus éclairé qu'un autre, qui ouvrira les yeux sur la cause de tant de défaites, et qui changera toute la face des affaires du monde entier. Les Moscovites étoient moins que les Turcs. Pierre le Grand a fait voir à toute la terre, qu'il naît des soldats partout où il naît des hommes, et que tout dépend de la discipline, de l'exercise, et de l'avantage des armes. Il ne faut pas croire qu'un tel changement soit plus difficile aux Turcs qu'aux Moscovites, dont les qualités pour la guerre sont fort au-dessous de celles des premiers."—Folard, " Polybe," vol. iii. p. 266, and vol. v. p. 180.

[1] "L'Empire des Turcs est à présent à peu-près dans le même dégré de foiblesse où étoit autrement celui des Grecs ; *mais il subsistera long-temps.* Car, si quelque prince que ce fût mettoit cet empire en péril en poursuivant ses conquêtes, les trois puissances commerçantes de l'Europe connoissent trop leurs affaires pour n'en pas prendre la défense sur-le-champ."—"Grandeur et Décadence des Romaines" (published in 1734), c. 23. Mr. Pitt referred to this passage in the debates on the Russian armament in 1792.

other districts between the Black and the Caspian Seas. The march of Tartar troops from the Crimea through the Caucasian territories for the purpose of co-operating with the Ottoman armies in the north of Persia, had been forcibly resisted by the Russians; and collisions had taken place, which gave an ample supply of pretexts for war to the Czarina, and her licentious favourite, Biren, by whom the councils of St. Petersburg were chiefly swayed. Turkey had also caused grave offence to Russia, by earnestly remonstrating, in 1733, against the iniquitous attacks of the Russians upon the independence of Poland. The Reis Effendi made an explicit protest against the occupation of that country and its capital by the Czarina's troops. He was met by the answer that the Russians had only entered Poland for the sake of enabling the Poles to proceed to the election of their new king in freedom, which France was endeavouring to disturb by her intrigues in favour of Stanislaus Leczynski. The Turk rejoined that the Sublime Porte did not concern itself as to whom the Poles chose for their king, but that it was resolved to uphold the national independence of Poland. The envoy of Russia then made a long catalogue of complaints against the Porte for permitting the Tartars to attack the Cossacks, for marching troops through the Caucasian territory, and for not delivering up a refugee from Russia, named Caluminski. These grievances were said to be the reason why Russia increased her forces in the south. These and similar recriminations were continued during the two next years; but Biren and the Czarina were resolved on war, which the ministers of the maritime powers vainly laboured to prevent.

So long as the hostile intentions of Russia were only manifested by conflicts with the Tartars along the ill-defined frontiers of Turkey near the Crimea and the Caucasus, the Porte continued to negotiate; but in May, 1736, intelligence reached Constantinople that the Czarina's army under Marshal Münnich had captured two Turkish fortresses near Azoph, and that Russian troops were actually besieging that important city. War was then (28th May, 1736), declared by a solemn Fetva against Russia, and on that very day Münnich stormed the lines of Perekop.

We possess in the memoirs of General Manstein,[1] who served under Marshal Münnich, and who was also frequently employed in the diplomatic service of the Russian cabinet, an unquestionable source of ample information respecting these Crimean campaigns, and also respecting the inveterate policy of Russia towards Turkey. General Manstein expressly states that Peter I., unable to stomach

[1] "Mémoires de Général Manstein."

the treaty of the Pruth, had long ago planned the war on the coasts of the Black Sea, which the Empress Anne undertook. He had formed vast magazines on the river Don, and had collected materials for a flotilla which was to waft his army down that river and the Dnieper. All was ready for the commencement of a campaign, when death cut short his projects (May 16, 1727). On the accession of the Empress Anne, in 1730, the design of a Turkish war was revived ; and General Keith was sent by the Court of St. Petersburg to Southern Russia, to inspect the state of the magazines which Peter the Great had formed, and to re-organise, so far as was necessary, his armaments for an attack on the Ottoman dominions. The troubles in Poland obliged the Empress to defer hostilities against the Porte ; but when, in 1735, the Russians had been completely successful against the independent party among the Poles, Münnich and his best troops were moved into the Ukraine ; and it was resolved to commence the campaign against Turkey by attacking Azoph, and to make also the greatest possible efforts against the Tartars of the Crimea, in order to conquer their whole country, and establish the Russian power over the Black Sea.[1]

Münnich made his preparations for the campaign while it was yet midwinter ; and he laboured earnestly to prepare his army for the hardships which he partly foresaw, and for resisting the numerous Tartar cavalry by which he knew that he would be surrounded. Each Russian regiment was ordered by him to collect a large number of waggons for the transport of its stores. Münnich also re-introduced the pike, a weapon which had for many years been entirely discontinued in the Russian service. Each regiment was by his command provided with 350 pikes, eighteen feet in length. The men in the second rank were armed with them ; but they were found to be useless in action, and extremely cumbersome to the troops when on march. Another device of the marshal's was far more successful. He supplied every regiment with twenty chevaux-de-frise two yards in length. These were found to be eminently serviceable, both as temporary defences against the enemy's horse, and as fortifications to the camp. When the army halted, the chevaux-de-frise were planted round the position, which was thus secured against surprise, and furnished with a barricade of no slight efficacy against the pressure of superior numbers. Münnich also made his officers and sergeants lay aside their spontoons and halberds, and carry instead of them the firelock and bayonet, as far more useful than their former weapons.

[1] Manstein, p. 123.

In the month of March, he advanced with six regiments of infantry, three of dragoons, and 3000 Cossacks of the Don, to St. Anne, a fortress which the Russians had erected about eight miles from Azoph. The Turkish governor of that city sent one of his officers to compliment the marshal on his arrival on the frontiers, and to express the Pacha's full belief that the Russian force had no design of breaking the peace which existed between the two empires. Münnich replied in terms of vague civility; but on the 27th of March he passed the River Don, and marched on Azoph with such speed and secrecy that he captured two of the outworks of the city before the main body of the Tartars knew of his approach. He then invested Azoph itself; and on the arrival of the Russian General Leontiew with reinforcements, Münnich left him to carry on the siege until the arrival of Count Lascy, for whom the command of the operations in that quarter was designed. Münnich himself on the 6th of April repaired to Zaritsinka, where the main Russian army was assembling, which was to effect the great enterprise of the campaign, the invasion of the Crimea.

The Russian forces for this operation, when concentrated at Zaritsinka, two leagues from the Dnieper, on the 19th of May, 1736, consisted of twelve regiments of dragoons, fifteen regiments of regular infantry, ten of militia, ten squadrons of hussars, 5000 Cossacks of the Don, 4000 Cossacks of the Ukraine, and 3000 Zaporogian Cossacks; amounting altogether to 54,000 men. Münnich had directed every regiment to take with it supplies of bread for two months; and the officers were bidden to make similar provision for themselves. Such ample magazines had been prepared, that even a larger supply might have been distributed; but the means of transport were deficient. Münnich was unwilling to defer operations until more waggons and beasts of burden could be collected; but he ordered Prince Troubetski to undertake that important duty, and to send forward continual convoys of provisions with the fresh regiments, which had not yet arrived, but were on their march to join the army. These orders of the marshal were ill-obeyed by the prince; and the invading forces suffered severely from his neglect.

Münnich formed his army in five columns, and marched down the left bank of the Dnieper, defeating some bodies of Tartar horse, which had advanced to reconnoitre the invaders; they then moved by Selnaya Dolina, and Tchernaya Dolina, to the banks of the little river Kolytschka. Thence he marched to the narrow isthmus which connects the Crimean peninsula with the continent, and on the 26th of May, 1736, the Russian marshal halted at a short distance from the celebrated lines of Perekop.

These lines were drawn across the isthmus a little to the north of the town of Perekop, at a part where the land is not more than five miles in breadth, from the Black Sea, to that recess of the Sea of Azoph which is called the Putrid Sea. The defences consisted of a trench about thirty-six feet wide, and twenty-five feet deep, backed by a rampart seventy feet high, if measured to its summit from the bottom of the ditch. Six stone towers strengthened the lines, and served as outworks to the fortress of Perekop, which stood behind them. The position was believed by the Tartars to be impregnable; and they assembled here under their Khan against Münnich to the number of 100,000, aided by a force of 1800 Turkish Janissaries, who garrisoned the towers.

Münnich sent a letter to the Tartar Khan, in which he reproached him for the depredations committed by his subjects in the Ukraine, and declared that the Empress of Russia had ordered the whole of the Crimea to be laid waste, in revenge for these misdeeds of its inhabitants. Still, the Russian marshal declared, such was the clemency of his imperial mistress, that the offending country should be spared, but only on condition of the Khan and all his people submitting to Russia and acknowledging themselves subjects of the Czarina. Perekop was to be instantly ceded, and to receive a Russian garrison; and, if this pledge of submission were given, Münnich professed his readiness to enter into negotiations. The Tartar Prince, in answer, denied the charge made against his subjects, and expressed his astonishment that the Russians should attack him without any declaration of war. He represented the impossibility of his severing the long connection between the Crimea and the Sublime Porte; and professed his inability to surrender Perekop, even if he were willing, inasmuch as it was occupied by Turkish troops. He implored the marshal to suspend hostilities, and to allow an opportunity of settling by negotiations any just cause of complaint that might exist. He added, that if attacked he should do his best to defend himself.

Münnich sent back a reply, that inasmuch as the Khan would not appreciate the gracious clemency of the Russian Court, he should soon see his country laid waste, and his cities given to the flames. The Russian army followed close upon the messenger who bore this fierce message to Perekop, and moved forward to the assault during the night before the 28th of May, 1736, in profound silence, halting about an hour before daybreak, at the distance of a quarter of a mile before the lines.

Münnich first sent a detachment of 2500 men and some pieces of artillery forward on his left (the side nearest to the Sea of Azoph), to make a false attack on that quarter and draw away the enemy's attention from the Russian right (the side nearest to the Black Sea), on which he designed the real assault to be given. The manœuvre was perfectly successful; and the Tartars, who had hurried to the eastern part of the lines to meet the Russian detachment that menaced them, were thrown into alarm and confusion when the main Russian force appeared, in six strong columns, advancing steadily and rapidly against the Tartar left, on the western part of their position.   No attempt seems to have been made to flood the ditch; and the Russian columns descended into it, crossed it, and began to clamber up the opposite rampart, while their batteries poured a heavy fire upon the parapet, and prevented the Tartars from forming so as to offer any effective opposition.   Terrified at seeing the enemy thus boldly passing through the works on which they had relied, the Tartars betook themselves to flight; and the Russians surmounted the rampart, and drew up on the southern side almost without resistance.   The Russian general, Manstein, who took part in the events of the day, remarks that it would probably have been impossible to force the lines in that manner against any other enemy than the Tartars. But he observes that the entrance into the Crimea would, nevertheless, have been practicable, inasmuch as the neighbouring part of the Sea of Azoph is so shallow in summer that it is easily fordable, and Perekop can thus be always turned, even if it cannot be stormed.   It does not appear that either party in this campaign endeavoured to avail themselves of the all-important co-operation, which a flotilla of heavily-armed gunboats would give, for the purpose either of attack or defence.

The tower and the city of Perekop were speedily captured by the victorious Russians; and Münnich then detached General Leontiew with 10,000 regular troops and 3000 Cossacks to attack the fortress of Kilburun or Kilbourn,[1] on the extremity of the

---

[1] Von Hammer (vol. iv. p. 323) says that the first syllable of Kilburun preserves part of the name of the Greek hero Achilles, who was in the classic times believed to have performed many exploits in these regions.   I wish I could share Von Hammer's faith, though I neither doubt the prevalence of the legends about Achilles which he refers to, nor the real personal existence of Achilles himself.   The legends were as old at least as the time of Euripides, who alludes to them in the "Iphigenia in Tauris," l. 436. The long, narrow spit of land that stretches from opposite Kilbourn nearly to the Crimea was called "The Course of Achilles," and he was worshipped here as Pontarches, or Lord of the Pontus. (See Clarke's "Travels," vol. ii.

tongue of land of the same name, which projects into the Black Sea near the mouth of the river Dnieper, and opposite to Oczakof on the mainland. This was on the 4th of June; and, on the same day, the marshal held a council of war, in which the future operations of the main army were considered. The greater number of the Russian officers were averse to entering farther into the Crimea; and they pointed out to the commander-in-chief that the army had now only twelve days' supply of bread. They urged that at least it would be prudent to halt until expected convoys of provisions arrived. But Münnich was eager for the glory of being the conqueror of the Crimea, and would not rest content with the capture of Perekop. He told his generals, that if they advanced boldly into the Tartar territory they would find the means of subsisting at the enemy's expense; and he refused to halt longer at the isthmus, and so give time for the Tartars to recover from their panic. The army accordingly moved forward across the steppes of the northern part of the Crimean peninsula; harassed incessantly by the Tartar cavalry, but protected against any serious attack by the skilful dispositions of the marshal. Münnich formed his force into one vast hollow square composed of several battalions, each of which was also formed in square. The baggage was in the middle. This arrangement has, since his time, been generally adopted by the Russian generals when acting in open countries with forces chiefly of infantry against large masses of hostile cavalry. As Münnich advanced, he kept up his communication with Perekop and the Ukraine by forming little redoubts in favourable positions, at a short distance from each other. Each of them was garrisoned by an officer, and ten or twelve regular foot soldiers or dragoons, and thirty Cossacks. A complete chain of fortified posts was thus formed, along which intelligence was readily transmitted. General Manstein observes, that it was astonishing to the army to find how vainly the Tartars endeavoured to assail their little citadels. Not one of them was captured; and it was only in a few instances that the Russian couriers failed to pass from post to post in safety. Besides thus preserving the army's communications, the soldiers who were posted along the

---

p. 362.) According to another legend, the White Island (now called the Isle of Serpents), off the mouths of the Danube, was given to Achilles by his mother, Thetis; and it was the chosen dwelling-place of the spirits of the hero and his friend Patroclus. Mariners, favoured by Heaven, were, when they approached the island, visited in dreams by Achilles and Patroclus, and instructed where to land. (See Clarke's "Travels," vol. ii. p. 397; and the notes to the Variorum edition of Euripides, vol. v. p. 86.)

line of march were charged with the useful service of making hay, and storing it up for the supply of the horses of the army on their return, when the herbage of the steppes was likely to be exhausted.

Thus arrayed, and with these precautions, the Russians moved on through the Crimea, taking also constant care to guard against the peril of fire, which they incurred from the Tartar custom of setting light to the long grass of the steppes, now dried by the fierce sunbeams of the Crimean summer.   Vessels of water were ordinarily carried in the numerous waggons that accompanied the army, for the refreshment of the soldiers while on the march ; and Münnich now ordered that every waggon and carriage should be provided with the means of putting out fire ; and whenever the army halted, the grass and soil were dug up, and removed for the breadth of three feet round the camp.   The town of Koslof, now better known as Eupatoria, on the western coast of the Crimea, was the first point on which Münnich marched on leaving Perekop. Koslof was considered at that time to be the richest commercial city in the peninsula.   It was taken and sacked by the Russians on the 17th of June.   Thence Münnich led his troops to Bakchiserai (the Palace of Gardens), the ancient residence of the Khans of the Crimea.   This city was also assaulted ; and after a short resistance, the Tartar garrison fled from their post.   Münnich then drew his Muscovites and Cossacks up outside the defenceless town, and sent in a quarter of his army at a time to pillage for a fixed number of hours.   The barbarous work was fully accomplished. Two thousand private houses, and all the public buildings were destroyed.   The vast palace of the Khans, the splendid library which Selim Gherai had founded, and that which had been collected by the Jesuit mission in the Crimea, perished in the flames. Simpheropolis, to the north-east of Bakchiserai, was next attacked by the Russians ; its inhabitants and its wealth were given up to the brutality and rapacity of the soldiers, its buildings to the flames.   Münnich then took the road towards Kaffa, with the desire of establishing the Russian force permanently in that advantageously situated city.   But his army, which had inflicted so much misery and devastation on the Crimea, was itself suffering fearfully ; and the marshal saw his ranks diminishing every day, not by battle, but by disease, want, and fatigue.   The Tartars laid waste the country wherever the march of the invading columns was pointed ; and the barbarous cruelties of the Russians themselves co-operated in increasing their privations.   General Manstein asserts that the Crimean campaign of 1736, cost Russia nearly 30,000 soldiers : and he justly censures the rashness of Münnich, who plunged with his army into the peninsula, on the sole hope that *perhaps* they would be able to subsist at the enemy's expense. He blames also the excessive severity of the marshal in discipline, and his recklessness in imposing unnecessary fatigues on the soldiers. He states that the Russians were so exhausted by their sufferings and trials, that men used to drop down stark dead on the march ; and that even officers died of famine and misery.[1]   Münnich returned to Perekop on the 17th of July ; and evacuated the Crimea on the 25th of August, having first razed a considerable portion of the defences of the isthmus. General Manstein observes as a proof of the severity of the losses which the invaders had sustained, that every Russian regiment which entered the Crimea in 1736, had its full complement at the beginning of the campaign—that is to say, each regiment of infantry was 1575 strong, and each regiment of dragoons 1231.   But when the army was reviewed at Samara by Münnich at the end of September, there was not a single regiment that could array 600 men round its colours.   Never in the annals of warfare had the sufferings of an invading force been more deeply deserved.   The whole campaign of the army under Münnich in the Crimea had been marked by the most atrocious cruelty, and the most savage spirit of devastation.   No mercy was shown by the Russians to age or sex.   Towns and villages were fired and their inhabitants slaughtered, even where no resistance was offered to the Russian troops. The monuments of antiquity were wantonly defaced ; libraries and schools were given to the flames ; and public buildings and places of worship were purposely and deliberately destroyed.   The whole enterprise (which was commenced without any declaration of war) was planned and conducted in a spirit of truly Scythian ferocity.[2]

Azoph had been captured by the Russian force under General Lascy within a short time of that officer's taking the command against the town ; and while Münnich's army was in the Crimea, the Kalmuck troops of the Czarina attacked the Tartars of the Kuban in Asia, and not only prevented them from crossing the straits of Kertch to aid their kinsmen and fellow-subjects of the Porte in the Crimea, but compelled large numbers of them to re-

---

[1] Manstein, p. 174.

[2] Von Hammer cites the indignant remarks on this invasion made by De Castelnau, in his " Essais sur l'histoire ancienne et moderne de nouvelle Russie," vol. ii. p. 60.   Von Hammer himself classes Münnich with the desolators of the Palatinate, with Louvois and Catinat.   Vol. iv. p. 324.

nounce their allegiance to the Sultan, and to acknowledge the Russian Empress as their sovereign. Kilbourn also capitulated to General Leontiew. Russian fraud and force were almost universally triumphant in the first year of the war.

The Sultan's arms were visited but by a single gleam of success. In November, when the survivors of Münnich's army were in winter-quarters, Feth Ghirai, the new Khan of the Crimea (his predecessor Kaplan Ghirai having been deposed by the Porte for want of vigour in opposing Münnich's invasion), made an inroad into the Ukraine, defeated a body of 500 Russians, and spread devastation throughout the province. The Tartar force returned to the Crimea with a living booty of no less than 30,000 Russian captives, whom they carried off into slavery.

The Ottoman court was solicitous to put an end to the war with Russia, and made frequent attempts to negotiate a peace, sometimes through the intervention of France and Sweden, and sometimes through that of Austria, which last was insidiously proffered in the hopes of retarding and arresting the preparations of the Turks for a new campaign. The Emperor Charles VI. was, in reality, eager to share with Russia the spoliation of the Turkish provinces: and in January, 1737, a secret treaty was made between the Courts of Vienna and St. Petersburg, which stipulated that the Austrian armies should invade Turkey in concert with the Russian forces. But it was wished that the Emperor's troops should have the same advantage of taking the Turks by surprise, which the Russians had obtained when they attacked Azoph and the Crimea without any declaration of war. The Austrian statesmen therefore feigned to be solicitous for peace ; and a congress was opened at Nimirof, in which the Czarina's and the Emperor's plenipotentiaries kept up the hollow show of negotiations till the November of 1737. Turkey was willing to make great sacrifices for the sake of peace ; but when at last the representatives of Russia and Austria were pressed into a declaration of the terms on which they were willing to grant it, their demands were such, as not even the farther humiliations and defeats of another century have yet brought the Ottoman spirit to regard as endurable.

Russia required, first, that all the former treaties between her and the Porte should be annulled ; secondly, that the Crimea, the Kuban, and all the countries inhabited by the Tartars, should be ceded to her ; thirdly, that Wallachia and Moldavia should be recognised as independent principalities under the protection and suzerainty of Russia ; fourthly, that the Porte should concede the title of Emperor to the sovereign ; fifthly, that the Russian fleets should have free passage to and from the Mediterranean, by the Black Sea, the Bosphorus, and the Dardanelles. Austria asked for fresh territories in Bosnia and in Servia, and for the extension of her Wallachian frontier as far as the river Doumbovisa. The Turkish plenipotentiaries rejected their arrogant claims with becoming indignation. But the language used by them was remarked as new from Ottoman lips, inasmuch as, besides their customary references to the Koran, they appealed to the Christian gospels, and to Christian writers on the law of nations, to prove the bad faith of their adversaries. On the other side, the Russian and Austrian ministers taunted the Ottomans with the precept of Islam which bids its followers offer to unbelievers the Koran or the sword. "How," said they, "can ye Moslems be sincere when you negotiate with Christians against your law?" The Turks answered that the text which had been cited, applied only to idolaters and heretics; and that the Mahometan sword ought to cease from smiting the confessors of the Old Testament, the Gospel, or the Tora, from the instant when they either submitted to pay the capitation tax, or asked for peace, which ought to be granted. They added that the Sublime Porte would make war or give peace, as was desired: and they appealed to the glory of their former victories at Mohacz and Cerestes, to prove the power of the House of Othman. They ended by asking if the Christian religion permitted the Austrian Emperor to break the peace, to which he had recently pledged his oath on the succession of Sultan Mahmoud? One of the Austrian ministers, confused by this appeal, muttered that ambassadors were the mere servants of their courts; and he cursed the authors of the war. He added that the Ottomans themselves had been the real causers of it by troubling Russia and making her put herself into a state of defence, so that the Emperor, as Russia's ally, was obliged to take part in the war. "It is on you, therefore, as the authors of the war," said the Austrian, "that all the miseries of this war will fall." "So be it," replied the Turk; "may the authors of the war bear the curses of the war! May God distinguish between the guilty and the innocent: and may the sword of His justice fall on the guilty only!" All present cried "Amen," and the congress terminated with this solemn anathema and international appeal of battle.

While the diplomatists of Russia and Austria had been spinning out the web of faithless negotiation, their armies had attacked the Turks with equal ambition, but with far different success.

Münnich took the field two months before congress had begun its meetings at Nimirof, with an army of 70,000 men, and a park

of artillery that numbered 600 pieces of different calibre. Münnich was high in favour with the court at St. Petersburg, which
cared little for the cruel sacrifice of troops by which the exploits
of the last campaign had been purchased; and the resources of the
empire were freely placed at the marshal's disposal for the new
operations which his daring ambition suggested. Münnich employed the early months of 1737 in the collection of stores, and of
waggons, in the formation of a flotilla of flat-bottomed gunboats,
and in perfecting the organisation and training of his army. His
severity was inhuman; but it is to him that the foundation of that
iron discipline is ascribed, by which the Russian armies have ever
since been distinguished.

Münnich left to General Lascy the renewal of the invasion of
the Crimea. His design for the main army under his own command was to advance down the north-western coast of the Euxine
and to capture the important city of Oczakof. He crossed the
river Boug on the 25th of June, without experiencing the least
opposition from the Turks, whose troops were slowly assembling
at Bender. On the 10th of July the Russian forces encamped
before Oczakoff. The Turkish generals had succeeded in throwing
a division of their best men into that city before Münnich had
arrived, and the Russian general found that he had to deal with a
garrison 20,000 strong, well provided with artillery and stores of
every description. The Turks fought bravely, and made many
desperate sallies, which from the number of troops engaged and
the heaviness of the slaughter, deserve to be considered regular
battles. Münnich's men suffered severely from want of provisions,
of fascines, and other ordinary materials for carrying on a siege.
Still Münnich persevered with fierce temerity, which his own
generals censured, and which the marshal's good fortune alone
crowned with success.[1]

After a cannonade of two days a fire was observed to break out
in the city, and Münnich instantly hurled his whole army on the
defences, without regard to the state of the fortifications in the
quarter where the assault was given, and without providing his
columns with ladders or fascines, or other usual means for passing
any obstacle that they might encounter. The Russians forced
their way to the foot of the glacis, and found there a deep trench,
which completely checked their farther advance. With unflinching, but useless bravery, they remained there nearly two hours,
under a heavy cannonade and musketry fire from the city, to
which they replied by useless volleys. At length they broke and

[1] Manstein, p. 210.

fled back in confusion ; and, had the Turkish commander followed up his success by a vigorous sally of the whole garrison, the siege must have been raised, and Münnich's army would have been almost certainly destroyed. But only a few hundred of the garrison followed the flying Russians, and Münnich was able before long to reform his men, and prepare for a renewal of the attack. The conflagration continued to spread in the city, and early on the morning after the first assault, the principal Turkish magazine of powder exploded, and destroyed 6000 of the defenders. The Seraskier, alarmed at this catastrophe, and seeing the flames within gathering still greater fury, and the Russians without re-assembling for the charge, hung out the white flag and capitulated, on the condition of surrendering himself and his forces prisoners of war. While the capitulation was being arranged, the Russian hussars and Cossacks of the Don forced their way into the city, and began to plunder it. The Seraskier and part of his troops had already marched out to surrender, but the Russian soldiery attacked them, slaughtered many, and drove the rest back into the town. The Seraskier sent again to Münnich to say that he surrendered at discretion, and to beg quarter for himself and men. The Russian commander then sent forward a regiment of guards, who conducted the Seraskier and between 3000 and 4000 of the garrison as prisoners to the Russian camp. But great numbers of the Turks were massacred without mercy, and many were drowned in a vain attempt to swim off to some Turkish vessels, which had been moored near the city during the siege, but which on seeing its capture weighed anchor, and sailed with the evil tidings to Constantinople. The bodies of more than 17,000 Turks were buried by the victorious Russians when they took possession of Oczakow. They had themselves lost in killed and wounded during their short, but sanguinary siege, nearly 4000 men. Disease, want, and fatigue were, as usual, still more deadly scourges to the invaders. Münnich found that his army was less strong by 20,000 men than it had been at the commencement of the campaign. He had projected a further advance upon Bender, but a report that the Turks had fired the steppes which it would be necessary to cross in a march upon that city, and the enfeebled state of his army, made him determine on returning to the Ukraine, after repairing the fortification of Oczakof, and leaving a strong garrison to secure his conquest.

In the meanwhile Lascy attacked the Crimea with a force of 40,000 men, supported by a fleet under Admiral Bredal in the Black Sea, and by a flotilla of armed rafts and gunboats, which.

Lascy caused to be constructed in the Sea of Azoph. The Khan of the Crimea had repaired the lines of Perekop with great care, and posted his army behind them, with the intent to defend them much better against Lascy, than they had been defended by his predecessor against Münnich. But Lascy marched his army along the narrow bank of land which extends from near Yenitchi on the mainland towards Arabat in the Crimea, nearly across the whole entrance of the Putrid Sea. He formed bridges of casks and rafts over the gaps in this perilous water, and entered the Crimea on the 23rd of July, 1737, without the loss of a single man.[1] He defeated the Tartars near Karasou Bazaar, and then led his men up and down through the devoted country, pillaging, burning, and slaying, after the manner of Münnich's troops in the preceding year. Lascy left the Crimea in August by a bridge, which he formed over the narrow part of the Putrid Sea near Schoungar. The Russians boasted that during this short invasion they had burnt 6000 houses, thirty-eight mosques, two churches, and fifty mills.

Austria commenced her treacherous attack upon Turkey in 1737, by suddenly assailing the city of Nissa, in imitation of Münnich's advance against Azoph in the preceding year. One Imperialist army, under Field-Marshal Seckendorf, entered the Ottoman territory in Servia in the month of July; and at the same time other Austrian forces were marched against the Turkish possessions in Bosnia. Nissa was captured without difficulty; and Seckendorf then sent part of his army against Widdin; but the Turks had time to strengthen the garrison of that city, and the invaders perished rapidly by disease and want in their marches and counter-marches along the banks of the Timok and the Danube. The Austrians had begun the war in a spirit of overweening pride in their own military skill and prowess, and in arrogant contempt of their enemy. Full of recollections of the triumphs of Eugene, they thought that the superiority, which under that great captain they had maintained over the Ottomans, was certain to continue, and that to advance against the Turks was necessarily to conquer.

---

[1] Lascy took this bold measure against the remonstrances of all his generals except one. They came in a body to his tent, and protested against the risk to which he was exposing the army. Lascy replied that there was risk in all military operations, and that they might return if they liked. He made his secretary write their passports, and even ordered out 200 Dragoons, who were to escort them to the Ukraine, where they were to remain until his return from the campaign. Awed by his firmness, the refractory chiefs gave way, but it was three days before Lascy would pardon them. Lascy was an Irishman.

The cabinet of Vienna was even more arrogant and rash than the officers whom it employed. When one of the generals proposed to the army-board at Vienna that the palpable weakness of the artillery force should be remedied by providing each battalion with two field-pieces, his request was rejected, on the principle that the Emperor's armies had always defeated the Turks notwithstanding any deficiency in cannon, and that the same would continue to be the case. The natural results of such a spirit in the camp and council were visible early in the campaign. It was found that the Turks fought with courage and skill; and rash attempts on the part of the Imperialists met with severe repulses. At the first appearance of reverse the Austrian generals began to quarrel among themselves, and the calamities of their troops soon increased. On the Turkish side the Grand Vizier took the command, ably assisted by the French renegade Bonneval, the fruits of whose military ability were manifested in the unusual accuracy of the manœuvrés of the Ottoman forces, and in the improved discipline of the troops. After a short and inglorious campaign Seckendorf led the remains of his army back into Hungary. The Turks recovered Nissa and penetrated at several points into the Austrian territories. In Bosnia the result of the campaign was similar. The Mahometan population of that province resisted the invading Imperialists with enthusiastic valour; and though the Austrian troops at first gained some advantages, they were before the close of the year driven back out of Bosnia with disgrace and loss.

In the following year the Emperor placed new generals at the head of his armies, and a new Grand Vizier, Yegen Mahommed Pacha, led the Ottomans against them. The Turks did not wait for the advance of the Austrians, but acted on the offensive in great force and with remarkable boldness. They took Meadia in Hungary, and laid siege to the important fortress of Orsova on the Danube. The Austrians were successful in an action at Kornia near Meadia (4th July, 1738) against Hadji Mahommed, but their loss of men was greater than that of the Turks; and the Grand Vizier coming up with fresh forces, drove the Imperialist army back, captured Semendria, and resumed the siege of Orsova, which surrendered to the Ottomans on the 15th of August. The Austrian commanders, disunited and disheartened, led their troops back in precipitate retreat within the walls and lines of Belgrade. The Turkish cavalry followed them, and occupied the heights near that city, where the Imperialist army lay shamefully inactive, and the prey of pestilential disorders. A body of Austrian

hussars that ventured to encounter the Turks, was routed with
severe loss; and the Grand Vizier, when he recalled his cavalry
from Belgrade, closed the campaign amid merited honours and
rewards, which the Sultan caused to be distributed to the general
and officers of the army, and to every private soldier who had distinguished himself by bravery and good conduct.

Though less brilliantly successful against the Russians, the Turks
during the year 1738, prevented those formidable enemies from
making any important progress along the coast of the Black Sea.
Marshal Münnich again led his army across the Dnieper and the
Boug, and defeated several bodies of Turkish and Tartar troops,
that encountered him near those rivers. But on arriving at the
Dniester he found a powerful Ottoman army strongly entrenched
in a position, which he was unable to force, and which barred his
intended advance for the purpose of besieging Bender. Several
conflicts took place, in one of which, according to one account, Sasi
Ghirai, the Seraskier of Boudjak, with 20,000 Tartars and an
equal number of Ottomans, dealt a severe blow on the Russian
army. In the inflated style of the Ottoman writers, "A great
number of the accursed ones, destined to hell, took the fatal leap
over the arch formed by the sparkling sabre of the True Believers,
into the infernal gulf." But disease and the want of supplies were
as usual much more deadly enemies to the Russians than either
Turkish or Tartar swords; and Münnich returned in the autumn
to the Ukraine, with an army that had accomplished little and
suffered much.

Marshal Lascy repeated the invasion of the Crimea in the July
of this year. He appeared with an army of from 30,000 to 35,000
men at the northern part of the Isthmus of Perekop; and the
Khan, who thought that the Russians now really meant to penetrate the Crimea by that route, prepared for an obstinate defence
of the lines. But Lascy turned them without the loss of a life.
The inlet of the Sea of Azoph (called the Putrid Sea) which adjoins
the eastern side of the Isthmus, is shallow at all times, and especially so in summer. The consequence is, that if the wind at that
season blows for a few hours strongly from the west, and drives
back the water, the passage from the mainland to the Crimea may
be effected without making use of the Isthmus of Perekop. On
the 7th of July the favourable wind sprang up; and Lascy instantly formed his army in a single line along the coast and
marched them across the bed of the gulf, before the wind had
lulled and the waves returned. A few baggage-waggons, that
followed in the rear, were lost, the wind having ceased to blow

from the west soon after the Russian troops had effected their passage. Lascy immediately took the Tartar position at Perekop in the rear. That city surrendered on the 8th; and the Russians were successful in an engagement on which the Tartars ventured against part of Lascy's army. Lascy's object in this campaign was to obtain possession of Kaffa, then the strongest place in the Crimea, and the mastery of which was considered to involve the conquest of the whole peninsula. But the ravages of the Russian armies in the preceding years had so wasted the country, that Lascy could not find the means of subsistence for his army. The Russian fleet, which was ordered to bring him supplies, was blown off the coast and severely damaged by a storm. After a few ineffectual marches and counter-marches the Russians were obliged to return to Perekop and thence to their own country.

Negotiations for peace had been frequently resumed during the war; and in the winter of 1738, fresh attempts to terminate hostilities were made under the mediation of France. But these were baffled by the exorbitant demands which the Russian Court continued to put forward. Marshal Münnich was the great inspirer of this ambitious spirit in the councils of the Czarina, and the vehement opposer of peace. He had repaired to the Russian capital at the close of the campaign of 1738, and employed all his influence to cause the continuance of the war, and to induce Russia to strike boldly for the conquest of Constantinople itself. He proposed to effect this not merely by Russian arms, but by raising the Christian subjects of the Turk against their master. He pointed out to the Court of St. Petersburg what was the true state of the Ottoman Empire in Europe, with its Mahometan population so many times outnumbered by the millions of Rayas, who had been oppressed for centuries, but who had never ceased to hate their conquerors, and who were now watching with anxious joy the progress of the Russian power. He told the Czarina that all the Greeks regarded her as their legitimate sovereign, and that the strongest excitement prevailed among them. " Now," he said, " now is the time to take advantage of their enthusiasm in our cause, and to march upon Constantinople, while the effect which our victories have produced is fresh and vivid. Such an opportunity may never be offered again."[1] The Empress Anne adopted readily this " Oriental project," as it was termed, of Marshal Münnich. The army in the south of Russia was largely recruited, and emissaries were sent into Epirus and Thessaly to prepare the

[1] Ruhiere, vol. i. p. 164; vol. iii. p. 286. Emerson Tennent's "Greece," vol. ii. p. 301.

inhabitants for a rising against the Turks. Münnich determined in 1739 to gain the right bank of the Dniester without exposing his troops to the sufferings and losses, which he knew by experience were the inevitable attendants of the march along the north-western coast of the Euxine. He accordingly led his army into Podolia, audaciously violating the neutral territory of the Polish State, in spite of the remonstrances that were addressed to him against this contemptuous breach of the law of nations. Spreading desolation round them as if in an enemy's country, Münnich's Muscovites and Cossacks traversed Podolia, and crossed the Dniester into Moldavia at Sukowza (12 August, 1739), about six leagues from the Turkish fortress of Khoczin. The Seraskier of Bender, Veli Pasha, took up a position in front of Khoczin, but was completely defeated on the 18th of August, and Khoczin surrendered a few days after the battle to the Russians. Münnich proclaimed Cantemir (a descendant of the former rulers of Moldavia), Prince of Moldavia under Russian protection, and Cantemir immediately raised the natives in arms against the Ottomans and the Sultan's viceroy. Münnich marched upon Jassy, the capital of the province, and he and Prince Cantemir entered that city without opposition. Thence the Russian general wheeled into Bessarabia, intending to reduce Bender, and the other strong places of that district, and so secure his base of operations before he advanced southward into the heart of European Turkey. But he was checked in the mid career of triumph by tidings of the disastrous defeats which his Austrian allies had been sustaining on the Upper Danube, and of the still more disgraceful terms on which they had begged peace of the common enemy.

Yegen Mohammed had given offence to Sultan Mahmoud, and had been superseded by Elhadj Mohammed Pacha. The new Grand Vizier, like his predecessor, took the command against the Imperialists ; and it may well be credited that he caused the best troops of Turkey, and especially the veterans who had returned from the Persian wars, to be enrolled in his own army, while the recruits and inferior regiments were given to the Pachas who commanded against the Russians. But the miserable imbecility of Generals Wallis and Neipperg (the two leaders whom the Emperor Charles VI. this year gave to his armies) is of itself sufficient to account for the difference of Austria's fortunes in the field from that which the Russians obtained under Münnich's guidance.

The main Austrian force was assembled near Peterwaradin in May. It amounted to 56,000 men, without reckoning the artillery-

32

men, or the hussars, and other light and irregular troops. Marshal Wallis intended to commence the campaign by the siege of Orsova, and he had positive orders from the Emperor to fight a pitched battle with the enemy at the first opportunity. The Austrians crossed the river Saave on the 27th of June, and marched along the right bank of the Danube towards Orsova. The Turkish army under the Grand Vizier Elhadj Mohammed Pacha, about 200,000 strong, advanced through Semendria, and took up a strong position on the high ground near Krotzka. Wallis on approaching Krotzka thought that he had only a detachment of the Turks to deal with, and hurried forward through a deep defile with only the cavalry of his army to the encounter. On debouching from the hollow way the Austrian horse regiments found themselves among vineyards and tracts of underwood, where it was impossible for them to form line or charge; and they were assailed in all directions by a heavy musketry fire from the Turkish infantry, which the Vizier had skilfully posted round the mouth of the defile. Unsupported by any foot or artillery, the Austrian cavalry suffered severe loss, and was driven back in disorder through the pass. The Turks advanced, occupying the heights on either side of the road, and assailed the right wing of the Austrian infantry. A furious engagement was maintained in this part of the field till sunset; when Wallis drew back his troops to Vinza. The Austrian loss in the battle of Krotzka was more than 10,000 in killed and wounded; and though the Turks also had suffered severely in the latter part of the action, they were in the highest degree elated by their victory. The Austrian general, whose despondency equalled his former presumption, soon fell back upon Belgrade. The Turks followed, and opened their batteries against the city, the soldiers exclaiming, "Let us take advantage of the panic and blindness which God has inflicted upon the unbelievers for having broken the peace of Passowitz."[1] Wallis and Neipperg now endeavoured to obtain terms from the Grand Vizier; and a series of negotiations ensued, in which the Austrian generals and plenipotentiaries showed infatuation, cowardice, and folly even greater than General Mack afterwards displayed in the memorable capitulation of Ulm. The French ambassador Villeneuve came to the Grand Vizier's camp near Belgrade to give the mediation and guarantee of France to the pacification which Wallis and Neipperg sought with almost shameless avidity. Preliminary articles were signed on the 1st of September, by which Austria was to restore to the Porte the city of

[1] Coxe, vol. iii. p. 213.

Belgrade, and all the districts in Bosina, Servia, and Wallachia, which the Emperor had taken from the Sultan at the peace of Passarowitz. As a security for the execution of these preliminaries, a gate of Belgrade was given up to the Turks. It was stipulated by the Austrians that Turkey should at the same time make peace with Russia; and messengers were sent accordingly to the camp of Münnich. The victorious Russian general received the intelligence of the convention of Belgrade with the greatest indignation; but he knew that it was impossible for him to resume his march upon Constantinople with the powerful and victorious army of the Vizier free to act against his flank; and Russia reluctantly consented to terminate a war, which had cost her such heavy sacrifices in treasure and in men, at the very time when her most ambitious schemes of conquest seemed to be on the eve of realisation.

The terms of the treaty of Belgrade, as finally arranged between the Porte and Austria, were substantially the same as those of the preliminary articles. The treaty between Russia and Turkey provided that the city of Azoph should be demolished, and its territory remain desert, as a border-land for the two empires. Russia was to be at liberty to erect a fortress on the Kuban, but Taganrog was not to be rebuilt. It was expressly provided by the third article of the treaty that Russia should keep up no fleet either in the Sea of Azoph, or in the Black Sea, and that she should build no vessels of war on the coast of any part of those seas.[1] She acknowledged the independence of the Kabartas; and a commission was appointed to fix the boundary line between the two empires. This gave Russia an increase of territory on the side of the Ukraine. Khoczin, and the other conquests of Russia in Moldavia and Bessarabia, were restored; and the treaty gave to the subjects of both the Turkish and Russian sovereigns assurance of pardon for anything done by them during the war.

Such was the peace of Belgrade, one of the most honourable and advantageous for Turkey that she has ever made with European powers. It marks the reign of Sultan Mahmoud I. with lustre, which is the more conspicuous from the contrast between this pacification, and the humiliating and calamitous character of the treaties, by which subsequent struggles of the House of Othman with its European neighbours have been concluded.

The evil day seemed now to be long deferred. A period of rest from the perils of war, unusually long in Ottoman history, intervenes between the signature of Turkey's treaties with Austria and

[1] See Von Hammer, vol. iv. p. 365.

Russia in 1739, and the calamitous renewal of her strife with the latter power in 1768. Not that these twenty-nine years were seasons of perfect calm. A war with Persia broke out in 1743, but was terminated in 1746 by a treaty which made little change in the old arrangements between the two empires, that had been fixed in the reign of Amurath IV. There were from time to time the customary numbers of tumults and insurrections in various territories of the Sublime Porte; and the governors of remote provinces occasionally assumed practical independence, disregarding the Sultan's commands, though professing allegiance to him, and handing down their power from father to son, as if they were hereditary potentates in their own right. These disorders were sometimes quelled, and sometimes overlooked, according to the relative strength and weakness, vigilance and supineness, of the central government and the insubordinate provincials.[1] The most serious of these internal disturbances of the empire were those that became chronic in Egypt, proving that the magnificent conquest of Selim the Inflexible was gradually passing away from the feeble grasp of his successors.

The latter part of the reign of Sultan Mahmoud I. is made memorable not only in Turkish history, but in the general history of Mahometanism, by the rise and rapid increase of the sect of the Wahabites in Arabia. These Puritans of Islam (of which they claimed to be the predestined reformers and sole true disciples) were so named after their founder, Abdul Wahab, which means " The Servant of the All-Disposer." Abdul Wahab, was born at Alaynah, in Arabia, near the end of the seventeenth century of the Christian era, and about the beginning of the twelfth century after the Hejira His father was Sheikh of his village, and young Abdul Wahab was educated in the divinity schools at Bassorah, where he made rapid progress in Mahometan learning, and at the same time grew convinced that the creed of the Prophet had been overlaid by a foul heap of superstition, and that he himself was called on to become its reformer. He returned to Arabia, where, fearless of danger, and unbaffled by temporary failure, he proclaimed his stern denunciations of the prevalent tenets and practices of the Mosque and State. He inveighed particularly against the worship of saints, which had grown up among the Mahometans, against their pilgrimages to supposed holy places, and against their indulgence in several pleasures which the Koran prohibited, especially that foul form of profligacy, which had become almost nationalised among the

[1] See Porter's Turkey by Larpent, vol. i. p. 270.

Turks and other chief peoples of the East. He at first met with ridicule and persecution from those to whom he preached; but he gradually made converts; and at length his doctrines were adopted by Mohammed Ben Sououd, the Sheikh of the powerful tribe of the Messalikhs, who at the same time married Abdul Wahab's daughter. The new sect now became a formidable political and military body: Abdul Wahab continuing to be its spiritual chief, but the active duties of military command being committed to Ben Sououd, who enforced the new faith by the sword, as had been done previously by the Prophet and the early Caliphs. Aziz, the son, and Sououd, the grandson of Mohammed Ben Sououd, continued the same career of armed proselytism with increased fervour; and the Wahabite sect spread through every region of Arabia. The attempts of successive Sultans and Pachas to quell this heresy and rebellion were vain, until the late Pacha of Egypt, Mehemet Ali, undertook the task. He overthrew the temporal empire of the Wahabites, and sent their last Emir in chains to Constantinople, where he was beheaded in 1818. But the Wahabite doctrines are said still to prevail among many of the Bedouin tribes.

The pacific policy maintained by Turkey towards Austria upon the death of the Emperor Charles VI. in 1740, is the more honourable to the Ottoman nation, by reason of the contrast between it and the lawless rapacity, which was shown by nearly all the Christian neighbours of the dominions of the young Austrian sovereign, Maria Theresa. The King of Prussia, the Elector of Bavaria, the Elector of Saxony, and the Kings of France, Spain, and Sardinia, agreed to dismember the Austrian Empire; and began the war of spoliation (called the war of the Austrian Succession), which was terminated by the peace of Aix-la-Chapelle, in 1748. Sultan Mahmoud not only scrupulously abstained from taking any part against Austria, the old enemy of his House, but he offered his mediation to terminate the hostilities which raged between the powers of Christendom. With equal justice and prudence the Turks took care not to become entangled in the other great European contest, which followed that of the Austrian Succession after no very long interval; and which, from the period of its duration (1756-1763) is known in history as the Seven Years' War.

Sultan Mahmoud I. had died (1754) before the outbreak of this last-mentioned contest; but his brother and successor, Othman III., adhered to the same system of moderation and non-interference which his predecessor had established; and he thus preserved peace for the Ottoman Empire during his three years' reign, from 1754 to 1757. He was succeeded by Sultan Mustapha III., the son of Sultan Achmet III. The name of Mustapha has always been accompanied in Turkish history by calamity and defeat; and we now approach the time, when, under the third Sultan of that inauspicious designation, the struggle between the Porte and Russia was resumed, with even heavier disasters to Turkey than those which she endured when she strove against Austria and Prince Eugene in the reign of Sultan Mustapha II.

The first years, however, of Mustapha III. were not unpromising or unprosperous. The administration of the affairs of the empire was directed by the Grand Vizier Raghib Pacha, a minister, not perhaps equal to the great Ottoman statesmen, Sokolli and the second and third Kiuprilis, but a man of sterling integrity, and of high diplomatic abilities. He turned the attention of the Sultan (who showed a perilous restlessness of spirit) to the construction of public works of utility and splendour. The most important of these undertakings was the project, so often formed, and so often abandoned, of making a canal which should give a communication between the Black Sea and the Gulf of Nicomedia, in the Sea of Marmora, without passing through the Bosphorus. For this purpose it was proposed to dig a channel from the eastern extremity of the Gulf of Nicomedia to the Lake of Sabandja; and to form another from the Lake of Sabandja to the river Sakaria, which falls into the Black Sea. The commercial advantages of such a canal would be great; and the Turks would be enabled to use the Lake of Sabandja as a naval depot of complete security, and of ample capacity for fleets of the greatest magnitude, which could rapidly issue thence as emergencies required either into the Euxine or the Propontis. This mode of uniting the two seas had been attempted before the commencement of the Ottoman Empire, twice by the Kings of Bithynia, and once by the Emperor Trajan. Three Sultans, Solyman the Great, Amurath III., and Mahomet IV., had commenced the same enterprise before Mustapha III. But it had never been completed; though the distances to be trenched through are inconsiderable, and the engineering difficulties presented by the character and elevations of the soil are said to be few and trivial. Sultan Mustapha abandoned the project in 1759, after having caused great interest and excitement among the French and English residents at Constantinople, who were anxious for the accomplishment of the design, and who in vain urged the Turks to persevere. Von Hammer observes that the realisation of this great work can then only be hoped for, when it is taken up by European energy and skill.[1]

The chief efforts of Raghib Pacha himself were directed to the strengthening of Turkey against the inveterate hostility of the courts of Vienna and St. Petersburg, by alliances with other states of Christendom. The results of the War of Succession, and of the Seven Years' War, had been to bring Prussia forward as a new power of the first magnitude in Europe. Prussia, from her geographical position, had nothing to gain by any losses which might befall Turkey; and both Austria and Russia had been bitter and almost deadly foes to the great sovereign of the House of Brandenburg, Frederic II. A treaty therefore between Prussia and Turkey seemed desirable for the interests of both states; and many attempts had been made to effect one, before Raghib Pacha held the seals as Grand Vizier. At length in 1761, the envoy of Frederic II. to Constantinople signed a treaty of amity between Prussia and the Porte, similar to treaties which the Turkish Court had already concluded with Sweden, Naples, and Denmark. But Raghib Pacha's design was to convert these preliminary articles into a treaty of offensive and defensive alliance. The English ambassador strove earnestly to forward this scheme, while the ministers of Austria and Russia endeavoured to retard and baffle it. Considerable progress had been made in the negotiations, when the death of Raghib Pacha in 1763 put an end to a project, which, if successful, would certainly have been followed by a new war with Austria. In that war the Prussians would have co-operated with the Turks, and it might have materially varied the whole current of subsequent Ottoman history.

[1] Von Hammer, vol. iv. p. 517.

CHAPTER XX.

RUSSIAN ATTACK ON POLAND—TURKISH REMONSTRANCES—WAR
WITH RUSSIA—OPINIONS OF EUROPE—DEFEATS OF THE TURKISH
ARMIES—RUSSIAN FLEET IN THE MEDITERRANEAN—BATTLE OF
TCHESME—EXPLOITS OF HASSAN OF ALGIERS—LOSS OF THE
CRIMEA — NEGOTIATIONS — WAR RENEWED — SILISTRIA AND
SHUMLA DEFENDED—DEATH OF MUSTAPHA III.—ABDUL HAMID
SULTAN—TREATY OF KAINARDJI.[1]

AFTER the death of Raghib Pacha in 1763, Sultan Mustapha III.
governed for himself. He was a prince of considerable industry
and talent, and honestly desirous of promoting the interests of
the Ottoman Empire ; but he was hasty and headstrong, and he
often proved unfortunate during the latter part of his reign in his
selection of councillors and of commanders. And the sceptre of
the power most inimical and most formidable to Turkey was now
grasped by one of the most ambitious, the most unscrupulous, and
also the ablest sovereigns, that ever swayed the vast resources of
the Russian Empire. Catherine II. (who has been termed with
such terrible accuracy both as to her public and private character,
the Semiramis of the North) reigned at St. Petersburg. A military revolution had placed her on the throne instead of her weak
and pacific husband ; and it was only by preserving the favour of
the Russian army, and by encouraging the fanaticism of the
Russian people, that she could hope to preserve her royalty or her
life. The military chiefs, by whom her husband had been murdered, and who were her own personal favourites, the Orloffs, and
their associates were eager for hostilities in which they might
gratify their rapacity and pride, and display the courage which
was their only merit. The Porte watched with anxiety and
alarm the aggressive but insidious policy, which was pursued
towards every weak state that was within the sphere of Russian
influence. That policy was to foment disturbances and civil war ;
to interfere in the pretended character of a friend of the weaker

[1] Von Hammer, books 70-72.

party; to sow the seeds of new and worse dissensions; and then to make the misery and anarchy, which Russian arts had produced, the pretext for the subjugation of the exhausted state by Russian arms.   It was in Poland, "that commonwealth of common woe,"[1] that this Muscovite Machiavelism was chiefly practised during the first years of Catherine's reign.   Prussia, unhappily for herself and Europe, became the accomplice of Russia against Poland.   Frederick II. no longer sought the alliance of Turkey against his old enemies at Vienna and St. Petersburg; but concluded, in 1764, a treaty with Catherine, by which the two parties mutually pledged themselves to maintain each other in possession of their respective territories; and agreed, that if either power were attacked, the other should supply an auxiliary force of 10,000 foot and 1000 horse.   But it was expressly provided that if Russia were assailed by the Turks, or Prussia by the French, the aid should be sent in money.   There was also a secret article to this treaty, which was directed against Polish independence, and which has earned for this confederacy between Russia and Prussia, the name of "the Unholy Alliance of 1764, whence, as from a Pandora's box, have sprung all the evils that have afflicted and desolated Europe from that time until the present day."[2]

The Ottoman Court protested continually but vainly against the occupation of Poland by Russian and Prussian troops; against the disgraceful circumstances of fraud and oppression, under which the election of Catherine's favourite, Stanislaus Poniatowski, as king, was forced upon the Poles; and against the dictatorship

---

[1] The phrase is Sir Walter Ralegh's, applied by him to Ireland.

[2] "This was that unholy alliance which, from 1764 till the present day, has proved the source of all the misfortunes of the European nations, because it has served as a model for all the treaties which have been since concluded, by means of which the fate and internal administration of the weaker states have become wholly dependent on the compacts, arms, and diplomatists of powerful nations.   This first treaty was against the Poles; and those by which it has been followed, and which have been drawn up after its model, have been concluded against the liberties of the nations; and in this way the seeds of discontent and discord between the governed and those who govern, have continued to grow and fructify till the present day.   As soon as the rights of the bayonet were once made good against Poland and Turkey, they were also regarded as good against the freedom and rights of the people. The oppressed have gnashed their teeth in despair, and waited for the visitations of the divine vengeance, which has followed close upon the footsteps of those insolent and tyrannical oppressors for five and twenty years, and will one day overtake them as sure as the world is under the superintendence of an overruling Providence."—Schlosser's " History of the Eighteenth Century."

which the Russian general Repnin exercised at Warsaw. The Turkish remonstrances were eluded with excuses so shallow, as to show the contempt with which the Russians must now have learned to regard their Ottoman neighbours, both in diplomatic and warlike capacities. Von Hammer expressly writes, that "the exchange of notes between the Turkish, Prussian, and Russian ministers on the affairs of Poland till January, 1768, is a singular proof of the simplicity of the Ottoman diplomacy, and of the duplicity of that of Russia and Prussia at this epoch. The Turkish Government, through their interpreters, continued from time to time to put the most pressing questions to the ministers of these courts, seeking for an explanation of the deeds of violence which were taking place in Poland. The Russian resident always pretended that he heard nothing of such events, or declared that these were merely measures for the protection of the freedom of the republic, and for the maintenance of solemn engagements."

Sultan Mustapha and his Viziers at last felt that they were treated as dupes and fools; and the indignation raised at Constantinople against Russia was violent. This was augmented by the attacks made by the Russian troops on the fugitive Poles of the independent party, who had taken refuge within the Turkish frontier; and who sallying thence carried on a desultory warfare against their enemies, which the Russians retaliated at every opportunity, without heeding whether they overtook the Polish bands beyond or within the Ottoman dominions. At last the Russian general Weissman followed a body of the confederated Poles into the town of Balta, on the confines of Bessarabia, which belonged to the Sultan's vassal, the Tartar Khan of the Crimea. The Russians besieged the town, took it by storm, plundered, and laid it in ashes. Turkey had received proofs of Russian hostility in other regions. There had been revolts in Montenegro and in Georgia, and there had been troubles in the Crimea, all of which were aggravated, if not created, by Russian agency. The Divan resolved, on the 4th of October, 1768, that Russia had broken the peace between the two empires, and that a war against her would be just and holy. But it was determined that the Grand Vizier should have a final interview with M. d'Obresskoff, the Russian minister at Constantinople, and inform him that peace might be preserved, but solely on condition that Russia should bind herself under the guarantee of her four allies, Denmark, Prussia, England, and Sweden, to abstain from all future interference with elections to the crown of Poland, or in the religious differences in that kingdom; that she should withdraw her troops from Poland, and no longer hinder the Poles from enjoying full liberty and independence. Obresskoff was summoned to an audience by the Grand Vizier, who interrupted the complimentary speeches of the Russian diplomatist by showing him a paper, by which Obresskoff had pledged himself on behalf of the Czarina, four years previously, that the Russian army of observation in Poland should be reduced to 7000 men, whereas it had been augmented to 30,000. Obresskoff replied, that this last number was exaggerated, but owned that there were 28,000 Russian soldiers in Poland.

"Traitor, perjurer !" cried the Vizier. "Hast thou not owned thy faithlessness ? Dost thou not blush before God and man for the atrocities which thy countrymen are committing in a land which is not theirs ? Are not the cannons, which have overthrown a palace of the Khan of the Tartars, Russian cannons ? "

The Vizier required him to sign instantly a paper containing the pledge on which the Divan had determined. Obresskoff replied that he had not sufficient authority for such an act. The declaration of war was then pronounced, and the Russian minister was sent to the prison of the Seven Towers ; an impolitic as well as unjustifiable act of violence on the part of the Turks, which enabled the Russian Empress to represent herself to the world as the injured party ; although the war had been sought by her, and all the acts of aggression which caused it, had been deliberately planned by the Russian Cabinet.

The general feeling of Europe was favourable to the Empress. England in particular, though she offered her mediation to prevent the Turkish war, was, at this period and for many years afterwards desirous of seeing the power of Russia augmented, and of uniting her with Prussia, Denmark, Sweden, Holland, and England herself, in a great Northern Alliance in opposition to the combination of France and Spain under the House of Bourbon. This design had been formed by Lord Chatham (then Mr. Pitt) during the Seven Years' War; and it continued to be a favourite project of English statesmen. The French minister Choiseul naturally regarded Russia with very different feelings. But that great statesman also discerned how necessary it was to watch jealously the growth of the Muscovite power, not only for the sake of French interests, but for the sake of the general commonweal of Europe. Choiseul now, at the outbreak of the war between Russia and Turkey in 1763, laboured anxiously to make the English ministry understand the true character of Russian power and ambition. His efforts were vain, but one of his state papers on

the subject deserves citation.   Referring to the well-known desire
of England for a Northern Alliance, Choiseul said :

"The English Secretary of State is in the wrong: he does not
look at these objects from the higher point of view, which should
engage the attention of a great minister.   Nothing can be more
dangerous for the happiness and repose of humanity, nor more to
be feared for the principal powers of Europe, than the success of
the arms and the ambitious projects of Russia.   Far from seeking,
on such a supposition, the alliance and the friendship of the Empress, it would become their most essential interest to unite to
diminish her strength and destroy her preponderance.   If the
balance of power, that unmeaning word, invented by William III.,
on becoming King of England, to raise all Europe against France,
could have a just application, and if this pretended balance of
power could be annihilated, it would be by the prodigious increase
of the material and moral strength of Russia.   She is now labouring to enslave the south ; and she will next encroach on the
liberty of the north ; unless an effective check is seasonably put
to her inordinate passion of despotism.

"Instead of contributing to the aggrandisement of Russia, the
principal courts ought jointly to restrain her ambition and her
cupidity, which may in some respects realise the chimerical idea,
once attributed to France, of aiming at universal monarchy."[1]

However just their cause, the Turks began the war too soon.
When Sultan Mustapha issued his declaration of hostilities against
Russia in the autumn of 1768, his anger had got the mastery over
his judgment.   He should have endured the affronts offered to
him a little longer, and not taken up arms before the summer of
the following year.   He might then have had the full force of his
empire in readiness to make good his threats.   But it was impossible to bring his Asiatic troops together during the winter ;
and the opening of the campaign on the Dniester and Danube was
thus delayed till the spring of 1769 ; a delay which enabled
the Russians to make ample preparations for assailing Turkey on
almost every part of her northern frontier, both in Europe and
Asia.   Neither were the Turkish fortresses in a proper state of
repair, nor sufficiently stored, when the war was proclaimed at
Constantinople.   The Ottoman government endeavoured to make
good these defects during the winter ; but the spring found the
Turkish equipments still far from a due state of efficiency.

One bold leader, on the side of the Moslems, and almost the

---

[1] Choiseul to Châtelet, April 16, 1769, cited in Bancroft's "America,"
vol. iii. p. 298.

only one who displayed any warlike abilities in support of the Crescent during the first years of this disastrous war, made a vigorous onslaught on the southern provinces of the Czarina's empire, long before the other generals on either side thought it possible to bring troops into the field.   This was the Tartar Khan of the Crimea, Krim Ghirai.   Before the end of January, 1769, the Tartar chief collected at the ruins of Balta, which the Russians had destroyed in the preceding summer, 100,000 cavalry.   With this vast force of hardy marauders, Krim Ghirai crossed the river Boug, and then sent one detachment towards the Doneck, and another towards Orel, while the main body under his own command swept over the Russian province of New Servia.   Khan Ghirai was accompanied in this expedition by Baron de Tott, one of the ablest (though not the least vaunting) of the numerous officers and agents, whom the French minister, Choiseul, had sent into Turkey to encourage and assist the Ottomans.   De Tott has minutely described the predatory activity and adroitness of the wild host which he marched with, and the stern discipline under which they were kept amid all the seeming license of the campaign by the military genius of their chief.   For fourteen days Krim Ghirai rode at his will through Southern Russia, with drums beating and colours flying, while his wild horsemen swept the land with an ever-widening torrent of devastation.   The Khan and his guest, the Baron, fared like the rest of the Tartars.   Their food was meat, sodden and bruised between the saddle and the horses' backs, a mess of fermented mares' milk, smoked horse-hams, caviare, boutargue, and other Tartar aliments ; but wine of Tokay was served to the guest in vessels of gold.   The Khan camped and marched in the middle of his army, which was arranged in twenty columns.   Before him waved, together with the Turkish and Tartar standards, the colours of the Ynad Cossacks, who had abandoned the Russian Empire in the time of Peter the Great, under the guidance of the Cossack Ignacius, and who had since been called Ygnad, or Ynad, which means the Mutineers.   By their influence, Krim Ghirai prevailed on the Zaporofkian Cossacks to revolt against the authority of the commandant of the fortress of Elizabethgrod.   A prince of the Lezghis also joined the Crimean Khan, and offered a reinforcement of 30,000 men to the Sultan's armies, on condition that certain honours should be paid him by the Sultan and the Grand Vizier, and that he should retain at the peace all the territories out of which he could drive the Russians.   Had Krim Ghirai lived a few years, or even months, longer, it is probable that his ascendency over the wild warriors of these regions, and his marvellous skill in handling irregular troops, would have materially changed the course of the war. De Tott admired the severe discipline which he maintained, while he permitted and encouraged his followers to develop against the enemy to the utmost their astonishing talent both for acquiring booty, and for preserving it when taken. But, woe to the Tartar who pillaged without the Khan's permission, or who offered any outrage against the Khan's command ! Some Noghai Tartars in the army having insulted a crucifix, received each a hundred blows of the stick in front of the church where they committed this offence ; and De Tott saw others, who had plundered a Polish village without orders, tied to the tails of their own horses and dragged along till they expired.

Krim Ghirai died within a month after his return from this expedition against Russia. It was believed that he was poisoned by a Greek physician named Siropulo, an agent of the Prince of Wallachia, against whom he had been vainly cautioned by De Tott. The Porte appointed, as the Khan's successor, Dewlet Ghirai, a prince without spirit or capacity. These were deficiencies, in which he too closely resembled the Grand Vizier and the other leaders of the Sultan's forces. Meanwhile, the Empress Catherine and her generals had been preparing for the war with their characteristic energy. One Russian army, 65,000 strong, was collected in Podolia, under the command of Prince Alexander Michailovitsch Gallitzin, who was directed to besiege and capture the city of Khoczin, and then to occupy Moldavia. The second, under General Count Peter Alexandrewitsch Romanzoff, was to protect the frontiers of Russia between the Dnieper and the Sea of Azoph, and to reconstruct the fortresses of Azoph and Taganrog, which had been razed in pursuance of the treaty of Belgrade. A third army of from 10,000 to 11,000 men was to occupy Poland, and prevent the Poles from giving any assistance to Turkey. A fourth army, under Major-General Medem, advanced from Zarizin into the Kabartas and the Kuban ; and a fifth, under General Todleben, was directed upon Tiflis, in order to attack Erzeroum and Trebizond in concert with the Georgian princes of Karthli, Mingrelia, Gouriel, and Imeritia, who had submitted themselves to the sovereignty of Russia. At the same time, money, arms, ammunition, and officers were sent to the Montenegrins : and those warlike mountaineers were set in action against the Turkish forces in Bosnia. While the Grand Vizier was slowly moving with the Sultan's main army from Constantinople to the Danube, Gallitzin passed the Dniester. and made an unsuccessful attempt upon

Khoczin; after which he retreated across the Dniester. Indeed, so far as Gallitzin was concerned, the sarcasm of Frederick II. of Prussia, on the conduct of this war, was well deserved. He called it a triumph of the one-eyed over the blind. But among the other Russian commanders and generals of division were Romanzoff, Weissman, Bauer, Kamenski, and, above all, Suwarrow, in whom Frederick himself would have found formidable antagonists.

The Turkish Grand Vizier, Emin Mohammed, was the Sultan's son-in-law. How far he was qualified for the duties of generalissimo, may be judged from the report of the proceedings at a council of war, which the Turkish historian, Wassif, has preserved. The Vizier had reached Isakdji (on the lower part of the Danube, near Ismail), early in May. He halted there twenty days, to complete his magazines of provisions and military stores. He then summoned his generals together and addressed them in these words :—" On what point do you think that I ought to direct the march of the army ? I have no experience in war : it is for you, therefore, to determine what are the operations which are fit for us to undertake, and which present the most favourable chances for the arms of the Sublime Porte. Speak, then, without reserve, and enlighten me with your counsels." All the generals sat for some time silent, and stared in astonishment at the Grand Vizier and each other. At length Schedh Osman Effendi began a long discourse, the pith of which was, that inasmuch as the enemy had made an unsuccessful attempt on the side of Khoczin, it was probable that they would next show themselves on the side of Bender. When the Grand Vizier comprehended the speaker's meaning, he interrupted his oratory by exclaiming, " Enough, enough ! everybody must have time to speak." Some of the officers then recommended a march on Khoczin, thinking that Oczakof and Bender were strong enough to be left to their own resources. Others thought that the wisest plan was first to pass the Danube, and then act according to circumstances. The Grand Vizier approved of this policy ; and the Turkish army crossed the Danube and advanced as far as Khandepé on the Pruth, between Khoczin and Jassy. The deficiency of provisions, and the swarms of gnats and musquitos which tormented the Turks in that locality, made the Grand Vizier change his line of operations and march towards Bender. They halted at Jassipede (June 9, 1769), where they found the supplies of food equally scarce, and the gnats and musquitos equally abundant as at Khandepé. Meanwhile, Gallitzin had reorganised his army, and received large reinforcements in Podolia. The wretched government of Poland had been compelled by the Russians to declare war against Turkey, and Sultan Mustapha and his Mufti issued a Fetva, by which the Turkish troops were directed to attack Poland and treat it as a hostile country. A series of operations and skirmishes in the neighbourhood of Khoczin followed, in which Prince Gallitzin and the Grand Vizier rivalled each other in imbecility. At last, the numerous complaints which the Sultan received against his son-in-law, made him recall Emin Mohammed, who was beheaded at Adrianople in August. Ali Moldowandji, who had distinguished himself in some engagements near Khoczin, succeeded Emin Mohammed in the Grand Vizierate. Ali had been a Bostandji, or gardener in the palace, and had been sent on an expedition against some gangs of robbers who infested the communicatio s between the northern European provinces and the capital. In that enterprise, Ali captured a number of Moldavian vagrant omen, whom, with their children, he sold as slaves. It was from this incident that he acquired his surname of Ali the Moldavian. On receiving the chief command of the Ottoman forces, he made several bold attacks on the Russians near Khoczin, and endeavoure l to penetrate into Poland. Ultimately, the Turks were unsucc ssful, and Khoczin surrendered on the 18th September, 1769. The Turkish army was now utterly disorganised, and hurried back to the left bank of the Danube, recrossing that river at Isakdji, y the same bridge of boats that had been constructed for their pa sage at the beginning of the campaign. The Empress had now recalled Gallitzin, and given the chief command to Romanzoff. Under that bold and able chief, the Russians speedily overran Moldavia, defeating the Turks at Galacz and at Jassy. Romanzoff entered the capital of the principality, and received there, in the name of the Empress Catherine, the homage of the Moldavian Boyards. The Russian influence speedily extended to Wallachia. On hearing of these events, the Sultan Mustapha, and his rash and violent adviser, the chief Mufti, published a Fetva commanding the slaughter of all Moldavians and Wallachians who had submitted to the enemy; and giving authority also for the confiscation of their property, and the selling of their wives and children into slavery. The chief effect of this foolish and tyrannical edict was, as the Turkish historian, Wassif, himself observes, to bind the Moldavians and Wallachians more firmly to the cause of Russia. Some of its immediate results were, that the Wallachian Boyards, at Bucharest, solemnly placed the insignia of government in the hands of Russian commissioners, took the oath of allegiance to the Empress Catherine, and sent a deputation to St. Petersburg to protest their loyalty and implore her Imperial protection.

The same Mufti, Pirizadi Osman Effendi, who was the author of the Fetvas against the Poles and the Moldo-Wallachians, endeavoured also in his rabid fanaticism to excite the Sultan to a general massacre of all the Christians in the empire. This atrocious project had twice before been mooted, in the reign of Selim I. and Mahomet III. It was now revived for the last time; but the Mufti found no seconders or sympathisers in the Divan. He was universally abhorred for his violence and cruelty; and his death at the end of the first year of the war was the subject of general rejoicing to his brethren, and to the great body of the Mussulman as well as the Christian subjects of the empire.

In Trans-Caucasia and Armenia the Russian generals Todleben and Medem had been uniformly successful, and had received in the Empress's name homage and oaths of allegiance from great numbers of the inhabitants. But Catherine had resolved on carrying out her project of conquering Turkey by means of its own Christian population on a bolder and grander scale in another part of the Ottoman dominions. The designs of Peter the Great and Marshal Münnich to arouse the Greeks against their Turkish master had never been forgotten at St. Petersburg, and Catherine now revived them with enthusiasm. The aged Marshal Münnich (who during the reign of the Empress Elizabeth had been banished to Siberia) was at Catherine's Court, and eagerly encouraged the Czarina to renew what had been termed his "Oriental Project." Russian emissaries had long been actively employed in the Morea, and other parts of Southern Turkey in Europe; and the Empress received numerous assurances of the devotion of the Greeks to the crown, and of their eagerness to rise against their Mahometan oppressors. The Empress and her favourites, the Orloffs, resolved not to wait till their land armies had effected the perilous and doubtful march from the Dniester to the vicinity of Greece, but to send a Russian fleet with troops into the Mediterranean, and thus assail the Sultan in the very heart of his power, at the same time that he was hard pressed on the Danube, in the Crimea, and in upper Asia. The state of Egypt, where Ali Bey had made himself virtual sovereign, and had discarded even the appearance of allegiance to the Porte, furnished an additional motive for the expedition. It was thought that Greece, Egypt, and Syria might be rent from the House of Othman in a single summer; and Constantinople itself was supposed not to be safe, if a sudden and bold attack were to be made through the ill-fortified channel of the Dardanelles and the Sea of Marmora. Towards the end of the summer of 1760 a Russian fleet of twelve ships of the line, twelve frigates, and a large number of transports carrying troops, left the port of Cronstadt for the Mediterranean. Count Alexif Orloff had the chief command of the expedition, and was nominated by Catherine, Generalissimo of the Russian armies, and High Admiral of the Russian fleets in the Mediterranean Sea. Admiral Spiridoff commanded the fleet under Orloff; but the real leaders in all the naval operations were Admiral Elphinstone, Captain Gregg, and other English officers, some of whom were to be found in almost every ship of the Czarina's fleet.[1] The equipment of this expedition was attended by great boasting and ostentation in the Russian Court, and in the numerous circles of the literary men of the age, with whom Catherine loved to correspond, and who debased their genius and their profession by heaping flatteries on her character, and rhapsodising glory to her arms. The report that a Russian fleet was on its way along the Atlantic to liberate Greece spread as far even as Constantinople. But the Turkish statesmen refused all credence to the rumour, and would not believe that there could be any communication between the Baltic and the Mediterranean Seas.

The fact of this astounding ignorance is attested by Wassif, the Turkish historian, himself. When afterwards, early in 1770, indisputable tidings reached the Divan that the Russian ships were actually approaching Greece, the Ottoman ministers made a formal complaint to the representative of Venice that the Venetian government had permitted the Russian fleet to pass into the Mediterranean by way of the Adriatic. Von Hammer, in recording this, mentions that a similar instance of Turkish ignorance came under his own notice in 1800, when he acted as interpreter to Sir Sidney Smith in an interview with the Grand Vizier Yousouf Sia, respecting the expulsion of the French from Egypt. That Ottoman grandee denied the possibility of the English auxiliaries from India reaching Egypt by the way of the Red Sea. How lamentably had the Turks of the eighteenth century degenerated from their ancestors in the time of Solyman the Magnificent, when Turkish admirals surveyed the Archipelago, the Mediterranean, and the Indian Seas, and published scientific

---

[1] Schlosser, "Hist. Eighteenth Century," vol. iv. The Russian fleet never could have reached the Mediterranean, had it not been for the assistance which it received in the English ports. See the full account of the expedition in Emerson Tennent's "Modern Greece," vol. ii., and see the Oczakof debates in the House of Commons in 1792.

as well as practical treatises on their geography, and on every matter connected with their navigation![1]

At the end of February, 1770, the Russian fleet was off the Morea; and Orloff landed among the Mainotes, who rose fiercely in arms against their Turkish masters. The force of Russian troops, which Orloff disembarked, was utterly insufficient to maintain order or discipline among those savage mountaineers and their countrymen from the rest of Greece, who also joined him in large numbers. They practised the most revolting cruelties upon all the Turks whom they could overpower in the open country or less defensible towns; Misitra, the chief place in Maina, in particular, was the scene of fearful atrocities, afterwards still more fearfully revenged. Four hundred Turks were slaughtered there in cold blood; and Ottoman children, torn from their mothers' breasts, were carried up the tops of the minarets, and thence dashed to the ground. At Arkadia the Turkish garrison surrendered to the Russian general, Dolgorouki, on the faith of articles of capitulation which guaranteed their lives. Dolgorouki's Greek followers slew them all, and burnt the town to the ground. In the stronger cities the Turks repelled all the assaults of Orloff and his Greek brigands. He was obliged to raise the siege of Modon and Coron; and on the 8th of April the Albanian troops, which several of the Turkish Beys had drawn together from beyond the isthmus, encountered the main body of the Russo-Greek force near Tripolitza. The Greeks thought themselves so sure of victory, that they had brought women with them, with sacks ready to be loaded with the spoil of the Mussulmans. But they were utterly defeated, and massacred without mercy in the flight. After having issued some vaunting manifestoes, in which he called on the Greeks to imitate the example of their fellow-Christians of the true church in Moldavia and Wallachia, who, he said, had risen to the number of 600,000 in defence of their faith and freedom, Orloff reimbarked his troops, and the Turkish Seraskier, Mouhinzadi, who had commanded at Tripolitza, assumed the title of "Fatihi Mora," which meant that he had reconquered the Morea.

At sea, the Russian undertakings were more successful, because (it is a German historian who makes the statement) they were under the direction of Englishmen. On the 7th of July, 1770, Orloff's fleet came in sight of the Turkish near the Isle of Scio. Sultan Mustapha had, throughout his reign, paid especial attention to his navy; and the Turkish Capitan Pacha, Hosameddin, had

[1] See *suprà*, p. 179.

now under his command a force which the Turkish writers describe as two corvettes, fifteen galleons, five xebecques, and eight galliotes; it comprised one ship of 100 guns, one of 96, four of 84, one of 74, one of 70, and six of 60. The Russians had eight ships of the line and seven frigates. The Turks were worsted in the action, which was chiefly memorable for the desperate bravery shown by one of the Sultan's admirals, named Hassan of Algiers. This man had been born on the frontiers of Persia, and was, while a child, sold as a slave. He had been a boatman, a soldier, a corsair, and had acquired such reputation in the Algerine squadrons as to be raised to the rank of Port Admiral of Algiers. A quarrel with the Dey sent him to Italy as a refugee. Thence he found his way to Constantinople, and acquired the favour of Raghib Pacha. At the battle of Scio, while his superior officer kept at a distance from the enemy, Hassan ran his ship alongside that of the Russian admiral, and fought yard-arm and yard-arm, till both vessels caught fire by the Russian hand-grenades, and blew up together. Spiridoff and Theodore Orloff escaped in the Russian ship's boats before the explosion, in which 700 of their men perished. Hassan kept the deck to the last; and, though severely injured, escaped with life, and swam to shore. The defeated Turkish ships took refuge in the port of Tchesmé, the ancient Cyssus, where the Roman fleet, B.C. 191, defeated that of King Antiochus. Seeing the Turkish ships cooped together in this narrow bay, the English officers on board Orloff's fleet formed and executed the bold project of attacking them and burning them as they lay on the very night after the battle. To use the words of the German historian, Schlosser, "The whole merit of the execution of this plan was due to the English. It was three Englishmen who conducted the whole of the exploit at Tchesmé; Elphinstone blockaded the Turkish ships, Gregg directed the cannonade, and Lieutenant Dugdale was intrusted with the dangerous commission of guiding the fire-ship by which the fleet was to be set in flames. At the very moment of departure, the Russians who were with Dugdale on board the fire-ship left him exposed to the danger, leapt into the water and swam away; he alone steered the ship, and set fire to one of the Turkish vessels, which rapidly conveyed the flames to the other ships of the fleet. Only one ship of fifty guns and five xebecques remained unconsumed, and these were carried away by the Russians. The small town of Tchesmé, also, with its fort, batteries, and cannon, was taken."

After this signal triumph (which procured for Count Orloff the

surname of Tschesmeski), Elphinstone proposed that the Russian
fleet should instantly sail for the Dardanelles, force the passage,
and then at once proceed to bombard Constantinople.[1] Such a
bold stroke would probably have been successful, as the panic
caused at Constantinople by the tidings from Tchesmé was
extreme, and the fortifications both of the straits and the capital
had been neglected. But Orloff hesitated and lost time, while
the Sultan despatched his late Vizier, Moldowandji (who had
been recalled from the Danube and deprived of the seals),
together with Baron De Tott, to strengthen and defend the Dardanelles.   The proceedings of the two officers were characteristic.
Moldowandji began by whitewashing the old walls of the forts, to
make the Russians think that the works, which looked so bright
and clean, must be new or newly repaired.   The Frank engineer
erected four batteries, two on the European and two on the
Asiatic side, so as to place any vessel, that endeavoured to pass,
under a cross fire.   An attempt which Orloff at last made to
destroy the first Turkish fort was ineffectual ; and the Russian chief
then resolved to make himself master of Lemnos, and formed the
siege of the castle of that island.   After sixty days' investment,
the Turkish garrison offered to capitulate ; and, according to some
accounts, the articles were actually prepared, and hostages given
for their execution, when a daring exploit of Hassan of Algiers
saved Lemnos, and drove Orloff discomfited from his prey.   After
the sea-fight off Scio, Hassan had gone to Constantinople to be
cured of his wounds.   As soon as he was capable of exertion, he
obtained an interview with the new Grand Vizier, and offered to
raise the siege of Lemnos.   He asked for no troops, or ships, or
artillery, but merely for permission to collect volunteers among
the population of Constantinople, for sabres and pistols to arm
them with, and for some light vessels to take them to Lemnos.
With 4000 such volunteers he said he would save the island.
Hassan's reputation was high among the Turks of all ranks ; and
the fanatic rabble of the capital enrolled themselves readily for
this service against the Giaours, under so valiant a chief of the
True Believers.   The French general De Tott felt it his duty to
remonstrate with the Grand Vizier against a proceeding, which
seemed to be so insane, and which was in such palpable contra-
vention of all the rules of war.   The Vizier answered that he also
thought Hassan's scheme absurd, but that it was sure to do good ;
as, if it succeeded, it would save Lemnos ; or, if it failed, it would
rid Constantinople of 4000 rogues and ruffians.   The event

[1] Eton, 186.   Emerson Tennent; vol. ii. p. 367.

showed that the Algerine corsair knew how such work was to be done, better than the Vizier and the Baron. Landing unperceived by the besiegers with his 4000 desperadoes on the eastern side of Lemnos, Hassan, in the grey of the morning of the 10th of October, fell suddenly upon Orloff's lines, sabre and pistol in hand, cut down Russian artillerymen, soldiers, and sailors, in the trenches ; and drove the rest in a panic to their ships, in which they re-embarked, and abandoned the enterprise.

Raised to the chief command of what remained of the Turkish navy, Hassan, within a short time after the deliverance of Lemnos, fought a severe action against Orloff near the port of Monderos, in which each admiral claimed the victory ; but, as Von Hammer observes, it is clear that the superiority was on the side of the Turks, as after the battle Orloff sailed away, having first given up, on Hassan's requisition, the hostages who had been placed in his hands by the garrison of Lemnos. The Russian armament in the Mediterranean effected little during the rest of the war, though it took possession of one of the Greek islands, frequently captured Turkish merchant-vessels, and impeded the communications between the maritime Pachalics and the capital. Orloff endeavoured to sustain the rebellion of Ali Bey of Egypt, and the Sheikh Tahir of Acre against the Porte. He concluded a treaty with the Egyptian insurgent, who at one time was not only master of Egypt and part of Arabia, but occupied Gaza, Jaffa, Jerusalem, and Damascus. Ali was preparing to march into Asia Minor against the Ottomans, where his brother-in-law Abouzeheb betrayed him, and revolted against his authority, as he had revolted against that of the Sultan. Ali Bey was defeated in Egypt by Abouzeheb, and then betook himself to Syria, where, aided by the Russian squadrons, and his friend the Sheikh Tahir of Acre, he maintained for some time the struggle against the Sultan's officers ; but he was at last defeated and taken prisoner in a battle near Sahiliè, where 400 Russians who were in his army perished to a man, except four officers, who were taken prisoners.

So went the war in the South ; but it was on the natural line of contest between Russia and Turkey, in the frontier lands of the weaker of the two empires, that the fortune of the combatants was decided. The inauspicious campaign of 1769 was followed there by others still more disastrous for the Ottoman arms. Moldavia was the scene of the early operations in 1770 ; and before the new Grand Vizier, Khalil Pacha, had reached that province, the Russian general Romanzoff had defeated the advanced bodies of the Turks and Tartars, and driven them in confusion back upon the army with which the Vizier was advancing. Khalil Pacha came in presence of the enemy near Kartal. The Vizier had led and rallied a force of about 30,000 effective troops : with these he intrenched himself in front of the Russian position, while a vast host of Tartars, under Kaplin Ghirai, the new Khan of the Crimea, collected on the other side. Romanzoff's troops were emboldened by repeated victories ; and he knew the disaffection and demoralisation which previous defeats had created among his adversaries.   He led his army in three columns against the Vizier's camp (August 1, 1770), stormed it with inconsiderable loss, and took possession of immense treasures and stores, with which the Ottomans had cumbered themselves, and of their whole artillery, amounting to 160 pieces.   The number of slain on the Turkish side was small, in consequence of the panic haste with which they fled.   The Vizier reassembled a part of his host on the southern side of the Danube ; and the Tartar Khan undertook to provide for the safety of the Turkish fortresses in the Dobruscha and Bessarabia.   But Kaplan Ghirai was as incompetent as his predecessor Dewlet had been ; and fortress after fortress fell before the Russians.   Kilia, Ackerman, and Ismail, surrendered after short sieges ; but at Bender, in Bessarabia, the Tartar population resisted desperately.   The siege lasted two months ; and when the final assault was given (27th September, 1770), although the Russians, by favour of a dark night and the laxity of the Turkish discipline, succeeded in escalading the walls by surprise, the conflict in the streets was maintained with equal fury on both sides for ten hours, and two-thirds of the population perished before the Russians won the town.   Their own loss is said to have been so severe, as to have drawn a caution from the Empress to Count Panin, that it was better not to take such a town than to win it at such a price. Brailow, or Ibrail, on the Danube, also made a gallant defence for eighteen days, and repulsed an assault of the Russians with heavy loss ; but there was no hope of relief for any of the Turkish garrisons on the Dniester or the Danube.   The Grand Vizier's army had disbanded ; and that high commander was left with about 3000 half-starved men to receive tidings of the successive capture of the bulwarks of the empire.   At the close of the campaign all the Turkish fortresses on the Lower Danube were in the power of the Russians, and the line of advance along the coast of the Black Sea was laid open.

A gleam of consolation came this year from the Crimea, where an attempt of the Russians to force the lines of Perekop was defeated. But in the following summer the armies of the Giaours were again directed upon the Crimean peninsula with fatal efficacy; and that splendid conquest of Mahomet II. was reft by Catherine II. from the House of Othman. Another new Khan had been appointed by the Porte, named Selim Ghirai; and the Turkish council of war judged his presence in his own country to be more important than it would be on the south of the Danube. Selim Ghirai accordingly left the Grand Vizier's camp, and repaired to Baghdjiserai, the Tartar capital of the Crimea, and the ancestral residence of its sovereigns. There Selim indulged in the pomps and pleasures of viceroyalty, until he was roused by the startling tidings that Prince Dolgorouki was before Perekop with a Russian army of 30,000 regular troops, and 60,000 Noghai Tartars, who had taken service under the Empress. Selim hurried to defend the isthmus; but the lines were stormed, a division of the Tartar army beaten by Prince Prosorofski, and the town of Perekop besieged and taken. While the siege of this place was proceeding, Selim Ghirai received intelligence that another Russian army 10,000 strong had attacked and captured Taman on the Asiatic side of the straits of Kertch; that they had entered the Crimea on its eastern point, and were in full march for Kaffa. Bewildered by these multiplied perils, the unhappy Khan quitted an intrenched camp which he had formed at Tuzla, and hastened to Baghdjiserai. He entered his capital, almost alone, and in such a state of agitation and terror, that he was incapable of giving any commands for defence. The Russians soon appeared before the walls; and Selim then fled to Mount Karadagh, where several members of his family had collected with their followers, and had formed a fortified post. Fearing to fall into the hands of his enemies, the Khan abandoned this refuge also without striking a blow, reached the coast, and embarked with a few friends in a vessel, which conveyed them to Constantinople. This ignominious flight of the Prince deprived the Tartars of the last ray of hope. Many sought the means of leaving their fatherland, which they saw about to become the dominion of the Giaours; and considerable numbers set sail for Anatolia. Others sought to make peace with the conquerors. Dolgorouki acted with consummate craft, and promised them independence under the rule of a prince of the royal House of Ghirai, and also under the protection of the Empress of Russia. They took the oaths of allegiance to the Russian Empress accordingly, and sent forty-eight deputies of their nation, and two sons of Selim Ghirai to St. Petersburg, to implore the imperial favour of Catherine.

Kaffa, Kertch, and Yenikale now opened their gates to the Russians. Eupatoria was captured; and the Turkish Seraskier in the Crimea, who vainly strove with his feeble force of Ottoman regular troops to stem the torrent of disaster and disaffection, was beaten in battle, taken prisoner, and sent to St. Petersburg. While waiting the gracious response of Catherine to her Crimean suppliants, Dolgorouki installed Shahin Ghirai as Khan. The Russian general received the surname of Krimski for this important conquest; and the Muscovites rejoiced that they had now completed their revenge for the ancient ignominies and oppressions which their race had formerly endured under the Tartars. Of the three great Tartar Khanates, which so long afflicted Russia, those of Kazan and Astrakhan had been overthrown by Czar Ivan the Terrible. It had been reserved for Catherine II. to strike down the last stem of the Tartar stock by subjugating the Khanate of the Crimea.[1]

This heavy blow to the House of Othman was poorly compensated by the successful resistance which both Oczakof and Kilburn made to the Russian forces which besieged them in the same year. On the Danube the Turks obtained some advantages in the beginning of the campaign of 1771. They recovered Giurgevo, which the Russians had taken in the preceding winter; and Mouhinzadi Mohammed, who had distinguished himself against the Russians and Greeks in the Morea, displayed equal energy and bravery as governor of Widdin, which important post was now confided to his care. He crossed the Danube, and camped at Kalafat, whence he pushed his troops as far as Crajova and Kalle. He defeated the Russian general Essen, who had endeavoured to regain Giurgevo, but was himself beaten in an attack which he made upon Bucharest. The Russian generals Miloradovitch and Weissman defeated bodies of Turks at Tuldja; and altogether the Russians maintained their superiority, though their general, Romanzoff, did not press the Turks with the vigour which usually characterised his movements. Probably the despatch of Dolgorouki's army to the Crimea weakened the Russians in Bessarabia and the Principalities; and it is also certain that Romanzoff was watching the progress of the negotiations for peace which had now been commenced.

The rapid progress of the Czarina's armies, the seemingly approaching ruin of the Ottoman Empire, and the establishment of Russian authority in Bessarabia and the Moldavian and Wallachian Principalities, had made even Austria desirous to interpose in behalf of her ancient Mahometan enemy, and to save herself

[1] See Levesque, "Histoire de Russie," vol. v. p. 357.

from the perilous proximity of her ambitious Muscovite friends. France, England, and Prussia had offered to mediate between the contending parties early in the war; but the Empress Catherine had made it a point of personal and national honour to allow no one to interfere between her and the Ottoman enemy. Romanzoff had caused an intimation to be conveyed to the Turkish government, that peace might be obtained on much easier terms by a direct application to the Empress herself, than would be granted if the agency of any third parties were employed. But the tangled web of diplomacy was still continued; Austria, Prussia, and France being the most active in its complication. The English ambassador at Constantinople, Mr. Murray, seems to have offended equally the Turkish and his own government by some maladroit attempts which he made to gain the especial favour of the Reis Effendi, and by his not being sufficiently convinced that "Russia was the natural ally of the British Crown."[1] Unhappily also for the interest and honour of himself and his empire, Sultan Mustapha thought highly of his own statecraft, and followed an eccentric tortuous policy, alike inconsistent with high principle or sound calculation. Indeed an universal spirit of selfish rapacity seems to have animated Russia, Austria, Prussia, and the Turkish Sultan in these negotiations; Poland being the victim which all four considered feeble enough to be plundered with impunity. It is certainly to be remembered that Turkey was at war with the nominal government of Poland; which makes the Sultan's policy towards her less execrable, than that of the three Christian powers, who were her nominal friends.

Frederick II. of Prussia, and Joseph II. of Austria (who was now associated with his mother, Maria Theresa, in the rule of that empire), had determined at a personal interview which took place between those two sovereigns, to interpose on behalf of Turkey;[2]

[1] See Von Hammer, and see Lord Rochford's despatch, censuring Mr. Murray, in the appendix to Lord Stanhope's "History of England," vol. v.

[2] According to Archdeacon Coxe it was on this occasion that Frederick proposed to Joseph the partition of Poland. He places the scene of those royal consultations at the Austrian camp at Neustadt in Moravia in 1770. He states that the Austrian statesman, Prince Kaunitz, who was present, endeavoured to persuade the Prussian King to join the House of Austria in opposing by force of arms the ambitious designs of Russia, and urged that such an union was the only sufficient barrier against the torrent from the north, which threatened to overwhelm all Europe. Frederick evaded this demand, and advised that they should rather invite Russia to join with them in the partition of Poland, and either persuade or compel her to accept a portion of that country instead of retaining Moldavia and Wallachia. See Coxe's "House of Austria," vol. iii. pp. 446, 447 (Bohn's Edition), and note.

but as they had not agreed on any joint line of action, their respective representatives at Constantinople, Zegelin and Thugut, made their offers of mediation in separate interviews with the Reis Effendi.   In a conversation between that minister and M. de Thugut, the Turks suddenly proposed that Austria and the Porte should enter into an offensive and defensive alliance against Russia.   The Reis Effendi added, " When the Russians are driven out of Poland, it will depend entirely on the pleasure of the Imperial Court whether it will place a King of its own choice on the throne of Poland, or divide the territories of that kingdom with the Porte."   To this project of Polish partition (of which Sultan Mustapha himself was the author) Thugut replied, that it was not a fit time for the consideration of so vast a project, which could only be effected by a great effusion of blood, whereas the object of his communications with the Porte was to put an end to a war which had already been too sanguinary.   At the same time that he was making these offers to Austria, the Sultan was treating with France for an active alliance against Russia.   The French Court offered the Porte to place at its disposal a fleet of fourteen or fifteen ships of war, in return for which certain annual subsidies were to be paid by Turkey.   France promised also to obtain similar assistance for the Sultan from Spain.   This project, which was called the Scheme of the Maritime Alliance, was not accepted by the Porte; though the French ambassador was requested, and promised to obtain from France ships of war, stores, and artillerymen, which were to be purchased and hired at a fixed rate of payment.   The Austrian minister, Thugut, obtained information of this project, and sought to conclude an engagement on the same principle between Austria and the Porte.   A convention was actually signed (July 6, 1771) by which the Porte bound itself to pay a subsidy of 20,000 purses (equal to 11,250,000 florins), to cede Little Wallachia to Austria,[1] to liberate Austrian commerce from all taxes, and to guarantee her merchant ships from all attacks by the Barbaresque powers.   Austria in return pledged herself to procure the restoration to the Porte of all the territories

---

Schlosser also (vol. v. p. 525) represents that Polish as well as Turkish affairs were discussed at Neustadt.   I think, however, that the account of Von Hammer, which I have followed, that the scheme of dismembering Poland was not formerly proposed by Frederick till 1771, is borne out by the dates and tenour of the documents, which Von Hammer cites and refers to.

[1] Von Hammer, vol. iv. p. 629 : Coxe's " House of Austria," vol. iii. p. 457.

that Russia had conquered in the war. An instalment of the money was paid to Austria; and the troops were put in motion towards the frontiers, where they served to overawe the Turks and Poles far more than the Russians.

Russia, on her part, again endeavoured to open negotiations for peace with the Porte on the understanding that no intermeddling by any other power should be permitted; and a categorical announcement was made to the Austrian-Court (September, 1771) that the Empress Catherine was determined to make the Crimea independent of Turkey, and to place an independent prince on the throne of Moldavia and Wallachia. Soon afterwards Frederick of Prussia notified to Austria that he designed to appropriate certain parts of Poland, especially Pomerelia; and that he should invite the Court of Vienna to take an equivalent portion of the Polish kingdom. This was in October; and about the same time the Russian Empress laid before the Austrian government a written scheme for dismembering the Ottoman Empire, in which Wallachia and Moldavia were allotted to Russia, while it was signified that the Austrians were welcome to take Bosnia and Dalmatia.[1]

The English ambassador had succeeded in obtaining a copy of the secret convention between Austria and the Porte, and had communicated it to the Courts of St. Petersburg and Berlin. Frederick was desirous of a peace between Russia and Turkey, both on account of his plans against Poland, and because his annual payment to Russia, by virtue of the treaty of 1766 (which bound him to supply certain sums in lieu of troops to Russia in a Turkish war), began to be burdensome. He saw in this secret treaty between Austria and the Sultan an engine for moving Russia to make peace with the Porte. The Empress Catherine, on the other hand, was more and more anxious for the Prussian money. But before January, 1772, though no progress had been made towards a Turkish peace, the common avidity of Russia and Prussia for the dismemberment of Poland had drawn those powers closer together; and a secret convention had been concluded, by which, in return for a promise of part of the Polish territory, Frederick bound himself to take arms against Austria, if Russia should be attacked by that power. But the same guilty bribe was now operating on the Court of Vienna. Austria joined the crowned conspiracy against Poland, and totally changed her position towards the Ottoman Court. She did not offer to return the Turkish money which she had received in part payment of her promised co-operation against Russia; but her ambassador was instructed to

[1] Von Hammer, vol. iv. p. 616.

memorialise the Porte in concert with the Prussian minister, and
to urge the necessity of convoking a congress for settling terms of
peace.   Catherine, by arrangement with her confederate spoliators
of Poland, now abated somewhat of her haughty pretensions to
sole action, and declared that she was ready to accept the good
offices of the Imperial Court.   An armistice by sea and land between the Turkish and Russian forces was agreed on; and during
the remainder of the year 1772, negotiations were carried on at
Fokschani and Bucharest.   They were prolonged into the following spring, when they were broken off, and hostile operations
resumed.   The Russian plenipotentiary, Obresskoff (who had been
released from the Seven Towers on the repeated and vehement
intercession of the other European ambassadors) delivered the
Empress's ultimatum on the 15th February, 1773.   It contained
seven articles, which stipulated—1. That Russia should be recognised as protectress of the independence of the Tartars : that the
fortresses of Kertch and Yenikale should remain in the hands of
the Russians.   2. That Russian merchant-ships, and ships of war,
should have free right of navigation in the Black Sea and the
Archipelago.   3. That all the other fortresses in the Crimea
should be given up to the Tartars.   4. That the Voivode of
Moldavia, Gregory Ghika, then in the hands of Russia, should be
reinstated in his principality as hereditary prince, with the obligation of sending a year's revenue once in three years as a tribute to
Constantinople.   5. That Russia should have a permanent representative at Constantinople.   6. That Kilburn should be ceded in
full property to Russia ; and that the fortress of Oczakof should be
razed.   7. That the Porte should allow to the sovereigns of Russia
the title of Padischah, and the right of protecting those inhabitants
of the Ottoman Empire who profess the religion of the Greek
Church.

The Reis Effendi and the Vizier submitted these articles to the
dignitaries and generals who were with the Turkish troops.   Their
unanimous answer was, that the principal object of Russia was to
possess the posts of Kertch and Yenikale; that the rest of the note
was mere verbiage and sophistry ; that it would be easy to come
to an understanding on the article respecting the navigation of the
Ottoman seas ; that it would be better to recognise the absolute
independence of the Tartars than to leave things in their actual
state, especially as in good time it would be possible to seize again
what was then given up ; that the sum of 50,000 purses, which
Russia threatened to exact for the cost of the war, if the articles
were not accepted, might be supplied ; but that, even if the war

26

were to go on for seven years, it would be impossible to win an advantageous peace. Atallah Bey was sent to Constantinople with these resolutions of the council of war. After a long discussion in the Imperial Divan it was resolved to reject the terms. The Turkish plenipotentiaries endeavoured to protract the negotiations, and to induce the Russians to relax some of their demands. The Sultan (who was sincerely desirous for peace) sent an autograph letter to the Reis Effendi, authorising him to offer to Russia a sum of 70,000 piastres if Russia would forego the possession of Kertch and Yenikale. Obresskoff replied: "You suppose that my court is almost in a state of bankruptcy; but I will pledge myself that we will, without further difficulty, forthwith pay you the same sum, if you will accept the articles." The required cession of the two extreme Crimean fortresses to Russia was the insuperable difficulty with the negotiations. All the Turkish Ulema protested against such a sacrifice, no matter what might be the consideration. The Sultan would have yielded to Russia, but he feared that the Ulema would raise an insurrection against him. He caused an intimation to be conveyed to the Turkish plenipotentiary at Bucharest, the Reis Effendi Abdurrisak, that he would do the state a signal service, if he would take it upon himself to agree to all the articles, and sign a treaty of peace; but Sultan Mustapha owned at the same time, that if such a treaty were to be followed by tumults at Constantinople, he should loudly disavow his minister's act, and banish Abdurrisak and all his family. The Reis Effendi declined to take upon himself so perilous a responsibility; and the congress at Bucharest was dissolved.

The breathing-time which these negotiations procured for the Turkish forces, had been well employed. At the end of the year 1771, Sultan Mustapha had again conferred the Grand Vizierate on Mouhinzadi Mohammed Pacha, who had signalised himself in 1770 by the recovery of the Morea, and afterwards by his energy when transferred from the chief command in Greece, to the important Danubian government of Widdin. Mouhinzadi had been Grand Vizier before the war; but he had offended the Sultan by advising him not to commence hostilities against Russia until his preparations for war were more complete. For this sound counsel, Mouhinzadi had been displaced from his high office: but the bitter experience of three campaigns taught the Sultan how unwise had been his haste both in attacking the Czarina, and in degrading his Vizier. In the inferior posts of Seraskier of the Morea, and Seraskier of Widdin, Mouhinzadi had made an honour-

able exception to the general incompetency of the Turkish commanders; and the Sultan turned to him as the man in his
dominions best fitted, both by his abilities in the field, and by his
sagacity in council, to bring the calamitous war to an end, or to
maintain it with better fortune for the empire.   Mouhinzadi had
striven hard to obtain a pacification at the Fokschani and Bucharest congress; but he had also throughout the fifteen months of
negotiations, neglected no available means for restoring the spirit
of the Ottoman troops, and for barring the further advance of the
Russians towards Constantinople.   He punished all acts of
brigandage with unrelenting severity, and beheaded a number of
officers who had set the example of cowardice in presence of the
enemy.   He reorganised the wrecks of the defeated armies, and
raised fresh troops, especially from among the Bosnians and the
other most warlike of the Mahometan populations of the empire.
He strengthened the garrisons and stores of the fortresses, which
the Turks yet retained on the Danube, especially of Silistria; but
he foresaw the necessity of being prepared to defend the inner
barrier of the Balkan against the Russians, and with this view he
made Shumla the head-quarters of his forces.

The city of Shumla (more correctly called Schoumna), which
has become so celebrated in modern wars between the Turks and
Russians, lies at the eastern foot of a group of hills which rise a
little in advance of the northern side of the Balkan.   These hills
curve forwards towards the north-east, and send out projecting
ridges like the extremities of a horse-shoe.   The town of Shumla
is situate in the basin formed by this curvature of high ground.
It is of little strength in itself, though it is provided with fortifications, and is partially screened from an enemy advancing towards
it from the Danube by a little range in its front of rising ground
of inferior altitude to that of the hills already mentioned, which
back and flank the city.   It is the plateau of these hills that forms
the position of Shumla.   This plateau is from eighteen to twenty
miles in area; the sides of it falling at first in precipitous walls of
rock, and then sinking more gradually.   The southward roads
from nearly all the towns on the lower Danube converge upon
Shumla; and from Shumla the roads or tracks radiate, which lead
farther southward through the chief passes of the Balkan.   Shumla
does not physically close any of these passes.   They might be
reached by circling it, but it would be very perilous for an invading army to attempt this in the presence of a large force encamped
on the plateau.   From the extent of the position, and the nature
of the country in the vicinity, it is almost impossible to invest

Shumla; and a strong defending army stationed there, if vigorously handled, can not only make the capture of the place impossible, but can deal heavy blows against any hostile troops operating in its vicinity, and can cut off their lines of communication, should they turn Shumla, and advance southward through the Balkan.[1] If invading troops from Russia endeavour to avoid the reach of the Turkish army which holds Shumla, and force a passage through distant parts of the Balkan, they must (by reason of the difficulties of the ground) emerge from the defiles of that mountain-range in disconnected detachments, and may be easily crushed, before they can re-unite, by the Turkish army of support, which they must expect to find stationed at Aidos, or some other suitable position in the rear of the mountain barrier. Such is Shumla, a position which the Turks have strengthened by field-works and redoubts wherever practicable, and which they have for the last century regarded as the position of paramount importance for the defence of their capital against the Russians, and as the grand pivot for a line of operations on the Danube.[2]

Two other places which have acquired an almost equal celebrity with Shumla in the Russo-Turkish campaigns of our own age, were the scenes of important operations in 1773 and 1774. These are Silistria and Varna.

Silistria is situate on the right bank of the Danube, nearly at the commencement of the Delta of that river. The town is built almost in the form of a semicircle, of which the river front forms the chord. There are high grounds in its vicinity on the landward (or Bulgarian) side, the military importance of which has been peculiarly exemplified in recent sieges. When Silistria became the object of attack in 1773, its principal defences were deep trenches surrounding the towns, which inclosed also suburbs, and spacious vineyards, and magnificent gardens of rose-trees. The possession of Silistria is considered indispensable for a successful invasion of Turkey through Bulgaria from Wallachia, as it lies on the immediate flank of any operation that can be undertaken against the line of the Balkan.[3] Varna (the scene of the great defeat of the Christian confederates by Amurath II. in 1444)[4] lies on the western coast of the Black Sea, about forty-eight miles eastward of Shumla, and is second only to that position in importance; as no hostile army can move with safety through the eastern passes of the Balkan, while Varna is uncaptured in its rear. The atten-

[1] Möltke, p. 118. Chesney, p. 86.   [2] Von Hammer, vol. iv. p. 625.
[3] Möltke, p. 285.   [4] See *suprà*, p. 69.

tion paid by Mouhinzadi to securing Varna, Silistria, and Shumla in 1773, is a high proof of the strategic talents of that Vizier, and the movements of Romanzoff also prove that the Russian general-issimo understood the value of these posts as well as they have been appreciated by his successors in more recent wars.

By fixing his head-quarters at Shumla, Mouhinzadi was enabled not only to provide best for the defence of the Balkan, but also to direct with the greatest efficiency operations either of defence or of attack along the Danube, as occasion might require. When hostilities recommenced in 1773, the arrangements of the Russian corps in Wallachia indicated a design to cross the Danube near Touldja. A Turkish force under Tcherkes Pacha was at Babatagh in the Dobruscha, and the Grand Vizier ordered them to watch with the greatest care every movement of the enemy. But the troops at Babatagh deserted their colours in disgraceful panic, and the Russians advanced as far as Karasou, and destroyed the forti-fications of Karakerman. Not dismayed by this reverse, the Vizier continued to direct and animate the commanders of his garrisons and advanced posts ; and a victory near Rustchuk was the first-fruits of this campaign for the Turkish arms. The Russians had grown over-confident from success, and advanced boldly against that place; but an Ottoman force under Daghistani Ali joined the garrison, and they completely defeated the attack-ing corps, taking 1500 prisoners, and capturing three of the Russian guns. On the other hand, General Weissman surprised and defeated the Turks under Bakht-Ghirai and Tcherkes Pacha at Karasou ; and took sixteen cannons from them (7 June, 1773). From Karasou the Russian general marched upon Silistria to sup-port the operations conducted by the generalissimo, Romanzoff, against that city.

Romanzoff crossed the Danube at Balia with the principal Russian army, which was commanded under him by Generals Stoupischin and Potemkin. Osman Pacha, the Seraskier of Silistria, endeavoured to prevent the passage of the river; but the flank movement of General Weissman protected the operation, and the Seraskier's troops, after fighting bravely, were repulsed and driven into Silistria. The importance of this post was keenly felt by the Sultan as well as by the Russian leaders ; and Ibrahim Pacha, who had commanded the Turkish vanguard in a late un-successful attack on the enemy, received a letter from Sultan Mustapha himself, which contained these laconic but emphatic orders : " If thy life is dear to thee, thou wilt rally thy beaten horsemen, and fly to the succour of Silistria."

Romanzoff battered the town with seventy cannons and a large number of mortars. The walls were soon trenched, and the Russian columns advanced to storm. 100 waggon-loads of fascines had been provided to fill up the outer ditches; and a murderous conflict took place, the Russians charging with their characteristic obstinacy, and the Ottoman garrison resisting with determined valour. Romanzoff continuously sent fresh troops forward; and the assault was renewed again and again for six hours, when at last the Turks gave way, the outer lines were passed, and the Russians poured into the suburbs, exulting at having won Silistria. But here Osman Pacha's troops, reinforced by all the male population, rallied, and fought with redoubled fury. The peculiarity in the sieges of Turkish towns (which has been so often remarked by military writers), that the chief resistance in them begins at the very crisis where all resistance in ordinary sieges terminates, was fully exemplified at Silistria in 1773.[1] The Russian columns were at last beaten back, and Romanzoff abandoned the siege with heavy loss. This victory of Osman Pacha, which was mainly due to his own courage, and to the gallantry of Essud Hassan Pacha, the commandant of the place, is the most brilliant exploit on the Ottoman side during the campaign of 1773.

Romanzoff formed his retreating army into three columns, two of which he led back across the Danube, while he placed the third under the orders of General Weissman, and directed him to retire to Babatagh in the Dobruscha. The Turkish force under Nououman Pacha endeavoured to intercept this column at Kainardji. The Russians were, as usual, formed in a system of squares; but Nououman's Janissaries charged with such spirit, that they broke through the Russian centre; and the whole

---

[1] Baron Möltke, at the close of his description of the siege of Brailow in 1828, remarks: "The Turkish commanders have the great merit of being blind to the weak points of places. Capitulations were not relished by the Divan, and those who made them risked their heads. The garrisons, too, were defending their own wives, children, and worldly goods within their walls, and fighting for their faith and for dominion over their Rayas. They make up for the want of outworks by a skilful use of the dry ditch, and their most vigorous defence commonly begins at the point where with the European troops it usually ends, from the moment when a practical breach has been effected. With us a large number of wealthy householders are a serious impediment to the protracted defence of a fortress; but in Turkey it is quite the reverse; every man capable of bearing arms is a soldier, and makes his appearance upon the walls daily. Thus, it is from the large towns, and from them only, that a very determined resistance is to be expected." P. 44. See ibid., pp. 102-104.

Russian force would have been destroyed, had it not been for the good conduct of their rear-guard, who charged the victorious Janissaries when in confusion, drove them back, and restored the formation of their own army. Eventually the Russians were successful, and captured twenty-eight Turkish guns; but their success was purchased by severe loss, including that of their brave and able general, who was shot dead at the very commencement of the battle. The beaten Turkish army was soon reinforced, and made an attempt to recapture Hirsova, but was repulsed with severe loss by Suwarrow, who commanded there. After this second defeat, Nououman Pacha was deposed by the Grand Vizier; and the command of his force was given to Daghistani Ali, the victor of Rustchuk. Promotions and rewards were at the same time liberally showered on Osman Pacha, Essud Hassan, and the other officers whose good conduct had been conspicuous.

The Russian generalissimo, Romanzoff, irritated at his failure at Silistria, was anxious to obtain some success on the right of the Danube before he placed his troops in winter quarters. Accordingly, he sent a column under Prince Dolgorouki across the Danube at Hirsova, and ordered General Ungern (who had succeeded to Weissman's command) to move from Babatagh, and co-operate in an attack on the Ottoman forces, which were again assembled at Karasou. This proved completely successful, and the greater part of the Turkish troops dispersed and fled towards Shumla. Elated with this triumph, the Russian generals separated their forces; and Ungern, with about 6000 infantry and 3000 horse, marched towards Varna in the hope of carrying that important place by a sudden attack, while the rest of the Russians moved upon Shumla. This division captured the town of Bazardchik after a feeble resistance, nearly all the garrison and inhabitants having fled. The facility of their conquest did not prevent the Russians from practising the most barbarous atrocities on the remnant of the population, which consisted almost entirely of feeble old men, and helpless women and children. But these cruelties were not long unpunished.

When it was known in the camp at Shumla that the army at Karasou had been routed, and that the enemy was marching towards the Balkan, the Grand Vizier assembled a council of war, and asked if there was any officer of spirit and resolution, who would undertake to rally the fugitives from Karasou and Bazardchik, and repair the calamity that had happened. The Reis Effendi, Abdurrisak, volunteered for the perilous duty, and his offer was gladly accepted by the Vizier and the other members of the council. Accompanied by Wassif Effendi (the Turkish historian), by the Mufti of Philippopolis, and by 400 men (nearly all being his own household retainers), the brave minister for foreign affairs set forward; and on the road to Kozlidje he succeeded in reuniting the fragments of the different Turkish corps which were scattered about the neighbourhood. At Kozlidje he attacked the Russian vanguard and beat it; and then hurrying forward, he fell upon the Russians in Bazardchik. They fled before him with precipitation, thinking that the whole Ottoman army was upon them; and leaving part of their baggage and stores, as trophies of Abdurrisak's daring exploit.

Meanwhile, General Ungern had received a severe repulse at Varna. The Turkish commander in the Black Sea, Kelledji Osman Pacha, was cruising with a small squadron near Varna when the Russian army approached the walls. He immediately landed his Kiaya with 600 marines to the succour of the place. The fortifications were weak, and the Russians after a short cannonade advanced to storm. But they were driven back in disorder from one part, which they had endeavoured to carry without having fascines for the ditches, or scaling-ladders for the walls; and the division, which at another part had made good its entrance and occupied the Christian quarter of the town, was attacked there in turn and driven out again by the Turks. Prince Dolgorouki, with part of the Russian force, retired to Babatagh; the rest, under General Ungern, retreated upon Ismail. The Russian loss at Varna amounted to nearly 2000 killed and wounded, and they left behind them 100 baggage-waggons and ten cannon. The successful defence of Varna, and the recovery of Bazardchik, were the two last events of the campaign of 1773; a campaign in which the balance of advantages was considerably on the side of the Turks.

They brought, however, inadequate consolation to the Sultan amid the general decline of the fortunes of the empire since the commencement of the war, and for the disappointment of the hopes which he had based on his own supposed pre-eminence in state policy. He had also, like many of his race, been a devotee to supposed occult sciences, to the kabala of the Moors and the astrology of the Egyptians. These had been to him, as he believed, sources of assurance that he should prosper in the war; and he now, in the bitterness of his heart, felt that either his cunning was foolishness, and he had been a visionary and a dupe, or that the stars had lied to him. Sick in body as in mind, he complained that he was weary of the mode in which his Seraskiers carried on war ; and when the news of the second defeat at Karasou reached Constantinople, Mustapha exclaimed that he would repair to the army in person.   His ministers represented to him that such an important step ought not to be taken without consulting the Divan ; and the Ulema declared that the departure of the sovereign for the army might be attended with evil consequences in the actual state of circumstances, especially having regard to the bad state of his health.   On this the Sultan deferred his journey to the camp until the restoration of his health, a time that never came.   The hand of death was already upon him ; and on the 25th of December, 1773, after many weeks of severe suffering, Sultan Mustapha III. expired.

He was succeeded by his brother Abdul Hamid, who had been shut up in the Serail for forty-three years, till called from the dreary monotony of a royal prison to the cares and fears of a royal throne.   He made few alterations in the government, and had the good sense to appreciate the merits of his Vizier, Mouhinzadi, and of his Capitan Pacha, Hassan of Algiers.   Above all, he was sincerely desirous of peace, as were his ministers, his generals, and every class of men in his empire, except the Ulema, who raised theological objections to the Sultan, as Caliph, abandoning his sovereignty over the Tartars, and against the cession of the Ottoman fortresses of Kertch and Yenikale to the Russian Giaours.   But the new campaign was soon marked by such reverses and perils, as silenced these orthodox demurrers ; and the dignitaries of the sword, who longed for peace, prevailed over the dignitaries of the law, who demanded warfare.

On the 14th of April, the Grand Vizier displayed the horse-tails with great pomp in front of his camp at Shumla.   A hymn on the birth of the Prophet was recited ; and a grand council was held, at which it was resolved to take the offensive, and drive the Russians from Hirsova.   But the Russian general at that place was Suwarrow ; and, instead of waiting to be attacked, he advanced towards the Turks, formed a junction with the division of General Kamenski, and brought the Turkish army, 25,000 strong, to action at Kozlidje.   He completely defeated them, captured their camp, baggage, and military stores, and twenty-nine cannon.   The defeated army dispersed over the country ; and when the Generals Kamenski and Milarodovitch advanced, after the battle, upon Shumla, the Grand Vizier found that he had but 8000 troops under him to defend that extensive position.   Even among these a faction-fight broke out ; and detachments of the Russians moved southward of Shumla to the very gorges of the Balkan.   In this

35

emergency the Grand Vizier sent an officer to the Russian camp, where the generalissimo, Count Romanzoff, now commanded in person, to request an armistice. This was refused, but the Vizier was invited to send plenipotentiaries to treat for peace. After a brief delay, during which Mouhinzadi obtained the sanction of the Sultan, the plenipotentiaries were despatched to treat with Prince Repnin, who acted on behalf of Russia, and the first conference took place on the 16th of July, at Kainardji.

The negotiations were carried on with military celerity; for both sides were sincerely anxious for a termination of the war. Notwithstanding the conquests and glory which Russia had achieved, she was suffering almost more severely than her beaten enemy.[1] Her losses in battle had been heavy; and, as is customary with Russian armies, the number of the soldiers that had perished by disease and privation, far exceeded the amount of the killed and wounded. At home, many of her provinces were ravaged by the plague. A district near Astrakhan had been left almost desolate by the migration of a horde of 400,000 Calmucks, who, irritated by the oppressive interference of the Russian government with their free customs, left the territories of the Czarina in 1771, and retired within the frontiers of the Chinese Empire. Still more formidable to the power of Catherine was the civil war raised against her by the remarkable impostor Pugatcheff, who, during 1773 and the greater part of 1774, spread desolation throughout Southern Russia. If, in addition to all this, it is remembered that the first great treaty for the partition of Poland, was made in 1773, and that there was deep need of Russian troops to coerce the anarchical but high-spirited population of that ill-fated land, we may appreciate at its true value the boasted magnanimity of Russia, in exacting no harsher terms of peace from Turkey, in 1774, than had been almost consented to in 1772.

After a discussion of only seven hours, the plenipotentiaries at Kainardji agreed, on the 17th July. 1774, to the minutes of the new treaty, that was to be made between the two empires; but the Russian generalissimo, Count Romanzoff, delayed the time for signature for four days, so as to make the treaty bear date on the 21st July, the anniversary of the Treaty of the Pruth. That day was thenceforth to be a day of humiliation and shame, not to the Muscovite, but to the Ottoman race. Nor was it by accident that the town of Kainardji was chosen as the scene of the conferences. The Russian General Weissman had been slain there by the Turks

[1] Levesque, "Histoire de Russie."

in the preceding year, and Romanzoff designed the treaty to be a votive offering to the memory of his brave companion in arms.

The peace of Kainardji consisted of twenty-eight public articles; to these were added two secret clauses, by which the Porte bound itself to pay to Russia, within three years, 4,000,000 roubles, and the Empress engaged that her fleet should be withdrawn from the Archipelago without delay. The twenty-eight public articles were the most important. They established that the Tartars of the Kuban, the Crimea, and the adjacent regions between the rivers Berda and Dnieper, and also of the countries between the Boug and the Dniester, as far as the frontier of Poland, were to be politically an independent nation governed by their own sovereign, of the race of Zenghis Khan, elected and raised to the throne by the Tartars themselves. It was expressly stipulated that "neither the Court of Russia nor the Ottoman shall interfere, under any pretexts whatever, with the election of the said Khan, or in the domestic, political, civil, and internal affairs of the said state, but, on the contrary, they shall acknowledge and consider the said Tartar nation, in its political and civil state, upon the same footing as other powers, who are governed by themselves, and are dependent upon God alone."

But from out of the natural territories of this newly organised Tartar nation Russia retained for herself the fortresses of Kertch and Yenikale in the Crimea, with their ports and districts; also the city of Azoph with its district; and the Castle of Kilburn at the north of the Dnieper, with a district along the left bank of the Dnieper. The opposite fortress of Oczakof, with a similar district, was to remain in the possession of the Turks. The two Kabartas were also to be Russia's; but the formal cession of them was to be made by the Khan and Ancients of the new independent Tartar nation. Russia was to withdraw her troops from the fortresses which she had conquered in Georgia and Mingrelia; and these provinces "were to be considered by Russia as belonging to those on whom they were formerly dependent; so that if, in ancient times or for a very long period, they have actually been under the Sublime Porte, they shall be considered as belonging to it." With the exception of Azoph, Kilburn, Kertch, Yenikale, and the Kabartas, Russia gave up all her conquests. The Porte confessed that it received back from her Moldavia and Wallachia on conditions which it religiously promised to keep—these were (in substance) "the grant of an amnesty for all offences during the war; free exercise of the Christian religion; humane and generous government for the future; and permission from the

Porte that, according as the circumstances of these two Principalities may require, the Ministers of the Imperial Court of Russia resident at Constantinople may remonstrate in their favour; and a promise to listen to them with all the attention which is due to friendly and respected powers."

A very important clause of the treaty (Art. VII.) respecting the Christian subjects of the Sultan, generally declared, that " The Sublime Porte promises to protect constantly the Christian religion and its churches, and it also allows the ministers of the Imperial Court of Russia to make, upon all occasions, representations, as well in favour of the new church at Constantinople, of which mention will be made in Article XIV., as on behalf of its officiating ministers, promising to take such representations into due consideration, as being made by a confidential functionary of a neighbouring and sincerely friendly power."[1]

The words of the XIVth section (referred to by the VIIth) were, " After the manner of the other powers, permission is given to the High Court of Russia, in addition to the chapel built in the minister's residence, to erect in one of the quarters of Galata, in the street called Bey Oglu, a public church, in which Christians may worship according to the Greek ritual, which shall always be under the protection of the ministers of that empire, and secure from all coercion and outrage."   And the VIIIth article stipulated that Russian subjects should have full liberty to visit the holy city of Jerusalem without being subjected to capitation tax, or other impost, and that they should be under the strictest protection of the laws.   Other articles provided that merchant ships belonging to the two contracting powers should have free and unimpeded navigation in all the seas which wash their shores; that merchants should have a right to such sojourn as their affairs required, " and," as the XIth clause of the treaty expressed it, "for the convenience and advantage of the two empires, there shall be a free and unimpeded navigation for the merchant ships belonging to the two contracting powers, in all the seas which wash their shores."

The same clause gave expressly to Russia the right of having resident consuls in all parts of the Turkish Empire, where it should think fit to appoint them; but no equivalent right was given to Turkey to have consuls in Russia.   The treaty merely said that the subjects of the Sublime Porte were to be permitted to carry on

---

[1] This is the clause on which Prince Menschikoff in 1853 founded the claim of Russia to the general protection of all the inhabitants of the Turkish countries who were members of the Greek Church.

commerce by sea and land in Russia, with all advantages of the most favoured nations.

It was formally declared by the fourth article, "that it is conformable to the natural right of every power to make, in its own country, such dispositions as it may consider to be expedient: in consequence whereof, there is respectively reserved to the two empires a perfect and unrestricted liberty of constructing anew in their respective states, and within their frontiers, in such localities as shall be deemed advisable, every kind of fortresses, towns, habitations, edifices, and dwellings, as well as of repairing and rebuilding the old fortresses, towns, habitations, &c."

By other clauses the Sultan was bound always to permit the residence of a Russian minister at the Porte, and to give the sovereign of Russia the title of " Padischah," which had hitherto been refused.[1] It was also declared that " the two empires have agreed to annihilate and leave in an eternal oblivion all the treaties and conventions heretofore made between the two states, including therein the Convention of Belgrade, with all those subsequent to it ; and never to put forth any claim grounded upon the said conventions, excepting, however, the one made in 1700 between Governor Tolstoi and Hassan Pacha, Governor of Atschug, on the subject of the boundaries of the district of Azoph and of the line of demarcations of the frontier of Kuban, which shall remain invariably such as it has heretofore been."

Finally, the whole treaty was drawn up and concluded without the insertion of a syllable relating to Poland, although the treatment of Poland by Russia had been one of the primary causes of the war. It was considered that this implied negation of all right in Turkey to interfere in Polish affairs, and also the circumstance that the treaty was concluded without any third power being allowed to be party to it as mediator between the Russian Empress and her defeated enemy, were not the least of the triumphs which were achieved for Catherine in the close of this contest.

Such in substance was the treaty of Kainardji ; in which one of the ablest diplomatists of the age saw not only the preparation of the destruction of the Mahometan Empire of the East, but also the source of evil and troubles without end for all the other states of Europe.[2] The German historian of the House of Othman

---

[1] See *suprà*, p. 98.

[2] "La position des deux empires a été totalement changée par le traité de Kaïnardjé, et par conséquent, s'il était encore possible de sauver la Porte, il conviendrait de trouver des mesures toutes nouvelles. . . . . Par l'adroite combinaison des articles de ce traité, l'Empire Ottoman devient dès

(whose guidance I have so long enjoyed, but must henceforth regret through this work) considers that treaty to have delivered up the Ottoman Empire to the mercy of Russia ; and to have marked the commencement of the dissolution of that empire, at least in Europe.   He sees in the articles of Kainardji " the germs of those of Adrianople."

---

aujourd'hui une sorte de province russe, d'ou la cour de Saint-Pétersbourgh peut tirer de l'argent et des troupes, &c. ; enfin, comme à l'avenir la Russie est à même de lui dicter ses lois et qu'elle a entre ses mains les moyens de forcer la Sultan à les accepter, elle le contentera peut-être,pendant quelques années encore, de régner au nom du Grand Seigneur, jusqu'à ce qu'elle juge le moment favorable d'en prendre possession définitivement. . . .   Si à ces exemples d'une frénésie incroyable, on ajoute la mauvaise administration de la Porte, qui viciée dans les fondemens prépare depuis quelque temps, comme à dessein et mieux que ne l'ont pu faire les armes de la Russie, la destruction de cet Empire d'Orient, on sera convaincu que jamais une nation prête à disparaître de la scène politique n'aura moins mérité la compassion des autres peuples que les Ottomans ; malheureusement les évènemens qui se passent en ce moment dans cet empire exerceront à l'avenir la plus grande influence sur la politique de tous les autres états, et feront naître des maux et des troubles sans fin."—Extraits des rapports de M. de Thugut, datés du 3 Septembre, 1774, et du 17 Aôut, 1774.

CHAPTER XXI.

ATTEMPTS OF GAZI HASSAN TO RESTORE THE EMPIRE—FRESH
ENCROACHMENTS OF RUSSIA—CONVENTION OF 1779—RUSSIA
ANNEXES THE CRIMEA—VAIN ATTEMPTS OF FRANCE TO INDUCE
ENGLAND TO ACT WITH HER AGAINST RUSSIA—CONVENTION OF
1783—SCHEMES OF AUSTRIA AND RUSSIA FOR THE DISMEMBER-
MENT OF TURKEY—WAR—RESISTANCE OF THE TURKS TO AUS-
TRIA—AUSTRIA MAKES PEACE—DISASTERS SUSTAINED BY THE
TURKS IN THE WAR WITH RUSSIA—ACCESSION OF SULTAN
SELIM III.—INTERVENTION OF ENGLAND AND PRUSSIA—TREATY
OF JASSY.

THE literary men of Western Europe and the Ulema of Turkey
alike regarded the treaty of Kainardji as consummating the glory
of Russia and the degradation of the House of Othman. The Encyclopædists of Paris[1] wrote felicitations to the Empress Catherine,
and to her generalissimo, Count Romanzoff, which were echoed by
all pretenders to enlightened opinions in other parts of Europe, who
recognised the centralisation of literary authority amid the circles
of the French metropolis.[2]

[1] See Capefigue, " Louis XVI.," pp. 13, 14, 93. There is too much foundation for his bitter remark at p. 14 on the influence of the Encyclopædists
and their admirers on the foreign politics of the Western Courts—" Il faut
reconnaître cette triste vérité, que si un gouvernement veut se perdre, il n'a
qu'à suivre l'opinion des écrivains, gens de lettres, sociétés savantes et
littéraires."

[2] One English literary man of this period deserves to be mentioned as an
honourable exception to the general adulators of Russia. Even before the
triumphs of Catherine II. in the war of 1765-1774, Oliver Goldsmith wrote
thus of Russia in his " Citizen of the World," published 1758:
" I cannot avoid beholding the Russian Empire as the natural enemy of
the more Western parts of Europe—as an enemy already possessed of great
strength, and, from the nature of the government, every day threatening to
become more powerful. This extensive empire, which both in Europe and
Asia occupies almost a third of the Old World, was, about two centuries
ago, divided into separate kingdoms and dukedoms, and from such a division consequently weak. Since the time, however, of Johan Basilides, it
has increased in strength and extent, and those untrodden forests, those innumerable savage animals, which formerly covered the face of the country,

In Constantinople devout followers of Islam looked wistfully to Asia as their refuge from the great infidels, as they termed the Russians; and sorrowfully recalled the old tradition that the city abounding in faith is destined to be taken by the Sons of Yellowness.[1] But still many among the Ottomans were superior to the torpor of despairing fatalism. They understood better both their duty to their empire and the precepts of their Prophet, who bade his followers not to lose heart at reverses in warfare, but to view them as visitations of Allah, designed to prove true believers; and who gave them the great maxim of " Fortitude in adversity, and Self-control in prosperity :" " Despond not, neither exult ; so shall ye prevail :" " God loveth those who persevere patiently :" " He turned you to flight before them that He might make trial of you :" " God giveth life and causeth to die ; and God seeth that which ye do :" " Oh, true believers, be patient and strive, to excel in patience, and be constant-minded and fear God, that ye may be happy."[2]

Foremost among these better spirits was the Capitan Pacha Hassan of Algiers, now commonly styled Gazi Hassan, for his glorious conflicts against the Giaours. Sultan Abdul Hamid placed almost unlimited authority in his hands ; and Hassan strove to reorganise the military and naval forces of Turkey, and to prepare her for the recurrence of the struggle against Russia,

---

are now removed, and colonies of mankind planted in their room. A kingdom thus enjoying peace internally, possessed of an unbounded extent of dominions, and learning the military art at the expense of others abroad, must every day grow more powerful ; and it is probable we shall hear Russia in future times, as formerly, called the ' Officina Gentium.'

"It was long the wish of Peter, their great monarch, to have a foot in some of the Western parts of Europe; many of his schemes and treaties were directed to this end, but, happily for Europe, he failed in them all. A fort in the power of this people would be like the possession of a floodgate : and whenever ambition entered, or necessity prompted, they might then be able to deluge the whole Western world with a barbarous inundation. Believe me, my friend, I cannot sufficiently condemn the politicians of Europe, who thus make this powerful people arbitrators in their quarrel. The Russians are now at that period between refinement and barbarity which seems most adapted to military achievement ; and, if once they happen to get footing in the Western parts of Europe, it is not the feeble efforts of the sons of effeminacy and dissension that can serve to remove them. The fertile valley and soft climate will be ever sufficient inducements to draw whole myriads from their native deserts, the trackless wild, or snowy mountain. History, experience, reason, nature, expand the book of wisdom before the eyes of mankind, but they will not read."

[1] Eton, 193. Thornton, 78.

[2] See the 3rd chapter of the Koran.

which all knew to be inevitable. He endeavoured to discipline the troops ; but finding that all attempts to introduce improved weapons and drill, or to restore subordination among the Janissaries and Spahis were fruitless, he gave up these schemes, but proposed a new order of battle, by which more effect was to be given to the fury of the wild Turkish onset. " He would have divided an army of 100,000 men into ten different corps, which were to attack separately, and so arranged that the retreat of the repulsed corps should not overwhelm and put in disorder those which had not attacked. He affirmed, that though the artillery of an European army would make great slaughter, yet no army could withstand ten Turkish attacks, which are furious but short if they do not succeed, and the attack of 10,000 is as dangerous as of 100,000 in one body, for, the first repulsed, the rest, on whom they fell back, immediately take to flight."[1]

This system of attacking in detail was never found practicable ; and probably the Capitan Pacha in proposing it was judging more from his experience of the capacities of squadrons of ships, than from any sound knowledge of the possible evolutions of troops in face of an enemy. The navy was a force which Hassan understood far better ; and his efforts to improve the Turkish marine were spirited and judicious, though some of his practical measures showed the true ruthless severity of the old Algerine sea-rover. Hassan possessed little science himself, but he respected it in others ; and his great natural abilities and strong common sense taught him how to make use of European skill, and of the most serviceable qualities, which the various seafaring populations of the Sultan's dominions were known to possess. The repairs and improvements which he sought to effect in the Turkish navy, extended to the construction of the vessels, the education of the officers, and the supply of seamen. Aided by an English ship-builder, Hassan entirely altered the cumbrous rigging of the Turkish ships, and equipped them after the English system. He lowered their high and unwieldy sterns ; and he gave them regular tiers of guns. He collected all the good sailors that he could engage from Algiers and the other Barbaresque states, and also from seaports on the eastern coast of the Adriatic : though he was still obliged to depend chiefly on Greek crews for the navigation of his fleets, as the Turks refused to do any duty on ship-board beyond working the guns. He compelled the commanders of vessels to attend personally to the good order and efficiency of their ships

[1] Eton, "Survey of Turkish Empire," p. 68.

and crews ;[1] and, by a still more important measure, he endeavoured
to keep a sufficient body of able seamen always ready at Constantinople to man the fleet in case of an emergency. It was usual
to lay up the ships from autumn till spring-time, and to dismiss
the sailors for the winter. Hassan pointed out the danger of
leaving the capital thus unprotected, and the ease with which the
Russians might at any time during the winter months sail down
from their new ports in the Black Sea, occupy the Bosphorus, and
destroy the Turkish marine in its harbours. He proposed that a
winter home for the sailors should be built at Constantinople ;
where they should be quartered, like troops in barracks. This
scheme met with great though secret opposition from the Grand
Vizier, and other high officers, who were jealous of the power
which the Capitan Pacha would acquire by having so large a force
at his disposal in the metropolis. As the supply of the necessary
funds for this design was continually retarded under various pretexts, Hassan formed an institution, such as he had projected, but
on a smaller scale, at his own expense. He also founded a naval
school for the scientific education of officers for the fleet. But all
these plans of the brave and sagacious admiral were thwarted, and
ultimately nullified, by the envy and prejudices of other officials
of the state.[2] Nor was Hassan more successful in an attempt
which he made at a thorough reform of the ancient but much
aggravated abuses of the Turkish feudal system, by which Ziamets
and Timars were given to court favourites, who trafficked in their
sale, and the Porte was deprived in time of war of the greater
part of its military resources.

The necessity of recovering for the Sultan some of the provinces,
which during the recent troubles of the state had cast off all

---

[1] "In 1778 the finest ship in the fleet foundered in the Black Sea ; being
too weak, she worked her caulking out, and leaked between all her planks.
The famous Capitan Pacha Hassan attributed it to the bad caulking, and
when the fleet came back into the port of Constantinople, he ordered all the
captains of the ships of war to attend in person the caulking of their own
ships, on pain of death. One of them, being one day tired of sitting by his
ship, went home to his house, not above a quarter of a mile off. The Capitan
Pacha happened to go himself to the arsenal to see the work, examined the
caulking, found fault, and asked for the captain ; the truth was obliged to
be told him : he sat down on a small carpet, sent one man for his blunderbuss, and another to call the captain ; as soon as the unfortunate man came
near him, he took up his blunderbuss and shot him dead, without speaking
a word to him. "Take and bury him," he said, "and let the other captains
attend him to the grave, and the caulking be suspended till they return,"—
Eton, p. 77.

[2] Ibid., pp. 66, 89.

allegiance, made it impossible for Hassan to be a regular resident in the capital ; and gave frequent opportunities for his enemies to countermine his policy during his absence. Against open foes in the field he commanded ably and successfully. He defeated the forces of Sheikh Tahir in Syria, besieged him in Acre, captured that important city, and reduced the district round it to temporary obedience to the Porte.

In 1778 he recovered the Morea, and destroyed or expelled the rebellious Albanians, who had been led into that peninsula in 1770 to fight against Orloff and the Greek insurgents ; and who had after the departure of the Russians established themselves there in lawless independence ; oppressing, plundering, and slaughtering both the Greek and Turkish residents, with ferocious impartiality.[1]

After relieving the Peloponnesus from this worst of all scourges, the tyranny of a wild soldiery, which had killed or deposed its officers, which had never known the restraint of civil law, and had shaken off all bonds of military discipline, Hassan was made governor of the liberated province, and exerted himself vigorously and wisely in the restoration of social order, and the revival of agriculture and commerce.[2] Subsequently to this he led a large force to Egypt against the rebellious Mamelukes. He had made himself master of Cairo, and had effected much towards the re-establishment of the Sultan's authority in that important province,[3] when he was recalled to oppose the Russians in the fatal war of 1787-1792 ; a contest still more disastrous than that which had terminated in the treaty of Kainardji.

The interval of fourteen years between the two wars had been marked by measures on the part of Russia as ambitious, and as inimical towards the Turks, as any of her acts during open hostilities. Even the writers who are the most unscrupulous in their eulogies of the Empress Catherine, and the most bitter against the Ottoman nation, avow that the Empress from the very beginning of her reign had constantly in view the expulsion of the Turks from Europe ; and that the vast design which she sought to accomplish, was the same which Peter the Great first entertained, and which the cabinet of St. Petersburg has never lost sight of during the succeeding reigns to this day.[4] A temporary peace was neces-

---

Emerson Tennent's " Greece," vol. ii. p. 376.
[2] Ibid., vol. ii. p. 378.
   Ibid., vol. ii. p. 379.   Eton, pp. 88, 383.
[4] See Eton, p. 407. The position occupied by Mr. Eton at the Court of St. Petersburg ; his intimacy with Count Potemkin, and other leading men

sary for Russia in 1774 ; but after Pugatcheff's rebellion was quelled, and the Russian grasp on the provinces which she had rent from Poland was firmly planted, Catherine scarcely sought to disguise how fully she was bent on the realisation of the "Oriental project." Her second grandson was born in 1778. He was named Constantine. " Greek women were given him for nurses, and he sucked in with his milk the Greek language, in which he was afterwards perfected by learned Greek teachers : in short, his whole education was such as to fit him for the throne of Constantinople, and nobody then doubted the Empress's design." Such is the testimony of Mr. Eton, an Englishman then resident at St. Petersburg, highly esteemed by the Empress and many of her favourite statesmen and generals, and strongly devoted to the cause of Russia. On his authority we also know that in the next year (1779) the Empress and Prince Potemkin formed a scheme for giving the King of England effective assistance against the Colonists in the American war, on condition of England giving the Empress aid in a renewed attack upon the Turks. The island of Minorca (then in the possession of the English) was to be ceded by this country to Russia, as a station for the Russian fleet in the Mediterranean, and a rendezvous for the insurgent Greeks. According to Mr. Eton, the details of this project were drawn up by Prince Potemkin, ready for presentation to the British ambassador at St. Petersburg, but the adroitness of Count Panin, the Russian minister for foreign affairs (who favoured the French interests against the English), prevented its being proceeded with further, and caused the Empress to adopt the anti-British policy of the Armed Neutrality. It is added that Prince Potemkin, to the last day of his life, regretted the failure of this scheme, and constantly affirmed that the success of the Russian enterprise against Turkey depended upon the alliance with Great Britain.[1]

The annexation of the Crimea to the Russian dominions was formally completed in the year 1783 ; but the plot for the subjection of that peninsula had been in progress from the very date of the treaty of Kainardji, by which Russia solemnly bound herself to treat the Crimean Tartars as an independent nation accountable to God only for their internal government, and to abstain from all

in the Russian councils, and his strong prejudice in favour of Russia, make him an unexceptionable witness as to the ambitious schemes of the Empress Catherine ; but his invectives against the Turks are to be received with great caution.

[1] Eton, p. 409.

interference in the election of their sovereign, or in other matters of their civil polity. Under the old pretexts of friendly mediation, and of relieving her frontier from the dangerous neighbourhood of anarchy, Russia soon made the Crimea a second Poland; except that in this case there were no accomplices with whom she was obliged to share the spoil. The Tartars had elected as their Khan, Dewlet Ghirai, who did not prove sufficiently subservient to the influence of St. Petersburg. The Russians, therefore, fomented disaffection and revolts against him, and made these troubles the pretext for marching an army into the peninsula for the ostensible purpose of restoring order. They sedulously disclaimed all projects of conquest, but they effected the abdication of Dewlet Ghirai, and the election in his stead of Schahin Ghirai, who had been a hostage at St. Petersburg, and was known to be most unpopular with the majority of his countrymen. The expected results soon followed. The new Khan, being threatened both by his own subjects and by the Turks (who justly regarded his election through Russian intervention, as a breach of the late treaty) sent a deputation of six of his Mirzas to St. Petersburg (1776) to implore the Empress's protection. This was graciously promised; and Romanzoff was ordered to collect troops on the Dnieper, to act, if necessary, against the Turks. But the Sultan felt himself too weak to renew the war. Some risings of the Tartars of Kuban against Russia were sternly quelled by Suwarrow; and, in 1779, a convention was signed between Russia and Turkey, by which the stipulations of the treaty of Kainardji were formally recognised and renewed, with the addition of explanatory clauses, by which the Sultan acknowledged the new Khan as lawful ruler of the Crimea, and bound himself to prompt performance of the religious formalities, by which it was necessary for him, as Caliph of the orthodox Mahometans, to give due spiritual sanction to the Tartar sovereignty.[1]

Schahin Ghirai, the object and unhappy instrument of Russian statecraft, was not suffered long to enjoy even the semblance of royalty. Prince Potemkin (who appears to have regarded the acquisition of the Crimea by force or by fraud as his peculiar function) placed dexterous agents at the Tartar Court, who persuaded the weak Khan to adopt Russian usages and costume (thereby offending the national pride and religious prejudices of his people), and also to commit numerous costly absurdities, which brought him more and more into public hatred and contempt. At

[1] Schlosser, vol. vi. pp. 124-127. The Convention (dated March 10, 1779) may be seen in Martens et Cussy's "Recueil des Traités," &c., vol. i.

the same time they secretly but sedulously encouraged the disaffection of his subjects. A revolt soon broke out; and the terrified Khan was persuaded by his Russian friends to call in the troops of the Empress to his assistance. Again the Russian soldiers occupied the Crimea in the guise of pacificators; but Potemkin and his imperial mistress now thought that they might safely appropriate the long-coveted prize. The Tartars, who opposed the Russian measures, were slaughtered or expelled without mercy; and, partly by threats, partly by bribes, Schahin Ghirai was induced to resign the crown of the Crimea and the Kuban to the Empress, and to attest that the individuals of his family, in which the throne was hereditary, were rightfully deposed for ever.[1]

In the Empress's manifestoes respecting the annexation of the Crimea, the Kuban, and the adjacent territories to Russia (which were published in April, 1783), the same spirit of grim hypocrisy was maintained, with which Europe was already familiarised by the sayings and doings of the Czarina and her confederates in the case of Poland. It was pretended that the Russian sovereign was only seeking to confer benefits on the Tartar nation. They were to be delivered by her from the miseries of civil war and internal anarchy; and were also to be relieved from the evils to which their former position between the frontiers of the Turkish and Russian dominions, exposed them in the event of any collision of those two powers. These flourishes of Russian liberality served the sophists and declaimers of Western Europe with materials for new panegyrics on the magnanimity of the Empress Catherine;[2] but the Tartars themselves felt the oppression of Russian conquest in all its bitter reality. Some of them took up arms for the independence of their country; and the chief men of the nation hardly sought to disguise their disaffection under Muscovite rule. General Paul Potemkin (the cousin of the Prince) put the malcontents to the edge of the sword, in a massacre, in which 30,000 Tartars of every age and sex are said to have perished.[3] Many thousands more were obliged to quit the country. Among the

---

[1] Clarke's "Travels," vol. ii. pp. 174-177.

[2] Schlosser, vol. vi. p. 128. Mr. Fox, in his advocacy of the proceedings of the Russian Empress, put the matter on a broader and a clearer basis. He said (in his speech in the House of Commons, March 29, 1791), "After the independence of the Crimea had been established by the peace of Kainardji, the Empress informed the Porte and other powers that she found it impossible to secure her old dominions if she was not complete mistress of Kuban Tartary and the Crimea; and, *by a kind of royal syllogism,* she said, 'And therefore I must have them.'"

[3] Schlosser, p. 129.

refugees from Russian tyranny were 75,000 Armenian Christians, all of whom, except 7000, perished from cold, hunger, and fatigue, as they endeavoured to cross the steppes on the eastern side of the Sea of Azoph.[1] Paul Potemkin was awarded for this carnage and his conquests by the dignity of Grand Admiral of the Black Sea, and Governor of the new Russian province of Tauris, as the Crimea and the adjacent territory on the mainland were now denominated. Prince Potemkin (under whose directions the general had acted) was signalised by the title of the Taurian.[2] The result of these injuries and violences was, that Russia increased her dominion by the possession of all the countries which had made up the independent Tartar kingdom, so formally recognised and guaranteed by herself in the treaties of 1774 and 1779. These countries were not only the Crimean peninsula itself, with its admirable harbours and strong positions, but also extensive regions along the north coast of the Euxine ; and, in Asia, the island of Taman, and the important Kuban territory, where the outposts of Russian power were now planted, ready for further advance against either the Turkish or the Persian dominions in Upper Asia.

The progress of this high-handed robbery excited the greatest indignation at Constantinople ; nor did Western Europe observe unmoved such inordinate aggrandisement of the Russian power. The American war was over. The House of Bourbon had gratified its ancient feelings of feud with England by aiding in the humiliation which the events of that war inflicted on this country. France for a brief period before her Revolution was at leisure to consider the general interests of the civilised world. Louis XVI. and his minister, M. de Vergennes, were sincerely desirous to check the ambitious career of Catherine, and to save the Turkish Empire from dismembermemt. Austria was found to be too much under Russian influence to be trusted; and the French Court addressed itself to that of England on the subject of the Crimea, even before the definitive treaty of peace between France and England was formally signed. In June, 1783, M. d'Adhémar, the representative of France at London, informed Mr. Fox (then Secretary of State for Foreign Affairs) that " The Most Christian King had just received from the cabinet of St. Petersburg the official notification that Russia had taken possession of the Crimea and the Kuban. Would England look on with indifference at such a spirit of conquest ?" The English minister replied by expressing a doubt of the fact of definite possession of those provinces having been taken by Russia: he said that Frederick of

[1] Clarke, vol. ii. pp. 179 n., 184.   [2] Schlosser, p. 129.

Prussia would make war sooner than allow it. Again and again, by orders from his court, M. d'Adhémar addressed Fox on the subject. He asked, " Would England see with indifference a Russian fleet in the Bosphorus ? was it wished that Constantinople should be given up to Catherine ? at any rate, could not some limit be imposed on the Empress's career of conquest ? might not the Kuban be conceded to her, so as on that cession to found a demand for her resigning the Crimea ? If France and England would join in a remonstrance, their voice must be attended to at St. Petersburg ; but, acting singly, France would not be heeded." Fox coldly replied that it was too late to interfere. " The annexation of the Crimea was now a *fait accompli.* Besides, England had engagements with the Empress which it was inconvenient to break." Thus repelled by the minister, M. d'Adhémar sought and obtained an audience from the King of England. He explained to George III. the importance of the Russian conquests ; he pointed out the political intimacy that was forming between Joseph II. of Austria and the Russian sovereign, and their evident intention to dismember Turkey, as the greater part of Poland had already been seized and partitioned. The honesty and strong common sense of George III. were moved ; and he exclaimed, with indignation, "If things are to go on in this fashion, Europe will soon be like a wood, where the strongest robs the weakest, and there will be no security for any one." But a King of England can only act constitutionally through his ministry and parliament. Fox persevered in his indifference to Turkey, or rather, in his partiality to Russia ; nor, indeed, is it probable that the English people, exhausted as they were by a long and unsuccessful war, would at that period have co-operated willingly with France in new hostilities. The irritation felt here against that country for the part which she had taken against England in the American contest was too bitter ; and the recollection of the combined fleets of the House of Bourbon riding supreme in the Channel was far too fresh and painful.

The French minister, by a despatch of the 8th of August, 1783, sorrowfully assured his court that there was no hope of obtaining the co-operation of England, and that Mr. Fox seemed bound to a false system ; but M. d'Adhémar added a prophetic expression of belief, that a nullification of the policy of England in so grave a matter could not be permanent ; and that sooner or later England would come to an understanding with France for the purpose of arresting the progress of the military and naval power of Russia, which threatened to overwhelm the East.[1]

[1] A minute and interesting narrative of these negotiations is given by M.

The Prussian King, when applied to by M. de Vergennes to act in concert with France in the Oriental question, merely replied by complaints against the alliance of 1756 between the Houses of Hapsburg and Bourbon; and he called on France to renounce her connection with Austria before she asked Prussia to take part with her.[1] Louis XVI. and his minister found the same selfish indifference to prevail both at the court of Turin and in that of Vienna.[2] It was, indeed, well known that Austria was conspiring with Russia for the spoliation of Turkey, and that her policy was to indemnify herself against the increase of the Russian power by seizure of territories for herself. A vain appeal was made to her sense of expediency by M. de Vergennes, who bitterly lamented that, according to the new system of European international policy, it was useless to talk of justice; and that self-interest was now openly recognised as the natural prime agent in the disposal of the affairs of the world.[3] The French ambassador at Vienna represented to the Austrian cabinet that "Austria could not desire to see her military and maritime interests sunk in the absorbing influence of Russia. Even if the Crimea and the Kuban were to be given up to the Empress, at least let an admission be required of her in behalf of the commercial and maritime interests of all nations. Let there be a stipulation that she is to have only merchant vessels in the Black Sea, or such vessels of war as mount less than twenty guns."[4] The same disregard was shown at Vienna, as at the other capitals of Western Europe, to the proposals of France; Louis XVI. judged it imprudent to act alone. The Sultan was informed that he must look for no aid from the West. He knew too well the strength of his northern adversary and his own. The Turkish preparations for the recovery of the Crimea were discontinued, and a new treaty was signed on the 8th of January, 1784, between Turkey and Russia, by which it was agreed that the new state of things in the Crimea, Taman, and the Kuban, should not disturb the peace between the two empires. The stipulation of the treaty of Kainardji, which assured to the Porte the sovereignty over Oczakof and its territory, was formally renewed; and the third article of the new convention provided that whereas the river Kuban was admitted as the

---

Capefigue in his recent historical work, entitled "Louis XVI., ses relations diplomatiques avec l'Europe, l'Inde, l'Amérique, et l'Empire Ottoman," pp. 195-209.   See also Mr. Fox's speech in the Oczakof debates of 1791, in the "Parliamentary History of England," vol. xxix. p. 63.

[1] Capefigue, p. 203.   [2] Ibid., pp. 204, 206.
[3] Ibid.   [4] Ibid., p. 206.

frontier in the Kuban, Russia renounced all sovereignty over the Tartar nations beyond that river; that is to say, between the river Kuban and the Black Sea.[1]

The pacific words inserted in this treaty, like those in the convention of 1779, were mere hollow formalities; for the Porte could not but cherish resentment for the wrongs to which it seemed to submit; and the aggressive ambition of Catherine was only stimulated by conquests and concessions. Austria was now entirely devoted to the interests of Russia; and a league was made between the two empires, by which each bound itself to aid the other.[2] In a triumphal progress which Catherine made in the early part of the year 1787 to her new Taurian province, she was joined by the Emperor Joseph at Kherson. He accompanied her to the Crimea, and, amid the festivities and frivolities of their journey, the imperial tourists sometimes argued, and sometimes jested on the details of the dismemberment of the Ottoman Empire, and on the questions of what was to be done with the Greeks, and what was to become of "those poor devils the Turks."[3] Batchiserai, the ancient capital of the deposed Tartar Khans, was the scene of many of these schemes and scoffs; and the downfall of the Sultan was gaily plotted at Sebastopol also, as Catherine's new city by the Gulf of Aktiar was pompously designated. The Empress and her guests saw there with pride and exultation a new Russian navy riding in the finest harbours of the Black Sea. Even then they boasted of the facilities which Sebastopol would give for a sudden and a decisive attack upon the Turkish capital.

It was the design of Catherine and Joseph to attack Turkey along the whole line of her northern frontier, from the Adriatic to the Caucasus. But, as it was wished by the Empress to keep up her character for magnanimity and equity in the literary world of Christendom, means were taken to provoke the Turks to be the first in declaring war. The emissaries of Russia excited disturbances in Moldavia, Wallachia, Greece, and other parts of the

---

[1] The treaty is printed in Martens et Cussy, vol. i. p. 345; and in Martens' "Recueil des Traités," vol. ii. p. 505.

[2] Coxe, vol. iii. p. 477.

[3] "Leurs Majestés Impériales se tâtoient quelquefois sur les pauvres diables de Turcs. On jetait quelques proposés en regardant. Comme amateur de la belle antiquité, et un peu de nouveautés, je parlais de retablir les Grecs; Catherine, de faire renaître les Lycurges et les Solons: moi, je parlais d'Alcibiade; mais Joseph II., qui était plus pour l'avenir que pour le passé, et pour le positif que pour le chimère, disait: 'Que diable faire de Constantinople?'"—Prince de Ligne, Lettres, &c., p. 55 (ed. 1810).

Ottoman Empire. Offensive claims were put forward on the part of the Empress to the province of Bessarabia, and the towns of Oczakof and Akerman, on the pretext that they had formerly been governed by the Khans of her new Taurida.[1] These and similar measures irritated more and more the haughty spirit of the Osmanlis, which had already been deeply incensed at the open insults put upon Turkey by the Russian and Austrian sovereigns during their progress to the Crimea, in which their hostility to Turkey had been so little veiled, that when Catherine and Joseph passed through the southern gate of her new city of Kherson, a pompous inscription, in the Greek language, was set up, announcing that this was the way to Byzantium.[2]

Had Gazi Hassan been at Constantinople in the summer of 1787, it is probable that the war would have been deferred, until Turkey had prepared herself to sustain it with more vigour. His policy was to complete the subjugation of the rebellious and disaffected provinces of the Sultan, before the renewal of the contest with the foreign enemy. In furtherance of this plan, he was, in 1787, occupied in the recovery of Egypt to his sovereign's power.[3] But, partly through the rivalry with which the Grand Vizier, Yusuf, and other Ottoman grandees regarded Gazi Hassan, and partly through the popular indignation at Constantinople, which the studied insults and aggressions of Russia excited, hostilities were declared by the Sublime Porte against that country on the 15th of August, 1787;[4] the Sultan unfurled the Sacred Standard of the Prophet, proclaimed a holy war, and summoned the True Believers to assemble round the banner of their Faith.

The first object of the Turks was to recover the fortress of Kilburn (which had been ceded to the Russians by the treaty of Kainardji, and so regain the mastery of the important embouchure of the rivers Boug and Dnieper. For this purpose, Gazi Hassan was recalled from Egypt, and placed in command of the Sultan's land and sea forces in and near the Black Sea. On the Russian side, Prince Potemkin (who chiefly directed the operations of the war) sent Suwarrow to defend the menaced fortress. A division of the Turkish army was posted at Oczakof, on the coast immediately opposite to Kilburn; and Gazi Hassan's design was to land part of these forces, and also the troops which his fleet had

---

[1] Schlosser, vol. vi. p. 141; "Parliamentary History," vol. xxix. p. 193; Emerson Tennent's "Greece," vol. ii. p. 401.
[2] Coxe, vol. iii. p. 515.
[3] Eton, p. 423.
[4] Ibid., p. 423; Coxe, vol. iii. p. 515; Schlosser, vol. vi. p. 141.

conveyed from Constantinople, on the Kilburn side, for the purpose of assailing the fortress by land, while the Turkish fleet
bombarded it from the sea.   Suwarrow's troops were few in
number, and Kilburn was then ill-fortified : but his generalship
and daring not only protected it, but nearly destroyed the assailants.   Kilburn has justly been called " Suwarrow's glory,"[1] down
to our own time.   Suwarrow erected a battery at the very
entrance of the Liman (as the embouchure of the two rivers,
which widens out after the passage between Oczakof and Kilburn,
is termed), and he drew together a strong force of Russian gunboats from Nicolaieff under the Prince of Nassau Siegen.   Suwarrow permitted the Turkish fleet to enter the Liman without moles-
tation ; and he remained inactive till the Turks had disembarked
from 6000 to 7000 men on the Kilburn shore.   He then made a
sudden and desperate attack on them with two battalions of
infantry, which he led on with fixed bayonets ; and when he had
broken them with this charge, he brought forward some regiments
of Cossacks to complete their rout.   All the Turkish troops that
had been landed on the Kilburn shore were slain.   At the same
time, the Russian battery at the end of the promontory opened its.
fire upon the Turkish ships, and the flotilla of the Nicolaieff gunboats assailed them in the Liman.   The greater part of Hassan's
armament was destroyed ; and thus, at the very commencement
of the war, the prestige of success (always important in war, but
doubly so when the contest is with Orientals) was fixed on the side
of the Muscovites.[2]

The approach of the winter season checked the progress of
hostilities during the remainder of 1787 : and in the following
year a seasonable diversion in behalf of Turkey was effected by
the war, which broke out between Sweden and Russia, and
which detained the Empress's best fleet and many of her troops
in and near the Baltic.   War had not yet been declared between
Austria and Turkey ; and the Emperor Joseph's internuncio at
Constantinople was instructed to offer the mediation of his sovereign to prevent the further effusion of blood.[3]   The cause of this
delay on the part of Joseph, was the troubled state of his dominions in the Netherlands ; but so soon as a temporary suspension
of these disturbances had been effected, the Austrian sovereign

[1] " Oh ! Kilburn, Kilburn, Suwarrow's glory, and my shame !" was the
exclamation of the Russian general on surrendering it to the combined
French and English armament in 1855.

[2] Schlosser, vol. vi. p. 142 ; Eton, p. 91.

[3] Coxe, vol. iii. p. 516.

resumed his hostile preparations against Turkey. He even endeavoured to obtain a treacherous advantage by surprising the important fortress of Belgrade, while he still affected the character of a peacemaker. This discreditable enterprise took place on the night of the 2nd December, 1787. But the Austrian troops, that were sent against the Turkish city across the Danube and the Saave, were delayed by natural obstacles, and by the want of due concert between their commanders. The morning found a detachment of them under the walls of Belgrade, who were exposed to certain destruction if the Turkish garrison had assailed them. But the Pacha, who governed there, pretended to be satisfied with the apologies of the Austrian officer in command and permitted him and his men to withdraw unmolested. This shameful violation of public faith and the law of nations on the part of Austria was met by the Ottomans with only a dignified appeal to the gratitude of the Emperor. They reminded him of the forbearance of Turkey in the time of Austria's distress after the death of Charles VI., and of the scrupulous honesty with which the treaties between the two empires had been observed by successive Sultans.[1] But cupidity and ambition had more influence on Austria than such feelings as gratitude or generosity, as honesty or honour; and on the 10th of February, 1788, Joseph published a declaration of war, in which he imitated the document by which the Emperor Charles VI. had commenced the war of 1737, even as he had imitated the treachery of his predecessor in attacking the possessions of a neighbour, while still professing peace and good-will.[2]

Joseph hoped to aggrandise his dominions by the conquest and annexation of not only Bosnia and Servia, but also of Moldavia and Wallachia. He began the war with an army of 200,000 men and a train of 2000 pieces of artillery; but what he effected in 1788 with this enormous force, was more in accordance with the scanty justice of his cause, than with the magnificence of his preparations. It had been arranged that a Russian army should enter Moldavia, and march thence to co-operate with the Austrians. But the breaking out of the Swedish war obliged the Empress to reduce the Russian corps that was to act with Joseph's troops to a division of 10,000 men under General Soltikoff. The same cause prevented the sailing of the intended Russian armament to the Archipelago. But the Empress's fleet on the Black Sea was now strengthened and well equipped, nearly all the

[1] Coxe, vol. iii. p. 516.
[2] Ibid., vol. iii. p. 516.

officers being foreigners. Russian troops, under Generals Tallizyn and Tamara made vigorous progress in the regions between the Black Sea and the Caspian; and the main army which was collected near the river Boug, under the favourite, Prince Potemkin, was numerous and efficient, though little activity was shown in its operations during the greater part of the year.[1]

On the Turkish side Oczakof was strongly garrisoned; and was regarded as the bulwark of the empire against Potemkin's army. Gazi Hassan commanded on the Black Sea, and the Grand Vizier assembled his forces in Bulgaria, to act as necessity required, either against the Russians, who were expected to advance by their old line of invasion, through Bessarabia and Wallachia; or against the Austrians, who threatened Turkey from the north-west. Joseph wasted the early part of the year in waiting for the Russians, and in unsuccessful intrigues with the Pacha of Scutari, and other Turkish commanders, whose customary insubordination towards their Sultan was erroneously thought convertible into traitorous co-operation with the enemies of their race and faith. When, at length, the Austrian Sovereign, ashamed at the ridicule which his indecision had brought on him, began to advance, he encountered an obstinate resistance from the Mahometan population of Bosnia; though in Servia the Rayas again welcomed the Imperialists, and formed armed bands that fought bravely against the Turks.[2] But the Grand Vizier, who found that there was no serious peril of a Russian advance upon the Balkan during that year, moved his whole force upon the flank of the Austrian line of operations. Joseph retired with precipitation. The Turks crossed the Danube; defeated an Austrian army under Wartersleben at Meadia; laid waste the Bannat; and threatened to invade Hungary. Joseph now gave the command of part of his forces, called the army of Croatia, to Marshal Laudohn, a veteran hero of the Seven Years' War, who instantly assumed the offensive,[3] defeated the Turks opposed to him at Dubitza, and, before the close of the campaign, had advanced into the heart of Bosnia, and besieged and taken the town of Novi. Joseph, himself, had marched with 40,000 men to relieve General Wartersleben and to protect Hungary. For

[1] Coxe, vol. iii. p. 517; Schlosser, vol. vi. p. 143.
[2] Coxe, vol. iii. p. 518. Ranke's "Servia," p. 91.
[3] "Laudohn had always disapproved of a defensive war; and his axiom was that more men are lost by sickness or desertion in inaction, than fall by the hand of the enemy in the most bloody battles."—Coxe, vol. iii. p. 518, note.

this purpose, he took up a position near Slatina, in the valley of Karansebes, where he closed his military career by inflicting upon himself one of the most remarkable defeats recorded in history.

The forces under his command amounted to 80,000 men. The Vizier's army was posted opposite to him at a little distance. Elated with the numbers and admirable condition of his troops, Joseph had resolved to attack the Turks, and to carry the war into Wallachia. The project was approved of by his generals; and an easy victory was anticipated at the cost of not more than 3000 or 4000 men. On the 20th of September all was prepared for the attack, and the generals were assembled in the Emperor's tent to receive their final orders : the troops were in the highest spirits, and everything seemed to promise a brilliant triumph to Austria. Suddenly the Emperor felt nervous and disquieted, and asked the veteran Marshal Lacy if he was sure of beating the enemy. The marshal replied (as any sensible man would under the circumstances),[1] that he expected victory, but that he could not absolutely guarantee it. This answer so discouraged Joseph, that he instantly abandoned the intention of attack, and resolved to fall back to Temeswar. The plan of retreat was arranged ; and, as an additional security, orders were given that the retrograde march should begin at midnight. The troops had proceeded a little distance, when Marshal Lacy discovered that the piquets of the left wing had not been withdrawn. He immediately directed that this should be done, and that the further movement of the main body should be checked, till it was joined by those detachments. The word of command to halt was passed and repeated loudly through the ranks ; and in the darkness and confusion some of the Austrian troops thought that it was the Turkish war-cry of "Allah" which they heard, and that the enemy was upon them. The panic spread rapidly. The drivers of the ammunition tumbrils urged their horses to full speed, in the hope of escaping. The infantry, thinking that the noise thus made was caused by the charge of the Turkish cavalry, clustered together in small bodies, and opened a musketry fire in all directions. At daylight they discovered their fatal error, and the havoc ceased, but not before 10,000 Austrians had fallen by the weapons of their own comrades. Order was then restored, and the army continued its retreat to Temeswar. But the Turks, whose courage was raised in proportion as that of their adversaries fell, captured part of the Austrian baggage and artillery ; and before the campaign was

[1] The words are Marshal Marmont's

terminated in November by an armistice for three months, 20,000 more of Joseph's best soldiers had perished by sickness, which was the consequence of his prolonged occupation of an unhealthy tract of country.[1] Altogether Austria lost in the operations of this year 30,000 men in killed and wounded, the greater part of whom fell at Karansebes or in desultory skirmishes; and 40,000 more, who were swept away by pestilential disorders.

On the north-western coast of the Black Sea, where Prince Potemkin commanded, the Russians effected little during the greater part of the year; though Oczakof was invested as early as August. At length Potemkin summoned the victor of Kilburn to urge on the siege, and the Russian arms made their customary progress under Suwarrow, though he was obliged by a wound to retire from head-quarters before the final assault was given. This took place on the 16th of December, 1788. Valour, maddened to ferocity, was shown on both sides. The Turks of Oczakof had, before the siege, surprised a Russian village in the vicinity, and mercilessly slaughtered all the inhabitants. Potemkin and Suwarrow caused the Russian regiments, that were to assault the town, to be first led through this village as it lay in ashes, and with its streets still red with the blood of their fellow-countrymen. With their natural stubborn savage courage thus inflamed by the longing for revenge, the Russians advanced on the 16th of December over the frozen Liman against the least fortified side of the city. Whole ranks were swept away by the fire of the besieged; but the supporting columns still came forward unflinchingly through musketry and grape; 4000 Russians fell; but the survivors bore down all resistance, and forced their way into the city, where for three days they revelled in murder and pillage. No mercy was shown to age or sex; and out of a population and garrison of 40,000 human beings, only a few hundreds (chiefly women and children) escaped, whom the exertions of the officers in the Russian service rescued from the indiscriminate fury of the soldiery.[2]

---

[1] See Marshal Marmont's account of the havoc of Karansebes at p. 11 of his Memoirs (Sir F. Smith's translation): see too Coxe, vol. iii. p. 520.

[2] Eton, p. 424; Schlosser, vol. vi. p. 164. Mr. Eton, who was with Prince Potemkin at Oczakof, describes a touching scene which he witnessed there, and which he cites as a proof of the "fortitude and resignation bordering upon apathy," with which the Turks bear evils of the greatest magnitude. He says (p. 115), "The Turkish women and children (in number about 400) who were brought out of Oczakof when the city was taken, to the head-quarters of the Russian army, were put all together the first night under a tent. No better accommodation could under the pressure of the

In the March of 1789, the Turkish Grand Vizier began the campaign against Austria with unusual activity. He left troops on the lower Danube to observe the enemy in Wallachia and Moldavia; he crossed the river at Rustchuk, with 90,000 men, whom he led in person. He advanced rapidly towards Hermanstadt in Transylvania, with the design of pressing forward and carrying the war into the hereditary provinces of the Emperor. Unfortunately for Turkey the death of Sultan Abdul Hamid at this crisis caused a change of Grand Viziers; and the able leader of the Turks was superseded by the Pacha of Widdin, a man utterly deficient in military abilities. The effect of this change was the abandonment of the late Vizier's plans for the campaign; and the Turkish troops were drawn back to the south of the Danube.[1]

Sultan Selim III., the successor of Abdul Hamid, ascended the Turkish throne on the 7th of April, 1789, being then twenty-seven years old. He was a young man of considerable abilities and high spirit; and his people gladly hailed the accession of a youthful prince, active in person, and energetic in manner, under whom they hoped to see an auspicious turn given to the long-declining fortunes of the empire. Selim had been treated by his uncle, the late Sultan, with far greater kindness, and had been allowed much

---

circumstances be made for them, though it froze exceedingly hard, and they suffered dreadfully from cold and nakedness, and many from wounds. As I spoke Turkish, I had the guard of that post, and the superintendence of them that night. I observed that there reigned a perfect silence among them, not one woman weeping or lamenting, at least loudly, though every one, perhaps, had lost a parent, a child, or a husband. They spoke with a calm and firm voice, and answered the questions I put to them apparently without agitation. I was astonished, and knew not whether to impute it to insensibility, or the habit of seeing and hearing of great vicissitudes of fortune, or to a patience and resignation inculcated by their religion; and at this day I am equally unable to account for it. One woman sat in a silent but remarkably melancholy posture, insomuch that I was induced to offer her some consolation. I asked her why she did not take courage and bear misfortune like a Mussulman, as her companions did. She answered in these striking words: '*I have seen my father, my husband, and my children killed; I have only one child left.*' 'Where is it?' I asked her with some precipitation. '*Here!*' she calmly said, and pointed to a child by her side, which had just expired. I and those with me burst into tears, but she did not weep at all. I took with me that night into my warm subterranean room as many of these miserable women and children, wounded and perishing with cold, as it would contain; they stayed with me twelve days, during all which time none of them either complained aloud, or showed any signs of excessive internal grief, but each told me her story (both young and old) as of an indifferent person, without exclamation, without sighs, without tears."

[1] Coxe, vol. iii. p. 521.

28

more freedom, both bodily and mental, than the non-reigning princes of the blood-royal were usually permitted to enjoy. One of his intimate associates was an Italian physician, named Lorenzo; and from him and other Franks, Selim eagerly sought and obtained information respecting the nations of Western Europe, their civil and military institutions, and the causes of that superiority which they had now indisputably acquired over the Ottomans. Selim even opened (through a confidential agent, Isaac Bey) a correspondence with the French King and his ministers Vergennes and Montmorin, in which he sought political instruction from the chiefs of what he was taught to regard as the foremost nation of the Franks.[1] He felt keenly the abuses which prevailed in his own country; and it is said that his father, Sultan Mustapha III., had bequeathed to him a memorial (diligently studied and venerated by young Selim), in which the principal events of Mustapha's unhappy reign were reviewed, the degeneracy of the Turkish nation discussed, and the great evils that prevailed in the state were pointed out, with exhortations to their thorough removal. Thus trained and influenced, Selim came an ardent reformer to the throne; but the war, which he found raging between his empire and the confederate powers of Austria and Russia, required all his attention in the beginning of his reign, which opened with the darkest scenes of calamity and defeat.

The great mass of the Austrian forces in 1789 was placed under the able guidance of Marshal Laudohn. The Prince of Coburg commanded the corps which was to co-operate with the Russians. Potemkin's army, after the destruction of Oczakof, occupied the country from the Dnieper to the Delta of the Danube; and Suwarrow (who had now recovered from his wound) was sent into Moldavia with the Russian division, which was to assist the Prince of Coburg.[2] Sultan Selim had recalled Gazi Hassan from the command of the fleet in the Black Sea, where he had experienced several reverses; and the old admiral was now placed at the head of the Turkish army, which was to act against Coburg's forces. Hassan advanced upon the Austrians, who were stationed at Fockshani, at the extreme point of Moldavia. He would probably have overwhelmed them, if they had not been succoured by Suwarrow, who marched his army no less than sixty English miles over a wild mountainous district in thirty-six hours.[3]

---

[1] Aleix. "Précis d'Histoire Ottoman," vol. ii. Article Selim III., "Biographie Universelle."

[2] Coxe, vol. iii. p. 521. Schlosser, vol. vi. p. 165.

[3] Marmont, p. 32.

Suwarrow reached the Austrian position at five o'clock in the evening of the 30th of July. Instead of waiting for Hassan's assault, he issued his order for battle at eleven o'clock the same night; and at two hours before daybreak the next morning, he led the allied armies forward against the Turkish fortified camp, in one of those bold bayonet attacks, which became national and natural to the Russian soldiery under his guidance.[1] The Turks were utterly routed, and all their artillery and baggage taken. Another and a larger army was collected by Selim's orders and exertions, which on the 16th of September encountered Suwarrow with the same result, though the contest was more obstinate. This great victory of the Russian general was gained by him near the river Rimnik, whence came the well-merited surname of Rimnikski, which was conferred on Suwarrow by his Empress.[2] The excitement and alarm of the Turks were now extreme; and Selim, in order to appease the popular tumult at Constantinople, disgraced himself by putting to death the gallant, though lately unsuccessful veteran, Gazi Hassan. The Ottoman forces in Bosnia and Servia experienced defeats almost as severe from the Imperialists under Laudohn. Belgrade and Semendria were captured; and the advance of the converging Russian and Austrian armies upon the Turkish capital seemed irrestrainable, when the Emperor Joseph was compelled by the disorder and revolts, which had broken out in almost every part of his dominions, to check the progress of his forces in Turkey, and to employ them against his own subjects. The death of the Austrian sovereign in 1790, relieved the Sultan from one of the most vehement, though not of the most resolute foes of the Ottoman power.[3] The succeeding Emperor, Leopold, alarmed at the perilous condition of many of his most important provinces, and menaced with war by Prussia, was anxious to conclude a secure and honourable peace with Turkey: and after some further operations on the Danube, in the course of which the Austrians captured Orsova, but were defeated by the Turks near Giurgevo, an armistice was agreed on, which was eventually followed by a peace: though the negotiations were protracted into the middle of the year 1791. The treaty of Sistova (as this pacification was termed) was signed on the 4th of August of that year. The Emperor relinquished all his conquests except the town of Old Orsova, and a small district in Croatia along the left

---

[1] Schlosser, vol. vi. p. 167, n.
[2] Coxe, vol. iii. p. 521. Schlosser, vol. vi. p. 168. "Biographie Universelle," tit. Souwarof.
[3] Coxe, vol. iii. p. 541.

band of the river Unna. With these slight variations the same boundary between Austria and Turkey was reconstituted in 1791 that had been defined by the treaty of Belgrade in 1739.[1]

Russia was a far more persevering and a far more deadly enemy to the Ottomans. The Empress Catherine made peace with Sweden in the August of 1790 ; but she long treated with haughty neglect the diplomatic efforts of England and Prussia in favour of the Turks.[2] Constantinople was the great prize which she sought to win at any cost, and at all hazards ; and she boasted that she would find there a capital for her empire, even if the Western powers were to drive her from St. Petersburg. In general, this design was veiled under the showy pretext of rescuing the Greeks from the Ottoman yoke, and reviving the classical glories of the Hellenic name. As in the preceding war, Russia now used every available method by which she might make the Greek population of the Turkish Empire fight her battles against the Sultan. Before hostilities commenced in 1787, Catherine had sent manifestoes to all parts of Greece, inviting the inhabitants " to take up arms and co-operate with her in expelling the enemies of Christianity from the countries they had usurped, and in regaining for the Greeks their ancient liberty and independence."[3] The Suliotes and other mountain tribes of Northern Greece (or rather Epirus) were leagued at her instigation in active insurrection against the Turks. The Swedish war at first, and afterwards the menacing attitude assumed by England towards Russia, detained in the Baltic the ships which the Empress had destined for the Archipelago and the Propontis ; but a Greek squadron of twelve vessels had been equipped by her orders in various ports in the Mediterranean ; and the Hellenic patriot, Lambro Canzani, sailed early in 1790 in command of this little force against the enemies of the Czarina. Lambro cruised for some weeks in the Archipelago, where he captured many Turkish vessels, made frequent daring descents on the mainland, and conquered the island of Zea, which he occupied with part of his crews. The Sultan was compelled to withdraw from the Black Sea part of the remaining Turkish navy to oppose these active enemies, and he sought and obtained also the more effectual aid of a squadron from Algiers. The united Ottoman and Barbaresque fleet, brought Lambro to action on the 18th of May, and succeeded, by the superiority of their numbers and the skilful gunnery of the

---

[1] Coxe, vol. iii. p. 550.　　　　[2] Schlosser, vol. vi. p. 170.
[3] Eton, p. 323. Emerson Tennent's "Greece," vol. ii. p. 401.

Algerines, in destroying the whole of his ships.[1] On land, the insurrection continued ; and the troops of the Pacha who attacked the Suliotes (the celebrated Ali of Yanina), met with repeated defeats. A general deputation of the Greeks was sent in the early part of 1790 to St. Petersburg, to implore the aid of "the most magnanimous of sovereigns," and to beseech that she would give to the Greeks, for a sovereign, her grandson Constantine.[2] This address was graciously received by the Empress, who promised them the assistance which they requested. They were then conducted to the apartments of her grandson, where they paid homage to the Grand Duke Constantine, and saluted him as Emperor of the Greeks (βασιλεὺς τῶν Ἑλλήνων). A plan for the military co-operation of the Greek insurgents with the expected advance of the Russians upon Adrianople was then discussed ; and the deputation was sent with the Russian General Tamaran to Prince Potemkin's head-quarters in Moldavia.

The great military event of the year 1790, was the capture of Ismail by Suwarrow. This important city is situate on the left bank of the Kilia, or northern arm of the Danube, about forty miles from the Black Sea. It was strongly garrisoned by the Turks, and presented an almost insurmountable barrier to the advance of the Russians through the coast districts of Bessarabia and Bulgaria. Potemkin besieged it in person for several months without success. He then retired to Bender, to enjoy his usual life of more than viceregal pomp and luxury, and sent the hero of Kilburn, Fockshani, and the Rimnik to reduce the obstinate city. His laconic orders to Suwarrow were, " You will take Ismail, whatever be the cost."[3] Suwarrow joined the besieging army on the 16th of December, and on the 22nd, Ismail was taken ; but at a cost of carnage and crime, for which the hideous history of sieges, ancient or modern, can hardly furnish a parallel.

An accomplished scholar and linguist, a highly scientific tactician, an acute and profound calculator, Suwarrow yet assumed the manners and appearance of a boorish humourist ; and encouraged the belief that each of his successes resulted rather from the happy inspiration of the moment, than from elaborate combinations and consummate military skill.[4] He acted this part

[1] Emerson Tennent, vol. ii. p. 407.

[2] Ibid., vol. ii. p. 405. Eton, p. 344, gives the Greek original of the address itself.

[3] Schlosser, vol. vi. p. 173. Castera, "Histoire de Nouvelle Russie," vol. ii. p. 205.

[4] See Marshal Marmont's account of Suwarrow, p. 29 of his Memoirs.

through his deep insight into human nature ; through his perfect understanding of the dispositions and inclinations of those around him, and especially through his knowledge of the character and capabilities of the Russian soldiers. The men, who would have misunderstood and perhaps suspected him, if he had displayed the high accomplishments which he possessed, loved him for the rough frankness and grotesque coarseness which he assumed. "Brother," was the term by which Suwarrow spoke to and of a Russian common soldier, to whom the sound of kindness from a superior was new ; and there was a thorough heartiness in this military fraternity. He was ever ready with the rude but cheering jest, as he mixed familiarly with the ranks in the drill, on the march, or in battle. He shared too in all the perils and privations which he required them to endure; and he knew how to address them in homely, spirit-stirring phrases, which roused at once the patriotism, the fanatic devotion to his creed and his sovereign, which the Russian recruit brings with him from his peasant-home, and the military pride which the Russian soldier soon acquires under the colours.[1]

However elaborate might be Suwarrow's strategy, his mode of handling his troops in action was most simple. "*Stuppai e Be !*" "Forward and Strike !" was his favourite maxim. He knew that his Russians were deficient in the alacrity and intelligent bravery, which the troops of some other European nations possess ; but he knew that he could rely on the same dogged obstinacy which had made Frederick II. exclaim that "Russians might be killed, but not routed." Suwarrow, therefore, led his men on in masses, which were taught always to attack, and to attack instantly and decisively. He discouraged long musketry firing, and evolutions in the presence of the enemy. His rules were: "Draw out the line immediately, and instantly attack with the cold steel,"—"Fire seldom, but fire sure,"—"Push hard with the bayonet : the ball will lose its way—the bayonet never !"—"The ball is a fool—the bayonet a hero !"[2] The Russian soldiers almost idolised him.; and, during his long military career he never met with a single defeat. At Ismail, the army, which had been preparing to abandon the siege in discouragement, returned to its duty with enthusiastic ardour, as soon as the men saw Suwarrow among them. He

[1] See for specimens of these phrases the extraordinary document called "Suwarrow's Catechism, or the Discourse under the Trigger." It is printed at the end of the second volume of Clarke's "Travels," and also at the end of Mr. Danby Seymour's valuable work on the Crimea.

[2] See the "Military Catechism," *ut suprà.*

drilled the young soldiers in person, and taught them how to use the bayonet against the Turkish sabre. Abandoning the tedious operations of a formal siege, Suwarrow ordered a general assault to be made on the Turkish defences, which, though not regularly breached, were not insurmountable. So far as the loss of life among his own troops was concerned, he probably judged well; as the protraction of the siege through the winter would have caused the death of far more men in the Russian lines, through cold, privation, and disease, than even the amount of the thousands who fell in the storming. But the slaughter of the brave defenders, and of the helpless part also of the population of Ismail, which stained Suwarrow's triumph, was horrible beyond the power of description. The assault was given at night, and it was not till after sustaining heavy loss, and frequent repulses, that the Russians forced the walls. But the fiercest part of the contest was within the city itself; every street was a battle-field; every house was a fortress, which was defended with all the wild energy of despair. It was near noon before the Russian columns, slaying and firing all in their way, converged upon the market-place, where a body of Turks and Tartars of the garrison had rallied. The struggle raged there for two hours, quarter not being even asked, till the last of the Moslems had perished. Fresh troops from the Russian camp, eager for their share of booty and bloodshed, continued to pour into the devoted city, the remnants of which were given up for three days to the licence of the soldiery. According to Suwarrow's official report to Potemkin, in the course of four days 33,000 Turks were either slain or mortally wounded, and 10,000 taken prisoners. According to other accounts, nearly 40,000 of the defenders were destroyed by the Russians at Ismail, and only a few hundreds survived as captives. No reckoning seems to have been taken of the thousands of feeble old men, and of women and children, who suffered death, and worse than death, in the annihilated city. Suwarrow, while the ruins yet reeked before him, wrote a despatch to the Empress, in which he announced, in a couplet of doggerel exultation, that Ismail was won. It is probable that this callous buffoonery was affected. He afterwards told an English traveller that when the massacre was over, he went back and wept in his tent. So Scipio wept over Carthage burning; but such tears cannot wash out such blood.[1]

[1] The Siege of Ismail is described in the "Annual Register" for 1791 by Dr. Lawrance, and Castera in the "Histoire de Nouvelle Russie." Large extracts from these and other authorities are given in the notes to Mr. Murray's late editions of Byron.

Many of the ablest Turkish generals and officers perished at Ismail; and the remaining part of the war was a series of uninterrupted calamities to the Ottoman Empire. Sultan Selim still found the means of sending forward fresh armies; but these dispirited and undisciplined levies only furnished the Russian generals with the materials for further triumphs. Kutusoff routed a Turkish army near Babadagh, in January, 1791, and in the following July the host of 100,000 men, which had been collected under the Grand Vizier, was scattered by 40,000 Russians under General Repnin. The death, however, of Potemkin in the October of this year, removed the most violent promoter of the war on the Russian side, and the remonstrances of Prussia and England began at last to command attention from Catherine. William Pitt was now Prime Minister of England; and he discerned, far more sagaciously than most of his contemporaries, the true interest of England with regard to Russia and Turkey. A triple alliance had been formed in 1788, between England, Holland, and Prussia; the immediate object of which was to terminate the internal dissensions of the United Provinces. But the alliance was maintained after that purpose had been effected. The powers that were parties to it, had interfered at the Congress of the Hague, in 1790, in the disputes between the Emperor Joseph and his Belgian subjects; and they also had compelled Denmark to withdraw the support which she had given to Russia against Sweden in 1788.[1] Prussia, in her extreme jealousy of the power of the House of Hapsburg, had offered, when the Austro-Turkish war broke out in 1788, to conclude a treaty of alliance, offensive and defensive, with the Porte; and articles had been prepared, by which the Prussian King was to guarantee the recovery of the Crimea."[2] These, however, were never executed; but the triple alliance mediated between Austria and the Porte in the Congress at Reichenbach, in 1790, the result of which was the peace between Austria and Turkey, signed at Sistova, in 1791.[3] Having succeeded in the case of Austria, Prussia and England endeavoured to induce the Court of St. Petersburg to negotiate with the Porte, on the same basis to which Austria had consented, which is called in diplomatic terminology, the basis of the *statu quo*, and involves the principle of a general restoration of conquests. This was refused on the part of Russia; and various modifications of the *statu quo* were insisted on by Catherine's representatives. One design which she communicated to the Courts of Berlin and London, was a project for erecting

[1] Wheaton's "History of Modern Law of Nations," p. 286.
[2] Schlosser, vol. vi. p. 170, and note.   [3] Wheaton, p. 280.

the provinces of Moldavia, Wallachia, and Bessarabia into an independent sovereignty, to be governed, as the Russian proposal
vaguely phrased it, by a Christian prince. Some supposed that
this sovereign was to be the Archduke Constantine; others, that
the new crown was designed for the Empress's favourite, Prince
Potemkin, who was actually ruling these regions with fully regal
pomp and power.[1] But, whoever might receive the title of King
of Moldo-Wallachia, the recent fate of the Crimea had shown that
the erection of such a state was the mere preliminary to its annexation with Russia. The proposal was rejected by England and
Prussia; and the Empress was obliged to abandon this not the
least cherished of her schemes. But she was peremptory in excepting Oczakof and its territory from the suggested rule for
negotiation, and in requiring that the Russian frontier should be
extended to the Dniester.[2] We have better means than the
majority of our countrymen possessed eighty years ago, for appre-
ciating the wise policy of the English minister, who wished to
prevent the Empress from converting the Liman of the Boug and
the Dnieper into a Russian lake, where armaments prepared at
Nicholaieff and other places on those rivers may be collected in
secrecy and security; and whence they may suddenly issue into
the Black Sea for decisive operation against Constantinople itself.
Pitt resolved to support his diplomatic remonstrances by the guns
of an English fleet in the Baltic; and the requisite forces for a
naval expedition were prepared accordingly in the English ports at
the close of the year 1790. But the project of a Russian war was
made unpopular in England by the violent and unscrupulous
exertions of Fox and other opponents of Pitt's ministry. In the
numerous debates on the subject, which took place in the English
Parliament in the session of 1791, Turkey was reviled by the
Opposition speakers as a barbarous country, which had no part in
the European state system, and the fate of which could have no
effect on the balance of power. The Empress was eulogised as the
most magnanimous of sovereigns; and the idea of any peril
accruing to Western Europe from the aggrandisement of Russia
was derided as chimerical. It was asserted by Mr. Fox that the
overthrow of the Ottoman Empire was improbable, and that, if it
happened, it would be an advantage. Mr. Whitbread said:
"Suppose that the Empress could realise all her imputed views

[1] Adolphus' "Hist. of England," vol. v. p. 5. Tomlin's "Life of Pitt,"
vol. ii. p. 236. "Parliamentary History," session 1791.
[2] "Parliamentary History," vol. xxix. *passim.* See also in Martens'
"Recueil des Traités," vol. v. p. 55, the various notes on this subject.

of ambition and get possession of Constantinople, and expel the Turks from all their European provinces, would any unprejudiced man contend that, by such an event, mankind would not be largely benefited ? " The Ministerialist speakers replied by pointing out how much cause England had for guarding against the inordinate aggressiveness of the Empress, and for taking care that the Russian maritime power should not acquire predominance first in the Black Sea, next in the Dardanelles, and then by a natural consequence in the Mediterranean, where it would assume its true and most formidable appearance. They exposed the real character of Catherine in her conduct towards weak foreign nations ; and protested earnestly against the influence of Great Britain in the pending negotiation being impaired by such party attacks as those which were resorted to by the British Parliamentary Opposition. Afterwards, in the debates of the subsequent session in 1792, when the English minister was at liberty to speak more freely than he could have prudently spoken while our relations with Russia were yet undetermined, Mr. Pitt and Mr. Jenkinson (afterwards Lord Liverpool) splendidly demonstrated that the principle, by which the foreign policy of this country should be directed, was the fundamental principle of preserving the balance of power in Europe ; and that the true doctrine of the balance of power required that the Russian Empire should not, if possible, be allowed to increase, nor that of Turkey to diminish."[1]

France at this time (1790, 1791) was in the early agonies of her revolution ; and no joint action against Russia, such as M. de Vergennes had proposed in 1783, could be hoped for now. But though thus deprived of what would have been the most effective co-operation abroad, and thus hampered by party warfare at home, Pitt continued his interposition in behalf of Turkey. The intended armament was not indeed sent to the Baltic, but the Empress thought it wise not to provoke its appearance there by increasing her demands for cession of Turkish territory ; though the victories which her armies continued to gain during the negotiations between the Court of St. Petersburg and those of London and Berlin, made her waver for a time, and almost resolve to brave England and Prussia, and place her grandson on the throne of Constantinople.[2] Ultimately, more prudent counsels prevailed,

---

[1] The debates on the Russian armament in the session of 1791, and the Oczakof debates (as they have been termed) of the session of 1792, deserve careful study at the present time. They are reported in the 29th volume of the " Parliamentary History of England."

[2] Eton, pp. 539, 560.

and it is probable that she was in no little degree induced to assume an appearance of moderation towards Turkey, by the state of affairs in Poland. Kosciusko and his compatriots had effected important reforms in that country, of which the Empress had openly expressed her disapprobation. She saw with anxiety the progress that was being made in reorganising the military force and general resources of the Polish provinces, which had not yet been deprived of independence, and she felt that she had need of her General Suwarrow, and her veterans from the Turkish wars, to consummate the final invasion and dismemberment of Poland, on which she had already resolved.

Preliminary articles of peace were agreed on between General Repnin and the Grand Vizier in the autumn of 1791; and regular conferences were opened at Jassv which ended on the 9th of January, 1792, in the peace between Russia and Turkey of that name.

By the treaty of Jassy, the dominions of Russia were extended as far as the Dniester; and that river was made the boundary line of the two empires. An article was inserted (the 5th) which in somewhat vague terms enjoined that the Turkish commandants on the north-eastern frontiers of the Ottoman Empire should cause no annoyance or disquiet under any pretext, either secretly or openly, to the countries and people, then under the rule of the Czar of Tiflis and Kartalinia; and that he should levy nothing from them. In order to show the full purpose of Russia in making this astute stipulation, it is necessary to explain that Catherine, like her predecessor Peter the Great, coveted the provinces that lie between the Euxine and the Caspian Seas, not only for their intrinsic value as acquisitions to the Russian Empire, but on account of the advantages, which the possession of them seemed to offer for attacks on the Turkish dominions in Asia, and also for wars of conquest against Persia. Catherine caused lines of fortresses to be constructed between the two seas, and she maintained a fleet on the Caspian. Russian emissaries continually tampered with the Christian Princes of Georgia, Immeritia, Mingrelia, and the other smaller principalities, to induce them to renounce their ancient allegiance to the Sultan, or the Shah, and to place themselves under the sovereignty of the Russian Empress. These practices had been especially successful with Heraclius of Georgia, who was styled Czar of Tiflis and of Khartil. He had become the pensioner, and acknowledged vassal of Russia as early as 1785. The effect of the 5th article of the treaty of Jassy was to make Turkey acknowledge Russia as the

protector of these important regions. The same policy, the same
design of Russia to appropriate the Caucasian provinces, had dictated the seemingly obscure 19th article of the treaty of Kainardji;
we shall recognise it presently more clearly in the provisions of
the treaty of Akerman.[1]

The pacification of Jassy was never regarded by the Russian
Empress as anything more than a temporary pause in her operations against Constantinople, until the thorough subjugation of
the Poles should be effected, and the Western powers should be
too much engaged in other operations to be willing and able to
interfere with her Oriental schemes. This was the case in 1796 ;
and she was then on the very eve of accomplishing what her
admirers term " the great design," when her death rescued the
Ottoman Empire from a more formidable attack than it had ever
experienced. We know, from Mr. Eton's pages, how she intended
to recommence the war, and how it was proposed to overwhelm
the Sultan by the combined operations of Russian armies in
Europe and Asia, and of a fleet and flotilla from Nicholaieff and
Sebastopol conveying a force across the Black Sea, which was to
strike at the Turkish capital itself. His words (proceeding from
a knowledge of facts acquired at St. Petersburg) deserve consideration. He says of Catherine immediately before her death, that
" She was now in possession of every resource she required in
Poland for her army, in acting against the Turks on the European
continent. The government of the acquired provinces was so
firmly settled, that she had no apprehension of disturbances ; her
army was so formidable, that she could have marched beyond her
frontiers at least 300,000 effective men ; and she had raised
150,000 men to recruit it. Her fleet in the Black Sea was much
superior to the whole Turkish navy, and there was a flotilla of
small vessels built for the purpose of landing troops in three feet
of water, which could have conducted, in three days, 60,000 men
within a few miles of the capital of the Turkish Empire. The
first blow would have been the destruction of the Ottoman fleet
in its own port, and the attack of Constantinople by land at the
same time. A great army had passed .Derbent ; an arrangement
would have immediately taken place with the Persian Khans, in
whose quarrels, without any apparent interest, she had inter-
meddled ; and this army would have fallen on the Turkish Asiatic
provinces, the consequence of which would have been, that all the
Asiatic troops which compose the garrison of their fortresses in

[1] Chesney, p. 2.   " Progress of Russia in the East," p. 30.

Europe would have quitted them, and fled to succour their own country, and have left the road to Constantinople defenceless.[1]

As we are now approaching the time when Turkey became involved in the great wars of the French Revolution, and also the commencement of the reforms which cost Sultan Selim his life, but which Sultan Mahmoud II. effectively resumed, it may be convenient to pause, and take a brief survey of the state of the Turkish Empire, as it was near the close of the last century, and before the changes which have been wrought in its inhabitants and institutions by the Nizam-Djinid and other innovations.

[1] Eton, p. 438.

CHAPTER XXII.

VIEW OF THE TURKISH EMPIRE BEFORE THE COMMENCEMENT OF
SELIM III.'S REFORMS — TERRITORIAL DIVISIONS ; EYALETS,
LIVAS, KAZAS—APPOINTMENTS OF THE PACHAS—THE AYANS—
EXTENT OF THE EMPIRE—ITS MISRULE AND MISERY—FEEBLE-
NESS OF THE SULTAN'S AUTHORITY—THE WAHABITES, DRUSES,
MAMELUKES, AND SULIOTES—REVOLTS OF THE PACHAS—
ABUSES OF THE FEUDAL SYSTEM—TYRANNY OF THE FARMERS
OF THE REVENUE—MILITARY WEAKNESS OF THE EMPIRE—
THE JANISSARIES AND OTHER TROOPS—THE HOUSE OF OTHMAN
AT ITS NADIR.

SULTAN SELIM III. reigned over twenty-six Eyalets (as the larger
divisions of the Ottoman Empire were named) in Europe, Asia,
and Africa.   These were parcelled out into 163 smaller departments called Livas ; and each Liva was again subdivided into
Kazas, or communal districts.[1]   Each Kaza had its own municipal
jurisdiction ; and it generally consisted either of a town and its
dependencies, or of a rural canton (Nahiya) which often comprised
small towns as well as villages.   An Eyalet was presided over
by a Pacha with three horse-tails, who had the rank of Vizier.
He had assigned to him as the special sphere of his government,
one or more of the chief Livas of his Eyalet, and he exercised a
general superior authority over the local rulers of the rest.
Seventy-two Livas were under the immediate command of Pachas
with two horse-tails, and these, as well as the Eyalets, were
generally, though not accurately, spoken of as Pachalics.   In
general the appointment to the Pachalics were annual ; though
the same individual often retained his post for many years, and
sometimes for life, if he was too strong for the Porte to depose
him, or if he provided a sufficient sum of money from time to
time to purchase his reappointment from the venal ministers of
the Imperial Divan.   Twenty-two of the Livas were held by
Pachas on life-appointments.

[1] This description of the Turkish Empire is chiefly taken from the 7th
vol. of the work of Mouradjea D'Ohsson.

The Turkish governor was supposed to be assisted in his administration by two or three individuals chosen by the inhabitants of his province, and confirmed in their functions by the Porte. These were called Ayans or Notables. Sometimes the office of Ayan was hereditary; but it was then requisite that the succession of the new Ayan should be ratified by the majority of the inhabitants. The Rayas also, or tributary subjects of the Porte, had officers called Codji Bachis of their own nations, who assessed upon individuals the tax imposed on the district.

The list of the twenty-six Eyalets was as follows :—Roumelia, Bosnia, Silistria, Djezaer (which included the greater part of Greece), Crete, Anatolia, Egypt, Bagdad, Ricca, Syria, Erzeroum, Sivas, Seide, Tchildeir, Djiddar, Aleppo, Caramania, Diarbekir, Adana, Trebizond, Moussoul, Taraboulous, Elbistan, Kars, Scherzroul and Van. There were also several districts and cities not included in any Pachalic or Eyalet. Such were the trans-Danubian principalities of Wallachia and Moldavia. Such also were the cities of Mecca and Medina; and many cantons of Kurdistan were under their own hereditary chiefs, and were merely bound to supply the Sultan with a certain number of soldiers. The political condition of six Turkoman cantons was the same. The Barbaresque regencies continued to hold the position relatively to the Sublime Porte, which has been before described when we were tracing the reign of Sultan Mahomet IV.[1]

Thus, although the Turkish power had, before the end of the last century, been reft of many fair provinces; though its Padischah had no longer dominion in Hungary, in Transylvania, in the Crimea, or along the northern coasts of the Black Sea and the Sea of Azoph, still, the empire over which the House of Othman claimed sovereignty, might have been deemed one of the amplest and richest in the world, if its natural advantages and capacities only were regarded. But the authority of Sultan Selim III. was scarcely recognised, even in name, in many of the best provinces of which he styled himself the ruler; and almost the whole of Turkey was in that state of official insubordination and local tyranny, in which the feebleness of the sovereign is commensurate with the misery of the people. The Wahabites were masters of all Arabia, except the two cities of Mecca and Medina, which they had not yet conquered. In Egypt, the Mamelukes treated the Sublime Porte and its officers with open scorn, though the Sultan's standard was permitted to float at Cairo. In Syria, the Druses and the Metualis of Mount Lebanon and the hill-country

[1] See p. 296, *suprà.*

of Palestine were practically independent tribes. So were the Suliotes, and others in northern Greece and Epirus. So were the Montenegrins, and the dwellers in the Herzegovene. Moldavia and Wallachia, though in form restored to Turkey, were in reality far more under Russian than Ottoman authority. And not only by these races (which though comprised within the populations that had submitted to the House of Othman, were aliens from that House in creed, in language, and in blood), but also by the most powerful of his Mahometan subjects the Sultan's authority was systematically disregarded, though the forms of allegiance and lip-worship might still be preserved. Revolt and civil war were the common practices of the chief Pachas. In Acre, Djezzar Pacha refused tax and tribute, put to death the Sultan's messengers, and tyrannised over the neighbouring country with a savage cruelty that procured him his surname of The Butcher. The Pacha of Bagdad was equally insubordinate, and for many years the Porte received no revenues from the rich territory which that potentate commanded. The same was the case with the Pachas of Trebizond, and Akhalzik.[1] In Widdin, the celebrated Passwan Oglou for many years defied the whole force of the Sultan, and made invasions of the adjacent provinces, like an independent and avowed foreign enemy. These are only some of the most conspicuous instances of viceregal revolt. It would be impossible to enumerate all the cases of local rebellion and civil war, of which the Pachas were the causes or the victims, or both; and it is hardly possible for the imagination to comprehend the character or the amount of the sufferings, with which these evils must have worn and wasted the population of the empire.

Even when the orders of the Central Government received obedience, the misery of the people was extreme. It has been already mentioned that the appointments of the Pachas (with some exceptions) were annual; and they were generally and notoriously obtained for money. It was seldom that the Turk, who intrigued among the officials and court-favourites at Constantinople for a Pachalic, was possessed of the necessary purchase and bribery-money. He usually borrowed the requisite sums from one of the wealthy Greeks of the Fanar, or from one of the Armenian bankers. The lender of the money became in reality the mortgagee of the Pachalic; and he may be said to have been a mortgagee in possession, inasmuch as his confidential agent accompanied the Pacha as secretary, and was often the real ruler of the province. As usually happens when a few members of an oppressed race

[1] Eton, p. 280.

purchase power under the oppressors, these Raya agents of
Moslem authority were the most harassing and merciless in their
policy towards their fellow-countrymen. The necessity which the
Pacha was under of re-purchasing his appointment at the end of
each year, prevented him, in ordinary cases, from shaking off this
financial bondage. Sometimes, before an appointment could be
obtained from the Porte, it was required that one of the Sarrafs,
or Armenian bankers, should become surety for the due transmission of the imperial revenue. The power thus given to the
money-lenders, who, by their refusal to continue their security,
could reduce the Turkish grandee to the state of a private individual, was a fresh source of exaction to the inhabitants of the
Pachalic. By these and similar other abuses, the greatest possible
amount of extortion and cruelty towards the subject was combined
with the smallest possible benefit to the Imperial Government: as
each of the agents and sub-agents who were employed in this
system of bribery, usury, and peculation, endeavoured to wring all
he could from those beneath him, and to account for as little as
possible to his superiors. The Ayans, or Provincial Notables,
who ought to have protected their fellow-countrymen from the
Pacha and his attendant harpies, became too often his accomplices.
If an Ayan was refractory and honest, it was an easy thing to ruin
him by a false charge brought before a Cadi, who had generally
purchased his appointment by the same means as the Pacha, and
was therefore equally venal and cruel.

As the Pachas had the power of life and death in their respective districts, and each maintained the pomp and luxury of an
Eastern court as well as the force of a camp, all of which had to
be paid for by the provincials, the motives to tyranny on the part
of the viceroy were infinitely multiplied, and the checks to it were
almost entirely absent. If the requisite amount of revenue was
regularly transmitted to Constantinople, no questions were asked
as to how it had been collected. Long and vehement complaints
against the cruelty of a Pacha might rouse the Sublime Porte to
punish him, especially if he was wealthy. But in such cases the
provincials obtained no redress for their past wrongs. The
treasures of the bow-strung Pacha were appropriated by the
Sultan; and those, from whom they had been extorted, only
gained a new governor, frequently more rapacious, because more
needy than his predecessor.

The power of the inferior Turkish officers, the Beys and Agas,
was like that of the Pacha in kind, both as to obtainment and
exercise, though less in degree. There were also throughout the

empire swarms of petty local tyrants, who farmed from the Porte the revenues of small districts of four or five villages each, under grants which were termed Mocattehs, if the lease was for life, and Iltezim, if it was for a term of years.[1] The misery, which the inhabitants of the Turkish Pachalics endured, may best be paralleled by referring to the descriptions which we possess, of the sufferings which were inflicted on the same regions, nearly 2000 years ago, by the Proconsuls and Publicani of the Roman Commonwealth in its last age of corruption.[2]

The weakness and disorder of the Turkish Empire were seriously increased by the enormous abuses of its feudal system, and by the infinite and antagonistic variety of dominations, princedoms, and powers, that had been suffered to grow up in many of its most important provinces. In describing the state of the Ottoman Empire when at its meridian of glory under Solyman the Ordainer,[3] I have drawn attention to the peculiar incidents of feudalism among the Turks in their best ages, and to the causes which prevented the growth of an insubordinate noblesse, like that which defied the throne and oppressed the commons throughout nearly all Christendom in the mediæval times. But before the close of the eighteenth century all this had been widely changed; and Turkey (especially in its Asiatic districts) abounded with mutinous hereditary feudatories, who generally were styled Dereh Beys or Lords of the valleys; and their lawless arrogance towards their sovereign and oppression of their dependents emulated the worst baronial and knightly abuses that ever were witnessed in Germany or France. A nominal deference to the Sultan and his Pacha might be professed; but an officer from Constantinople who endeavoured to enforce any order of the Sublime Porte in the stronghold of a Dereh Bey, would have met with the same treatment that an emissary of the Emperor Frederick III. might have expected in the castle of a German baron on the Rhine, or as the

---

[1] See Browne's Travels, published in Walpole's "Turkey."

[2] "Surrounded by an army of officials all engaged in the same work of carving out fortunes for themselves and abetting their colleagues, the proconsuls had little sense of responsibility to the central government, and glutted their cupidity without restraint. The tithes, tolls, and other imposts from which the public revenue was drawn, were farmed by Roman contractors, belonging generally to the order of knights, who had few opportunities of rising to the highest political offices at home; and the connivance of their superiors in the province, backed by the corrupt state of public feeling in Rome, shielded to a great extent the sordid arts by which they defrauded both the state and its subjects," &c.—Merivale, vol. i. p. 25.

[3] Page 203.

messengers of Charles the Simple would have received, if they had carried threat or mandate to Brittany or Rouen.

It is impossible to supply any adequate description of the number and nature of the minor local powers, that struggled with each other and with the central government of Turkey, during this period of " her wild misrule of her own anarchy." The account which Sir John Cam Hobhouse (afterwards Lord Broughton) gave of a single province, Albania, as seen by him a few years after the close of the last century, may serve as an example. He says, " Specimens of almost every sort of government are to be found in Albania. Some districts and towns are commanded by one man, under the Turkish title of Bolu Bashee, or the Greek name of Capitan, which they have borrowed from Christendom ; others obey their elders ; others are under no subjection, but each man governs his own family. The power in some places is in abeyance, and although there is no apparent anarchy, there are no rulers. This was the case in our time at the large city of Argyro Castro. There are parts of the country where every Aga or Bey, which, perhaps, may answer to our ancient country squire, is a petty chieftain exercising every right of the men of the village. The Porte, which in the days of Ottoman greatness divided the country into several small Pachalics and commanderies, is now but little respected, and the limits of her different divisions are confused and forgotten."

In the nominally central government at Constantinople, the Grand Vizier was still the Sultan's principal officer in temporal affairs, both civil and military ; and the Mufti, as head of the Ulema, continued to be next in spiritual rank to the Sultan, whc as Caliph, was and is, the religious chief of all Sunnite Mahometans. Under the Grand Vizier, besides his Kaimakan or lieutenant, were the Kehaya Bey, who attended to the home department, and also to the war office. Foreign affairs were the special province of the Reis Effendi. The Tchaoush Baschi was vice-president of the Grand Vizier's judicial tribunal, and chief of the police force of the capital. He also acted as the Lord High Marshal. Besides these, there were the Nischandyis or secretaries, the Defterdars or treasurers, and the holders of the other ancient offices that have been described when we examined the Turkish system of government in the times of Mahomet the Conqueror.[1] And, without attempting to enumerate or analyse the prolix catalogue of ceremonious courtiers and speculating placemen, who are described by those who wrote seventy or eighty years ago on Turkish matters, it

[1] Page 96, *et seq.*

may be generally stated, that, both in quantity and character, they were such and so many, as are usually found to multiply in decaying empires, especially in empires of the East.

The Imperial Divan was now generally convened not oftener than about once in six weeks. The ordinary Divan of the Grand Vizier sate much more frequently : and formed a court of justice, at which, besides the Vizier, the Capitan Pacha, the two Kadi-askers, and the Nischandyis and Defterdars attended. On important occasions a grand council was summoned, consisting of nearly forty members, and comprising the chiefs of all the orders in the State. In extreme emergencies the members were called together to what was termed a standing Divan, and deliberated without taking seats.

The power of the Ulema, and especially of the head of them, the Mufti (which has been before alluded to),[1] had increased and was increasing. So was the amount of ecclesiastical property, the Vakoufs.[2] And though the system of permitting so large a proportion of the landed property of the empire to be held in mortmain was unquestionably evil, it was made to act in some degree as an alleviation of other evils, which generally affected the possessors of property under the extreme misgovernment of Turkey. Not only private estates, but whole districts and cities were the properties of mosques or other ecclesiastical foundations ; and the occupier of them, on paying the stipulated quit-rents (which were usually light), lived in undisturbed possession, and in immunity both from the imposts of the central government, and the exactions of the local functionaries. Similar privileges were often enjoyed by those who dwelt in districts, that were the special property of the Sultana Validé and other high individuals. There were also many places, where, by ancient custom or royal grant, the Raya lived almost free from the intrusion of any of the dominant race ; and where it was absolutely forbidden for any Turk to become a resident. It was to the existence of these and similar privileged localities in the empire—to the protection which the Frank residents enjoyed under their own laws and consuls—to the exceptional good government of just and able men who sometimes became Pachas—and also to the stern order sometimes enforced in their provinces by some of the most ferocious Pachas, who would tolerate no crimes but their own, that Turkey was indebted for what little commercial activity and wealth was to be found in her at the period of which we are speaking.

If we look to the means which the Sultan possessed of asserting his authority against domestic rebels or foreign invaders, we shall find the military system of the empire so wretched, that instead of wondering at the success of the Christian powers against it, there seems to be rather cause for surprise at the Russians and Austrians not having completed its overthrow. The classification of the Turkish troops which Thornton has adopted in his "Treatise on the Ottoman Empire" (published in 1807) seems to be authentic and convenient. There were the paid troops, called generally the Kapikouli (which means, literally, slaves of the Porte), and the unpaid troops, who were termed Toprakli. The largest and by far the most important part of the paid troops was the once renowned·corps of the Janissaries. In one of the earlier chapters of this work we have traced the institution of this soldiery by the councils of the Vizier Alaeddin and Black Khalil Tschendereli in the reign of Orchan, the second sovereign of the House of Othman. We have seen the increase of their numbers and the excellence of their discipline under Mahomet the Conqueror, and Solyman, the Lord of his Age ; their growing insubordination under the subsequent Sultans ; the change in the system by which they were recruited ; the increase of their numbers ; and the decrease of their military efficiency. At the close of the eighteenth century they were computed to consist of 150,000 registered members, who were settled in the various towns of the empire, where they arrogated authority and military pre-eminence, and at the same time followed various trades. But the large number of those, who procured the enrolment of their names as Janissaries for the sake of the privileges and immunities which were thereby acquired, was no proof that any force of corresponding amount could be relied on by the State for actual service. The grossest frauds as to the character and capacity of the individuals who were placed on the muster-rolls, were practised by the private Janissaries themselves, and still more extensively by officers, who also enriched themselves by drawing pay for non-existent hundreds and thousands. Still, the Janissaries formed a large community in the empire, and one of the greatest importance both in war and in peace. They were conspicuous for their bigotry as Mahometans ; and, as they knew the suspicion with which they and their predecessors had been regarded by successive Sultans, they in turn watched every innovation and reform with jealousy and hatred, and were ready even to rise in each other's aid to exercise the right of oppressing the Rayas who were beneath them, and what they deemed their still more sacred right of insurrection against the authorities that were over them.[1]

Besides the Janissaries, there was a force of artillerymen, called Topidjis, said to be 30,000 in number, but dispersed, like the Janissaries, in the chief cities of the empire, and bound to join their standards on receiving orders.[2] The Bostandjis, or gardeners, of the Imperial palaces of Adrianople and Constantinople, continued to be enrolled and armed, and formed a kind of body-guard for the Sultan. There were other small bodies of regular infantry; and the old cavalry corps of the Spahis and the Silih-dars were still preserved, though in little numerical strength or efficiency. The irregular forces, the Toprakli, consisted chiefly of the old feudal contingents which the holders of Ziamets and Timars were bound to supply; but which, owing to the abuses in these institutions, were now uncertain in amount and inferior in quality; nor could the services even of those who appeared beneath the horse-tails, be relied on for the continued operations of a war. There were also in time of hostilities, levies of troops called Miri-Askeris, which received pay while in the field. When a Turkish town was besieged, the Mahometan inhabitants were enrolled as a kind of national guard for service while the peril lasted, and were called Yerli Neferats. The other irregular volunteers that joined a Turkish army were termed Guenullus.

Besides the forces of the Sultan, regular and irregular, that have been mentioned, there were also corps of provincial troops called Serratkuli, who were levied and paid by the Pachas. These were not kept permanently embodied, but were only called together in time of war, or during the march of an army. They consisted of Azaps, or pioneers, of Lagunjis or miners, and His-sarlis, who assisted the Topidjis in the artillery service.[3]

Great assemblages of armed men from these various sources were sometimes arrayed under the Ottoman standards, especially in the early part of a war. At the opening of a first campaign, the Porte could set in motion 300,000 sabres; and if the war was a successful one, there was no lack of volunteers to recruit the armies. But these large hosts were for the most part mere heaps of irregular troops, incapable of discipline, and destitute of experience. They were seldom even nominally enrolled for more than six months, and, on the first serious reverse that the army met

---

[1] See as to the number, composition, &c., of the Janissary force (besides D'Ohsson), Ranke's "Servia," pp. 41, 100; Thornton's "Turkey," p. 180; Eton, pp. 27, 66; Porter, vol. i. p. 273.

[2] Thornton, p. 183. [3] Ibid p. 186.

with, they disbanded by thousands, and dispersed towards their homes, generally plundering the provinces in their way, whether hostile or friendly, Christian or Mahometan. Behind walls or entrenchments, and in confused engagements in broken countries, the native valour of the individual Turk, and his skill in the use of the sabre, made him a formidable opponent; and the wild charge of the Ottoman horse, often over ground which no other cavalry would dare to traverse, was still more destructive to a shaken or unready enemy. But, as compared with the steady movements and intelligent organisation of the forces of European Christendom, a Turkish army was (as Napoleon termed it) a mere Asiatic rabble. Two astonishing but indisputable facts both attest and account for this. Throughout the Turkish infantry and cavalry there was now no regulation whatever as to what weapons should be used, nor were any of them ever drilled together, or instructed to act in bodies in the commonest military evolution.[1] Each armed himself as he pleased; and, when an action had commenced, each may be said to have fought as he pleased. The French General Boyer well describes the Turkish soldiers of this time as " without order or firmness: unable even to march in platoons, advancing in confused groups, and falling on the enemy in a sudden start of wild and savage fury."[2]

The barbarous custom of receiving pay for the heads of fallen enemies, and the consequent eagerness of the Turkish soldiers to obtain "these bloody testimonials,"[3] tended not a little to increase the disorder and the heedlessness of mutual support, in which they combated. More than once the advantage which Ottoman armies gained at the beginning of a battle, was lost in consequence of the men dispersing to gather these hideous trophies, and to obtain head-money for them at the Seraskier's tent.

The condition of the navy, notwithstanding the exertions of Gazi Hassan, and of the Capitan Pacha Hussein, who succeeded him, was even worse than that of the army. And altogether it may be safely asserted that the Turkish Empire had reached its nadir of misery and weakness about three-quarters of a century from the present time. With the commencement of Sultan Selim's reforms a new era was opened. It is true that Turkey has since then suffered from defeats and revolts—she has lost armies, fleets, and provinces; but a new spirit has been infused

---

[1] D'Ohsson, vii. pp. 345-370.
[2] "Intercepted Correspondence from Egypt," p. 183. Adolphus' "History of England," vol. v. p. 112.
[3] See Sir Walter Scott's observation, "Life of Bonaparte," vol. iv. p. 126.

into her rulers and statesmen, which, though often checked, has never been extinguished ; and which, whatever may be her ulti- mate doom, has falsified the confident predictions of Volney and other writers at the close of the last century, according to whom " the Sultan, equally affected with the ignorance of his people, was to continue to vegetate in his palace ; women and eunuchs were to continue to appoint to offices and places ; and govern- ments were still to be publicly offered for sale.   The Pachas were to pillage the subjects, and impoverish the provinces.   The Divan was to follow its maxims of haughtiness and intolerance.   The people to be instigated by fanaticism.   The generals to carry on war without intelligence, and continue to lose battles, until this incoherent edifice of power, shaken to its basis, deprived of its support, and losing its equilibrium, should fall, and astonish the world with another instance of mighty ruin."[1]

This vaticination of Volney's may well be compared, both with that of Sir Thomas Roe, in 1622,[2] and with many of the present day.   Threatened states, like threatened men, sometimes live long ; especially if the threatenings make them forewarned and forearmed.

---

[1] Volney, "Considerations sur la Guerre actuelle des Turcs."
[2] See *suprà*, p. 245.

CHAPTER XXIII.

SELIM'S REFORMS—THE NEW TROOPS—NAPOLEON ATTACKS EGYPT
— WAR BETWEEN TURKEY AND FRANCE — ALLIANCE WITH
RUSSIA AND ENGLAND—DEFENCE OF ACRE—FRENCH EVACUATE
EGYPT—GENERAL PEACE—TROUBLES IN SERVIA—THE DAHIS—
KARA GEORGE—WAR WITH RUSSIA AND ENGLAND—THE PAS-
SAGE OF THE DARDANELLES—TRUCE WITH RUSSIA—SELIM III.
DEPOSED BY THE JANISSARIES — MUSTAPHA IV. SULTAN—DE-
POSED BY MUSTAPHA BAIRACTAR — MAHMOUD II.—DEATH OF
BAIRACTAR — TRIUMPH OF THE JANISSARIES, AND APPARENT
END OF REFORMS — RUSSIAN WAR CONTINUED — TREATY OF
BUCHAREST.

RELIEVED from the immediate pressure of Russian war by the
peace of Jassy, and from the imminent peril of its renewal by the
death of the Empress Catherine, Sultan Selim earnestly applied
himself to the difficult and dangerous duty of internal reform.
To meet the multitude of evils that distracted the State, he projected manifold and extensive changes in almost all its departments. The abuses of the feudal system were to be dealt with by
abolishing feudality itself. The Ziamets and Timars were to be
resumed by the sovereign on the deaths of their holders; and
their revenues were thenceforth to be paid into the royal treasury,
and appropriated to the maintenance of a new military force. The
administration of the provinces was to be ameliorated by curtailing
the powers of the Pachas. Each ruler of an Eyalet or a Liva was
to be appointed for three years; and at the expiration of that
term, the renewal of his office was to depend on his exertions to
give satisfaction to the people over whom he ruled. Another
reform was proposed, from which the provincials would have
derived still greater benefits. All farming of the taxes was to be
abolished; and the revenue was to be collected by officers of the
Imperial treasury. In the General Central Government the Grand
Vizier's power was to be restrained by making it necessary for him
to consult the Divan on all important measures. The Divan was
to consist of twelve superior ministers; one of whom was bound

to attend especially to the collection of the funds by which the new troops were to be kept on foot.[1] The spread of intelligence, and the advancement of education among all classes of his subjects were earnestly encouraged by Selim III. The printing establishment which had been founded in the reign of Achmet III., was revived; and many European works on tactics and fortification were translated from the French and published by the Sultan's orders, under the inspection of the Turkish mathematician, Abdurrhahim Effendi.[2] Selim also showed favour and patronage to the establishment of schools throughout his dominions. It was especially among the Greeks that new educational institutions sprang up, and old ones regained fresh energy under the Sultan's auspices;[3] and when it was found that the revolutionary party among the Greeks availed themselves of this intellectual movement to excite their fellow-countrymen against the Turks, Selim, instead of closing the Greek schools and printing-offices, established a Greek press at Constantinople, and sought to counteract the efforts of those opposed to the Turkish Government, by employing the pens of the Greek clergy of the capital in its favour.[4] He designed to provide a certain number of his Ottoman subjects with a better political education than could be acquired at Constantinople, by attaching them to the permanent embassies which he sought to establish at the chief European courts. Turkish missions were received at London, Paris, Vienna, and Berlin; but the Cabinet of St. Petersburg artfully avoided Selim's proposal to accredit a regular ambassador to the Russian Empire.[5]

However needful were these and other measures for improving the civil and social condition of the inhabitants of the Turkish Empire, and however valuable they were likely to prove, if carried into effect, Selim well knew that a properly disciplined and loyal armed force was as indispensable for the enforcement and maintenance of internal reform, as it was for preserving the integrity of the empire from further attack from without. The example of Peter the Great of Russia, who, by means of the new troops that Lefort trained for him on the model of the armies of Western Europe, overthrew both domestic and foreign foes, was ever before the eyes of Selim; and the inquiring Turkish Sovereign may have been aware that almost the highest political authority of the West had deliberately pronounced that " whoever

---

[1] See Ranke's "Servia," p. 100, and the authorities therein.
[2] White's "Three Years in Constantinople," vol. ii. p. 205.
[3] Emerson Tennent, vol. ii. p. 423.
[4] Ibid., vol. ii. p. 521, note.   [5] D'Ohsson, vol. vii.

examines with care the improvements which Peter the Great introduced into the Russian Empire, will find that they almost all resolve themselves into the establishment of a well-regulated standing army."[1]   Among the prisoners made by the Turks during the last war, there was one who was a Turk by birth, but had long been in the Russian service, in which he had attained the rank of lieutenant, and the reputation of a good officer.   The Grand Vizier, Yussuf Pacha (by whose troops he had been taken), was fond of conversing with him on the military systems of the two nations; and was at last persuaded to allow a little corps (consisting chiefly of renegadoes) to be armed and drilled on the European plan.   The Vizier used to amuse himself with seeing them go through their exercises; and when he left the camp at the end of the war, he took the little company with him, and stationed them at a village at a short distance from Constantinople. The Sultan, hearing of them, expressed a wish to see " how the infidels fought battles," and went to one of their parades.   He instantly saw the superiority of their fire to that of the ordinary Turkish troops, and appreciated more than ever the advantages which the arms and discipline of his Christian enemies had long given them over the Ottoman troops.   The little band was kept on foot; and Omar Aga, as its chief was called, was enabled to recruit it by enrolling other renegadoes, and also a few indigent Turks, who consented to learn the exercise and wield the weapons of the Giaour.[2]   The Divan was required by the Sultan to consider the policy of introducing the new system among the Janissaries; but this produced a mutiny, which the Sultan appeased for the time by fair promises, and by desisting from any further measures, though Omar Aga's company was still kept together.[3] In 1796, General Albert Dubayet arrived at Constantinople as ambassador from the French Republic.   He brought with him, as a new and acceptable present to the Sultan, several pieces of artillery, with all their appointments and munitions, to serve as models, and a number of French artillerymen and engineers, who were to instruct the Turkish Topidjis, and to aid in the management of the Ottoman arsenals and foundries.   The ambassador was accompanied also by drill-sergeants from the French horse and foot regiments, who were to give lessons to the Spahis and Janissaries.   The efforts of the French artillerymen were well received; and marked improvements in the fabric, and the equipment, and the working of the Turkish guns was effected by them.   Some progress

---

[1] Adam Smith.   [2] Eton, p. 92; Ranke, p. 99.
[3] Ranke, p. 168; Eton, p. 93.

was made in arming and training a squadron of horse on the European system; but the Janissaries again absolutely and angrily refused to adopt the arms or learn the manœuvres of Frankish infantry; and Dubayet's drill-sergeants were only able to serve the Sultan by improving the discipline of Omar Aga's men. Albert Dubayet died within a few months after his arrival at Constantinople, and many of his officers then left Turkey. But the Capitan Pacha, Hussein, who, like the Sultan, saw the value of the new system, took some of them into his own service, and by high pay and patronage induced a few more Mussulmans to enter into Omar's corps. These new troops were about 600 in number, when war broke out between France and Turkey, in 1798, in consequence of the attack which the French Republic, or rather Napoleon Bonaparte made on Egypt.[1]

It had been the anxious wish of Sultan Selim to keep clear of the conflicts which the French Revolution had produced in Europe. He knew the paramount necessity of reorganising his empire, and the impossibility of this being effected while it was involved in the jeopardies of war. But the tidings which reached Constantinople in July, 1798, that a French army, 30,000 strong, under the most celebrated general of the Republic, had suddenly landed in Egypt and taken the city of Alexandria by storm, left the Sultan no alternative. It was true that the Turkish authority in Egypt was little more than nominal; and that the Mamelukes, the real lords and tyrants over that country, were as deeply hated by the Sublime Porte as by the Copts and the Fellahs whom they oppressed. It was true also that Napoleon professed hostility against the Mamelukes only, and put forth proclamations, in which he vaunted the sincerity of the alliance between the Turks and the French, at the very time that he was ordering all the severities of military execution against the Turkish Janissaries who had defended Alexandria. But the intention of the French General to conquer and retain Egypt for France, or rather for himself, was self-evident; nor could the Porte forego its rights of dominion over that province, where its Pacha was still titularly the supreme ruler, and which it had made vigorous efforts to reduce to effective obedience so lately as 1787, when the outbreak of the Russian war checked Gazi Hassan in his successful performance of that duty. We know from Napoleon's own memoirs that he expected to overawe Constantinople by means of the magnificent fleet which had brought the French army to Egypt.[2]

[1] Juchereau de Saint Denis, "Révolution de Constantinople."
[2] Montholon's "History of the Captivity of Napoleon," vol. iv. p. 195.

His victory over the Mamelukes at the battle of the Pyramids on the 21st of July, and the submission of Cairo six days after that battle, seemed to ensure the realisation of the dazzling visions which had led him across the Mediterranean. But on the 1st of August Nelson destroyed the French fleet in the battle of the Nile. This at once removed all considerations of alarm, which might have made the Sultan pause. An alliance was concluded between Turkey, Russia, and England, and war was solemnly declared against France. An Ottoman army and a fleet were forthwith ordered to be assembled at Rhodes, and another army was collected in Syria. The formidable Pacha of Acre, Djezzar Pacha, though contemptuously independent of his Sultan in times of peace, consented to act as his Seraskier against the Giaours of Franghestan, and took the command of the Syrian forces. It was designed that the Syrian army should cross the desert and attack the French in Egypt early in 1799, and that the armament from Rhodes should act simultaneously with it by landing 16,000 of the best Turkish troops under Mustapha Pacha at Aboukir. The activity of Napoleon disconcerted these projects. Instead of waiting to be thus assailed in Egypt, he anticipated his enemies by crossing the desert into Syria during the winter, and carrying offensive war into that important province. In his own words, he expected that "according to this plan, the divisions of the army of Rhodes would be obliged to hasten to the aid of Syria, and Egypt would remain tranquil, which would permit us successively to summon the greatest part of our forces to Syria. The Mamelukes of Mourad Bey, and of Ibrahim Bey, the Arabs of the Egyptian desert, the Druses of Mount Lebanon, the Metualis, the Christians of Syria, the whole party of the Sheiks of Azor in Syria might join the army when it was master of that country, and the commotion would be communicated to the whole of Arabia. These provinces of the Ottoman Empire in which the Arabian language was spoken, desired a great change, and only waited for some one to bring it about. Should the fortune of war be favourable, the French might, by the middle of summer, reach the Euphrates with 100,000 auxiliaries, who would have as a reserve 25,000 veteran Frenchmen of the best troops in the world, and numerous trains of artillery. Constantinople would then be menaced; and if the French could succeed in re-establishing friendly relations with the Porte, they might cross the desert, and march upon India towards the end of autumn."[1]

These dreams of Oriental conquest were finally dissipated before

[1] Montholon's "History of the Captivity of Napoleon," vol. iv.

St. Jean d'Acre. Djezzar Pacha had proved himself in readiness and energy no unworthy opponent of the great victor of Italy and Egypt; and English skill and gallantry now co-operated with the stubborn valour of the Turks. Djezzar had sent Abdallah, the Pacha of Damascus, forward with the advanced guard of the Syrian forces as early as January, 1799. Abdallah garrisoned Gazi and Jaffa, and proceeded as far as El Arisch, which is the key of Egypt on its Syrian side. Napoleon commenced his march in February. He took, without difficulty, El Arisch on the 15th of February, and Gaza in a few days afterwards. Jaffa resisted more obstinately, but was breached and stormed on the 3rd of March. 2000 Turkish soldiers, who were made prisoners here, were on the following day put to death in cold blood. As the best biographer of Napoleon relates this fearful scene:—
"The body of prisoners were marched out of Jaffa, in the centre of a large square battalion. The Turks foresaw their fate, but used neither entreaties nor complaints to avert it. They marched on silent and composed. They were escorted to the sand-hills to the south-east of Jaffa, divided there into small bodies, and put to death by musketry. The execution lasted a considerable time, and the wounded were despatched by the bayonet. Their bodies were heaped together, and formed a pyramid, which is still visible, consisting now of human bones, as originally of bloody corpses."[1]

Napoleon then advanced upon Acre, which was the only place that could stop him from effecting the complete conquest of Syria. The siege began on the 20th of March, and was maintained with the greatest vigour and determination on both sides until the 20th of May, when Napoleon reluctantly abandoned his prospects of an imperial career beyond the Euphrates and the Indus, and retreated with the remains of his forces upon Egypt. In this siege, no less than eight assaults were given by the French, and eleven desperate sallies made by the defenders. The operations of Napoleon were greatly retarded in the first weeks by his deficiency in heavy artillery. Sir Sydney Smith, who was cruising off Syria with two English ships of the line, captured the flotilla which was conveying the French battering train along the coast; and he aided the defenders of Acre still more effectively by landing gunners and marines from his own ships, and also the emigrant French officer, Colonel Philippeaux, who took the command of the engineer force in the city. Philippeaux, and many more brave men perished during the defence; and the French

[1] Scott's "Life of Napoleon."

obtained in April some mortars and heavy guns which their Rear-admiral Perrée landed near Jaffa. A large army also which the Pacha of Damascus assembled in Syria for the relief of Acre, was completely defeated and dispersed by Napoleon, and two divisions of his troops at the battle of Mount Thabor; while the remainder of his force maintained the position before the besieged city. But it was impossible for him to prevent Djezzar Pacha from receiving reinforcements by sea; and on the 7th of May a Turkish squadron landed 12,000 men in the harbour. These included the new troops, armed with musket and bayonet, and disciplined on the European system, who have been already described. This body signalised itself by gallantry and steadiness during the remainder of the siege, and attracted the notice of the besieging general as well as of the Turks. Napoleon had received further supplies of artillery, and the greater part of the defences of Acre became a mass of blood-stained ruins. But every attempt of the French to charge through the living barriers of the garrison and their English comrades was repulsed with heavy loss. The number of Napoleon's wounded who lay at Jaffa and in the camp, was 12,000; and the plague was in his hospitals.[1] His retreat was conducted with admirable skill and celerity; and Napoleon soon found that his presence in Egypt was deeply needed to quell the spirit of insurrection that had arisen there, and to encounter the Turkish army from Rhodes.

This army, commanded by Mustapha, the Pacha of Roumelia, and escorted by Sir Sydney Smith's squadron, landed at Aboukir on the 11th of July. It consisted of about 15,000 infantry, with a considerable force of artillery, but without horse. Mustapha Pacha assaulted and carried the redoubts which the French had formed near the village of Aboukir, put to the sword the detachment of Marmont's corps which he found there; and then, in expectation of an attack from the main French army, he proceeded to strengthen his position with a double line of entrenchments. Napoleon collected his forces with characteristic rapidity, and on the 25th of July was before the peninsula of Aboukir. The action that ensued was well contested but decisive. Napoleon cut off some detached bodies of the Turks, and carried their first line without much difficulty. But behind the second line the Pacha's troops resisted desperately; and aided by the fire of the English gunboats in the bay, they drove the French columns back with considerable loss. At this critical moment, the Turks left their entrenchments and dispersed about the field to cut off

[1] Montholon, vol. iv. p. 286.

the heads of their fallen enemies. Napoleon took instant advantage of their disorder. He sent his reserves forward ; and Murat, with the French cavalry, dashed through an opening between the redoubts into the midst of the Ottoman position. Murat forced his way to Mustapha Pacha's tent, and had exchanged blows with the Turkish general, each slightly wounding the other, before the Pacha, seeing the inevitable ruin of his army, consented to surrender.[1] Pursued at the point of the bayonet by the victorious French, the mass of the Turks was thrust into the sea, the whole bay appearing for a few minutes to be covered with their turbans, until they sank by thousands, and perished beneath the waves. After this victory, which restored to the French, for a few months, the undisputed possession of Egypt, Napoleon departed from that country to win empire in the West, though it had eluded him in the Eastern world.

General Kléber, who was left in command of the French force in Egypt, entered into a convention with Sir Sydney Smith, the English Commodore, for evacuating the province, but the English Admiral, Lord Keith, refused to ratify the terms ; and a large Turkish army, under the Grand Vizier, entered Egypt early in the year 1800. Kléber completely defeated this host at the battle of Heliopolis, on the 20th of March ; and it was ultimately by the English expedition under Abercrombie and Hutchinson that Egypt was wrested from the French.

On the western frontier of the Ottoman dominions in Europe some territorial acquisitions were made in consequence of the war between the Porte and France, and of the alliance of the Sultan with Russia and England, which that war produced. France had, by the treaty of Campo Formio, between her and Austria, in 1797 (when these two powers agreed that the republic of Venice should be extinct), obtained possession of the Ionian Islands and their dependencies on that continent, Prevesa, Parga, Vonitza, Gomenitza, and Butrinto, which had formed portions of the Venetian dominions. Immediately that the war was declared against France by the Porte, in 1798, Ali Pacha, the celebrated Vizier of Epirus, marched troops upon Prevesa, Vonitza, and Butrinto, and won these cities from the French. Soon afterwards,

---

[1] "Mustapha Pacha was taken, and carried in triumph before Bonaparte. The haughty Turk had not lost his pride with his fortunes. 'I will take care to inform the Sultan,' said the victor, meaning to be courteous, 'of the courage you have displayed in the battle, though it has been your mishap to lose it.' 'Thou mayst save thyself the trouble,' answered the prisoner haughtily ; 'my master knows me better than thou canst.' "—Scott.

a Russian fleet from the Black Sea sailed to the Bosphorus, where it was joined by a Turkish squadron, and the combined armament entered the Mediterranean, where it conquered the Ionian Islands, and afterwards endeavoured to aid the enemies of the French on the coasts of Italy; which then witnessed the strange spectacle of the forces of the Sultan and the Czar co-operating to support the Pope.[1]

The Ionian Islands were at first (1801) placed under the joint protectorate of the Russians and Turks. Disputes naturally followed: and it was agreed in 1802 that one of these ill-matched guardians should resign. It was left to the Greek inhabitants of the islands to make the selection. They chose to retain the Russian Emperor as their protector, and the Turks withdrew accordingly. The acquisition of these islands was always a favourite project with Ali Pacha: more, however, with a view to aggrandise himself than from any desire to strengthen his master. But he never succeeded in obtaining them. They passed, in 1807, from Russian to French sovereignty, and were afterwards captured by the English, who were for many years the supreme rulers of what was termed the Septinsular Republic.

The possession of the old Venetian districts on the mainland was confirmed to Turkey by agreement between her and Russia in 1800. Butrinto, Prevesa, and Vonitza, which had been taken by Ali Pacha, were retained by him; but Parga, which was garrisoned by a body of hardy Suliotes, refused to submit, and nobly maintained her independence for fourteen years. During four more years she was protected by England; and when that protection was withdrawn, and the city given up to the Pacha, the inhabitants (like the Phocæans of old) abandoned their homes rather than become the subjects of an Eastern despot. We have been glancing far forward, while speaking of the fate of these relics of the old Venetian Empire in Greece, in order that they may not again require our notice. But we must now revert to the early part of the nineteenth century. It has been mentioned that the Turks, in the year 1802, gave up to Russia their share of the protectorate of the Seven Islands; and in the October of that year the influence of Russia obtained a Hatti-scheriff from the Sultan in favour of the inhabitants of Moldavia and Wallachia; by which the Porte pledged itself not to remove the reigning Hospodars of those principalities without previous reference to Russia, and not to allow any Turks, except merchants and traders, to enter either territory.[2] The November of the preceding year,

[1] See Ranke's "Servia," p. 210.   [2] Ibid., p. 145.

1801, had been a still more important epoch. It was then that a general though brief pacification throughout Europe was effected, in which the Ottoman Empire was included, so far, at least, as regarded foreign powers. By a treaty between France and Turkey (negotiated concurrently with the peace of Amiens between France and England), Napoleon, then Chief Consul, acknowledged the sovereignty of the Porte over Egypt and its other dominions in full integrity; and the Sultan renewed the ancient privileges which the French had, under their kings, enjoyed in Turkey. The old policy of France, in seeking the friendship of the Ottoman Court, was now revived: and, before long, the skill of Napoleon's ambassadors, Generals Brune and Sebastiani, restored the French influence at Constantinople.

Selim had now a second respite from war with any European power, until he was attacked by Russia in 1806. But this was no period of tranquillity for the Turkish Empire. The Wahabites renewed their attacks on Syria; and in 1802 they captured the cities of Mecca and Medina, so that all Arabia was now in their possession. The loss of the Holy Cities, the indignities with which the Wahabites treated the sanctuaries and reliques of Mahometanism, and the cruelties practised by them towards the Hadjis, or pilgrims, especially those of the Sunnite persuasion, excited a profound sensation throughout the Ottoman Empire, and tended to prejudice the Turkish part of the population against their innovating Sultan, whose reign was marked by such visitations. In Egypt, the remnant of the Mamelukes long kept at bay the troops by which Selim endeavoured to bring that province under effectual control. In Syria, Djezzar Pacha resumed his old attitude of haughty insubordination towards the Porte, and exercised independent tyranny until his death, in 1804. On the Danube, Passwan Oglou maintained himself against all the forces that the Sultan could employ for his reduction; until, at last, the Porte, in 1806, made peace with its stubborn rebel, confirmed him in all the power which he had usurped, and sent him the insignia of a Pacha of the highest rank.

The troubles in Servia deserve more careful consideration, as their ultimate effect was to withdraw that important province from the practical authority of the House of Othman, and to convert it into an independent Christian State. The narrative of this is also closely connected with that of the contest between the Janissaries and the Sultan, and it gives fearful proof of the stern necessity under which Selim and Mahmoud acted in all their measures against that force.

It has been mentioned, while tracing the events of the war of the Emperor Joseph II. against Turkey, that the Austrian forces, which entered Servia, were actively assisted by the Rayas of that province. The Servians formed a considerable force, both of horse and foot, which rendered excellent service to the Emperor, and defended many important districts from the attempts made by the Turks to reconquer them. When the peace of Sistova gave Servia back to the Porte, with merely a provision for an amnesty in favour of such of the inhabitants as had acted against the Sultan, Turkish commissioners were sent from Constantinople to take possession of the province : their surprise was extreme, and not unmingled with apprehension, when they found the change that had taken place in their Christian subjects, whom they had been accustomed to regard as " a weaponless and submissive herd." One of them exclaimed to the Austrian officers, when a Servian troop, fully armed and accoutred, marched out in military array from one of the fortresses, " Neighbours, what have you made of our Rayas ?"[1] The Servian regiments were disbanded, and the Turks returned to their old dominion ; but the military spirit which had been called into action among the Rayas could not be easily extinguished.

It was, however, not against, but in aid of the Sultan, that the Servians next appeared in arms. The turbulent tyranny of the Janissaries was the cause of this strange phenomenon. At no place had the members of that body proceeded to such lengths of lawless outrage, as at Belgrade, where their commanders already styled themselves Dahis, in imitation of the rulers of the Barbaresque States, who had originally been raised to independent power from among a mutinous soldiery.[2] The Janissaries of Belgrade, and the other Servian towns robbed and murdered not only the Rayas, but their fellow-countrymen, the Spahis—the feudal lords of the land. The Pacha's authority was so insignificant, that the Austrians, during the war, treated with the Aga of the Janissaries instead of with the legitimate viceroy of the Sultan. As this state of insubordination and violence was renewed in Servia after the peace, Selim determined to act vigorously against these rebels ; and Ebu Bekir was sent to Belgrade as Pacha, with a firman which commanded the Janissaries to quit that city and the entire pachalic. According to the too common policy in the East of using the basest crimes to punish criminals, the chief leader of the Janissaries was removed by assassination, and the firman was then published and enforced. The expelled Janissaries joined Passwan Oglou, the rebel of Widdin ; and at their instigation, Passwan's

[1] Ranke's "Servia," p. 84.　　[2] Ibid., p. 104.

forces invaded Servia. In this emergency, Hadschi Mustapha (who had succeeded Ebu Bekir as Pacha of Belgrade) called on the Servians to take up arms in defence of the province. Both Hadschi Mustapha and Ebu Bekir had governed Servia with justice and humanity, and the country had flourished and become enriched by commerce with Austria under their rule. The Servians gladly obeyed the summons of the Pacha against their old tyrants, the rebel Janissaries, and victoriously defended the pachalic. But the other Janissaries of the empire, and especially those at Constantinople, received the tidings of the events in Servia with the highest indignation, with which the Ulema and the Mahometan population in general largely sympathised. "The pride of the Mussulmans revolted at the idea that old Moslems of the True Faith should be banished from the pachalic, and that Rayas and Giaours should be armed and set up against them."[1] Selim found it necessary to give way; Hadschi Mustapha received an order of the Divan to re-admit the Janissaries to Belgrade. They were restored accordingly; and they recommenced their sway there by murdering one of the chief Servian officers, and soon proceeded to overpower and murder the Pacha. They condescended to ask for a new Pacha from the Porte; but their intention to keep the sovereign power in their own hands was evident. Four of their chiefs assumed the title of Dahis, and allotted the country between them. Each was the Tetrarch of a district; but Belgrade was their common capital, where they met and deliberated. As the number of the Janissaries of Belgrade seemed insufficient to uphold their power, they formed another armed force of Mahometans from Bosnia and Albania, who flocked together to the pillage of Servia. It was not only the Rayas over whom they tyrannised—the old Turkish feudal proprietors, the Spahis, were expelled by them from the province, and the Janissaries now established themselves as absolute lords of the soil.

In Bosnia Ali Bey Widaitsch of Sumnik made himself master of a large territory in the same manner, and entered into close alliance with the Dahis of Belgrade. Passwan Oglou also (who was still in rebellion against the Porte) was their confederate; and thus a Mahometan brigand league was formed nearly across the whole north of European Tartary, in direct antagonism to the House of Othman. The exiled Spahis of Servia implored the Sultan's aid; and the Rayas, whose sufferings were now infinitely multiplied, also called on him as their sovereign to rescue them from these oppressors. The Servian Kneses (as the Christian local

[1] Ranke, p. 112.

anagistrates were termed) sent an address to Constantinople in which they recapitulated some of the wrongs which they endured. They said they were not only reduced to abject poverty by the Dahis, but "they were attacked in their religion, their morality, and their honour; and no husband was secure as to his wife, no father as to his daughter, no brother as to his sister. The church, the cloister, the monks, the priests, all were outraged." They demanded of the Sultan—"Art thou still our Czar? then come and free us from these evil-doers; or, if thou wilt not save us, at least tell us so, that we may decide whether to flee to the mountains and forests, or to seek in the rivers a termination of our miserable existence."[1]

The Porte was at this time destitute of means to crush the Dahis. It could only threaten. An intimation was sent to Belgrade, that unless the Janissaries amended their conduct, the Sultan would send an army against them; "but not an Ottoman army, for it would be a grievous thing to cause true believers to fight against each other; but soldiers should come against them of other nations, and of another creed; and then such evil should overtake them as had never yet befallen an Osmanli."[2]

On hearing this, the Dahis said to one another, "What army can the Padischah mean? Is it to be of Austrians or Russians? Nay, he will not bring those foreigners into his empire." "By Allah," they exclaimed, "he means the Rayas." They believed that the Sultan would send a general to arm and lead the Servians under their Kneses against them. They resolved to prevent this by a massacre of all such Rayas as, from their position or spirit, might prove dangerous. Each Dahi repaired for this purpose to his own district; and, in February, 1804, they simultaneously commenced the work of horror. Great numbers of the chief Servians were at first surprised and slaughtered; but some received timely warning and fled. The Dahis and their emissaries continued to murder; and the belief grew general in Servia that it was intended to extirpate the entire Christian population.[3] But there was still bold and able men among them; and too high a military spirit had been created by recent events in the Servian Rayas for them to perish without resistance. At first the shepherds and peasants, who fled from their homes and joined the Heyducs, or robbers, in the mountains, did so merely to save their lives, or to gain a chance of taking life for life. Their next thought was how they could return to their homes in safety. But soon came the reflection that, in order to be safe, they must put down their

[1] Ranke, p. 118.   [2] Ibid., p. 119.   [3] Ibid., p. 121.

oppressors; and that this could only be done by a national war throughout the country. Such a war was soon organised in Servia. The Heyduc chiefs came forward zealously in the good cause; and there were many other men of capacity and courage, who combined the peasantry of the various districts in a general rising. The bands of the Dahis were rapidly driven from the open country, from the villages, and from all the smaller towns; and, in a few weeks, all Servia was in the hands of Servians, except Belgrade and some of the other strong fortified places.

The Servians now determined to choose a commander-in-chief of their nation. They offered the supreme dignity to George Petrowitcsh, called Czerny George by his countrymen, and Kara George (both meaning Black George) by the Turks. The name of Kara George is that by which he is most conspicuous among the heroes of revolutionary warfare.

Kara George was the son of a Servian peasant named Petrowni, and was born at Vischessi between 1760 and 1770. He served in the corps of Servian volunteers against the Turks in the Austrian war of 1788-91; and after the peace of Sistova, he was for some years a dealer in swine, one of the most profitable and respectable employments in Servia. When the Dahis began their outrages, Kara George left his forests and swine-droves, and betook himself to the mountains, where he became one of the most redoubtable of the Heyducs. When the war of independence broke out, he showed himself as eminent for skill in command, as for personal bravery in action. He despised pomp and parade; and, in the days of his highest prosperity, when sovereign of Servia, and of more than Servia, he was always seen in his old herdsman's garb, and his well-known black cap. He was in general kindly disposed; but was easily irritated, and was terrible in his wrath. He would cut down or shoot the offender with his own hand; and he made no distinction between friend and foe, between stranger and kinsman. But, though cruel, he was not vindictive; and if he could be brought once to promise forgiveness, he pardoned with the heart as well as with the lip. It is recorded of him with truth that he shot his own father and hanged his own brother; but it ought to be added that he shot the old man in order to prevent his falling into the power of enemies, who would have put him to death with lingering tortures; and that his brother, presuming on his relationship with the Commander of Servia, had acted with violence and licentiousness, which Kara George for a time overlooked; but at length the young man committed a gross outrage on the honour of a family, which complained loudly, saying that it was for such crimes the

nation had risen against the Turks.   Kara George instantly had
the offender hanged at the door of the house, and forbade his
mother to wear mourning for her son.[1]

Kara George knew the fierceness of his own character, and so
did the Servian people before they chose him to rule over them.
When he was proposed in the assembly, he at first excused himself
on the ground that he did not know how to govern.   The Kneses
replied that they would give him counsel.   He then said, "I am
too hasty of mood for the office.   I cannot stop to take counsel.
I shall be inclined to kill at once."   They answered that "such
severity was needed at that time."[2]

Such was Kara George; and thus did he become Commander
of Servia.   He afterwards styled himself "Supreme Ruler."   However arbitrary we may think his acts, and however ferocious his
energy, he unquestionably saved his country, and for many years
maintained her independence with matchless resolution and ability.
And yet, such is the inconsistency of genius, that ultimately this
very man, while still in the prime of life, wavered and grew fatally
weak of heart, at a crisis and in a situation where even ordinary
men might have been expected to be firm.   But in 1804 none
could foresee the ignominious termination of his career; and all
eyes were directed to him, as the victorious patriot, and as the
establisher of the principle of the emancipation of the subjected
Christian races from the government and power of the Mahometans.

It was not in a single year that the liberation of Servia was
accomplished.   The Dahis had been surprised and driven out of
the open country at the first uprising of the patriots, but they were
not thoroughly overcome without a formidable struggle.   They
called to their aid their confederate Ali Bey of Bosnia; and they
enrolled among their supporters many of the bands called Krid-
schalies, formed of adventurers of every description, creed, and
class, who had fought in the late wars, and who were leagued
together, like the Free Companies of the Middle Ages.

On the other hand, the Servians received help from an unexpected ally.   The Pacha of Bosnia came to their assistance with
the Sultan's forces from that province : and Turkish recruits
appeared in the Servian camp.   The Porte was now firmly resolved that the Janissaries of Belgrade, as the most turbulent of
that turbulent body, should, if possible, be crushed; and the arms
of the Servians were to be employed, together with those of loyal
Mahometans, for that purpose.   The union was again successful;

[1] Ranke, p. 206.   [2] Ibid., p. 127.

but the Servians this time insisted that the destruction of their tyrants should be made sure. The Dahis and their followers were not to be exiled, they were to be slain. The Pacha felt little anxiety to interpose in their favour. Such as could not escape to Passwan Oglou, were cut down without mercy; and the heads of the four Dahis were displayed in the Servian camp. The Pacha now pronounced the object of the war to be gained. The rebellious enemies of the Sultan had been punished; and the old order of submission by Rayas to Turks was to be restored. He directed the Servians to disarm, and return to their flocks and herds. But the command was issued not to spiritless and powerless Rayas, like those of the olden time, among whom humility before the Moslems had become a second nature; but to practised and victorious soldiers, who had fought and beaten the most renowned of the old Ottoman troops; who had stormed Turkish fortresses, and had torn down Mahometan standards. The Servians regarded as their real chiefs, not the Pachas and the Spahis, but Kara George and the other leaders of their own race and creed—men who had shared in the extremity of the land's distress, and had been foremost in fighting their way out of it. These were the commanders, whose words alone were heeded; and their words were not words of submissiveness. The Servian chiefs were men who had created their own strength and power; they were surrounded each by his band of resolute partisans, called Momkes, ready for any service; and they were not disposed to resign the pleasure of commanding, which they so recently had enjoyed.[1] The original objects of the uprising of Servia had been merely to obtain protection for life and honour against the bloodthirsty and brutal Dahis; but, in the course of that struggle, a national feeling had been evoked, and a national power evolved, which made it impossible that Servia should not now aspire to a higher destiny, than she had known since Sultan Amurath II. overthrew the Prince George Brankovitch and his Christian confederates at Varna.[2]

The struggle which the Servians had hitherto maintained against the Sultan's Mahometan rebels, was now to be continued against the Sultan himself. They determined to seek the aid of one of the great powers of Christendom. Austria was first thought of. Many of them had fought under her banner; and many of their kindred tribes were already under the sovereignty of the Kaiser of Vienna. But it was remembered that the Austrians, though they had more than once occupied Servia, had

[1] Ranke, p. 141.   [2] Page 69, *suprà.*

always given back the country and the people to the Turks. Moreover, Austria was known to be now directing all her energies to the conflict, which was approaching on her western frontiers between her and the French, by whom she had been twice humbled during the last few years.   But there was another great Christian Empire near Servia.   Russia was strong and active, and undefeated by either Turks or French, both of whom her famous general, Suwarrow, had repeatedly vanquished.   The Russians, moreover, were, like the Servians, Christians of the Greek Church ; and they had shown their zeal for their co-religionists by their repeated and formidable intercessions with the Porte in behalf of the Moldavians and Wallachians.   The Servians accordingly, in August, 1804, sent a deputation to St. Petersburg, which returned, in February, 1805, with a favourable answer.   But the Russian Emperor advised the Servians first to prefer their requests at Constantinople, promising to support them by all his influence with the Sultan.[1]

The Servians, in obedience to this direction, sent, in the summer of 1805, an embassy to Constantinople, which was instructed to demand, that in future all the fortresses of their country should be garrisoned by Servian troops ; and that, in consideration of the sufferings of the province during the recent troubles, all arrears of taxes and tribute should be remitted.   The first article was the most important, and the one respecting which most difficulty was anticipated, especially as, at the time when it was preferred, Belgrade and other strong places in Servia were still in the power of the Moslems.

The period when these demands were laid before the Porte, was an important crisis in Selim's reign.   The rival influences of France and Russia in the Divan, and also the conflicting spirits of reform and conservatism in the Ottoman nation, were now engaged in a trial of strength, with which the Servian question became closely connected.[2]

Russia was at this time at war with France ; and was redoubling the efforts, which she had been making for several years, to gain such a paramount authority in Turkey, as should render the populations and resources of the Ottoman Empire subservient to the Czar's schemes of aggrandisement against his Western enemies, as well as in the Eastern world.   Selim had made large concessions to Russia since they had become allies in 1798 : concessions which the Turkish nation viewed with anger and alarm.   Her fleets had been permitted to pass and repass the Bosphorus and the Dar-

[1] Ranke, p. 146.   [2] Ibid., p. 150.

danelles, after as well as before the general pacification in 1801. This had caused great indignation among the Turks in Constantinople; and the Sultan had been obliged to declare that such permission should not be repeated, if Russia were at war with any nation friendly to the Porte. By means of the squadrons which she thus sent from the Black Sea to the Adriatic, Russia had largely increased her force in the Ionian Islands; and she further augmented that force by levying troops among the Albanians of the mainland, notwithstanding the remonstrances of the Turkish authorities.[1] We have already noticed her successful claims regarding Moldavia and Wallachia in 1802; and in the early part of 1805 the influence of Russia over the Sultan was still more strikingly displayed on the south-eastern coasts of the Black Sea. The Porte consented that the Russians should have the free navigation of the river Phasis in Mingrelia, and erect fortresses, and place garrisons on its banks for the better security of their flotillas. The Pacha of Erzeroum was ordered to assist the Russians in establishing these posts, and in any other operations that might be of use to them, for the purposes of the war with Persia, in which Russia was then engaged.

The Russians took more than full advantage of this permission by occupying districts at some distance from the Phasis, seizing the fortress of Anakria, and building another on the coast of the Black Sea. At last, when Russia was about to join Austria and England against Napoleon in 1805, her ambassador, M. Italinski (Suwarrow's son) formally declared to the Reis Effendi, that his government found it necessary, owing to the state of affairs in Europe, to require that Turkey should forthwith enter into an offensive and defensive alliance with Russia; that all the subjects of the Sultan, who professed the faith of the Greek Church, should thenceforth be considered to be under the protection of the Emperor of Russia, and that, whenever they were molested by the Turks, the Porte should be bound to do right upon the representations of the Russian ambassador.[2] These requisitions of M. Italinski were made at the same time that the demands of the Servian deputation were laid before the Sultan on the avowed recommendation of Russia.

It is said that when Sultan Selim heard that Russia required the Protectorate of all the inhabitants of the Turkish Empire, who professed the faith of the Greek Church, he shed tears of anger and humiliation. For many days he remained in silent gloom: he then called to him such members of the Divan, as were not

[1] Alix. vol. iii. pp. 154, 169.   [2] Ibid., 170.

notoriously influenced by Russian bribes, and he took counsel with
them in this emergency.   All agreed that it would be better to
bury themselves beneath the ruins of Constantinople, than to sign
a treaty which would annihilate the Ottoman power.   But when
they reflected that the troops of Russia then assembled in her ports
on the Black Sea, could in eight days be under the Serail; that
the forces which she had gathered in the Ionian Islands could
instantly land in Albania, and, joined by the insurgent Arnauts and
Greeks, march without resistance upon Adrianople; that her army
in Georgia, which had been victorious over the Persians, could
advance upon the Turkish capital through Asia Minor; that on
the Danube she could join her troops with the revolted Servians,
and at once overrun Bulgaria;—when Selim and his advisers
thought over these things, on the strength of the enemy which
thus grasped them, and on their own weakness, they resolved that
they must not venture to return a direct refusal to the demands of
Russia, but must temporise, and negotiate, and make any sacrifice
of treasure or territory, if absolutely needed, rather than consent
to a term so fatal.[1]

The Turkish ministers succeeded in gaining time in their conferences with Italinski; but it was necessary to come to a prompt
decision as to what line the Porte should follow in dealing with
the Servians.   There were strong inducements to endeavour to win
their loyal devotion to the Sultan by a frank concession of their
wishes.   Selim had now made considerable progress in his military
reforms.   The Topidjis (the artillerymen) had been trained to a
promising extent by French officers; and they were placed on a
footing superior to that of the Janissaries.   Omar Aga's little
corps, which had acquired so much credit in the defence of Acre,
had further signalised itself by destroying some formidable bands
of brigands or free companions, which had ravaged Bulgaria and
Roumelia, and defeated the Janissaries, whom the Pachas of those
provinces led against them.   Selim increased the number of new
troops.   Two regiments of the Nizam Djidites, uniformly armed
and accoutred after the most approved French models, were now
seen performing the same evolutions as those of the best European
troops.   Special funds were provided for their pay: a few of the
Pachas—especially Abdurrahman of Caramania—adopted zealously
their Sultan's views; and in 1805, Selim ventured on the bold
measure of issuing a decree, that in future, the strongest and
finest young men should be selected from among the Janissaries

[1] Alix. vol. iii. pp. 168-171.

and other corps in the empire, for the purpose of serving in the Nizam Djidid.[1]

This was at the time when the power of the Janissaries in Belgrade had been broken by the Rayas; but in other parts of the empire they gave terrible proofs of their strength. At Adrianople they gathered together in resistance to the Sultan's edict to the number of 10,000. A Cadi who endeavoured to enforce the royal orders, was seized by them and strangled; and in the greater part of the empire it was found impossible, at least for the present, to carry out the reforms which had been decreed. The services of a brave and well-armed Raya, like the Servian, would have been invaluable to Selim, if he could have been sure that they would have loyally preferred the cause of the Sultan to that of Russia; and if he could have employed them against the Janissaries of Adrianople and the capital, without raising in rebellion the great mass of his Mahometan subjects, already deeply incensed at the means which had been used against the Dahis of Belgrade. Threatened as Selim was at this very time by Russia, and in hourly expectation of being obliged to appeal to the fanatic energy of the Moslem population of his empire for a final effort of despair against the invading Giaours, he abandoned the thought of winning the friendship of the Servian Rayas, and determined to treat them as foes, whom he must deprive of the means of injuring him. The Servian deputies at Constantinople were arrested; and Afiz, the Pacha of Nissa, was ordered to enter Servia and disarm the Rayas. Kara George met him at the frontier of the province and defeated him; and when, in 1806, Servia was attacked by two of the Sultan's armies on different sides of the province, the Servians (who had now become altogether a warlike people, every man bearing arms) defended themselves heroically. They drove back their invaders with heavy loss; and by capturing Belgrade and the other fortresses, which had hitherto been garrisoned by Turks, they made themselves completely masters of their own country. The generalship displayed by Kara George during this campaign was of the very highest order. Under him, Servia, in 1806, completed her independence, without foreign interference, and by the weapons of her own sons alone. But before another year's warfare commenced, she obtained important assistance through the outbreak of avowed hostilities between Russia and the Porte.

While the Russian ambassador, Italinski, had pressed the Porte with demands, which, if complied with, would have made the

[1] Ranke, p. 151. Juchereau St. Denys.

Sultan the mere vassal of the Czar, the French minister had been equally earnest in encouraging Selim to resist, and in endeavouring to induce him to acknowledge Napoleon as Padischah, or Emperor of France. The British ambassador, as well as the Russian, strongly opposed this recognition of their great enemy by his new Imperial title; and war was plainly threatened by both these powers in the event of any closer connection being formed between France and Turkey. The successes gained by Napoleon over the Austrians and Russians, in the autumn and winter of 1805, materially augmented the influence of the French minister at Constantinople, and diminished the dread with which Russia was regarded. The effect of the French victories round Ulm and in Moravia, was practically felt in the Black Sea and the Bosphorus. A corps of 15,000 Russians, which had been collected at Sebastopol to overawe or attack Turkey, was withdrawn into central Russia, to replace the troops which it was necessary to march westward against the advancing French.[1]

Italinski grew more moderate in his demands on the Porte, which were heard with increasing indifference, while those of France were listened to with more and more attention.

The treaty of Presburg, by which Napoleon on the 26th December, 1805, triumphantly concluded his war with Austria, transferred to the French sovereign, among other territories, Dalmatia and part of Croatia; so that the French was now in contact with the Ottoman Empire. Napoleon is said to have made it a point of primary importance thus to advance his dominions to the frontier of Turkey, and acquire the means of keeping a force ever ready to act promptly and effectively, either in supporting Turkey, or in seizing on a share of her provinces, as circumstances might make it expedient.[2] A copy of the treaty of Presburg was promptly laid before the Grand Vizier by M. Ruffin, the French minister, who dilated on the advantage which it would be to the Sultan to secure the friendship of the great Conqueror, who had now become his neighbour. The effect of this was speedily displayed in a Hatti-scheriff, by which the titles of Emperor and Padischah were solemnly given to the Ruler of the French; and when in the summer of 1806 General Sebastiani arrived at Constantinople, as an ambassador extraordinary from Napoleon to Selim, that able military diplomatist persuaded the Sultan to take measures, which were almost certain to lead to a war between Turkey and Russia. Such a war was then most desirable for

[1] Alix., vol. iii. p. 174.
[2] Ibid., p. 175, and note. **Marmont's** " Memoirs," pp. 85, 148.

Napoleon's purposes, as it was calculated to make an important diversion of part of the Russian forces from the great scene of conflict in Prussian Poland, where the Czar Alexander was striving to support King Frederick William of Prussia against the armies of victorious France.

At Sebastiani's instigation, the Sultan deposed the Hospodars of Wallachia and Moldavia, Prince Moroutzi and Prince Ipsilanti, who were more than suspected of being the pensioned agents of the Russian Court. This dismissal of the Hospodars without any previous notification to St. Petersburg, was a violation of the pledge given in the Hatti-scheriff of 1802; and the Russian ambassador at Constantinople protested angrily against it. He was joined in his remonstrances by the ambassador of England; and they informed the Porte that " the armies and fleets of the Allies were about to receive a new impulse." This meant that a Russian army would be marched into Moldavia, and that an English fleet would sail against Constantinople.[1] Selim offered to repair the breach of his engagement respecting the government of the Principalities; and an order was issued to reinstate Moroutzi and Ipsilanti as Hospodars. But before this could be accomplished, the tidings reached Constantinople that Russian troops had entered Moldavia and advanced as far as Jassy. The Emperor Alexander had promptly seized on the pretext, which the intelligence of the dismissal of the Hospodars gave him, for an attack upon Turkey; and 35,000 men under General Michelson were ordered into Moldavia and Wallachia, without even the formality of a declaration of war. The Russians speedily overran the Principalities, and beat back the scanty forces with which the Turkish commanders of the neighbouring Pachalics had endeavoured to check their progress. On the 27th of December, Michelson entered Bucharest; and it was announced that his troops would speedily cross the Danube.

A declaration of war by the Sublime Porte against Russia was the natural and inevitable result of the indignation which these things excited at Constantinople; nor was the Turkish government awed into submission by the threats of the British minister, Mr. Arbuthnot, who required that the Porte should instantly renew its alliance with Russia and England, and dismiss the ambassador of France; and who menaced Turkey with an attack by the combined English and Russian fleets, as well as by the Russian armies, in case of non-compliance with his demands. The Reis Effendi returned an answer of much sense and dignity, in which

[1] Lord Broughton's " Travels," vol. ii. p. 390.

he recapitulated the exertions which Turkey had made to preserve peace, and especially alluded to the late humiliation which Sultan Selim had voluntarily undergone in reinstating the two traitorous Hospodars.   He stated that in making war with Russia after her attack on Turkish provinces and Turkish troops, the Sultan was only repelling force by force.   He expressed a hope that a great and enlightened nation like the British, would appreciate the sacrifices which the Sublime Porte had made for the sake of amity, and the spirit which now made it act in self-defence. "But if Great Britain was determined to aid Russia in attacking the Sultan, he would repel force by force, and would trust in God for deliverance from the most unjust of aggressions.   And if, after all," said the Turkish statesman, "Turkey is to perish, she will perish in the defence of her capital : and the English nation will, above all others, experience the irreparable mischief that will follow the downfall of the Ottoman Empire."[1]

On receiving this reply, the English minister repaired to the fleet, that was then moored off Tenedos, under the command of Admiral Duckworth.   The admiral's instructions were to proceed forthwith to Constantinople, and to insist on the surrender of the Turkish fleet, or to burn it and bombard the town.[2]   On the 19th of February, 1807, the fleet (consisting of seven ships of the line and two frigates), favoured by a strong wind from the south, sailed through the formidable straits of the Dardanelles with little or no loss.   A Turkish squadron of one sixty-four gun ship, four frigates, and some corvettes, that lay in the Sea of Marmora, was destroyed by the English ; and, if Constantinople had been promptly assailed, it could not have been defended with any prospect of success ; so defective were the fortifications, and such was the panic caused by the forcing of the straits.   But the English wasted time in negotiations ; while the Turks, roused from their temporary consternation, and excited and directed by Sultan Selim and General Sebastiani, laboured energetically at the defences of the capital, until the English commander became convinced that it would be impracticable for him to make any impression on them.[3]   Accordingly, the English fleet withdrew from the Sea of Marmora, and on the 3rd of March repassed the Dardanelles, but not without a dangerous contest and severe loss. The Turks on the first occasion had been negligent, surprised, and dismayed.   They were now well-armed and prepared.   Under the direction of French engineers, whom Sebastiani had sent

---

[1] Alix., vol. iii. p. 229.   [2] Lord Broughton, vol. ii. p. 515, n.
[3] See the Appendix to Lord Broughton's "Travels," vol. ii. p. 510.

down from the capital, they had repaired the old batteries and erected new ones. Even the huge granite-shooting guns, that had lain inactive opposite each other on the European and Asiatic shores for centuries, were now employed, and with no inconsiderable effect. Several of the English ships were struck and seriously injured by the 800 lb. globes of stone which these cannon discharged. One result of the expedition was certainly to destroy the belief, which had long prevailed, that the Dardanelles gave an infallible protection to the Holy City against the fleets of the Infidels from the south; but altogether the appearance and ultimate retreat of the English force raised greatly the spirit of the Mahometan population of Constantinople and the neighbouring provinces. Unhappily for Sultan Selim, the same events raised also the fanatic hatred of that population towards all who were supposed to favour the Giaours and their usages, and who were said to be traitors to the good old faith and the good old institutions of the true believers.

An English expedition against Egypt was undertaken almost immediately after that against Constantinople, and was still more unsuccessful. A small British force, utterly inadequate for such an enterprise, was landed near Alexandria. It occupied that city, and endeavoured also to reduce Rosetta, but was ultimately obliged to retire from Egypt, after much loss, both of men and reputation.

In the Archipelago, a Russian squadron, under Admiral Siniavin, gained some advantage over the Turkish fleet; but the Turkish Capitan Pacha was able to retire into the Dardanelles and protect the capital: and altogether in the south the fortune of the war in 1807 was not unfavourable to the Ottomans. In the north, the Russian and Turkish forces on the Danube carried on the contest without either side gaining a decided superiority over the other. Indeed the war which began at the close of 1806, and was terminated by the treaty of Bucharest in 1812, is, of all the struggles between Turkey and Russia, the least interesting and the least important. Neither party put forth its full strength against the other. Hostilities were suspended for a considerable time by the truce of Slobosia; and, even while they were being carried on, Russia was obliged to employ her chief force either to combat or to watch a far more formidable enemy. She had only the use of her left hand against the Turk. On the Ottoman side, the revolts, the civil wars, and the revolutions of this period, were almost incessant. At the commencement of hostilities, the Pacha of Caramania (who was a partisan of Sultan

Selim's reforms) while leading a force, trained on the new model, towards the seat of war on the Danube, was intercepted at Babaeska on the Yena by a large force of Janissaries and other troops opposed to the change of system. A battle ensued, in which the Caramanians were utterly defeated.

It was evident that Selim was the weakest in the balance of physical power between himself and his malcontent subjects, and that a decisive struggle was fast approaching. He had neither the military ability nor the cruelty, which the part of Cleomenes required; and he was soon destined to sustain that of Agis. The death (early in 1807) of the Mufti, who had been a devoted friend to Selim, and had aided in all his undertakings, was a heavy blow to the Sultan. The Ulema, as a body, were most inimical to his reforms; and their new chief entered into an active alliance with the leading Janissaries against the throne. But the individual who did most to overthrow Selim, was the Kaimakan, Mousa Pacha. This man had, during twenty years of court intrigue, been the seemingly meek instrument of the ambition of others, and was generally despised as a submissive drudge of office. Djezzar Pacha of Acre had alone discovered the vindictive venom, that sweltered under Mousa's guise of patient humility. Djezzar foretold that he would be the cause of many troubles to the state. Selim gave Mousa Pacha the important office of Kaimakan, in the hope that its real powers would be dormant in his hands, and that he would be abundantly content with the mere pageantry of high station. Mousa used the opportunity of his office to instigate the mutinous spirit of the Janissaries and other malcontents, while he at the same time retained the confidence of the Sultan by the outward show of simple-minded loyalty. An order that was given by Selim in May (not much more than two months after the departure of the English fleet) for some changes in the equipment of the garrison of the forts on the Bosphorus, was the immediate signal for the fatal revolt. The garrison mutinied; and the Janissaries of the capital, who were in co-operation with them, repaired to the Etmeidan (the head-quarters of Janissary sedition for centuries), and there overturned their camp-kettles, in token that they would no longer accept food from Sultan Selim. Under the influence, and on the lying assurance of the traitorous Kaimakan, the Sultan tried to appease the storm by concession, and by the sacrifice of his best ministers, instead of sending for his new troops who were near the capital, and defending the seraglio with his body-guard until their arrival. The natural result was a resolution of the mutineers

3 I

to depose their sovereign. They obtained a fetva from the Mufti sanctioning their proceedings; and, headed by the traitor Mousa, who now threw off the mask, the Janissaries forced their way into the palace, and placed Mustapha, the eldest son of the late Sultan, Abdul Hamid, on the throne. Selim retired with dignity to the prison apartments, and there employed the brief remainder of his life, not vainly, in instructing his young cousin, Prince Mahmoud, afterwards Sultan Mahmoud II., how to rule the empire; and in holding out his own fate as a warning against the weakness, which the Sultan, who would reform Turkey, must discard, in order to save both her and himself.

Mustapha IV., whom the Janissaries and their accomplices then made Padischah of the Ottoman Empire (May 29th, 1807), was at this time about thirty years old. He was a prince of imperfect education, and slender capacity. During the few months for which he was the titular sovereign of Turkey, the armed multitude who had appointed him were its real rulers. But the deposed Sultan had friends: and a bold effort to restore or at least to avenge him, was speedily and sternly made. The Pacha of Rustchuck, Mustapha Bairactar, owed his elevation to Selim; and as soon as the truce of Slobosia with the Russians (August, 1807) enabled him to move his forces from the frontier, Bairactar marched upon Constantinople. At the end of 1807 he was at the head of 40,000 soldiers, chiefly Bosnians and Albanians, who were encamped on the plains of Daoud, about four miles from the capital. He summoned to his camp many of the chief men of the empire, who assembled at his bidding and swore to aid in abolishing the Janissaries, and in restoring good government to the empire. Sultan Mustapha remained in his palace, little heeded and little honoured, even in semblance, for a space of six months, during which Mustapha Bairactar, from his tent on the plains of Daoud, exercised the chief authority in the Ottoman Empire. At length he led his Albanians to the capital itself, with the design of dethroning Mustapha and reinstating Selim III. The adherents of Mustapha (or rather the partisans of the Janissaries and the Ulema) closed the gates of the Serail against him. Bairactar had brought with him from the head-quarters of the army of the Danube the sacred standard of Mahomet. He unfurled this before the Serail, and demanded that the gates should be opened to admit him and his brave soldiers, who were bringing back the holy banner from the wars. The chief of the Bostandjis replied from the wall, that the gates could not be opened but by command of Sultan Mustapha; "Talk not of

Sultan Mustapha," shouted Bairactar with fury, "let us see Sultan Selim, our Padischah and thine, false slave." He gave orders for an immediate assault; an entrance into the palace was soon effected, but, brief as the delay was, it proved fatal to Selim. On hearing the demand of Bairactar, Mustapha ordered that Selim and his own brother, Mahmoud, should be instantly seized and strangled. By their deaths he would have been left the sole representative of the House of Othman, whom no Osmanli would dare to destroy or depose. The executioners found and murdered Selim, though not till after a desperate resistance, which was maintained by the unhappy prince almost long enough to save his life; for at the very time when he was expiring under the bowstring of Mustapha's mutes, Bairactar's Albanians had forced the outer gate. As Bairactar pressed forward to the inner gate, it was suddenly thrown open, and Mustapha's eunuchs cast the body of Selim before him, saying, "Behold the Sultan whom ye seek." Bairactar bent over the corpse of his benefactor, and wept bitterly; but his confederate, the Capitan Pacha, Seid Ali, shook him by the shoulder and exclaimed, "This is the time for vengeance, not for tears." Bairactar roused himself, and they rushed into the presence-chamber, where Sultan Mustapha had placed himself on the throne, in the hope of awing the insurgents by the display of legitimate royalty. But Bairactar dragged him down, exclaiming, "What dost thou there? Yield that place to a worthier."

Mustapha had almost gained the security of being the last of the Othman Princes. The mutes and eunuchs who had murdered Selim, sought eagerly after young Mahmoud, who had been secreted by a vigilant and faithful slave in the furnace of a bath. While the ministers of death were searching the very apartment in which he was hid, the shouts of the victorious Albanians rang through the palace, testimonies not only of life preserved, but of royalty acquired for Mahmoud. Before the night had closed in, the cannon of the Seraglio announced to the people of Constantinople that Mustapha had ceased to reign, and that Mahmoud II. was Padischah of the Ottoman world. (July 28, 1808.)

Bairactar assumed power as the Grand Vizier of the new Sultan, and acted for a time with vigour and success against the party that had dethroned Selim. Mousa Pacha and other traitors were executed; and a plan was commenced for superseding the Janissaries by a new armed force under an old name. The troops, whom Bairactar designed to arm and train on the European system, were to be called Seymens, the title of an ancient corps in the Ottoman service. The Vizier's measures were received with simulated, which he mistook for real, submissiveness, by the Janissaries and the Ulema. In fatal confidence he dismissed his provincial army, retaining not more than 4000 European soldiers on whom he could rely, in the capital; but Cadi Pacha, who was his friend, was encamped near Scutari with 8000 Asiatic troops. On the second night after the departure of the Bosnian and Albanian forces, a large body of the Janissaries surrounded the Palace of the Porte, where the Vizier resided, and set fire to the building. Bairactar escaped into a stone tower, which was used as a powder magazine. There he defended himself desperately, but, either by accident or design, the tower was blown up, and the Vizier perished, before he could collect his adherents or communicate with Sultan Mahmoud. The whole Janissary force of the capital now assailed the Seymens. But these were aided by Cadi Pacha, who led his 8000 Asiatics across from Scutari, and commenced a furious engagement with the Janissaries, which raged for two days in the streets of Constantinople with varying fortune. The Capitan Pacha, Seid Ali, co-operated with Cadi Pacha; and caused a ship of the line, that lay in the harbour, to fire repeated broad-sides upon the part of the town where the Janissaries' barracks were situated. Several extensive districts of Constantinople, and immense magazines of military stores, were set on fire during this fearful conflict, which was still maintained on the morning of the 17th of March, 1809, when the Galiongi and the artillerymen, who had hitherto been neutral, pronounced in favour of the Janissaries, and determined the victory. The Sultan and his attendants had kept the palace gates closed; and the deposed Sultan, Mustapha, had been put to death in his apartments, while the result of the civil war in the streets was still doubtful. It is uncertain who gave the order for Mustapha's execution, but it is certain that if he had been left alive, the victorious Janissaries would have restored him to the throne, and have murdered Mahmoud. As sole scion of the House of Othman, Mahmoud knew that he bore a charmed life. But he was obliged to yield, at least in appearance, to the demands of the victors. An imperial edict was issued in favour of the Janissaries. All the customs of the Franks, and all the late innovations were solemnly cursed and renounced; and the old system, with all its abuses, seemed to be re-established more firmly than ever. But there were men of judgment and action among the Turks, who had seen all these things, and who saw in them only the sterner proof of the necessity of sweeping changes. They were obliged to think in silence ; but they were preparing themselves for the time when their thought might be embodied in deed.   Above all, the Sultan himself watched from year to year, as Amurath IV. had watched under not dissimilar circumstances,[1] for the hour and the means of ridding himself and his country from these worst, these home-oppressors of his race.

We must now turn again to the provinces near the Danube, that were the scenes of the war between the Porte and Russia. No great advantages had been obtained by the forces of the Czar over those of the Sultan ; and Kara George, though victorious in defence of Servia, had been unsuccessful in an attempt to conquer Bosnia, when, in consequence of the peace of Tilsit, between Alexander and Napoleon on June 7, 1807, the French general, Guillemot, negotiated a cessation of hostilities between the Turks and Russians, which was agreed to at Slobosia in the August of the same year.   One of those terms of the treaty of Tilsit, which were made public, stipulated that the Russians should evacuate Moldavia and Wallachia, but that the Turks should not re-enter those provinces until a peace between them and the Emperor Alexander was finally arranged.   There was a show of attempting to make this the basis of a treaty at Slobosia, but nothing was definitively settled, although an armistice was agreed on, in which the Servians were included.   Hostilities were in fact suspended for nearly two years, when the irritation caused among the Turks by the evident design of Russia to retain Moldavia and Wallachia, and the belief that their interests had been sacrificed by the French Emperor led to the renewal of the war.   It was not without cause that the sincerity of Napoleon's professions of friendship for the Sublime Porte was suspected.   In the interviews between him and the Emperor Alexander, when those two great potentates dazzled each other with the scheme that they should form an Imperial Duumvirate of the world, each gave up his weaker allies. As the Triumvirs who divided the Roman world, when they met on the little island on the Rhenus, sacrificed each his own friends to the ambition and wrath of the others, so Alexander and Napoleon, on their raft on the river Niemen, sacrificed friendly nations.   Spain was to be abandoned to the French Emperor in return for his leaving Turkey at the mercy of the Muscovite.   It was formally provided by a secret article of the treaty of Tilsit, that if the Porte did not comply with the private recommenda-tions of France and Russia, her European provinces, except

[1] See *suprà*, p. 247.   The account of the Revolutions 1807-1809 is chiefly taken from Lord Broughton, and from Juchereau St. Denis.

Roumelia and Constantinople, should be withdrawn from the vexation of Turkish government;[1] and it was arranged between the two Emperors, that the provisions in the public treaty for the evacuation of Moldavia and Wallachia by the Russians should be practically disregarded. Afterwards, Napoleon, in the negotiations of his ministers with Alexander, and in their subsequent interviews at Erfurt, sought to effect a dismemberment of Turkey, by which some of her best provinces should fall to his own share. Two plans were discussed; by one of which the Turks were to be allowed to retain their Asiatic, and part of their European territories; by the other, the Ottoman Empire was to be almost annihilated. The first scheme assigned to Russia the Danubian Principalities and Bulgaria. The Balkan was to be the boundary. France was to have Albania, Greece, and Candia. Bosnia and Servia were to be transferred to the Austrians, as a compensation to them for seeing the Russians established at the mouth of the Danube. According to the second project, Austria was to be bribed by receiving not only Bosnia and Servia, but Macedonia also, except the town and harbour of Salonica. France was to take (besides Albania, Greece, and Candia), all the islands of the Archipelago, Cyprus, Syria, and Egypt. Russia's portion was to be Wallachia, Moldavia, Bulgaria, Thrace, and the Asiatic provinces nearest to the Bosphorus. The Turks, thrust back beyond Mount Taurus, might still worship Mahomet on the banks of the Euphrates.

This last gigantic scheme of national robbery involved the cession of Constantinople to Russia; and to this Napoleon would not consent. His minister, M. Caulaincourt, proposed to obviate the difficulty by making Constantinople and the shores of the straits a neutral territory, a kind of Hanseatic free state, like Hamburgh or Bremen. The Russian negotiator, M. de Romanoff, was tenacious as to Constantinople, the city of St. Sophia, the true metropolis of the Greek Church, and the natural capital of the empire of the East. Caulaincourt hinted that Constantinople might perhaps be given up by France, but only on condition of her occupying the Dardanelles and the coasts of those straits, as the proper means of passage for her armies into Syria by the old route of the Crusaders. The Russian would not yield the Dardanelles, and stated that the Czar would prefer the first, the limited scheme of partition, to any arrangement that would give France the keys

---

[1] The text was, "Soustraire les provinces d'Europe aux vexations de la Porte, excepté Constantinople et la Roumilie." See Thiers, "Histoire du Consulat et de l'Empire," vol. vii. p. 668.

of the passage between the Euxine and the Mediterranean.[1] Thus wrangled they over the ideal proceeds of an uncommitted crime, little thinking that Moscow was soon to blaze, with French invaders for her occupants, and that Paris, in a few more years, was to yield to Russian cannon, while the House of Othman proceeded to complete its fourth century of unbroken dominion at Constantinople.

However much Alexander and Napoleon in 1807 and 1808 differed in their theories respecting the future of Turkey, the Russian Emperor had this practical advantage, that he retained possession of Wallachia and Moldavia ; and it became evident to the Austrian as well as to the Ottoman Court, that he had no intention of retiring from them.   Austria regarded the establishmen of the Czar's dominion in these Danubian Principalities with the utmost anxiety and alarm.   Justly suspecting that France and Russia were leagued together against the integrity of Turkey, Austria employed her mediation to reconcile the Porte with England, as the only power that could effectually withstand the project of the Cabinet of the Tuileries and St. Petersburg.[2]   Aided by this influence, Sir Robert Adair, the English ambassador, concluded the treaty of the Dardanelles with Turkey, in January, 1809.   The imperious menaces, by which France and Russia endeavoured to prevent the Porte from making peace with England, only incensed the Turkish nation more and more against Russia.   The national cry was loud for war ; and the Ottomans demanded that it should be war in earnest, and not broken by armistices to suit the convenience of false foes and falser friends. Volunteers for the campaign came forward readily from the Mahometan populations of every part of the empire ; but such was the extreme disorganisation, which the recent revolution had caused, that there was no concert, no subordination, and sometimes not even the semblance of superior authority, among the Turkish commanders.   Sir R. Adair, the English ambassador at Constantinople, in a despatch to his government, dated June 3, 1809, gives a striking sketch of the disorders, which had then prevailed for several months, and which, though abated at the time when he wrote, were soon revived.   The Janissaries had refused for a considerable time to accept the Grand Vizier whom the Sultan nominated, and until their consent was gained, that high officer did not venture to appear in Constantinople.   Sir R. Adair pro-

[1] Thiers, vol. viii. p. 440.   See also " Montholon," vol. iv. p. 229, and De Garden, "Histoire des Traités," vol. x. p. 243, *et seq.*
[2] Schlosser, vol. viii.

ceeds to state : " During this long period, from the death of Mustapha, the Ottoman Empire may be said to have been without a government. The heads of the different departments confined themselves to the details of their several charges. No man would undertake the responsibility of a general measure. Public business in all its essential parts was at a stand. The disorders in the provinces continued with as little intermission. Government, indeed, appeared everywhere to be fallen into such a state of relaxation, as to have lost the means of acting right, even when it was supported by the public sentiment. Nothing can so truly characterise both the nature and the source of these disorders as what has passed at the frontiers upon the renewal of hostilities with Russia. I have already had the honour of informing you to what degree the spirit of the people was roused by the insolent demand made at the end of March by that power. Some degree of vigour seemed also to have been inspired into the ministry on that occasion. Great activity prevailed in all the war departments. The fleet was ordered to be fitted out ; and, in fact, ten sail of the line have been equipped with uncommon expedition. Troops and provisions were ordered to the fortresses ; and numbers of men were seen to pass the Bosphorus, day after day, taking their route for the frontiers. Unhappily, when they reached the Danube, instead of being embodied into an army to oppose the enemy, finding no leader to command them, they enlisted under one or the other of two ferocious chiefs, who, in the very sight of the Russian tents, were desolating their country with civil war. There is an Ayan of Schumla, and a chief named Pehlivan Aga, under whose banners all the new comers engaged, and who have already had many desperate encounters, to the unspeakable injury of the public cause."[1]

About the same time that hostilities between the Turks and Russians recommenced on the Danube, the Austrian Empire began its calamitous war of 1809 with France ; a war in which Russia, in pursuance of her confederacy with Napoleon, took part against Austria. It is true that the Emperor Alexander's troops entered but languidly into that struggle ; for the general feeling among the Russians towards Napoleon was already one of jealousy and dislike. But the prevalence of those very feelings, in which the Czar himself ere long fully shared, kept the attention of Russia fixed more on her perils from the West, than on her prospects in the South ; and neither her best nor her largest armies were drawn away from the Polish to the Danubian provinces. Still, before

[1] Adair, " Mission to Constantinople," vol. i. p. 206-7.

the end of 1809, her general, Prince Bagration, had taken Isaktja, Tulosch, and Hirsowa, on the right bank of the lower Danube. The Servians and the Turks of Bosnia again fought with varying success, neither party being able to make any serious impression on the territories of the other.

In the next year the Russians captured Silistria on the 10th of June; but they failed in a series of operations against the Grand Vizier's camp at Shumla; and on the 3rd of August they sustained a sanguinary overthrow in an assault made by them upon Rustchuk. The Russians owned to a loss of 8000 killed and wounded in this obstinate contest. If the Turkish commander, Bosniak Aga, had followed up his success by a vigorous sally upon his defeated enemy, the whole army of the besiegers would have been destroyed.[1] But Bosniak Aga was, like many of the Ottoman commanders during the war, rather an independent Mahometan potentate, than an officer of the Sultan. He had succeeded Mustapha Bairactar as Governor of Rustchuk; and, after Bairactar's death, he disregarded all orders from Constantinople, and reigned as petty autocrat of Rustchuk and its territories. When the Russians advanced against the city, Bosniak Aga resisted them heroically; but when he had saved Rustchuk from the Giaours, he remembered that he might have to save himself from the Grand Vizier, who regarded him as a rebel. He avoided, therefore, the risk of weakening his force by any operations against the Russians in the open field.[2] Afterwards, when reconciled to the Porte, he fought loyally and bravely in the last campaigns of the war; but this incident is a fair example of the manner in which the contest was often conducted on the Turkish side. In the autumn of 1810 the Russians obtained some important successes. A large Turkish army was entirely defeated at Battin, on the 7th of September, with the loss of camps, artillery, and baggage. Sistova, Rustchuk, and other strong places, were yielded to the Russians; but all their attempts at penetrating through Shumla, across the Balkan, were unsuccessful. In the following year, the Russian generals on the Danube were ordered to act only on the defensive; so evident and so imminent was the gathering storm from the West against Russia. The Turks boldly carried the war to the left bank of the Danube, and fought with great gallantry in several engagements; but through the incompetency of their commanders, they were beaten in detail, and one whole army was obliged to surrender to the Russian general, Kutosoff, as prisoners of war. Russia was now most anxious to conclude peace with the Porte, in order

[1] Valentini, p. 104.   [2] Ibid., pp. 64, 104.

to have the full means of defending herself against Napoleon. Several attempts at negotiating a treaty were made in 1811, but without success; as the Emperor Alexander required the annexation of not only Bessarabia, but Moldavia and Wallachia, to his empire: terms which Sultan Mahmoud peremptorily refused. But the growing pressure of the danger from France made the Russians abate their demands, and consent to restore Moldavia and Wallachia, but on condition that Bessarabia should remain in their possession. Napoleon now recognised, when too late, the error which he had committed in sacrificing the friendship of Turkey to the hope of propitiating or duping Russia. He directed his ambassador to urge the Sultan to advance with the whole strength of his empire on the Danube; and promised in return, not only to secure Moldavia and Wallachia, but to obtain also the restoration of the deeply regretted Crimea to Turkey. But this "war-breathing message"[1] arrived too late. The Porte had already resolved on a cessation of hostilities with Russia. The envoys of the Emperor Alexander and the English ministers (who zealously promoted the pacification between the Czar and the Sultan) found means to give the Turks full information as to the designs which Napoleon had encouraged and brought forward for the dismemberment of their empire; so that Sultan Mahmoud now naturally disregarded the interests of the French, and sought only to obtain an alleviation of the miseries which his own nation was enduring. By the treaty of Bucharest, which was signed on the 28th of May, 1812, the river Pruth was made the boundary between the Russian and Turkish Empires, from the point where it enters Moldavia to its confluence with the Danube. All Moldavia to the right of the Pruth, and the whole of Wallachia, were given back to the Sultan, who bound himself to maintain and respect all the former conventions and stipulations in favour of the inhabitants of the restored countries. The Eighth Article of the treaty relates to Servia. It recited that, "though it was impossible to doubt that the Sublime Porte would, according to its principles, act with gentleness and magnanimity towards the Servians, as to a people that had long been under its dominion, still it was deemed just, in consideration of the part taken by the Servians in the war, to come to a solemn agreement respecting their security." A full amnesty was therefore granted to the Servians. The regulation of their internal affairs was to be left to themselves, and only moderate imposts were to be laid on them, which were not to be farmed, but received directly by the treasurers of the Porte. But

[1] Scott.

the Servian fortresses were to be given up to the Sultan, and were
again to be occupied by Turkish garrisons. The Servian statesman, Cunibert, who has lately become the historian of his adopted
country, rightly comments on the selfishness with which Russia
acted in this negotiation ; on her eagerness to obtain Bessarabia
for herself, and her indifference as to the fate of her Servian allies.
He observes that the vagueness of the stipulations in the treaty,
as to the future relative positions of the Turks and Servians, was
probably intentional on the part of the Russians; who knew well
that disputes and conflicts would ensue, which would furnish pretexts for Russian intervention at a more convenient season. " Such
conduct might promote the ulterior designs of Russia in the East ;
but it showed little justice and little generosity to Servia."[1]

[1] " Essai Historique sur les Révolutions et l'Indépendance de la Serbie,"
vol. i. p. 46.

CHAPTER XXIV.

CHARACTER OF MAHMOUD II.—MEHEMET ALI—OVERTHROW OF
THE MAMELUKES AND THE WAHABITES—FRESH TROUBLES IN
SERVIA — MILOSCH OBRENOWITCH — GENERAL EXCITEMENT
AMONG THE RAYAS—THE HETÆRIA—THE GREEK REVOLUTION
—MAHMOUD DESTROYS THE JANISSARIES—RUSSIA, UNDER
NICHOLAS I., FORCES THE TREATY OF AKKERMAN ON TURKEY
—FRANCE, ENGLAND, AND RUSSIA INTERFERE ON BEHALF OF
THE GREEKS—BATTLE OF NAVARINO—WAR WITH RUSSIA—
TREATY OF ADRIANOPLE—REVOLT OF MEHEMET ALI—BATTLE
OF KONIEH—RUSSIAN TROOPS PROTECT THE SULTAN—TREATY
OF UNKIAR SKELESSI—FRESH WAR WITH MEHEMET ALI—
DEATH OF MAHMOUD—THE TURKS DEFEATED—SULTAN ABDUL
MEJDID AIDED BY ENGLAND AGAINST MEHEMET ALI—SETTLE-
MENT OF DISPUTES WITH EGYPT.

PERIL from Russia, peril from England, peril from France, peril
from mutinous Janissaries and factious Ulemas; peril from many-
headed insurrection among Wahabites, Mamelukes, Servians, Albanians, Greeks, Druses, Kurds, Syrians, and Egyptians; peril from
rebellious Pachas, who would fain have founded new kingdoms on
the ruins of the House of Othman—such were some of the clouds
that hung over the reign of Mahmoud, the second Sultan of that
name, and the thirtieth sovereign of his dynasty. He braved
them all. Though often worsted by fortune, he never gave up the
struggle; and his memory deserves the respect of those, who are
capable of judging historical characters according to the rule laid
down by the great statesman and orator of antiquity; [1] according
to the principle of giving honour to sage forethought and energetic
action, whether favoured by prosperous or baffled by adverse circumstances. The time has not yet come when a full biography of
Mahmoud may be written. Our knowledge (in Western Europe
at least) of the details of many parts of his career is imperfect.

* Τὸ μὲρ γὰρ Πὲρας ὡς ἂν ὁ δαίμων βουληθῇ πάντων γίγνεται· ἡ δὲ Προαίρεσις
αὐτὴ τὴν τοῦ συμβούλου διάνοιαν δηλοῖ, κ. τ. λ.—Demosthenes, "De Coronâ,"
vol. i. p. 292, l. 18. Ed. Reiske.

But the general features of his character are plainly discernible. He was neither coward nor fool; nor was he a selfish voluptuary like Louis XV., who could understand the growing miseries of a state, and the approaching overthrow of a monarchy, but rest content with the calculation, that the means and appliances of pomp and indulgence were safe for his life at least, and that after him might come the deluge. The evils that Mahmoud saw around him were gigantic, and he gave up the repose of his seraglio to grapple with them in the true heroic spirit. It would be absurd to assert that he fell into no errors; it would be rash to maintain that he was sullied by no crimes; but, take him on the whole, he was a great man, who, amid difficulty, disappointment, and disaster, did his duty nobly to the Royal House whence he was sprung, and to the once magnificent empire, which it was his hard lot to govern.

It is observable in the early part of Mahmoud's reign, that two formidable classes of his enemies were swept away by the instrumentality of a high officer, who afterwards became himself the most formidable of all the foes who crossed the Sultan's path. The Mamelukes were destroyed, and the Wahabites completely conquered by Mahmoud's Egyptian Pacha, Mehemet Ali, himself one of the most remarkable men that the Mahometan world has produced in modern times.

Mehemet Ali was born in Macedonia, about the year 1765. He served in the Turkish army against the French in Egypt, and learned there the superiority of the arms and tactics of Western Europe over those of the Turks and Mamelukes. He afterwards distinguished himself greatly in the repulse of the English expedition against Egypt in 1807. Having attained the rank of Pacha of the province, he strove sedulously to free the country and himself from the lawless tyranny of the Mamelukes. He effected this in 1811 by a stroke of the vilest treachery and most ruthless cruelty. Under the show of reconciliation and hospitable friendship he brought those formidable cavaliers to his palace; and then caused them to be shot down by his Albanian guards, while cooped helplessly together in a narrow passage between high walls.[1]

[1] The following account (in " Walpole's Travels," p. 32), of the massacre of the Mamelukes, was written by an English gentleman who was at Cairo at the time:

"Nothing can be imagined more dreadful than the scene of the murder. The Mamelukes had left the Divan, and were arrived at one of the narrow passages in their way to the gates of the citadel, when a fire from 2000 Albanians was poured in on them from the tops of the walls, and in all directions. Unprepared for anything of the sort, and embarrassed for want

The Mamelukes were effectually exterminated by this atrocious massacre; and Mehemet Ali rapidly consolidated his power within his province, and also extended it beyond the Egyptian territory. His armies, under his sons, carried on a series of campaigns against the Wahabites in Arabia, at first with varying success; but at last the power of those fierce sectaries was completely broken. The holy cities and the rest of Arabia were recovered; and Abdullah Ibn Saud, the last Emir of the Wahabites, was made captive. Mehemet sent him to Constantinople, where he was beheaded on the 19th of November, 1819. The Egyptian Pacha next conquered Nubia and Sennaar, and annexed those regions to his dominions. He had formed an army on the European model, trained and officered by European military adventurers, chiefly from France, whom the cessation of the great wars in Christendom after 1815 set at liberty, and who were tempted to Egypt by the high pay and favour which Mehemet offered. Equal care was taken in preparing and manning a naval force, in the improvement of harbours, the construction of docks and roads, and all those other territorial improvements, which are at once the emblems and the engines of what is called enlightened despotism. The people of Egypt suffered bitterly under Mehemet's imposts, and still more under the severe laws of conscription, by which he filled the ranks of his army. But, arbitrary and oppressive as was Mehemet's system, it succeeded in gaining him the great object of his heart, a permanent and efficient military force; as was well proved when he aided the Sultan against the Greeks, and still better proved at a later period, in the campaigns

---

of room, they were capable of scarcely any resistance; a few almost harmless blows were all they attempted; and those who were not killed by the fire were dragged from their horses, stripped naked, with a handkerchief bound round their heads, and another round their waists, they were led before the Pacha and his sons, and by them ordered to immediate execution. Even there the suffering was aggravated, and instead of being instantly beheaded, many were not at first wounded mortally. They were shot in different parts of their bodies with pistols, or stuck with daggers. Many struggled to break loose from those who held them, some succeeded, and were killed in corners of the citadel, or on the top of the Pacha's harem. Others, quite boys of from twelve to fourteen years, cried eagerly for mercy; protesting, with obvious truth, that they were innocent of any conspiracy, and offered themselves as slaves. All these, and, in short, every one, however young and incapable of guilt, or however old and tried in his fidelity, the more elevated and the more obscure, were hurried before the Pacha, who sternly refused them mercy, one by one, impatient until he was assured the destruction was complete. Here then is an end of the Mamelukes, and this is the Pacha who piques himself upon his clemency!"

which Mehemet's son, Ibrahim Pacha, conducted against the generals of the Sultan himself.

Before, however, we consider these last-mentioned events, we must revert to the affairs of Servia, and the other northern provinces of European Turkey. It has been observed, how vague and unsatisfactory were the stipulations respecting the Servians, that were introduced in the treaty of Bucharest. One natural result of this was, that Kara George, and the other Servian chiefs, were desirous of having some definite provisions made for the security of their people, before the Turks took possession of the fortresses; whereas the Sultan's officers insisted on Belgrade and the other strongholds being given up to them immediately. While these and other differences were pending, Molla Pacha of Widdin who (like the former chief of that pachalic, Passwan Oglou) was in active rebellion against the Sultan, proposed to the Servians that they should ally themselves with him against the Porte. The Servians declined this offer, in compliance with the advice of the Russians, who were endeavouring to induce Turkey to join the confederation against France (Napoleon not yet having been completely overthrown), and were consequently at that time desirous to save the Porte from embarrassment.[1] The disputes between the Turks and Servians continued to increase, and, in 1813, Turkish armies assailed, and overran the country. Kara George (who had made himself absolute ruler of the Servians, and from whom at least the example of courage was expected) now betrayed his self-assumed trust. He buried his treasure, which was considerable, and fled across the frontier into Austria. Once more Servia seemed hopelessly bowed down beneath the Turkish yoke, but the gallantry of one of her Kneses, Milosch Obrenowitch, once more preserved her. Animated and guided by him, the Servians rose in arms in 1815, and before the close of the year the Turkish troops that had occupied the country were broken and dispersed; though the fortresses remained in the occupation of the Sultan's garrisons. Two formidable Ottoman armies advanced upon Servia in the succeeding year; but instead of overwhelming her, they halted on the frontier, and offered to negotiate. This hesitation on the part of the Ottomans was caused by the universal excitement then prevailing throughout the Christian populations of Turkey, who expected an intervention in their behalf to be made by the confederate sovereigns of the Holy Alliance, and were ready to rise throughout the empire at the first signal of encouragement. The Porte also had watched with

[1] Cunibert, vol. i. p. 47.

anxiety and alarm the proceedings of the Congress at Vienna, to which no representative of the Ottoman Empire was admitted; and the league of the three sovereigns of Russia, Austria, and Prussia, as " Holy Allies," seemed eminently menacing to the excluded Ottomans. Under these circumstances the Sultan was averse to entangling and risking his whole available military force in a war against the Servian Rayas. No resolute attempt was made to conquer Servia; but a series of embassies and treaties occupied several years; during which Milosch made himself absolute ruler of the Servians, much after the manner of his predecessor, Kara George. Kara George himself, who ventured to return to his country, was seized and shot by the commands of Milosch, on the requisition of the Turks. Milosch observed the external semblance of obedience to the Porte; which had reason at that period to be content that a chief should rule the Servians, who would keep them in control, and whose self-interest would deter him from joining in revolutionary projects for the total overthrow of the Ottoman Empire.[1] But it is not probable that, after the Holy Alliance had clearly shown its disinclination to interfere in the affairs of the East, Mahmoud would long have acquiesced in the real independence of the Grand Knes of Servia, had it not been for the grave difficulties that were brought upon the Sultan by the Greek insurrection, and other circumstances connected with that celebrated event.

Many causes combined to originate and to sustain the Greek War of Independence. The first, and the most enduring, were unquestionably those feelings which are among the noblest of our nature; and which the national historian of modern Greece refers to, when he claims peculiar glory for his country, " because from the very commencement of the struggle, her purpose, proclaimed before God and man, was to break the yoke of the stranger, and to raise again from the dead her nationality and her independence. She took up arms that she might by force of arms thrust out of Greece a race alien to her in blood and in creed, a race that had by force of arms held her captive for ages, and that regarded her to the last as its captive, and as subject to the edge of its sword."[2] To these public feelings were added, in the bosoms of many, the

---

[1] Ranke, p. 365.

[2] Ἡ Ἑλλὰς καὶ προέθετο καὶ ἐκήρυξεν ἐνώπιον Θεοῦ καὶ ἀνθρώπων ἐξ ἀρχῆς τοῦ ἀγῶνός της, ὅτι ὡπλίσθη πρὸς συντριβὴν τοῦ ξένου ζυγοῦ καὶ πρὸς ἀνέγερσιν τοῦ ἐθνισμοῦ της, καὶ τῆς ἀνεξαρτησίας της· νὰ ἐξώσῃ διὰ τῶν ὅπλων ἐκ τῆς Ἑλλάδος μίαν ξένην καὶ ἀλλόθρησκον φυλὴν, ἡ ὁποία διὰ τῶν ὅπλων τὴν ᾐχμαλώτευσε πρὸ αἰώνων, καὶ τὴν ἐθεώρει μέχρι τέλους αἰχμάλωτόν της, καὶ ὑπὸ τὴν μάχαιράν της. Tricoupi, tom. A. p. 2 and p. 1,

remembrance and the sense of intolerable private wrong. More-over, the general diffusion of knowledge among the Greeks, and the impulse that had been given to education and literary pursuits since the time of Selim III., powerfully contributed in arousing the courage as well as the intelligence of a long oppressed and much enduring people.[1] Many also of the Greeks had acquired both wealth and habits of energetic enterprise by the advancing commerce of their nation; and the insular and seafaring popula-tion of the country had generally shown the greatest activity and skill in availing themselves of the opportunities, which the state of Europe for the first fifteen years of the century gave them, for securing a large share of the carrying trade of the Levant. While Greece thus possessed admirable materials for a national maritime force, she had also better resources for an immediate military struggle on land, than nations, which have been subject to others for centuries, can usually command. Her bands of Klephts, or robbers, were numerous, well-armed, and brave; and such an occupation in a country in the condition of Greece before the revolution, implied no greater degree of discredit than was attached in England during the early Norman reigns to the "bold outlaws" of Sherwood, or in Greece herself in the Homeric ages to the avowed sea-rover and pirate.[2] There was also in central and northern Greece another important class of armed natives, forming a kind of militia, which had been originally instituted and sanctioned by the Turks themselves for the purpose of main-taining order and repressing the Klephts. These national guards (as they might be termed) were composed exclusively of Greeks, and were officered by Greeks, but they acknowledged the authority of the Pachas of their respective districts. They frequently con-sisted of Klephts, who had come in from the mountains, and made terms with the government, and who were thenceforth denominated "Tame Klephts" (Κλέφται ἥμεροι); but the regular name of the defensive troops was the Armatoli. The Porte had for some years before the Greek Revolution been jealous of the numbers and organisation of the Armatoles; and violent efforts had been made to reduce their strength, which chiefly resulted in driving them into open rebellion, and increasing the power of the Ἄγριοι Κλέφται, the armed, or wild Klephts. Another circumstance, which favoured still more the insurrection of Greece, was the density and homogeneousness of its Christian population, far ex-ceeding the usual proportions to be found in the Turkish Empire.

[1] See Emerson Tennent, vol. ii. p. 561.
[2] Tricoupi, vol. A. p. 15: and Thucydides as there cited.

Napoleon had remarked, in one of his conversations at St. Helena on the subject of the East, that the Sultans had committed a great fault in allowing so large a mass of Christians of the same race to collect together, and in such numerical preponderance above their masters, as in Greece; and he predicted that "sooner or later this fault will bring on the fall of the Ottomans."[1]

Such were the impulses and resources which Greece possessed within herself for her War of Independence, which must, however, have been ultimately unsuccessful (notwithstanding the gallantry with which it was waged) had it not been for the sympathy which the Greek cause excited among all the nations of Europe : " a sympathy such as had never been known before, in which recollections of the classic ages, liberal tendencies, and an universal Christian feeling were united."[2]   Unhappily, other motives, selfish and sordid motives, tended not a little to throw the sword of Christian Europe into the scale against the Turks in the Greek war.[3] The ambition of one great power was predominant, and used as its most effective, though unconscious instrument, the enthusiastic generosity of others.

Ever since the ineffectual rising with Russian help, which took place in 1770,[4] the Greeks had been incessantly scheming fresh attempts. Their national poet, Rhiga (whose lyrics powerfully contributed to keep up the flame of freedom in the hearts of his countrymen), towards the close of the last century formed the project of uniting the whole Greek nation in a secret confederacy for the overthrow of their Turkish masters. Thus was originated and first organised the celebrated Hetæria. It made rapid and extensive progress under Rhiga; but it decayed after his death in 1798. It was revived in 1814 among the Greeks of Odessa, by Nicholas Skophas. He termed it the Society (or Hetæria) of the Philikoi,[5] and, by engrafting it on a Literary Society, which was flourishing at Athens, he obtained the means of spreading it with rapidity among the most intelligent Greeks, and at the same time of masking it from the suspicion of the Turks. The association soon comprised many thousand members. A great number of officers in the Russian service were enrolled in it : and it was sup-

[1] Montholon, vol. iv. p. 229.   [2] Ranke, p. 365.
[3] That strong-minded and strong-spoken man, William Cobbett, said that the Greek Revolution was "a war got up by poets and stock-jobbers for the benefit of Russia."
[4] See p. 391, *suprà*.
[5] Ἐταιρία τῶν Φιλικῶν, seems meant for "Society of Friends." But Tricoupi censures the name as Ὀνομασίαν ἀρκοῦσαν μόνην νὰ χαρακτηρίση τὴν μικρὰν γνῶσιν τοῦ συζητοῦ καὶ αὐτῆς τῆς μητρικῆς γλώσσης του.

posed to identify Russian policy and Greek interests more closely
than really was the case ; a supposition highly favourable to its
advancement ; as the belief that they were acting under Russian
authority, and were sure to receive Russian aid in time of need,
naturally increased the numerical strength and boldness of the
confederates. The association had its hierarchy, its secret signs,
and its mysterious but exciting formalities. Its general spirit
may be judged of by the oath administered to the initiated in the
third of its seven degrees :—"Fight for thy Faith and thy Fatherland. Thou shalt hate, thou shalt persecute, thou shalt utterly
destroy the enemies of thy religion, of thy race, and of thy
country." The Hetæria had its branches and agents in every
province of European Turkey, in the chief cities of Asia Minor,
and in every foreign state where any number of Greeks had
settled. Early in 1820 its chiefs were making preparations for a
general insurrection, which could not have been much longer delayed. But the event, which was the immediate cause of the
rising, was the war between the Sultan and Ali Pacha, which
broke out in the spring of that year, and offered the Greeks the
advantage of beginning their revolution while the best troops of
the Porte were engaged against a formidable enemy—against one,
who long had been himself one of the strongest and cruellest
oppressors of the Greek race, but now seemed driven by self-
interest to become its most valuable ally.

Nothing certain at this time was known in the Divan at Constantinople of the danger that was gathering against the Ottoman
power in the Hetæria of the Greeks ; and Sultan Mahmoud had
determined on commencing one of the many difficult tasks of his
reign, that of effectually putting down the over-powerful and
rebellious vassals, who had long maintained their empires within
his empire, and who overshadowed the majesty of his throne. None
of these was more insolently independent, or had given juster cause
of alarm or offence to the Porte, than Ali of Epirus, the Pacha of
Jannina, whose name has already often occurred to us, but who
requires more special notice in considering the recent history of the
Ottomans and their subject-races.

Ali Pacha was an Albanian, and his family belonged to one of
the tribes, that had long embraced Mahometanism. His ancestors
had, for several generations, been hereditary chiefs of the little
fortified village of Tepelenè, where Ali was born about the year
1750. His father (who died before Ali was fourteen) had been
deprived of nearly all the possessions of the family, in a series of
unsuccessful feuds with the neighbouring chieftains. Ali's mother,

Khamko, trained the lad up to make revenge and power the sole objects of his existence. He formed a band of freebooters, at the head of which he sometimes won plunder and renown, and sometimes experienced extreme reverses and peril. On some occasions he sought refuge in the mountains, where he wandered as a solitary Klepht or robber, till he again gathered comrades, and struck for power as well as for existence. After some years of romantic but savage adventures, Ali had recovered the greater part of the territories of his family, and had acquired fame throughout Albania as a bold and successful chieftain. He did good service in the armies of the Porte against the Austrians in 1788; and partly by the reputation thus gained, but still more by bribery, he obtained from the Divan the Pachalic of Tricala, in Thessaly. By unscrupulous and audacious craft and crime, he afterwards made himself Pacha of Jannina, in Epirus, which thenceforth was the capital of his dominions. Gifted with great sagacity, and embarrassed by no remorse and little fear, Ali triumphed over rival Beys and Pachas, and almost accomplished the subjugation of the neighbouring mountain tribes; though he experienced from them, and especially from the gallant Suliotes, a long and obstinate resistance. Every forward step of Ali's career was stained by the foulest treachery and the most fiendish cruelty. But the cities and lands under his rule obtained peace, security, and commercial prosperity. Ali watched eagerly the conflicts and changes, of which nearly all Europe was the scene for many years after the breaking out of the first French Revolution. He had frequent negotiations with Napoleon and other rulers of the West, who substantially, though not formally, recognised him as an independent potentate. It is said[1] that "his scheme was, to make himself master of all Albania, Thessaly, Greece, and the Ionian Islands; and the Gulf of Arta, a bay with a narrow entrance, but spacious enough to contain the united fleets of Europe, was to become the centre of this new empire. His Albanians were the best soldiers in Turkey; the forests of Jannina and Delvino abound with excellent timber, and Greece would have furnished him the most enterprising sailors in the Mediterranean." Ali never could realise this project; but he maintained and increased his dominion until 1819, when the acquisition of Parga was his last triumph. Mahmoud had long resolved to quell his insubordinate Pacha, whose haughty independence was notorious throughout Europe; and a daring crime committed by Ali, in February, 1820, gave the

---

[1] "Biographical Dictionary" of Useful Knowledge Society; title, "Ali Pacha."

immediate pretext for his destruction. Two of Ali's agents were detected in Constantinople in an attempt to assassinate Ismail Pacha Bey, who had fled from Jannina to avoid the effects of the Pacha's enmity, and had been employed in the Sultan's own court. A Fetva was forthwith issued, by which Ali was declared Fermanli (or outlaw), and all loyal viziers and other subjects of the Padischah were ordered to make war upon the rebel. In the conflict which ensued, Ali had at first some success; but Mahmoud inspired his generals with some portion of his own energy; and by sternly declaring that he would put to death any one who dared to speak in favour of the outlaw, the Sultan checked the usual efficacy of the bribes which Ali dispensed among many members of the Divan. Cooped up in Jannina, Ali prolonged his resistance till the beginning of 1822, when he was lured into the power of his enemies by pretended terms of capitulation, and put to death by Churchid Pacha, who commanded the besieging army.

But while the "old Lion of Jannina" (as Ali was called) thus long held at bay the Sultan's forces, and detained one of the ablest, though most ferocious, of the Sultan's generals,[1] almost all Greece had risen and beaten back the Ottomans; and a similar insurrection had been for a time successfully attempted in the trans-Danubian provinces. In February, 1821, Ipsilanti, a Greek who had obtained high distinction in the Russian army, and who was then the chief of the Hetæria, crossed the Pruth into Moldavia with a small band, and called on his countrymen throughout the Turkish Empire to take up arms. Unhappily, the very first acts of the Greek liberators (though Ipsilanti was not personally responsible for them) were the cruel and cowardly murders of Turkish merchants, in the towns of Galatz and Jassy.[2] The tidings of these things, with the addition of much exaggeration and many false rumours, soon reached Constantinople. The consequent indignation, and the alarm of the Mahometans at the wide-spread confederacy of their Rayas against them, which was now suddenly revealed, produced a series of savage massacres of the Greek residents in the capital; and these were imitated or exceeded by the Turkish populations, and especially the Janissaries, in Smyrna and other towns. Indeed, throughout the six years' war that followed, the most ferocious, and often treacherous cruelty, was exhibited

---

[1] See the powerfully-drawn character of Churchid Pacha in Tricoupi, vol. A. p. 67.

[2] Tricoupi, vol. A. p. 53. He expressly speaks of the murder of the Turks at Galatz, as of Αἱμοσταγοῦς ταύτης πράξεως τῆς πρώτης πράξεως τοῦ ὑπὲρ ἐλευθερίας καὶ εὐνομίας ἀγῶνος.

on both sides. But many acts of heroism, worthy of the best days of ancient Greece, cast a lustre on the cause of the insurgents, and added to the sympathy with which the peoples of Christian Europe regarded their efforts ; sympathy, which was shown in the accession of frequent volunteers to the Greek armies, and in liberal contributions by individuals and private societies to their funds, before the kings of Christendom interfered in the conflict. In Moldavia and Wallachia, the Turks destroyed Ipsilanti's force, and put an end to the insurrection at the battle of Drageschan, on the 19th of June, 1821. But in Greece, and on the Greek seas, the bands and light squadrons of the insurgents were generally victorious over the Turkish armies and fleets, until, in 1825, Sultan Mahmoud summoned to Greece the forces of his Egyptian Pacha, Mehemet Ali. The effect of superior arms and discipline was at once apparent. Ibrahim Pacha, at the head of his father's regular battalions, defeated the Greeks in every encounter, laid waste their territory at his will, and gradually reconquered the cities and fortresses which had been won from the Turks : Missolonghi (which was regarded as the great bulwark of Western Greece) falling after a noble resistance, on the 22nd of April, 1826, and Athens surrendering in the June of the following year.

While the Egyptian troops were thus maintaining a decided superiority by land, the squadron sent by Mehemet Ali had combined with the Turkish, and a powerful fleet of heavily-armed and well-manned ships was thus collected under the Sultan's flag in the Greek waters, with which the lighter vessels of the insurgents were utterly unable to cope. The usual curses of a liberal cause, when the fortune of arms goes against it—disunion and civil war—now raged among the Greek chiefs ; and despite of the general gallantry of the nation, and of the high abilities and boundless devotion displayed by some of the leaders, Greece must have sunk in 1827, if the forces of the Three Great Powers of Christian Europe had not appeared with startling effect on the scene.

Before, however, we consider the final catastrophe of the Greek war, we must revert to the intervening transactions between the Porte and the Court of St. Petersburg on the subject of Servia and the Principalities ; and also to the bold measures by which the Sultan, in 1826, struck down the long-hated, and long-dreaded power of the Janissaries, and revolutionised the military system of his empire. The destruction of the Janissaries is the greatest event of Mahmoud's reign. While considering the state of Turkey in the first years of Selim III.,[1] we have seen how indispensably

---

[1] Page 475, *suprà.*

necessary it had become, both for the internal amelioration of the
empire, and for strengthening it against attacks from without,
that there should be a thorough change in the composition, the
organisation, the discipline, and the arms of the regular troops.
We have seen how obstinately the Janissaries resisted all improvements, and the savage fury with which they destroyed the sovereign and the statesmen who endeavoured to effect the requisite
alterations. Since those events the worthlessness of the Janissaries
in the field had been further proved, not only in the campaigns on
the Danube, in 1810 and 1811, but still more conclusively in their
repeated failures against the Greek insurgents. On the other
hand, the victorious progress of the Egyptian troops in Greece
demonstrated that the European discipline could be acquired by
Mahometans, as well as by natives of Christendom, and that the
musket and bayonet were as effective in the hands of a Copt or
Arab, as in those of a Muscovite or Frank. The comparison between the troops sent from his Egyptian provinces, and those
supplied by other parts of his empire, was at once inspiriting and
galling to the Sultan. He saw that Mehemet Ali had realised
in Egypt the very projects, which had hitherto been beyond the
power, and almost beyond the daring of the Padischahs of the
Ottoman world. Mahmoud determined that this contrast should
cease to shame him, and that the Janissaries should no longer survive the Mamelukes. But he knew well the numerical strength
and the unscrupulous violence of the body which he was about to
assail. Scarcely a year of his reign had passed, in which some
part of his capital had not been destroyed by fires caused by malcontent Janissaries, or in which it had not been necessary to make
some concession to their turbulent demands. It was impossible to
collect and destroy them by any stratagem, such as Mehemet Ali
had used against the Mamelukes; nor, indeed, is there any act of
Mahmoud's life, which justifies us in suspecting that he would have
been willing to employ such treacherous artifices, even if they could
have availed him. Mahmoud foresaw that a battle in the streets
of Constantinople must decide the question between him and the
Janissaries; and he diligently strengthened himself in the arm of
war, which is most effective in street-contests. It is said that
when he heard of the manner in which Murat, in 1808, used cannon to clear the streets of Madrid of the insurgent populace, it
made such an impression on the Sultan's mind, that it never was
forgotten.[1] He sedulously improved the condition of his own
artillery force, and by degrees officered it with men on whose

[1] Ranke, p. 369.

loyalty and resolution he could rely. When, in the eighteenth year of his reign, he made ready for the final struggle with his Janissaries, he had increased the force of Topidjis, or artillery-men, in and near Constantinople, to 14,000, and he had placed at their head an officer of unscrupulous devotion to his sovereign's will. This general of Turkish artillery was named Ibrahim; but his conduct on the day of the conflict, and his swarthy complexion, made him afterwards known by the grim title of Kara Djehennin, or "Black Hell." Mahmoud also had taken an opportunity to appoint as Aga of the Janissaries themselves, Hussein, who was ready to carry out all the Sultan's projects. The Grand Vizier was staunch to his sovereign, and a man of spirit; and a large body of trustworthy Asiatic troops was encamped at Scutari, which could be brought into action at the fitting moment. Mah-moud also reasoned, not unsuccessfully, with the leading Ulema on the folly of their abetting by their influence the obstinate dis-loyalty of the Janissaries, who might once have been the truest champions, but were now clearly the worst enemies of Islam. He had a little before this time raised to the dignity of Chief Mufti a man who would support him; and he determined to proceed in strict accordance with every recognised formality and law, so as to throw upon the Janissaries the odium of being the first to appeal to brute force. In a great council of Viziers and Ulema, held in June, 1826, it was resolved that it was only by encountering the infidels with a regularly-disciplined army that it was possible for the Moslems to regain the advantage over them; and a Fetva was drawn up, and signed by all the members of the council, which ordered a certain number out of each Orta of the Janissaries to practise the requisite military exercises.[1] After some murmurings and partial tumults, the whole body of the Janissaries of the capital assembled on the 15th June, 1826, in the Etmeidan, overturned their camp-kettles (the well-known signal of revolt), and advanced upon the palace, with loud cries for the heads of the Sultan's chief ministers. But Mahmoud was fully prepared for them. He un-furled in person the Sacred Standard of the Prophet, and called on all True Believers to rally round their Padischah and their Caliph. The enthusiasm of the people was roused into action on his side; and he had ready the more effectual support of his artil-lerymen and Asiatic troops. As the Janissaries pressed forward through the narrow streets towards the Serail, "Black Hell" and his gunners showered grape on them; and round shot cut lanes through their struggling columns. They fell back on the Etmei-

[1] Ranke, p. 369.

dan, and defended themselves there with musketry for some time with great steadiness and courage. After many had perished, the remnant of the sons of Hadji Beytasch retired in good order to their barracks, which they barricaded, and they prepared themselves to offer the most desperate resistance to the anticipated assault. But Mahmoud and his officers risked no troops in such an encounter. The Sultan's artillery was drawn up before the barracks, and an incessant storm of shot and shell was poured in on the devoted mutineers. Some of the most daring of them sallied out, sabre in hand, but were all shot or cut down as they endeavoured to escape. Some few begged for mercy, which was sternly refused. The artillery of Kara Djehennin continued to thunder upon the buildings till they were set on fire and utterly destroyed; and the last of the Janissaries of Constantinople perished among the blazing and blood-stained ruins.

The number of those who fell on this memorable day has been variously estimated.[1] The most accurate calculation seems to be that which gives 4000 as the number of the Janissaries killed in the battle. Many thousands more were put to death afterwards in the various cities of the empire; for Mahmoud followed up his victory with unremitting vigour and severity. The Janissary force throughout the Ottoman dominions was abolished, their name was proscribed, their standards destroyed; and the assemblage of new troops, on a new system, was ordered; which were (in the words of the Sultan's proclamation), to sustain the cause of religion and of the empire, under the designation of the "Victorious Mahometan Armies."

At this point in Sultan Mahmoud's career, it was not without reason that he was "aroused into courageous self-confidence, and animated with high and promising hopes."[2] The endurance, and the preparations of eighteen years had gained their reward. He had accomplished the task which had baffled so many of his predecessors; he had swept away the military tyranny under which the empire had groaned for centuries. At last the Sultan felt real freedom for himself, and real sovereignty over his kingdom. He now formed an army of upwards of 40,000 men, clothed, armed, and disciplined after the European system. It was expected that this force would by degrees be raised to the number of 250,000. True it is, that Mahmoud found no adequate aid from among enlightened members of his own nation, that nearly everything had to be done "by the Sultan's own iron will."[3] But that will had

[1] See Marshal Marmont's remarks on this, p. 77.
[2] Ranke, p. 371.   [3] Möltke, p. 13.

already worked wonders; and each success gave him tenfold means for achieving others. In the provinces, the most formidable of the rebellious Pachas, who had set at nought the authority of the throne in the beginning of his reign, were now dead or deposed; and, above all, the head of Ali of Jannina had been shown by Mahmoud himself, in stern triumph, to his submissive Divan. The Wahabites were crushed, the Mamelukes exterminated. Mehemet Ali had hitherto committed no overt act of insubordination. Rebellion had been trodden out in Moldavia and Wallachia; and though it had blazed more fiercely and more enduringly in Greece, it seemed about to be extinguished there also by the victorious Turco-Egyptian forces of Ibrahim Pacha. All that Mahmoud now required from fortune, was immunity from attack by foreign powers during the period of transition, through which it was necessary for Turkey to pass between the abolished old, and the yet uncreated, or immature institutions, under which he designed her to flourish. It is the opinion of one of the ablest historians of Mahmoud's reign,[1] that, "if Turkey had enjoyed ten years of peace after the destruction of the Janissaries, Sultan Mahmoud's military reforms might in that time have gained some strength; and, supported by an army upon which he could depend, the Sultan might have carried out the needful reforms in the administration of his country, have infused new life into the dead branches of the Ottoman Empire, and made himself formidable to his neighbours. All this was prevented by Russia, which nipped the Sultan's military reforms in the bud." And the strongest possible proof of the wisdom with which Mahmoud's measures were planned, of the beneficial effects which they actually produced in Turkey, and far greater benefits which they would have conferred if Russia had not hastened to attack her while those measures had scarce begun to ripen, is to be found in the despatches of the chief statesmen of Russia during the war of 1828-29, in which they take credit for their sagacity in discerning in Mahmoud's reforms the necessity for prompt hostilities on the part of Russia; and in which they own that Turkey had displayed, under the stern guidance of Mahmoud, a degree of energy and power higher than she had long previously possessed; and they felicitate themselves in not having waited until the new Turkish forces, which even in their infancy were so hard to conquer, had acquired consistency and mature strength.[2]

[1] Möltke, p. 456.
[2] See the Despatches of Count Pozzo di Borgo, and the Prince di Lieven, cited *infra*, p. 515.

It was singularly unfortunate for Sultan Mahmoud, that only a few months before he struck the decisive blow, which destroyed the principal old military force of Turkey, there was a change of emperors at St. Petersburg. In Alexander I., the abhorrence of revolution had predominated over every other sentiment. He therefore kept aloof from the side of the Greek insurgents ; and he was in the latter part of his life (which was clouded with melancholy and sickness) indisposed to the energetic action which wars of conquest require in a sovereign. But on the 24th of December, 1825, he was succeeded on the Russian throne by Nicholas, a prince of many high merits, but a genuine representative of Russian national feeling, and, as such, ready and willing for a war in support of the Christians of the Greek Church, against the "old arch-enemy" of Muscovy.[1] Moreover, the civil strife which had broken out at St. Petersburg on the accession of Nicholas, at the end of 1825, and the disquiet which had not ceased to pervade the Russian nation, and especially the army, made the statesmen of St. Petersburg consider a Turkish war most desirable for their own empire's internal security.[2] The negotiations which had been long pending between Russia and the Porte respecting Servia, the Principalities and other matters, were resumed in a far more peremptory tone by the ministers of Nicholas, than had previously been employed towards the Ottomans. In the August of 1826 (two months after the destruction of the Janissaries) the Russians insisted that the Porte should forthwith give up certain fortresses in Asia, which were alleged to have been ceded by the treaty of Bucharest ; that the Moldavians and Wallachians should be restored to their full privileges, as before the revolt of 1821 ; and that the confirmation of the political rights of the Servians should be no longer delayed. The Turks at first received these demands with avowed indignation ; but in the utterly unprepared state of Turkey at that crisis of internal change, the Sultan felt himself obliged to give way ; and on the 7th of October, 1826 (the very last day which Russia had allowed for deliberation), the treaty or convention of Akkerman was signed.

It ratified the treaty of Bucharest; and ordained that the Moldavians and Wallachians should thereafter enjoy all the privileges conferred by the fifth article of that treaty, and also those bestowed by the Hatti-scheriff of 1802. The future Hospodars of the provinces were to be elected by the Boyards from among their own body for a period of seven years. No Hospodar was to be deposed by the Porte without the consent of Russia.

[1] Möltke, p. 3.   [2] Ibid., p. 3.

The Moldavian Boyards, who had been implicated in the insurrection of 1821, and obliged to take refuge in Russia, were now to be at liberty to return, and to resume their rank, estates, and possessions. With respect to Servia, the Porte and a body of deputies from the Servian nation were to settle the necessary regulations for the future government of the province, which were to be forthwith published in an imperial Hatti-scheriff, and become part of the treaty between Russia and Turkey. It was stated that among the privileges of the Servians, which were to be thus guaranteed, were religious liberty, free choice of their chiefs, independent internal self-government, the re-union of the districts that had been detached from Servia, the consolidation of the various imposts in a single charge, freedom of commerce, the establishment of hospitals, schools, and printing-offices, and an edict that no Mahometan should be allowed to reside in Servia, except those belonging to the garrisons of the fortresses. The treaty of Akkerman contained many other stipulations, all to the disadvantage of Turkey ; such as that the Porte should be obliged to indemnify Russian merchants for depredations committed by the Barbary corsairs ; and that in granting the free navigation of the Black Sea to nations which had not yet obtained that right, the Porte would do so in such a manner as to cause no injury to Russian commerce.

Bitter as was the humiliation which the necessity of accepting the treaty of Akkerman imposed upon Mahmoud, he was soon to experience heavier blows from the same quarter, and also from powers which he had hitherto regarded as sure friends. On the 6th of July, 1827, a treaty was signed at London between Russia, England, and France, the object of which was declared to be to stop the effusion of blood, and to effect the reconciliation of the Turks and the Greeks.

The mediation of the three high contracting powers was offered for this purpose : and the basis of pacification was to be the practical independence of Greece ; the Sultan retaining only a nominal sovereignty, and receiving a fixed annual tribute, to be collected by the Greeks themselves. An armistice was to be insisted on before the discussion of terms ; and if the Porte rejected this intervention, the three powers were to form international relations with the Greeks, by sending and receiving consuls, and thereby recognising the insurgent province as an independent state. The offer of these terms was eagerly accepted by the Greeks, then in their extreme distress, but indignantly rejected by Sultan Mahmoud. He stated that the country, which it was proposed to

withdraw from his rule, had for centuries formed part of the Ottoman Empire ; and that those, whom powers, professing friendship
to the Porte, designed to treat with and recognise as a Greek govern
ment, were mere brigands and rebels to their lawful sovereign.
The Sultan appealed to history as offering no example of such interference in violation of all principles of legitimate authority, and
also to the law of nations, by which every independent power has
a right to govern its own subjects without the intervention of any
foreign power whatever.   He declared finally his inflexible resolution never to renounce his rights.

The statesmen of Christendom, who interposed on behalf of the
Greeks, had great difficulty in justifying their intervention under
any generally recognised principle of the law of nations, especially
after the forcible manner in which the chief continental Christian
potentates had lately concurred in upholding the legitimate right
of ancient sovereignty against the revolutionists of Italy and Spain.
They shrank from openly professing a broad general principle that
it is lawful and laudable to aid the oppressor against the oppressed.
They might have quoted against the Turks the authority of their
own renowned Grand Vizier Ahmed Kiuprili, who (as we have
seen)[1] thus justified in 1672 the interference of Turkey in behalf
of the Cossack subjects of the Polish Republic.   But such a mere
argumentum ad hominem would have been of little value : and the
principle of foreigners interfering with an established government
because the foreigners think the conduct of that government
towards part of its subjects cruel and iniquitous, is certainly a
principle liable to gross abuse ; and it is one little likely to be
favoured by despotic rulers, or by states in which one race is
dominant over other races.[2]

[1] See p. 287, *suprà*.

[2] See as to intervention by a foreign state on behalf of oppressed subjects, Grotius, lib. 2, xii. 40 ; lib. 2, xxv. 8 ; Wheaton's "Elements," vol. i.
p. 87 ; Kent's Comment., vol. i. p. 25 ; Phillimore, vol. i. p. 441 ; Count
Mamiami, p. 359 ; Mackintosh's "Review of the Causes of the Revolution of
1688," c. ix. ; Vattel, livre i. c. 4, secs. 51-54, and livre iii. c. 18, sec. 296.
I have examined this subject in "The First Platform of International Law,"
p. 297, *et seq.*, more fully than can be done in the present volume.

The national historian of modern Greece, Spiridion Tricoupi, takes a
natural pride in the peculiar circumstances under which the great Powers
of Christendom saved his country.   He boasts that the intervention put an
end to the principle of the Holy Alliance, which condemned all political
changes, if sought by revolt and force of arms ; that it disturbed the balance
of power in Europe ; and that it tended to destroy an ancient empire, to
which he, as might be expected, applies severe epithets :

Τὰ ἀποτελέσματα τῆς Ἑλληνικῆς ἐπαναστάσεως ἐδείχθησαν γιγανταῖα καὶ κατ'
ἄλλον τρόπον· διότι ἀνέτρεψαν τὰς πολυθρυλλήτους ἀρχὰς τῆς Ἱερᾶς Συμμαχίας,

We find accordingly that this principle of intervention was very faintly and hesitatingly put forward by the diplomatists of the great powers, in 1827. They did, indeed, state that one of the reasons for their proceedings was to stop the effusion of blood : but this might have been explained as being no more than a common formula of negotiation.[1] They appealed to another justification, which was the fact of their mediation having been solicited by one of the contending parties. But the request of one only of two disputants is no sufficient ground for interference, especially if that party consist of revolted subjects. The main ground on which the intervention was vindicated, was the alleged

καταδικαζούσης πᾶσαν πολιτικὴν μεταβολὴν ἐνεργουμένην δι᾽ ἀποστασιῶν καὶ δι᾽ ὅπλων, διότι ἐτάραξαν τὸ πολυθρύλλητον σύστημα τῆς ἰσορροπίας, τὸ ὁποῖον περὶ πολλοῦ εἶχεν ἡ Εὐρωπαϊκὴ πολιτική, καὶ διότι, ἀνακαλέσαντα εἰς τὴν δόξαν καὶ εἰς τὴν πολιτικὴν ζωὴν ἓν ἔθνος, τὸ ὁποῖον ἐρρίφθη πρὸ αἰώνων εἰς τὸν τάφον τῆς ἀδοξίας καὶ τῆς δουλείας, συνέτρεξαν καὶ εἰς τὸ νὰ διαλύσωσι μίαν μεγάλην καὶ παλαιὰν αὐτοκρατορίαν γεννηθεῖσαν, ἀνδρωθεῖσαν, γηράσασαν καὶ ἀποθνήσκουσαν ἀνεπιστήμονα ἀντικοινωνικὴν καὶ βάρβαρον.

[1] At one period in the war the Duke of Wellington was prepared to recommend forcible intervention to check atrocious violations of the laws of war, such as were alleged against the Turks. " When, in 1826, Ibrahim Pacha was rapidly reconquering the Morea, besides the continuance between him and his armed opponents of the same merciless spirit on both sides, which had characterised the contest from its commencement, it was imputed to the Egyptian commander that in every district and town which he won from the Greeks, he seized the Greek male children for circumcision and forcible conversion to the Mahometan faith, and that he had declared and was beginning to act on a system of transplanting the remains of the Greek population to Egypt, and of repeopling the Peloponnesus with colonies of Copts and Arabs. Atrocities of similar character may be found in the histories of ancient and of mediæval Oriental conquerors ; but even if anything of the kind had ever been practised by any of the civilised nations of the West, certainly many centuries had passed away without European warfare being sullied by such abominations. It is to be remembered that the Ottoman Turks had long before the Greek war of independence, on more than one occasion, appealed to the European laws of nations, and had recognised the principles and usages which those laws established. Even if this had not been the case, it is not likely that civilised European communities would have tolerated the obtrusion into their continent, or into any part of the world where their usages predominated, of such hideous barbarism. The Duke of Wellington urged that these charges against Ibrahim Pacha should be investigated ; and the Duke maintained that, if true, they gave third states the right to intervene in the war." (See the Wellington Despatches, 3rd series, vol. iii. p. 75.) " But the Egyptian commander denied the truth of these charges. No proof of them was given or found ; and consequently other grounds for intervention, besides a general statement that the war was carried on by the Turks in a ferocious manner, were put forward by England and her allies, when intervention actually took place in the October of 1827." —(" First Platform of International Law," p. 439.)

necessity of affording protection to the subjects of other powers who navigated the seas of the Levant, in which for many years atrocious piracy had been exercised, while neither Turkey nor revolted Greece was, *de facto,* either able or willing to prevent the excesses springing out of this state of anarchy. But, unfortunately for the validity of this pretext, the three powers intervened at the very crisis, when the Sultan had acquired a decided ascendency in the war; and when it was clear that in a short time the contest would be over, and the condition of the Levant restored to what it had been for centuries. Moreover, if the suppression of piracy in the Turkish waters had been the genuine object of England, France, and Russia, they might have effected it with a tenth part of the force employed at Navarino; and in order to effect it, there was not the least occasion for them to burn the Sultan's men-of-war, or to land troops to reduce his fortresses in the Morea.

On the 20th of October, 1827, the combined squadrons of England, France, and Russia, entered the Bay of Navarino, in which the Turco-Egyptian fleet was moored. The avowed object of the allies was to compel Ibrahim Pacha to desist from further hostilities against the Greeks. Their force amounted to ten ships of the line, ten frigates, and some smaller vessels. It was much superior to that of the Sultan, which, though it comprised a large flotilla of small barks, and nineteen frigates, presented only five line-of-battle ships. It is probable that the ministers of England and France (who could have no wish to see Turkey weakened for purposes of Russian ambition) hoped to the very last that such an imposing demonstration of force would awe the Sultan or his officers into submission, and that Greece might thus be saved without her old masters being further injured.[1] But the stern, unbending spirit that nerved Sultan Mahmoud, was fully shared by his admirals, the Capitan Pacha, Tahir Pacha, and Moharem Bey. An engagement was the inevitable result of the entrance of the allied fleet into Navarino; an engagement in which the Turco-Egyptians fought for four hours with desperate valour, until the whole of the Sultan's magnificent armament was destroyed, except a few insignificant barks that were left stranded on the shore. The consequences of the battle were immense; far, indeed, beyond what the better part of the conquerors either designed or desired. It was not merely that the Greek question was virtually decided by it; Ibrahim gladly retiring from the Morea to Egypt with the chief part of his army, and a division of French troops, under Marshal Maison, completing the deliverance of the Greek terri-

[1] See Möltke, p. 6.

tory; but Turkey was by this "untoward event," as the Duke of
Wellington truly termed it, left defenceless before Russia. Men
said, that "the Sultan had destroyed his own army; and now his
allies had destroyed his navy."[1] Still Mahmoud and his people
would not bend to the stranger and to the rebel; nor would the
Divan, even after Navarino, accept the treaty of London, which
the ministers of the three powers, especially of Russia, now pressed
in more and more peremptory tone.   But the Turkish statesmen
knew their peril, and endeavoured to induce the ambassadors to
remain at their posts, and to communicate to their respective
courts the offers of the Porte respecting the future treatment of
Greece.   These were, a complete pardon and amnesty : a remission
of all arrear of taxes and tribute : a restoration of confiscated
property : a re-establishment of all privileges : and, finally, a
pledge of milder government.[2] The ambassadors refused to accept
any terms but those of the treaty, and on the 8th of December,
left Constantinople. An attempt was made by the Reis Effendi
to reopen negotiations; but the Russian minister (to whom the
communication was sent) returned no answer; and the preparations for war on the Russian frontier showed clearly that the
design of the Emperor Nicholas was not to bring about a reconciliation, but to force a quarrel.   Though Russia was nominally at
peace with all the world (her Persian war having ended by a convention in November), she was calling out new levies of conscripts,
concentrating troops in Bessarabia, and collecting military stores
and transports in her harbours in the Black Sea in readiness for
an invasion of the Ottoman dominions.   There were also many
topics of dispute between the Sultan and the Czar as to certain
Asiatic fortresses wrongfully retained by Russia, and those never-
failing sources of difference, the affairs of the Principalities and of
Servia.   Convinced that his great enemy intended to attack him
in the spring, the Sultan took the bold step of being the first to
declare war; and a Hatti-scheriff was issued on the 20th of December, in which, addressing the Pachas and Ayans of his empire,
the Sultan recited the wrongs which he had endured from Russia,
among which he classed the unjust extortion of the treaty of Akkerman; and he called on all true Mussulmans to show again the
determined valour, with which the Ottomans had in ancient times
established in the world the true religion, and to resist the foe,
whose object was to annihilate Islam, and tread the people of
Mahomet under foot.

In the ensuing war the vigour shown by Mahmoud astonished

[1] Möltke.   [2] Chesney, p. 15.

both friends and foes. Russia employed in the first campaign about 100,000 troops of all arms in European Turkey. The number might easily have been greater; but she judged it prudent to retain large armies in Poland, Finland, and the Ukraine, and a far less spirited resistance on the part of the Turks was expected, than that which was actually encountered. In Asia, her general, Count Paskievitsch, led an army 30,000 strong into the Turkish provinces, besides having a reserve of 16,000 more. At sea her superiority was incontestable. She had sixteen line-of-battle ships in the Black Sea, besides frigates and smaller vessels; and in the Archipelago she had the fleet which had aided in destroying the Turkish navy at Navarino. Throughout the war this command of the sea was of infinite importance to her; and in particular, the operations against Varna in 1828, and the decisive movements of Diebitsch in 1829, were only rendered possible by her uncontrolled possession of the Euxine. Mahmoud had only been able to collect an army of about 48,000 troops trained on the new system. These were principally mere lads, who were selected in the hope that their prejudices against the Frankish innovations would not be so violent as generally prevailed among the elder Turks. The Prussian General, Baron Möltke, who served with the Turks throughout the war, and our countryman, Colonel Chesney, describe vividly the disheartening spectacle which this infant force presented, and its difference from the aspect of the old Ottoman troops. "The splendid appearance, the beautiful arms, the reckless bravery of the old Moslem horde had disappeared;" but the German writer adds, "yet this new army had one quality which placed it above the numerous host which in former times the Porte could summon to the field—it obeyed." Besides these troops, the Sultan was obliged to call together the feudal and irregular forces of his empire, chiefly from Asia; for throughout European Turkey the deepest discontent with their sovereign's reforms prevailed among the Ottomans. Bosnia, a remarkably warlike and strongly Mahometan province, sent no troops at all; and many of the officers, whom he was obliged to employ, were attached to the old order of things, and were almost as bitter in their disaffection to the Sultan, as in their antipathy to the Russian Giaours. But the artillery force was numerous and loyal; and the armed Turkish inhabitants of the towns, which the enemy assailed, showed as usual the greatest spirit in self-defence, and contributed greatly to the prolongation of the war, which was (in its first campaign, at least) principally a war of sieges.

In the operations of 1828, in Europe, the Russians occupied the

Principalities with little opposition, and crossed the Danube early in June. Brailow (or Ibrail) was taken on the 15th of June, but not till after an unexpectedly long and obstinate defence, which cost the invaders 4000 men, and much valuable time. The Russians then advanced on Shumla and Varna. Before Shumla they gained no advantage ; and suffered several severe blows. But Varna fell after a gallant defence, which was, however, ultimately tarnished by the treachery of Yussuf Pacha, the second in command, who went over to the enemy with nearly 5000 men. Silistria repulsed the Russian corps that besieged it ; and altogether, at the close of the European campaign, the position of the combatants was such, that in the words of the ablest military critic of the war,[1] "If we consider the enormous sacrifices that the war cost the Russians in 1828, it is difficult to say whether they or the Turks won or lost it. It remained for a second campaign to decide the value of the first."

In Asia, the genius of Paskievitsch had gained far less chequered advantages for the Russian Emperor. Besides Anapa (which was captured by the Russian armament that afterwards co-operated in the siege of Varna) the Turks lost in Asia during 1828, Kars, Akhalkhaliki, Hertwitz, Akhaltzikh, and other important fortresses. They were beaten also in a pitched battle ; and Paskievitsch obtained an admirable position for an advance into Asia Minor in the following year. But it was to the Danube and the Balkan that the statesmen of Europe looked most attentively ; and the general feeling (especially in Austria) was, that Russia had been overrated, that the Sultan was unexpectedly powerful, and that the war was likely to be prolonged without any heavy catastrophe to the Turkish Empire. Russia herself felt keenly the need of recovering her prestige by more signal success in another campaign, which she resolved to make a decisive one. The Russian ministers at the courts of the other European powers watched anxiously the probabilities of any mediation being attempted. It was thought that France would be kept quiet through the well-known predilection of her King, Charles X., for Russia ; and that the domestic troubles, which the Duke of Wellington, then Prime Minister of England, had to deal with in the Catholic question and other matters, diminished the risk of any activity in foreign politics on the part of England. Prussia was sure to be inactive. Austria was known to be more suspicious and jealous of Russia ; but she was dull of discernment, and slow in action ; and if the Russians could gain such a sudden supe-

[1] Möltke.

riority in the war over the Turks, as to force on and hurry to
conclusion, a negotiation between the two belligerent powers only,
the Russian court believed that the rest of Europe, however much
it might dislike the terms of such a treaty, would not take up
arms to set it aside.[1]

Accordingly, in 1829, more numerous and better appointed
forces crossed the Danube, and they were led by Marshal Diebitsch,
a general who thoroughly entered into the spirit in which his
imperial master wished the war to be conducted and concluded.
"He besieged one fortress, and fought one battle; but this
brought him into the very heart of the hostile empire. He
arrived there followed by the shadow of an army, but with the
reputation of irresistible success."[2]   Such is the expressive eulogy in
which Baron Möltke epitomises the Turkish campaign of Marshal
Diebitsch, thence surnamed Sabalskanski, that is to say, the
Crosser of the Balkan.   In Asia the Emperor Nicholas was
equally well served by the genius and bravery of Marshal Paskievitsch, the victor of the battle-field of Akhaltzikh, and the captor
of Bayezid, Khart, and Erzerum.

The main Turkish army of Shumla, emboldened by the partial
successes of the last year, commenced operations in 1829, by

---

[1] See the remarkable despatch of Count Pozzo di Borgo to Count Nessel-
rode of 28th Nov., 1828, and another from the Prince de Lieven of the 16th
January, 1829.   They are in the third volume of Murhard, Nouveau Supplement, pp. 340, 383.   The following passage from Count Pozzo di Borgo's
despatch is remarkable for the unintentional proof it gives in favour of Sultan Mahmoud's reforms, and for its avowal of the motives that made Russia force on the war:

"Lorsque le cabinet impérial a examiné la question si le cas était arrivé
de prendre les armes contre la Porte à la suite des provocations du Sultan,
il aurait pu exister des doutes sur l'urgence de cette mesure aux yeux de
ceux qui n'avaient pas assez medité sur les effets des réformes sanglantes que
le chef de l'Empire Ottoman venait d'executer avec une force terrible, et
sur l'intérêt que la consolidation de cet empire inspirait aux cabinets de
l'Europe en général, et notamment à ceux qui sont moins bien disposés
envers la Russie; maintenant l'expérience que nous devons faire doit réunir
toutes les opinions en faveur du parti qui a été adopté.   L'Empereur a mis
le systême turc à l'épreuve, et sa majesté l'a trouvé dans un commencement
d'organisation phisique et morale qu'il n'avait pas jusqu'à présent.   Si le
Sultan a pu nous opposer une résistance plus vive et plus regulière, tandis
qu'il avait à peine réuni les eléments de son nouveau plan de réforme et
d'amélioration, combien l'aurions-nous trouvé formidable dans le cas ou il
aurait eu le temps de lui donner plus de solidité et de rendre impenetrable
cette barrière que nous avons tant de peine à franchir, quoique l'art ne soit
encore venu qu'imparfaitement au secours de la nature." — Murhard.
Nouv. Rec. de Traités, Nouv. Supp., vol. iii. p. 342.

[2] Möltke, p. 476.

attempting (17th May) to recover Pravadi from the Russians.
While the Grand Vizier's army was engaged in this enterprise
(which was conducted with great valour but little skill, and admirably opposed by the Russian generals Roth and Rudiger),
Marshal Diebitsch, who had commenced the siege of Silistria on
the 18th of May, moved the greater part of the Russian force
from before that fortress ; and by a series of rapid and brilliant
movements, placed himself in connection with Roth and Rudiger
in a position between Pravadi and Shumla. This brought on the
battle of Kulewtsha, on the 11th of June ; in which, after several
fluctuations of fortune, the Turks were entirely defeated ; but the
Russian victory was far more caused by the superiority of
Diebitsch as a general to Redshid Pacha, the Turkish Grand
Vizier, than by any inferiority of the Turkish troops to the Russians.
The Grand Vizier reassembled some of the fugitives at Shumla ;
but his force there was, in his judgment, so inadequate to defend
the place, that, in the belief that the Russian general designed to
capture Shumla before attempting any forward movement, the
Turkish commander called in the greater part of the detachments
which were watching the passes of the Balkan : a fatal error,
which left Diebitsch at liberty to break through the hitherto impenetrable barrier. As soon as Silistria fell, which was on the
26th of June, Diebitsch was joined by the Russian corps, which
had previously been detained before that important fortress, and
he now prepared for the daring march which decided the war.
But even with the advantages, which the Russian Marshal's
generalship had secured, the march across the Balkan would not
have been hazarded, if the Black Sea had not then been a Russian
lake ; and if friendly fleets had not been stationed both in that
sea and in the Ægean, ready to co-operate with such troops as
the generals of the Emperor Nicholas might lead across the mountains to either coast. Sizeboli on the western shore of the
Euxine, and to the south of the Balkan chain, had been surprised
and occupied by a Russian armament in February ; and in July a
squadron of the Czar's fleet, under Admiral Greig, with a great
number of vessels carrying stores and provisions, cast anchor in
the Bay of Bourgass ; so that Diebitsch's army might move lightly
equipped, and unincumbered by waggons through the mountains,
and, when it came down from them, find all things that were
necessary for its support, and a secure basis for further operations.
The losses of the Russians during the campaign had been so enormous (far more perishing by privation and disease than in battle),
that after leaving 10,000 men to watch the Grand Vizier in

Shumla, Diebitsch could not muster more than 30,000 for his advance through the Balkan on the Turkish capital.   But he reckoned justly on the moral effect already caused by the battle of Kulewtsha, and the capture of Silistria, and on the still greater panic, which the sight of a Russian army to the south of the trusted barrier would produce.   It was known that the greatest excitement and disaffection prevailed in Constantinople and the other great Turkish cities, and among the commanders of the troops in Albania and Roumelia.   Emboldened by these considerations, Diebitsch suddenly and secretly moved his columns on the 11th of July from the neighbourhood of Shumla upon the gorges of the Balkan, and in nine days he reunited his force to the south of the mountains.   The feeble Turkish detachments, which were encountered in the passes, offered but a desultory and trifling resistance.   As the Russian soldiers came down from the heights of the eastern Balkan, and saw "the flags of their ships flying over the broad shining surface of the Bay of Bourgass,"[1] a general shout of joy burst from the ranks.   Their progress was now one continued triumph; but a triumph rendered very hazardous by the ravages of dysentery and plague, which the invaders brought along with them, and which reduced their numbers by hundreds and by thousands.   But this weakness was unknown to the Turks, who believed that at least 100,000 men had crossed the Balkan, and that they must have destroyed the Grand Vizier's army before they left Shumla.   An officer, whom the Pacha of Missivri sent forward to reconnoitre Diebitsch's force, came back with these words: "It were easier to count the leaves of the forest than the heads of the enemy."   Missivri, Bourgass, and the important post of Aidos were occupied by the Russians, almost without opposition.   Striking inland towards Adrianople, Diebitsch pursued his resolute career, and on the 20th of August, the ancient capital of European Turkey capitulated to a pestilence-stricken and exhausted army of less than 20,000 Russians.   With admirable judgment as well as humanity, Diebitsch, in his occupation of the Turkish cities, and throughout his march in Roumelia, took the most effectual measures for protecting the inhabitants from the slightest military violence.   The Christian population received the Russians with enthusiasm; and even the Moslems returned to their peaceable occupations, when they found that there was full protection for property, person, and honour, and that neither their local self-government nor their religious rites were subjected to interruption or insult.   Diebitsch thus

[1] Möltke.

saved his sickly and scanty army from being engaged in a guerilla warfare, in which it must inevitably have been destroyed; and he continued to impose upon the terrified enemy by the appearance of strength, and by well-simulated confidence, amid rapidly increasing weakness, and the deepest and most serious alarm.   He could not hope to keep up the delusion of his adversaries about the number of his army, if he advanced much nearer to the capital ; and the amount of the Turkish troops now collected in Constantinople, the strength of the fortifications of that city, and the fanatic bravery of its armed population (which the appearance of a Russian army would be sure to rouse into action), made all hope of an ultimate success by main force utterly chimerical.   Moreover, in his rear, the Vizier's army, that held Shumla, was superior to the Russian corps of observation left in front of it ; and on his flank there was Mustapha, the Pacha of Scodra, with 30,000 excellent Albanian troops.   This officer had hitherto refused to obey orders from the Porte, but it was impossible for Diebitsch to reckon on the continuance of such insubordinate inactivity.   The only alternatives for Diebitsch were to obtain a peace, or to be destroyed; and in order for him to obtain peace, it was necessary to keep up the boldest semblance of waging war.   Fortunately for him, not only were the panic and disorder at Constantinople extreme ; but both the Turkish statesmen and the ministers of the European powers there knew nothing of the real state of his army.   An insurrection of the partisans of the Janissaries had been organised, but Sultan Mahmoud was beforehand with them ; and it was suppressed by Chosreef Pacha, his chief of the Police, by a wholesale execution, with very little heed as to how many hundreds of innocent persons suffered, provided only the guilty did not escape.[1]   But though discontent was thus silenced, it was known to be wide-spread and intense ; and a general outbreak was daily expected, in which it was too probable that Constantinople would be destroyed by her own populace, aided by the mutinous bands of soldiery, who had escaped to the capital from the defeated armies and captured fortresses.   Even the European ambassadors at Pera believed that Diebitsch was at the head of 60,000 efficient troops; and they joined the Sultan's ministers in urging him to save the empire from total destruction, by negotiating instantly with the Russian general, and obtaining peace at almost any sacrifice.   Mahmoud is said long to have resisted their pusillanimous advice; and well would it have been for him and his empire, if a single faithful friend had then been near him, to

[1] Möltke.

support his sovereign with manly counsel. At length the Sultan yielded to the importunities of all around him; and plenipotentiaries were sent to the Russian camp, who concluded with Marshal Diebitsch, on the 28th of August, 1829, the treaty of Adrianople.

By this treaty Russia obtained the sovereignty of part of the left bank of the Lower Danube, and of the Sulina mouth of that river. She was thus enabled to control that important artery of the commerce of Central Europe, especially of Austria. Her other European conquests were restored, and also those in Asia, with the material exception that the Russian Emperor retained as part of his dominions the important fortresses of Anapa, Akhaltzikh, Akhalkhaliki, and several valuable districts; and the treaty recognised, by way of recital, that " Georgia, Imeritia, Mingrelia, Gouriel, and *several other provinces of the Caucasus,* had long been annexed in perpetuity to the Empire of Russia." A separate article (but declared to be read as part of the treaty) stipulated in favour of the Moldavians and Wallachians, that the Hospodars should be thenceforth elected for life; that no Turkish officer should interfere in their affairs, and that no Mussulman should be allowed to reside in any part of their territories. Nothing but a nominal sovereignty, and an annual tribute, was reserved to the Porte; and the tribute was not to be exacted for the two years following the war.

In behalf of the Servians, the Sixth Article of the Treaty of Adrianople provided that all the clauses of the separate act of the Convention of Akkermann relative to Servia, should immediately be carried into effect, and ratified by a Hatti-scheriff of the Sultan, which was to be communicated to the Court of St. Petersburg within a month. The passage of the Dardanelles was to be open to Russian merchant vessels; an indemnity for injuries done to Russian commerce was to be paid in eighteen months; and another sum, amounting to nearly £5,000,000 sterling, was to be paid to the Russian Government for the costs of the war. Moreover, by the Tenth Article of the Treaty, the Sultan declared his adhesion to the stipulations of the Treaty of London, and of a subsequent convention of the Three Powers respecting Greece. The result of this branch of the negotiations was the erection of Greece into an independent kingdom, comprising all Continental Greece south of a line drawn from the Gulf of Arta to the Gulf of Volo, thus leaving Thessaly and Albania as the Sultan's frontier provinces. The islands of Eubœa, the northern Sporades, and the Cyclades, also became members of the new State; the Ionian Islands remaining under British Government, while Crete and the islands off the Thracian and Asiatic coasts, were still allowed to appertain to Turkey.

It is said that Sultan Mahmoud's wonted firmness failed him for a time when he signed the Treaty of Adrianople. He shed bitter tears, and for weeks shut himself up in his palace at Therapia, almost crushed in spirit.[1] His misery must have been severely augmented when he heard the truth as to the amount of force which his victors really possessed at Adrianople. So rapid had been the progress of disease among the Russian ranks, that at the moment when the peace was concluded, Diebitsch could not command more than from 15,000 to 17,000 bayonets;[2] and at a grand review of the invading army in November, before they quitted Adrianople, scarcely 13,000 men of all arms could be brought together.[3] The mortality among the rest of the Russian forces employed in the European campaign of 1829 was almost equally terrible; and it is computed that not more than 10,000 or 15,000 Russians ever recrossed the Pruth; so that their army was in fact nearly destroyed during the second campaign.[4] After the peace was concluded, the Pacha of Scodra (who had been a Janissary, and vainly hoped that the Sultan's exigencies would make him beg aid from his subjects on condition of restoring the old abuses), refused for a time to recognise the treaty; and threatened the Russians with a force of 30,000 Albanians, which would have ensured their destruction if more speedily employed. Had this man been loyal, or if, even without a sabre having been raised against Diebitsch's army, no negotiation had been opened, and the Russians had been left to die of disease, the campaign must have closed more triumphantly for Turkey than even that of the Pruth. Invigorated by such success, she could (notwithstanding the Asiatic exploits of Paskievitsch) have maintained the struggle against Russia during 1830; and, before that year was over, the second French Revolution had broken out, Poland had risen against the Emperor Nicholas, and the obstinate struggle had commenced, in which Diebitsch perished, and in which the full power of Russia was taxed to the utmost, even by the unaided Poles. The whole current of the world's history would have been changed. Poland might now be an independent state; there would have been no Egyptian revolts; the name of Hunkiar Iskelessi would be unknown in the West; and France and Eng-

[1] Möltke, p. 770.   [2] Colonel Chesney, p. 255.
[3] Colonel Chesney. He was present at the review.
[4] Möltke, Appendix.

land might never have been required to join in a Russian war, if a single messenger of truth from Adrianople could have been heard in the Divan, or at Pera, in the August of 1829 ; or, if Sultan Mahmoud, in happy obstinacy, had resisted a little longer the solicitations of those who urged on him " Peace, peace," when there should have been no peace.

In the year after the treaty of Adrianople, the French seized and occupied Algiers (July 4, 1830), which, though practically independent, had still acknowledged the titular supremacy of the Sultan, and was governed by a Dey, who professed to be his officer.   The injury which the conquest of a Mahometan province by the Frankish Giaours inflicted on the general authority of Mahmoud in the world of Islam, was increased by the proclamation of the French General, Marshal Bourmont, who stated that he came to deliver Algeria from the yoke of the Turks.   The Sultan was in no condition to interpose, or even to remonstrate ; for far worse evils and convulsions in the integral parts of the Ottoman Empire showed how violent was the shock which it had sustained from the Russian war, and how much the spirit of disaffection and revolt had been increased by the issue of that contest.   The unfortunate are generally unpopular : and the very pride of the Turks made them impute the disasters of their sovereign to his Frankish innovations and abandonment of the old usages of the empire.   The bonds of loyalty to the Head of the House of Othman grew weaker in proportion to the strength of Mahometan feeling ; and, of the numerous insurrections that broke out in 1830, and the two following years, in European Turkey, none were more violent than those of the eminently warlike and fanatic Bosnians, and of the Mussulman tribes of Albania.   They were quelled by the resolute spirit of Mahmoud, and the abilities of his Vizier, Redschid Pacha ; but they exhausted more and more the resources of the heavily-burdened State.   Asia was not much less mutinous ; but it was in Egypt that the most deadly storm was gathering.   Mehemet Ali had resolved on founding an hereditary dominion on the ruins of the apparently doomed empire of the Sultan.   He had restored his navy after its destruction at Navarino ; he possessed a veteran and admirably-disciplined army, chiefly officered by Frenchmen ; and, above all, he had a general of science, experience, prudence, and energy, in his son, the celebrated Ibrahim Pacha.   He had obtained the Pachalic of Crete from the Porte, but had been refused that of Syria.   He determined to take it by force.   A personal quarrel with the Pacha of Acre gave him a pretext for attacking that officer.   The command of the Sultan that this civil war between his servants should cease, was contemptuously disregarded ; and Ibrahim besieged Acre with an army of 40,000 men, and a fleet of five ships of the line, and several frigates. The key of Syria was captured by him on the 27th of May, 1832, and for seven years Mehemet Ali was the real sovereign of that important country. The disaffected armies of raw recruits, badly officered, and worse generalled, which the Sultan sent against the rebel Egyptian chief, were beaten by Ibrahim in three great battles, at Ems, in Upper Syria, on July 6, 1832 ; at Beylan (in Cilicia, near the ancient battle-field of Issus), on the 29th of the same month ; and at Konieh, in Asia Minor. on the 29th of October. The positions of these places indicate the rapid progress and bold designs of the Egyptian commander ; who seemed to annex Asia Minor to Mehemet's dominions with the same ease as Syria ; and whose advance upon Constantinople in the coming spring appeared to be inevitable and irresistible. In this agony of his House and empire, the Sultan sought aid first from England, but none unhappily was accorded. The execrable policy of paring down our military and naval forces, so as to effect the temporary saving of farthings, and to involve the ultimate expenditure of millions of pounds, besides sacrifices and risks of imperial character, for which no money can compensate, was then prevalent in this country ; and the answer returned to the Turkish application was an expression of regret that England had not the means of supplying the required assistance. Russia was watching eagerly for the opportunity which English folly thus threw in her way. Her troops, and her transports, and her ships of war were ready at Sebastopol and Odessa; and when at last Mahmoud humbled himself to express to his ancient enemy a wish for a protecting force, prompt messengers were despatched to the great Crimean depot of Muscovite power, and a Russian squadron of four ships of the line set sail from Sebastopol, and landed 6000 of the Emperor's troops near the mouth of the Bosphorus, on February 20, 1833.

Meanwhile, the forward march of Ibrahim had been temporarily stayed by a messenger from Admiral Roussin, whom the French Government had sent with a fleet to aid the Sultan. A negotiation was entered into, but broken off after a few days ; and in the beginning of March Ibrahim again pointed his columns towards the Bosphorus. But a second Russian armament from Odessa now had reached those straits, and on the 5th of April, 12,000 soldiers of the Czar Nicholas were encamped on the Giant's

Mountain, near Scutari. Ibrahim felt that any further advance
on his part would be madness ; and occupied himself in procuring
the largest possible increase to his father's power in the negotiations that followed, in which England and France (now thoroughly
alarmed at the advantages gained by Russia) took part with
anxious zeal.

The terms of compulsory reconciliation between the Sultan and
his over-powerful vassal were embodied in a Firman of May the
6th, 1833, by which the Porte confirmed Mehemet Ali in his
governments of Crete and Egypt, and added to them those of
Jerusalem, Tripoli, Aleppo, Damascus, and Adana. This was
virtually a cession to the Egyptian of nearly all the countries
which the victories of Selim I. had incorporated with Turkey,
besides the important island of Candia, which it had cost the
Porte a twenty years' war to wrest from Venice. At such a bitter
cost was Mahmoud compelled to purchase the removal from Asia
Minor of his insurgent Pacha ; and before he could obtain the
withdrawal of his equally formidable Russian friends, he was
obliged to sign the treaty of Hunkiar Iskelessi on the 8th of July,
1833, which, by its public articles, bound him to an offensive and
defensive alliance with Russia, and by a still more important
secret article, provided that the Ottoman Porte should, when
required by the Russian Emperor, close the straits of the Dardanelles against the armed vessels of all other foreign powers.

It was the general opinion in Europe at this time, that Turkey
was irretrievably ruined ; and that the attempts of her reforming
sovereign to resuscitate her power had been the mere galvanising
of a corpse. Many, indeed, thought that Mahmoud had accelerated the empire's downfall, by destroying the lingering sparks of
vitality in the old system, without being able to replace them by
new life. And, indeed, had Mahmoud not been a man of the
noblest energy, and of high genius, he might well have despaired
of his country after such a Cannæ as Konieh. First, the foreign
invader, and next, the home-rebel had crushed his armies, had rent
from him his dominions, and had bowed him beneath the humiliation of treaties, worse even than those of Carlowitz and Kainardji.
It might well have seemed, even to himself, that " he had failed
in the object for which he had striven all his life. Rivers of blood
had been shed, the old institutions and sacred traditions of his
country had been destroyed, the faith and pride of his people had
been undermined for the sake of reform, and that reform was
condemned by the event."[1] But Mahmoud was one of the few

[1] Möltke, p. 451.

really great men, whom disappointment in a well-judged enterprise unnerves not, but rather rouses to more vigorous exertion. He knew that the old path of the Turkish government was the sure path to destruction, and refused to consult his own repose by letting his ministers return to it. He knew, too, the resources of his empire. He discerned and appreciated, even amid the general show of discontent, the deep layers of true allegiance, of bravery, and of national spirit, which the hearts of his Moslem subjects contained. He had also the wisdom and the magnanimity to value rightly the importance of conciliating the affections of the Rayas, by giving them equal and just laws, in defiance of the prejudices of his own, the long-dominant race. Sultan Mahmoud continued, amid good repute and evil repute, to re-organise the troops, the fleets, and the finances of his empire : to encourage education : to promote commerce : to give security for person and property : to repress intolerant distinctions ; and to remove by degrees the most galling of the burdens and prohibitions, which pressed upon his Christian subjects. The strong and almost unanimous testimony which English travellers from the East bore in favour of the policy of the Turkish Sultan, and their statements respecting the rapid improvement of the inhabitants of his empire, caused a marked reaction in the public feeling of England with respect to Turkey. When war broke out again in 1839, between the Sultan and the Egyptian Pacha, Turkey was supported by England, not only for the sake of English interests, but with the respectful cordiality which is only felt towards those who evince a sense of self-respect, and who prove that they are ready and willing to aid themselves. This new war was caused by the indignation of Mahmoud at the undisguised designs of Mehemet Ali, to convert the vast provinces, which he governed, into an hereditary monarchy for his own family. Mehemet declined to continue the payment of tribute to the Porte; and his removal of the Turkish guards from the Prophet's Tomb, and substitution of his own Arab soldiers, con- stituted a still more open denial of the sovereignty of the Sultan, as chief of Islam. Attempts at negotiation only led to mutual complaints and recriminations ; and the Sultan at last sent a final summons to the Pacha, requiring him to re-establish the Turkish guards at the Tomb of the Prophet, to pay regularly his tribute, and to renounce all sovereignty over Egypt, save so far as the Sultan might concede it to him. On obedience to this being refused, Mahmoud directed his generals and admirals to attack his refractory vassal. A numerous and well-appointed Turkish army had been collected at Bir on the Euphrates ; and by the strenuous exertions of many years, a well-disciplined and well-manned fleet of thirty-six vessels of different rates, twelve being ships of the line, had been formed and collected in the harbour of Constantinople. But venality and treachery baffled all the preparations of the Ottoman sovereign. When his army under Hafiz Pacha met the Egyptian under Ibrahim, at Nezib, on the 25th June, 1839, whole battalions and squadrons, whose officers had taken the gold of Egypt, deserted the Sultan's standard, and ranged themselves with the enemy. The remainder was hopelessly routed, with the total loss of artillery, camp, baggage, and military stores of every description. Still fouler was the fate of the fleet. The Capitan Pacha, the infamous Achmet Fevzy, on the 8th of June knelt before his imperial benefactor, Mahmoud, received the Sultan's parting benediction, and with solemn oaths renewed his assurances of loyalty and devotion. On the 6th of July following, the imperial fleet was seen in full sail for Alexandria, and on the 13th the traitor who commanded it, brought it into the port of that city, and delivered it up to Mehemet Ali. It is some consolation to know that Sultan Mahmoud was spared the anguish of hearing of these calamities, especially of Achmet Fevzy's ingratitude. His health had long been undermined by continued anxiety and toil. On the 1st of July, 1839, before the messenger from Nezib reached Constantinople, Sultan Mahmoud II. died: and as gallant a spirit left the earth, as ever strove against the spites of fortune—as ever toiled for a nation's good in preparing benefits, the maturity of which it was not permitted to behold.[1]

Before we consider the personal qualities of his successor, Sultan Abdul Medjid, and the constancy with which the reforming policy of Mahmoud has been maintained, it will be convenient first to trace rapidly to its conclusion the Egyptian war, which seemed to darken with such fatal disasters the opening of the young sovereign's reign. A difference of opinion as to the amount of power which should be secured to Mehemet Ali, existed for a time between France and the other great powers of Europe, which at one period threatened to cause a general war. England, France, and Austria, concurred as to the necessity of arranging the Turco-Egyptian question, and of not leaving to Russia an opportunity

---

[1] A report was industriously circulated in the East, and also in Europe, that Sultan Mahmoud's death was caused by habitual drunkenness. The official report of his regular medical attendants, Drs. Macarthy and Constantine Caratheodeori, completely refutes this calumny; and it contains strong incidental evidence of the Sultan's steady industry and high intellectual powers. See their "Relation Officielle de la Maladie, et de la Mort du Sultan Mahmoud II." Paris: J. B. Baillière, 1841.

of sole intervention, such as that which she gained in 1833.   But France was no party to the treaty of July 15, 1840, between Turkey, England, Russia, Austria, and Prussia, which defined the terms on which the disputes between the Pacha and his sovereign were to be arranged.   Mehemet Ali (who probably expected aid from France) refused for some time to accede to the requisitions of Turkey and the Four Powers; and an English fleet, under Admirals Stopford and Napier, proceeded to wrest from him his strongholds on the Syrian coast.   Beyrout was bombarded on the 29th of August, 1840; its Egyptian garrison was expelled, and the Turkish troops, which had been conveyed on board the English fleet, took possession of the ruins in the Sultan's name. By a still more splendid achievement of the British navy, Acre was bombarded and captured on the 3rd of November.   The other Syrian fortresses fell rapidly; and, aided by the British seamen and marines, and also by the native populations (which had found their Egyptian bondage far more grievous than the old Turkish rule), the Sultan's forces were, by the close of November, completely masters of Syria.   Menaced in Alexandria with the fate of Acre, the Pacha at last gave way.   He restored the Sultan's fleet.   He withdrew his forces from Candia, and from the few Asiatic districts which they still retained; and negotiations, in which France (now directed by the wise statesmanship of M. Guizot) took part, were opened for the final settlement of these long-continued dissensions.   The Sultan's final Firman (Feb. 13, 1841) gave and confirmed to Mehemet Ali for himself and descendants in the direct line, the Pachalic of Egypt : one fourth of its revenues to be paid as tribute to the Porte, and certain naval and military contingents to be supplied on demand. In the summer of the same year, a convention of great importance with regard to the right of Turkey to control the navigation of the Dardanelles, was agreed to by the representatives of England, Austria, France, Prussia, Russia, and the Porte.   The first and second articles of this convention, which was signed at London on July 13, 1841, were as follows :

" Art. I.— His Highness, the Sultan, on the one part, declares that he is firmly resolved to maintain for the future the principle invariably established as the ancient rule of his Empire, and in virtue of which it has at all times been prohibited for the ships of war of foreign powers to enter the Straits of the Dardanelles and of the Bosphorus ; and so long as the Porte is at peace, his Highness will admit no foreign ships of war into the said straits.

" Art. II.—And their Majesties, the Queen of the United Kingdom of Great Britain and Ireland, the Emperor of Austria, King of

Hungary and Bohemia, the King of the French, the King of Prussia, and the Emperor of all the Russias, on the other part, engage to respect this determination of the Sultan, and to conform themselves to the principle above declared."

This formal recognition of the Dardanelles and the Bosphorus being mere Turkish streams, and not highways for the fleets of all nations (as seas in general are), was of great value for Turkey. But still the convention of 1841 did not free the Porte from the chain by which the treaty of Hunkiar Iskelessi had bound it to Russia. That liberation was not to be effected without the aid of the armed force as well as of the diplomacy of the Western powers. It was fortunate for the Ottoman Empire, that a pacific period of twelve years intervened before the struggle for that liberation commenced ; and, that time was given for the develop-ment of measures of internal reform.

CHAPTER XXV.

REFORMS OF SULTANS MAHMOUD II. AND ABDUL MEDJID—
ABOLITION OF THE COURT OF CONFISCATION—POWER OF LIFE
AND DEATH TAKEN FROM THE PACHAS—THE VAKOUFS—THE
TIMARS AND THE ZIAMETS ABOLISHED—THE DEREH BEYS PUT
DOWN — FINANCIAL REFORMS — EDICTS IN FAVOUR OF THE
RAYAS—REFORM OF THE CENTRAL ADMINISTRATION—ACCES-
SION OF ABDUL MEDJID—ARMY REFORMS—THE TANZIMAT—
RUSSIAN AGGRESSIONS—THE CRIMEAN WAR—PEACE OF PARIS
—HATTI-Y-HUMAYOUN—ACCESSION OF SULTAN ABDUL-AZIZ—
CRETAN WAR—ROUMANIA AND SERVIA MADE INDEPENDENT
STATES—SULTAN VISITS ENGLAND—RUSSIA REPUDIATES THE
TREATY OF PARIS AS TO THE BLACK SEA—TROUBLES IN
HERZEGOVINA—NATIONAL INSOLVENCY—DETHRONEMENT AND
DEATH OF ABDUL-AZIZ—MURAD V., MADE SULTAN, DEPOSED
— AHMED HAMID II. PRESENT SULTAN—SERVIAN WAR —
MENACES OF WAR WITH RUSSIA — HOPES OF PEACE NOT
EXTINCT.

AMONG the many services rendered to his country by Sultan
Mahmoud II., was his careful education of the young princes, who
were likely to succeed him on the throne. The eldest survivor of
these, at the time of Mahmoud's death, Prince Abdul Medjid, was
only sixteen years of age. But, providentially for Turkey, her
youthful sovereign possessed not only eminent natural abilities,
but a thoughtful earnestness of character beyond his years. The
last charge of his father to him had been, that he should persevere in the completion of those remedial measures, the principles
and importance of which had been fully taught him, and in
the enlightenment and amelioration of all classes of his subjects.

A detailed account of the various changes introduced into every
part of the polity of the Turkish Empire by Mahmoud would
exceed the due limits of this chapter. But the main points of the
more momentous measures may be advantageously surveyed

together; and among the first in value as well as in date (next to the all-important army reforms, which will be separately considered), are the edicts, by which Sultan Mahmoud, soon after he was emancipated from the military tyranny of the Janissaries, closed the Court of Confiscations, and took away the power of life and death from the Pachas. Previously to the first of these Firmans, the property of all persons banished or condemned to death was forfeited to the crown; and a sordid motive for acts of cruelty was thus kept in perpetual operation, besides the encouragement of a host of Delators of the vilest kind. By the second, it was rendered no longer in the power of a Turkish governor to doom men to instant death by a mere wave of his hand; but the Pachas, the Agas, and other officers, were enjoined that "they should not presume to inflict themselves the punishment of death on any man, whether Raya or Turk, unless authorised by a legal sentence pronounced by the Cadi, and regularly signed by the judge." Even then an appeal was allowed to the criminal to one of the Kadiaskers of Asia or Europe, and finally to the Sultan himself, if the criminal chose to persist in his appeal.[1]

About the same time that Mahmoud ordained these just and humane changes, he set personally an example of reform, by regularly attending the Divan, instead of secluding himself from the labours of state, according to the evil practice, which had been introduced so long ago as the reign of Solyman Kanouni, and which had been assigned as one of the causes of the decline of the empire by a Turkish historian nearly two centuries before Mahmoud's time.[2] Mahmoud redressed some of the worst abuses connected with the Vakoufs, by placing the revenues under the administration of the state; but he did not venture to apply this vast mass of property to the general purposes of the government. With the military fiefs, the Timars and the Ziamets, he dealt more boldly. These had long ceased to furnish the old effective military force, for the purpose of which they were instituted; and by attaching them to the public domains, Mahmoud materially strengthened the resources of the state, and put an end to a host of corruptions. One of the most resolute acts of his reign was his suppression of the Dereh Beys, the hereditary local chiefs (with power to nominate their successors in default of male heirs), who, by one of the worst abuses of the Turkish feudal system, had made themselves petty princes in almost every province of the empire. The reduction of these insubordinate feudatories was not

---

[1] Sir G. Larpent, vol. ii p. 25.   [2] See p. 210.

effected at once, or without severe struggles and frequent insurrections. But Mahmoud steadily persevered in this great measure; and ultimately the island of Cyprus became the only part of the empire in which power, not emanating from the Sultan, was allowed to be retained by Dereh Beys. In dealing with the complicated questions caused by the embarrassed finances of his empire, and by the oppression and vexatiousness with which certain imposts pressed upon particular classes, Mahmoud showed the best spirit of the best of the Kiuprilis. A Firman of February 22, 1834, abolished the vexatious charges which public functionaries, when traversing the provinces, had long been accustomed to make on the inhabitants. By the same edict all collections of money, except at the two regular half-yearly periods, were denounced as abuses. "No one is ignorant," said Sultan Mahmoud, in this document, "that I am bound to afford support to all my subjects against vexatious proceedings; to endeavour unceasingly to lighten, instead of increasing their burdens, and to ensure their peace and tranquillity. Therefore, those acts of oppression are at once contrary to the will of God, and to my imperial orders."

The kharatch, or capitation-tax, though moderate in amount, and exempting those who paid it from military service,[1] had long been made an engine of gross tyranny, through the insolence and misconduct of the government collectors. The Firman of 1834 abolished the old mode of levying it, and ordained that in future it should be raised by a commission composed of the Cadi, the Mussulman governors, and the Ayans, or municipal chiefs of the Rayas of each district. Many other financial improvements were effected, the narration of which would be too long for introduction here. By another important series of measures, the central administrative government was simplified and strengthened; a large mass of sinecure offices was abolished, and the Sultan set a valuable personal example of good sense, and economy, by re-organising the imperial household, and mercilessly suppressing all titles without duties, and all salaried officials without useful functions.

I do not propose to prolong the regular history of the Ottoman Empire in this volume beyond the reign of Mahmoud II. But the reader may not be unwilling to have brought briefly before

[1] The Greek Armatoli who rendered military service, did not pay the kharatch. On the other hand, the Turks of Volo and Baba, and some few other places, who by special custom did not serve as soldiers, paid the kharatch.

his notice here some of the principal civil and military events affecting that empire, which have occurred during the reign of Mahmoud's two nearest successors.

On the 3rd November, 1839, Sultan Abdul Medjid issued an organic statute for the general government of the empire, commonly named the Hatti-scheriff of Gülhanè (the imperial palace where it was first proclaimed), and sometimes called the Tanzimat.

In this very important document[1] the Sultan stated that he designed

" to attempt by new institutions to obtain for the provinces composing the Ottoman Empire the benefits of a good administration, and that these institutions would principally refer to these topics :

" '1. The guarantees which will insure our subjects perfect security for their lives, their honour, and their property.

" '2. A regular method of establishing and collecting the taxes.

" '3. An equally regular method of recruiting, levying the army, and fixing duration of the service.' "

Some of the most important clauses are as follows :

" In future, the cause of every accused party will be tried publicly, in conformity with our divine law ; and until a regular sentence has been pronounced, no one can put another to death, secretly or publicly, by poison, or any other form of punishment.

"No one will be permitted to assail the honour of any one, whosoever he may be.

" Every person will enjoy the possession of his property of every nature, and dispose of it with the most perfect liberty, without any one being able to impede him : thus, for example, the innocent heirs of a criminal will not be deprived of their legal rights, and the property of the criminal will not be confiscated.

" These imperial concessions extend to all our subjects, whatever religion or sect they may belong to ; and they will enjoy them without any exception.

" Perfect security is, therefore, granted by us to the inhabitants of the empire, with regard to their life, their honour, and their fortune, as the sacred text of our law demands.

" With reference to the other points, as they must be regulated by the concurrence of enlightened opinions, our Council of Justice (augmented by as many new members as may be deemed necessary), to whom will be adjoined, on certain days which we shall appoint, our Ministers and the notables of the empire, will meet for the purpose of establishing the fundamental laws on those points relating to the security of life and property, and the imposition of the taxes. Every one in these assemblies will state his ideas freely, and give his opinion.

" The laws relating to the regulations of the military service will be

---

[1] " The whole of it will be found in Hertslet's " Map of Europe by Treaty," vol. ii. p. 1002.

discussed by the Military Council, holding its meetings at the Palace
of the Seraskier. As soon as a law is decided upon, it will be presented
to us, and in order that it may be eternally valid and applicable we
will confirm it by our sanction, written above it with our imperial hand.

" As these present institutions are solely intended for the regenera-
tion of religion, government, the nation, and the Empire, we engage
to do nothing which may be opposed to them."

On the 15th of July, 1840, the convention between Great
Britain, Austria, Prussia, Russia, and Turkey was signed for the
pacification of the Levant (see Hertslet, vol. ii. p. 1008) which was
followed by Firmans of the Sultan giving the hereditary government of Egypt to Mehemet Ali and his family, and fixing the
tribute to be paid therefor to the Porte.

Some mention must be made of the military reforms effected by
Sultan Abdul Medjid. We have seen that Sultan Mahmoud was
obliged to wage his Russian and Egyptian wars with hasty levies
of compulsory recruits, taken from among the younger parts of the
Moslem population. After the promulgation of the Hatti-scheriff
of Gülhanè, a regular system of recruiting the army was established ; but it was in 1843, when Riza Pacha was Seraskier or
commander-in-chief, that the remodelling of the military force of
the empire was completed. The army was divided into the
troops in active service, called the Nizam, and into those who had
fulfilled their terms of active service, and thenceforth formed a
reserve, called the Redif. A specified number of troops is
required from each district ; and this is filled up partly by volunteers, partly by conscription, to which all young men of twenty or
upwards are liable. The period of active service in the Nizam is
five years. After that, the soldier is permitted to return home,
but is then incorporated for seven years longer in the Redif of his
district. This force is summoned together for drill and exercise
at stated periods, and is liable to be embodied for service in case
of war or other emergency. All writers on Turkish subjects concur in eulogising the sobriety, patience, obedience, and bravery of
the Turkish common soldiers ; and in censuring the venality and
incompetency which are frequent among the officers. But these
are evils which a wise administration could gradually remedy ;
for, when bravery and aptitude for military discipline are general
national qualities, and where the state provides schools of military
education (both of which requisites already exist among the
Ottomans), there must be an abundant material for good officers.
All that is needed, is that the higher authorities shall watch carefully for intelligence and merit ; and shall reward those qualities,

when found, by prompt and liberal promotion. But the conscription has pressed severely on the Ottoman part of the population, which alone has supplied the armies. An edict, which was issued authorising the military service of the Christians, had little practical operation.

Sultan Abdul Medjid was in two important points more fortunate than his father Mahmoud. He found in Omar Pacha an excellent general, who put down the various insurrections that were attempted against the Sultan's reforms in Albania, Kurdistan, and Bosnia, and other provinces; and in the suppression of those movements Omar showed not only valour and military skill, but also humanity and sound judgment. And Abdul Medjid, during the years which intervened between the conclusion of the Egyptian war in 1841, and the outbreak of the Russian war in 1853, obtained that necessary period of quiet for the " strengthening of his military creations, and carrying out needful reforms," which, as we have seen, was denied to his predecessor. During this period of twelve years, the advancement of the commercial and general prosperity of the empire was marked and rapid. A similar amelioration had been visible even to foreign statesmen during the latter part of Sultan Mahmoud's reign; and in 1853, Lord Palmerston, in the British House of Commons, bore the most emphatic testimony in favour of the two reforming Sultans, by declaring that Turkey had made more progress and improvement during the last twenty years than any other country.

Other and less friendly eyes were watching the revival of strength in the Ottoman Empire. But the prudence of Abdul Medjid's government gave Russia no occasion for quarrel; and when the revolutionary fervour of 1848 extended to Moldavia and Wallachia, the moderation and fairness with which the Porte acted towards the malcontents, presented a striking contrast to the eagerness with which a Russian army was marched across the Pruth. The forces of the Emperor Nicholas, to the number of between 40,000 and 50,000, continued to occupy the Principalities till 1850, when they were withdrawn, after lengthened negotiations on the subject with both the Turkish and British cabinets. But while the Porte was thus wisely pacific and conciliatory in its general conduct towards foreign powers, a memorable and noble proof was given in 1849, that Sultan Abdul Medjid had not degenerated from the high honour and chivalrous generosity of the ancient race of Othman and of Ertoghrul, "The Right-hearted Man."[1] When the united forces of Russia and Austria put an end

[1] See page 1.

to the Hungarian war of independence, many of the chiefs, who had been most active in the Magyar cause, escaped into Turkey, and received hospitable shelter in the Sultan's dominions. The Courts of Vienna and St. Petersburg peremptorily demanded, first, their extradition, and afterwards their expulsion from Turkey. Sultan Abdul Medjid met these demands and the threats with which they were accompanied, with a dignified and firm refusal to violate the laws of hospitality, and betray the old principles of his race and creed. The two Emperors menaced more and more loudly, but in vain. Diplomatic relations between Russia and Turkey were suspended; and, for a time, war seemed certain; but England showed her intention to aid the Ottoman Empire if thus attacked; and the British fleet, under Sir William Parker, was ordered to Besika Bay in October, and in the next month entered the Dardanelles. Russia and Austria thought it prudent to abstain from hostilities; and the diplomatic relations which had been broken off were renewed. True to the old policy of Potemkin, that Russia's conquest of Turkey must be effected with the acquiescence of England,[1] the Emperor Nicholas sought more than once to induce the English Cabinet to participate in his schemes. Some overtures of this kind were made by him during his visit to this country in 1844; but the most remarkable proof of the continual designs of Russia for the dismemberment of the Ottoman Empire, is to be found in the well-known conversations of the Emperor Nicholas with Sir Hamilton Seymour, the British ambassador at St. Petersburg, in the early part of 1853.[2] In these strange dialogues the sovereign of Russia invited the repre sentative of this country to discuss with him the partition of Turkey, offering Egypt and Crete to England. "The Principali ties," said the Czar, "are, in fact, an independent state under my protection: this might so continue. Servia might receive the same form of government: so again with Bulgaria."

In another part of the same conversation the Emperor referred to the possession of Constantinople as the most difficult question to settle. He disclaimed any design that it should be permanently held by Russia, though he said that circumstances might cause its temporary occupation by his troops. He stated his fixed resolution that that city should never be held by the English, or French, or any other great nation. "Again," said he, "I never will permit an attempt at the reconstruction of the Byzantine Empire, or

[1] See p. 420, supra.
[2] See Eastern Papers, part v., laid before the Houses of Parliament in 1854.—House of Commons' Papers, No. 88.

such an extension of Greece as would render her a powerful state : still less will I permit the breaking up of Turkey into little republics, asylums for the Kossuths and Mazzinis, and other revolutionists of Europe : rather than submit to any of these arrangements, I would go to war, and would carry it on as long as I have a man and a musket left." The Czar spoke of Austria as identified in interest with Russia, and in a manner which seemed to infer that he regarded her as entirely subservient to his policy. He professed indifference as to what part France might think fit to take in Eastern affairs, so that there was a good understanding between Russia and England. Turkey was treated by him throughout these conversations as an expiring empire ; and he assured the British minister, that his Government must have been deceived if it had been led to believe that Turkey retained any elements of existence. " The sick man is dying. We have on our hands a sick man—a very sick man, and he may suddenly die on our hands." Such was his reiterated expression : and the sum and substance of his revelations and hints may be fairly characterised as a proposal, that the two strongest neighbours of the sick man should walk into his house and strangle him, and forthwith divide his goods and chattels between themselves. These overtures were properly met by the ambassador and ministers of England with sincere disclaimers of any desire to participate in the spoils of the Ottomans, and with an expression of belief that " the sick man" was not dying ; that (in the words of Lord Clarendon's despatch of March 23, 1853) " Turkey only requires forbearance on the part of its allies, and a determination not to press their claims in a manner humiliating to the dignity and independence of the Sultan—that friendly support, in short, which among states as well as individuals the weak are entitled to expect from the strong—in order not only to prolong its existence, but to remove all cause of alarm respecting its dissolution." It is impossible to read the narrative of these communications between the Russian Emperor and the English statesmen, without being convinced that Sir Hamilton Seymour judged rightly, when he stated to his court that " It can hardly be otherwise but that the Sovereign who insists with such pertinacity upon the impending fall of a neighbouring state, must have settled in his own mind that the hour, if not *of* its dissolution, at all events *for* its dissolution, must be at hand." And, could there have been any doubt in the beginning of 1853, that the Czar designed an attack on Turkey, that doubt must have been removed by the full knowledge which since has been obtained of the immensity of the Russian stores and preparations in their great arsenals in the Crimea, far exceeding anything which purposes of defence or precaution could require, and evidently collected in readiness for a sudden and overwhelming assault on the heart of the Turkish Empire.[1]

Of the war which actually broke out in 1853, and which was practically terminated by the capture of Sebastopol in 1855, it would be useless and unbecoming to attempt a formal narrative here. The immediate pretext for it was caught from a revival of the old dispute between the Latin and Greek Christians in Palestine, respecting the custody of the Holy Places.[2]   An interposition of the French Emperor, on behalf of the Roman Catholic subjects of France resident in the East, was at one time misconstrued into a general claim of protection for all members of the Latin Church, but such an assumption was promptly and explicitly disavowed by M. Drouyn de Lhuys, the French minister. But this was made a handle for the interference of Russia, and for a demand (among others) which her envoy, Prince Menschikoff, preferred in the most arrogant and domineering manner—a demand of a general protectorate by Russia of all inhabitants of the Turkish Empire, who profess the creed of the Greek Church. This is the same requisition which Russia had twice made before, but to which the Porte, even under the pressure of the greatest calamities, had never yielded. It had been preferred in the negotiations of 1773, before

[1] The following remarkable proof of the designs of Russia against Turkey, and of her oppressive influence on the Sultan's Government, was communicated to me by Sir P. Colquhoun, who was resident at Constantinople, as representative of the Hanse Towns, at the time in question :

"Two artillery officers were sent out by the English Government in 1840 with an artificer of Congreve rockets and other projectiles, a bombardier, and some workmen, to assist the Porte in fortifying the Bosphorus. But the Russian envoy, M. Titow, interfered to prevent the execution of the works which those officers designed ; and such was the influence of Russia in the Divan, that the Porte dared not fortify the passage from the Black Sea to the Turkish capital, against the will of the Emperor Nicholas. The English officers and engineers remained for five years at Constantinople, during which time repeated attempts were made by them and the British ambassador to cause their plans to be carried out. At last, one of these officers returned to England with the engineering staff and the unused designs, and the other was employed on the Turco-Persian frontier. Every one in Constantinople, down to the smallest merchant, knew at that time the object of Russia in keeping the Bosphorus unfortified, and was aware that the Porte was obliged to obey her commands."

[2] Very full and clear information on this subject, and on the various treaties made by various Christian Powers (especially France) with the Porte as to the Holy Places, will be found in Phillimore's "International Law," vol. i. p. 577 *et seq.*

the conclusion of the peace of Kainardji.[1] It had been again pressed on Sultan Selim in 1805, a little time before the Russian general, Michelson, occupied the Principalities. All that had ever been admitted into the treaties between the two empires, amounts (as well stated by an eminent jurist, Dr. Phillimore) to no more than—

"1. That pilgrims, ecclesiastics, and travellers may visit, safely and untaxed, Jerusalem and the Holy Places.

"2. That certain new chapels may be built in a particular quarter of Constantinople—*à l'example des autres puissances*—besides the Ambassadorial Chapel, then existing. There is a similar provision in the French Treaty of 1740.

"3. That the Sublime Porte, not the Emperor of Russia, shall continue to protect the Christian religion; the interference of *the Emperor* being in the same clause limited to the making representations in favour of a particular church and its clergy, to which the Porte, on the ground of friendship alone, engages to listen."

On the refusal of Sultan Abdul Medjid to transfer the sovereignty over thirteen millions of his subjects to the Emperor Nicholas, the armies of Russia (3rd July, 1853) passed the Pruth, and occupied Moldavia and Wallachia, "as a material guarantee" for the fulfilment of the Czar's demands. On the 9th of the same month, a manifesto of the Emperor Nicholas to the Russian nation appeared, in which he stated to his subjects that the solemn oath of the Sultan had been perfidiously broken, and appealed to their religious feelings against their old Mahometan adversary. On the 1st of October, the Porte declared war, which was carried on during the ensuing winter on the banks of the Danube by the Turkish army under Omar Pacha, with remarkable spirit and success. Instead of waiting, as in former wars, to be attacked, the Turks crossed the river, and gained victories at Oltenitza (November 4) and at Citate (November 5). The loss on either side in these actions was not heavy; but they were of incalculable importance in demonstrating to Turkey, to Russia, and to Europe, the reality of the improvement which had been effected in the Ottoman military system: and they tended materially to augment, in the Turkish ranks, that self-confidence and self-respect which are material elements of success in war. The aid of France and England was, from the very commencement of the war, given frankly and zealously to the Sultan. Their fleets entered the Dardanelles in September; and in the spring of the next year, each of the great European nations of the West had landed

[1] See p. 401, *suprà.*

auxiliary armies in European Turkey, and had occupied the Baltic as well as the Euxine with its navy; thus compelling Russia to retain large portions of her force in the north-west for home defence against the allies of the Porte. In Turkey, the great feature of the war, during the first half of the year 1854, was the siege of Silistria by the main Russian army, under the command first of General Schilders, and afterwards of Marshal Paskievitsch. The defence of that fortress by the Ottomans under Moussa Pacha (who was killed near the end of the siege), and two English officers, named Butler and Nasmyth, is one of the noblest examples of heroic valour and endurance that are recorded in military history. The Russians were repeatedly repulsed in a series of desperate and murderous assaults; and finally recrossed the Danube on the 15th of June, with immense loss of men and military stores of every description. The Turks passed the Danube in pursuit of the retreating Russians, and had gained further advantages, when hostilities in Moldavia and Wallachia were checked by Austria marching her troops into those Princi-palities, and by the belligerents acquiescing in a convention for their being left in her temporary occupation. The French and English armies, that had been hitherto prepared to defend Varna if Silistria fell, now assumed the offensive; and, in September, the memorable expedition to the Crimea was undertaken.

That Peninsula became now the region, to which the anxious interest of all Europe was for more than a twelvemonth directed. The allied armies landed near Eupatoria, and took possession of that city on September 14, and on the 20th the victory of the Alma opened to them the road to Sebastopol. The siege of that renowned stronghold began in the same month, and was prolonged with almost unexampled bravery and resolution on both sides until the 8th of September, 1855, when the victorious assault was delivered, in which the French column captured the long-coveted Malakoff Tower, and on the following day the city was in the possession of the allies.

In Asia, the incompetency of the Turkish commanders gave several easy triumphs to the Russians; but the important city of Kars was nobly defended by the garrison and armed citizens under their English leaders, Williams and Teesdale, and the Hungarian Kmety. On the 29th of September, they gained a signal victory over the Russian army under General Mouravieff; but they were unable to break the blockade: no relief came from without, and at last, on the 25th of November, the worn and wasted band of heroes was starved into surrender.

Negotiations were opened, on the intervention of Austria, early in 1855, between Russia and the powers in alliance against her, consisting of Turkey, England, France, and Sardinia. The Russian Court consented that the following five propositions should be taken as the basis of a pacification:

" 1. *Danubian Principalities.*—Complete abolition of the Russian protectorate. The Danubian Principalities shall receive an organisation conformable to their wishes, to their wants, to their interests ; and this new organisation, respecting which the population itself will be consulted, shall be recognised by the contracting Powers and sanctioned by the Sultan as emanating from his sovereign initiative. No state shall be able, under any pretext whatever, under any form of protectorate, to interfere in the question of the internal administration of the Principalities ; they shall adopt a definitive permanent system demanded by their geographical position ; and no impediment shall be made to their fortifying, in the interest of their safety, in such manner as they may deem advisable, their territory against foreign aggression.

" In exchange for the strong places and territories occupied by the Allied armies, Russia consents to a rectification of her frontier with Turkey in Europe. It would commence in the vicinity of Choytm, follow the line of the mountains, which extend in a south-easterly direction, and terminate at Lake Sasik. The line (*trace*) shall be definitively regulated by the general treaty ; and the conceded territory would return to the Principalities and to the suzerainty of the Porte.

" 2. *The Danube.*—The freedom of the Danube and of its mouths shall be efficaciously assured by European institutions, in which the contracting Powers shall be equally represented, except the particular positions of the lords of the soil on the banks (*des riverains*), which shall be regulated upon the principles established by the act of the Congress of Vienna as regards the navigation of rivers. Each of the contracting Powers shall have the right to keep one or two small vessels stationed at the mouths of the river, destined to assure the execution of the regulations relative to the freedom of the Danube.

" 3. *Neutralisation of the Black Sea.*—This sea shall be open to merchant vessels, closed to war navies (*marines militaires*) ; consequently, no naval military arsenals shall be created or maintained there. The protection of the commercial and maritime interests of all nations shall be assured in the respective ports of the Black Sea by the establishment of institutions conformable to international law, and to the customs sanctioned in such matters. The two Powers which hold the coast engage themselves to maintain only the number of light vessels, of a fixed force, necessary for their coast service. This convention, concluded separately between these two Powers, shall form part as an annex of the general treaty after receiving the approval of the contracting parties. This separate convention cannot be annulled or modified without the consent of the signataries of the general treaty. The closing of the Straits will admit the exception applicable to the stationary vessels mentioned in the preceding article.

" 4. *Christian Subjects of the Porte.*—The immunities of the Raya subjects of the Porte shall be religiously preserved, without infringement on the independence and dignity of the Sultan's crown. As deliberations are taking place between Austria, France, Great Britain, and the Sublime Porte, to assure to the Christian subjects of the Sultan their religious and political rights, Russia shall be invited, when peace is made, to associate herself thereto.

" 5. The belligerent Powers reserve to themselves the right which appertains to them of producing in an European interest special conditions over and above the four guarantees."

Paris was selected as the place for the conference; and there accordingly assembled the Plenipotentiaries of France, England, Russia, Turkey, and Sardinia, which last-mentioned country had, during the latter part of the war, co-operated gallantly with the two Great Powers of the West in the common cause of justice and of national independence. Austria, as the mediating power, took part by her diplomatic representatives in the whole proceedings of the Congress. Prussia, which had at first stood aloof, was induced, at the end of the discussions, to become a party to the terms on which the others had debated and resolved. At last, on Sunday, the 30th of March, 1856, a treaty, framed in accordance with the propositions that have been cited, was signed by the ministers of the Seven Powers, and peace was restored.

The terms of the Treaty of Paris may be seen at length in " Hertslet," second volume, page 1250. Those, which it seems material to cite here, were as follows :

By Article VII. the Sublime Porte was declared by the other signatory Powers to be admitted to participate in the advantages of the Public Law and System (*concert*) of Europe. The Christian sovereigns engaged, each on his part,

"to respect the Independence and the Territorial Integrity of the Ottoman Empire ; guarantee in common the strict observance of that engagement ; and will, in consequence, consider any act tending to its violation as a question of general interest.

" *Mediation in event of Misunderstanding between the Sublime Porte and one or more of the Contracting Powers.*

" ART. VIII. If there should arise between the Sublime Porte and one or more of the other Signing Powers, any misunderstanding which might endanger the maintenance of their relations, the Sublime Porte, and each of such Powers, before having recourse to the use of force, shall afford the other Contracting Parties the opportunity of preventing such an extremity by means of their Mediation.

" Amelioration of Condition of Christian Population of Ottoman Empire.

" ART. IX. His Imperial Majesty the Sultan having, in his constant solicitude for the welfare of his subjects, issued a Firman which, while ameliorating their condition without distinction of Religion or of Race, records his generous intentions towards the Christian population of his Empire, and wishing to give a further proof of his sentiments in that respect, has resolved to communicate to the Contracting Parties the said Firman, emanating spontaneously from his Sovereign will.

" Non-interference of Allies in Internal Affairs of Ottoman Empire.

" The Contracting Powers recognise the high value of this communication. It is clearly understood that it cannot, in any case, give to the said Powers the right to interfere, either collectively or separately, in the relations of his Majesty the Sultan with his subjects, nor in the Internal Administration of his Empire.

" Closing of Straits of Bosphorus and Dardanelles.

" ART. X. The Convention of 13th of July, 1841, which maintains the ancient rule of the Ottoman Empire relative to the Closing of the Straits of the Bosphorus and of Dardanelles, has been revised by common consent.

The Act concluded for that purpose, and in conformity with that principle, between the High Contracting Parties, is and remains annexed to the present Treaty, and shall have the same force and validity as if it formed an integral part thereof.

" Neutralisation of the Black Sea.

" ART. XI. The Black Sea is Neutralised ; its Waters and its Ports, thrown open to the Mercantile Marine of every Nation, are formally and in perpetuity interdicted to the Flag of War, either of the Powers possessing its Coasts, or of any other Power, with the exceptions mentioned in Articles XIV. and XIX. of the present Treaty.

" Commercial Regulations in the Black Sea.

" ART. XII. Free from any impediment, the Commerce in the Ports and Waters of the Black Sea shall be subject only to Regulations of Health, Customs, and Police, framed in a spirit favourable to the development of Commercial transactions.

" Military Maritime Arsenals not to be established or maintained on Coasts of Black Sea.

" ART. XIII. The Black Sea being Neutralised according to the terms of Article XI., the maintenance or establishment upon its Coast of Military Maritime Arsenals become alike unnecessary and pur-

46

poseless ; in consequence, his Majesty the Emperor of All the Russias, and his Imperial Majesty the Sultan, engage not to establish or to maintain upon that Coast any Military-Maritime Arsenal.

"*Russian and Ottoman Naval Force in Black Sea.*

"Art. XIV. Their Majesties the Emperor of All the Russias and the Sultan having concluded a Convention for the purpose of settling the Force and the Number of Light Vessels, necessary for the service of their Coasts, which they reserve to themselves to maintain in the Black Sea, that Convention is annexed to the present Treaty, and shall have the same force and validity as if it formed an integral part thereof. It cannot be either annulled or modified without the assent of the Powers signing the present Treaty."

By the Convention of the same date referred to in the treaty, and referred to in it, it was declared that—

"*Prohibition to Foreign Ships of War to enter the Bosphorus and the Dardanelles.*

"Art. I. His Majesty the Sultan, on the one part, declares that he is firmly resolved to maintain for the future the principle invariably established as the ancient rule of his Empire, and in virtue of which it has, at all times, been prohibited for the Ships of War of Foreign Powers to enter the Straits of the Dardanelles and of the Bosphorus; and that, so long as the Porte is at Peace, his Majesty will admit no Foreign Ship of War into the said Straits.

"*Agreement of Six Powers to respect this Prohibition.*

"And their Majesties the Queen of the United Kingdom of Great Britain and Ireland, the Emperor of Austria, the Emperor of the French, the King of Prussia, the Emperor of All the Russias, and the King of Sardinia, on the other part, engage to respect this determination of the Sultan, and to conform themselves to the principle above declared.

"*Admission, under Firman, of Light Vessels in Service of Foreign Missions.*

"Art. II. The Sultan reserves to himself, as in past times, to deliver Firmans of Passage for Light Vessels under Flag of War, which shall be employed, as is usual, in the service of the Missions of Foreign Powers."

Another convention of the same date, between Russia and Turkey, fixed the number of light vessels to be maintained by each Power in the Black Sea.

By a treaty of the 15th April, 1856, between Great Britain, Austria, and France, these three contracting parties bound themselves to maintain the integrity of the Turkish Empire, as follows:

"*Guarantee of Independence and Integrity of the Ottoman Empire.*

"ART. I. The High Contracting Parties Guarantee, jointly and severally, the Independence and the Integrity of the Ottoman Empire, recorded in the Treaty concluded at Paris on the 30th of March, 1856.

"*Any Infraction of Treaty of 30th March,* 1856, *to be considered as a* casus belli.

"ART. II. Any infractions of the stipulations of the said Treaty will be considered by the Powers signing the present Treaty as a *casus belli.* They will come to an understanding with the Sublime Porte as to the measures which have become necessary, and will without delay determine among themselves as to the employment of their Military and Naval Forces."

While the negotiations for the close of the Crimean war were in progress, Sultan Abdul Medjid put forth another important state document, called the Hatti-y-Humayoun, addressed to his Grand Vizier, Alati Pacha, by which he bound himself to maintain the franchises and securities given by the Hatti-scheriff of Gülhanè to all classes of his subjects, without distinction of rank or religion. It contained numerous directions for the summoning of local councils of each Christian community for local self-government, for ensuring free exercise of religion, for providing mixed tribunals in matters where the litigants were of different religious persuasions, for raising contingents of Christian troops, and for numerous improvements in administration of legal and of commercial matters.

The execution of these orders has not equalled the excellence of their design.

By another edict of the same year, the Sultan forbade the further importation of slaves into his empire.

There continued to be numerous discussions between Russia and Turkey as to the government of Moldavia and Wallachia. England and France and other Powers took part in some of these, and in 1858 a treaty[1] was executed by which these two Principalities were recognised as united, but under the suzerainty of the Sultan. Practically, they were made a free state, under the government of an elective Hospodar.

In 1860 the disturbances that took place in Syria, in the districts of Lebanon, grew so serious, as to attract the anxious notice of the chief Powers of Europe. There was actual civil war between the Druses and the Maronites; and the troops of the Turkish Government, instead of repressing these disorders, took part with the Mahometan portion of the combatants in plundering Maronite villages, and slaughtering the inhabitants. There

[1] Herts., vol. ii. p. 1330.

was also an outbreak of the fanatic fury of the rabble of Damascus; and the authorities there connived at, if they did not promote, foul plunder and massacre, of which the Christians of that city were the victims. A convention was agreed to by Great Britain, Russia, France, Austria, and Prussia, to which it is to be carefully observed that the Sultan was a consenting party, in pursuance of which a French army of 10,000 men was sent to Syria to restore order. But the Porte, alarmed at the probable effects of this apparent confession of its imbecility, took energetic measures, while the French expedition was yet on its way, to restore order and to punish the chief offenders. Fuad Pacha executed this mission with such strenuous severity, that the French, on their arrival, found the province pacified; and they returned to France, after occupying the chief military posts in Syria for a short period.

On the 25th of June, 1861, Sultan Abdul Medjid died, and was succeeded by Sultan Abdul Aziz.

The important Island of Crete now became the part of the Ottoman dominions that caused general disquiet in Europe. A wide-spread insurrection against the Turkish rule broke out there, which was aided and maintained almost undisguisedly for a considerable time by the government of Greece. It was generally believed that Greece herself was encouraged to this aggressive policy by help and by promises of support given by another far stronger empire. The Cretan war continued until 1867, when the Porte formally insisted on the Greeks giving up their co-operation with the insurgents. Diplomatic relations between Greece and Turkey were broken off; and there seemed to be every probability of open war between these two states—a war in which other and stronger belligerents would probably have soon taken part. But the Great Powers (Britain, Austria, France, Italy, Prussia, and Russia) concurred in a formal declaration (20th January, 1869; see Hertzlett, vol. iii., 1864), which expresses regret and censure as to the conduct of Greece, and pronounces that " It is indeed unquestionable that the principles of International Law oblige Greece, like other nations, not to allow that bands should be recruited on her territory, or that vessels should be armed in her ports to attack a neighbouring state." In obedience to this requisition by her expected coadjutor, as well as by the other great states of Christendom, Greece became a party to the convention; and diplomatic relations between her and Turkey were restored. Some concessions were made by the Sultan's government to the demands of the Cretan chiefs, and the insurrectionary movements in that island terminated.

It has been mentioned that Turkey, in Sultan Abdul Medjid's reign, consented to the reunion of Moldavia and Wallachia as a single dominion, practically independent of the Porte. In 1866 the ruling dynasty of these principalities (now generally spoken of under the collective name of Roumania) was changed ; and Prince Charles of Hohenzollern was invested by the Sultan as their hereditary prince. The close family connection of Prince Charles with the monarch of Prussia, whom the Seven Weeks' War with Austria has made Emperor of Germany, gives an unusual degree of interest to this change of princely dynasty on the northern bank of the Danube.

Continual complaints had been made by the party in Servia, which was under the influence of the Sultan's enemies, that the liberty of that country was incomplete, so long as Belgrade and other Servian fortresses were occupied by the Sultan's soldiers. In April, 1867, the Porte, by the advice of France and England, endeavoured to obviate all risk of hostilities against Turkey being any longer fomented in that quarter, by issuing a Firman (see Hertslet, vol. iii. p. 1800), in consequence of which the Turkish garrisons were withdrawn ; and Servia was made a completely independent power, so far as regarded her former masters.

While the troubles connected with the Cretan insurrection were still unsettled, Sultan Abdul Aziz travelled beyond his dominions for a pacific visit to some of the chief states of Christendom. He was in London in 1867. No other Turkish Sultan ever took a similar journey.

The Porte took no part direct or indirect in the war of 1870, between France and Germany ; but the disasters which befell France in that struggle were of calamitous importance to Turkey. While France was strong, she was both willing and able to co-operate with England in securing the substantial observance of the conditions, on which the Crimean war had been terminated. The most important of these, for the safety of the Ottoman Empire, was the convention for neutralising the Black Sea. This restriction on the aggressive power of Russia was now repudiated by the Russian Government.

I shall repeat here some of the observations lately made on this subject in my work on International Law, as they appear to me, on reflection, to be fully warranted by the facts and by the justice of the case.

"In 1856, after the fall of Sebastopol, peace was made between Russia and the Allies by the general Treaty of Paris of the 30th of March, 1856. That treaty contained many provisions as to many subjects; but its most important stipulation was an engagement on the part of Russia to limit her naval forces and armaments on the Black Sea to a defined minimum. This limitation of the Russian forces in this quarter had been one of the main objects of the war; and it was especially in order to effect it that the Crimean expedition had been planned and persevered in by France and England.

"So long as the strength of both these two great Western Powers remained unimpaired, Russia made no protest against this treaty, and preferred no claim to be released from any part of it. But near the end of 1870, when the military force of France had been crushed by her defeats in the war with the Germans, when Paris was besieged, and the submission of France to her invaders was obviously only a question of time, the English Government were informed by the Russian Minister, in the name of the Emperor, that 'His Imperial Majesty cannot hold himself bound by the stipulations of the Treaty of 18th (30th) of March, 1856, as far as they restrict his sovereign rights in the Black Sea.' The Russian Note, containing this 'Denouncement' of the Treaty of Paris, will be found in the 3rd volume of Hertslet's 'Map of Europe by Treaty,' p. 1892. It should be read through, as should also l e the 'Further Russian Note' which follows it, by all who wish to be satisfied as to the real character of these transactions.

"It will be seen that Prince Gortchakoff complains of the stipulations about Black-Sea armaments pressing hardly upon Russia; but he sets the chief pretext for Russia's conduct in the following words: 'The Treaty of 18th (30th) of March, 1856, has not escaped the modifications to which most European transactions have been exposed, and in the face of which it would be difficult to maintain that the written law, founded upon the respect of Treaties as the basis of Public Right, and regulating the relations between States, retains the moral validity which it may have possessed at other times.' He goes on to complain, first, of some changes of government which had occurred in the Principalities of Moldavia and Wallachia; and secondly, of foreign men of war having been suffered to enter the Straits and the Black Sea. As to the first of the matters thus particularised, it is obvious that the affairs of the Principalities had nothing to do with the stipulations as to the Euxine; they were of no real importance in themselves, and the mention of so frivolous an excuse shows the weakness of the Russian case. As to foreign ships of war passing the Dardanelles and Bosphorus, it appeared, from inquiries made by the British Government, the result of which was published in a Parliamentary Paper, that in sixteen years eight ships of war only had so passed; that one of these was Russian, only three French or English, and that no infraction of treaty had taken place as to any of them.

"The really important new facts which had occurred between the spring of 1856 and the winter of 1870, and which to the Muscovite

mind ' modified the moral validity' of the Treaty of Paris, were, first
the temporary prostration of France after the catastrophes of Sedan
and Metz, and her consequent inability to side with England in
upholding the treaty which had been the result of their joint efforts
in the Crimean war ; and secondly, the determination which the
German and Austro-Hungarian Powers had formed not to co-operate
with England in any armed resistance to Russia's project for nulli-
fying the protection to the independence of Turkey, which that
Treaty of 1856 had created, when it limited the Russian armaments
in and near to the Euxine.   The English Government had ascertained
this ; and the English Premier informed the House of Commons in
the Debate on the Address in 1871, that " We should not have had
a single ally among the Neutral Powers if we had proposed simply
to insist on the neutralisation of the Black Sea.'   There can be no
doubt that Prince Gortchakoff had learned with equal accuracy
what policy Austria and other Powers intended to pursue if England
went to war for the sake of the denounced treaty.

" Under these circumstances the British Foreign Secretary sent a
reply to the Russian Notes protesting against Russia declaring as a
general doctrine that a single party to a treaty might destroy the
treaty at pleasure ; but containing the following invitation :—' If
instead of such a declaration the Russian Government had addressed
her Majesty's Government and the other Powers who are parties to
the Treaty of 1856, and had proposed for consideration with them
whether anything had occurred which could be held to amount to an
infraction of the treaty, or whether there is anything in the terms
which, from altered circumstances, presses with undue severity upon
Russia, or which, in the course of events, had become unnecessary for
the due protection of Turkey, her Majesty's Government would not
have refused to examine the question in concert with the cosignataries
to the treaty."[1]

" The hint was taken.   Russia condescended to admit that ' it is an
essential principle of the Law of Nations that no Power can liberate
itself from the engagement of a treaty, nor modify the stipulations
thereof, unless with the consent of the Contracting Powers by means
of an amicable arrangement.'[2]   This ceremonious admission was made
by a proctocol signed on the 17th of January at London, and by a
treaty signed there on the 13th of the following month, the articles
of the Treaty of Paris as to the navigation of the Black Sea were
abrogated, and Russia gained her purpose of discarding the restraints
she had submitted in 1856."[3]

In 1875 the turbulence and armed strife which for centuries
have been chronic in Herzegovina and the districts near its ill-
defined frontiers, broke out into unusual violence, and were soon
accompanied by open insurrection against the Sultan by the great
majority of the Herzegovenes.   Armed bands also from Monte-

[1] Hertslet, vol. iii. p. 1200.   [2] Ibid., p. 1904.   [3] Ibid., p. 1919.

negro were engaged in frequent and active attacks on the Turkish forces, and in Mahometan districts ; nor have there been wanting sure proof of substantial sympathy with the insurgents, or, at least, of enmity towards the Ottoman on the part of much more formidable powers. Tumults, amounting to civil war, were excited in many districts of Bosnia, where the population is partly Mahometan, and partly Christian. Insurrectionary societies were actively at work in Bulgaria ; and the Sultan's Government was placed in difficulties, of which a disastrous confession was made to Europe by an official announcement that the interest due to the public creditors of Turkey could not be provided.

The Turkish National Debt was an evil novelty in the institutions of the empire, which had come into existence during the Crimean war, and had rapidly grown into perilously large proportions. Only a small portion of the money had been borrowed at home. The great mass had been raised by successive loans contracted with the capitalists of Western Europe, and chiefly in the London Market. It amounted in 1876 to 195 millions. The first decree on the subject, in October, 1875, promised speedy payment of half the interest, and securities for the residue ; but these, like most other promises of the kind, proved worthless ; and in July, 1876, it was frankly announced that payments in respect of the National Debt must cease, while the state troubles continued. This declaration of insolvency on the part of Turkey did more than anything else to create a wide-spread belief that the speedy downfall of the Ottoman Empire was to be expected ; and it also did much to create the disfavour, with which the Turks have lately been regarded in England, compared with the general zeal in their behalf, which was generally felt here when Turkey was attacked by Russia in 1854. Defaulters are always unpopular.

On the 30th of May, 1876, Sultan Abdul-Aziz was formally but forcibly deposed. On the 4th of June following, he was found dead in the place of confinement to which he had been removed.

Murad (or Amurath) V. was proclaimed Sultan in his stead ; but the new sovereign proved hopelessly imbecile, and he was in turn deposed on the 31st of August. His brother, Abdul Hamid II., was then proclaimed Sultan, and at present continues to hold that station.

The troubles and hostilities in the north-western districts of the empire and in Bulgaria assumed more and more alarming proportions. Servia, which had no ground of complaint whatever against Turkey for aught that had occurred during the present generation, and which had received complete independence when Belgrade and her other fortresses were evacuated by the Ottomans, took undisguised part in aiding the Herzegovines, and in exciting the Bulgarians to insurrection. The movements in Bulgaria were quelled by the Turkish Government; but it was done by the employment of irregular troops, who committed cruelties and outrages, the report of which filled western Christendom with horror, and did more harm to the Turkish cause than could have been produced by any reverses in the field, or by the loss of whole provinces.

In July, 1876, Servia and Montenegro declared war against Turkey. The Servian armies were largely recruited by Russian soldiery, and were chiefly officered by Russians, who took part in the campaign with the full knowledge and sanction of their government. The Turks were almost uniformly successful in this war, and were only checked from a victorious advance on the Servian capital by the peremptory interposition of Russia. An armistice was agreed to on the 31st of October. Against the Montenegrins the Turks were generally unsuccessful. Hostilities in this region also were suspended at the close of the autumn by an armistice.

There have been numerous changes of ministers at Constantinople, which it is needless to discuss here : nor is it necessary to examine the details of the constitutional decree put forward in the name of the new Sultan, which purports to be still more liberal than even that of Gülhanè, and the Hatti-y-Humayoun. After years must show whether it has to have any practical value, if indeed the opportunity of putting it in practice be ever allowed to the House of Othman.

In November the Emperor Alexander made a public speech to the local authorities at Moscow, in which he announced that if Turkey did not give due guarantees for the better government of its Christian subjects, he would enforce them, either in concert with his allies, or by independent action. In the same month he ordered the mobilisation of part of his army ; and large masses of Russian troops were concentrated in Bessarabia, ready to commence the invasion of Turkey at the Czar's command.

[*In January*, 1877, *the Representatives of the Great Powers met in Conference at Constantinople, and on the* 15th *of that month presented their demands to the Porte, by whom they were rejected three days afterwards.*

Peace was formally concluded between Turkey and Servia on the 1st *of March, and, through the intervention of the European Powers, on terms very favourable for Servia.*

In March the first Turkish "Parliament" was opened, conducted by constitutional forms, &c., on English principles.

The winter being over, and the Russian preparations being nearly completed, the Czar, encouraged by the apparent division of feeling in England, and the outcry raised by Mr. Gladstone, considered the time had come when he could carry out his scheme for the partition of Turkey. On the 23rd of April, 1877, diplomatic relations were broken off between Russia and Turkey, and on the following day the Russian armies crossed the Pruth, war being declared at the same time.

Towards the close of May Prince Charles of Roumania issued a proclamation, declaring the independence of that State.

The Turkish forces in Europe (under command of Abdul Kerim) remaining inactive, the Danube was crossed, towards the end of June, by the Russian forces at two points, near Galatz and at Sistova; and, after a slight conflict at Biela, the Russian armies were established in Bulgaria. In the middle of July their advance guard, under General Gourko, pushed across the Balkans and reached Kezanlik and Eski-zagra, but was afterwards defeated and driven back with great loss across the mountains.

Osman Pasha, hurrying up from Widdin to oppose the invading forces crossing the Danube, seized a strong position at Plevna on the 19th of July, driving out a detachment of the enemy's troops. Whilst engaged in fortifying this position he repulsed several attacks in force made by the Russians, towards the end of July, with great loss to them.

The campaign in Asia had been a varied one at the outset. The Turkish forces, being much out-numbered, were driven slowly back from the frontier to the heights before Erzeroum, leaving Kars to be invested by the enemy. The Ottoman forces were further reduced by a large detachment being sent to Soukoum Kaleh to the aid of the insurgent subjects of Russia, but which place they had to evacuate in September. Having been reinforced, Muktar Pasha advanced towards the latter part of June, and after a severe engagement at Zewin compelled the Russians to retreat again to their own frontier, and re-entered Kars in triumph on the 9th of July. The Russian forces having being re-organised and strengthened, gave battle to Muktar Pasha at Aladja Dagh on the 15th of October, totally defeating him, and driving his forces in great confusion back upon Erzeroum. On the 19th November the Russians obtained possession of Kars by treachery; and the campaign in Asia was virtually at an end.

At Plevna Osman Pasha gallantly held out against the combined forces of Russia and Roumania. During September a terrific but unsuccessful bombardment took place, and the Roumanians, after a most obstinate struggle, obtained possession of one of the outworks—the Grivitza Redoubt. In consequence of these defeats General Todleben (the defender of Sebastopol) was now summoned from Russia, and Plevna was invested on all sides by the vastly superior forces of the enemy. Cut off from all supplies of food and ammunition from the outer world, Osman still held out in the hopes of being relieved by his brother general in the field.

These hopes being found vain, and all his provisions being consumed during the many months the investment had lasted, on the 10th of December,

1877, *after an heroic but unsuccessful attempt to cut their way through the enemy's entrenchments, the Turkish forces were compelled to capitulate unconditionally, their commander himself being wounded in the final sortie. The investing force consisted of upwards of 100,000 men ; those who capitulated of about 30,000 men, including the sick.*

Plevna having fallen, Servia, oblivious of the terms of peace so recently granted to her by Turkey, found it safe to declare war against her Suzerain, and united her forces with those of the Czar.

The Russian forces were now at liberty to cross the Balkans, capturing on their way a Turkish corps d'armée in the defiles of the Shipka Pass. Adrianople fell into their hands, and their advance was only arrested by an armistice, when in sight of Constantinople and Boulair (Gallipoli).

Terms of peace were subsequently arranged between Russia and Turkey at San Stefano, March 3, 1878.

The terms of the Treaty of San Stefano, ably criticised in a circular issued by Lord Salisbury, alarmed the European Powers, discovering as they did the elements of a future complete destruction of the Ottoman Empire, and the transfer of its finest provinces to the Russian Power. In England the eyes of the public were completely opened to the error committed by Mr. Gladstone, and a revulsion of feeling set in in favour of the policy originally started by Lord Beaconsfield ; and which, had he been suffered to carry it out, unchecked by the " Bulgarian Atrocities " cry, might have wholly prevented the war.

Fortified by the support of public opinion, Lord Beaconsfield took his stand on the Salisbury Circular. The attitude of Russia, from being aggressive towards this country, immediately the national division excited by Mr. Gladstone had ceased, became more conciliatory, and a Congress of the leading Powers was agreed to, which met at Berlin in June and July, 1878, under the Presidency of Prince Bismarck. According to the terms of the treaty drawn up at the Berlin Congress (to replace those of the Treaty of San Stefano, which was now set aside) Roumania, Servia, and Montenegro, all somewhat enlarged, were declared to be independent ; the greater portion of the country between the Balkans and the Danube was erected into an autonomous state, to be called Bulgaria, under a prince chosen by the people, but under the Suzerainty of the Sultan, to whom tribute was to be paid ; all the fortresses in Bulgaria (including Rustchuk, Silistria, Varna, Schumla, etc.) were to be razed to the ground, and a new autonomous state called Eastern Roumelia was formed south of the Balkans, but subject to the direct rule of the Sultan.

The provinces of Bosnia and Herzegovina were to be administered by Austria-Hungary, and Roumania was made to cede to Russia that portion of Bessaberabia removed from the dominion of the Czar in 1856, receiving in exchange for it the Dobrudscha.

In Asia, Kars, Batoum, Ardahan, and the surrounding country were ceded to Russia.

By a separate treaty, negotiated between Great Britain and Turkey in June, 1878, the island of Cyprus was given up to the former Power for so

*long as Kars, Batoum, and Ardahan remained in the hands of Russia, in
return for which Great Britain guarantees the integrity of the existing
Asiatic dominions of the Sultan.   Cyprus was taken possession of by the
English in July,* 1878.]

INDEX.